THE
POLITICAL ECONOMY
OF DEVELOPMENT

THE
POLITICAL ECONOMY
OF DEVELOPMENT

THEORETICAL AND EMPIRICAL
CONTRIBUTIONS

EDITED BY

NORMAN T. UPHOFF AND WARREN F. ILCHMAN

UNIVERSITY OF CALIFORNIA PRESS
BERKELEY,   LOS ANGELES,   LONDON

University of California Press
Berkeley and Los Angeles, California

University of California Press, Ltd.
London, England

Copyright © 1972, by
The Regents of the University of California
ISBN: 0-520-02062-6

0-520-02314-5 (paperback)
Library of Congress Catalog Card Number: 77-161999
First Paperback Edition 1973
Printed in the United States of America

CONTENTS

PREFACE

In our book *The Political Economy of Change*, we attempted to formulate a social science framework useful for assisting persons making public policy. Although "the new political economy" was thought to apply generally, our focus was on the countries of Africa, Asia, and Latin America. In that book, we begged all questions about "development," having in mind a sequel that would explore this subject in political economy terms.[1] We deliberately avoided using the term "development" because it is probably one of the most depreciated terms in social science literature, having been used vastly more than it has been understood. We did not want to muddle our model by associating with it the ambiguities and abstractions that are all too common in contemporary thinking and writing about "development."

Economists have addressed themselves more explicitly and usefully to questions of development policy and strategy than have other social scientists, but as will be suggested later, they have missed important aspects by failing to distinguish clearly between growth and development. With respect to other social science disciplines, we would note Herbert Blumer's conclusion, after making a survey of the literature, that "the idea of social development is hopelessly vague and confused," [2] and Lucian Pye's observation that "there is still considerable ambiguity and imprecision in the use of the term 'political development.' " [3] Recognizing these problems with the term "development," we chose to speak in our first book only of "change."

Our question-begging on issues of development was prompted by a great concern rather than a lack of concern. The political economy model was first conceived while Professor Ilchman was teaching social and political science to economic planners from Third World countries who came to the Center for Development Economics at Williams College. Its extension to encompass analytically the phenomena of economic, social, and political development resulted from Professor Uphoff's study of the use of foreign aid in Ghana to promote development there.[4]

---

[1] Ilchman and Uphoff, *The Political Economy of Change* (1969), p. 48.

[2] "The Idea of Social Development," *Studies in Comparative International Development*, II:1 (1966): 10.

[3] "The Concept of Political Development," *The Annals of the American Academy of Political and Social Science*, 358 (March 1965): 4.

[4] See Uphoff, "Toward a Supradisciplinary Theory of Development," *Studies in Comparative International Development*, VII:2 (1972); this is a revised version of a paper presented at the 1970 meeting of the American Political Science Association in Los Angeles. This is a synopsis of the longer study, *Ghana's Experience in Using External Aid for De-*

The immensity and gravity of development problems and processes did not repel us; rather they attracted us, but we wanted to withhold any discussion of the subject until we thought we could clarify it significantly and usefully.

The political economy approach leads readily to a consideration of development since both are concerned with *productivity*. In political economy, choices are compared and made according to their aggregate productivity, not simply in economic terms but in terms of the various values sought. And while persons may disagree on the exact definition or criteria of development, few would disagree that development stands in the final analysis for increases in productivity, however this is conceived or measured. That which is more developed is more productive, and vice versa. This is understood intuitively and implicitly if not always explicitly and analytically. We wish to contribute to an explicit and analytical understanding of development in productivity terms.

In working on "the political economy of development," we discovered a significant number of studies which we thought contributed to an emerging view of development that was supradisciplinary and quite relevant to policy choices. The contributors to this view included political scientists, economists, sociologists, and anthropologists, some already well known and others just beginning their careers, some indeed coming from Third World countries. Rather than present these contributions through paraphrases or short citations, we concluded that it would be better to present them more fully, along with our own statements on development in political economy perspective.

The resulting work resembles a "reader," but we think it goes beyond the usual social science reader in its objective and consequence. As the subtitle suggests, a synthesis of theoretical and empirical contributions to "the political economy of development" is sought. What emerges is a general statement on development in which, we think, the sum is greater than its parts. The theoretical and empirical contributions extend each other's significance, and in the process a common, supradisciplinary perspective and terminology are fashioned. The aims and claims suggested for this approach are, admittedly, ambitious, but we see important opportunities here for making social science more relevant to public policy concerns.

We have not suggested and do not suggest that the new political economy constitutes a theory of politics, economics or society. Formally, it is only a model. Substantively, it is an approach or a perspective that we think is shared by others and that lends itself to further improvement and refinement. In Part I, we attempt to articulate this approach or perspective, which relates to more than "development" and deals generally with social science as an enterprise. The reader who is interested specifically in "development" may choose to devote little attention to this first Part. The conceptual framework of "the political economy of development" is presented in Part II, illustrated and extended by the empirical studies that accompany it. Then analyses and articles dealing with four principal areas of development strategy and policy are offered in Part III, followed by a discussion in Part IV of problems of measurement and modeling of development processes.

We appreciate, and wish the reader to appreciate, that the articles presented as readings in this book were in most cases written with different purposes and au-

velopment, 1957–1966: Implications for Development Theory and Policy (Berkeley: Institute of International Studies, 1970), which is being revised for publication under the title: *Foreign Aid and the Political Economy of Development in Nkrumah's Ghana.*

diences in mind. It has therefore been frequently necessary to excerpt the presentation in order to focus on the points we would like to see emphasized with reference to development. We wish to thank the many authors for their generosity in allowing us to include their material and to make such excerptions. We also wish to thank other authors whose work is in the political economy tradition and who had given us permission to use their work, but which owing to the trade-off between length and cost of the book could not be included in the final version: Irma Adelman, Samir Amin, Adam Curle, David S. French, Jack Gray, James Heaphey, Guy Hunter, Anne O. Krueger, Edward J. Mitchell, William C. Mitchell, Cynthia Taft Morris, Norman Nie, Jeffrey Paige, G. Bingham Powell, Kenneth Prewitt, and Edward Tufte. Drafts of our sections were read by numerous colleagues and students, and we wish especially to acknowledge Matthew Edel, Eldon Kenworthy, Ann Seidman, and the members of the University of California International Planning Seminar. Manuscript preparation was assisted by the Center for International Studies of Cornell University.

This book and its royalties are dedicated to the American Friends Service Committee.

Norman Thomas Uphoff
Warren F. Ilchman

Ithaca, New York
Berkeley, California
May 1972

PART I

THE NEW POLITICAL ECONOMY

The time has come to recognize the professional respectability as well as the practical essentiality of the ancient and honorable hybrid discipline of "political economy." JAMES S. COLEMAN

THE POLITICAL ECONOMY of which we speak is an integrated social science of public choice. It is political in that its subject matter is the exercise of authority and the competition for authority within a community. Purely private aims and activities that do not impinge upon the use or possession of authority remain outside the purview of political economy. It is economic in that it treats with the allocation and exchange of scarce resources, including political and social resources as well as those generally dubbed economic. Inasmuch as alternative activities or choices present differing combinations or balances of cost and benefit, and insofar as persons seek to gain net benefits or advantages, behavior is assumed to be purposeful and "economizing." There can be political or social profits and losses just as surely as economic ones if we are willing to recognize them as such. The recognition and explication of these relationships is the task of the new political economy.

A SUPRADISCIPLINARY SOCIAL SCIENCE

As a supradisciplinary approach to social science, political economy is pertinent for the analysis of any issue or policy of public relevance and can simulate the perspective and situation of any participant in political life. Depending on the purpose of analysis, it can deal with individual, group, or aggregate conditions, employing the same factors at micro and macro levels. While equally relevant for political actors in industrialized and rich nations, in the pages and contributions to follow, political economy is addressed to persons in the nonindustrialized and

1

impoverished nations of the world and to their public efforts to improve their lot.[1]

The current interest in political economy, evidenced by many persons in addition to ourselves, is not a matter of fashion or fad. What we are seeing is a revival of interest in an approach to public problems that has persisted since formalized analysis began, as James S. Coleman points out in his contribution presented here on pages 30–39. Though eclipsed in recent decades by the popularity of continental historical and macrosociological analyses, though undermined by a psychology and an anthropology that separated private motive from public action, and though hampered by the widely accepted divisions of labor in academic life, political economy has nevertheless survived as an intellectual discipline because of its utility for thinking about public choices and its distinctiveness as a mode of analysis. Like the political economy of the past, our supradisciplinary approach is intransigently linked to values and preferences. In an era when the value-neutrality of social science is much proclaimed, political economy is intended to be value-relevant, seeking to illuminate the costs and consequences of alternative courses according to the values one holds for individual and community welfare.

The version of political economy offered here, however, is somewhat different from that proposed by a Mill in 1848 or a Keynes in 1919. Today there is disagreement among many political economists about the scope of their subject and the borrowing of insights from the formal disciplines of economics or political science. Some would restrict political economy to the political effects of economic decisions or the economic effects of political choices. We would not be so restrictive, for all public choices, whether explicitly "economic" or not, affect the distribution of resources and the productive possibilities of members of the community. We would agree with Robert Mundell that "economics is the science of choice," and therefore we would adopt and adapt economic modes of analysis to multitudinous problems of public choice.[2] For us, the continuous exchanges required for achieving public purposes, together with their consequences, whether called economic, social, or political, constitute the subject matter of political economy.

Other political economists would emphasize more the borrowing of formal intellectual instruments from the discipline of economics, such as indifference curves or rates of discounting future returns. However, given our interest in policy choices in the real world, formalistic tools hold less attraction for us. We appreciate the strengths and weaknesses of economics as a discipline, some of which are suggested by Kenneth Boulding in his essay reprinted below. We borrow directly the

---

[1] We are sorry that we cannot take up here the estimable challenge posed by Kenneth Boulding in his review of our book *The Political Economy of Change* (1969): "This work is an important landmark in the development of an integrated social science, and everyone who reads it seriously will profit by it. It is perhaps a little unfortunate, in its illustrative material at least, that it concentrates so heavily on the problems of the poor countries and of development, because the principles which it expounds are of complete generality and indeed the applications to the rich countries may be of even greater interest. Perhaps the authors will consider this in the future" (*American Political Science Review*

64 [June 1970]: 604. Our forte unfortunately is not in the analysis of the richer countries, but we anticipate that others will be attempting this application of political economy.

[2] Robert A. Mundell, *Man and Economics* (1968), p. i. Professor Mundell is editor of the *Journal of Political Economy*. In his book, he applies economic reasoning even to things like voting for President and choosing a spouse. For an exploratory application of economic modes of analysis to military strategy, see Bernard Brodie, "Strategy as a Science." *World Politics* 1, no. 4 (July, 1949), especially pp. 475–484; also Kenneth Boulding, *Conflict and Defense* (1962).

concepts of resources and exchange, though we broaden these beyond the conventional realm of economics. We borrow also the bedrock assumption of economics, that the value of resources depends on the demand for them and that this demand depends on their scarcity in relation to their productivity for achieving people's purposes. Although we would aspire to the rigor of economic analysis in this new political economy, we would borrow from any discipline insofar, and *only* insofar, as this aided in the assessment of public choices.[3]

Aggregate Optimality.

Owing to the isolation of political science from economics in the recent past, two distinct and discrete perspectives have emerged: an economic perspective concerned with the most efficient use of economic resources, and a political perspective similarly concerned with the use of political resources. From each perspective, the other's concern is seen more as a constraint than as a variable. The political economy perspective, in contrast, incorporates both and seeks to evaluate potential trade-offs. The differences in perspective can be illustrated by suggesting a matrix of different policy choices judged as optimal, acceptable, or unacceptable from an economic or a political point of view.

	Optimal Politically	*Acceptable Politically*	*Politically Unacceptable*
Economically optimal	A	B	C
Economically acceptable	D	E	F
Economically unacceptable	G	H	I

Whereas an economist would arrive at choice B and a political scientist at choice D, a political economist would, with his modes of analysis, aim at a policy corresponding more closely to choice A. What is sought is an *aggregate* optimality. A choice approximating A might be less desirable in economic terms than B, and less so in political terms than D, but the total benefit achieved would be greater than that from either of these other two choices.

This point cannot be adequately understood through such typological models, however. Optimizing in political economy terms goes beyond "splitting the difference" between economic and political optima. Since political economy embraces the entire range of resources used in public exchange, there are situations where combinations of resources have variable efficiencies for achieving a public purpose, which are quite different from the efficiency suggested by either conventional economics or political science. Let us illustrate this with an example.

Consider a situation in which public resources available for expenditure on

[3] We would concur in the generally held view that economics is the most advanced of the social sciences in terms of the development of theory and would attribute this in large measure to the long-standing involvement of economists with policy analysis. At the same time we would draw attention to the view of an eminent economist, C. P. Kindleberger, that once one goes beyond elementary analytical problems, economists' analyses are not necessarily much more precise or conclusive than those of political scientists. See *Power and Money* (1970), p. 4.

education can be used to improve the *quality* of education offered (by hiring more teachers, by training them better, or by other means) or to increase access to education, that is, the *quantity* of education made available. For the sake of discussion, let us consider the first use as basically *economic,* inasmuch as better education could be expected to raise labor-force productivity, and the second use as *political,* in that expanded enrollments would be expected to increase support for the regime and involve more people in the common values of the nation. Neither direction is purely economic or purely political; each is some combination of these. Moreover, each has some "social" advantages or disadvantages as well. But let us describe these uses, respectively, as economic and political.[4]

An analysis and evaluation of alternatives from an economic *or* a political perspective would be incomplete, at least for policy purposes, where one wants to ascertain the allocation of resources that is optimal in some aggregate sense. The following graph clarifies the problem of choice if one has a limited amount of economic resources to apply toward making an educational system more productive, by improving the quality of instruction and/or increasing enrollments. The coordinates identified on the graph correspond to the choices represented within the matrix above.

At *B* there is the greatest improvement in quality satisfying the minimum "political" requirement of increase in enrollment, while at *D* enrollment is increased maximally subject to the "economic" constraint of some minimum improvement in quality of education. Our interest is the location of point *A,* which lies somewhere between *B* and *D*. Political economy would not suggest splitting the difference and locating it midway between the two suboptimal points.

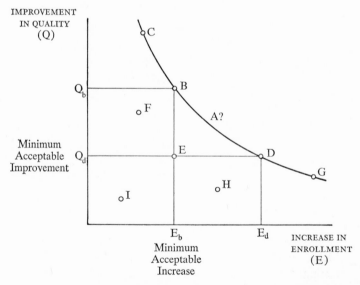

[4] Here we exemplify the proposition advanced by William C. Mitchell that political economists are willing to trade "realism" for "simplicity," in order to explicate complicated situations. Mitchell suggests that political economists—knowing that they normally cannot have more of one of these two analytical virtues without some sacrifice of the other—in contrast to political sociologists, will prefer greater simplicity. See "The Shape of Political Theory to Come: From Political Sociology to Political Economy," in S. M. Lipset (ed.), *Politics and the Social Sciences* (1969), pp. 130 ff. We would stress, as Mitchell does not, that political economists with a concern for policy will sacrifice "realism" reluctantly and only temporarily, doing so only to advance their understanding of unsimple problems. In

Whether one emphasizes improvements in quality or increases in enrollment will depend on the value attached to each, relative to the other.[5] Under conditions of low labor productivity and adequate regime support, A will be closer to B than to D; if political stability is a short-run problem, resources should be allocated so that the combination of improvements and increases is that represented by locating A closer to D.[6] The exact location would depend on the situation, on the interaction between resources and needs and between political and economic factors. That neither political nor economic calculations in themselves would offer sufficient guidance to choice is evident from this example.

Few would contest the desirability of having a supradisciplinary social science that encompassed economic, social, political, and other relevant factors.[7] The difficulty involved is that of conceiving and establishing it. In our view, and in that of other social scientists such as William Mitchell, the best prospects for success lie with a framework that relates economic modes of analysis to wider political and policy problems. Simplified models are needed, but they should be open to a number and variety of pertinent variables. This we think the new political economy allows.

A POLICY-ORIENTED SOCIAL SCIENCE

The distinction commonly made in the physical sciences between pure and applied science is hardly appropriate for the social sciences. There is little to be said for "pure" social science, however virtuous those who practice it may be. We would

---

this essay, Mitchell cites others who are contributing to the development of a "new political economy."

[5] Making this a two-dimensional graph—or choice—simplifies the analysis, perhaps too much. This becomes a three-, four-, or n-dimensional graph if one admits other objectives into the analysis, so that the value of increased enrollments or quality improvements is considered vis-à-vis other aims as well.

[6] This could be represented graphically by indifference curves in the following manner, with curve I standing for the first condi-

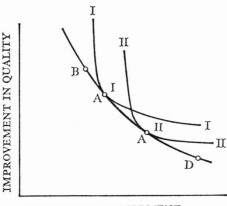

INCREASE IN ENROLLMENT

tion described, and curve II for the second. We do not suggest this, at least in the text, because in a choice situation such as this one, indifference curves only *portray* the preferred solution in graphic terms; they do not reveal it. The shape of such curves is derived from estimations of the marginal rate of substitution (of increases in enrollment for decreases in quality, or vice versa) at any particular level of either. We are interested only in the preferred position between B and D, which we can estimate if we know the marginal rate of substitution over this limited range. Drawing indifference curves would make the solution appear more elegant, but they would be no better or determinant than the estimates we already had. If more than two objectives are involved and we wish to introduce indifference curves, we confront n-dimensional surfaces that boggle the mind and do not tell us more than we already know.

[7] Two quite different supporting views come from Fred Riggs, *Administration in Developing Countries* (1964), chap. 2, concerning a "pan-disciplinary approach," and from George C. Homans, *The Nature of Social Science* (1967). Homans contends that the social sciences "are in fact a single science. They share the same subject matter—the behavior of man. And they employ, without always admitting it, the same body of general explanatory principles" (p. 3).

contend that the relevant categories for social science are *applied* and *applicable*. This view does not derive from any positivist orthodoxy concerning the social role of social science. Rather it stems from a recognition of the theoretical backwardness of the social science enterprise and of the need to put all theoretical propositions to the test.[8] What is needed are opportunities for establishing causal relationships in the realm studied by social scientists. Applied research, even if the less prestigious enterprise in the physical sciences, should be the preferred enterprise in the social sciences.[9] Applicable social science would include those theoretical and analytical endeavors which had not been but could be applied, which is to say that they were unverified but nevertheless verifiable.

Policy as the Test of Theory.

At the outset of this discussion, we should state that our concern with public policy is not prompted solely by intellectual curiosity. The findings, or non-findings, of social scientists can have, and do have, great import for people's well-being.[10] However, as social scientists we are concerned with policy because the only test of social science theory is human activity, spontaneous or induced. The opportunities for systematically and rigorously studying spontaneous action are, practically by definition, limited. Public policy is the major source of induced activity and ought therefore to be of major interest to social scientists.

[8] For a lucid and telling critique of the present state of social science theory, we would refer the reader to the essay by Marion J. Levy, Jr., " 'Does It Matter If He's Naked?' Bawled the Child," in Klaus Knorr and James Rosenau (eds.), *Contending Approaches to International Politics* (1969), esp. pp. 89–93. We would ourselves disagree with him that the essence of science is the establishment of a generalized system of theory in which the more abstract and parsimonious the variables, the better. We prefer William of Occam's rule (Occam's razor) concerning parsimony: that one should not multiply entities (variables) unnecessarily. He was not referring to the number of variables employed but to the use of abstract concepts for explaining phenomena. See B. A. G. Fuller, *A History of Philosophy, Vol. I: Ancient and Medieval* (1945 edition), pp. 419–420 for pertinent exegesis.

[9] We would note and endorse Kenneth Parsons' view on this question:

> To accept the distinction between "pure" and "applied" economics as generally valid and fundamental is not only to accept the view that "theory" in its pure form can have an independent career but that it can be validated in some way other than by "application" . . . The crux of the issue is simply this: that the only alternative which we have to the *validation of inquiry by problem solving* is a reliance either upon self evidence of fact or principle as the foundations of knowledge—or upon revelation. Both of the latter alternatives are incompatible

with a genuinely scientific viewpoint (emphasis added). "The Logical Foundations of Economic Research," *Journal of Farm Economics* 31 (November 1949): 664 and 674; cited by Dorner below.

For a pointed conclusion about "pure" research in political science, see Lucien Pye's statement about "the dead end of [a] science without engineers" in Austin Ranney (ed.), *Political Science and Public Policy* (1968), pp. 259–262.

[10] We share with Marion Levy his apprehension of the imminence of what he calls "the stupidity death":

> . . . long before we fall heir to the "entropy death" or to "fertility drowning," if we don't get cracking on these problems, we shall die the stupidity death, the ignorance death. The world we inhabit gets more highly interdependent every day. As it does, the level of knowledge requisite for adequate planning mounts. As interdependence increases, the probability that any particular stupidity will have increasingly large catastrophic implications also mounts. If the curve of knowledge produced by social thinkers falls below that curve of requisite knowledge, avoidance of catastrophe is a function of luck (*op. cit.*, p. 90).

Perhaps because we are political economists rather than sociologists, we are not so concerned about the implications of interdependence as we are about inadequacies of production and inequities of distribution.

Of the social sciences, only economics has fastened upon policy as the focus of research and analysis. It is no coincidence that economics is also the most theoretically advanced of the social sciences; its hypotheses are continuously tested by real-world choices. For instance, when the Federal Reserve Board alters its policy for the creation of currency, there is not only an effect on the public; there is as well some additional evidence gained confirming or challenging the generally accepted theoretical explanation of inflation. The adequacy of theoretical "mousetraps" is continually scrutinized, and potentially better ones are devised and tried whenever conventional ones appear to be ineffective.

Yet, despite its successes, as Boulding points out, economics has shortcomings, and these are instructive for the development of a policy-oriented political economy. The *modus operandi* of economics, and the various models and measures employed, analytically screen out the impact of "noneconomic" factors. As an analytical expedient this may be necessary and fruitful, but only as an approximation of reality. For policy purposes, more factors must be considered. Political economy would adopt the operating methods of economics without the confined ambit of that discipline.[11]

The best test of hypotheses and confirmation of theory in social science is public policy. The aim of political economy is to develop propositions about the outcome of exchanges of resources, noneconomic as well as economic ones. These resources determine one's ability to get compliance, whether achieved through negative sanctions or positive inducements. Policies are combinations of resources that maintain or alter an exchange relationship between the regime and various sectors, or among sectors.

Public policy is controlled and focused exchange taking place within discrete periods of time, and it thus permits cumulative proposition-building. When certain authority is granted to a sector by the regime, how much is the regime's legitimacy increased or its expenditure of coercion decreased? Or what happens to legitimacy or coercion when certain authority is withdrawn from a sector by the regime? What kinds of incentives reduce or increase bureaucratic corruption? What are the limits to pure coercion when compliance is sought? At what point do other resources increase or diminish the efficiency of coercion? Or, from the point of view of sectors, what is the productivity of violence for achieving certain objectives? What allocations of resources can increase the solidarity of family units or decrease the solidarity of tribal ties?

The answers to these questions are not universal. Conditions differ from community to community, so one must study the effects of variations in sectors, resources, values, propensities, and objectives. Often only limited generalizations can be made, but the answers to questions such as these yield a kind of knowledge that is more valuable than the kind of abstract reasoning now so common in the social sciences.[12] Unfortunately, the currently modish formulations of social science

[11] A more fundamental shortcoming, and one less often recognized and conceded by economists, is the relativity of theory to certain institutional or structural conditions. This is argued, we think persuasively, in Peter Dorner's piece reprinted on pages 41–46. Despite economists' efforts to achieve the greatest possible generality for their theory, it has not escaped the influence of the time and places in which it was formulated. Appreciation of this influence should not deter social scientists from theoretical endeavors; but it should convince them that they need to test their theories continually against particular conditions and problems in order to ascertain the validity of these theories.

[12] We would note here Homans' commentary on propositions and generalizations: "But

theory—concerning broad systemic changes over generations and centuries, with subsystems differentiating in time and space—defy this-worldly confirmation and elude application to achieve public purposes more effectively. Such formulations may be impressive but they are inutile. More important for social science, they can be neither true nor false.

When we say that public policy is the test of propositions or theory, we mean that public policy is the most effective way of determining whether causal models or inferences can be confirmed—that is, whether they enable one to make reliable predictions. We have previously stated our agreement with Boulding that the most essential element of the scientific process is prediction, not "experiment," as is sometimes suggested.[13] Astronomers have developed a science without any laboratory experiments, by studying movement and interaction and by formulating theory on the basis of predictive models. Students of public policy, while they lack the laboratories of a physicist or a psychologist, are fortunately closer to the movement and interaction that interests them than are astronomers, and they do have opportunities for at least quasi-experimentation to the extent that they associate their inquiry with policy actions.

Optimal Ignorance.

A social science consisting of tested political economy propositions would be useful for those charged with making public decisions. In this capacity, political economy becomes an *ex ante* calculus of the outcomes of political choices. To achieve this capacity, the political economist must simultaneously develop an *ex ante* calculus of the productivity of knowledge. This second calculus would evaluate knowledge in terms of its problem-solving potential and would be grounded in the controversial assumption that the truth of a proposition derives not from its generality of application but from its explanatory power.

We can illustrate this view by suggesting in matrix form four combinations of generality and explanatory power.

	Productivity of Knowledge	
Generality of Knowledge	*Results Conform Largely to Explanation*	*Results Conform Little to Explanation*
Explanation covering the greatest number of cases	A	B
Explanation covering the fewest number of cases	C	D

There would probably be agreement that propositions fitting category A—those covering the greatest number of cases with great predictive power—are most preferred, and that those fitting category D have nothing to commend them. Our position would be (and here we might encounter disagreement) that propositions cor-

---

let us not worry much at the moment about the degree of generality of propositions. To have stated and tested a proposition of any degree of generality is no mean achievement. Let us remember Mr. Justice Holmes' dictum: 'I always say that the chief end of man is to form general propositions,' and let us not al-

together forget what he added: 'And no generalization is worth a damn'" (*op. cit.,* pp. 9–10).

[13] See Ilchman and Uphoff, *op. cit.,* pp. 258–260; and Kenneth Boulding, *The Impact of the Social Sciences* (1966), pp. 13–14.

responding to category C are preferable to ones matching category B. Propositions need not be general to be productive, and general propositions may be quite unproductive.[14]

The reasons for this are several. First, the most encompassing explanations of phenomena are bound, in clear probabilistic fashion, to manifest deviant cases. Of more interest to us is the probability that an explanation encompassing fewer cases will, if acted upon, be more predictive of outcomes and is likely to be more consonant with the levels of resources available to be expended, with the time horizons governing a particular choice, with the calculation of foregone opportunities, and with the aspirations of the relevant constituencies for a policy.

An *ex ante* calculus of the productivity of knowledge may be best developed with an eye toward what we call "optimal ignorance," an assessment of what one does *not* need to know in order to decide upon a course of action.[15] If one bears in mind that not all additional knowledge adds equally to problem-solving capacity, and that some knowledge does not add as much in value as the cost of acquiring and using it, one concludes that some amount of "ignorance" must be judged beneficial in any particular situation. The idea of optimal ignorance suggests that the productivity of knowledge is a function of the problems it helps to solve; that there are diseconomies as well as economies of scale in formulating all-encompassing or exhaustive explanations; that there is some point of maximum returns associated with the collection of information or additional cases and that beyond this point, diminishing returns set in with respect to acquiring and utilizing further data.

As a rule, there are diseconomies involved in explanations that account for a very few or a great many cases. Economies in explanation lie within the range of generalization where the behavior of a particular target group can be predicted with some certainty and where the available resources can be effectively used. Little can be gained from explanations that encompass unnecessarily large groups, because the larger a group is the more deviant cases there will be, as a rule. Neither will anything be gained from explanations that require more resources to effect desired change than are attainable. This range of optimal information or explanation cannot be ascertained *a priori*, since it depends on the extent of one's ends and the extent of one's means. But it needs to be considered explicitly, and no apologies need be made for taking the position that the most ambitious or encompassing explanation is not necessarily the best one.

Levels of Explanation.

Implicit in our view is the premise that "truth" is neither monolithic nor immutable. What may be thought of as "truth" is universal and unchanging only at the most abstract level. Phenomena can be explained, with varying utility, at different

---

[14] If our topic were explanation in social science as a general concern, we would expand this statement to contend that knowledge can be fallacious but fruitful. The idea, for example, that man is a "rational" being—an idea central to the development of Western civilization—was widely believed to be "true" until assaulted during the last hundred years by psychologists and philosophers. Yet this "myth of rationality" gave impetus to the scientific and technological as well as cultural and aesthetic accomplishments of Western civilization, which have so greatly enriched our lives, in medicine, engineering, architecture, literature, music, and other fields. That we now appreciate the "irrationality" in man cannot take away the productive accomplishments of this civilization. To paraphrase Marion Levy, things can be true but trivial, and fruitful but false.

[15] This idea was introduced in Ilchman and Uphoff, *op. cit.*, pp. 261–262.

levels. We are concerned that the most productive levels be chosen, both in terms of problem-solving and theory-evolving, the two being, we think, reinforcing. Explanations at the "highest" level are those employing the most abstract variables, being intended to encompass the largest number of cases. We would argue not for explanation at the "lowest" level, to be sure, but rather for explanations that treat with the number and range of cases affected by policy choices and do not interpose abstract macro variables beyond the knowledge or time horizon of persons involved.[16]

An example of the problem of selecting among levels of explanation is the one posed in an attempt to explain the responsiveness or unresponsiveness of peasants to innovations in agricultural production. Two impressive, alternative, and contending approaches have been suggested by Kusum Nair and Theodore Schultz.[17] In *Blossoms in the Dust,* Mrs. Nair presents a picture of rural Indians as staunchly "traditional" and resistant to change. Farmers are content with four acres when they could cultivate thirty. "I am satisfied," one of them says. Emaciated cows are lovingly tended as objects of adoration rather than production. Meager savings are spent on bangles and urban amenities, rather than invested in tube wells or equipment. People do not desire change, therefore no change comes about. Values are considered to be the independent variable governing behavior. Deep-rooted, pervasive cultural factors are considered determinant by Mrs. Nair and independent of opportunities. Agricultural development can come about only after these factors are changed, and changed throughout the population.

The behavior of peasant farmers described by Professor Schultz, on the other hand, is quite different. He finds that growers of maize in Central America, for example, despite their use of "traditional" production techniques, have allocated their limited resources of land and labor quite efficiently, or rationally in economic terms, so that the marginal products of each are approximately equated under prevailing market conditions. In his book, Schultz presents evidence that the marginal productivity of labor in underdeveloped countries such as India is not zero or negative, as is often argued or assumed. Where innovations have not been adopted, it is because of peasants' perception of higher true costs than those estimated by outsiders, or because peasants considerably discount the proffered benefits. They place a high premium on avoiding the risk of crop failure, a reasonable decision rule when they live close to the subsistence level and will suffer great hardship if an innovation does not produce the anticipated results; they cannot afford to bet "double or nothing." In Schultz's view, peasants are surprisingly "rational" in the economic sense, responding to economic incentives when these can be satisfactorily demonstrated. Opportunities become the independent variable, with economic rather than cultural factors shaping behavior.

It would not make sense to argue that one of these authors is "right" and the other "wrong." Both derive their conclusions from empirical data; both would acknowledge that there is neither total stagnation nor complete receptivity to change in the real world. One emphasizes and explains static elements in agriculture; the

[16] The problem of "levels of explanation" is discussed with reference to stimulating entrepreneurship and controlling bureaucratic corruption in Ilchman and Uphoff, *op. cit.,* pp. 260–272. This relates to our concern with "scope of explanation," or the number of cases one seeks to include in his study and generalizations.

[17] Nair, *Blossoms in the Dust: The Human Factor in Indian Development* (1962); and Schultz, *Transforming Traditional Agriculture* (1964).

other, dynamic elements. The most significant difference in their two analyses, however, is the level of explanation adopted.[18]

The cultural mode of explanation is all-encompassing, is practically totalistic in scope, and presumably affects all persons equally. To alter cultural values would require great effort and expenditure, and if it could be done, it would also require a long time. The more economic explanation, on the other hand, is more partial, almost particularistic in scope. Some individuals are more and others less responsive to economic incentives. In any case, they are not necessarily barred from responding by a culturally determined set of values. The modification of incentives can be quick, selective, and to the degree necessary to achieve some desired change in behavior. This micro explanation of behavior is "economic" in the general as well as the specific sense of the word.

This does not make Schultz "right" and Mrs. Nair "wrong," to reiterate the point made above. It is a matter of choice which kind and level of explanation one will employ in analysis. Both authors can claim to be shown at least partially right by recent developments in Indian agriculture. The "Green Revolution," the application of new agricultural technology that can double or triple yields, has been given impetus by only a minority of Indian farmers. Most are still cultivating by traditional methods and with traditional seeds. Mrs. Nair's generalizations about widespread unresponsiveness to opportunities has not been disproven thus far, though some would argue that those farmers who have remained "traditional" have not had effective opportunities to respond; indeed, the demand for these new inputs has been steadily growing.

What is significant for policy purposes are the *exceptions* to the rule. This minority of farmers has brought India, after centuries of intermittent famine and food shortages, within sight of self-sufficiency in cereals (wheat and rice in particular).[19] These farmers, supporting Schultz's analysis, have been quite responsive to economic incentives, so responsive, indeed, that they have begun to create economic, social, and political problems. Tenants are being put off their land, which landowners now find profitable to operate themselves; laborers are being put out of work by mechanization; and tensions are mounting as a consequence of increasing inequality of incomes.

To achieve the goal of raising food production in India, it has not been necessary to replace traditional cultural values with "modern" ones or to affect the value preferences of all Indian farmers.[20] Significant change could be brought about with more selective and specific measures than those indicated by a cultural explanation of

[18] Little attention has been paid to the consequences of adopting one level of explanation rather than another. One exception is the study of bureaucratic values and behavior in Malaysia by James C. Scott, *Political Ideology in Malaysia* (1968). On the basis of field research, Scott finds serious deficiencies in psycho-cultural modes of explanation, such as that offered by Lucien Pye in *Politics, Personality and Nation Building: Burma's Search for Identity* (1962). Scott opts for a more rationalistic model of behavior, drawing upon and extending Edward Banfield's analysis of behavior in southern Italy (see *The Moral Basis of a Backward Society*, 1958) and

George Foster's explanation of peasant behavior (see "Peasant Society and the Image of the Limited Good," *American Anthropologist*, April 1965).

[19] For an analysis of this, see Lester R. Brown, *Seeds of Change: The Green Revolution and Development in the 1970's* (1970).

[20] In her more recent book, *The Lonely Furrow* (1969), Kusum Nair acknowledges the differential receptivity of Indian farmers, going an interesting step farther to show that receptivity to change is *also* differentially distributed among American farmers. Many of the latter are just as risk-avoiding and conservative in their attitude toward innovation

behavior. For purposes of policy, emphasis is on sufficient, rather than on necessary conditions for change. Particular explanations covering execptions can be more valuable than universal ones stating the rule. One wants to know not so much what is "necessary" as what is "possible" and at what cost. Some levels of explanation make this easier and others make it quite difficult. Many of the popular social, cultural, and psychological explanations are of the latter sort, as Joseph Elder's article reprinted below suggests.[21] In it he shows how few conditions are "necessary" and many things "possible."

As will be discussed later in this introduction, the search for general rules and explanations covering the largest possible number of cases derives its impetus from the nature of the real world, as well as from certain philosophical preconceptions of it. The ubiquitous existence of deviant cases seems to impel social scientists to higher and higher levels of explanation—that is, to more and more abstract analysis. The desire for rules without exceptions leads them to move from analyzing individuals acting to promote their purposes, to larger categories of persons, to even larger categories, and eventually to macro structural and personality explanations of purpose. Extrinsic rather than intrinsic sources of motivation are imputed, and one ends up with explorations of prenatal environments, transcendent historical or cultural forces, and metaphysical concepts such as "function" and "equilibrium."

Policy-oriented social science, in contrast, adopts levels and kinds of explanations that can be tested and verified as a consequence of public choice. It seeks those levels and kinds which can increase the degrees of freedom or expand the opportunities for choice. Political economy is a dismal science when no such degrees or opportunities can be discovered. But our contention is that more such discoveries will be made when levels of explanation are adopted that explore the considerations made by persons themselves and that examine direct causal connections rather than connections that are remote in time and space.

The Variable Productivity of Knowledge.

The common propensity of social scientists to seek higher and higher levels of generality for explanation is associated with a propensity to gather more and more information, in specific research projects and for social science generally. This has been lamented poetically by T. S. Eliot: "Where is the wisdom we have lost in knowledge? Where is the knowledge we have lost in information?" [22] Concerned as we are with the amounts, quality, and meaning of data used in research, we have formulated the rule of "optimal ignorance." This was done to focus attention not only on what one may need to know to give reliable and valid answers to questions relating to public policy, but also on what one may *not* need to know. Ignorance may or may not be bliss, but certain amounts of it are economic, in the broader sense of the word, and therefore advisable. It is interesting that social scientists who have been impressed with the value of sampling theory in statistics

---

as their Indian counterparts. This finding argues, first, for less ethnocentrism in the analysis of development problems and, second, for less preoccupation with cultural differences.

[21] Though we have reason to disagree with Fred Riggs's formulation and analysis of de-velopment problems in numerous respects, we concur completely with his finding that cultural or psychological explanations of behavior in underdeveloped countries are of little use, or even useless. *Administration in Developing Countries*, pp. 66–67 and 84–86.

[22] From *The Rock*, Part I.

have often failed to apply its lessons to their nonstatistical work. Asking what one does *not* need to know is valuable for setting limits and standards of utility for social science inquiry.

Our concern with this matter is prompted in part by the indeterminate—some might say, indiscriminate—collection of information now being urged for social science. Information is not as neutral or transitive as the term "data" suggests. The categories used for organizing data are not equally useful for different purposes. The concrete cases included within a category vary qualitatively and quantitatively, and sometimes both ways. Interpretation of data becomes a serious problem once one moves beyond elementary or superficial analysis. Even "simple" things become complex once one starts analyzing them—for example, what constitutes a "marriage"? The legal definition and official statistics tell us little about the phenomena and consequences associated with this social institution. Voting statistics, the stock in trade of some political scientists, tell us how people voted but not why they voted as they did, and the latter is a matter of equal or greater importance. Economists' data—even on national product or employment, basic and relatively tangible things—depend on the definitions used. All this is said to stress the relativity of information, even that which looks like "hard data." [23] Information has to be considered relative to the analytical purposes it is supposed to serve.

All pursuit of knowledge, and all exposition of it, have costs as well as benefits.[24] There are costs of collecting, collating, and evaluating information, and the phenomenon of diminishing marginal productivity relates to information as it does to other resources. As more and more information is gathered with respect to a particular topic or problem, diminishing returns invariably set in at some point. In any productive enterprise, information is one of the complementary factors of production; increasing it out of proportion to the other resources available for using the additional information means that its productivity begins to decline beyond some point. To some extent, information can substitute for other resources, but the convertibility is limited. Where further increments of information cease to increase one's ability or accuracy in problem-solving, it is hard to see how accumulating or presenting more information can be justified. We cannot, and do not, suggest any general rules for determining this "optimizing" point, which is entirely relative to the particular inquiry and the costs and benefits of information for it.[25] But we be-

[23] On this point we would like to cite a report from the Inter-University Consortium for Political Research, based at the Survey Research Center of the University of Michigan. Referring to the problems of comparing variables from diverse political units (using only demographic and election data), it was noted that "variables often measure only approximately the same thing in different nations, or indeed within a nation at different times. . . . The Consortium has, through its several years of archival data collection, found that prior expert opinion about the condition of data and its documentation has been quite astoundingly wrong." Cited by Charles Metzner, "Data Banks: Fundamental Considerations," *American Journal of Public Health* 60 (October 1970): 1988.

[24] We are not including here consideration of certain "costs" of knowledge which Albert Hirschman treated in his book, *Development Projects Observed* (1967). He suggested that foreknowledge of all the risks, costs, and uncertainties involved in development projects would inhibit decision-makers from going ahead with projects which, once undertaken, they could salvage, make productive, and even learn from so as to promote subsequent development more effectively. If they had full knowledge, they would not attempt what they ought to. Hirschman does not argue for complete ignorance of risks, costs, and uncertainties; this would lead to undertaking some unsalvageable projects. Rather, he is arguing for what could be called "optimal ignorance."

[25] This problem has been explored in microeconomic terms for business enterprises, using econometric analysis to estimate the point where the costs of obtaining additional infor-

lieve that even one's awareness of the hypothetical existence of such a point will improve research design and implementation.

Our arguments in favor of "optimal ignorance" should not be taken to exclude all "basic" research in social science—that is, descriptive examination of economic, social, political, and other phenomena. Clearly, prescription cannot be attempted usefully without considerable prior description. But, we would contend, the process of description itself benefits from the discipline imposed by an orientation to policy considerations. Description justified for its own sake can lead to excessive amounts of information that is of little use to anybody. Relating it to policy studies provides some guidance to how much information is needed and whether the concepts and categories employed have any utility in particular situations. If there is little or no utility to be derived from them, one can question how correct they are. But this concern leads us beyond consideration of levels of explanation and amounts of information most advisable for social science inquiries to a consideration of the epistemological foundations of social science.[26]

AN EXISTENTIAL SOCIAL SCIENCE

There appear to us to be two contending and hitherto insufficiently examined intellectual traditions in social science: essentialist and existential. They stem from different epistemological solutions to the problem of comprehending the real world in all its complexity, ambiguity, and uncertainty.[27] The first, which has been dominant in social science, inclines one to abstract, generalize, and seek "first causes," to account for outcomes in terms of the *essence* of things rather than their interaction. The second tradition is oriented more toward problems of *choice,* taking into account the goals and capabilities of persons as well as the uniqueness of situations in which persons find themselves.

Both traditions involve analysis, and both are concerned with causation; but the first orients work toward description, while the latter orients it toward prescription. The first views outcomes as determined *ex ante,* before the fact, because of the "nature" of the actors and system; the latter sees them rather as being "necessary" only *ex post,* or after the fact. Actors always face constraints, but these are not

---

mation to improve decisions exceed the benefits from that information. See W. J. Baumol and R. E. Quandt, "Rules of Thumb and Optimally Imperfect Decisions," *American Economic Review* 54 (March 1964): 23–46.

[26] The term "epistemological" and its noun, "epistemology," may sound imposing or complicated to those unfamiliar with them, but they are reasonably straightforward, referring to the theory of knowledge. Put less formally, they refer to how we know what we know (or how we know that we know what we think we know). Such considerations are commonly ignored by social scientists. A related term, "ontology," is also important, referring to the theory of being or to consideration of what is the nature of things in the real world. Do they "exist" in their own right or only in our perception of them? Are they ephemeral or lasting? One need not become preoccupied with such questions, but one's ontological premises, often implicit and unexamined, greatly influence inquiry into social phenomena.

[27] The two traditions can be traced and attributed to Plato and Aristotle, respectively, and their contending views of what constituted the "essence" of a thing—that quality which it shared with all other things like it (its ideal form) or those qualities which made it individual, concrete, and unique. Elaboration of this as well as other epistemological issues pertaining to the distinction between essentialist and existential social science would sidetrack our consideration here, and we will deal with this elsewhere. For a concise and critical examination of the Platonist-Aristotelian difference, see B. A. G. Fuller, *A History of Philosophy,* Vol. I, esp. pp. 128–135 and 367 ff.

necessarily physical ones. Rather they commonly arise as a matter of values. Does it "cost" too much to achieve a particular end? The interaction of actors' alternatives and valuations is complex, and it is possible that estimations of net cost or benefit—and willingness to undertake or abstain from certain action—can be affected *ex ante*. In both traditions, probabilities are weighed, but in one these are regarded as relatively fixed. In the other, existential social science, these are regarded as dependent variables to be affected rather than as independent variables determining outcomes.

In the final analysis, the distinction we make between the two traditions is, indeed, more analytical than concrete, and in fact our effort to distinguish between them is an "essentialist" exercise. The relationship is more dialectical than polar, but we find that many shortcomings of contemporary social science can be illuminated by posing the distinction, which has been demonstrated so potently by Albert Hirschman in the article reprinted on pages 64–73.

For an understanding of the real world some abstraction and generalization are necessary exercises. Concepts, models, and general rules have their uses; this we do not question.[28] The question is, what use shall be made of them? We believe that social scientists working in the essentialist tradition are inclined to use them too broadly, in the process often obscuring more of importance than they explain. Although they are only products of the mind and have no concrete existence or meaning, concepts like "one-party state," "traditional values," or "subsistence farmers" are generally accorded reality by social scientists and take on a life of their own.

We would distinguish between concepts and categories, preferring the latter as analytical tools, though recognizing that the distinction itself is a matter of definition and thus essentialist.[29] Categories can be misused also, but one is usually less inclined to reify categories, unless they are as concrete as "male" and "female." The instrumental nature of categories, seen as convenient and illuminating aggregations of phenomena, is, we think, not so easily forgotten. Thus, in the new political economy, we are dealing with categories that group concrete activities, attitudes, and relationships, rather than with concepts that introduce abstractions into the analysis.

For example, grouping states with only one party in order to analyze any common consequences involves fewer assumptions about the homogeneity of the cases thus categorized than conceptualizing them and postulating in effect "one-party-state-ness" as significant in itself, having certain necessary consequences due to the essence of one-party states. No such essence is sought or discovered in existential social science. Cases are grouped for purposes of analysis, to ascertain predictable patterns or outcomes, but the latter are seen as more contingent than necessary, not flowing from any intrinsic abstract nature which the cases have in common.

There should be no assumption that states with only one legal political party are necessarily intolerant of civil liberties, for example. Although intolerance may be a common concomitant, there are exceptions, and the circumstances under which

---

[28] Although the argument can be extended to justify rampant essentialism, we would note our agreement with Karl Deutsch that "we are using models, willingly or not, whenever we are trying to think systematically about anything at all" ("On Communications Models in the Social Sciences," *Public Opinion Quarterly* 16 [Fall 1952]: 356).

[29] Myrdal noted some years ago that even heretics cannot avoid using orthodox terms in formulating their heresies. *Economic Theory and Under-Developed Regions* (1957), pp. 129 ff. We see our views as heterodox rather than heretical, but still cannot criticize essentialist social science without employing essentialist reasoning.

such exceptions are found are interesting and important, not abnormal or aberrant. Nothing is gained by conceptualizing "democratic one-party states" as contrasted to "authoritarian one-party states" in order to handle anomalous cases. This leads to an infinite proliferation of terms whose explanatory power is purchased by giving up the generality that is the basic rationale for concepts.

Neither should there be any assumption that "traditional values" are antithetical to change or that "subsistence farmers" are not efficient producers. If one wishes, he may group certain values in a category called "traditional," or farmers in one called "subsistence," for analytical purposes. But he need not and should not assume that this categorization accounts for the phenomena, that exceptions are somehow illegitimate, or that the generally observed relationships are "natural" or immutable. Nothing in the "essence" of "traditional values" or "subsistence farmers" determines present or future behavior conclusively. Those social scientists concerned with development especially need intellectual tools that do not foreclose change by presuming that whatever "is" is necessary.

This position does not imply that the social universe is indeterminate with no knowable causation. The problem for social scientists is one of establishing the source of causation. There is no question that choices and actions can be traced always to individuals, but by focusing on interaction rather than on essence, one assesses opportunities and constraints in terms of persons' valuations rather than treating the values as somehow determinant, so that choices and actions are a function of the "kind" of person or group involved.

There is also no question that some aggregation, some generalization, are necessary for deriving some predictive knowledge about the world in order to act to affect outcomes *ex ante*. But this is done quite instrumentally, and the attributes of a class of things that they have in common are not deemed important in themselves so as to mitigate other aspects or aspirations. The attributes according to which one groups cases, such as "single-party systems," represent only one aspect of the individual or phenomenon. When these attributes are taken to stand for and to determine the whole, the problems of reification and tautology arise.

These problems are the cardinal sins of social science, which an existential perspective should avoid by minimizing the role of conceptualization and definition in analysis. The focus on interaction of alternatives and valuations, on choices and consequences, gives a quite different slant. Though in the absence of any significant change in the existing environment there may be a .8 probability of a particular outcome, what social science should seek to establish are what actions will raise that probability if the outcome is desired, or reduce it if undesired. In the "sociosphere," unlike the laboratory, outcomes can be affected by modifying people's estimations of their net costs or benefits from a particular course of action. Thus, the knowledge sought is pertinent to an *ex ante* calculus of economic, social, and political consequences of choice.

Existential social science involves more rather than less of our intellectual faculties. The role of reason is not diminished by reducing the place of abstraction in social analysis. Indeed, by disallowing the oversimplification and overgeneralization which abstraction encourages, the role of reason is, we think, enhanced. Uses of ideal-types, dichotomous or trichotomous 4-, 6-, or 9-cell matrices, correlation coefficients, or factor analyses, with a view to description rather than prescription, tax the mind with respect to their elegance but not their relevance. Examples of a more "existential" approach in social science can be pointed to, but they are as yet unfortunately not very numerous.[30]

TWO SOCIAL SCIENCE PITFALLS

Two concomitants of the prevailing social science that bear on the analysis of development should be considered before concluding this introduction. Economists, sociologists, and political scientists have often, we think, misconstrued development in various ways. They have approached problems of development from only one disciplinary perspective; they have been concerned with "pure" and not "applied" social science; and they have adopted essentialist epistemology and methodologies. A further reason is that they have either accepted or propounded explanations that we would consider "intellectually neo-colonial," or they have succumbed to the compulsions of the "religion of development." Both pitfalls can be avoided, and they can more easily be avoided if social scientists share and employ the perspective and orientation we have been advocating.

Intellectual Neo-Colonialism.

In trying to explain differences among nations with respect to wealth and political well-being, many social scientists in the 1950s and 1960s assumed that poverty and political instability in the Third World originated in some defects in local character or in the failure of "native" institutions. At the same time, they assumed that the Western world's productivity and political stability, exemplified by affluence and a presumed absence of violence, were the consequence of Western virtues or of the genius of Western institutions. Too little achievement motivation, not enough universalism, too much affectivity and ascription, insufficient interest aggregation and articulation, or blocked throughputs were thought to distinguish poor nations from rich ones and to explain the difference.

We would concur with Gunnar Myrdal's indictment in *Asian Drama* of this transference of responsibility from the rich to the poor. The concepts and methodology used in Western social science research have been "well fitted to the rationalization of opportunistic interests both in the developed Western countries and among the influential intellectual elite of the underdeveloped countries themselves." Exaggerated emphasis on presumed "impediments" to change, he says, has served Western interests. "It explained away their responsibility for the backwardness of colonial peoples and their failure to try to improve matters." [31]

---

[30] Albert Hirschman's work, *Development Projects Observed,* has contributed as thoughtfully as any work to an understanding of how foreign aid can contribute to the processes of development. He employed neither detailed case studies nor typological models of a general sort, unostentatiously bridging the gap between the particular and the general. (See esp. pp. 3–8.) We would point also to Michel Crozier's work on the French bureaucracy, *The Bureaucratic Phenomenon* (1964), from what he calls a "phenomenological" perspective. (See p. 3.) Hans Morgen-

thau's now-classic work, *Politics Among Nations* (5th ed., 1965), presents a powerful intellectual justification for what we would consider an "existential" perspective in social science. (See chaps. 1 and 2.)

[31] Myrdal reproaches social scientists for not taking seriously the "sociology of knowledge" in their own profession. Of particular concern are inappropriate conceptual categories, derived and imported from Western studies, which often obscure the most salient problems and relationships. These categories when used to gather statistics introduce further errors;

Too seldom have economists, sociologists, and political scientists thought through the implications of their theories of development in terms of their justification of the status quo—the existing economic and political stratification of nations and of groups within nations—or their rationalization of intervention by the strong in the affairs of the weak. Too often these theories have contributed to intellectual neo-colonialism, even if the effect was unintended. Economic theories stressing capital formation, even if this means suppressing incomes of the poor, can be seen to have this effect if we compare them, as Myrdal does, with long-discredited mercantilist theory.[32] Sociological and psychological theories that emphasize the "uniqueness" of people and cultures in Third World countries have a similar effect, blaming the impoverished for their poverty.[33]

The neo-colonizing effect of various political theories is less obvious, but the premise that the majority is unable to govern itself and that an elite must "lead the way" can be seen to legitimate the dominance of educated, wealthy, and generally privileged groups within Third World countries. These elite groups commonly have close connections with foreign countries and promote the latters' interests, as well as their own, more effectively than the interests of the "masses" in these countries. These "masses" are regarded as inert, incompetent, or unruly, according to the situation, but invariably as "wards" of the elite.[34]

Like the evangelical ministers in the early nineteenth century who told the London poor that they were so because of defects in their character or imperfections in their faith, many political scientists, sociologists, and economists have argued that Third World countries are backward because of defects in the character or beliefs of their peoples. Rather than consider the proposition, for instance, that India is poor in spite of caste (or that in the context of great poverty caste assured a relatively more equitable distribution of wealth), the argument has been made and widely accepted that India's poverty had its origins in the caste system and

---

"the resulting mountains of statistics have either no meaning or a meaning other than that imputed to them. . . . The very fact that the researcher gets figures to play with tends to confirm his original biased approach." See Myrdal's Prologue in *Asian Drama,* "The Beam in Our Eyes," pp. 5–35, esp. pp. 16–24.

[32] Colonial economic policy was greatly influenced by mercantilism, says Myrdal, pointing out that in both, the main purpose of labor policy was "to assure employers of an adequate labor force available on favorable terms." He cites Edgar S. Furniss's observation that "the Mercantilist did not perceive that the poverty of the majority was incompatible with the wealth of the whole; quite the contrary; he came to believe that the majority must be kept in poverty in order that the whole might be rich" (*The Position of the Labourer in a System of Nationalism* [1920], p. 7). See Myrdal, *op. cit.,* pp. 966 ff. Many contemporary Western economists have found different and less direct reasons for reaching this same conclusion.

[33] Rarely in the literature on underdeveloped countries has uniqueness been argued or demonstrated without some imputation of inferiority vis-à-vis the West. A prominent example

of this is Pye's book, *Politics, Personality and Nation Building,* which offers an encompassing explanation of Burmese political and administrative behavior in psycho-cultural terms. For a critique of such approaches, see Myrdal, *op. cit.,* pp. 981 ff. It is ironic and unfortunate that, despite his very perceptive critique, Myrdal himself cannot avoid showing a "beam" in his own eye from time to time, however sophisticated the rationale, e.g., pp. 61–62.

[34] A stark formulation of this view is presented in I. R. Sinai, *The Challenge of Modernisation* (1964), in which he speaks of "a new elite of reformers and innovators" who can impose very heavy costs upon their people, force-marching them into the modern world. Most statements of elitist development strategies are more circumspect. Surprisingly few critiques of their premises or consequences are to be found in the literature. For polemical but serious critiques, see Frantz Fanon's discussion of the "national bourgeoisie" in *The Wretched of the Earth* (1962); and Paul Baran's consideration of the comprador elite in *The Political Economy of Growth* (1957), pp. 205 ff.; also Noam Chomsky, *American Power and the New Mandarins* (1968).

attendant institutions and values. A range of factors more closely linked to India's colonial past and its consequences is virtually excluded from consideration.[35]

We are not prepared to maintain that India's poverty should be blamed wholly on British colonization. The few empirical studies of the economic consequences of colonialism have had conceptual or methodological flaws or have shown mixed results. But neither are we prepared to ignore, as is too often the case, the extent to which India's poverty and Britain's wealth are related. More is involved than simply the respective values and institutions of the two countries. And where in the Third World no colonial relationship exists or has existed, poverty still has various sources other than simply culture and personality. One should not ignore the asymmetry of bargaining power in world trade between rich and poor countries in which the benefits from trade accrue more readily to the former than to the latter.

Intellectual neo-colonialism, then, by placing responsibility for underdevelopment wholly on the people, culture, and institutions of underdeveloped countries, has the consequence of justifying the existing economic and political stratification of the world. We would not argue that this responsibility rests wholly with the developed countries; the blame for underdevelopment is widely shared. Ascertaining the balance of blame is not our intention. We are interested in the mechanics of development to the end that it can best be promoted. However, we are concerned that social scientists working at abstract levels of explanation and inundated with "information" may not recognize or face up to the consequences of their work, which contributes to scholastic fatalism and immobilism.

We would agree with most of the criticisms made of American social science by Moskos and Bell, but we would not attribute its faults so definitely to the ideologies of American social scientists.[36] Rather we would argue that the epistemology they have adopted has diverted attention from the real world and its real problems. The counsel inferred from social science which is oriented to "first causes" and "fundamental" explanations is likely to advise only very large changes, suggesting that the character, culture, and consciousness of millions of people must be altered, not just modified. Partial or incremental measures giving these people greater incentives or greater means are eschewed as "superficial," since changing their *capacity* to act is judged less important than changing their *will* to act. If these people are given greater means, it is thought that they will not choose to act in a proper or productive way, hence tutelary relationships of one sort or another are justified, and hence our designation of this thinking or analysis as "neo-colonial."

There are epistemological as well as practical reasons for not seeking "first causes." We have no way of knowing that the extended family, Hindu values, or Burmese children's toilet training account for the situations we find today, or that altering these will have the desired intended effects. A policy orientation is advised for social scientists because it prompts them to look at what policies—of colonial and independent governments—have done in underdeveloped countries and at what policies can do to make situations correspond more to preferred conditions. This is not to say that effective policies can invariably be devised or pursued, but

---

[35] Myrdal lays considerable emphasis on factors associated with caste in India, but he does point out how Britain's colonial economic policies disadvantaged India vis-à-vis the "mother country." As if it were not enough that India's industrial development, which had begun prior to colonization, was held back by discriminatory colonial policies, most of the burden for financing colonial rule was also imposed upon Indians. See pp. 453 ff. in Myrdal, *op. cit.*

[36] See Charles Moskos and Wendell Bell, "Emerging Nations and Ideologies of American Social Scientists," *The American Sociologist* (May 1967), pp. 67–72.

it does put aside the fatalism and immobilism which can make social science generally more dismal than economics.

The Religion of Development.

A second concomitant of the prevailing orientation of social science is what may be called, admittedly somewhat facetiously, "the religion of development." Like any religion, the religion of development provides its believers with a world view that defines empirical situations in terms of saints and sinners, transcendent moving forces, appropriate and inappropriate acts, and the sequence of activity most laudable and rewarding. By simplifying reality, the religion allows its adherents to confront this reality more confidently, if not necessarily more effectively. Moreover, it gives them scapegoats; failures can be charged off to various devils or to faults in character.

We can best illustrate the essential features of this "religion" by suggesting parallels between it and other sacred or secular religions in table 1.[37] The analogy is proposed, not to proclaim the existence of a religion of development, but rather to consider how certain "religious" qualities of contemporary "belief" in development doctrine serve to limit the effectiveness of social science. That the analogy is weak in several respects is itself instructive.

TABLE 1

SUGGESTIVE SCHEMATIC PARALLELS AMONG SACRED AND SECULAR RELIGIONS

	Christianity	Communism	Nationalism	Development
The Force of Creation (Alpha)	Jehovah	Dialectical materialism	Destiny of the nation	Science and technology
The Source of Salvation	Messiah	Karl Marx	The "Father of the Country"	Industrialization
The Recipients of Grace	Elect	Proletariat	Colonized	Poor and under-privileged
The Source of Opposition	Devil	Capitalists	Colonialists	(see text)
The Agency for Progress	Church	Party (Communist)	Nationalist movement	Planning Commission (USAID)
Decisive Event	Second Coming	Revolution	Independence	Economic takeoff
The Show-down	Last Judgment	Expropriation of the expropriators	Expulsion of colonialists	(see text)
The Final Age (Omega)	Millennium	Communist commonwealth	National sovereignty	High-consumption mass society

[37] This table was prepared with inspiration from, and apologies to, Lord Bertrand Russell; see *The History of Western Philosophy* (1946), p. 383.

While there is great clarity about Good in this scheme—higher gross national product, longer life expectancy, full employment, or universal education—there is some ambivalence about Evil in this "religion." Whereas other faiths, Christianity, Communism, and nationalism, define the obstacles to spiritual, economic, or political progress as persons, the religion of development tends to focus on impersonal enemies such as "tradition" and "backwardness." True, feudal oligarchies and landed aristocracies are regarded as "bad," but most attention is given to institutions or resource deficiencies such as the extended family or a shortage of mineral fuels.

As sects within this religion, planners and social scientists have each somewhat different rituals and dogmas, but so do Catholics and Protestants, or Stalinists and Trotskyists. Planners are unlikely, for very practical reasons, to put themselves in opposition to powerful, privileged groups within their societies. Thus, concentrating on hunger, disease, and illiteracy as impersonal enemies has considerable rationale. Resources are expended in an effort to eliminate these, while economic, social, and political structures are either ignored or disturbed only marginally. Social scientists, on the other hand, have less salient reasons for not dealing with questions of power and privilege and for seeking "first causes" that divert attention to the macro variables of culture or personality as obstacles to development. These factors, which are beyond the reach of planners' "good works," suggest a modern version of the credo "salvation by faith alone." Faith in "modern" patterns of thought and social organization is preached, but little can be done directly, since these things cannot be readily altered by available policy instruments. There is accordingly little deliberate impact on the status quo.

The religion of development fails to match the others as a religion in that it arouses much less fervor, except perhaps among the "priesthood" of planners and social scientists. The absence of personalized enemies can account for this at least in part; it is more difficult to mobilize persons against an impersonalized evil than against a personal one. More significant an explanation, however, may be the lack of success thus far in bringing development's succor to the majority of persons. In the first years when the "gospel of development" was preached, some popular passion was aroused. But it now appears that the populace has little faith either in the doctrines of the religion or in the rituals of its practitioners. The latter continue, nevertheless, to manifest considerable commitment to the various orthodoxies of development.

It is these orthodoxies which we find objectionable, not any external resemblances to religion such as we have suggested. What we take to be the religion of development prejudges the world, favoring that which is "modern" and castigating that which is "traditional," exalting the elite and deprecating the "backward" masses. The world is not seen or understood in terms of maximizing opportunities or of making them. Orthodoxy drives out innovation; it makes for unwillingness to form unusual alliances, to pursue unorthodox policies, or to pursue orthodox ones in novel sequences. In promoting development, persons previously judged to be "sinners" need sometimes to be treated as "saints," and vice versa.[38] In some situations or under some circumstances, it is quite possible that extended families would encourage savings and investment, that tribal associations would provide modern social services, or that the modernizing elite of a country would be factionalized or

[38] Two of the most interesting recent books in this regard are Lloyd I. Rudolph and Susanne Hoeber Rudolph, *The Modernity of Tradition: Political Development in India* (1967); and C. S. Whitaker, *The Politics of Tradition: Continuity and Change in Northern Nigeria, 1946–1966* (1969).

self-serving. The compulsive policies advocated by adherents of the religion of development may produce martyrs and achieve some measure of "salvation" for these adherents, but the policies may well contribute little or nothing to relieving the poverty of nations.

That so many well-meaning and intelligent social scientists should have contributed to intellectual neo-colonialism and the religion of development, when their objective was supposed to be assistance to underdeveloped countries, requires some explanation. Our intention here is neither to impugn nor exonerate the work of other social scientists, since we are more concerned here with the consequences than the motivations of choice. By making clearer the implications of certain kinds of analysis, we expect that more beneficent and productive modes of analysis will subsequently be chosen.

A feature which intellectual neo-colonialism and the religion of development have in common is a prejudgment of situations on the basis of fixed attributes and predetermined courses, reflexive casting of actors in "modernizing" or "traditional" roles, with *a priori* preference or exclusion of certain policy options. We are very much in accord with Albert Hirschman's analysis of "Obstacles to Development: A Classification and a Quasi-Vanishing Act" and have reprinted it on pages 55–62 because it puts so well the case for a social science that avoids prejudgment of problems and solutions.

This long discourse on social science has been an extended introduction to our ideas and others' on development. It has been presented to make clear our perspective on the analysis of development and to advocate a particular approach to social science, one that will make it more justifiable not only to social scientists but also to the contemporary equivalents of philosophers and kings.

•

Toward a
Supradisciplinary
Social Science

•

"ALL THE social sciences are studying essentially the same system, which I have called the 'sociosphere,'" writes Kenneth Boulding. In "The Legitimacy of Economics" below he discusses the origins of political economy and the specialized discipline of economics. He considers the shortcomings of this latter discipline when problems of the "sociosphere" and even of the "econosphere" are dealt with, and he attributes its deficiencies to the narrow delimitation of the discipline and to the excessive use of abstraction.

Boulding's analysis of "legitimacy" by way of introduction to his critique of economics is also important for our consideration in that he treats legitimacy as a resource, in effect as a factor of economic, social, or political production. Possession of legitimacy enables persons to get goods and services, esteem and deference or compliance without (or with less) expenditure of other resources. The elaboration and testing of Boulding's analysis could lead to a body of theory pertaining to legitimacy as a factor of production analogous to capital theory or labor theory in economics. His analysis here is a good example of supradisciplinary endeavor.

There are important contemporary reasons for rediscovering and refurbishing "the ancient and honorable hybrid discipline" called political economy. James Coleman accepts the definition of political economy as "a modern social science dealing with the interrelationship of political and economic processes," but he is not averse to extending it to include social processes as well. In his conclusion he advocates a joint analysis of economic and political feasibility, leading to what we have called "aggregate optimality." This requires a perspective such as that acquired with the new political economy.

THE LEGITIMACY OF ECONOMICS

KENNETH E. BOULDING

University of Colorado

The problem of legitimacy has been surprisingly neglected by social scientists, and especially by economists. This is perhaps because legitimacy is something which we take for granted, when we have it, almost without question and when we do not have it the system falls apart with such rapidity that there is no time to investigate it. The whole dynamics of legitimacy is subject to "step functions" and sharp, discontinuous changes. Here, indeed, *natura facit saltum,* and the economist who is accustomed to continuous functions and smooth changes finds himself in very unfamiliar territory.

I am using the word legitimacy to cover a fairly wide range of social phenomena, all of which, however, center around the concept of acceptance of an institution or an organization as right, proper, justified and acceptable. Without legitimacy no institution or organization can exist, and no continuous series of like operations can be conducted. I am thus using the term in a much wider sense than it is sometimes used in political science, in the sense of formal legitimacy, for instance, the succession of a monarch. It is a wider concept also than that of legality, even though legality and legitimacy are closely related. An institution can be legitimate, however, without being legal, and it can be legal without being legitimate, although unless the law is legitimate, it cannot really function as an organizer of society.

Legitimacy has two aspects, internal and external. Internal legitimacy is roughly equivalent to morale, or "nerve" in the sense in which the word is used in the expression "the loss of nerve." Internal legitimacy is the belief on the part of an individual actor that the role which he is performing is acceptable and justified to himself. A loss of internal legitimacy leads to disorganization of behavior and an inability to perform an assigned role. Unless a person feels that what he is doing is justified he cannot continue to do it, and if he is forced to do it through threats he will sabotage his own behavior, even unconsciously.

Internal legitimacy has both a short-run and a long-run aspect. In its long-run aspect a person may feel that his whole life is legitimate, successful, and gratifying by his own standards, or he may feel quite the reverse. Even a person who has a low opinion of his whole life pattern, however, may feel that what he is doing on a particular day or a particular week may be entirely legitimate and he may function effectively in the short run. The relationships here can be enormously complex because of the different levels of self-awareness and self-examination, each with a value pattern of its own. Thus, at one level, a person may believe himself to be a "heel," at another level he may feel quite justified in being a heel and act correspondingly with high morale.

The other aspect of legitimacy is external legitimacy, that is, acceptance on the part of persons in the environment. Every organization exists in an environment of persons, and unless on the whole they regard it as legitimate it cannot survive. An institution like the stock exchange, for instance, can survive in the United States because it is fairly widely regarded as legitimate. In the Soviet Union it cannot survive because it is regarded as illegitimate. Internal and external legitimacy are of course related in complex ways. A strong sense of internal legitimacy tends to create external legitimacy. A person who has confidence in himself tends to create confidence in others. Self-hatred, on the other hand, tends to produce hatred on the part of others. Conversely, if external legitimacy declines—if an institution becomes less acceptable to people in its environment —internal legitimacy will probably decline also.

The distinction between internal and external legitimacy can be applied not only

From *Western Economic Journal* (September 1967), pp. 299–307. Reprinted by permission.

to persons but to any subsystem of the total society. Thus an organization or even a profession may be said to have high or low morale, simply because there are widely shared attitudes on the part of those people who are associated with it.

The dynamics of the system of legitimacy depends very much on information flows among persons and segments of the society and is particularly affected by cognitive dissonance. If a person's image of himself is different from the image which he infers from the behavior of others, a strain is set up in the system, and if this strain becomes large enough the system will change. The discontinuities which are so apparent in the history of legitimacy, especially the sudden collapses, arise because internal legitimacy has very strong inner defenses. It can stand therefore a large amount of cognitive dissonance before it finally breaks. The stronger the internal defenses, however, the more dramatic the break when it finally occurs.

In a previous paper [1] I have outlined six possible sources of legitimacy as follows:

1. Positive payoffs. An institution or an organization which is perceived as having positive payoffs both for its participants and for the people in its environment is more likely to achieve legitimacy, especially in the long run, than institutions with low or negative payoffs. Where the positive payoffs are clear and obvious, legitimacy is easily established and hard to threaten.

2. Negative payoffs. The situation unfortunately is enormously complicated by the fact that, especially where payoffs are complicated, ambiguous, and hard to perceive, negative payoffs as well as positive payoffs may establish legitimacy. An institution which is legitimate has the capacity to demand sacrifice, that is, negative payoffs. This means, however, that we easily fall into what I have called a "sacrifice trap." If we once begin making sacrifices for something, the admission that the sacrifices were in vain would be a threat to our internal legitimacy. Hence we tend to create the integrative relationship which would justify the sacrifices.

People make sacrifices, for instance, for a king, or for their country, or for their religion. Even though these sacrifices may originally have been made in the expectation of eventual positive payoffs, where these payoffs are vague, abstract, hard to perceive, or perhaps in the distant future, the sacrifices have to be justified in the present in terms of the establishment of what might be called a legitimacy of sacredness. Sacrifices create sacredness and sacredness justifies sacrifices. In this way the blood of the martyrs becomes the seed of the church, the blood of the soldiers becomes the seed of the state, the tears of the children the seed of the family, the anguish of education the seed of the professions, and so on.

The sacrifice trap phenomenon again contributes to the discontinuity of legitimacy. The pattern here is that sacrifice creates legitimacy, which demands more sacrifice, which creates more legitimacy, and this process goes on building up until somebody finally says, "To hell with it," and the whole institution collapses. We saw this happen to the medieval church in the Reformation, we have seen it happen to the institutions of monarchy and empire. We see it begin to happen in the Communist Party; we may even see this happen in the national state. A sacred institution which says, "Ask not," can get away with it for a long time, until finally somebody asks!

3. Another dimension of legitimacy is the time dimension itself. Here we seem to have a nonlinear relationship; the new thing has a certain legitimacy of its own, simply because it is new. As time goes on it loses legitimacy and becomes old-fashioned. If it can survive this trough, however, it will eventually become an antique and its legitimacy will rise again. Any institution that has been around for a long time has legitimacy simply because of habit. A good deal depends on the general attitudes of the society. There are societies in which age is venerated and societies which are worshippers of youth. There are societies in which things are regarded as good simply because they are old, and societies in which things are regarded as good simply because they are new. The question as to what produces these progressive or conservative attitudes is a puzzling one, and as far as I know little work has been done on it.

4. Another source of legitimacy is mystery and charisma. We often regard as legitimate what we do not understand or what we only dimly understand. Both church, state, and the professions derive

a certain amount of legitimacy from this source.

5. Another source of legitimacy which is closely related to the preceding source is communication through the accepted symbols of legitimacy. This is closely related to what Adam Smith called "state" in the sense of the word "stately." Impressive buildings, rituals, clothing, incense, music, dance, art, architecture, and so on are devoted in no small part to creating the symbols of legitimacy. An economist might almost define a legitimacy industry as a segment of the economy engaged in producing these symbols. Here again, however, the relationship between the source and the product may be quite nonlinear. Up to a point expenditure on the symbols of legitimacy produces it; beyond it, however, it may destroy it, and there seems to be a certain tendency for institutions to overreach themselves in this regard. The magnificence of St. Peter's in Rome may have contributed to producing the Reformation. A king frequently builds himself a magnificent palace just before he is deposed. The university that builds itself a cathedral of learning may soon find itself in severe financial trouble. The *nouveau riche* who builds himself a magnificent mansion may live to regret it.

6. The sixth source of legitimacy consists of alliances and associations with other legitimacies. Legitimacy, as it were, is something that rubs off, and if a less legitimate institution can ally itself with a more legitimate one, the legitimacy of both may even be increased. The frequent alliance of church and state is an example of this phenomenon. The Pope crowns the Emperor; the Archbishop crowns the King; and even the President of the United States is sworn in on the Bible.

This has been a very long introduction but we now have enough in the way of a theory of legitimacy to apply it to the specific problem of this paper, which is the problem of the legitimacy of economics as a science or a discipline, and the legitimacy of economics as a profession. As a discipline, economics is certainly not much more than 200 years old and as a profession about 150 years old. Perhaps we should credit Sir James Steuart with the invention of the idea of political economy as a discipline, but we must certainly credit Adam Smith with being its founder.

The first economists were those who first read *The Wealth of Nations*. For a generation these perhaps represented rather widely scattered individuals. In the early years of the 19th century, however, these individuals came together into an "invisible college" linked by personal friendship and epistolatory communication. Ricardo, Malthus, James Mill, Nassau Senior and a number of lesser lights formed an intellectual community arising very largely out of the stimulus provided by Adam Smith's *Wealth of Nations*. They constituted, as it were, a kind of "early church" of economics.

Legitimization comes fairly rapidly. The first professor of political economy is Nassau Senior at Oxford, and from this point on professors of political economy multiply. Eventually, departments of economics are formed. In less than a hundred years we have the Royal Economic Society, the American Economic Association and now we have an International Economic Association. The various councils of economic advisers which have sprung up in almost all the western countries, at least, since the end of the Second World War represent what might almost be called a Constantinization of economics.

What we have witnessed, therefore, is a constant rise in the legitimacy of economics, interrupted, however, by what might be called the great schism under Karl Marx, who established another line of legitimacy, denying the legitimacy of the older line. The parallels with the history of almost any religion are quite striking, and we can see the rise of economics as a dynamic process, within what I have elsewhere called the integrative system, following the patterns of many such processes.

If now we ask ourselves what have been the sources of this rise in legitimacy the previous analysis may be helpful. In the first place, economics unquestionably produced a complex network of positive payoffs. In an intellectual movement intellectual payoffs themselves are important, and *The Wealth of Nations,* for instance, unquestionably provided these. Even today reading *The Wealth of Nations* carefully can produce intellectual rewards in terms of insight, answers to questions which have been previously puzzling, and even the sheer intellectual pleasure of watching a very great mind at work, which are by no

means negligible. These intellectual rewards depend a good deal on a kind of
"readiness" but the men of the enlightenment were clearly ready for Adam Smith.
The alliance with other legitimacies is
noticeable here, as in a sense Adam Smith
represents an alliance of the social sciences
with the great legitimacy of the Newtonian
system. Enlightenment itself is an enormous payoff, and in association with other
enlightenments is a great source of legitimacy.

There were payoffs also to people outside the profession which created external
legitimacy. Adam Smith not only had an
enormous self-confidence and a great deal
of internal legitimacy, but he also acted as
a legitimizer for classes in the society
whose power was rising. It is a paradox,
indeed, that Adam Smith acted as a legitimator for many people whom he regarded
as rather illegitimate, such as the rising
merchant class, which was, on the whole,
despised by Adam Smith himself. Nevertheless, the notions of natural liberty which
fitted so clearly into the Newtonian system of a cosmic order were highly gratifying to the new merchants and manufacturers of the Industrial Revolution who
chafed at medieval restrictions and who
used the great lamp of the Enlightenment
to rout out the creatures of medieval mystery and darkness. Legitimacy is often a
matter of being in the right place at the
right time with the right idea. In this regard
Adam Smith was lucky. If he had come
100 years earlier, his ideas would have
fallen on deaf ears.

A similar happy combination of time,
place and idea accounts for the rise of the
legitimacy of the Keynesian economics.
This came along at a time when the system of neo-classical economics in the western countries seemed quite incapable of
producing payoffs in the way of solving
the problem of unemployment. Keynes
again produced "an enlightenment," a kind
of Copernican revolution which seemed to
make soluble a problem which had previously been regarded even by the professionals as virtually insoluble. In those societies where development had proceeded
far enough that the Marxist solution was
unacceptable, the Keynesian ideas came as
an enormous relief, and their payoffs have
certainly been considerable. If anyone
doubts this, he has only to contrast the

experience of those twenty years after the
First World War with the twenty years
after the Second. The first period, in which
economic policy was guided largely by
neo-classical considerations, was a disastrous failure. The second period at least
has been a modest success, in some countries, indeed, a spectacular success, and
while we cannot attribute all of this to the
Keynesian economics, at least this is a
major difference between the two periods.

Sacrifice has played a very small role in
establishing the legitimacy of what might
be called the main line of western economics (Adam Smith-Ricardo-Mill-Mar-
shall-Keynes), although it may have had
some impact in establishing the legitimacy
of Marxism. As far as I know, economics
has produced practically no martyrs. The
main sacrifices are involved in understanding the subject, and in the painful process
of learning. It may be therefore that some
of the very vices of the masters may contribute towards establishing their legitimacy.
The obscurities and confusions in Adam
Smith unquestionably aroused people's interest and may even contribute towards his
legitimacy. This is even more true of
Ricardo. Anybody who thinks he really
understands Ricardo has put a great deal
of investment and sacrifice into the process, and he is not likely to give it up
lightly. Economists therefore, like almost
all the other professions, are a tribe united
by the memory of painful rites of initiation,
and this contributes quite substantially to
their internal legitimacy and morale.

The contribution of sacrifice to the legitimacy of Marxian economics is very great.
It is not only that Marx himself was a
writer of great obscurity and difficulty, so
that the sacrifice involved in understanding
him is considerable, and represents an investment not lightly to be given up. Marxism, however, legitimated a Revolution,
whereas classical economics legitimated an
establishment. Marxism therefore has personal martyrs in a sense in which western
economics does not. Where the Revolution
has been successful, however, as in the
Socialist countries, Marxist economics le-
gitimates itself by the political success of
its exponents, even though it may ultimately be threatened by inadequate positive payoffs, unless it can produce its own
Keynesian revolution.

Any movement that survives beyond the

lifetime of its originators can draw upon antiquity as a legitimator, and even though economics is not much more than 200 years old, the fact that it has classical writings and that it looks back on a history beyond the lifetime of any of its practitioners gives it a certain legitimacy from the sheer passage of time.

Economics draws relatively little on mystery or symbolism to maintain its legitimacy. Every profession, of course, which has a distinction between the priesthood and the laity makes some use of mystery in legitimating itself, and economists like every other profession derive a certain amount of legitimacy from the fact that they are not understood. This is a much less important source of legitimacy of economics than it is say, for the medical profession, or even the law, which indulges in rather deliberate obfuscation in the interest of establishing a clear distinction between the priesthood and the laity. Economists have not only been singularly free from "the wretched spirit of monopoly" but one likes to think they have been free also from deliberate obscurity, although one has doubts about this.

Certainly economics owes no legitimacy to the splendor of its trappings. It is a pretty fair generalization, indeed, that the economics department occupies the worst slum on the campus, but this itself is a tribute to the extent of its legitimacy derived from other sources. It is the business school that has to establish its legitimacy by splendid buildings and halls of fame, because it is a parvenu, whereas the ancient legitimacy of the economics department is strong enough to permit it to live in any old buildings.

It may be, however, that some of the passion of the younger economists, especially for mathematization beyond the call of duty, is a result of subconscious desire for more legitimacy than they already have. The use of mathematics to establish legitimacy indeed is a very interesting case because it draws not only upon mystery, but also it represents a strong alliance with an older, larger legitimacy of mathematics itself. Even quantification and the use of computers might be thought of in part as a search for legitimacy through alliance.

A question of great interest, the answer to which, however, may be almost embarrassing, is that of the relation of the legiti-

macy of an intellectual discipline to the truth of its content. In the ideal model of science, truth should produce its own legitimacy, for the satisfaction of intellectual curiosity is supposed to be the only payoff. The real world of the scientist however is rarely as simple as this, and we have to admit that a large complex of other factors, as we have discussed above, are active in increasing or diminishing the legitimacy and along with the legitimacy the support and the prosperity of any branch of science or intellectual activity.

This problem is particularly difficult where the testing process is more complicated and especially where it involves programs covering long periods of time. Economists have always prided themselves on being the defenders of the long run and have criticised politicians and political processes for throwing up short-run solutions, for being too much influenced by short-run payoffs which may turn out badly in the long run. Economists themselves, however, are open to the criticism that their long-run propositions are very hard to test, and indeed most of them are untested. This is particularly true of propositions relating to economic development and long-run change. We may not all be dead in the long run, but the prophets are; hence the payoffs do not accrue to the people who make the decisions, and this is a bad system for producing truth.

It may be, therefore, that economics is in for some long-run trouble because of the long run. Even in the short run, the problem of the testability of many of the propositions of economics is a tricky one. The main difficulty here is that economic theory is essentially a parametric system, that is, a system of relationships which assume certain constant parameters, and that in the real world these parameters frequently shift. The magnitude of parameters can only be detected, however, if they do not change, so that in the face of parametric shift many of the economists' propositions are extremely hard to test.

This is perhaps one reason why the weakest part of economics is that which deals with technological change and economic development. Economics starts with an equilibrium system which assumes certain technological coefficients to be constant; in fact, of course, these coefficients are undergoing constant change, and the problem of detecting a further parametric system with reasonably constant parameters which can describe and predict the change of production coefficients has turned out to be very difficult.

In conclusion, we may ask ourselves whether there are any changes in the future that might threaten the legitimacy of economics as a separate discipline. An institution which does not rely on sacrifice or on mystery, ritual, age or primarily on alliances with other legitimacies, can only derive legitimacy ultimately from its positive payoffs. Its internal legitimacy may be derived from certain internal payoffs in the sense of intellectual satisfaction; the economic support of the discipline, however, comes primarily from its external environment, and it is therefore its external legitimacy that is really significant, especially among the more significant aspects of its external environment.

In part, economics exists in the market environment, in part in what might be called the budget environment in the matrix of larger organizations such as the university or the corporation. Some disciplines can survive within the university, even though there is virtually no market for their products at all, simply because they represent a body of knowledge which the university regards as an essential part of its total *Gestalt* and which must therefore be transmitted from generation to generation. Economics, however, is not in this category; it has a large external market, and the demand for learning economics far exceeds what would be necessary simply to replace its teachers.

There is indeed a kind of multiplier effect here in that an external demand creates a larger demand for teachers to transmit the knowledge to new teachers. Hence the expansion or contraction of economics as a discipline may depend much more on the external demand for it than on the internal demand. This external demand comes mainly from government and business firms who increasingly seem to believe that economists as such have skills that are valuable to them and which have to be paid for.

The critical question facing the profession is perhaps whether the system of training by which it reproduces itself is in fact going to satisfy this external demand. Up to now it has certainly done so fairly well,

and the demand for economists in both governments and businesses has been increasing in the last generation by leaps and bounds. We learn, however, not by success but by failure, and the very success of economics as a profession may present it with hidden dangers. The teaching of every profession produces a certain amount of what Veblen called "trained incapacity" and we should certainly look with a critical eye at economics to see if we are not doing this.

If the training of the economist leads to his neglecting certain important aspects of the world around him, once he is in a position to give advice and to have this advice taken, disasters might easily ensue. It may be indeed that economics will turn out to be another example of a new adage which I have been promoting a good deal lately, that nothing fails like success because we do not learn anything from it. Certainly economists have learned a good deal from the failures of the great depression and indeed learned more from this than from the smooth intellectual successes of Marshallian equilibrium.

If failures are to come out of economics in the present or succeeding generations, it may well be because of its very success as an abstraction. Economics certainly has strong claims to be the most successful and it is certainly the most prestigious of all the social sciences. There is, after all, a Council of Economic Advisers; there is no Council of Sociological Advisers or Psychological Advisers. To some extent economics had achieved this position because of its capacity for abstracting the most easily measurable element out of the total social system, namely, that aspect of it which deals with exchange and which is therefore subject to the measuring rod of money. The very success of the abstraction, however, leads to dangers of neglect of what it has been abstracted from.

All the social sciences are studying essentially the same system, which I have called the "sociosphere." This is the total sphere of all human beings, their inputs and outputs, their organizations, their images, behaviors and so on. The "econosphere" is an abstract segment of the sociosphere; it is not divided from the rest of it by any difference in systems level. The social sciences are divided from, shall we say, physiology, by a fundamental difference in the level of the system itself. They are not divided from each other by any differences in the systems level, however, because they are all essentially studying the same system. Consequently, an abstraction which is too successful presents real dangers because it may lead to the neglect of the other elements of the system.

The neglect by economists, for instance, of the dynamics of legitimacy itself could lead them into very serious misapprehensions about the nature of society. Economists tend to assume, for instance, that the "success" of government is measured by the rate of increase of the gross national product. There are many cases, however, in which countries have had quite successful development from this point of view, but where the legitimacy of the whole process has been undermined simply by failure to pay attention to the dynamics of legitimacy itself. Cuba is probably a good case in point. There have been some notorious cases, indeed, where visits by economists to developing countries have been associated with internal disturbances, riots, or even the overthrow of the government.

When one is giving advice, therefore, about a system that involves the total society, it is extremely dangerous to be over-trained in a certain abstract element of the total process. If we run into enough of this we may find indeed a widespread reaction against economics and a withdrawal of legitimacy from it. It is my own view frankly, at this point, that we must move towards a more integrated and perhaps even a rearranged social science, that the existing departmental and disciplinary lines often mask real problems, and that economics may even have to lose its life in order to save it.

Certainly, if economists maintain the haughty and superior attitude which many of them have towards the other social scientists, they may be heading for some rude shocks. No matter how internally satisfactory a structure of thought is, no matter how useful it may be for passing examinations and for creating internal morale, if its external payoffs are low, retribution will eventually come upon it. The very elegance and self-sufficiency of economics, therefore, may be a long run threat to it. The more successful we are, the more humble we need to be.

1. "The Legitimation of the Market," speech given at Midwest Economic Association, April 20, 1967 (C. Woody Thompson Memorial Lecture).

THE RESURRECTION OF POLITICAL ECONOMY

JAMES S. COLEMAN

Institute for Development Studies, Nairobi

The time has come to recognize not only the professional respectability but the practical essentiality of the ancient and honorable hybrid discipline of "political economy." There are at least three compelling reasons in support of this proposition. One is that the ever-increasing specialization of political scientists and economists has tended to reify what is after all nothing more than an artificial boundary between two categories of social scientists each concerned with only analytically different aspects of a single concrete whole, namely, human society. In drawing attention to the artificiality of disciplinary boundaries in the social sciences we do not deny the critical importance of specialization and all that it implies, rather we are merely affirming a non-purist—and, incidentally, an historically validated—concept of what con-

From *Mawazo* (June 1967), pp. 31–40. Reprinted by permission of author. Some sections have been omitted.

stitutes an academic discipline, much along the lines of the late Frederick Dunn's definition:

A field of knowledge does not possess a fixed extension in space but is a constantly changing focus of data and methods that happen at the moment to be useful in answering an identifiable set of questions. I¹ presents at any given time different aspects to different observers, depending on their point of view and purpose. The boundaries that supposedly divide one field of knowledge from another are not fixed walls between separate cells of truth but are convenient devices for arranging known facts and methods in manageable segments for instruction and practice. But the foci of interest are constantly shifting and these divisions tend to change with them, although more slowly because mental habits alter slowly and the vested interests of the intellectual world are as resistant to change as those of the social world.¹

Such a flexible concept of a discipline validates the continuing process of disciplinary hybridization so marked in recent and contemporary social science. There is, for example, widespread acceptance of such hybrids as "political sociology" and "social psychology." Thus, recognition of the hybrid discipline of political economy is supported not only by history—it is after all the oldest of the hybrids—but by current fashion as well.

A second argument is that those comparatively unique historical situations of fairly pure laissez-faire which once encouraged and perhaps even gave some justification for sharp differentiation between the two disciplines have long since been transcended by varying but substantial forms of *etatisme*, either of the "developed" welfare state, or of the modernizing state variety. In either type of polity—indeed, in all intermediate types as well—sound and successful public policy requires the specialized competence and collaboration of both groups of disciplinarians. The interdependence of political, administrative and economic aspects of modern statecraft must be matched by an interdisciplinary perspective among those scholars essaying to comprehend, analyze and provide policy guidance for national development.

The third reason is that there already are a significant number of practitioners in both disciplines concentrating in the hybrid area, but unlike such proud hybridists as political sociologists and social psychologists they seem reluctant to declare their special identity. This is true despite the legitimating and fortifying definition in Webster's Third New International:

political economy 1: an 18th century branch of the art of government concerned with directing governmental policies toward the promotion of the wealth of the government and the community as a whole; 2a: a 19th century social science comprising the modern science of economics but concerned principally with governmental as contrasted with commercial or personal economics; *b:* a modern social science dealing with the interrelationship of political and economic processes.

The principal reason for their reluctance is that in the course of the evolution of political science and economics as separate and increasingly specialized disciplines, the term political economy has tended to become the distinctive appellation for a special branch of economics (*i.e.,* definition *2a*), and modern politico-economic hybrids have, as a consequence, sought to avoid guilt by association. However, as their number and the need for them increases— as inexorably it will—the most logical name for their interdisciplinary identity will and must be reclaimed, and Webster's definition *2b* allowed to prevail.

THE TREND TOWARDS CONVERGENCE

Independent, but complementary and frequently identical, developments have occurred or are in gestation in both disciplines which have greatly facilitated the relaxation of the boundaries that ever-greater specialization over the years has tended to erect. The impact of the Soviet Union and other socialist systems, and more recently the developing areas, has led to a greater convergence of scholarly interest and concern in the two disciplines. The interdependence of economy and polity in such systems is in theory and fact so close that the nature of the relationship could not be ignored even by the arch purists in both disciplines. Moreover, whether specializing in such systems or not, all political scientists and economists *qua* social scientists are, or ought to be, comparativists; thus an explicit concern with the economy-polity relationship in differing systems has been virtually inescapable.

Political Science has always been more or less amenable to giving consideration to the effect of non-political variables upon politics. This is partly due to the tendency of its practitioners to regard their profession as the "umbrella" discipline, and partly to the weaker impact of the scientific perspective upon them. The result has been fuzzy boundaries, lack of focus, and extraordinary diversity in schools, approaches, and methods. As a leading political scientist has lamented, at mid-century

if political scientists are agreed on anything, it is probably on the muddled state of their science. Political scientists are riding off in many directions, evidently on the assumption that if you don't know where you are going, any road will take you there.[2]

During the past two decades, among a new and more scientifically-oriented generation of political scientists, there has been a quite extraordinary expansion of interest in and commitment to the developing areas. Already disposed and, by their permissive discipline, allowed to study anything politically relevant (and in the tempestuous decade of terminal colonialism almost everything was politically relevant), they became the proponents and carriers, on a rather massive scale, of an entirely new orientation in the discipline. This orientation was marked by an intensification among them of the macropolitical perspective (national elites, national parties, and the nation-building process tended to be the main foci), and by an explicitly interdisciplinary commitment derived in part from contact with the structural-functionalism of anthropological colleagues in the field, and from their perception of the obvious importance of the social, economic and cultural setting of politics.

Their intensive personal exposure to the realities of the developing areas not only strengthened their macropolitical (nation-building) and holistic perspective, as well as their sensitivity in general to the relevance of the setting of politics; it also brought the scholars concerned into direct contact with the major problem of public policy of the postcolonial period, namely, economic development. In due course one or another aspect of the politics of economic development emerged to the fore as dissertation topics and research pro-

posals by a second wave of postwar younger political scientists coming to Africa.

In the meantime other major reorientations in the discipline of political science were already well under way: (1) the impact of "group theorists"; (2) the increasing popularity within the discipline of functionalism and "systems" theory; (3) the shift from static to dynamic modes of analysis for the study and comparison of patterns of political development in both historical and contemporary perspective; and (4) the reconceptualization of the nature of the polity from that of ultimate physical compulsion to the idea of the creative, purposive mechanism through which societal goals are determined and pursued. Each of these has had evident implications for the role of economic variables in political analysis.

The "group theorists" alerted political analysts to the significance of economic (pressure) groups in the political system and provided a basic analytical tool for assessing the functioning of the system. The concept "political system" has compelled political scientists to think of the political universe analytically (i.e. as encompassing all politically relevant activity in all institutional spheres) rather than confining the "political" to the narrower concept of "state" and concrete political and governmental structures such as parties, legislatures, and courts. The shift from static or "equilibrium" analysis to dynamic and developmental analysis also nudges political scientists into taking exogenous variables into consideration in their analysis and into relating patterns of development in the polity to those in the society and economy.

Finally, although it has been some time since governments in Western countries accepted a continuing responsibility for the function of providing welfare, planning the economy, and using the power of the state to seek and achieve new goals, political scientists until very recently continued to define the political realm either in the simplistic nineteenth century law-and-order terms of Max Weber: "monopoly of the legitimate use of physical force within a given territory," or in such equilibratory Parsonian terms as "pattern maintenance," "adaptation," or "integration."

As J. Roland Pennock put it, "political systems develop their own autonomous political goals and . . . the attainment of these collective goals is one of their major functions, providing an important measure of their development. . . . I shall call these goals 'political goods' . . . (and) . . . the degree to which a political system achieves these political goods may be considered yet another dimension of political development." [3] And one of Pennock's four "political goods" (the other three being the classical maintenance of "law and order," "justice," and "liberty") is "the promotion of economic growth, either indirectly by supplying the necessary infrastructure, by providing conditions that encourage the immigration of foreign capital and expertise, or more directly by governmental 'planning' and enterprise." Today this is accepted as a proper function of government; and therefore as an integral part of the political scientist's concept of the polity.

The first significant contrast between economics and political science is the greater scientific rigor (both attempted and achieved) of the former. The self-image of most—but not all—economists is that they are the only really "hard" social scientists with a predictive capability. This they can rightly claim, but at a price. It has meant, among other things, a reluctance to include non-economic variables in their analysis, and an avoidance of being stigmatized as area specialists. The avoidance of non-economic variables is deliberate. As one leading economist put it, "Society has an economic aspect and this is the element economic science purports to explain, leaving others to other disciplines." The avoidance of the non-economic realm is brought out in economist Karl de Schweinitz's interesting distinction between economic "development" and "growth," which deserves being quoted at length.

[Economic] *growth* may be defined as increasing output (GNP) per capita. [Economic] *development* has broader reference to the building of institutions, new lines of production, and the dissemination of attitudes essential for self-sustaining growth. . . . It must be acknowledged at once that economics is concerned more with growth than development and so, paradoxically, does not have much to contribute to the explanation of the origins of growth. Recently it has been taken to task for this

"failure," the charge being that while appropriate for growing systems the narrow concerns of economics do not explain much where growth is not taking place. . . . These critics ask too much of economics. Unlike Marxian analysis, which attempts to encompass the totality of behaviour, it does not pretend to be a complete science of society. Economics is concerned with market phenomena in nationally-integrated economies. Where these do not exist, its analytical techniques are nonoperative. . . . However imperfect economics, it is further advanced as a policy science than the other social sciences. And if it has not been more effective in helping new states realize growth objectives, it is because so many of them have not yet developed institutions conducive to growth. For explanations of this lack of development, however, one should look to political science or sociology, rather than to economics.[4]

Another reason for the economists' tendency to avoid political variables is their close and more continuous link with governments as policy advisers. De Schweinitz's claim that economics is a more highly developed policy science is undoubtedly correct: economists know it, employing governments know it, and other social scientists know it. As a result economists are more acceptable, indeed, more sought after, as social science technicians in the policy formulation process. One obvious consequence—a tendency characteristic of anyone in the Establishment—is to avoid or ignore political variables, usually by the convenient phrase *ceteris paribus*.

This tendency is underscored by the fact that even those development economists who readily acknowledge the relevance of the social and cultural context of development, or even psychological variables, frequently exclude those of a political character. Some economic advisers claim that they do not and cannot ignore such variables; they assess them "on the job," so to speak, and react accordingly. What they do reject is the need for the development of a set of integrative theoretical conceptions concerned with politico-economic phenomena. It is our contention here that the hybrid discipline of political economy requires such a theoretical framework.

The imperative of disciplinary purity and the constraints of their advisory role help to explain all evident reluctance by economists in the past to involve themselves explicitly with the non-economic environment. Nevertheless, at least three major re-orientations in economics have nudged economists toward a more interdisciplinary perspective. It is, also, particularly interesting and relevant that these parallel three of the new orientations in political science previously discussed, suggesting the operation of certain generic forces in the social sciences.

These new emphases in economics are (1) the macro-economic perspective emerging from the Great Depression and the Keynesian Revolution and reinforced by the impact of the developing areas; (2) the shift in focus from static equilibrium models to development; and (3) acceptance of the unavoidability of taking into account the setting or context ("exogenous factors") within which economic growth occurs.

By the end of World War II macro-analysis in economics was well-established. The development of Keynesian ideas made it possible for economists to consider major aggregate variables and to look at an economy as a whole, in the same sense that postwar political scientists were nudged by systems-analysis and structural-functionalism to look at the polity as a whole. Moreover, Keynesian economics favoured a very considerable degree of government regulation and direction of the economy, a point of view highly congruent with the transformative "social engineering" ideology of the political elites of the new states emerging from colonialism. The new holistic orientation in economics was thus linked with their acceptance of the idea that the polity had a creative, purposive and goal-seeking function.

The second major re-orientation has been what Walter Newlyn has described as the "significant shift in the 'centre of content' of the subject of economics itself." A postwar phenomenon, he describes it as follows:

By excessive concentration on . . . static analysis, economists have lost touch with the bold generalisations of Adam Smith, Ricardo, Malthus and Marx about the basic growth variables. . . . Indeed, during this century economists have had sadly little to say about the "causes of the wealth of nations." The significant shift in the centre of content of the subject . . . has taken place, like many previous changes in

the emphasis of economic thought, in response to the social problems of the time. (The latter, including the "immensity of the task of transforming the economies of the underdeveloped countries") . . . has turned economists away from their preoccupation with the fluctuations of activity in industrial societies to the problems of growth of primitive societies. Economists became once more interested in growth *as a process* to be examined and explained . . . all economists have suddenly become "development" specialists and, as a result, have become interested in comparative studies of growth . . . this specialisation necessarily means that their comparative method must be applied to the economy as a whole.[5]

Third, many economists, like political scientists, have also come to admit the relevance of the "setting" for economic growth. The decisively persuasive factor has been their encounter with the realities of the developing areas. The first wave of economists drawn to the developing areas saw capital formation as the chief problem, but this simple model of growth inevitably had to be modified because of its woeful inadequacy. Economists were thus compelled, as Manning Nash put it, "to confront the social and cultural system, so to speak, head on," to take systematic account of the context of economic development. This broadening of the spectrum of the economists' world is associated with the work of Walt Rostow (Stages of Economic Growth), Arthur Lewis (Theory of Economic Development), as well as the various writings of Gunnar Myrdal, Bert Hoselitz, Everett Hagen, Simon Kuznets, Albert Hirschman, and many others. They have all turned at some point or other in their analyses to anthropologists, sociologists, and psychologists for a stipulation of the context of development.

THE POLITICAL PRECONDITIONS OF ECONOMIC
DEVELOPMENT

The most striking new emphasis in discussions on the nature of politics and the problem of economic development in the developing countries, and particularly in Africa, is the almost unanimous agreement on what has come to be known as the "primacy of the polity." The arguments asserting polity primacy over other institutional spheres tend to fall into two categories:

(1) the argument of African cultural continuity, and (2) the argument of situational necessity.

The argument that the primacy of the political sphere in contemporary Africa is rooted in African culture is advanced by Professor Lloyd Fallers:

. . . in traditional Africa goods and services, both as symbols and as facilities, circulate primarily in terms of political relations, for it is the polity that dominates stratification. . . . Traditional African societies . . . have characteristically exhibited patterns of role differentiation in which political specialization has been more prominent than economic. The ambitions of their members have been directed primarily toward attaining authority, and economic processes have commonly been dominated by the political needs of individuals and groups. Although direct cultural continuity may be difficult to achieve, some characteristic features of the traditional systems may perhaps persist and give a distinctly African character to the new independent nations. For example, in the new African nations, as in the old, political structures seem likely to continue to dominate economic ones, and political elites to retain their pre-eminence. To be sure, the place of economic processes in society has changed greatly. Whereas in traditional societies an essentially static economy was manipulated for political ends, the new independent states make rapid economic development the principal aim of public policy. . . . The traditional cultural emphasis upon authority coincides with, and perhaps helps to produce, modern conceptions of planning for economic development.[6]

Most anthropologists are reluctant to generalize in this manner about "traditional African culture," largely because of the enormous diversity of indigenous institutional forms and the fact that they personally are intimately familiar with only one or two societies. They are equally averse to generalize about cultural continuities. However, this particular hypothesis stands as an exciting challenge to the behavioral sciences to validate, qualify or disconfirm.

The main burden of the argument for the priority of the political sphere over the economy in the developing countries is, however, based on situational necessity. The major elements in this argument are now fairly well known. Walter Newlyn has argued, for example, that the peculiarity of the development problems which face the primitive economies of Africa has convinced economists of the "need for deliberate planning and for governments to play a major role as entrepreneurs in the transformation of the modes of production of such economies." Charles Wolf argues that another reason for the dominance of the political factor is that nationalists in many colonial areas perceived the relationship between political and economic power in causal terms, namely, whoever possesses political power has, and ought to have, control over the economy.

A strongly interventionist economic tradition is a major element in the Western colonial legacy to new states. Moreover, in areas of almost total expatriate domination of the economy the determination to use newly-won political power to "indigenize" economic power has been understandably strong, indeed, inevitable. This could be done only by an interventionist policy since the "free play of the market" would serve only to perpetuate expatriate domination of the economy. Fairly comprehensive interventionism has also been a consequence of the determination of insecure political elites in new states to maximize their control over what S. N. Eisenstadt has called "free-floating resources." The political value of various forms of patronage (i.e., control over public employment and loans), and of a monopoly over central planning are self-evident.

One of the most explicit and detailed arguments rationalizing the priority of the political realm in the developing areas is that made by economist Wilfred Malenbaum. He notes that in the first decade of discussion regarding economic development in the newly independent countries it was universally assumed that economic growth was mainly a technical and virtually autonomous process, the independent variable affecting all other spheres. Painful experience convinced many economists that the relationship was precisely the reverse. Out of this ordeal of frustration, he affirms the following proposition:

We now know that the primary ingredient of *economic* growth is motivational more than material. [We also know] that the motivation for change in a nation demands some national expression. The attitudes and desires of parts of the nation—including, where relevant, the demands of the market place—must somehow combine to serve as the national expression. This task of combination extends far beyond tasks of organization or of administration. It is essentially and fundamentally a political task, reflecting skilled leadership. . . . [Economic growth is not possible] . . . unless the political structure, including its leadership, seeks their attainment as explicit and major goals.[7]

. . . Much of the recent literature on economic development reflects near unanimity on the absolute essentiality of an effective system of public administration. The point need not be labored, it is both obvious and well known. Yet there is not complete consensus. Referring to John Kenneth Galbraith's list of four preconditions (one of which was "a reliable apparatus of government and public administration"), Albert O. Hirschman observed that

. . . whenever development occurs, it does so invariably in the absence of one or several of these "required" components or preconditions. In nineteenth century Germany, it occurred without much primitive accumulation of capital and in Italy without the Protestant ethic, to mention some of the earlier theories on prerequisites; and during the postwar period, Brazil experienced development in the absence of monetary stability, and Colombia even in the absence of public order, not to speak of land reform. . . . Therefore, I continue to advocate that in their research the experts pay special attention to the emergence and possible rationality of new or inverted sequences. When they discover an "obstacle," such as poor public administration . . . their job does not consist in merely advising its removal; they ought to explore also how, by moving the economy forward elsewhere, additional pressure (economic and political) could be brought on the obstacle to give way.[8]

This is useful wisdom distilled from the comparative study of conditions normally associated with economic development, but does it not ignore the peculiarity of the African problem of economic development referred to by Newlyn? Here the need for central, planned and directed economic development is so manifest, and the dependence of such a process upon an efficient and trained bureaucracy so clear, that while one can share Hirschman's and Gershen-kron's scepticism that history provides little guidance, one can also insist that the overpowering logic of the African situation makes effective public administration a precondition for economic development.

Economists and political scientists are not only concerned with the identification of political and administrative preconditions of economic development, but also with the nature of political constraints and the latitude of political feasibilities in concrete situations. Some of these are generic to African as well as other societies. As they are multi-ethnic societies political leaders must be acutely sensitive to the imperative of ethnic arithmetic not only in the allocation of jobs, but also in the geographical allocation of resources and in the distribution of the product of economic growth. Heeding this imperative frequently plays havoc with economic rationality, but it is a political constraint of such pervasiveness and magnitude, because it strikes at the very heart of the legitimacy of the governing regime, that economists neglect it at peril to themselves as well as the political leaders they advise.

THE POLITICAL CONSEQUENCES OF ECONOMIC
DEVELOPMENT

Political economists are concerned not only with how political variables and constraints affect economic development, but also with how the latter, as an independent variable, affects political behavior and institutions. This latter dimension will be examined with reference to three rather well-known issues: (1) economic development and political competitiveness, (2) rapid economic growth and political instability, and (3) uneven economic development and political integration.

The statistical evidence (how reliable it may be is still in dispute) unquestionably suggests a close connection between economic development and political competitiveness (a situation close to but not completely synonymous with democracy). Higher degrees of economic development are associated with greater political competitiveness; and, conversely, the lowest levels of economic development tend statistically to be linked with authoritarianism. These studies suggest, be it noted, only a statistical correlation, and not a causal nexus.

The hypothesis that economic growth and political competitiveness are positively correlated has been challenged by Morris Janowitz:

. . . this type of analysis appears to have limited relevance for understanding, on a comparative basis, the dynamic relationship between economic development and political forms . . . there is no basis for asserting that, with higher levels of economic development, there is a movement toward more competitive political systems. In fact, among those nations with the highest level of economic development, the absence of democratic competitive systems is more noteworthy than their presence, since competitive systems are concentrated in the middle level of economic development. . . . But the analysis is not without meaning if the general hypothesis is abandoned and the underlying process examined. Authoritarian-personal regimes are heavily concentrated among the nations with low economic development, for these nations are just embarking on economic development. (However) the basic conclusion is that, with higher economic levels, the outcome is as likely as not to be in the direction of military oligarchy, and perhaps somewhat more likely.[9]

Another critic, Harry Eckstein, has argued that between the great extremes of economic development and economic underdevelopment there is a "large no-man's land where apparently any governmental order, from stable democracy to totalitarianism can exist." [10] We are clearly in the presence of an issue that cannot be definitively resolved, at least not until there is a vast improvement in our statistical data and a greater consensus on the definition of political forms.

There is far greater consensus on the proposition that *rapid* economic growth has political destabilising consequences. It has this effect because it increases the number of individuals who are *déclassé* ("detribalized" in old Africanist jargon) and most disposed to lead or to follow in a revolutionary movement; it markedly increases the number of gainers (the insatiable *nouveaux riches*) and losers (the bitterly resentful *nouveaux pauvres*), both of whom tend to become alienated; and it vastly expands the numbers caught up in the "revolution of rising expectations." [11] Hagen, however, rejects the contention that there is a positive correlation between economic growth and political instability. The "awakening of the masses," their growing awareness of the possibility of change, he argues has been brought to them "by the course of history; it is surely almost entirely independent of economic growth." [12] But even if economic growth is one of the contributory causes of this awakening, the remedy is not to curtail or to forego growth. On the contrary:

. . . awareness that they are not powerless will surely reach the peasant and worker in the absence of economic change, even if slightly late, and their reaction will be the more extreme if nothing has previously been done to indicate that the world has regard for them. Opportunities for economic growth that reach the discontented groups are surely a counteragent to political instability, though they may be an insufficient counteragent if the accumulated bitterness has grown too great.[13]

The foregoing argument overlooks the disposition and the capacity of individuals and groups to accommodate themselves to the hard realities of life. The "revolution of rising expectations" may indeed lead to a "revolution of rising frustrations," but the latter does not necessarily lead to actual revolution. Any number of examples —historical and contemporaneous—can be found of individuals and categories of persons who, by all objective criteria, should be on the brink of revolutionary violence or bitterly alienated, but who are nonetheless disposed and capable of adjusting themselves to disappointment and only partial fulfillment of their original expectations. This imponderable in human nature is all too frequently overlooked. In the painful choices political leaders must make it is admittedly a calculated risk to base decisions on the assumption of accommodation rather than revolution, but dedicated and inspired (and inspiring) leadership itself can frequently ensure that the dice are loaded in favour of accommodation.

The third selected issue concerns the effect of economic growth upon political integration. This has been brilliantly examined by economist Elliot Berg in his effort to explain postwar political developments in former French West Africa, and particularly to explain why differential political choices were made at certain critical junctures. He found the economic factor unquestionably dominant at each crisis point. Underlying these complex political events, he argues, "is a set of economic circumstances which have given shape to the political decisions made; in West Africa, as elsewhere, political choice is conditioned by the nature of the economic environment in which it takes place." [14] The unequal economic development among the various territories of French West Africa was the decisive factor in the political choices which resulted in the subsequent political fragmentation of that vast stretch of the African continent.

Economic growth can also have a politically dysfunctional effect as a result of its uneven impact in an ethnically pluralistic context. It can not only perpetuate, but all too frequently it intensifies, tensions among different ethnic, regional, and parochial groups. Before planned economic growth is launched existing groups and regions are not only at a different level of economic development, but they have differential capacities for further development. Those already more developed have an inherent advantage over those that are less developed. As Adam Curle has noted, "It is a sad fact that, once the process of development starts in one sector of a society, the inequalities within that society tend to increase. . . . Trade, labour and enterprise are apt to move towards the progressive areas, leaving the poor zones still poorer." [15] The net result of this natural operation of economic forces invariably tends to be heightened ethnicity, and sometimes even political separatism.

It is equally clear that certain patterns of economic growth can and do lead to new class differentiations. [Here Coleman contrasts the development strategies of regimes in Kenya, Uganda, and Tanzania, elaborated in Aaron Segal's article in Part II. Eds.]

The high degree of de facto *etatisme* characteristic of most new states elevates the process of economic-policy-making to a position of central importance. Economic policies are highly determinative of the achievement or prevention of particular economic, political or social consequences. But economic policies themselves reflect conscious political decisions. Thus, once one accepts the importance of political decisions for economic growth, the way in which economic policies are determined is obviously of crucial significance. The comparative study of this process should provide insight into the kinds of decisions and policies that are *politically* as well as *economically* feasible.

The foregoing issues illustrate the many areas of public policy and problems of nation-building where the practical and the theoretical concerns of the political scientist and the economist converge. They provide a basis for a potentially fruitful dialogue, in which one would hope the purism of the economist and the dilettantism of the political scientist might be somewhat reduced. Whether there is enough there yet to resurrect the hybrid discipline of political economy is a question that can be answered only by the practitioners themselves.

1. Frederick S. Dunn, "The Scope of International Relations," *World Politics,* 1 (Oct., 1948), p. 142.

2. "Political Science," in Bert F. Hoselitz (ed.), *A Reader's Guide to the Social Sciences* (Free Press, 1959), p. 91.

3. J. Roland Pennock, "Political Development, Political Systems, and Political Goods," *World Politics,* XVIII (April, 1966), p. 420.

4. Karl de Schweinitz, Jr., "Economics and the Underdeveloped Economies," *American Behavioral Scientist,* IX I (Sept., 1965), pp. 3 and 5. Italics added.

5. Walter T. Newlyn, "The Present State of African Economic Studies," *African Affairs* (Spring, 1965), p. 39.

6. Lloyd A. Fallers, "Social Stratification and Economic Processes," Melville J. Herskovits and Mitchell Harwitz (eds.), *Economic Transition in Africa* (Northwestern University Press, 1964), pp. 126, 127, 129, 130.

7. Wilfred Malenbaum, "Economic Factors and Political Development," *The Annals* (March, 1965), pp. 42–43.

8. Albert O. Hirschman, "Comments on 'A Framework for Analyzing Economic and Political Change,'" in The Brookings Institution, *Development of the Emerging Countries* (Washington, 1962), p. 41.

9. Morris Janowitz, *The Military in the Political Development of New Nations* (University of Chicago Press, 1964), pp. 21 and 23.

10. Harry Eckstein, *A Theory of Stable Democracy* (Princeton University Press, 1961), p. 39.

11. Mancur Olson, Jr., "Rapid Growth as a Destabilizing Force," *Journal of Economic History,* XXIII (December, 1963), pp. 530–531.

12. Everett E. Hagen, "A Framework for Analyzing Economic and Political Change," in The Brookings Institution, *op. cit.*, p. 37.

13. *Ibid.*, p. 37.

14. Elliot J. Berg, "The Economic Basis of Political Choice in French West Africa," *American Political Science Review*, LVI (1960), pp. 391–405.

15. Adam Curle, *The Role of Education in Developing Societies* (Ghana University Press, 1961), pp. 7–8.

•

Toward a
Policy-Oriented
Social Science

•

THE RELATIVITY of economic theory to particular historical and institutional contexts, despite the aspiration of economists for the universality of their explanations, is suggested by Peter Dorner in the essay below. He argues that only by accepting the historical and institutional relativity of their theory can social scientists develop better and more useful theory.

Dorner's contention that social science theory has been developed from the study and eventual resolution of major policy issues in the past is of profound importance, since it suggests how time-bound our theories are. To keep social science theory up-to-date, social scientists need to be continually engaged in the study of contemporary policy problems. In this context it is clear that policy is the best and perhaps the only test of social science theory. A part of this article, dealing with more specific developmental issues, is contained in Part II.

Socio-cultural determinism, a mode or level of explanation of late in vogue in social science pertaining to development, is called into question by Joseph Elder, a sociologist with experience in India. He challenges the dichotomous view of "tradition" and "modernity" that regards the former as inimical to development. Elder shows how variable are the effects of different cultural and social factors.

In the promotion of agricultural development through public policies, there are many possibilities for success and failure. General rules are of limited value; the particular conditions need to be considered carefully and empirically so that policy measures can be fashioned which achieve the "critical total" effect that brings about developmental change.

The article by Albert Hirschman was one of the first in the development literature to challenge the prevailing but facile analysis of "obstacles to development." The policy implication of such analysis was that one should spare no effort in eliminating or overcoming these presumed "barriers." Hirschman's classification gives impetus to policy-oriented analysis that considers how so-called "obstacles" can be ignored or even turned to advantage in development programs.

The real world Hirschman describes contains possibilities foreclosed by conventional social science. In the course of his analysis, he exposes some of the tenets of of what we have called "the religion of development," which is inclined to damn or doom too categorically. Hirschman thereby encourages a healthy heterodoxy of approaches to development.

40

NEEDED REDIRECTIONS IN ECONOMIC ANALYSIS FOR AGRICULTURAL DEVELOPMENT POLICY: I

PETER DORNER

University of Wisconsin

I

Within the past several decades, especially the one just ended, agricultural economists have become increasingly concerned with agricultural *development* policies. I stress development because this is a new emphasis.[1] Agricultural economics and the related rural social sciences emerged as academic disciplines at about the turn of this century, after U.S. agriculture was far along the road to modernization. Initially, agricultural economists were concerned with problems of farm management and tenancy. Later, problems of marketing, credit, price and income protection, resource conservation, and aggregative characteristics of demand and supply became subfields of specialized interest and research. Since the discipline "grew up" after the basic economic, social, and political institutions of production and distribution were established, policy issues of concern to researchers were essentially those dealing with imperfections of the system—obstacles and barriers (to the free flow of information and resources) inhibiting the most efficient use and combination of *given* resources [24, pp. 725–729; 35, p. 83; references listed by number at end of article].

A look at the "growth of government in agriculture" [1, 39, 41] reveals a fairly close correspondence between policy issues in U.S. agriculture and the development of specialized areas of research.[2] The shape of agricultural economics as a discipline reflects the range of issues that arise in agricultural policy. Organized systems of thought are the result of man's efforts to cope with experienced difficulties. The configuration of such a system of thought will be different if establishment of basic institutions is a key issue, in contrast to the system of thought that emerges from inquiry into policy issues that arise *within*

an established and accepted institutional framework [14, p. 4].

At the time of United States' independence, economics was just emerging as a recognizable, separate branch of moral philosophy. A major policy issue in the late 18th and early 19th century was the nature of economic organization to establish in agriculture. The resulting system of family farms was rationalized more in terms of political theory (a major reaction to European feudalism) than economic theory [16].

The system of economic, social, and political organization was firmly established by the time problems of agricultural policy attracted the attention of professional economists. Had our earlier policies fostered a feudal hierarchy or communal ownership of land instead of fee simple ownership and family farms; had our social organization developed around the extended family or the tribe instead of the nuclear family living in relative isolation on its farmstead; had our political system been one of centralized control and management of the economy with all transactions involving land, labor, capital, and commodities regulated by central political authority instead of the local autonomy and free private enterprise of individuals in their economic activities; much of our theory of the firm, of markets, of pricing, and of equilibrium would be irrelevant. In fact, we most likely would not have them. *They could be developed and perfected only within a particular political and institutional context.* They provide no analytical insight into a system whose institutions are different.[3]

Thus, there is little reason to believe that the concepts and hypotheses derived from our theories are entirely relevant to all of our country's currently recognized problems; they are even less relevant to prob-

From *American Journal of Agricultural Economics* (February 1971), pp. 8–11, 15–16. Reprinted by permission. Part III of article appears separately below.

lems facing the poor, agricultural countries. The need, it would seem, is to understand institutional systems and the nature of public policy issues.

On some problems our theories and professional economic analyses are serving reasonably well in the United States and in other industrialized countries. The relevant questions are being asked and the data needed for analyses are being generated. But the categories in our census and other statistical series are not accidental.[4] They too are products of the policy issues and the theoretical formulations developed through the interaction of problems and ideas.

On other important policy questions, however, present theories provide little insight even on U.S. issues: environmental quality, poverty, race relations, a more acceptable distribution of economic and political power, congested cities, rural development, automation, and basic changes in the structure of resource ownership. Present theories do not seem to encompass these issues; they do not help us to formulate the right questions; hence, appropriate data are not available, and fundamental policy questions tend to fall outside the boundaries of traditional academic disciplines.[5]

II

A basic question is whether economics, or any other social science, has anything significant to say on matters of development policy. More fundamentally, are the social sciences capable of generating guidelines for public policy that are in some sense "better" than those formulated by other means and criteria? Or are the value questions of public policy subject only to political compromise or the dictates of dogma, coercion, and personal tastes?

This depends, it seems, on one's view of the role of theory, how it is developed, and the manner in which it is tested. If one assumes that economic theory develops in some pure form independent of policy issues existing within a specific institutional matrix, it follows that theory can have an "independent career" and be set apart in a separate domain.[6] This view may not be too harmful with respect to those aspects referred to by Kuhn as "nor-

mal science" or the "mop-up work" growing out of established theory.[7]

Another position, taken in this paper, is that as major changes occur in society, the existing body of theory (developed through the study and eventual resolution of major policy issues) becomes inadequate and fails to comprehend the new policy issues that confront society. The major breakthroughs and theoretical syntheses in economics have come about from attempts to deal with major policy crises. Smith, Ricardo, Marx, and Keynes were all deeply immersed in the policy issues of their time, and their theoretical advances resulted from their inquiry into the possible resolution of questions central to economic policy.[8] Advances in theory have always been constructed on the basis of detailed and specific research into the very issues that could not be forced "into the preformed and relatively inflexible" boxes available from existing theory [22, p. 24].

Emphasizing the need for research on policy issues does not mean that the goals of policy are set by politicians, bureaucrats, or pressure groups and that the role of research is merely to seek the most efficient means of arriving at such predetermined goals. Rather, it means that the investigator must be concerned with both ends and means. "Since development is far from being achieved at present, the need is not, as is generally assumed, to accelerate economic growth—which could even be dangerous—but to change the nature of the development process" [36, p. 3].

This view holds certain dangers. For example, it raises the question of objectivity in research.[9] This is perhaps why many social scientists deny that they are working on policy questions and maintain that —as scientists—their only concern is establishing value-neutral relationships. This latter function is of great social significance, and most social scientists will be engaged only in such studies. Indeed, new theoretical breakthroughs are impossible without them [22]. But without direct attention to relationships not prescribed by present theories, some of the most pressing public policy questions are ignored.

It may be helpful at this point to note a fundamental difference between the physical and the social sciences. Both physical and social scientists can carry on much of their normal science under laboratory conditions, but social scientists will always conduct some of their research within the context of human society. When a crisis in policy emerges, when accepted theories fail to offer insights into phenomena readily observed, when these anomalies become so obvious that they can no longer be ignored, a new theory cannot be validated except as it is tested in practice.

In physical science this can still frequently be done under laboratory conditions; but in economics it requires new directions in policy. Its measured consequences must then serve as the experimental test. They Keynesian reformulation of the 1930's is perhaps the best and most recent example in the field of economics. Today, many economists are indeed engaged in the normal science that is not directly concerned with ends or values. But this is made possible by the new Keynesian paradigm which has once again (for the industrialized, capitalist countries) relegated many evaluative or "normative" issues to the level of assumption, removing them for the time being from the immediate field of inquiry. This makes possible the common practice of reading prescriptions for public policy directly from the refined Keynesian models (a practice which Keynes himself did not recommend).[10] But such prescriptions could not command the respect they do if the new theoretical constructions had not been tested—in the only meaningful terms possible—through their practical influence in shaping public policy and resulting in measured and anticipated consequences.

In the United States we have begun to accept as a measure of progress the number of people lifted from the misfortune of being poor. There is a growing recognition that developmental problems are not confined to some far-off "less-developed country," and people are beginning to realize that development is more than capital, investment, and markets. It is a complicated process of institutional change, redistribution of political power, human development, and concerted, deliberate public policy efforts for redistributing the gains and losses inherent in economic growth [7, p. 291].

Despite such recognition, these issues are still often treated as "fringe problems," outside the mainstream of economic policy. And development economics, so far as I

can determine, does not incorporate these issues into its analysis. As a result, the relevancy of development economics to development is being questioned [36, 4]. . . . There is, it would appear, a crisis situation developing in economics (and perhaps in the social sciences generally) in the sense defined by Kuhn—"Crisis and the Emergence of Scientific Theories" [22, pp. 66–76]. Unless some key development issues, presently ignored, are directly addressed in research, this crisis may challenge the very legitimacy of economics [2].
(Section III appears on pages 129–34.)

IV

What conclusions are to be drawn from the arguments set forth in this paper? First, we need additional criteria by which to assess development. This means inclusion of presently less measurable and quantifiable variables than the commonly accepted ones in use today. Second, both ends and means must be incorporated as variables in the analysis rather than accepting certain ends implicit in standard economic theories. Finally, distributional questions must be given higher priority on the research agenda.

Present theories may have much more relevance once we understand better the institutional context of specific country development problems and the "special case" out of which our own theories were constructed. If new theoretical extensions can accommodate the enlarged context, present theories may become more useful in guiding research in the very situations in which they are at present unsuccessful.[11]

New developments in theory are not simply willed into existence. The hypothesis suggested in this paper is that only as research concentrates on presently neglected policy issues within specific institutional contexts of individual countries can more adequate theories of agricultural development be constructed. It is obviously asking a great deal of a man to be guided by present theories and preconceptions and yet to be continuously suspicious and to question them at every stage in his research. Nevertheless, this would seem to be the nature of the present challenge.

1. Development is here viewed in the broad sense of expanding opportunities and the human capacities needed to exploit them, along

with a general reduction of mass poverty, unemployment, and inequality [36, 31].

2. Note also current policy issues (poverty, resource and environmental management, population, urban congestion, agricultural development, etc.) and the corresponding growing interest and research specialization (including new institutes and professional journals) in all of these areas.

3. N. Georgescu-Roegen has observed, "As soon as we realize that for economic theory an economic system is characterized exclusively by institutional traits, it becomes obvious that neither Marxist nor Standard theory is valid as a whole for the analysis of a non-capitalist economy, i.e., of the economy of a society in which part or all of the capitalist institutions are absent. A proposition of either theory may eventually be valid for a non-capitalist economy, but its validity must be established *de novo* in each case. . . . Even the analytical concepts developed by these theories cannot be used indiscriminately in the description of other economies. Among the few that are of general applicability there is the concept of a production function together with all its derived notions. But this is due to the purely physical nature of the concept. Most economic concepts, on the contrary, are hard to transplant. . . ." [13, pp. 147–148].

4. Seers has noted that "lack of data on poverty, unemployment and inequality reflects the priorities of statistical offices rather than the difficulties of data collection. The conceptual problems of these measures do not seem to be more formidable than those of the national income. We have just grown accustomed to ignoring (them)" [36, p. 3].

5. "Nowhere," says John Gardner, "can the operation of vested interests be more clearly seen than in the functioning of university departments . . . (the department) assesses the significance of intellectual questions by the extent to which they can be answered without going outside the sacred territory" [12, p. 98].

6. "To accept the distinction between 'pure' and 'applied' economics as generally valid and fundamental is not only to accept the view that 'theory' in its pure form can have an independent career but that it can be validated in some way other than by 'application.' . . . The crux of the issue is simply this: that the only alternative which we have to the validation of inquiry by problem solving is a reliance either upon self evidence of fact or principle as the foundations of knowledge —or upon revelation. Both of the latter alternatives are incompatible with a genuinely scientific viewpoint" [30, pp. 664 and 674]. (See also [6].)

7. "Mopping-up operations are what engage most scientists throughout their careers. They constitute what I am here calling normal science. Closely examined, whether historically or in the contemporary laboratory, that enterprise seems to attempt to force nature into the preformed and relatively inflexible box that the paradigm supplies. No part of the aim of normal science is to call forth new sets of phenomena; indeed those that will not fit the box are often not seen at all. Nor do scientists normally aim to invent new theories, and they are often intolerant of those invented by others. (Here Kuhn cites Bernard Barber, "Resistance by Scientists to Scientific Discovery," *Science* 134:596–602, 1961.) Instead, normal scientific research is directed to the articulation of those phenomena and theories that the paradigm already supplies" [22, p. 24].

8. "One of the results of any survey of the development of economic doctrines is to show that in large measure the important departures of economic theory have been intellectual responses to changing current problems' [25, p. 13].

9. The problem-solving approach to inquiry "easily and naturally frays out into a mere servicing of practical judgments. In fact, it requires strenuous intellectual effort to avoid this very outcome. Under such circumstances we gradually drift into an acceptance of the 'problems' as formulated by our constituency. The next step is simply that of making 'investigators' the mere tools of various interests. . . . Yet the issue must be faced. The argument seems inexorable, that there is no other alternative in genuinely scientific inquiry to having both the roots of inquiry and the final tests of validity in practical problem solving" [30, pp. 675–676].

10. "The object of our analysis is, not to provide a machine, or method of blind manipulation, which will furnish an infallible answer, but to provide ourselves with an organised and orderly method of thinking out particular problems; and, after we have reached a provisional conclusion by isolating the complicating factors one by one, we then have to go back on ourselves and allow, as well as we can, for the probable interactions of the factors amongst themselves. This is the nature of economic thinking" [21, p. 297].

11. See concluding paragraphs by Dudley Seers [36, p. 6; presented in Part II].

1. Benedict, Murray R. *Farm Policies of the United States, 1790–1950.* New York: The Twentieth Century Fund, 1953.

2. Boulding, Kenneth. "The Legitimacy of Economics," *Western Econ. Journal* 5:299–307, 1966–67 [reprinted above].

3. Buse, Rueben C. "Some Comments on Government Policy in Under-developed Countries," paper presented at AID Spring Review

of the High Yielding Cereal Varieties, Washington, D.C., May 1969.

4. Currie, Lauchlin. "The Relevance of Development Economics to Development," paper presented at a Workshop on International Development at the University of Wisconsin, Nov. 1965.

5. Day, R. H. "The Economics of Technological Change and the Demise of the Sharecropper," *Am. Econ. Rev.* 57:425–449, June 1967.

6. Dewey, John. *Logic: The Theory of Inquiry.* New York: Holt, Rinehart and Winston, 1938.

7. Dorner, Peter. "Fourteen Million Rural Poor" (book review of *The People Left Behind,* report by the President's National Advisory Commission on Rural Poverty), *Yale Rev.* 58:282–292, Winter 1969.

8. ———. "Human Progress is Basic to Agricultural Growth," *Internat. Agr. Dev.* (a monthly newsletter, USDA, IADS) 35:12–15, Sept. 1967.

9. Dovring, Folke. "The Share of Agriculture in a Growing Population," *Monthly Bul. Agr. Econ. and Stat.* 8(8/9):1–11, FAO, Rome, Aug.–Sept. 1959. (Also in *Agriculture in Economic Development,* ed. Carl K. Eicher and Lawrence W. Witt. New York: McGraw-Hill, 1964, pp. 78–98.)

10. Eagly, Robert V., ed. *Events, Ideology and Economic Theory.* Detroit: Wayne State University Press, 1968.

11. Eckaus, R. S. "The Factor Proportions Problem in Underdeveloped Areas," *Am. Econ. Rev.* 5:539–565, Sept. 1955.

12. Gardner, John W. *No Easy Victories.* New York: Harper and Row, 1968.

13. Georgescu-Roegen, N. "Economic Theory and Agrarian Economics," *Oxford Econ. Papers* (New Series) 12:1–40, Feb. 1960. (Also in *Agriculture in Economic Development,* ed. Carl K. Eicher and Lawrence W. Witt. New York: McGraw-Hill, 1964.)

14. Gerschenkron, Alexander. "History of Economic Doctrines and Economic History," *Am. Econ. Rev.* 59:1–17, May 1969.

15. "Global Fallacies," *The Economist* 233 (6586):75, Nov. 15, 1969.

16. Griswold, A. Whitney. *Farming and Democracy.* New Haven: Yale University Press, 1948.

17. Heady, Earl O. *A Recipe for Meeting the World Food Crisis.* CAED Report 28, Iowa State University, 1966.

18. Hirschman, Albert O. *Development Projects Observed,* Washington, D.C.: The Brookings Institution, 1967.

19. Johnston, Bruce F., and J. Cownie. "The Seed-Fertilizer Revolution and Labor Force Absorption," *Am. Econ. Rev.* 59:569–582, Sept. 1969.

20. Johnston, Bruce F., and John W. Mellor. "The Role of Agriculture in Economic Development," *Am. Econ. Rev.* 51:566–593, Sept. 1961.

21. Keynes, John Maynard. *The General Theory of Employment, Interest and Money.* New York: Harcourt, Brace and Company, 1936.

22. Kuhn, Thomas S. *The Structure of Scientific Revolutions.* Chicago: University of Chicago Press, 1964.

23. Kurihara, Kenneth K. "The Dynamic Impact of History on Keynesian Theory," in *Events, Ideology and Economic Theory,* ed. Robert V. Eagly. Detroit: Wayne State University Press, 1968, pp. 127–146.

24. Long, Erven J. "Some Theoretical Issues in Economic Development," *J. Farm Econ.* 34:723–733, Dec. 1952.

25. Mitchell, Wesley. *Types of Economic Theory.* New York: Augustus M. Kelly Publishers, 1967.

26. Nair, Kusum. *The Lonely Furrow: Farming in the United States, Japan, and India.* Ann Arbor: The University of Michigan Press, 1969.

27. Owen, Wyn F. "The Double Developmental Squeeze on Agriculture," *Am. Econ. Rev.* 56:43–70, March 1966.

28. ———. "Structural Planning in Densely Populated Countries: An Introduction with Applications to Indonesia," *Malayan Econ. Rev.* 14:97–114, April 1969.

29. Paddock, William, and Paul Paddock. *Hungry Nations.* Boston: Little Brown and Co., 1964.

30. Parsons, Kenneth H. "The Logical Foundations of Economic Research," *J. Farm Econ.* 31:656–686, Nov. 1949.

31. ———. "Poverty as an Issue in Development: A Comparison of United States and Underdeveloped Countries," *Land Econ.* 45:1–14, Feb. 1969.

32. Prest, A. R., and R. Turvy. "Cost-Benefit Analysis: A Survey," *Econ. J.* 75:683–735, Dec. 1965.

33. Raup, Philip. "Land Reform and Agricultural Development," in *Agricultural Development and Economic Growth,* ed. Herman M. Southworth and Bruce F. Johnston. Ithaca: Cornell University Press, 1967, pp. 267–314.

34. Schultz, T. W. "Investment in Human Capital," *Am. Econ. Rev.* 51:1–17, March 1961.

35. Schumpeter, Joseph A. *Capitalism, Socialism and Democracy,* 3rd ed. New York: Harper Torchbooks, 1962.

36. Seers, Dudley. "The Meaning of Development," *Internat. Dev. Rev.* 11(4):2–6, Dec. 1969 [reprinted below].

37. Singer, H. W. "The Distribution of Gains Between Investing and Borrowing Countries," *Am. Econ. Rev.* 40:473–485, May 1950.

38. Southworth, Herman M., and Bruce F.

Johnston, eds. *Agricultural Development and Economic Growth*. Ithaca: Cornell University Press, 1967.

39. Taylor, Henry C., and Anne D. Taylor. *The Story of Agricultural Economics in the United States 1840–1932*. Ames: Iowa State University Press, 1952.

40. Todaro, Michael P. "A Model of Labor Migration and Urban Unemployment in Less Developed Countries, *Am. Econ. Rev.* 59:138–148, March 1969.

41. Wilcox, Walter W., and Willard W. Cochrane. "The Growth Government in Agriculture," ch. 25 in *Economics of American Agriculture*, 2nd ed. Englewood Cliffs: Prentice-Hall, Inc., 1961.

CULTURAL AND SOCIAL FACTORS
IN AGRICULTURAL DEVELOPMENT

JOSEPH W. ELDER

University of Wisconsin

Six or eight years ago I would have found it easier to discuss "Cultural and Social Factors in Agricultural Development" than I do today. For six or eight years ago there seemed to be a kind of consensus about how cultural and social factors *do* affect agricultural development. It was a consensus based, to be sure, on a certain amount of guesswork and inference. But the guesswork and inference seemed reasonable, and at that time there was little else to go on.

Today, alas, the consensus has all but vanished. In its place stands an array of nonfitting cases, increases and decreases in agricultural productivity that seem to defy explanation, and studies that indicate that the links between cultural and social factors and agricultural development are far more complex than we ever dreamed.

In order to see where we have come in these last few years, let us take a look at where we used to be and then examine why we have had to abandon that position.

A few years ago it seemed possible to talk about the phenomenon "traditionalism." In those days, "traditionalism" was seen as an interrelated collection of social institutions and cultural beliefs that blocked the path of progress. For example, in 1962

Everett Hagen described the world view of traditional societies as follows:

The image of the world of the simple folk and elite classes alike includes a perception of uncontrollable forces around them that restrict and dominate their lives. . . . The lines of dependence extend upward to the spiritual powers, to whom the members of the society appeal for protection against the physical forces. . . . Each individual finds his place in the authoritarian hierarchy of human relationships . . . the simple folk find satisfaction in both submissiveness and domination; their personalities as well as those of the elite are authoritarian. . . . In these societies, except for struggles within the class of elite itself, class relationships are fixed.[1]

This world view, according to Hagen, inhibits economic growth:

A society is traditional if ways of behavior in it continue with little change from generation to generation. Where traditionalism is present . . . behavior is governed by custom, not law. The social structure is hierarchical . . . and at least in the traditional state so far in the world's history, economic productivity is low.[2]

Gunnar Myrdal, in his recent *Asian Drama*, describes the clash between the

From *Development and Change in Traditional Agriculture: Focus on South Asia*, Asian Studies Center Occasional Paper, South Asia Series #7, Michigan State University, November 1968, pp. 40–51. Reprinted by permission.

"modernization ideals" and "traditional valuations." According to Myrdal, when certain traditional valuations are held by members of government and those participating in shaping government planning, they act as *inhibitions* to development. When these valuations are held by the majority of the people, they serve as *obstacles* to development:

. . . All the traditional valuations, including those on the most intellectualized level, are static. Even when they are of such a nature as to lend support to the modernization ideals, they themselves are not the driving force.[3]

This "traditional-modern" dichotomy sets the stage for an apparently logical deduction: "The removal of traditionalism is a necessary condition for economic development."

Sure enough, one can find social scientists who have made virtually that deduction. Bert Hoselitz, for example, identifies differences in the basic value orientations of "underdeveloped" and "advanced" societies. He then suggests that for an "underdeveloped" country to become "advanced," it must change its value orientations:

The very needs of economic advancement must bring about a gradual replacement of ascription as a standard by achievement, and associated with this a replacement of functional diffuseness by functional specificity and particularism by universalism.[4]

Hoselitz suggests that along with needing to undergo a basic change in value orientations, "underdeveloped" societies must transform certain traditional institutions, such as their family system, if they are going to "advance":

A change in the pattern of family organization has been observed to accompany all really far-reaching instances of economic growth. . . . It may even be argued that the abolition of certain aspects of the traditional joint family is necessary, because with them the demands of the new economic order could not be adequately met.[5]

Were I to have prepared this paper six or eight years ago, this, then, would have been my major argument: Traditional societies are characterized by cultural values and social institutions that preserve the status quo. Only if these values and institutions are changed can development occur. To elaborate this argument, I would have looked for instances where traditional beliefs or practices inhibited or blocked economic growth—of farmers refusing to use fertilizers or steel-tipped plows because they believe fertilizers "burn the soil out" and steel poisons it; of farmers giving up the cultivation of high-yield corn because they didn't like its taste; of farmers abandoning irrigation because it was too much trouble to keep the pumps in working order; or of farmers preventing a school or credit union from being established in their village for fear a rival faction might receive some benefit.

What has happened in the intervening six or eight years that makes me less sure of that argument? The answer is: a growing body of empirical evidence the argument cannot explain.

Take, for example, the suggestion that traditional values must change if there is to be economic growth. How does one explain the increase in agricultural productivity observed by Albert Mayer and his associates in Etawah District? [6] Were there dramatic shifts in villagers' values during this period? Or what does one do with the rapid increase in agricultural development in West Pakistan in the 1960's? Is it reasonable to suppose that the West Pakistanis have undergone a major value change within the last decade? Or how, indeed, would I explain the increase of agricultural production in my own village of Rajpur in U.P. following the Consolidation of Holdings Act? [7] In this instance I *knew* that the farmers involved had changed very little save that they were now double-cropping their fields instead of single-cropping them. Yet if an abandonment of traditional values is a necessary condition for agricultural development, these farmers should have undergone a value change.

When there are too many exceptions to even a tentative generalization, that generalization must be abandoned. This is what happened to the generalization that traditional values must change if there is to be economic growth.

Or take the widely-accepted view that the traditional, joint family system inhibits economic growth. According to *a priori* reasoning, joint families are ruled by their oldest and hence most conservative members. Therefore they will not be innovative. Reasonable though the view seems, evidence from both Bailey and Ross [8] shows that, in the farming areas where they worked, joint families were more innovative and produced higher yields than did smaller family units.

Furthermore, leaving the realm of agricultural activity for a minute, Gadgil's and Lamb's studies of industrial development in India also underscore the part that traditional joint families have played in innovative, entrepreneurial business activity.[9] In short, the dictum that the removal of traditionalism is a necessary condition for economic development needs revision.

One can ask why the dictum was accepted in the first place. Anybody who has played with intellectual history knows how easy it is to link one "plausible" variable with another. This, I believe, is what happened in social scientists' efforts to link social and cultural variables to economic indices. Observers saw societies with traditional attitudes, traditional institutions, and low productivity. And they assumed that they were all causally linked.

Just as with other fields of inquiry, additional evidence has broken down the earlier tidy formulation, and we must rework both our concepts and our formulations. First of all, the concept of "traditionalism" needs recasting. At present it incorporates such a welter of different phenomena as to render it almost useless for rigorous analysis. The "traditionalism" of North India differs from the "traditionalism" of South India.[10] The "traditional joint family" is one institution in Kerala, another in the Tamilnad, another in U.P., and another in Assam.[11] Even the "traditionalism" of one caste group can differ from that of another, for example, the "traditionalism" of the brahmans and the "traditionalism" of the banias.[12] In the future we are going to have to specify what particular *aspect* of "traditional" cultural attitudes or social institutions we are referring to.

Second, we are going to have to specify more rigorously what the exact relationships are between attitudes and institutions, on one hand, and particular types of economic activity on the other. Because of the complexity of variables, what "works" in one place and time may not "work" in another place and time. Furthermore, what "works" somewhere may not be the *only* thing that would work there. Perhaps the same results can be obtained two or three other ways.

In short, in the following discussion I shall try to delineate clearly what "traditional" cultural and social factors are being discussed, and I shall try to specify what precise relationship these factors appear to have to what aspects of agricultural development.

ONE INDEX OF AGRICULTURAL DEVELOPMENT

In order to narrow the discussion to somewhat manageable proportions, I shall consider only one index of agricultural development—*the increase of yield per acre.* I could have chosen other indices—for example, the increase of yield *per labor unit,* or even the increase of yield *per national capita.* The increase of yield per labor unit is relevant if one is interested in the efficient utilization of manpower by means of the adoption of farm machines, tractors, etc. But it is not a key consideration in a country like India, where there already is a labor surplus. The increase of yield per national capita is relevant from the point of view of long-range national policy, export and import considerations, and family planning to limit population. But an examination of all these variables would take us into problems far removed from farmers and why they work their fields the way they do. But confining our analysis to increase of yield per acre, we shall be dealing with only *one* point where cultural and social factors affect agricultural development. However, especially in India, it seems to be a crucial point.

The broad question we shall be asking is: What makes farmers increase their output per acre? Why is it that some farmers (those not only in India, but also in countries such as Japan, Israel, the United States, and the Soviet Union) are continually looking for ways to increase their crop productivity—new seeds, crop rotation, pesticides and fertilizers, additional irrigation facilities, etc. And why is it that other farmers—even though they may have the necessary knowledge and facilities—will continue their low level of production year after year? If one wants illustrations of the two ends of the continuum, one might choose on the maximum end the Japanese farmers who moved to the northern island of Hokkaido and who, despite expert advice that rice was not suitable to Hokkaido, experimented with new seeds and cropping procedures until they *made* rice not just a suitable but also a prolific crop in Hokkaido. On the minimum end, one might choose the Mysore farmer, Meerappa, described by Kusum Nair, who did not irrigate his fields from the Tungabhadra Project, even though the irrigation channel passed through his fields.[13] Neither he nor many of his neighbors took steps to increase their productivity, even though the means were literally almost at their doorsteps.

Some years ago, I read an article in one of the popular magazines of "success" in marriage. The author contended that 10 percent of the population could be happy with anyone they married and 10 percent could *never* be happy with anyone they married; so the remaining 80 percent would be the focus of his concern. Perhaps we have something analogous with increasing crop yields per acre: 10 percent of the world's farmers will always try to increase their yields regardless of the obstacles; another 10 percent will never do anything to increase their yields no matter how simple the required steps; and the remaining 80 percent will or will not increase their yields, depending on a host of impinging factors. Let us now focus on some of these factors.

In keeping with the title of this paper, I shall divide the variables into two broad categories: social and cultural. However, there is going to be a considerable overlapping, as the two are so closely interrelated. By social factors I shall generally mean institutional factors involving patterned interactions, roles, positive and negative sanctions, etc. To some extent the social factors provide the setting to which the farmer responds. By cultural factors I shall generally mean shared benefits, values, meanings, and attitudes, although at times I shall also bring in individual beliefs, values, meanings, and attitudes. To some extent the cultural factors provide the perspectives the farmer himself brings to the setting.

Social Factors Increasing Yield Per Acre

In looking over the range of social factors that have at times been associated with increasing yields per acre, I am struck by the fact that none of them appears to be indispensable. Furthermore, each particular factor appears able to take various forms. So the final picture is a highly complicated one in which causal links are difficult, if not impossible, to establish. The most we can say is that each of the social factors

I shall list has, in certain instances, contributed to increasing agricultural yields per acre.

Accessible markets. One factor that can encourage increased production is the existence of a pool of persons ready to consume whatever the farmers can produce. Obviously many technical features are involved in the accessibility of markets: roads, bridges, beasts of burden, carts, trucks, railway lines. Yet the presence or absence of these technical features is often related to the ideologies and programs of planners as well as the aspirations of farmers. So even here one is concerned with cultural and social factors.

"Accessible markets" might refer to American gourmets who develop a taste for Kerala cashew nuts or Malihabad mangoes, or it might refer to neighbors down the lane who have decided to augment their diet with more *dal* or tomatoes. Or it might refer to the government's guarantee to purchase all grains that cannot be sold at a certain market price on the open market. Regardless of what particular form the "accessible market" takes, that the market is there and that farmers know they can sell any increased quantity they produce mean that farmers may try to get higher yields from their land in order to benefit from the accessible markets.

Irrigation facilities. Another factor that can encourage higher yields per acre is the availability of irrigation facilities. Complex technical problems may be involved in bringing water hundreds of miles by canal, or sinking tube wells and lacing an area with distribution channels. But alongside the technical problems are the institutional ones: How will the tube well or canal clerks be selected? How will prices be determined? How will they decide who gets priority on the water? How will farmers file requests? To whom can they complain? How can corruption be checked? All of these problems need to be worked through, and on the nature of their solution will rest, to a certain extent, the degree to which irrigation facilities will be used to increase yields per acre.

Of course, it is not essential that irrigation facilities be provided by government departments. Farmers in many parts of India can invest in their own irrigation wells and lifting devices, as they did during the 1965–67 drought in Bihar, when hundreds of farmers installed their own wells to try to save their crops, or as in my U.P. village following the consolidation of the village's fields.

Power (e.g., electricity) facilities. Closely related to irrigation are power facilities such as electricity. An available source of electricity makes it possible to install electric pumps for government and private wells. As with the irrigation facilities, there are institutional questions. Who will decide who gets priority with the electricity? How will prices be determined? How will farmers file requests for using electricity? And how can corruption be checked? To the degree these problems can be solved, electric facilities can play a significant part in increasing agricultural productivity.

Electrical facilities are like so many other factors we are discussing. Obviously they are not sufficient conditions for increased productivity, since electricity can be introduced into an area without any guarantee that agricultural productivity will swing upward. Equally obvious is that electrical facilities are not necessary conditions. If a farmer wants to run a pump, he can just as well do so on diesel fuel. Nonetheless, in the study of 108 villages in Andhra, Maharashtra, and Bengal done by Fliegel, Roy, *et al.,* the presence of electric power facilities was significantly associated with the more successful agricultural change programs.[14]

Fertilizer and seed facilities. Increases in food productivity in West Pakistan and, more recently, in certain districts of India, can sometimes be traced directly to the use of new types of high-yield seeds coupled with the effective use of fertilizers. Although an individual farmer can produce his own fertilizer by composting and green manuring and can develop his own variant of high-yield seed through careful selection from his own fields, more efficient fertilizers and more highly-productive seed varieties *are* known and *can* be made available through either government or private channels. If the decision is made to provide fertilizers and seed facilities, the next questions are: By whom? Under what payment terms? How can the farmers protect themselves against adulterated fertilizers or seeds? How can an excess of demand over

supply be handled without resorting to corruption or favoritism?

Land reform. In my study of the increase of yield per acre in my Uttar Pradesh village, the key antecedent variables I identified were the 1951 Zamindari Abolition Act and the 1953 Consolidation of Holdings Act.[15] Each of the seven farmers who had installed his own irrigation facilities mentioned that the consolidation of his holdings was a major factor in his decision to construct his own well. And the overall increase in productivity in that area following consolidation suggested that drawing together many scattered plots into a few consolidated plots introduced other efficiencies that contributed to higher yields.

In my study, the net effect of abolishing *zamindari* and making former tenants into owners was lost in the shuffle. However, it is frequently assumed—and there is some evidence for it—that converting a farmer from a tenant to an owner contributes directly to his concern for productivity and yields per acre, since now he gets to keep any surplus he produces instead of having to turn it over to the landlord.

Although in my study I looked at only two forms of land reform, other varieties of land legislation may also increase productivity per acre. For example, one way in which farmers who are beginning to prosper frequently expand their wealth is by buying additional land. The farmer prospers, to be sure, because he now has greater acreage. However, typically there is no net increase in productivity per acre. The only change is that the harvest goes to a different farmer.

In view of these findings, it might be advantageous to prohibit farmers of a certain scale from buying additional land. If they want to maximize their profits, they would then be forced to turn their efforts to the more intensive farming of their own fields. The result might be an overall increase in food produced—not merely a different distribution of the same quantity of food.

Once again, legislation is not an indispensable condition for increasing yields per acre. A farmer can decide to crop more intensively whether he is a tenant or an owner, whether his fields are scattered or consolidated, and whether he can buy more land or not. However, land legislation can encourage or discourage certain types of behavior. In the aggregate, it can contribute to increasing productivity per acre.

Credit facilities. In its formal structure, this factor cross-cuts some of the factors already discussed. For example, if a farmer can secure an advance on irrigation water, electrical facilities, or fertilizers and seeds on the basis of his expected higher yields, he may be able to obtain those higher yields. Likewise, if he can secure a sizable loan to enable him to dig his own well, it too might be a key factor in his decision to put in such a well. So long as the terms are manageable and the loaning officials honest, whether he acquires his loan from a credit union, a governmental department, a bank, or even a money lender makes little difference. Should none of these agencies be available, a farmer might still be able to obtain credit from his extended family or caste fellows. In fact, in some ways this "traditional" family institution can be the most "streamlined" in its loaning procedures; it requires less collateral and less red tape simply because it holds wide-ranging powers over the farmer. If he does not fulfill the terms of his agreement the caste can ostracize him with a finality no bank could manage. Once again we have a case of half a dozen agencies that can perform the same function, while the function itself is not indispensable for increasing agricultural productivity.

Communication agents. Many of the studies done on increasing agricultural production in India focus on communication agents—particularly community development workers.[16] Their general conclusion is that such communication agents (with varying degrees of success) do contribute to increasing agricultural productivity. Virtually all of them acknowledge how slow the going is, and all of them indicate that, for certain farmers or in certain villages, the net influence of communication agents is virtually nil. Nevertheless, in the Fliegel, Roy, *et al.*, study of 108 villages, change agents who were willing to demonstrate modern practices were one of the most consistent variables associated with the adoption of more efficient agricultural practices.

Although these studies typically focus on community development workers, it is quite possible for other persons to serve as communication agents—distant family members, one's own schoolchildren, neighboring farmers, relatives back from the army, etc. These communication agents, since they are frequently in touch with details of the immediate area, may actually be more effective communicators than the professionally-trained outsiders.

Village leadership. One of the variables identified in the Fliegel, Roy, *et al.*, study was what they termed a "secularly-oriented leadership." Those villages scoring high on the adoption of agricultural innovations also tended to have "secularly" oriented leaders. The secular orientation of the leaders was determined by a series of questions on caste and disease asked of from six to ten village leaders. Admittedly, there is a slight operational complication here, since six of the seventeen items used to score adoption of agricultural innovations dealt exclusively with the adoption patterns of the leaders. Despite this possibility of a built-in bias, it is still a relevant observation that villages in which there is a greater adoption of agricultural innovations also tend to have leaders(panchayat presidents, village co-op presidents, schoolmasters, priests, etc.) who are more critical of caste and less likely to believe in the magical prevention of diseases. To the extent that leaders set patterns for others to follow, their actions as well as their attitudes may be imitated by others in the village.

Once again, the farmer who decides to increase the yields on his acreage does not need to have heard village leaders expressing secular ideas to have watched them increasing the yields from their own farms. However, apparently in the larger picture it helps to have such leaders in one's village.

One can probably find additional social (institutional) factors that are associated with increasing yields per acre. However, perhaps this list of eight gives some indication of the wide range of factors that might contribute to larger farm output. But we must still keep in mind that none of these factors seems to be the magic key that always unlocks greater productivity.

We now turn to the other set of factors defined in this paper—the cultural factors, these we have earlier defined as shared beliefs, values, meanings, and attitudes, although we shall stretch the definition to include *individual* beliefs, values, meanings, and attitudes. These cultural factors, in a sense, are the perspectives the farmer himself brings to the setting.

Cultural Factors Increasing Yield Per Acre

The range of differing speculation in the recent development literature concerning cultural factors has been greater than that concerning social factors. On one extreme we have the view that only with a radical shift in value orientations can one get a marked change in traditional economic practices. On the other extreme we have the view that in any traditional society there is an ample supply of necessary values, in fact, almost any set of values can be harnessed to increasing productivity if the appropriate institutional infra-structure is there. And there is a spectrum of opinions between the two extremes. From this spectrum I have selected three views for closer scrutiny:
1. Basic value changes are essential if there is to be economic development;
2. Ideological changes are essential if there is to be economic development;
3. No particular value changes are essential for economic development.
Let us examine each one briefly.

Basic value changes are essential if there is to be economic development. This is the view supported by Everett Hagen, David McClelland, and Bert Hoselitz.[17] Whereas Hoselitz simply states that fundamental value orientations must change from particularistic to universalistic, ascriptive to achievement, etc., Hagen and McClelland go into the child-rearing mechanics of how such a change must be brought about. Of the two, Hagen has the most elaborate theory, beginning with traditional societies having authoritarian fathers who implant authoritarian personalities into their sons and thereby prevent them from being creative, moving through a transitional stage wherein the upper classes lose their traditional status, and fathers become unsure of themselves and pass their insecurity and concern for their sons' future welfare on to their sons, who rebel against their fathers and engage in innovative and creative behavior. For the cycle to be completed takes a generation or more.

Although one may question the validity of Hagen's chain of hypotheses, one might agree that the creative personalities he de-scribes or the high-need-achievers McClelland describes would indeed engage in vigorous development activities *regardless* of the institutional infra-structure. Perhaps farmers imbued with these qualities would correspond to the 10 percent of the population who could be happy with anybody they married. These might be our Hokkaido rice farmers whom nothing could stop. And perhaps farmers *totally* lacking in these values would correspond to the 10 percent of the population who could never be happy with anyone they married. These might be Meerappa and his neighbors who wouldn't dig an irrigation channel in order to benefit from the Tungabhadra Project. But the majority of people in any society lie between the range of total commitment to change and total commitment to non-change. We still have the 80 percent in the middle to consider.

Ideological changes are essential if there is to be economic development. In this category one could place Max Weber, the German sociologist, with his view that dramatic economic innovation could hardly take place without some suitable ideological undergirding such as the this-worldly asceticism advocated by certain Protestant sects.[18] W. W. Rostow in his analysis of the stages of economic growth also suggests that certain ideological considerations may be preconditions for economic take-off.

The idea spreads not merely that economic progress is possible, but that economic progress is a necessary condition for some other purpose judged to be good: be it national dignity, private profit, the general welfare, or a better life for the children.[19]

In this context of ideological change contributing to economic development, one can place two of the strongest ideological forces at work in the mid-twentieth century: communism and nationalism. If one looks at countries that have in the recent past performed impressively in raising both industrial and agricultural productivity, one notes such countries as Israel and China where strong ideological forces have been at work.

One needs to stress the variety of possible ideologies that can contribute to economic growth. Horatio Alger, who rises from rags to riches through free enterprise, Ivan Ivanovitch, who exceeds his quota of prairie land brought under cultivation in

Siberia, Lin Chu, who works on the commune farm all day and teaches adult literacy classes each night, these cultural heroes can and do serve as models for the economic behavior of real people.

No particular value changes are essential for economic development. John Lewis, Eugene Staley, and Morris Morris have all suggested that cultural or attitudinal variables have been considerably overemphasized in analyses of India's economic position.[20] They indicate that Indians on almost any level have an ample supply of positive aspirations that can be harnessed to increasing productivity. Even such "traditional" wants as the desire to go on pilgrimages, or to marry off one's daughter with a large dowry, or to give gifts to priests, or to endow temples can serve to motivate hard work, thrift, plowing back profits into increasingly efficient production, and so forth. Even such mundane but widely prevalent desires as the wish to have a brick home or to send one's children to school can stimulate economically-productive behavior. And if these typical positive aspirations are not enough to stimulate agricultural development, there are negative fears that can prod farmers into more intensive cultivation practices: their concern over higher taxes that will leave them with less income unless they increase their yields; their worries about numerous children for whom the same fields will not produce enough unless their yields are increased; their awareness that available land is disappearing from the market so that, if they want to become richer, they have to force higher yields from their present lands.

These aspirations or fears require no radical alteration in child-rearing practices. Nor do they require mass propaganda and the pressures to sustain a high level of ideological commitment. Lewis, Staley, and Morris all suggest that what is needed for agricultural development is less concern over attitudes and more concern over an institutional infra-structure. Man may not be *homo economicus,* but there is enough of the economically rational in most men so that if they see some way in which they can better their lot, they will. Pointing to such countries as Japan or West Pakistan or to such progressive states in India as the Punjab, these theorists indicate that the motivational resources are all around; they need only be harnessed into productive activities.

CONCLUSIONS

Concluding a paper like this poses peculiar problems. The emphasis has been on multiple variables, functional equivalence, and the dispensability of factors certain theorists have held to be indispensable. Such an emphasis does not lend itself to tidy conclusions. However, a number of points I think can be made by way of tying things together.

1. There seems to be ample evidence that so-called "traditional institutions" (such as the joint family, traditional religion, caste, etc.) are not necessarily detrimental to increasing yields per acre.

2. The evidence is also ample that so-called "traditional attitudes" (strong ties to family members, concern over life after death, desire for conspicuous consumption, and expenditure at ritual occasions, etc.) are not necessarily detrimental to increasing yields per acre.

3. There appears to be a variety of social institutions the addition of which can induce higher yields per acre.

4. Certain persons may be either so committed to change (Hagen's creative personalities, McClelland's high-need achievers) or so committed to non-change (Nair's Meerappa) that they are impervious to the institutional innovations. However, I would suggest that such persons at the most compose a small segment of the total population.

5. Many persons, to varying degrees, respond positively to ideological and institutional innovations. Numerous attitudes and ideological streams (such as nationalism, communism, family advancement, etc.) can be tapped, just as numerous institutional factors (such as credit, fertilizer, and improved-seed facilities) may be utilized. For the present, it is difficult to see one—or even several—clear patterns. Perhaps some kind of "critical total" is necessary for any given farmer to change his ways. If none of the ideological or institutional factors is present, one might predict *no* change in low-yield agriculture. If more of the factors are added (development ideologies, irrigation facilities, power facilities, land reform, communication agents, etc.) more and more of the farmers may

reach their "critical total" and begin increasing their yields per acre. Then, when all the social factors are added, virtually all the farmers (with the possible exception of the 10 percent) will engage in high-yield farming. From that point on, one might have reached a type of "take-off" in agricultural development, with farmers demanding further developments of the infra-structure, and the infra-structure developments enabling the farmers to increase their yields still further.

Obviously a great deal of comparative empirical work is required as well as considerable re-conceptualizing of variables before anything like a clear picture emerges concerning the relationships between cultural and social factors and agricultural development. Perhaps the first step is to realize how complex the picture is.

1. Everett Hagen, *On the Theory of Social Change* (Homewood, Illinois: Dorsey Press, 1962), pp. 83–84.

2. *Ibid.*, pp. 55–56.

3. Gunnar Myrdal, *Asian Drama*, Vol. 1 (New York: Pantheon Books, 1968), p. 73.

4. Bert Hoselitz, *Sociological Aspects of Economic Growth* (Glencoe: The Free Press, 1960), p. 47.

5. *Ibid.*, p. 45.

6. Albert Mayer, in collaboration with McKim Marriott and R. L. Park, *Pilot Project India: The Story of Rural Development at Etawah, Uttar Pradesh* (Berkeley: University of California Press, 1958).

7. Joseph W. Elder, "Land Consolidation in an Indian Village: A Case Study in the Consolidation of Holdings Act in Uttar Pradesh," *Economic Development and Cultural Change*, Vol. XI, No. 1 (October, 1962), pp. 16–40.

8. Frederick G. Bailey, *Caste and the Economic Frontier* (Manchester: University of Manchester Press, 1957); Martin H. Ross, "Family Organization and the Development of Agrarian Capitalism in a North Indian Village," unpublished Ph.D. dissertation, University of Wisconsin, 1968.

9. D. R. Gadgil, "Origins of the Modern Business Class: An Interim Report" (New York: International Secretariat, Institute of Pacific Relations, 1959), pp. 1–44; Helen B. Lamb, "The Development of Modern Business Communities in India," in Robert L. Aronson and John P. Windmuller (eds.), *Labor, Management, and Economic Growth; Proceedings of a Conference on Human Resources and Labor Relations in Underdeveloped Countries, November 12–14, 1953* (Ithaca, New York: Cornell Institute of International Industrial and Labor Relations, 1954), pp. 106–121.

10. See, for example, Joseph W. Elder, "Regional Differences in Family and Caste Attitudes: North and South India," in Robert I. Crane (ed.), *Regions and Regionalism in South Asian Studies: An Exploratory Study* (Durham, N.C.: Duke University Program in Comparative Studies in Southern Asia, Monograph No. 5, 1967), pp. 232–257.

11. See, for example, Irawati Karve, *Kinship Organization in India*, rev. ed. (New York: Asia Publishing House, 1965).

12. See, for example, Milton Singer (ed.), *Traditional India: Structure and Change* (Philadelphia: American Folklore Society, 1959), Sec. 1, "The Social Organization of Tradition."

13. *Blossoms in the Dust: The Human Factor in Indian Development* (New York: Frederick A. Praeger, 1962), pp. 46–51.

14. Frederick C. Fliegel, Prodipto Roy, Lalit K. Sen, and Joseph E. Kivlin, *Agricultural Innovations in Indian Villages* (Hyderabad: National Institute of Community Development, 1968), p. 104.

15. Joseph W. Elder, "Land Consolidation in an Indian Village, pp. 20–40.

16. See, for example, Albert Mayer, *op. cit.;* S. C. Dube, *India's Changing Villages; Human Factors in Community Development* (London: Routledge and Kegan Paul, 1958); G. R. Madan, *Changing Pattern of Indian Villages (With special reference to Community Development)* (Delhi: S. Chand and Co., 1959); Kusum Nair, *op. cit.;* B. Mukerji, *Community Development in India* (Bombay: Orient Longmans, 1961); and *Seventh Evaluation Report on Community Development and Some Allied Fields* (New Delhi: Government of India, Planning Commission, 1960).

17. Everett E. Hagen, *op. cit.;* David C. McClelland, *The Achieving Society* (Princeton: D. Van Nostrand, 1961); and Bert F. Hoselitz, *op. cit.*

18. See Max Weber's *The Protestant Ethic and the Spirit of Capitalism,* tr. by Talcott Parsons (New York: Charles Scribner's Sons, 1958); *The Religion of India, The Sociology of Hinduism and Buddhism,* tr. by H. H. Gerth and D. Martindale (Glencoe: The Free Press, 1958); *The Religion of China, Confucianism and Taoism,* tr. by H. H. Gerth (Glencoe, Illinois: The Free Press, 1951); *The Sociology of Religion,* tr. by E. Fischoff (Boston: Beacon Press, 1963).

19. Walter W. Rostow, *The Stages of Economic Growth; A Non-Communist Manifesto* (Cambridge: Cambridge University Press, 1961), p. 6.

20. John P. Lewis, *Quiet Crisis in India* (New York: Doubleday (Anchor paperback), 1964); Eugene Staley, "The Role of the State

in Economic Development," in Myron Wein-
er (ed.), *Modernization* (New York: Basic
Books, 1966), pp. 294–306; and Morris D.
Morris, *The Emergence of an Industrial La-*
bor Force in India: A Study of the Bombay
Cotton Mills, 1854–1947 (Berkeley and Los
Angeles: University of California Press,
1965).

OBSTACLES TO DEVELOPMENT: A CLASSIFICATION
AND A QUASI-VANISHING ACT

ALBERT O. HIRSCHMAN
Harvard University

One could think of several ways of classifying obstacles: natural (lack of resources) and man-made (lack of law and
order, lack of capital), objective (lack of
resources or of capital) and subjective
(lack of entrepreneurship and risk-taking,
lack of a desire for change, contempt for
material success), internal (all the factors
so far named) and external (exploitation
by a foreign power), etc.

I find it useful, however, to adopt a classification which is grounded in the concept
of "obstacle" itself and which, in the process, questions its solidity from the outset.
It is a principal contention of this note that
the concept is far from solid, that it is not
possible to identify either a finite number
of "reliable" obstacles to development or a
hierarchy among these obstacles which
would permit us to arrange them neatly
into boxes marked "basic," "important,"
"secondary," etc.

The traditional method of identifying an
obstacle to development points immediately
to the conceptual weakness we have in
mind. The method consists in looking up
the history of one or several economically
advanced countries, noting certain situations that were present at about the time
when development was brought actively
under way in one or several of these countries (a temperate climate, a population
belonging to the white race, "primitive"
accumulation of capital, coal deposits, law
and order, widespread literacy, a group of
Schumpeterian entrepreneurs, a fairly effi-

cient and honest civil service, agrarian reform, the Protestant Ethic, etc., etc.), and
then construing the *absence* of any of these
situations as an obstacle to development.
This procedure could lead one to conclude
that the more countries develop, the more
difficult does it appear for the remainder
to do the same, for each successfully developing country does so under a set of
special conditions, thus lengthening the list
of obstacles (i.e., the absence of these conditions) which have to be "overcome."

Fortunately, this conclusion is as implausible as it is dismal. The usual way of
escaping from it is by the successive substitution of a newly discovered *fundamental*
obstacle for those that held sway before
the latest theoretical or historical insight.
In this paper we shall proceed in a more
empirical vein and attempt to classify obstacles in the order of their greater or
smaller *reliability* as obstacles, on the basis
of what evidence we have been able to
collect.

Suppose some specific situation or condition can be shown to have been essential
for the development of country X at time t;
in other words, the absence of this condition performed as an insuperable barrier
to the development of X. Now it is possible that the development experience of
other countries confirms that of X; on the
other hand, one can think of the following
ways in which the barrier or obstacle would
fail to perform as such in other countries:
(1) The obstacle does not constitute an

From *Economic Development and Cultural Change* (July 1965), pp. 385–389. Reprinted
by permission.

absolute barrier in the case of country *Y;* certain forward moves are available to this country, and the obstacle, while still exerting a negative influence on development, can be dealt with, perhaps more easily, at a later time.

(2) The alleged obstacle, in view of another set of circumstances, turns out not to be an obstacle at all and therefore does not need to be removed, either now or later.

(3) The alleged obstacle, in view of yet other circumstances, turns into a positive advantage and asset for development.

In justifying each of these possibilities— and, in the process, discovering several other variants—we shall invert the order in which they have been cited and thus start with the most extreme case.

AMBIVALENCE: ALLEGED OBSTACLES THAT TURN INTO ASSETS

How difficult it is to classify certain concrete situations as unequivocally hostile or favorable to economic development is well illustrated by the institution of the *extended* or *joint family*. Several Western economists belonging to quite different schools of thought have taken the position that the extended family dilutes individual incentives and that its demise and replacement by the nuclear family is required for dynamic development to occur.[1] This is, of course, a highly ethnocentric argument. Westerners who hold this view find it difficult to imagine that any one would want to exert himself if the fruits of his labors accrue largely to what they consider as distant relatives; implicit in the idea that the extended family is a bar to economic progress is therefore the judgment that no one in his right mind can really care for the welfare of his third cousin.

But suppose "they" do? In that case the argument against the extended family not only falls to the ground, but one can immediately perceive of several advantages in an arrangement in which the basic economic decision-making unit is not the nuclear family, but a wider grouping. For one, the special relationship existing among the members permits them to undertake new tasks requiring cooperation without prior mastery of such complications as hiring labor and keeping accounts.[2] Furthermore, the members may pool their resources not only for consumption, but equally for investment purposes; and thus it may be possible for them to finance business ventures as well as advanced education for the more gifted among them.[3]

Can we save the proposition for the rather special situation where the extended family still exists as a formal behavior code but can no longer command the full loyalty of the individual member of the society and is perhaps actively resented by him? In that case the strictures of our economists would seem to apply fully. Yet, such is the variety of possible situations that even here we must tread with care. For example, the very desire to withhold extra earnings from one's family may deflect the more enterprising members of the family from a bureaucratic career (where earnings are fixed and a matter of public knowledge) into a business career (where earnings are uncertain and can be concealed).[4] Moreover, if there is any time lag between the newly won affluence of the individual and the famous moving-in of all the relatives to share in his newly won riches, then the institution of the extended family combined with the desire to escape from it provides a stimulus to ever new spurts of temporarily relative-exempt entrepreneurial activity.[5] Hence, even if the sharing implicit in the extended family system is resented, the obligation to share may act like those taxes that stimulate individuals to greater effort at securing non-taxable gains (and at tax evasion).

Our point is strengthened by the observation that, just as the extended family cannot be held to stunt growth under all circumstances, so the nuclear family will not always promote development. If the economic operator perceives no possibility of common interest, action, or gain with anyone outside his immediate blood relatives, then economic advance is likely to be severely hamstrung, as I have explained elsewhere and as has been documented by several empirical studies.[6]

A more general remark is in order at this point. We have said that an obstacle to development may usually be defined as the absence of a condition that was found to be present in a country which subsequently developed. But in many cases the question that ought to have been asked is *how much* of this condition was present. Too much may be just as deleterious as too little. It is too much rather than too little individualism and entrepreneurship and too little willingness to work with discipline in a hierarchical organization that plagues much of Southeast Asia and also other underdeveloped lands.[7] Too much law and order may be as stifling as too little is disruptive.

Let us arrange the possible states of society along a horizontal scale with two such extremes at opposite ends. Suppose we measure the chances for development along the vertical scale. In most cases, then, these chances will seriously drop off at *both* ends of the scale, but they may well be tolerably good during a wide stretch in the middle. In other words, societies that are *all* individualistic entrepreneurship or that are *all* hierarchical discipline will both be hard put to develop, but in the real world we are likely to encounter predominantly individualistic and predominantly hierarchical societies that contain some, perhaps well hidden, ingredients of discipline and of entrepreneurship, respectively; hence, they may both be capable of development, even though the paths on which they will set out toward this goal are likely to be very different.

We have dwelt at some length on the extended family, since it illustrates well our notion of ambivalence of alleged obstacles. We shall now give a few more examples, rapidly and at random, to suggest the wide spectrum of situations to which the notion applies.

In Europe the tradition of very high craftsmanship was initially most helpful in the development of new mechanical methods. But the rapid pace of development in the United States in the 19th century has been explained in part by the *absence* of such a tradition in the new continent and by the relative scarcity of skilled labor which stimulated the introduction of capital-intensive, skilled-labor-saving techniques.[8]

Lack of social mobility ranks high as an impediment to economic progress because it sets limits to individual achievement and prevents the best utilization of manpower resources. In Japan, however, the rigid social barriers which kept the merchants and their sons from joining the bureaucracy or from becoming landlords have been hailed as one of the sources of private entrepreneurship and have been contrasted with

the harmful effects of the ease with which such transitions were effected by the successful merchants of China.[9]

What could be more inimical to the accumulation of material wealth than the ascetic ideal? Yet, as soon as this ideal extends to combating indulgence in *leisure* (in addition to indulgence in food, drink, and sex), capital accumulation through self-denying work is a likely, if surprising, result.[10]

Law and order and the absence of civil strife seem to be obvious preconditions for the gradual and patient accumulation of skills, capital, and investors' confidence that must be the foundation for economic progress. We are now told, however, that the presence of war-like Indians in North America and the permanent conflict between them and the Anglo-Saxon settlers was a great advantage, because it made necessary methodical, well-planned, and gradual advances toward an interior which always remained in close logistic and cultural contact with the established communities to the East. In Brazil, on the contrary, the backlands were open and virtually uncontested; the result was that once an excessively vast area had been occupied in an incredibly brief time span the pioneers became isolated and regressed economically and culturally. Jacques Lambert, author of this observation, sums up his remarks in the following sentence: "In contradiction to a deeply entrenched legend, which paints the Anglo-Saxon colonizers as individualists and adventurers and the Iberians as colonial functionaries without initiative, Brazil is now paying dearly for the taste of adventure of the Portuguese and for their excess of initiative." [11]

ALLEGED OBSTACLES WHOSE ELIMINATION
TURNS OUT TO BE UNNECESSARY

We turn now to a somewhat less paradoxical type of situation: the presumed obstacle no longer changes colors and become a blessing in disguise; its existence simply leads to the charting of a hitherto unfamiliar path to economic progress, and the resulting, economically more advanced society exhibits a profile that is "different" because of the survival of certain institutions, attitudes, etc., which were originally thought to be incompatible with development. These situations can be difficult to distinguish clearly from the preceding ones, for if the presumed obstacle has at all survived, then one can frequently show that it is not only tolerated, but actually lends strength to the new state of affairs. Nevertheless, there is a difference, at least initially, between an obstacle that is being turned or neutralized and one that turns out not to be an obstacle at all, but a factor that promotes and propels development.

The confusion on this score is due to the somewhat shapeless notion of "challenge." Any difficulty or obstacle can be transmuted by a sort of semantic hocus pocus into a challenge which evokes a response. But these Toynbeean terms are not helpful, for they dissolve the concepts of difficulty and obstacle altogether, instead of permitting the differentiated analysis we are aiming at here. To recall an example from our preceding section, it is incorrect to say that the existence of the extended family is a "challenge" to developers; it is rather a real trouble-maker in some respects and some situations and a valuable asset in others, as we have shown. The notion of challenge is similarly ineffectual in the case, now under consideration, of obstacles which have no positive dimension, but which do not preclude development via some "alternate route" (alternate to the removal of the obstacle).

Let us take a country which lacks an important natural resource such as coal or whose history has not permitted any sizeable "primitive accumulation of capital"; when such countries substitute hydroelectric energy for coal, or bank credit and state finance for private equity capital,[12] they are not "responding" to a "challenge." They are merely encountering a different way of achieving growth which, of course, they might never have discovered had they been more "normally" endowed. "Believe me," says the Marquise de Merteuil in Laclos' *Les Liaisons Dangereuses,* "one rarely acquires the qualities he can do without." Yet, to acquire these very qualities is less a matter of responding to a challenge than of discovering one's comparative advantage. In doing so a country may not even have been aware of the fact that the lack of a certain natural resource, institution, or attitudinal endowment constituted a special difficulty, an obstacle, or much less, a "challenge."

If a country lacks one of the conventional "prerequisites," it can overcome this lack in two distinct ways. One consists in inventing its own substitute for the prerequisite; as just mentioned, Gerschenkron has given us an exceptionally rich and convincing account of such substitution processes for the Marxian prerequisite of primitive accumulation of capital. The other possibility is that the purported "prerequisite" turns out to be not only substitutable, but outright dispensable; nothing in particular needs to take its place, and we are simply proven wrong in our belief that a certain resource, institution, or attitude needed to be created or eradicated for development to be possible. In other words, the requirements of development turn out to be more tolerant of cultural and institutional variety than we thought on the basis of our limited prior experience.

Recent research shows this to be the case in various parts of the world. A revealing study of the Japanese factory by Abegglen has shown in considerable detail how "rationalization and impersonalization are not necessary to the adoption from the West of an industrial economy."[13] Here we are admittedly only one step away from our previous category, where the negative factor is transmuted into a positive one. A study of Argentine entrepreneurship takes this step explicitly.

Analysts of entrepreneurship hold certain of the Latin American characteristics to be deterrents to success in the development of industry. Granting that [Di Tella, the founder of the firm under study] neither could nor wanted to break the emotional patterns of an inward-looking individualism, a reliance on *personalismo,* or the claims of the family . . . he skillfully neutralized these assumed deterrents or turned them into positive assets. He used themes and relationships such as *personalismo, dignidad, simpatia, confianza,* and the *patrón*-client relation for the development of [his firm].[14]

In a somewhat different vein, a study of Indian village life has shown that the social, political, and cultural changes that come with development may be of sharply different dimensions depending on the precise way in which economic opportunities arise. The study deals with two villages and the way in which they have taken advantage of irrigation. Change is shown to be more extensive and comprehensive in the dry village whose lands are close to, but not right in, the irrigation district than in the wet village. In a perceptive introduction, Sir Arthur Lewis remarks: "What we need to know is just how powerful a solvent the love of money is. The answer seems to be that it dissolves what stands in its way, but nothing more. How much is changed depends partly on how much is compatible, and partly on how closely interrelated the various institutions are." [15] It appears from the studies here surveyed that a variety of non-Western institutions are either more compatible with economic development (Sir Arthur's "love of money") or less interrelated with those that are incompatible than has been believed by those who look at each social situation as an "interrelated whole." [16]

OBSTACLES WHOSE ELIMINATION IS
POSTPONABLE

We are now ready for those obstacles which we come closest to recognizing as such, those that refuse to turn mysteriously into assets or to be accommodated in an unexpected fashion within an economically progressive society. They stubbornly remain factors detrimental to development which ought to be eliminated. In many cases, however, and this is the point of the present section—the priority which this task commands can be shown to be less rigidly defined than had been thought.

I am returning here to a theme which I have set forth at length in my previous writings. I have drawn attention to "inverted" or "disorderly" or "cart-before-the-horse" sequences that are apt to occur in the process of economic and social development; and I have argued that, under certain circumstances, these sequences could be "efficient" in the sense of making possible the achievement of stated goals of economic expansion within a briefer time period or at a smaller social cost than would be possible if the more orderly sequence were adhered to.[17]

The implication of this approach for the notion of barrier and obstacle is evident. While it grants that insufficient electric power, inadequate education, or the absence of agrarian reform are serious defects, it is suspicious of theories that erect the elimination of such defects into *prerequisites* for *any* forward movement; in

addition to the head-on assault on these defects, it will evaluate, look for, and scrutinize ways in which the economy can be moved forward elsewhere and how thereby additional pressure can be brought to bear on the acknowledged obstacles. If they are truly hindrances, then any forward move that can be instigated in spite of them is going to make it even more imperative than before to get rid of them; if, on the other hand, this additional pressure is not generated, then perhaps these obstacles are not to be taken quite so seriously, and they belong, at least in part, in our second category (assumed obstacles that, as it turns out, can be accommodated into an economically progressive society).

Rather than repeat my earlier argument and cite a series of examples to which it applies, I shall limit myself here to one particular type of inverted sequence which seems to me of considerable interest and with which I have not dealt before.

As the search for the conditions of economic development has been unremittingly pursued by social scientists over the past years, increasing attention has been given to the role of attitudes, beliefs, and basic personality characteristics favorable to the emergence of innovation, entrepreneurship, and the like. While these theories, with their expeditions into psychology and psychiatry, are frequently fascinating, the message they leave behind is almost as dismal as that of the very first theories of development which attributed a decisive role to such unalterable factors as race, climate, and natural resources. Rooted, as they are purported to be, in childhood experiences and transmitted unfailingly from one generation to the next, the deplored attitudes or personality structure appear to be similarly refractory to any but the most radical treatment.

We have already seen, in our first two sections, that a good many attitudes which, on the basis of some previous experiences, had been believed to be detrimental to development can, in different settings, be neutralized or even be put to positive use, as the case may be. But let us accept now the premise that some residual attitudes, beliefs, and personality characteristics are really and truly incompatible with sustained economic advance—must we then accept the conclusion that *all* our efforts should be concentrated on extirpating them, and that no other road to progress is available?

Fortunately, while the behavioral scientists have become depth psychologists, the psychologists have come up with the discovery that attitudinal change can be a *consequence* of behavioral change, rather than its precondition! From a variety of approaches exploring this nexus, I shall single out the *Theory of Cognitive Dissonance*, which was originated in 1957 by Leon Festinger in a book bearing that title. Since then the theory has been widely investigated, tested, and discussed; much of the empirical evidence which has been gathered, together with a chapter on the applicability of the theory to problems of social change, can be found in a volume by Jack W. Brehm and the late Arthur R. Cohen, *Explorations in Cognitive Dissonance* (New York, 1962).[18]

Briefly and in non-technical language, the theory states that a person who, for some reason, commits himself to act in a manner contrary to his beliefs, or to what he believes to be his beliefs, is in a state of dissonance. Such a state is unpleasant, and the person will attempt to reduce dissonance. Since the "discrepant behavior" has already taken place and cannot be undone, while the belief can be changed, reduction of dissonance can be achieved principally by changing one's beliefs in the direction of greater harmony with the action.

The theory thus predicts significant shifts in attitude consequent upon commitment to discrepant behavior, and its predictions have been verified empirically. In a classical experiment, for example, college students are asked to write an essay supporting the side opposite to their private view on a current issue. It turns out that after writing the essay (and to some extent even right after committing themselves to write it and before actually writing it), the students' attitude shifts away from what they used to consider their position on the issue. An interesting refinement of the experiment consists in varying the reward given to the students for writing the essay; it then appears that, in contrast to the usual ideas about refinement, highly rewarded students change their opinion much *less* than the lowly rewarded ones, the reason being that dissonance and hence the extent of the shift is highest when the discrepant

behavior cannot be explained away and dismissed by the ego as having at least some pleasurable result.

This theory has been of practical use in helping us understand the processes of "thought reform" or "brainwashing" as applied, for example, to U.S. prisoners of war by their Chinese captors during the Korean War; in a more constructive vein, the theory has contributed to illuminate the psychological processes leading to acceptance of racial integration. A further fruitful field of application of the theory may be the process of attitude change which is required in the course of economic development. The following quotations from the Brehm-Cohen volume are suggestive:

> The theory is different in its essential nature than most other theoretical models in psychology. Where the major concern in other theories has been largely with the guidance of behavior—that is, with what leads to a given behavior or commitment —dissonance theory deals, at least in part, with the *consequences* of a given behavior or commitment (p. 299).
>
> Dissonance theory attempts to understand the conditions under which behavioral commitments produce cognitive and attitudinal realignments in persons (p. 271).

In other words, dissonance theory deals with the possibility of replacing the "orderly" sequence, where attitude change is conceived as the prerequisite to behavioral change, by a "disorderly" one, where modern attitudes are acquired *ex post*, as a consequence of the dissonance aroused by "modern" type of behavior which happens to be engaged in by people with non-modern attitudes. One question will, of course, be asked, namely: how can a commitment to "modern" behavior be obtained from people whose values and attitudes preclude in principle such behavior? Actually, however, this is not much of a problem among *late coming* societies surrounded by modernity and by opportunities to transgress into or try out modern behavior; at one time or another, it is likely that the late-comer will stumble more or less absent-mindedly into such behavior as pursuit of individual profit, entrepreneurial risk-taking, promotion according to merit, long-term planning, holding of democratic elections, etc.; dissonance will thus arise and will then gradually lead to those changes in attitude and basic beliefs which were thought to be prerequisites to the just-mentioned modes of behavior. The art of promoting development may therefore consist primarily in multiplying the opportunities to engage in these dissonance-arousing actions and in inducing an initial commitment to them.[19]

One observation will conclude this section. A country which achieves economic advance and modernization through the process just described, i.e., where behavioral change paces attitudinal change, is likely to exhibit a personality rather different from the country whose elite right at the outset of the development journey is imbued with the Protestant Ethic and saturated with achievement motivation. Because, in the case of the former country these motivations are being laboriously acquired *ex post* and en route, its path will be more halting and circuitous and its typical personality may well be subject to particularly strong tension between traditional and modern values.[20] While a country can well develop without being endowed at the outset with all the "right" values and attitudes, its development profile and experience cannot but bear the marks of the order and manner in which it accomplishes its various tasks.

CONCLUSION

This is the end of our exercise in classification. It goes without saying that its purpose was not to destroy entirely the notion of barrier, obstacle, or prerequisite. In the first place, the classification was not meant to be exhaustive, and there may well exist a residual category of obstacles which by no stretch of the imagination can be considered as assets, which cannot be accommodated or neutralized, and whose removal must be accomplished before any other forward step can be usefully attempted. Secondly, if certain alleged obstacles turn out to be blessings in disguise, quite a few factors, hitherto considered as wholly favorable to development, are likely to function in some situations as *curses* in disguise.

Finally, and most important, while our exercise points to many ways in which obstacles can be made into assets or lived with or turned, it says nothing about the *ability to perceive these possibilities* on the part of the policy-makers in developing

countries. If this ability is strictly limited, as is often the case, then this very limitation emerges as a super-obstacle, which commands and conditions the existence and seriousness of the more conventional obstacles. And it can now be told that the survey here presented was really aimed at loosening the grip of this central difficulty.

1. P. T. Bauer and B. S. Yamey, *The Economics of Under-Developed Countries* (Chicago, 1957), p. 66; and Benjamin Higgins, *Economic Development* (New York, 1959), p. 256.

2. C. S. Belshaw, *In Search of Wealth: A Study of the Emergence of Commercial Operations in the Melanesian Society of South-Eastern Papua* (Vancouver, 1955), chaps. 5 and 7.

3. Peter Marris, *Family and Social Change in an African City* (London, 1961), p. 138. The importance of kinship ties in the early spread of banking and mercantile enterprise in the West is of course well established.

4. *Ibid.*, p. 139.

5. "The fact that, under the customary rules of inheritance, individual property was always in process of conversion to family property provided individuals with a great incentive to acquire additional lands, over which they had, for some time at least, unlimited control." Polly Hill, *The Migrant Cocoa-Farmers of Southern Ghana* (Cambridge, 1963), p. 16.

6. A. O. Hirschman, *The Strategy of Economic Development* (New Haven, 1958), pp. 14–20; Edward C. Banfield, *The Moral Basis of a Backward Society* (Glencoe, Ill., 1958); Clifford Geertz, *Peddlers and Princes* (Chicago, 1963), pp. 42–47, 73 ff., 122 ff.

7. "Malaya probably suffers from an excess of enterprise, since this is a factor which tends to disintegrate existing business." T. H. Silcock, *The Economy of Malaya* (Singapore, 1956), p. 44.

8. H. J. Habakkuk, *American and British Technology in the 19th Century* (Cambridge, England, 1962), pp. 116, 128–29.

9. M. J. Levy, Jr., "Contrasting Factors in the Modernization of China and Japan," in S. Kuznets et al., eds., *Economic Growth: Brazil, India, Japan"* (Durham, N.C., 1955), pp. 496–536.

10. Karl F. Helleiner, "Moral Conditions of Economic Growth," *Journal of Economic History* (Spring 1961), pp. 97–116.

11. Jacques Lambert, *Os dois Brasís* (Rio, 1959), pp. 116–17.

12. Alexander Gerschenkron, *Economic Backwardness in Historical Perspective* (Cambridge, Mass., 1962), chaps. 1 and 2.

13. James G. Abegglen, *The Japanese Factory* (Glencoe, Ill., 1958), p. 141.

14. Thomas C. Cochran and Reuben E. Reina, *Entrepreneurship in Argentine Culture: Torcuato Di Tella and S.I.A.M.* (Philadelphia, 1962), pp. 262–63. Abegglen also occasionally takes this step, arguing that certain elements of traditional Japanese culture are not only compatible with the new order, but actually lend strength to it: "The principle of family loyalty and cohesion, when successfully symbolized and incorporated into military, industrial and financial organizations, may have become an important source of energy and motivation for the transition to industrialization." *Op. cit.*, pp. 136–37.

15. T. S. Epstein, *Economic Development and Social Change in Southern India* (Manchester, 1962), p. x.

16. ". . . (various) studies suggest that the impact of economic modernization upon the total social system is not necessarily as revolutionary and all-embracing as it has sometimes been described; or, put somewhat differently, a modern economic system may be compatible with a wider range of noneconomic cultural patterns and social structures than has often been thought." Geertz, *op. cit.*, p. 144. For an interesting essay on the compatibility of certain traditional values (as distinct from "traditionalism") with progressive economic development, see Bert F. Hoselitz, "Tradition and Economic Growth," in Braibanti and Spengler, eds., *Tradition, Values and Socio-Economic Development* (Durham, N.C., 1961), pp. 83–113.

17. See, e.g., *The Strategy of Economic Development*, pp. 80–81, 93–94, 154–55; *Journeys Toward Progress: Studies of Economic Policy-Making in Latin America* (New York, 1963), p. 260.

18. It should be pointed out that the theory is by no means universally accepted. For a highly critical appraisal, see N. P. Chapanis and A. Chapanis, "Cognitive Dissonance: Five Years Later," *Psychological Bulletin* (January 1964), 1–22.

19. If one were to extend the above-mentioned "refinement" of the theory to the development context, one would conclude that the conditioning of foreign aid on internal reform can do positive harm at the stage when an underdeveloped country is about to commit itself to new types of "modern" or reform actions; to reward such perhaps partly dissonant behavior would lead to less cumulative change than if the behavior could not be dismissed by the actors as something they did just to get hold of the aid funds. In this way, the theory throws some light on the difficulties of using aid as a means of promoting internal reform which have beset the Alliance for Progress since its inception. Besides many other constructive uses, foreign aid may be helpful in promoting reform and will serve as a reinforcing agent when it is conceived and presented as a means of reducing the cost of a reform to which the policy-makers in the recipient country are already firmly committed; but it is cast in a self-defeating role if it is proffered as a *quid pro quo* for the reform commitment itself.

20. In *Journeys Toward Progress*, pp. 235 ff., I have drawn a related difference by distinguishing between societies which, in the process of tackling their problems, let motivation to solve problems outrun their understanding, and those that do not usually tackle problems unless the means to solve them are close at hand. Here also the two styles of problem-solving are shown to result in sharply differing development experiences.

•

*Toward an
Existential
Social Science*

•

WHAT Albert Hirschman calls "cognitive styles" in this review article refers to the epistemological stance taken toward the real world. James Payne's analysis of Colombian politics represents an application of essentialist thinking, while John Womack's treatment of the Mexican Revolution demonstrates a more existential approach.

Hirschman's castigation of "paradigms" refers more to the typological mode of analysis than to models as such. For one thing, he has himself employed paradigms, though he has done so to explore and explicate possibilities rather than to foreclose them.[1] For another, he recognizes the importance of making some simplification in analysis in order to achieve some predictive capabilities. This is not possible without some degree of generalization or some use of models.

The endorsement of Womack's concern with "feeling" as an aid to understanding is not, we think, an endorsement by Hirschman of subjectivism in social science. Rather it is a recognition on their part of the need to attain some understanding of the perspective of the actors involved and of the realities of the particular situation.[2] Research that ignores actors' perceptions and intentions and treats particular cases as an approximation of some general case cannot obtain the insight needed to trace real causal connections and to make apt, if limited, generalizations from the case under consideration.

Hirschman is concerned with the problems of causation and prediction in social science. But this leads to a search for the configurations of variables and the transformation of parameters into variables that make change possible and achievable. It leads away from generalization and abstraction for the sake of "science" and leads, instead, toward the study of consequences of action. In addition, Hirschman points out some manifestations of "intellectual neo-colonialism" that affect contemporary thinking about underdeveloped countries.

[1] See Part II of his book, *Journeys Toward Progress: Studies of Economic Policy-Making in Latin America* (1963).

[2] We would note that Womack's account is replete with the terms used in our model of political economy: resources—money, services, status, prestige, respect, legitimacy, authority, information, violence, coercion, etc.; political capital, debts, investment; even sectors and infrastructure. These things, even if not all material, have definite tangibility from the perspective of political actors seeking to achieve competing ends.

THE SEARCH FOR PARADIGMS AS A
HINDRANCE TO UNDERSTANDING

ALBERT O. HIRSCHMAN

Harvard University

In a recent issue of this journal, Oran Young argued forcefully against the "collection of empirical materials as an end in itself and without sufficient theoretical analysis to determine appropriate criteria of selection." [1] The present paper issues a complementary critique of the opposite failing. Its target is the tendency toward *compulsive and mindless theorizing*—a disease at least as prevalent and debilitating, so it seems to me, as the one described by Oran Young.

While the spread of mindless number-work in the social sciences has been caused largely by the availability of the computer, several factors are responsible for the compulsion to theorize, which is often so strong as to induce mindlessness. In the academy, the prestige of the theorist is towering. Further, extravagant use of language intimates that theorizing can rival sensuous delights: what used to be called an interesting or valuable theoretical point is commonly referred to today as a "stimulating" or even "exciting" theoretical "insight." Moreover, in so far as the social sciences in the United States are concerned, an important role has no doubt been played by the desperate need, on the part of the hegemonic power, for shortcuts to the understanding of multifarious reality that must be coped with and controlled and therefore be understood *at once*.

Interestingly enough, revolutionaries experience the same compulsion: while they are fond of quoting Marx to the approximate effect that interpreting the world is not nearly as important as changing it, they are well aware of the enormous strength that is imparted to revolutionary determination by the conviction that one has indeed fully understood social reality and its "laws of change." As a result of these various factors, the quick theoretical fix has taken its place in our culture alongside the quick technical fix.

In the following pages, I do not have a central epistemological theorem to offer that would permit us to differentiate between good and bad theorizing, or between fruitful and sterile paradigmatic thinking. My accent throughout is on the kind of *cognitive style* that hinders, or promotes, understanding. I introduce the topic by a critical look at two books that exemplify opposite styles. Subsequently, I make an attempt to delineate various areas in which an impatience for theoretical formulation leads to serious pitfalls. Theorizing about Latin American society and economy, on the part of both Latin Americans and outside observers, receives special attention because it has been particularly marked by the cognitive style I find unfortunate.

I

John Womack's *Zapata and the Mexican Revolution* [2] and James L. Payne's *Patterns of Conflict in Colombia* [3] are the two books I shall use to open the argument. They have in common that they are both by young North American scholars; both, in fact, were originally written as doctoral dissertations; and they were both published early in 1969. But this is where any possible resemblance ends. At this point I should state that both books aroused in me unusually strong feelings: I found Womack's way of telling the Zapata story extraordinarily congenial, while I was strongly repelled by Payne's book in spite of its crispness, cleverness, and occasional flashes of wit.

There are of course many striking contrasts between the two books that can account for these opposite reactions, not the least perhaps being that Womack obviously fell in love with revolutionary Mexico and the Zapatistas whereas Payne's treatment exudes dislike and contempt for Colombians in general, and for Colombian poli-

From *World Politics* (April 1970), pp. 329–343. Reprinted by permission.

ticians in particular. But the more important, and not necessarily related, difference is in the cognitive styles of the two authors.

Within the first few pages of his book Payne presents us triumphantly with the key to the full and complete understanding of the Colombian political system. The rest of the book is a demonstration that the key indeed unlocks all conceivable doors of Colombian political life, past, present, and future. Womack, on the other hand, abjures any pretense at full understanding right in the Preface, where he says that his book "is not an analysis but a story because the truth of the revolution in Morelos is in the feeling of it which I could not convey through defining its factors but only through telling of it." "The analysis that I could do," so he continues, "and that I thought pertinent I have tried to weave into the narrative, so that it would issue at the moment right for understanding it" (p. x). And indeed what is remarkable about the book is the continuity of the narrative and the almost complete, one might say Flaubertian, absence from its pages of the author who could have explained, commented, moralized, or drawn conclusions.

Yet whoever reads through the book will have gained immeasurably in his understanding not only of the Mexican Revolution, but of peasant revolutions everywhere, and Womack's very reticence and self-effacement stimulate the reader's curiosity and imagination. Payne's book, on the contrary, obviously explains far too much and thereby succeeds only in provoking the reader's resistance and incredulity; the only curiosity it provokes is about the kind of social science that made an obviously gifted young man go so wrong.

Here, then, is the experience behind the title of this paper: understanding as a result of one book without the shadow of a paradigm; and frustration as a result of another in which one paradigm is made to spawn 34 hypotheses (reproduced, for the convenience of the reader, in the book's appendix) covering all aspects of political behavior in Colombia and, incidentally, the United States as well.

Perhaps I should explain briefly what Mr. Payne's basic "insight" or paradigm consists in: politicians in Colombia, he has found out through questionnaires, interviews, and similar devices, are motivated primarily by status considerations rather than by genuine interest in programs and policies, as is predominantly and fortunately the case in the United States. He uses the neutral-sounding terms "status incentive" and "program incentive"; the former characteristically motivates Colombian political leaders whereas the latter animates their North American counterparts.

In plain language, occasionally used by the author, Colombian politicians are selfish (p. 70), ambitious, unscrupulous, unprincipled, exceedingly demagogic—interested exclusively in increasing their own power, always ready to betray yesterday's friends and allies, and, to top it all, incapable of having friendly personal relations with anyone because they feel comfortable only with abject supplicants (p. 12). On the other hand, there is the politician with a program incentive whose preferred habitat is the United States of America. He enjoys working on concrete policies and achieving a stated goal; hence he is principled, willing to defend unpopular causes, always ready to come to constructive agreements, hard-working, and generally lovable.

For a North American to contrast Colombian and United States politicians in terms of such invidious stereotypes is, to say the least, a distasteful spectacle. We must of course allow for the possibility that truth, as unearthed by the scholar, turns out to be distasteful. But Payne does not betray any sense of realizing the unpleasantness of his discovery. On the contrary, he evidently draws much satisfaction from the edifice he has built and takes good care to make sure that there will be no escape from it.

At various points he assures us that Colombians are like that; that, as he put it in a subtitle, they are not "on the brink of anything"; that it is futile to expect any change in the pattern of Colombian politics from such incidental happenings as industrialization or urbanization or agrarian reform: like the three characters in Sartre's *Huis Clos,* the 20 million Colombians will just have to go on living in their self-made hell while Mr. Payne, after his seven-month diagnostic visit (from February to September, 1965, as he informs us in the preface), has returned to his own, so much more fortunate section of the hemisphere.

It is easy to show that the Payne model

is as wrong as it is outrageous. In the first place, it is unable to explain the very wide swings of Colombian politics; after all, during almost all of the first half of the twentieth century Colombia stood out as a "stable" democracy with peaceful transfers of power from one party to another; throughout the Great Depression of the thirties when almost all other Latin American countries experienced violent political convulsions, constitutional government continued in spite of much social unrest.

This experience is hard to explain by a theory that holds that vicious political infighting, untrammeled by any concern with programs or loyalty, holds continuous sway throughout the body politic. Moreover, such a theory ought to take a good look at—and give a special weight to—the body's head: if Payne had done that he might have noticed that his stereotype, the politician with a status incentive, simply does not apply to a number of the most outstanding leaders and recent presidents of Colombia—there is no need to mention names, but it is amusing to quote, in contrast, from a recent portrait of a contemporary President of the United States: "His preoccupation seems to have been success—in this case the achievement of power rather than its use for political purposes." [4]

Supposing even that the diagnosis is essentially correct and that politicians in Colombia are more interested in the quest for power *per se* than in the use of this power for the carrying out of specific programs— what does this "insight" explain? Suppose that we find, as Payne indeed does, that those self-seeking politicians frequently switched sides or vote for demagogic measures, does this finding teach us anything fundamental about the political system, its ability to accommodate change, to solve newly arising problems, to assure peace, justice, and development? It does nothing of the sort, but at best leaves us with the proposition, which incidentally is both platitudinous and wrong, that if the politicians are vicious, the ensuing politics are likely to be vicious too!

Let us pass now from the paradigms of James Payne to John Womack, who has rigorously excluded from his universe any semblance of a paradigm. It is of course impossible to do justice to his narrative. I shall refer here only to one particular turn of the events he describes in order to show how he invites speculation and thereby contributes to the possibility of understanding.

It has perhaps not been sufficiently remarked that the book has *two* protagonists: Zapata dominates the action during the first nine chapters, but in the important last two chapters (80 pages) the leading figure is Gildardo Magaña who became Zapata's ranking secretary after mid-1917 and, after a brief fight for the succession, the chief of the Zapatista movement following Zapata's death in April, 1919. Womack honors Magaña with one of his too-rare character portraits: "From these stresses [of his youth] Gildardo Magaña somehow emerged strong and whole. What he had learned was to mediate: not to compromise, to surrender principle and to trade concessions, but to detect reason in all claims in conflict, to recognize the particular legitimacy of each, to sense where the grounds of concord were, and to bring contestants into harmony there. Instinctively he thrived on arguments, which he entered not to win but to conciliate" (p. 290).

Womack then relates the exploits of Magaña as a resourceful negotiator of ever new alliances and contrasts him with the rigid and sectarian Palafox, Zapata's earlier principal secretary, who "seemed in retrospect the individual responsible for the Zapatistas' present plight—the man they could blame for their disastrous involvement with Villa in 1914, their alienation of worthy chiefs in the constitutionalist party, and their abiding reputation as the most intransigent group in the revolutionary movement" (p. 306).

After the murder of Zapata, Magaña maneuvered tactfully and successfully among the various chiefs. After six months, the succession crisis was over and Magaña was recognized as commander-in-chief, with the movement virtually intact. Womack then traces the complex events through which the Zapatistas, as he puts it in the title of his last chapter, "Inherit Morelos"—that is manage, by alternately fighting and negotiating and by backing Obregón at the right moment, to pass from outlaws into local administrators and members of a national coalition. "So ended the year 1920, in peace, with populist agrarian reform instituted as a national policy, and with the Zapatista movement established in Morelos politics. In the future through thick and thin these achievements would last. This was the claim Zapata, his chiefs, and their volunteers had forced, and *Magaña had won and secured"* (p. 369; italics added).

Twice Womack implies that this outcome was due not only to the presence of Magaña, but perhaps also to the absence of Zapata from the scene. There is first the "extraordinary maneuver" by which Magaña offered the Carranza government the Zapatistas' support when United States intervention threatened in the Jenkins case in 1919. Womack says here flatly, "Had Zapata lived, Zapatista strategy could not have been so flexible" (p. 348). Then again at the celebration of Obregón's victory, on June 2, 1920, "twenty thousand Agua Prieta partisans marched in review through the Zócalo, among them the forces from Morelos. And watching with the honored new leaders from a balcony of the Palacio National . . . stood the squat, swarthy de la O, frowning into the sun. From an angle he looked almost like Zapata, dead now for over a year. (If de la O had been killed and Zapata had lived, Zapata would probably have been there in his place, with the same uncomfortable frown, persuaded by Magaña to join the boom for Obregón but probably worrying, as Magaña was not, about when he might have to revolt again.)" (p. 365).

Out of these bits and pieces, there emerges a proposition or hypothesis that must have been on Womack's mind, but that he allows the reader to formulate: did the comparative success of the Morelos uprising within the Mexican Revolution rest on the *alternating* leadership, first of the charismatic, revolutionary Zapata and then of the skillful, though highly principled, negotiator Magaña? And what are the "lessons" of this story for other revolutions and, in particular, for revolutionary movements that are confined to a limited portion or sector of a nation-state?

The historian is probably ambivalent about such questions. He revels in the uniqueness of the historical event, yet he constantly intimates that history holds the most precious lessons. And I believe he is right on both counts! Perhaps the rest of this paper will show why this is not a self-contradictory position.

II

First let me return briefly to the comparison of Payne and Womack. What strikes the reader of the two books most is, as I said before, the difference in cognitive style: Payne, from the first page to the last, breathes brash confidence that he has achieved complete understanding of his subject, whereas Womack draws conclusions with the utmost diffidence and circumspection. His respect for the autonomy of the actors whose deeds he recounts is what gives his book its special appeal and probably contributed to the spectacular accolade he received from Carlos Fuentes in the *New York Review of Books*.[5] For it is today a most unusual restraint. I believe that the countries of the Third World have become fair game for the model-builders and paradigm-molders, to an intolerable degree.

During the nineteenth century several "laws" were laid down for the leading industrial countries whose rapid development was disconcerting to numerous thinkers who were strongly affected by what Flaubert called "la rage de vouloir conclure."[6] Having been proven wrong by the unfolding events in almost every instance, the law-makers then migrated to warmer climes, that is, to the less developed countries. And here they really came into their own. For the less developed, dependent countries had long been objects of history—so that to treat them as objects of iron laws or rigid models from whose working there is no escape came naturally to scholars who turned their attention to them.

Soon we were witnesses to a veritable deluge of paradigms and models, from the vicious circle of poverty, low-level equilibrium traps, and uniform stage sequences of the economist, to the traditional or non-achievement-oriented or status-hungry personality of the sociologist, psychologist, or political scientist. A psychologist may find it interesting some day to inquire whether these theories were inspired primarily by compassion or by contempt for the underdeveloped world.

The result, in any case, is that the countries of Latin America, for example, appear to any contemporary, well-read observer far more constrained than, say, the United States or France or the USSR.

Latin American societies seem somehow less complex and their "laws of movement" more intelligible, their medium-term future more predictable or at least formulable in terms of clearcut simple alternatives (such as "reform or revolution?"), and their average citizens more reducible to one or a very few stereotypes. Of course, all of this is so exclusively because our paradigmatic thinking makes it so. Mr. Payne is merely the latest in a long line of "law"-makers, model-builders, and paradigm-molders who have vied with one another in getting an iron grip on Latin American reality. And it must now be said that Latin American social scientists have themselves made an important contribution to this headlong rush toward the all-revealing paradigm.

Elsewhere I have described as "the age of self-incrimination" one phase of the efforts of Latin Americans at understanding their own reality and the lag of their countries behind Europe and the United States. Incidentally, traces of this phase can be found in a few contemporary Latin American intellectuals, and they, jointly with their bygone confrères, provide Payne with some telling quotations about the despicable character of Colombian politicians and politics. By and large, the phase has fortunately passed; it has, however, been replaced by a somewhat related phase that might be called the age of the *action-arousing gloomy vision:* on the basis of some model or paradigm, the economic and social reality of Latin America is explained and the laws of movement of economy and society are formulated in such a way that current trends (of terms of trade, or of income distribution, or of population growth) are shown to produce either stagnation or, more usually, deterioration and disaster. The art of statistical projection has made a potent contribution to this type of forecast, which is then supposed to galvanize men into action designed to avert the threatened disaster through some fairly fundamental "structural changes."

Now I believe that this strategy for socioeconomic change has sometimes been and can on occasion again be extremely useful in just this way. But for several reasons I would caution against the exclusive reliance on it that has recently characterized Latin American social and economic thought.

There is a world of difference, by the way, between this action-arousing gloomy vision and the Marxian perspective on capitalist evolution. In the Marxian perspective, events in the absence of revolution were not at all supposed to move steadily downhill. On the contrary, capitalist development, while punctuated by crises and accompanied by increasing misery of the proletariat, was nevertheless expected to be going forward apace. It was in fact the genius of Marxism—which explains a large part of its appeal—that it was able to view both the advances and the setbacks of economic development under the capitalist system as helping toward its eventual overthrow.

My first criticism of the vision ties in directly with my dislike of paradigms laying down excessive constraints on the conceivable moves of individuals and societies. Why should all of Latin America find itself constantly impaled on the horns of some fateful and unescapable dilemma? Even if one is prepared to accept Goldenweiser's "principle of limited possibilities" in a given environment, any theory or model or paradigm propounding that there are only two possibilities—disaster or one particular road to salvation—should be *prima facie* suspect. After all, there *is,* at least temporarily, such a place as purgatory!

The second reason for which I would advocate a de-emphasis of the action-arousing gloomy vision is that it creates more gloom than action. The spread of gloom is certain and pervasive, but the call to action may or may not be heard. And since the theory teaches that in the normal course of events things will be increasingly unsatisfactory, it is an invitation *not* to watch out for possible positive developments. On the contrary, those imbued with the gloomy vision will attempt to prove year by year that Latin America is going from bad to worse; a year like 1968—and this may hold for 1969 as well—when the economic performance of the three large and of several small countries was little short of brilliant, will come as a distinct embarrassment.

Frequently, of course, the theories I am criticizing are the result of wishful thinking: wouldn't it be reassuring if a society that has been unable to meet some standard of social justice or if an oppressive political regime were *ipso facto* condemned to economic stagnation and deterioration? For that very reason we should be rather on our guard against any theory purporting to *prove* what would be so reassuring.

But the propensity to see gloom and failure everywhere is not engendered only by the desire to reprove further an oppressive regime or an unjust society. It may also be rooted in the fact that one has come to expect his country to perform poorly because of its long history of backwardness and dependence; hence any evidence that the country may possibly be doing better or may be emerging from its backwardness is going to be dissonant with previous cognitions and is therefore likely to be suppressed; on the contrary, evidence that nothing at all has changed will be picked up, underlined, and even greeted, for it does not necessitate any change in the pre-existing conditions to which one has become comfortably adjusted. This is so because people who have a low self-concept and expect failure apparently feel some discomfort when they suddenly perform well, as psychologists have shown.[7] In this manner, social psychology provides a clue to a Latin American phenomenon that has long puzzled me, yet has struck me with such force that I have invented a name for it—the "failure complex" or "fracasomania."

Finally the paradigm-based gloomy vision can be positively harmful. When it prevails, hopeful developments either will be not perceived at all or will be considered exceptional and purely temporary. In these circumstances, they will not be taken advantage of as elements on which to build. To give an example: the rise of the fishmeal industry in Peru and the similarly spectacular growth of banana planting in Ecuador from about 1950 to the mid-sixties contradicted the doctrine that the era of export-promoted growth had ended in Latin America. As a result, economists first ignored these booms, then from year to year predicted their imminent collapse.

It is quite possible that particularly the latter attitude held down the portion of the bonanza that the two countries might otherwise have set aside for longer-term economic and social capital formation; for

why bother to exert oneself and, in the process, antagonize powerful interests if the payoff is expected to be so limited and short-lived? More recently, another theory of gloom has been widely propagated: it seems that now the opportunities for import-substituting industrialization have also become "exhausted" even though it can be argued that, just as earlier in the case of *desarrollo hacia afuera,* there is still much life left in *desarrollo hacia adentro.*[8] Again, if the exhaustion thesis is wholly accepted it may weaken the search for and prevent the discovery of new industrial opportunities.

In all these matters I would suggest a little more "reverence for life," a little less straitjacketing of the future, a little more allowance for the unexpected—and a little less wishful thinking. This is simply a matter, once again, of cognitive *style.* With respect to actual socioeconomic analysis, I am of course not unaware that without models, paradigms, ideal types, and similar abstractions we cannot even start to think. But cognitive style, that is, the kind of paradigms we search out, the way we put them together, and the ambitions we nurture for their powers—all this can make a great deal of difference.

III

In trying to spell out these notions in greater detail I shall now make three principal points. In the first place, I shall explain why the gloomy vision is in a sense the first stage of any reflections about a backward reality and shall make a plea for not getting stuck in that stage. I shall then attempt to show that in evaluating the broader social and political consequences of some ongoing event we must be suspicious of paradigms that pretend to give a clearcut answer about the desirable or undesirable nature of these consequences. And finally I shall suggest that large-scale social change typically occurs as a result of a unique constellation of highly disparate events and is therefore amenable to paradigmatic thinking only in a very special sense.

The initial effort to understand reality will almost inevitably make it appear more solidly entrenched than before. The immediate effect of social analysis is therefore to convert the real into the rational or the contingent into the necessary. Herein, rather than in any conservatism of "bourgeois" social scientists, probably lies the principal explanation of that much commented-upon phenomenon—the conservative bias of social science in general, and of functional analysis in particular. This very conservatism takes, however, a strange turn when the target of the social scientist is a society that is viewed *from the outset* as backward or unjust or oppressive. For analysis will then make it appear, at least to start with, that the backwardness, injustice, and oppression are in reality far more deep-rooted than had been suspected. This is the origin of all the vicious-circle and vicious-personality theories that seem to make any change impossible in the absence of either revolution, highly competent central planning with massive injection of foreign aid, or massive abduction of the young generation so that it may be steeped elsewhere in creativity and achievement motivation.[9]

Interestingly enough, then, the same analytical turn of mind that leads to a conservative bias in the case of a society that we approach *without* a strong initial commitment to change, leads to a revolutionary or quasi-revolutionary stance in the case of societies that are viewed from the outset as unsatisfactory. In the case of the former, the analyst, like the ecologist, often becomes enamored of all the fine latent functions he uncovers, whereas in the latter case he despairs of the possibility of change (except for the most massive and revolutionary varieties) because of all the interlocking vicious circles he has come upon.

Fortunately these initial effects of social science analysis wear off after a while. In the case of the backward countries, the realization will dawn that certain so-called attributes of backwardness are not necessarily obstacles, but can be lived with and sometimes can be turned into positive assets. I have elsewhere attempted to bring together the accumulating evidence for this sort of phenomenon.[10] This evidence, then, should make us a bit wary when *new* vicious circles or *new* development-obstructing personality types or *new* deadends are being discovered. Though such discoveries are bound to occur and can be real contributions to understanding, they carry an obligation to look for ways in which they

may play not a reinforcing but a neutral or debilitating role in so far as system maintenance is concerned.

Perhaps social scientists could pass a rule, such as has long existed in the British Parliament, by which an M.P. proposing a new item of public expenditure must also indicate the additional revenue through which he expects the nation to finance it. Similarly it might be legislated by an assembly of social scientists that anyone who believes he has discovered a new obstacle to development is under an obligation to look for ways in which this obstacle can be overcome or can possibly be lived with or can, in certain circumstances, be transformed into a blessing in disguise.

IV

A related element of the cognitive style I am advocating derives from the recognition of one aspect of the unfolding of social events that makes prediction exceedingly difficult and contributes to that peculiar *open-endedness* of history that is the despair of the paradigm-obsessed social scientist. Situations in which the expertise of the social scientist is solicited frequently have the following structure: some new event or bundle of events such as industrialization, urbanization, rapid population growth, etc., has happened or is happening before our eyes, and we would like to know what its consequences are for a number of social and political system characteristics, such as integration of marginal or oppressed groups, loss of authority on the part of traditional elites, political stability or crisis, likely level of violence or of cultural achievement, and so on.

Faced with the seemingly reasonable demand for enlightenment on the part of the layman and the policy-maker, and propelled also by his own curiosity, the social scientist now opens his paradigm-box to see how best to handle the job at hand. To his dismay, he then finds, *provided he looks carefully,* that he is faced with an embarrassment of riches: various available paradigms will produce radically different answers. The situation can be compared, in a rough way, with the quandary the forecasting economist has long experienced: the magnitudes that are of most interest to the policy-makers, such as the prospective deficit or surplus in the balance of payments or the budget, or the inflationary or deflationary gap, or the rate of unemployment, are usually—and maddeningly—*differences* between gross magnitudes. Hence even if the gross magnitudes are estimated with an acceptable margin of error, the estimate of the difference may be off by a very large percentage and may easily be even of the wrong sign.

The hazards in forecasting qualitative social events on the basis of perfectly respectable and reliable paradigms can be rather similar. Take the question: what is the effect of industrialization and economic development on a society's propensity for civil war, or for external adventure, or for genocide, or for democracy? As with the effect, say, of accelerated growth on the balance of payments, the answer must be: it depends on the *balance* of the contending forces that are set in motion. Industrialization creates new tensions, but may allay old ones; it may divert the minds of the elite from external adventure while creating new capabilities for such adventure, and so forth.

Thus the outcome is here also a *difference* whose estimate is necessarily subject to a particularly high degree of error. This ambiguous situation, incidentally, characterizes also less crucial, more "middle-range" causal relationships. An example is the effect of bigness and diversity of an organization on innovation. As James Q. Wilson has argued, bigness and diversity increase the probability that members will conceive of and propose major innovations; but they also increase the probability that any one innovation that is proposed will be turned down. Again the net effort is in doubt.[11]

Wilson's dilemma is the sort of cognitive style in paradigmatic thinking that is not often met with; ordinarily social scientists are happy enough when they have gotten hold of *one* paradigm or line of causation. As a result, their guesses are often farther off the mark than those of the experienced politician whose intuition is more likely to take a variety of forces into account.

v

Finally, the ability of paradigmatic thinking to illuminate the paths of change is limited in yet another, perhaps more fundamental way. In the context of most Latin American societies, many of us are concerned with the bringing about of *large-scale* change to be carried through in a fairly brief period of time. But ordinarily the cards are stacked so much against the accomplishment of large-scale change that when it happens, be it a result of revolution or reform or some intermediate process, it is bound to be an unpredictable and nonrepeatable event, unpredictable because it took the very actors by surprise and nonrepeatable because once the event has happened everybody is put on notice and precautions will be taken by various parties so that it won't happen again.

The uniqueness and scientific opaqueness of the large-scale changes that occur when history "suddenly accelerates" have often been remarked upon. Womack brings them out as well as anyone in his narrative of the Mexican Revolution. I shall invoke the authority of two recent commentators belonging to rather different camps. The first is the anthropologist Max Gluckman, who addresses himself to "radical change" after having defended anthropology against the charge that it is not interested in change. He writes, "The source of radical change escapes these analyses [of other kinds of change]. Perhaps this is inevitable because social anthropology aims to be scientific. Scientific method cannot deal with unique complexes of many events. The accounts of the actual course of events which produce change therefore necessarily remain historical narratives. . . ."[12]

Perhaps a more significant witness, because as a Marxist he should be an inveterate paradigm-lover, is Louis Althusser. In his remarkable essay, "Contradiction and Over-determination," Althusser makes much of some striking statements of Lenin's about the unique constellation of events that made possible the Russian Revolution of 1917. The key passage from Lenin is: "If the revolution has triumphed so rapidly it is exclusively because, as a result of a historical situation of extreme originality, a number of completely distinct currents, a number of totally heterogeneous class interests, and a number of completely opposite social and political tendencies have become fused with remarkable coherence."[13]

On the basis of Lenin's testimony Althusser then proceeds to explain that revolutions never arise purely out of the basic economic contradictions that Marx stressed, but only when these contradictions are "fused" in some unique manner with a number of other determinants. This fusion or embedding is the phenomenon he calls "overdetermination" of revolutions. Actually this is a poor term (as he himself recognizes) for it could imply that, had one of the many circumstantial factors not been present, the revolution would still have taken place.

But the whole context of the essay, and certainly the quotations from Lenin, exclude this interpretation. On the contrary, it is quite clear that even with all these converging elements the revolution won by an exceedingly narrow margin. *Thus, while a surprising number of heterogeneous elements almost miraculously conspired to bring the revolution about, every single one of them was still absolutely indispensable to its success.* Uniqueness seems a better term for this phenomenon than overdetermination.

Incidentally, this interpretation of revolutions undermines the revolutionary's usual critique of the advocacy of reform. This critique is generally based on the *high degree of improbability* that a ruling group will ever tolerate or even connive at the elimination or destruction of its own privileges, the only way to achieve this end is by smashing the "system" through revolutionary assault. But with the view of revolutions as overdetermined or unique events, it turns out to be a toss-up which form of large-scale change is more unlikely—so we may as well be on the lookout for whatever rare openings in either direction appear on the horizon.

In sum, he who looks for large-scale social change must be possessed, with Kierkegaard, by "the passion for what is possible" rather than rely on what has been certified as probable by factor analysis.

This view of large-scale social change as a unique, nonrepeatable and *ex ante* highly improbable complex of events is obviously damaging to the aspirations of anyone who would explain and predict these events through "laws of change." Once again, there is no denying that such "laws" or paradigms can have considerable utility. They are useful for the apprehending of many elements of the complex and often are stimuli to action before the event and indispensable devices for achieving a be-

ginning of understanding after the event has happened. That is much but that is all.

The architect of social change can never have a reliable blueprint. Not only is each house he builds different from any other that was built before, but it also necessarily uses new construction materials and even experiments with untested principles of stress and structure. Therefore what can be most usefully conveyed by the builders of one house is an understanding of the experience that made it at all possible to build under these trying circumstances. It is, I believe, in this spirit that Womack makes that, at first sight rather shocking, statement, "the truth of the revolution in Morelos is in the feeling of it." Perhaps he means not only the truth, but also the principal lesson.

1. Oran R. Young, "Professor Russett: Industrious Tailor to a Naked Emperor," *World Politics,* XXI (April 1969), 489–90.

2. New York.

3. New Haven and London.

4. Nora Beloff and Michael Davie, "Getting to Know Mr. Nixon," *The Observer,* February 23, 1969.

5. March 13, 1969.

6. I have long looked for a good translation of this key concept into English. It now strikes me that an apt, if free, rendering of Flaubert's meaning would be "the compulsion to theorize"—which is the subject and might have been the title of the present paper.

7. Elliott Aronson, "Dissonance Theory: Progress and Problems," in R. P. Abelson and others, eds., *Theories of Cognitive Consistency: A Source Book* (Chicago, 1968), p. 24.

8. See my article, "The Political Economy of Import-Substituting Industrialization in Latin America," *Quarterly Journal of Economics,* LXXXII (February 1968), 1–32. The Spanish terms *desarrollo hacia afuera* and *desarrollo hacia adentro* are convenient shorthand expressions for growth through the expansion of exports and of the domestic market, respectively.

9. It is only fair to note that, in his more recent work on achievement motivation, David McClelland has changed his earlier views on these matters. Thus he writes (after having given cogent reasons for doing so): "To us it is no longer a self-evident truth that it is easier to produce long-range personality transformations in young children than it is in adults." David C. McClelland and David G. Winter, *Motivating Economic Achievement* (New York, 1969), p. 356.

10. "Obstacles to Development: A Classi-

fication and a Quasi-Vanishing Act," *Economic Development and Cultural Change,* XIII (July 1965), 385–9.

11. James Q. Wilson, "Innovation in Organization: Notes Toward a Theory," in James D. Thompson, ed., *Approaches to* *Organizational Design* (Pittsburgh, 1966), pp. 193–218.

12. *Politics, Law and Ritual in Tribal Society* (Oxford, 1965), p. 286.

13. As quoted in Althusser, *Pour Marx* (Paris, 1967), p. 98.

PART II

DEVELOPMENT IN THE PERSPECTIVE OF POLITICAL ECONOMY

> Since development is far from being achieved at present, the need is not, as generally imagined, to accelerate economic growth—which could even be dangerous—but to change the nature of the development process.
>
> DUDLEY SEERS

THE POLITICAL ECONOMY of development is proposed as an improvement, in both theoretical and practical terms, on the conventional disciplinary approaches to the analysis of development. Although in political economy we analytically distinguish economic, social, and political development from one another, they are viewed as aspects or manifestations of a generic process affecting levels of aggregate productivity. As John Montgomery has put it, "development is a seamless web without clear lines of distinction among its cultural, social, economic and political strands."[1] This process involves alterations in human activities and attitudes such that what are called economic, social, and political relations become more productive and for more people. The political economy approach should permit us to unify as we explicate social science theory on development. At the same time, it should help us and others to devise, test, and choose among strategies and policies more efficacious for development.

We will not deal much with what might be considered deficiencies in the conventional wisdom about development to be found in most of the present literature of economics, sociology, and political science. What we will try to present is an approach which has foundations in the present literature but which leads explicitly to a supradisciplinary, policy-oriented, and existential social science. Rather than describe the empirical footings of the approach and delineate its connections to the literature,[2] we propose a model of development and relate it to the work of many other social scientists working on these problems. Such a model cannot be "true"

---

[1] "The Quest for Political Development," *Comparative Politics* (January 1969), p. 286.

[2] This would be instructive but unfortunately not conclusive given the nature of the problem. Such a description and delineation has been presented in N. T. Uphoff, *Ghana's Experience in Using External Aid for Development, 1957–1966: Implications for Development Theory and Policy* (Berkeley: Institute of International Studies, 1970).

or not; it can only be useful or not. We offer the approach here so that others may consider it and, we hope, contribute to its refinement. This is not a matter of asking others to do our work for us, since we are engaged in such work. But we are soliciting involvement in an endeavor which, though it has already been given impetus by the work of social scientists such as those represented in this book, lacks explicit identification and rationale such as that which would engage the energies and intellect of others in the effort.

It will be readily apparent to readers that in our analysis of development we do not try to avoid completely the use of abstraction or generalization. We do try to use these carefully, keeping always in mind the perspective of actors and the problems of choice they face. The only justification for our use of abstraction or generalization can be that it enables persons to choose more wisely with respect to development. We do not suggest that our work is *the* explanation or *the* theory of development, as we do not think such an explanation or theory would be tenable. Although we equate development with productivity, we do not construct a definition of development or dwell on its "essence." There can always be disagreements on what constitutes development or productivity. We try to clarify the issues involved in each, but ultimately, value preferences as to the goals and routes of development are crucial. We find the model well grounded in the empirical record of development and consistent with most value preferences stated for development, but it is ultimately an intellectual paradigm rather than a "scientific" creation. To be sustained, it must prove helpful to students and practitioners of the development enterprise. We advance it at this time expecting that it will direct research and activity in more fruitful ways.

PRODUCTIVITY AS THE CRITERION OF DEVELOPMENT

Various criteria of development have been proposed in economic, social, and political terms: per capita national product, structural differentiation, political system capability or stability. None appear to us as defensible or as basic as the criterion of *productivity*. It is the prior condition for a higher GNP per capita; structural differentiation is presumed to increase it; the usual rationale for political stability is that it promotes the conditions for productivity. In commonsense terms, one usually equates development with high productivity, and underdevelopment with low productivity in each particular case. The difficulties involved in the definition and measurement of productivity are substantial in all but the most narrow technically defined processes. However, this does not alter the general understanding that productivity, regardless of definition or measurement, is a fundamental and perhaps a determining feature of development.

There are several sources of difficulty in measuring productivity. Measuring *production*, though not always easy or indisputable, involves some actual output; ascertaining *productivity*, which involves *capacity* or *potential* for production, is more difficult, and production is therefore often taken as an indicator for it. Productivity, however, is a more complex and more significant thing than production, which can be consumed or exhausted.[3] Productivity represents capability over time to satisfy

[3] This argument is well made with reference to economic development by Hans Singer, who says that the problem is not creation of wealth but creation of *capacity* to produce

human needs and desires, not only materially with goods and services, but in other respects as well. It presents social scientists with perhaps their greatest challenge: how they can aid in increasing this capability for human satisfaction in various dimensions.

It is difficult to ascertain and demonstrate incremental gains in productivity because of the fact that few changes result in benefits for some or all persons without entailing some costs or disadvantages for other persons.[4] Even a given gain or loss is valued differently by different people, some judging it more, and others judging it less significant. Since the gain of one person can seldom be objectively judged greater or less than the loss of another person, comparing aggregate benefits and costs of a change entails wide margins for error. Major changes in which there are a great many gainers and very few losers can be regarded as productive with some margin of confidence, and those with a great many losers and very few gainers, as unproductive. But estimations of net benefit or cost are made difficult by the fact that "net" is a difference between aggregate costs and benefits, both terms having margins for error; subtracting one from the other is as likely to compound error as to reduce it.

Such considerations, however, should not deter us from an analytical concern with productivity.[5] Though a concept, it is not just a fabrication of the mind. The problem is one of explicating productivity and finding factors accounting for it. Productivity relates to more than economic development. Just as the level and composition of economic activity can be made more productive for satisfying human needs and desires through the production and exchange of goods and services, so can social relations become more productive in terms of the esteem and deference people receive and the satisfaction or security gained from these. Similarly, politics can be more or less productive for the persons engaged in it or affected by it. While the distinction among economic, social, and political processes is ultimately an analytical one, the productivity of each is of more than theoretical concern.

The Political Economy Perspective.

In social science, as presently organized, the gross distinction between *production* and *distribution* is commonly made too firmly and applied to the disciplines. Economics is thought to be primarily concerned with production, and politics, with distribution. Economists meliorate their preoccupation with production functions to some small extent by sustaining the subdiscipline of welfare economics, which is concerned with the consequences of the distribution of goods and services. Political scientists have been almost exclusively preoccupied with distributional questions— who gets what?—and have paid little attention to the productivity of politics, or at least its productive potential.

What should be clear, and without much reflection, is that production and dis-

---

wealth. See "The Notion of Human Investment," *Review of Social Economy* (March 1966), pp. 1–14.

[4] The solution offered by Pareto to the problem of comparing costs and benefits (utilities and disutilities) affecting different persons is seldom applicable. Any measure that benefits somebody without reducing the benefits enjoyed by anybody else will indeed increase total welfare, or aggregate productivity, but such measures are rare.

[5] We would share Robert Lekachman's critical view of the retreat, in recent decades of economists, from making interpersonal comparisons of welfare on the ground that "subjective" value judgments are involved.

tribution are separable only analytically and even then often inappropriately. Any serious consideration of productivity has to take into account the varying productivity of different distributions of what is produced and the fact that different modes of production lead to differing distributions. Production and distribution are aspects of a single process, each affecting the other. Examining them separately is useful only if they are linked conceptually. Each profoundly affects the other.

The identification of politics with distribution has some basis in that government plays or can play a redistributive role within any community. In the absence of political intervention in the production and distribution of various resources, not just economic ones, they will go to those who possess the factors of production. We find that social and political processes can usefully be analyzed in such terms, analogous to those used in economic analysis which relate distribution to production and vice versa. In particular we are concerned with the consequences for productivity of different allocative political choices.

Just as production and distribution have been too readily separated and contrasted in the social sciences, so too the terms *process* and *structure*. The idea of structure as something solid and static is inappropriate for social scientists. As used in the new political economy, the two terms are both dynamic and closely related. What are generally considered economic, social, and political processes each involve activity and exchange; at the same time, what are generally called economic, social, and political structures result from these activities and exchanges and significantly affect them. To suggest that this relationship is like that between the chicken and the egg is to appreciate the heart of the matter.

Economic, social, and political relations are in effect *exchanges* between persons of things having economic, social, or political value. These things, which we call *resources,* are valued for what they can produce, in terms of immediate satisfaction through consumption, consequent satisfaction from using them for producing something else or from getting something else in exchange, or deferred satisfaction by saving or investing them. Resources may be quite tangible materially or may be intangible, but in the latter case, they are only considered if they have some tangible effects for other persons; otherwise they can and should be ignored. Resource exchange is the nexus between structure and process. Our efforts to analyze these two terms, in this and in the following section, are prompted not by an interest in conceptualization or definition but by our concern with making human interaction more productive for satisfying people's needs and wants.

Resources: The Factors of Production.

A concern with the analysis of productivity should lead one logically to a consideration of *resources,* or those things which are the principal *factors of production.* The analytical power and versatility of economics depends heavily on its paradigm of resources. The things used as inputs in economic production are diverse, but they have been and can be usefully categorized as land, labor, or capital, just as outputs are categorized as goods or services. Within each of these categories there is a wide range of real things or activities. What the categories have made possible is the analysis of economic production and distribution at any level, macro or micro, and in any historical or cultural context, medieval or modern, American or Armenian. The quantity and quality of actual inputs can vary widely, but the analysis of factors of production lends itself to both description and prescription where economic productivity is involved.[6]

Social relations can also be viewed as more or less productive, for individuals and groups or for the whole community. *Status* represents social wealth, yielding social income flows of esteem and deference, which are the social analogues of economics' goods and services. The attributes that confer status vary from community to community—membership in a particular caste, family or religion, age, wisdom, economic wealth, political power—but the phenomena and consequences of social interaction are similar everywhere in terms of the differential derivation of satisfaction from social exchanges.

The use of economic concepts or categories in analyzing social relations is somewhat metaphorical and does not exhaust the full range of meaning in such relations, but we think it helps to clarify issues of aggregate social productivity. *Status* is viewed as the principal factor of social production in that possessing more of it entitles a person to more esteem and deference in social relations. It is also a product of social interaction, so that it is an output as well as an input, available for consumption or for other uses. We would not draw the analogy with economics in all respects, since social phenomena differ in various ways from economic ones. Yet status resembles wealth, and as social *capital* it is not necessarily used up in exchange. Rather, esteem and deference are consumed or converted into something else, like goods and services in economic exchange.

Status can appreciate or depreciate in value and may require other resources to maintain its value. Prestige performs many of the functions that money does in economic activity, and is therefore considered to be social currency. In the process of social interaction, prestige and consequently status can be acquired or diminished, so that one's claims on the esteem and deference of others are increased or decreased over time. We will take up later the question of whether social production, or aggregate social product, is fixed in amount and value and whether it can be expanded. Here we are simply introducing the ideas that suggest how status fits into the political economy framework of analysis.[7]

The political process is more complex than the economic and social processes because it can subsume or influence both of them and because the factors of political production are more numerous and complicated. The same dynamic, however, prevails in politics as in economics and social interaction. Political production (out-

---

[6] There is not unanimous agreement on what constitutes the factors of economic production. Some economists suggest that organization or entrepreneurship or managerial skills should also be regarded as factors. We would hold to a more limited conception of resources, i.e., those things which can be *allocated* as inputs or as outputs of the economic, social, and political production processes. We regard these other things as important—as will be shown below—though not as resource factors of production.

[7] The factors contributing to or encompassed by status are various and differ from situation to situation, but then so do the factors included under the rubric of economic resources. In a given situation, "land" will include some combination of these: soil, water, mineral, and other natural resources; "labor"—professional, managerial, supervisory, skilled, and unskilled services; "capital"—machinery, equipment, credit, and cash on hand. What we call a factor of production is really a *category* of various concrete factors, the mix of which changes according to the particular circumstance. Heterogeneity within categories of factors will not bother us if some analytically useful purpose can be served by the categorization, which is, we think, the case. Status and other factors are discussed at some length in chapter 3 of Ilchman and Uphoff, *The Political Economy of Change* (1969).

puts) will be distributed among those persons who possess and provide political resources (inputs). The factors of political production we have suggested are economic resources, social status, information, authority, legitimacy, and force. The concepts and categories of economic analysis are not in every respect analogous for political activity, but we find that they are approximate enough to provide insights into the problems of assessing political productivity.

What distinguishes political interaction from economic and social interaction is the factor of *authority*. This is the right to speak on behalf of the government and declare public policies. It derives from the occupancy of authority roles which have been established to accomplish some division of political labor whereby certain persons make decisions binding on all other members of the community. Activities and attitudes that affect or are affected by the exercise of authority are political.[8]

Interaction involving only goods and services, and which has neither effects on authority nor effects from authority, can be considered strictly economic. Similarly isolated interaction involving only esteem and deference qualifies as purely social. But to the extent that economic or social activities affect the acquisition or exercise of authority or are influenced by authority, they are also political. We would not want to erect these distinctions into typological ones. Rather we want to simplify some of the complexity of human interaction so that productivity can be better understood and increased. Political economy, encompassing as it does a wider range of productive factors than does economics, sociology, or conventional political science, is concerned more with the common characteristics of economic, social, and political factors than with their dissimilarities.

Information is a resource, or factor of production, that is important to economic, social, and political processes. It differs from other resources in that it is not scarce or limited in the way the others are. These are costs to the acquisition of information, but one can share it with others without diminishing one's own possession of it. (To be sure, its value is often dependent on its scarcity; something that is widely known will net its possessor little in the way of other resources in exchange.)[9] Information is productive in that it can lead one more economically to the acquisition of other resources, and in that it can reduce the costs of production in economic, social, and political activity. Other resources can be used to acquire information, and it in turn can be used to acquire them. *Education*, it is noted, is not the same thing as information, but educated persons generally have more information and can acquire it more readily. Thus education can often be considered a proxy for information.

The resource of *legitimacy* has been introduced analytically by Kenneth Boulding above. Legitimacy is not exchanged in behavioral terms and cannot be overtly observed, which makes its measurement and analysis difficult. However, it has tangible and significant effects in economic, social, and political interaction and thus

[8] For elaboration of our definition of "political" and our treatment of authority as a resource, see *ibid.*, pp. 50–51 and 81–86. For an extended analysis of authority, not explicitly in political economy terms but nonetheless supporting our analysis, see Richard Rose, "Dynamic Tendencies in the Authority of Regimes," *World Politics* (July 1969), pp. 602–628.

[9] Where the value of certain information derives from monopoly possession of the information, its value is decreased and possibly even destroyed by sharing it. Yet this does not in any way diminish the *volume* of information in question. For further discussion, see Ilchman and Uphoff, *op. cit.*, pp. 67–70; also Kenneth Boulding, "Knowledge as a Commodity," in National Institute of Social and Behavioral Science, *Symposia Studies Series* (1960), No. 11, pp. 1–6.

needs to be considered seriously. If a person believes that an institution or organization—or, we might add, an authority role, a person possessing authority, or a policy decision—should be accepted as "right, proper, justified and acceptable," he accords it legitimacy. Figuratively, what he does is transfer some "credit" into the implicit account he keeps in his mind for that institution, organization, authority role, authority wielder, or policy. When he is expected, asked, or ordered to comply with a specific request, part or all of the compensation he receives for his contribution of resources is the legitimacy he has accorded the source of the request. To the extent that he continues to accord it legitimacy, he can replenish or even increase the "credit" it has with him.

Legitimacy can be a factor of production in economic or social processes. Persons according others legitimacy will comply more readily with the requests of others for goods and services or esteem and deference. Such persons will comply with less compensation received than if they did not accord as much, or any, legitimacy to others. In many ways, legitimacy is like status as a resource. Both are "soft" resources in that they are not freely convertible into resources from persons other than those who accord the status or legitimacy. In effect, bilateral or "blocked" accounts are created that can be drawn on only by the person to whom one accords status or legitimacy.

The primary importance of legitimacy is in political processes because of the value which legitimacy adds to the possession of authority. Not all claims of authority are considered legitimate by all persons subject to that authority. To the extent that they do accord legitimacy to authority roles, to persons in authority and/or to policy decisions, they will comply with policies made by persons in these roles more readily and "cheaply." Fewer of other resources—economic resources, status, information, or force—are required to obtain a given level of compliance to the extent that the policy-maker possesses greater legitimacy, not in his hands but in people's minds. A highly and widely legitimated government or activity is, as a rule, a productive one. It must be meeting a significant number and range of people's needs or wants in order to warrant the legitimacy it receives. From the regime's point of view, the receipt of legitimacy means that the ratio of output to other inputs is considerably increased.

We include physical *force* as a factor of production in our analytical framework even though when used in exchanges it subtracts from the welfare of the recipient (rather than adding to it, as is the case with other resources). Force is a fact of economic, social, and especially political life, and however one may reject it on normative grounds, it must be taken into account in any realistic model. Because force is negatively valued, when it is used in exchanges the loss of one party (the recipient) must be subtracted from the other's gain in a consideration of the net productivity of such exchange. For this reason, it figures less centrally than do other resources in our analysis of development, which is concerned with raising the level of aggregate productivity. Nevertheless, very often when political interventions are made to alter the distribution of resources in society, force is involved, and one needs to be able to incorporate it and its consequences into the analysis. This can be done in political economy terms by considering violence and coercion as political resources.[10]

All of these various resources are sources of *power,* or the ability to get com-

[10] We generally identify force used by a regime against others as *coercion;* force used by persons not having authority (or any official claim to legitimacy in the use of force) is

pliance with one's demands. Economic resources and status confer economic and social power, as information represents the power of knowledge. Force, similarly, is physical power, and legitimacy represents the power that normative or moral beliefs can engender. Authority, the term most often equated with power in social science vernacular, stands for political power, which is only one kind of power. Indeed, it is a conditional and variable power, deriving from those other resources which can be commanded and allocated through the political process by persons possessing authority.[11] As has been suggested, and as will be elaborated next, all of these resources can, under various conditions, be exchanged for or converted into other resources. What need to be considered are the *processes* of exchange and conversion, and for this we have extended the economic concept of the market.

Exchange: The Metaphor of Markets.

The idea of a market was initially quite specific and concrete, referring to a time and to a place where people came to trade or buy and sell. The idea has since been extended and freed from its temporal and spatial limitations, so that it refers to a process of exchange over time. What delimits a market is the *scope* of exchange. A market is as broad or as narrow, as extended or as restricted, as the number and location of persons who participate in it, and who offer factors of production or finished products for sale and purchase these for use in production or consumption. The idea, while an abstract one, ultimately refers to real persons and real exchanges.

In the new political economy, we have proposed that three markets be distinguished analytically. The *economic market* is the one most people think of when they think of markets. It is the nexus between persons acting as producers and persons acting as consumers. Inputs and outputs of economic production are bought, sold, or bartered. As economic analysis has moved to the macro level, sectors of the economy—which is synonymous with the national economic market—have been distinguished from one another in terms of their outputs and in terms of their demand for certain inputs. The agricultural sector requires certain land, labor, and capital and produces foodstuffs for consumption as well as certain raw materials for industrial processing. The economic market is made up concretely of many people, but analytically of various sectors.

Depending on one's analytical purposes and the extent of one's data, one can analyze an economy in terms of 2 sectors (e.g., products for domestic consumption and for export); 3 sectors (e.g. agricultural, industrial and service sectors); 10

---

usually called *violence*. Withholding of economic resources or status from persons is often called, colloquially, coercion, but we think it more useful to restrict the term to the use of physical force, thereby distinguishing this use from the use of other resources. Threats serve as the currency for force, having the same relation to it as money has to goods and services; they can serve as a medium of exchange, a store of value, a standard of deferred payment, and/or a measure of value. For a more extended discussion, see Ilchman and Uphoff, *op. cit.*, pp. 70–73.

[11] It is common, but misleading, to speak of a person or a regime as being "in power" or "out of power." What is meant is that someone possesses authority or does not, is "in authority" or "in authority roles" or is not. It is possible to have authority and very little power, if the processes and structures of political exchange do not provide much in the way of other resources. Persons lacking authority can have considerable power, deriving from wealth, status, or physical force, for example. To the extent that possession of authority confers legitimacy and other resources on "the authorities," they will have significant power within the community.

sectors; or 250. Following the pioneering work of Wassily Leontief, economists have constructed models of national economies that describe the flows of inputs and outputs among sectors, which are both consumers and producers of economic resources.[12] The *structure* of an economy is represented by the *pattern of resource flows* at any particular time. This is a conveniently static portrayal of a dynamic *process* in which one finds some combination of stability and change according to the balance or imbalance of people's needs and capabilities for production.

We would suggest a similar model for social exchange, that of a *social market* in which esteem and deference are exchanged between persons and in which social capital is accumulated or expended. For analytical purposes, people have always been aggregated into groups, families, clans, castes, classes, or strata. Sociologists have not reached agreement on the most appropriate aggregate category for analysis, as one might expect, since different sizes and kinds of groupings are appropriate for treating different problems. Some have upon occasion used the economic term *sector*. We find it useful because it can be used for differentiating society into two or two hundred groupings and because it implies no presuppositions about group genesis, cohesion, or relationship to other groups.

The common and conventional analysis of "elite" and "mass" is a two-sector model of society, often implying, to be sure, more than just status relations between the two. A complicated analysis of Indian caste relations amounts to a model involving hundreds of differentiated sectors differentially producing and consuming esteem and deference. The common notion of *social structure* is indeed quite similar to the input-output conception of economic structure just described. In using the idea of a social market, one should not reify it or import all the assumptions commonly made about an economic market, many of which are much oversimplified and mistaken. The main purpose of our drawing the analogy is to introduce possibilities for considering the question of aggregate productivity in social relations.

The analogy of a *political market* is proposed for a parallel purpose, the examination of political productivity. Because the factor of authority is involved in political relations, the model includes, distinguished from the various sectors, a *regime* that is composed of those persons claiming to possess authority. It may delegate some of its authority to other persons, or give other persons *influence* on the use of authority.[13] But in the final analysis, it has the prerogative to make policy decisions allocating resources among sectors and to itself. Whether this prerogative was granted to the regime by all, some, or a few of the sectors, or was simply claimed on the basis of superior power, will affect the sources and volume of political resource flows, but it does not alter the fact that authority is possessed by those persons occupying the highest authority roles.

As in economic and social analysis, the number and composition of sectors will vary according to the problem being considered and the available information, on differing interests, ideologies, propensities, time horizons, and resource capabilities.

---

[12] For a short exposition of input-output analysis, which is of central importance in the political economy of development, see Leontief's article, "Input-Output Economics," *Scientific American* 185 (October 1951): 15–21; for a longer, more detailed analysis, see H. B. Chenery and P. Clark, *Interindustry Economics* (1959).

[13] Influence amounts to a currency for the resource of authority. Like money vis-à-vis goods and services, it is a *claim* on this resource, and it is worth no more than the value of the authoritative decisions into which it can be converted (which themselves convey certain resources from the regime or sectors). See Ilchman and Uphoff, *op. cit.*, pp. 84·85.

Individuals differ considerably in terms of these variables, and so do groupings of individuals. In political economy one explicitly avoids the assumptions, often made in economic analysis, that there is "perfect competition" among participants in the market and that they differ primarily with respect to tastes rather than their relative power deriving from *endowments* of the factors of production. Sociological analysis has generally been sensitive to inequalities, and its paradigm has been one of stratification. Political economy combines the paradigms of sociology and economics to arrive at the paradigm of the *stratified market,* in which sectors are seldom if ever equal in their factor endowments or in their relation to one another.

There is in political and economic relations a sector ranking, akin to social stratification, deriving from differing endowments of the factors of economic, social, and political production—economic resources, status, information, legitimacy, authority, and force.[14] Because resources are to a significant extent convertible, one into the other, there is considerable congruence of economic, social, and political stratifications. This has been widely observed, though the dynamic accounting for this has been much less widely examined. It is taken into consideration in the political economy of development.

We would suggest that, other things being equal, exchange is a productive activity although since some resources are used up in the process of exchange, these costs must be subtracted in reckoning the net productivity of exchange. The principal effect and justification of infrastructure is in its reduction of these costs. The volume of resources is not in the short run increased by exchange, but their value can be. In *voluntary* exchange between two partners having relatively equal bargaining power, so that the terms of trade do not particularly favor one person or the other, each person gains something he values more by giving up something he values less.[15] What are not equal in most exchanges are the supply of or demand for resources, thus the margin of benefit may not be positive for both persons; and where coercion is involved, one person will be giving up something of benefit to him without receiving in return anything he values positively. Recognizing that exchange does not add invariably to aggregate productivity, we nevertheless point to the potential benefits to be derived from exchange. Further, the greater the margin of benefit that persons derive from exchange, the more incentive they have to increase their production. Thus, mutually beneficial exchange can in the longer run increase the volume as well as the value of available resources.

One of the principal factors affecting the margin of benefit from exchanges is the scope of exchange. As the scope within which exchange can take place expands, there is more opportunity and more incentive to devote resources to their most productive use, partly because there are more alternative uses to choose from and partly because there is likely to be more competition, unless such expansion of scope

[14] For an analysis and a terminology of political stratification, see *ibid.,* pp. 42–47.

[15] We would note here Joseph J. Spengler's formulation of this proposition: "Exchange does not, of course, increase the amount of what is allocated, at least in the short run. But it does increase the amount of service or utility derivable by exchanging individuals from a given amount of scarce resources; it is thus a positive-sum game." "Allocation and Development, Economic and Political," in Ralph Braibanti (ed.), *Political and Administrative Development* (1969), p. 633. We would qualify this by noting that involuntary exchanges or exchanges of "bads" are not positive-sum games. On this, see Kenneth Boulding, "On the Pure Theory of Threat Systems," *American Economic Review* (September 1963), pp. 809–810.

is oligopolistically encouraged and controlled. Gains in productivity can also result from the division of labor and specialization, which are made feasible by extending the scope of exchange. This was argued nearly two hundred years ago by Adam Smith in *The Wealth of Nations*. There can be diseconomies as well as economies from specialization in different productive activities, but the latter generally outweigh the former, the net difference contributing to the productivity of exchange.

The metaphor of markets has particular relevance to the analysis of development because of the problems of relating local communities to the national community. Whether one is thinking in economic, social, or political terms, there exist in underdeveloped countries numerous small-scale local markets. When economists talk of "subsistence" economies, they are referring to communities in which everything consumed is produced locally (and vice versa). There is practically no exchange with the national economy, which is an economy generating surpluses because of its higher productivity. The scope of exchange is something greatly affecting economic productivity, and we see an important analogy for social and political relations.

The small community that is isolated socially is similarly a "subsistence" social market in which esteem and deference are produced and exchanged only within the community. For example, consanguinity or clan membership may be thought the only valid criterion for according esteem and deference. These would be neither received from nor accorded to persons outside the particular—particularistic—community. Few communities nowadays are completely self-contained, autonomous from what may be thought of as the national social market, in which the criteria for status are widely shared and esteem and deference can be widely exchanged. Yet, just as few communities are completely self-sufficient economically, so the relationship between central and peripheral social markets is an important one to consider.[16]

Analogously, there are, in an underdeveloped polity, numerous small-scale local political markets. In these, political resources are exchanged between the authorities and participants in the local market, and few if any resources are sent to or received from persons outside the particular community. The volume of resources that can be aggregated, and likewise the public purposes that can be achieved, are limited, just as resource mobilization and diversified production are quite limited in a subsistence economic market. Within a larger-scale national political market, authority extends over more persons and can allocate more resources. The exercise of such authority can achieve a broader range of purposes.

In drawing these analogies, we do not wish to divorce economic, social, or political relations from the whole process of human interaction. We are separating each set of relations analytically in order to explore the ways in which the scope of exchange affects the productivity of human interaction. For the sake of analysis, this interaction is considered in terms of economic, social, and political processes, which involve the exchange, respectively, of goods and services, esteem and deference, and any resources relating to the exercise of authority. The developmental

[16] For an interesting though differing treatment of this relationship, see Edward Shils, "Centre and Periphery," in *The Logic of Personal Knowledge: Essays in Honour of Michael Polanyi* (1961), pp. 117–130.

implications of an extended scope of exchange are addressed below with respect to integration of central and peripheral markets.

Infrastructure: The Facilitation of Resource Exchange.

In economic analysis, infrastructure was initially understood in quite concrete terms. Included in the category were telephones and radio, roads and harbors, electricity and other facilities for communication, transportation, and power. Infrastructure lowers the costs of production and thereby increases the amount of production, to the extent that it reduces the time or cost of gaining information about the availability and productivity of resources, of moving resources from one place to another, or of converting resources from one form to another. In other words, infrastructure contributes to the *predictability* of resource flows, to the *mobility* of resources, and to their *convertibility*.

As the processes and dynamics of economic production have become better understood, the conception of infrastructure has been extended beyond the physical forms of infrastructure cited above to include social and organizational forms as well. Investments that raised the productivity of labor—education, training, health, and housing—have come to be considered part of social overhead capital, and banks, credit unions, labor exchanges, and other institutions have also been viewed in infrastructural terms. Activities that involve some present use of resources with the expectation of increasing productivity fall within the general category of investment. The function of infrastructure is to elicit and channel the flow of resources by increasing the margin of benefit that people receive from resource use. This is made possible by providing them with more and better information on alternative sources or uses of resources, by making it easier or cheaper to procure inputs and dispose of outputs, and by providing an adequate supply of power for production.[17]

The structuring of resource flows so as to facilitate and expand the exchange and use of resources surely is not limited to the economic market. A social stratification system mobilizes and regularizes the exchange of esteem and deference, just as a political party or civil service elicits and channels political resources. Application of the idea of infrastructure to social and political relations is easy once one has an understanding of resource exchange in its broader context of human interaction. But to move beyond metaphor, social scientists need a better understanding of "structure" and its relation to "process." This, we think, is provided by an explication of the difference between "growth" and "development," a difference that arises from questions of structure and structural change.

DEVELOPMENT AS STRUCTURAL CHANGE

An improved understanding of the development process is of critical importance, as Dudley Seers suggests. To persevere with policies derived from present models

---

[17] We will not go into the matter of *external economies* here, important though they are to the operation, or even definition, of infrastructure. We are more concerned initially with the nature and consequences of infrastructural activities than with who pays the costs and who receives the benefits.

and theories can well have adverse consequences, as he shows in his article, re-printed on pages 123–129. The faults of these models and theories derive from the usual isolation of disciplinary analyses from one another, from the common prefer-ence for "pure" research as opposed to "applied" work on policy concerns, and from the general neglect of the concrete effects of theories and policies on the lives of individuals. We have undertaken to elaborate a conception of development that can have both intellectual rigor and practical application. We recognize that we are confronting difficult problems of measurement with respect to productivity, and problems of normative judgment with respect to questions of distribution. However, we prefer to face up to these even if we cannot resolve them definitively, because they are crucial to addressing the intellectual and practical problems involved in directing development efforts in more fruitful ways.

The Distinction Between Growth and Development.

The distinction that concerns us here is commonly made intuitively but seldom rigorously. When dealing with biological organisms, we see growth manifested more clearly than development. The first shows up in increases in size, while the latter is evident only when the relationships between various parts of the organism are analyzed to show changes over time. Growth and development have an intimate and dialectical relationship to one another in the realm of biology. The structure of an organism changes considerably during its lifetime; indeed, if the organism simply grows without any change in structure, it becomes a freak, overgrown and usually unviable. Structural change permits viable growth to occur, and growth provides the material for subsequent structural change.

The terms *growth* and *development* are commonly applied to social aggregates, but we must not extrapolate terms uncritically from the level of individual or-ganisms to the level of communities of organisms. Social scientists can learn from biological scientists, but their subjects are qualitatively different. The former face considerably greater complexity and indeterminacy. In our thinking about growth and development we have had the biological model in mind, but our attention focused initially on economic phenomena. These are more tangible than social or political phenomena, and the economic literature is more extensive on the subject of growth vis-à-vis development, even if economists have commonly minimized the distinction.[18] Some, influenced perhaps most by the work of Joseph Schumpeter, have considered the difference, and their attention has centered on questions of structural change.[19] We would like to propose a number of distinctions, which are

[18] In their extensive survey of the economic literature, F. H. Hahn and R. C. O. Matthews document the dominance of savings and cap-ital investment theories, noting that these fail to account adequately for the phenomena un-der consideration. "The Theory of Economic Growth," *Economic Journal* (December 1964), pp. 779–902. In his classic work on the subject, *The Theory of Economic Growth* (1956), W. Arthur Lewis explicitly chooses to deal with "growth" rather than "develop-ment." See p. 9. A similar position is taken by W. W. Rostow in *The Stages of Economic Growth* (1960). In her effort to deal with this problem, *Theories of Economic Growth and Development* (1967), Irma Adelman adopts a production function (or growth) model for analysis of the various theories, though in the end she comes to use an entre-preneurial/structural (or development) mod-el for explaining change.

[19] Schumpeter's book *The Theory of Eco-nomic Development* (1934) is the classic work in this field. "Development in our sense," he says, "is a distinct phenomenon, entirely foreign to what may be observed in the cir-cular flow [of resources] or in the tendency towards equilibrium. It is spontaneous and

clearest if thought of in economic terms but which we will explicitly apply to social and political phenomena as well.

The distinction between growth and development is, in the final analysis, an analytical one, since we are dealing with a complex process having many facets and elements. Yet we think it useful to identify growth with *production,* and development with *productivity.* The one concerns actual production; the other, potential production or capacity for production, which has the greatest impact over time. We need to think in terms of *structures of production,* which acquire inputs, convert them into outputs, and distribute the latter among those who contributed the former. To achieve growth, one takes the structure of production as given and increases outputs basically by increasing inputs. Thus, growth is a *quantitative* phenomenon.

To achieve development, on the other hand, one has to change the structure so as to raise its productive capacity. This is done by introducing new outputs, establishing new sources of inputs or new uses for them, finding new demands for outputs or new techniques for converting inputs into outputs. Forging new links between inputs and outputs or altering existing links is essentially a *qualitative* undertaking. Development involves changes *in structure,* while growth involves changes *in scale.* Growth policies, it should be noted, treat distribution as a function of production, rewarding those who possess factors of production. Development policies, on the other hand, treat production as a function of distribution; they increase and, to the extent productivity can be thereby raised, redistribute the factors of production available to the population.

The Ubiquity of Structures.

Social scientists have long recognized that the term *structure* can be usefully applied to relationships between persons. The model for the term is drawn from biology or, originally, engineering, and implies something solid and essentially static. But in social science usage, structure is applied to many things that are immaterial and commonly dynamic. We have spoken already of the *structure* of an economy as a pattern of resource flows at any particular time. The idea of a country's *social structure* refers to the differentiated and differential flows of esteem and deference between and among individuals and sectors. Indeed, what is conventionally called the "power structure" of a country describes the pattern of possession and exchange of political resources. One can readily see how economic, social, and political macro structures can be considered and analyzed in terms of resources and exchange, but the same terms can be applied as well to intermediate and micro structures.

In economic analysis, one talks about the structure of a sector like agriculture or of a particular firm, as well as of tax structures, trade structures, structures of capital, labor force, and land tenure. Sociologists consider class structures, group

---

discontinuous change in the channels of the flow . . ." and he adds in a footnote as an ironic exemplification of his argument, "Add successively as many mail coaches as you please, you will never get a railway thereby." The structure of a railroad must be estab-

lished and developed; incremental increases can yield growth, but only if the structure already exists (p. 64). The best, most recent work extending this line of economic analysis is, we think, Raymond Mikesell, *The Economics of Foreign Aid* (1969).

structures, and also the structure of the family. In political science, party structures have received considerable attention, as have the structures of bureaucracies, armies, judiciaries, and electorates. One can talk as well about an educational structure or the structure of knowledge. All represent identifiable patterns of resource possession and exchange, of resource stocks and flows—if we can think in terms of social and political as well as economic resources.

Stocks are easier to measure than are flows, and largely for this reason conceptions and descriptions of structures have tended to be more static than dynamic. Both stocks and flows are involved, however, and the latter are more significant except in the very short run because the strength or stability of a structure depends primarily on whether the rate at which resources are being acquired is greater than, or at least equal to, the rate at which they are being expended. Viewed in this way, structures not only are dynamic, or at least in dynamic equilibrium, but they extend more into time and space than is usually apparent.

The sources of resource inputs and the sources of demand for resource outputs, if not nominally part of the structure that uses and produces resources, figure significantly in the maintenance and extension of any structure.[20] Even if not as evident as in economic input-output analysis, structures of all sorts represent the productive linking of inputs and outputs. Some of these may be quite tangible and others rather intangible, but the common feature of structures is that they provide sufficient benefits to enough persons so that the necessary efforts are made to sustain the supply of inputs and perpetuate the production of outputs.

Structural Change.

When thinking of development in terms of structural change, it is necessary to bear always in mind the criterion of productivity. Not all changes in structural relationships result in more productive structures, and some changes that are productive for certain persons or sectors are not productive for others. We would, for example, decline to identify structural *differentiation* with development, as some political scientists have done.[21] The multiplication of distinct roles and therefore of exchange relationships may provide opportunities for augmenting the productivity of a structure, just as diversification within an economy's structure does this. But productivity can decline as a result of differentiation if more resources are consumed than produced as a result. Dividing a ministry into two, or creating three specialized jobs in place of a general position filled by three persons, may not produce more output or satisfactions. What is important is not the fact of role

[20] In much of organization theory and systems analysis, the "environment" is regarded as a relatively undifferentiated space from which the structure or system draws inputs and to which it provides outputs. Even at our most abstract level, we would not regard "environment" in this way. Rather we view the persons providing inputs and receiving outputs (often the same persons) as extensions of the structure. "Boundaries" are defined not abstractly but in terms of the interaction people undertake, occurring where such interaction declines markedly or disappears.

[21] The Social Science Research Council's Committee on Comparative Politics, representing the thinking of Gabriel Almond and Lucien Pye among others, stressed this question of differentiation. For a discussion of this, by a political scientist who has himself stressed the same thing, see Fred W. Riggs, "The Theory of Political Development," in James C. Charlesworth (ed.), *Contemporary Political Analysis* (1967), pp. 328–331 and 337 ff.

or structural differentiation but the consequences of it, if any, for productivity. Efforts frequently made to relate differentiation to the *capacity* or *capability* of a system (or structure) reflect a concern about productivity, but there is no justification for assuming that differentiation in itself necessarily yields greater productivity, which is presumably what development is all about.[22]

Schumpeter's conception of development in economic terms—as the carrying out of new combinations—can be related to development more generally. The discovery and establishment of a new use for present inputs (the production of a new output), a new demand for present outputs (the opening up of a new market), a new source of supply for inputs, a new method of production, and a new organization or reorganization of production—all raise productivity through alterations in the structure of production.[23] They involve qualitatively different, even discontinuous processes, which should permit new and/or more needs to be satisfied as a result of the change in structure.

In talking about structural change, then, we are talking about changes in the *pattern* of resource possession and use by persons. Proportional changes in possession and use do not alter the pattern; they affect the *scale* of each. This is not to say that changes—in particular, increases—in scale are not important. Indeed, they are the proof that productive structural changes have been made and development has been promoted. But scale changes are facilitated or constrained by the existing *pattern* of resource stocks and flows, and it is this to which we would direct attention. Development policies and strategies aim at creating those structures, or patterns of resource possession and use, which can elicit, channel, and transform resources most satisfactorily to meet people's needs more fully.

Several examples of development illustrate the relationships of which we speak. The Peruvian village of Huayopampa, studied by Whyte and Williams, manifested rapid transformation of its economic structure during the 1950s and 1960s. Resources were shifted from production of livestock, corn, potatoes, and other crops to growing fruit, which could be sold in urban markets because of the road which the people of Huayopampa had built to connect their village to the highway in the valley below. New markets were cultivated for their produce, and new products such as fertilizer and insecticide were imported for use as inputs. The people were willing to make investments in part because they accepted deferred gratification, expecting and preferring greater rewards in the long run, and also because they had organized themselves in the community so as to have confidence in their ability to achieve these future goals. Whyte and Williams report that the agricultural shift "was but one of a series of innovations in activities and in economic, political and social organization that our associates have traced back over a period of almost a hundred years." [24] The transformation of Huayopampa they

---

[22] Analyses equating structural differentiation with structural capacity are bolstered (tautologically) by specifying that there be concomitant structural "integration," i.e., differentiation without integration does not increase capacity. See *ibid.* Such manipulation of concepts is an example of essentialist social science. This "whole system" approach using concepts like "differentiation" obscures the benefits and costs accruing to individuals and groups that give the "system" its dynamic (or stagnating) character, its *raison d'être* if there be any. Issues of productivity, how much and for whom, keep analysis attuned to real factors.

[23] See Schumpeter, *op. cit.,* pp. 66 ff.

[24] See William F. Whyte and Lawrence K. Williams, *Toward an Integrated Theory of Development: Economic and Non-Economic Variables in Rural Development* (1968), pp. 4 ff; the various studies of Huayopampa are noted on p. 4.

take to illustrate the interrelation of economic and noneconomic variables, but it also shows the relevance of Schumpeterian analysis to both kinds of variables.

A comparative study of two villages in Mysore, India, points up the central importance of structural change for development, according to Guy Hunter.[25] In one of the two, a new irrigation scheme was introduced, making the traditional pattern of agriculture more profitable. The social structure of the village and the traditional rules were reconfirmed. The prestige, and power, of the large land-holder was further increased. The opposite happened in the neighboring village, where no irrigation was introduced. There, villagers established a sugar mill, carted the sugarcane from their neighbors' irrigated field, and took jobs in the more prosperous neighboring town, all because they did not have the immediate economic opportunities of their neighbors. Consequently, men in this second village grew more prosperous in new ways through employment in new activities. Instead of the traditional symbols of prestige, new ones came into fashion, things like transistor radios, which could be displayed not in the home village but in the neighboring one. New types of men emerged, Hunter says, not farmers but entrepreneurs, who disturbed the balance of political power in the village.

Two conclusions were drawn from this study. First, that there exist reserves of initiative and ability, which can be mobilized by some major change, even within a traditional economy. Second, and more significant for our discussion here, investment (or change) that simply enriches the existing tradition (or pattern of activity), by making the same type of activity more profitable, may bring temporary benefit in terms of individual incomes, but it may also freeze the social situation in ways that will make change more difficult later on. Income gains can be easily absorbed by subsequent population increases, so that no long-run benefits may result from short-run growth. Hunter concludes that " 'more of the same,' without structural change, is not a long-term policy by itself," and defines structural change as a change in the pattern of occupations and in the pattern of social, and by implication, political relationships.[26] We would include more than this under the rubric of structural change, but the thinking corresponds to the framework we have been presenting. Whether the first village will some decades hence still be less productive than the second in aggregate terms is something we cannot say. It is the kind of question, however, that must be addressed in our studies of development policy.

There is disagreement about whether development is a gradual process or a profound departure from existing conditions; whether the changes associated with it are incremental or discontinuous; whether it is "evolutionary" or "revolutionary." The question is not, we suggest, whether development is one or the other of these, but rather, whether and how these contribute to increased productivity. More productive patterns of resource possession and use can be established through "evolutionary" or "revolutionary" means. Differential incremental changes will, over time, change a pattern and can lead to greater productivity. This occurs, however, more slowly than with discontinuous new combinations or new relationships.

According to the framework we have proposed, one can consider and identify

[25] See Guy Hunter, *Modernizing Peasant Societies: A Comparative Study in Asia and Africa* (1969), pp. 43 ff; Hunter is considering the study by T. S. Epstein, *Economic De-velopment and Social Change in South India* (1962).

[26] *Op. cit.,* pp. 44 and 48.

"growth without development"—increases in the scale of production without changes in the structure of production—and "development without growth"— changes in structure without increases, at least in the short run, in scale.[27] To be sure, if no increases of any sort resulted from the change in structure, such structural change would not qualify as development. The common expression *laying foundations* conveys the idea of development without growth. When "foundations are laid," an investment is made in structural change of some sort; nothing may "happen" for some period of time, but it is expected to yield subsequent increases, whether in the value or the volume of outputs of any kind.

Many things are involved in development: markets, resources, infrastructure, organization, entrepreneurship, and investment. We think that all of these can be related to one another in a coherent and useful framework applying to social and political as well as economic relationships. The problem is that of ascertaining increases in productivity, of knowing whether certain changes in economic, social, or political structures contribute to greater production over time and therefore promote development. This is the problem we address in political economy terms.

BASIC CONDITIONS FOR DEVELOPMENT

We recognize that by identifying development, on the one hand, with increased productivity, on the other, we are faced with all the problems of measuring or estimating changes in productivity. There are two aspects to this term, volume and value. The first is reasonably objective and measurable, at least in principle. Increases in the volume of output are conventionally identified with the phenomenon of growth. The second aspect, value, is essentially subjective and therefore intrinsically difficult to measure. Increases in volume do not always yield an increase in value, and redistribution of a given volume of output may result in greater aggregate value, so the first cannot be taken as an infallible proxy for the second.

Are we in an analytical cul-de-sac when confronting questions of productivity? If we cannot handle questions of productivity using acceptable quantitative analyses at the present time, we think it still possible to agree on a conception of development that can guide policy choices in the absence of thoroughgoing quantification. The distinction between growth and development is helpful insofar as it separates out the class of changes that are simply scale changes, or growth. We are left with the problem of trying to make judgments about what changes will contribute to aggregate productivity, and hence to development.

Our work suggests that there are several *relatively objective conditions* that *make greater productivity possible,* whether viewed in economic or social or political terms. We think an understanding of these basic conditions offers criteria for development strategy and policy and at the same time links the analysis of economic, social, and political factors in a way that is useful and not really possible within other conceptual approaches.

[27] Two books that have greatly influenced and assisted our thinking on this problem are Robert W. Clower, George Dalton, Mitchell Harwitz, and A. A. Walters, *Growth Without* *Development: An Economic Survey of Liberia* (1966), and Robert S. Szereszewski, *Structural Changes in the Economy of Ghana, 1891–1911* (1965).

The method used in arriving at this conception of development involved no factor analysis, no structural-functional models, no detailed historical studies. It did involve thinking through the process of economic development in its most basic terms. It was found that these could be readily applied to social and political development if we adopted an expanded conception of markets, resources, and structure. Such reasoning from analogy is not infallible, but the methodology was not simply deductive, inasmuch as we were checking our conclusions, as students of comparative development, against a wide range of country experiences and cross-national data.[28] We recognize that we must engage in some abstraction and generalization, thus making ourselves liable to the kind of criticism made in Part I of other approaches. However, we maintained a steady focus on the activities and attitudes of individuals and groups, interposing no abstract concepts that departed from human experience or motivation. Some of the terms, such as *market integration* and *factor endowment,* derived from economic analysis, are not common layman's terms, but neither are they jargon. An understanding of them should contribute greatly to an understanding of development.

We concluded that the structural changes involved in development were generally of two sorts, though we would not erect typological classifications, since we know we are focusing on different parts or aspects of a complex process manifesting variations in degree more than in kind. We suggest that *incremental* structural change results from the extension and integration of markets and from the increase in persons' endowments or possession of the various factors of production—economic, social, informational, and political resources. *Innovative* structural change is achieved through the establishment or organization of new exchange relationships and through the exercise of entrepreneurship, which mobilizes resources for productive collective enterprises. Promoting these conditions constitutes the political economy of development.

The Integration of Markets.

The first characteristic of development involves the linking up of local or peripheral markets with and into a *national or central market,* thereby extending the scope of exchange. We have already suggested that such an extension can contribute to increased productivity, first, by allowing resources to be put to more productive uses, and second, by eliciting greater provision of productive factors as a consequence of the increased opportunity for beneficial exchange.[29] This involves something quite different from "enclave development," where a new activity, productive within its narrow boundaries, is introduced, though with few linkages to the rest of the community.[30]

[28] Moreover, the impetus for this analytical effort came from detailed studies at the micro level of development projects that had generally failed to increase productivity in Ghana by any significant amount. Thus, this was not a speculative undertaking but one growing out of a need to account for concrete outcomes of activities intended to promote development.

[29] Hunter writes of the primary "need for new institutions which will give to the self-

isolated village community a reliable and growing contact with the outside world— the market, technical knowledge, social and political support" (*op. cit.,* p. 138). Barrington Moore comments inter alia on market integration and development. *The Social Origins of Democracy and Dictatorship* (1967), pp. 467–468.

[30] For an instructive analysis of "enclave development," see Ruth C. Young, "The Plantation Economy and Industrial Development

The matter of *linkages* is the basic element here, with resource flows being patterned or structured to turn inputs into outputs, and vice versa.[31] Too much attention has been given, we would argue, to the acquisition of inputs in order to achieve given production targets. This kind of "production-function thinking" neglects the importance of marketing and of having sustained demand for the outputs of production.[32] A concern with market integration leads to the linking up of productive structures—markets and enterprises—thereby providing incentive for persons to increase their activity and to employ or generate more resources.

We would not want to suggest, however, that market integration is a sufficient condition in itself for facilitating development. Extending the scope of exchange will not raise productivity in a continuing and dynamic fashion unless there are increases in factor endowments. Also, as Griffin points out in his article, reprinted below on pages 203–213, if the partners to an exchange are unequal in resources and, therefore, in bargaining power, exchange can work to the detriment of the weaker partner. Whyte and Williams, as a result of their research into rural development in Peru, emphasize that the distribution of benefits from exchange "depends very much upon the distribution of political power," and in such countries, the most salient feature of much exchange is its coercive nature.[33] Certainly, we do not suggest that involuntary exchanges, however wide their scope, add necessarily to aggregate productivity, or to development, since the gain of the stronger stems from the loss of the weaker. This means that we have to consider concomitantly the level and distribution of factors of production.

The Increase in Factor Endowments.

The second characteristic of development involves increased possession and utilization of resources. If development enables people better to satisfy their needs, it is in part because the scope of exchange is expanded, and, perhaps more important,

---

in Latin America," *Economic Development and Cultural Change* (April 1970), pp. 342–361. The hacienda or latifundia system in Latin America, with rural subsystems isolated from the larger social and political systems of the nation-state, was debilitating as far as national development was concerned. See John Duncan Powell, "Agrarian Reform or Agrarian Revolution?" in Arpad von Lazar and Robert R. Kaufman (eds.), *Reform and Revolution: Readings in Latin American Politics* (1969), pp. 269 ff.

[31] The most notable statement on linkages is to be found in Albert O. Hirschman, *The Strategy of Economic Development* (1958). Szereszewski's input-output analysis of the Ghanaian economy in 1960 revealed that only 8 percent of outputs were used by other sectors as inputs. This minimal integration of productive activities, with little "value added" to final products, "is perhaps the very essence of underdevelopment," he suggests in W. Birmingham, I. Neustadt, and E. N. Omaboe (eds.), *A Study of Contemporary Ghana, Volume I: The Economy of Ghana* (1966), esp. pp. 66–68.

[33] For two excellent studies examining the relationship between development and markets, see N. R. Collins and R. H. Holton, "Programming Changes in Marketing in Planned Economic Development," *Kyklos* (January 1963), pp. 123–135; and William P. Glade and Jon G. Udell, "The Marketing Concept and Economic Development: Peru," *Journal of Inter-American Studies* (October 1968), pp. 533–546. Collins and Holton see marketing institutions and the distributive sector as changing demand and cost functions in agriculture and industry to encourage their expansion. Glade and Udell conclude that without "adoption and implementation of the marketing concept, it is doubtful that Peru or any other developing nation will be able to improve substantially its relative position in the wealth of nations" (p. 546).

[33] See Whyte and Williams, *op. cit.* (n. 24 above), pp. 26 ff. They point to the prevalence of forced barter, rigged prices, and disadvantageous arrangements for transporting goods to urban markets. The extent to which middlemen cream off a larger share of the total value is inversely related, however, to the extent to which political influence is widely distributed, they add.

because they have more resources to exchange. Increased productivity in the long run requires increases in the endowment of factors of production, especially for those persons presently less or least well endowed.

It is important to note the often-neglected fact that in poor countries not everyone is poor. Indeed, some proportion of the population, let us say the top 10 percent, will have incomes comparable to those of most persons in the more developed countries. These persons, whom we shall call *the few,* have command over factors of production—natural resources, capital, or skills—comparable to those commanded by persons in developed countries.[34]

The aggregate difference in income, or productivity, between rich and poor countries results primarily from the differing productivity, or factor endowment, of the lower 90 percent of the population—let us call them *the many.* Closing the economic gap between rich and poor countries ultimately entails raising the productivity of this large majority of the population. In doing this, factor endowments are made somewhat more equal, at least in relative terms.[35]

It is no accident that income inequality is generally greater in underdeveloped countries and less in more developed countries. Relative disparities in factor endowment have been reduced in the latter countries essentially by upgrading the endowments of the many. It has been suggested that the relative equalization of income is a consequence of development.[36] It appears more plausible to regard such equalization more as a cause than a concomitant of development. It is increases in the factor endowment of the many which raise their productivity and income, which in turn will raise production and income in the aggregate.

Mercantilist theorists of development, stressing the accumulation of gold if need be at the expense of the poor, or the many, did not comprehend this dynamic.[37] Unfortunately, however, neither did classical or neo-classical economists. Enamored

[34] See Simon Kuznets, *Modern Economic Growth: Rate, Structure, and Spread* (1966), pp. 425–426; also Elias Gannage, "The Distribution of Income in Underdeveloped Countries," in Jean Marchal and Bernard Ducros (eds.), *The Distribution of National Income* (1968), pp. 326–347. This latter volume was prepared under the auspices of the International Economics Association.

[35] Practically all comparisons of income distribution in more and less developed countries show greater inequality in the latter. See the works cited in n. 34, and also two longitudinal studies by L. C. Solton, "Long-Run Changes in British Income Inequality," *Economic History Review* (April 1968), pp. 17–29, and "Evidence on Income Inequality in the United States, 1866–1965," *Journal of Economic History* (June 1969), pp. 229–277. It is an open question whether the relationship between development and income equalization is linear in the long run. Some current statistical evidence in the U.S. and U.K. suggests the possibility that inequality may increase again at higher levels of per capita income. For a discussion of this question, see paper by Norman Uphoff and L. L. Wade, "The Paradox of Affluence for Political Development: A Political Economy Perspective," annual meeting of the American Political Science Association, Chicago, 1971. We are prepared to consider the possibility that a relationship observed over a certain range would be nil or reversed at higher levels. This would not, however, invalidate the analysis and conclusions drawn from looking at the relationship over a range of national incomes from, say, $50 to $3,000 per capita.

[36] See, for example, Irving B. Kravis's consideration of the greater equality of incomes in the more developed countries. He concludes that "forces . . . operate [there] to make the income distribution more equal." "International Differences in the Distribution of Income," *Review of Economics and Statistics* (December 1960), p. 414.

[37] See statement by E. S. Furniss cited in n. 32 in Part I above. Adam Smith's view, unfortunately neglected by most of his intellectual successors, was that "no society can surely be flourishing and happy of which a far greater part of the members are poor and miserable." Cited by W. Howard Wriggins, in *The Ruler's Imperative: Strategies for Political Survival in Africa and Asia* (1969), p. 180. Smith was arguing against mercantilist economic theories at the time.

with the efficiency, and consequently the productivity, resulting from *competition,* they neglected the fact that no such benefits accrue to anyone unless he has something with which to compete, that is, unless he has something to contribute to the production process. Raising factor endowments is thus a prior condition for achieving benefits, individual or aggregate, from exchange.

The level and distribution of factors of production critically affect the levels of production that can be achieved and the manner in which outputs are distributed. Raising the factor endowments of the many has the effect of "enfranchising" them economically, and also socially, politically, and intellectually insofar as the level and distribution of more than economic factors are affected.[38] It should not be necessary to say this, but the prevailing theories of development with their impersonal macro views of society commonly evade the issue: aggregate productivity depends on individual productivity, and the latter cannot be increased without raising people's economic, social, political, and intellectual means—or resources.[39] This has the effect of raising their incomes in these various respects, but only secondarily. The primary action is to raise, and in many ways to equalize, *factors of production.*

The Organization of Resource Flows.

Any analysis of development needs to look beyond resources and their exchange and to include structures, which represent the patterning of resource exchange. Although usually either ignored or simply discussed in abstract terms, structures are of great significance for development and have tangible if not always material effects. They are subject to deliberate creation or modification, and thus they constitute a focus for efforts to promote development. Whether economic, social, or political, or some combination of these, structures have in common the consequence of making resource exchange more profitable or predictable, and this contributes to greater productivity.[40]

---

[38] Thomas Balogh argues along these lines of "enfranchisement," stating that "a more equal distribution of incomes . . . is good not only for moral reasons but also for purely economic reasons." "Land Tenure, Education and Development in Latin America," in UNESCO-IIEP, *Problems and Strategies of Educational Planning: Lessons from Latin America* (1965). Similar arguments are made by Thomas F. Carroll of the Inter-American Development Bank in H. M. Southworth and B. F. Johnston (eds.), *Agricultural Development and Economic Growth* (1967), pp. 317–320.

[39] The preoccupation with physical capital accumulation is often justified as the means of raising the productivity of human resources for transforming natural resources into economically valuable outputs. This justification is clear enough if considered in these delimited instrumental terms. But capital in most contemporary models of development has become reified, taking on a life and purpose of its own. Further, as is argued in John Gurley's article on pages 145–152, labor productivity is

a function of much more than capital. Increased skills and incentives are probably more significant factors. See E. F. Denison, *The Sources of Economic Growth in the U.S. and the Alternatives before Us* (1962); and Harvey Leibenstein, "Allocation Efficiency versus 'X-Efficiency,'" *American Economic Review* (June 1966), pp. 392–415.

This emphasis on skills and incentives does not address itself to, though it is congruent with, the psychologically oriented view of development that stresses self-fulfillment or self-actualization. We would not quarrel with this view but generally find it too "consumption-oriented." We favor a more "productivity-oriented" view inasmuch as increases in an individual's productivity should benefit not only himself but others as well. For statement on "self-actualization" as a criterion of development, see Henry S. Kariel, "Goals for Administrative Reform in Developing States," in Ralph Braibanti (ed.), *Political and Administrative Development* (1969), pp. 143–165.

[40] Whyte and Williams describe the problem of development as one of converting the de-

We are concerned with structures at all levels and with their alteration in more productive directions, but in particular we are interested in *infrastructure* and *organization*. Both pattern resource flows, but they differ in terms of who uses and benefits from them and, therefore, who invests in them. Infrastructure provides external economies for various sectors and thus patterns their resource flows. Organization, on the other hand, facilitates the aggregation and utilization of resources for a particular group or sector. The differences in scale and in beneficiary are important, but the two levels of structure are otherwise similar in many respects.

We have already discussed infrastructure above as a basic part of the political economy perspective. The principal means for integrating markets, it should be noted, have usually been the creation of infrastructure. By reducing the cost or time involved in movement of resources, a greater volume of resources will usually be elicited for productive purposes, resulting in greater aggregate output. Not just any structure designated as infrastructure will promote development, however. Only that which increases the flow of resources into more productive uses than they previously found contributes to development by raising aggregate productivity. Particularly those patterns of resource exchange which provide broadly distributed benefits should persist and expand.[41]

The principal means for raising factor endowments has been, through the years, the creation of organizations, which are in effect infrastructure at the micro level. Robert Michels observed more than fifty years ago that organization is "the weapon of the weak in their struggle with the strong."[42] Only by pooling their resources, even meager ones, could the less advantaged make their needs and demands carry weight within the community. The principle of organization applies, however, to any group and its resources.[43] By enabling individuals to aggregate and concert their resources, the productivity of existing resources can be raised. Through organization, the distribution of resources in a society can be altered, though it must be noted that this change can be in a direction not enhancing aggregate satisfactions.

Because organization can be used, through monopolization and coercion, to restrict the scope of exchange and manipulate factor endowments, it is often an ambiguous instrument of development. This, however, does not disqualify organization from contributing to the achievement of higher levels of aggregate productivity than would be possible in the absence of organization. Not everyone will benefit equally from organization, nor will everyone enter as readily into organizations.[44] But the principle of organization as a means of raising factor endowments

---

sires that people have into "established pathways of interaction and activity." Their view corresponds very closely to that presented here. See *Toward an Integrated Theory of Development* (n. 24 above), pp. 61 ff.

[41] One of the most insightful treatments of the civil service and public administration as infrastructure is found in Hunter, *Modernizing Peasant Societies* (n. 25 above), chap. 8. He sees administration as providing, among other things, "new institutional channels through which new forms of relationship can flow" (p. 195). See also his article, "Development Administration in East Africa," *Journal of Administration Overseas* (January 1967), pp. 6–12.

[42] See *Political Parties* (1959 edition), p. 21. For discussion of organization as a political strategy, see Wriggins, *op. cit.*, chap. 6.

[43] Gaetano Mosca explained the political power of the few over the many as a consequence of the common fact that the former are organized and the latter are not. See discussion of this in T. B. Bottomore, *Elites and Society* (1964), pp. 9 ff.

[44] Henry Landsberger considers the significance of *organization* for the economic, social, and political advancement of the peasantry in Latin America. One qualification he makes is that it usually benefits the relatively better endowed. "The first among industrial low-status groups to organize were the upper

and of increasing the satisfactions people get from their economic, social, and political interaction should be evident.[45]

It should also be clear that there is no unambiguous distinction between incremental and innovative structural change. The establishment of structures can result from cumulative activities and attitudes, few of which were intended to create an infrastructure or organization. Most often, however, there is deliberate initiative taken to create or change a pattern of resource exchange that will yield greater aggregate satisfaction. As was suggested before, *policies* represent allocations of resources, and the net benefits they provide to persons can produce some continuation or expansion of certain patterns of exchange. Also, as was already suggested, *investments* represent uses of resources intended to yield greater future benefits, and most investments concern the establishment or improvement of structures, of one sort or another. With either means, it is a matter of eliciting and channeling resource flows. This involves providing sufficient incentive to the persons involved; otherwise, the flows will not be maintained. Even if we talk of structures in terms of resource flows, structures are not impersonal abstractions but are always based, in the final analysis, on persons and their needs and desires.

The Exercise of Entrepreneurship.

The establishment of structures by innovative means involves usually some entrepreneurship. Whether this is thought of as economic, social, or political entrepreneurship depends on the primary structures and resources affected by entrepreneurial activity. Such activity is noted for its widening the scope of exchange by extending and integrating markets, for mobilizing and aggregating factors of production, and for using factors to create infrastructure and organizations which make economic, social, and political enterprise more profitable.[46]

There is in the political sphere the same question as in economics, whether the pursuit of entrepreneurial profit serves to increase total welfare. We would not equate entrepreneurship with collective benefits in any unqualified way. But our first qualification is that entrepreneurship is as relevant to public or group activities

---

strata, those higher in income and occupational level. Thus, printers and other craftsmen were organized many decades before textile workers. . . . One of the reasons for this phenomenon is that the organization of low-status groups, even of its better-off sectors, generally takes place against the wishes of superior social strata. The kind of irreplaceability which goes with plying a skilled trade and the cushion of economic resources provided by a somewhat better income are necessary to overcome the resistance of these higher strata" (*Latin American Peasant Movements* [1969], p. 39).

[45] Hunter describes the formation of cooperatives as performing a basic function, that "of organizing the *first* flow of production and marketing, because this flow is originating from tiny units, from producers with the slimmest resources, with no insurance, with no wide view of the market, with little or no cap-

ital, from ignorant and powerless people who need to combine for protection and for access to capital which is beyond their single means" (*op. cit.,* p. 157). Such organization is not a cure-all, he says, however; many other structural changes need to be made, particularly in what we call resource endowments. See also Whyte and Williams, *op. cit.* (n. 24 above), pp. 37 ff.

[46] Our thinking is influenced and abetted, as was already noted, by the work of Joseph Schumpeter, especially his *Theory of Economic Development.* The idea of "political entrepreneurship" has been frequently if not often analytically used by political scientists, such as Apter, Banfield, Dahl, and Zolberg, to name a few. The analogue of "social entrepreneurship" has been less considered, though it would clearly apply to innovators in social relations such as Mohandas Gandhi and Dr. Martin Luther King, Jr.

as it is to private or individual ones. Thus what is "profitable" can be, and commonly is, collectively defined. Second, what distinguishes entrepreneurial activity from other kinds of activity is not primarily the outcome of profit but the orientation of activity toward invention, innovation, initiative, and investment. These, after endowments activities serve to extend markets, alter factor endowments and organize in more productive ways the resource flows under consideration.

The reader will agree that these four conditions are not independent or autonomous, just as economic, social, and political factors interact in the real world. Each condition affects the others, and it is not easy empirically to separate a particular development measure's effects on the different conditions. But what is seen from this conception of development is the interaction of effects and the multiple consequences of a particular measure.[47]

This interdependence is not one pointing to some equilibrium. Rather it points out how one could begin to raise productivity by changing any one of the conditions, which would in turn ramify on other conditions of development. Insofar as this is an equilibrium model of development, it is very much a dynamic equilibrium model, one allowing for rapid change and also for change that has negative rather than positive consequences. The political economy of development is neither unidimensional nor unidirectional. Factor endowments can decline, just as the scope of exchange can contract; organization can deteriorate and entrepreneurship dwindle. The crucial element, the dependent variable, is productivity. These conditions contribute to it, and from this they derive their importance for development.

DEVELOPMENT AS A GENERIC PROCESS

Just as there is interaction among the conditions for development, so too with the different aspects of development. It is common to talk of economic development, social development, and political development as separate processes. For purposes of elucidation, this separation can be useful, but we would contend that the process of development is a generic process, the different aspects of which manifest similar relationships under the guise of various factors. The interaction of which we speak is similar to that cited above, in which no fixed equilibrium is found or anticipated. Changes in economic, social, or political factors can occur or be introduced autonomously, and changes in some set of factors may occur slowly or to a limited extent. Any interdependence arises from the ramifications which the factors we conventionally characterize as economic, social, or political have on each other.

---

[47] Although this analytical framework is derived from economic theory and concepts, it is worth noting that two sociologists working on development problems, Henry Landsberger and Dov Weintraub, address themselves to these same conditions for development, although in more sociological terminology. Landsberger considers *horizontal .differentiation and integration* and *vertical assimilation* in terms parallel to our market extension and integration and our increased factor endowments. He is concerned also with the factors of organization and leadership. See *Latin American Peasant Movements*, pp. 15 ff. The main theme of Weintraub's analysis is the relationship between the "center" and the "periphery," which corresponds to our analysis of markets. He cites also resources, organization, and initiative as critical factors for development. "Rural Periphery, Societal Center, and Their Interaction in the Process of Agrarian Development: A Comparative Analytical Framework," *Rural Sociology* (September 1970), pp. 367–376. Both sociologists see their analysis as extending to more than sociological variables.

The parallels between economic growth and development, on the one hand, and social or political growth and development, on the other, have been widely observed and frequently represented in metaphorical terms. We find that the resource-exchange analysis of structures permits analysis of the three major aspects of development in analogous and conceptually substantial terms, such that the processes of social and political development can be better understood and also promoted through public policies. The purpose of the following analysis is to move beyond metaphors and to specify in each sphere the elements of development that can make human interaction more productive for its participants.

Economic Development.

The significance of the different conditions for development—expanded scope of exchange, increased resource endowments, the organization of resource flows, and the application of entrepreneurship—has already been stated, largely with respect to economic development. Thus, little more need be said here. That economic development requires, in the final analysis, structural changes such that aggregate production of goods and services is increased, few persons would dispute. What is or should be evident by now is that attention must be given to more than increasing the supply of production inputs. The demand for and distribution of outputs is equally important. Whole structures of production—the structure of the economy at the macro level, and the structures of sectors, markets, and firms at the micro level—need to be changed over time so that they can more adequately and efficiently meet the needs of those participating (or wishing to participate) in the production process.

The fixation of many economists on capital accumulation or formation as the leading factor in economic development is not so much refuted as it is greatly qualified by political economy analysis. The contribution made by physical capital to development is in its increasing the availability and efficiency of natural and human resources. Especially when it is used to create structures—infrastructure in particular—capital can elicit and expand the various flows of resources into and out of structures of production. The linking up of markets is commonly facilitated by the application of physical capital, so the role of capital in development is clearly important. But there is little to be said for capital accumulation in the abstract. The significance of capital lies in the productivity of the structures it creates or improves, in eliciting inputs, and in the increase or wider distribution of outputs. Thus, quantitative measures of capital are not necessarily very meaningful and are possibly misleading.[48]

Attention needs to be given to the *linkages* created, maintained, and increased, connecting inputs to outputs and these in turn to other productive uses. In this,

[48] What demonstrated this to us and pushed us to think of development in these more fundamental terms was the fact that Ghana maintained between 1957 and 1965 a 20 percent rate of capital formation in real terms. (This is twice as great as the 10 percent target set by W. W. Rostow for a "take-off into self-sustained growth" in his book, *The Stages of Economic Growth*.) Yet real economic growth per capita *declined* in Ghana from 1964 to 1969. Clearly there are structural conditions to be met, not merely input conditions—of capital in particular—if a country is to make economic progress. For a view that gives more emphasis to capital than we do, see Sayre P. Schatz, "The Role of Capital Accumulation in Economic Development," *Journal of Development Studies* (October 1968).

entrepreneurship is crucial, in finding opportunities for the productive use of resources, in mobilizing the needed factors of production, in establishing certain patterns of resource use (structures), and in providing products to a wider range of persons than previously. Economic development involves, then, we think, the four conditions, not in any necessary sequence or proportions but in a definite set of interactions that increase factor endowments and the aggregate output of goods and services.

Social Development.

Viewed within the analytical framework of political economy, social relations can be considered in terms of their aggregate productivity. Just as a gross national product (GNP) in economics represents the aggregate value of goods and services produced and exchanged, so an analogous "gross social product" would result from the aggregate value of esteem and deference produced and exchanged in interpersonal relations. In the same way that national product and national income are equated by economists, the total social *product* and total social *income* would be equivalent in magnitude. The rate of growth and the distribution of social income are matters that should be of concern to policy-makers in the same way that they deal with economic income.

The analogy has many implications. Just as some portion of goods and services is consumed and another portion used in further productive activities, so the esteem and deference received by individuals can be used for consumption (immediate satisfaction) or for production (to gain other things of value). Esteem and deference may be used in present-oriented activities or in ways that increase future income (economic, social, or political) as a consequence of investment. We appreciate that such a formulation of status relations is like a line drawing of a rich and varied social picture. But the elementary ideas of social income and social product justify, we think, the simplification because they focus attention on the productivity of social interaction for individuals.

We have already suggested the productive consequence of extending the scope of social exchange within a country. Social markets are integrated as a consequence of the establishment of common criteria for esteem and deference. This is a process akin to monetization in economic relations, and it has been analyzed in terms of "social mobilization" by Karl Deutsch.[49] The effect of this is to encourage the exchange of esteem and deference among more people, thus increasing the aggregate social product. Just as esteem and deference are granted to more people, so more is received from others, and thus social incomes should rise. Not everyone is entitled to one's esteem and deference, just as not everyone receives one's goods or services; but the widened scope of exchange increases the productive capacity of social structures, making possible an enlarged gross social product (GSP).[50]

An increase in gross social income, equivalent to GSP, is generally made possible by increases in individuals' endowment of status, the principal factor of social production. The amount of esteem and deference one receives is largely a function of

[49] See "Social Mobilization and Political Development," *American Political Science Review* (September 1961), pp. 493–514.

[50] This is an economic way of putting what Daniel Lerner described in terms of "empathy" in his study of modernization in the Middle East, *The Passing of Traditional Society* (1958).

one's status, and the value of the esteem and deference one accords to others is largely determined by one's status. In a social market where a few people have much status and most have very little, the aggregate value of social income or product is limited, because while the few receive esteem and deference from many persons, it has a very low value per unit, and at the same time, the many receive very little esteem and deference because of their low status. Where most people are esteemed and entitled to deference, no individual may have as high a social income as in the inegalitarian situation, but the majority will have reasonably high social incomes, representing a greater social product in the aggregate.

If, as some sociologists hold, status is something determined strictly in hierarchical, or relative, terms, changes in status are "zero-sum," with someone's gain in status necessarily being someone else's loss. In this sense of the term, if everybody has equal "status," nobody has any. This relative view would suggest, however, not only that the total amount of status is nil in an egalitarian society but that it is at a maximum where one person receives esteem and deference from everybody else and they receive none at all. It is ludicrous to suppose that social interaction is most productive of satisfactions when status is most unequally distributed.

The view that status is something real rather than simply relative derives from the analogy we find between esteem and deference, on one hand, and goods and services, on the other. The amount of esteem and deference received by individuals can increase without *necessarily* detracting from the esteem and deference others receive. Relative and even invidious distinctions affect, and often detract from, esteem and deference, to be sure. But the satisfaction derived from esteem and deference comes not simply or necessarily from others not receiving them. Esteem and deference may be more appreciated if not shared with others, but invariably, receiving more of these is preferred to receiving less. We hold that, in the aggregate, the volume and value of "social goods and services" can increase as criteria for according esteem and deference to more people come to be more widely accepted or as more people come to satisfy the prevailing criteria.[51]

The significance of organization for social development derives from the contribution which organization makes to raising resource endowments. Organization per se does not necessarily affect social development directly, since the productivity of social relations need not increase as a consequence of organization. Esteem and deference can be withheld from others by organized groups, and organized groups may have esteem and deference withheld from them. What organization can do is to enable less well endowed persons to acquire a greater share of income or authority, so that they become entitled also to more esteem and deference than previously.[52]

[51] For a thoughtful consideration of this and related questions, see Lloyd A. Fallers, "Equality, Modernity and Democracy in the New States," in Clifford Geertz (ed.), *Old Societies and New States* (1963), pp. 158–219. See also the detailed study of Indian conditions by L. I. Rudolph and S. H. Rudolph, *The Modernity of Tradition: Political Development in India* (1967), especially the section on "The Future of Equality," pp. 103–131. Readers interested in ascertaining empirically how the allocation of status can change are referred to the UNESCO study by A. Bopegamage and P. V. Veeraraghavan, *Status Images in Changing India* (1967).

[52] The "Black Power" movement in the U.S. represents a use of organization to acquire more income and authority for an underendowed sector but also to raise its status directly. Caste associations in India have been making similar efforts. See Rudolph and Rudolph, *op. cit.*

Perhaps because social relations are generally very much "decentralized" in terms of the decisions about criteria of "worth" and "estimability"—such decisions are seldom made explicitly, and they are made mostly by individuals or small groups—entrepreneurship appears to be less important for social development than for economic or political development. Leaders like Gandhi or Martin Luther King do mobilize resources in order to restructure the allocation of status and the flows of esteem and deference within a society. But such entrepreneurship, we would conclude, is rarer in social relations than in economic or political relations except at the micro level. As a rule, incremental changes are likely to be more significant than innovative changes in the process of social development.

Political Development.

To the extent that the productivity of political activity is increased for members of a political community, political development is being promoted in that community. However, measuring political productivity is more complicated and ambiguous than is economic or social productivity. It requires, therefore, more inference and "triangulation." If inductive proof is less feasible, deductive reasoning must take up the slack. Consideration of the several basic conditions for development will, we think, provide means with which to deal with this difficult problem of analysis. The common features of the development process viewed in political economy terms give insights into political development that support and elaborate upon the analysis of this problem by a number of political scientists.

The idea of "nation-building" has been presented by Emerson, Bendix, Deutsch, and others.[53] The presumed refinements on this idea by Almond, Huntington, Halpern, and still others, introducing terms such as *capabilities, institutionalization,* and *capacity,* have moved to a higher level of abstraction, unfortunately adding little clarity to the process whereby these characteristics are achieved.[54] These all relate to the process of political market integration, linking peripheral markets to a central one. What is involved is the establishment of exchange relationships—resource flows of economic goods and services, esteem and deference, information, legitimacy, authority, and force—all used to make, affect, or implement public policy.

Organization in the form of political and administrative infrastructure—political parties, constitution, elections, bureaucracy, armed forces, police, and the like—is essential to this process, though not all kinds of infrastructure are equally important or productive under particular circumstances. Extension of the scope of political exchange permits greater aggregation of political resources to achieve public purposes than is possible with a restricted central market and a multiplicity of unconnected peripheral markets. However, market integration does not contrib-

[53] See Rupert Emerson, *From Empire to Nation* (1960); Reinhard Bendix, *Nation-Building and Citizenship* (1964); and Karl Deutsch and William Foltz (eds.), *Nation-Building* (1963).

[54] See Gabriel Almond, "A Developmental Approach to Political Systems," *World Politics* (January 1965), pp. 183–214; Almond and G. Bingham Powell, *Comparative Politics: A Developmental Approach* (1966); Samuel P. Huntington, "Political Development and Political Decay," *World Politics* (April 1963), pp. 384–430; Huntington, *Political Order in Changing Societies* (1968); Manfred Halpern, "Toward Further Modernization of the Study of New Nations," *World Politics* (October 1964), pp. 157–181.

ute unambiguously to political development. If the level and distribution of political resources available to the public are not improved, the productivity of politics is only increased in terms of the values and objectives of those persons occupying positions of authority. To have a more balanced view of political development, it is necessary to consider individuals' endowments with the factors of political production.

To the extent that persons possess more political resources, they will be able to participate more effectively in the political process, contribute more to it, and make political interaction more productive for themselves. Since increases in an individual's endowment of economic resources and status have important ramifications for his ability to gain more from political activity, it is clear that economic and social development affect political development. However, there is also an effect vice versa, since gains in one's possession of a resource like authority can enhance one's economic resources and status. Thus, increased resource endowments are both cause and consequence of political development.[55]

Just as we think it useful to conceive of a gross social product for a society, so we suggest consideration of the implications of a polity's gross political product (GPP). As in an economy, there is an identity between product and income, such that GPP is equal to gross political income. This latter term represents the return to factors of political production, inasmuch as political resources go into making the total political product or output, which is distributed primarily among those persons providing the inputs.[56]

Valuation of political product is extremely difficult, since persons place different values on given outputs, and there is no common political denominator, such as money in economic valuation. However, one can expect that the greater the aggregate endowment of factors of political production, the greater will be the aggregate political product and income from the political system. To the extent that resources such as status and authority derive some of their productivity from relationships of superiority-inferiority, the increase in product will be less than proportional to that in factor endowments. Nevertheless, our contention is that politics become more or less productive not in the abstract but in terms of the increased or decreased ability of persons to gain satisfactions from political interaction.

Thus, we would suggest that more attention be given to individuals' political capabilities (in terms of resources) than to "system capabilities." The latter, we

---

[55] One of the most interesting explorations of some of these interactions is T. H. Marshall, *Class, Citizenship and Social Development* (1965).

[56] Gabriel Almond has expressed doubt that something like GPP can be measured. See "Political Development: Analytical and Normative Perspectives," *Comparative Political Studies* (January 1969), pp. 447–470. The difficulties he perceives stem in large measure, however, from the framework he has adopted for political analysis. Karl de Schweinitz shows how GPP could be estimated in terms of political outputs, though he gives no attention to what we consider gross political income. "On Measuring Political Performance," *ibid.* (January 1970), pp. 503–511. We think

that a political economy framework mitigates some of the problems posed by functionalism. Some of the same distinctions made in economic national accounting can be made, at least in principle. One could distinguish *net* from *gross* political product by subtracting the resources expended simply to maintain the amount and productivity of political capital, including infrastructure. Similarly, *domestic* political product (or income) could be distinguished from *national* political product (or income) by adjusting for the receipt of (or payment for) political resources coming from outside the political system. This adjustment is obviously important for most underdeveloped polities.

believe, following the logic of economic analysis, cannot be regarded as something independent of the former. A political system in which persons have more economic resources, status, information, and particularly authority should more adequately meet their needs than one in which they have less of these various political resources. Changes in political structures can increase the productivity of existing available resources, to be sure, but the fundamental variable would be the level and distribution of resources themselves.

Increasing the political factor endowments of the many, the underendowed majority, has the effect of equalizing political participation and the rewards gained therefrom. This phenomenon of "equalization" has been observed and commented upon by a good many persons writing on political development. The terms used vary, but the import is the same.[57] The analysis proposed here in terms of political resources and factor endowments gives, we think, greater substance to the variable in question and permits more instrumental activity to promote political development than is indicated by other approaches. The greater equity, equality, or participation that analysts have associated with political development stems from raising the political factor endowments of the many.

The contribution of political organization to the promotion of political development should be apparent from the foregoing analysis and discussion. We have already considered political and administrative infrastructure as macro organization, eliciting and patterning resource flows within the polity. Political organizations at the micro level serve similar purposes. They can extend the scope of political exchange by aggregating a greater volume of resources that can be used for more things than an individual would be able to seek. More important, organization can increase the volume of resources at the disposal of the less well endowed. Persons having few resources are individually very weak in setting the terms of political exchange, but by the pooling of resources to be given or withheld, more favorable terms can be achieved for persons who otherwise receive little benefit, and possibly even lose, from political exchange.

Political entrepreneurship, bringing innovation, initiative, and investment to political interaction, can raise the productivity of the political process by establishing new linkages within the polity.[58] Mobilization of political resources can be

[57] See discussions of political development by Lucian Pye, *Communications and Political Development* (1963), pp. 13 ff., and "The Concept of Political Development," *Annals of the American Academy of Political and Social Science* (March 1965), pp. 1–13; also Fred Riggs, "The Theory of Political Development," and Karl von Vorys, "Use and Misuse of Development Theory," pp. 353–354, both in James C. Charlesworth (ed.), *Contemporary Political Analysis* (1967); Frederick Frey, "Political Development, Power and Communications in Turkey," in Pye, *Communications and Political Development*, pp. 298–326; S. N. Eisenstadt, "Modernization and Conditions of Sustained Growth," *World Politics* (July 1964), pp. 576–594; J. Roland Pennock, "Political Development, Political Systems, and Political Goods," *World Politics* (April 1965), pp. 413–434; Alfred Diamant,

"The Nature of Political Development," in Jason Finkle and Richard Gable (eds.), *Political Development and Social Change* (1966), esp. p. 92; Ralph Braibanti, "External Inducement of Political-Administrative Development" in Braibanti, *Political and Administrative Development* (1969), esp. pp. 47–52; and Dankwart Rustow, *World of Nations* (1967).

[58] We would note here Charles Anderson's observation that a reformmonger or entrepreneur "can tip the equilibrium of power, amass power in his own behalf both to make his own intentions more credible, his decision-making processes more precise, and to enhance the prospects for successful implementation of public programs . . . [through] the intentional creation of a relevant 'political infrastructure'" ("Reformmongering and the Uses of Political Power," *Inter-American Economic Affairs* [1965], pp. 38 ff.).

ephemeral, more so than with economic resources because the former include more attitudinal resources; but to the extent that persons contributing resources to new uses, or new resources to existing uses, find these beneficial, there is some basis established for continuing and even expanding the pattern of exchange. It is even possible that while a political entrepreneur himself may go bankrupt others will benefit from the more or less formal structures he has brought into being. He can gain only from internalized benefits, but others can have their situation improved by resulting external economies. Entrepreneurship is to be judged, like the other conditions, in terms of what it contributes to the raising of aggregate political productivity.

The Dynamics of Development.

In treating separately with economic, social, and political development, we have tried to show not so much the differences among them as the similarities manifested by a process of development. The interaction among economic, social, and political factors has been discussed and needs no further comment here except to note the dynamic relationships among them. Changes in one set of factors, whether increasing productivity or not, will have ramifications for other sets; this is clear. Although we have not discussed here the role and dynamics of *informational* development, it is also part of this process, adding under various circumstances to the productivity of different resources and prompting more extensive exchange.

The readings that follow address themselves in various ways to the dynamics of development. Observations on markets and exchange, resources and power, infrastructure, organization, and leadership run through these pieces like a set of threads. Rather than point them out and draw them together for the reader, which he or she should be able to do in thinking through the experiences and ideas presented below, we would highlight here two general themes.

The first, *participation,* pertains to the micro level, to the activities and capacities of individuals.[59] Persons need resources in order to be able to participate productively in economic, social, and political interaction. Resources give one some capacity to make others meet one's own needs, and at the same time give one some capacity to meet the needs of others. We noted above Thomas Balogh's concept of "enfranchisement" in economic, political, moral, and intellectual terms, which is the same as our idea of endowment or that of empowerment.[60] The reciprocal nature of interaction makes productivity something which must be increased at the individual level if it is to be increased at all. The Vicos experiment in Peru, reported by Allan Holmberg on pages 219–226, gives dramatic empirical testimony to this. Though the lessons learned from it were not applied elsewhere, it did

[59] We would note here a statement on development and participation which came out of an FAO seminar on land reform: "Development does not mean only economic growth for the limited purpose of attaining a quantitative increase in production capacity . . . [but involves] the reorientation of political and social power of all sectors of the population in social and political institutions. To this end, development in Latin America must be approached as a process of structural change involving modifications in production as well as in institutions and requiring the creative participation of the entire people." Cited in Solon Barraclough and Jacobo Schatan, "Technological Policy and Agricultural Development," unpublished manuscript (May 1970), p. 6.

[60] See n. 38 above.

show how the reallocation of economic, social, political, and informational resources could raise aggregate productivity for a community.[61]

The second, *responsiveness,* relates to the macro level, to the flexibility of structures and their ability to provide for people's needs.[62] Structures are not in the
final analysis inanimate objects, however impersonal may be the patterns of exchange which outline them. Rather, structures can be reduced to the resources
which *persons* have and desire. Certain patterns of resource possession and flow
can be rather rigid, relatively unresponsive even to effective demands backed by
resources offered for exchange. Greater multiplicity of resource flows within and
between structures is likely to make, other things being equal, for greater flexibility and responsiveness in structures. There are more alternative points of exchange where flows can be increased or modified. In this sense, "differentiation"
may be seen as contributing to development. It is possible, however, for "specialization" accompanying differentiation to have negative effects if it impedes the flow
of resources through a resulting insularity or monopolization in economic, social,
or political relations. Specialized or differentiated structures facilitate development
insofar as they increase participation for individuals and responsiveness for the
market or system as a whole.

We would not contend that development is a consequence strictly of the size
of markets or the amount of resources available. Productivity is the definition of
development, not bigness or quantity per se. It may be that the relationship between markets and resources, on the one hand, and development, on the other, is
more curvilinear than linear. The largest possible market may not be the most
productive. At some point, the diseconomies of scale are likely to outweigh the
economies. Similarly, the diminishing marginal productivity of resources may be
such that the greatest volume of resources may not yield the greatest value. When
we address ourselves to problems of "development" in this work, we are considering a range of possible relationships, from those presently prevailing in underdeveloped countries to some more productive set. In them, moving from present
conditions to some more desirable future state involves, we believe, market integration and increased factor endowments, with organization and entrepreneurship as
productive causes or concomitants.

It is quite conceivable that the size of economic, social, or political markets

[61] In 1952, Holmberg, on behalf of Cornell
University, purchased the hacienda at Vicos
and transformed the feudal manor into a self-
governing community, which operated as a
producers' cooperative. Whyte and Williams
report that while the hacienda owner reported
he was losing money on the operation prior
to 1952, "the Indians were able to pay annual
installments of between $4,000 and $7,500 out
of their agricultural surpluses," so as to acquire clear ownership to the land. Whyte and
Williams conclude that despite the limited
economic potential of the region, "the Vicos
case does indicate that reorganization of the
structure of human relations and provision of
greater incentives for the Indians could provide substantial improvements" (*Toward an
Integrated Theory of Development,* pp. 46–

47). See also the March 1965 issue of *American Behavioral Scientist,* from which the
Holmberg article is taken. No comparable
efforts were made in other areas of Peru or
other countries, so there was no spread effect
from the experiment to justify calling it a
contribution to *national* development, but
there was development in terms of the community itself, and this demonstration is illuminating.

[62] For a statement on this with respect to
economic structures of production, see Wolf-
gang Stolper, "Planning and Flexibility in
Underdeveloped Countries," *Kyklos* (1967),
pp. 841–883. Inflexible productive structures,
which do not adapt readily to changes in the
world market, are seen as the principal economic problem facing these countries.

could become "too big." Sociologists, for example, have for some time now been concerned with anomie, which results from a decline in social income, that is, in the receipt of esteem and deference from valued others, as a consequence of much enlarged social markets. A political system can expand to the point where people's needs become less well known and consequently less well satisfied through the operations of government. "Bureaucratization" represents an unproductive distribution of authority prompted often by the enlarged scope of public decisions. Overcentralization is by definition unproductive in satisfying people's needs, and some reduction in the scale of government operations would be warranted in this situation and would contribute, consequently, to political development. The *distribution* as well as level of resources affects productivity, and this is the decisive criterion for development.

We have not considered thus far the implications of "revolution" for development. An analysis of the political economy of revolution would require and be worth another whole volume. The structural changes associated with development may be achieved through some combination of "evolutionary" and "revolutionary" means. When profound changes in the overall distribution of wealth, status, and authority occur, these qualify as revolutionary. Because such changes are made voluntarily only in the rarest of cases, revolutions are as a rule "violent." Usually the political resource of violence is required to alter the allocation of wealth, status, or authority to any great extent. (The resource of information is much less amenable to redistribution by the use of force, as many revolutionaries have discovered the hard way; "expertise" resists rapid transfer.)

The productivity of revolutionary change cannot be assumed *a priori*. The productive potential of revolution, on the other hand, should not be dismissed as readily as most defenders of the status quo are inclined, for obvious reasons, to do. When the factor endowments of the many are enhanced, their capacity for contributing to and receiving from economic, social, and political processes of production is correspondingly increased. The important question is always, how much? In many situations, far-reaching structural change cannot be accomplished without the utilization of violence. But the successful employment of violence is itself problematic, as Hirschman argues on pages 71–72. The contingencies for success require extensive analysis, which can be done best, we think, in political economy terms. But this is beyond our scope here. The development strategies and policies we consider are mostly in the range of "reformist" to "radical," though we include some consideration of the Chinese revolutionary development strategy and experience. We recognize that revolutions can have developmental ramifications, but exploring these amply would extend too broadly the limits of our endeavor, which are already stretched rather wide.[63]

DEVELOPMENT STRATEGY AND POLICY

No single development strategy or policy could be optimal for all situations. Our appreciation of existential realities in the Third World prompts this basic premise.

[63] Mark Selden has undertaken such an analysis in "Revolution and Third World Development," in Norman Miller and Rod Aya (eds.), *National Liberation: Revolution in the Third World* (1971), pp. 214–248.

At the same time, we think that the political economy mode of analysis leads to some general principles of development, which deserve elaboration. The specifics of a particular development strategy or policy would have to be worked out with reference to certain developmental objectives in the context of definite sectors and structures having different interests, capabilities, and capacities. The political economy model provides the appropriate analytical categories for this, we think. As has been made clear already, we are indisposed to isolate economic from political analysis. But in our consideration below, we find it helpful to focus, in turn, on economic and on political factors as independent variables in development activity. Because social factors are much more often dependent rather than independent variables, we leave them aside from this discussion of strategy and policy.

Economic Factors.

The basic strategy for development as far as economic factors are involved is one of mobilizing resources and structuring resource flows so as to satisfy more needs of more people more adequately. Since production and distribution are connected processes, it involves also allocating resources so as to ensure these objectives. This may not appear very different from what is advocated in conventional economic analysis. But the difference is that more attention is paid to structures and processes of production, and less to standard production functions and physical capital accumulation.

The aims of development go well beyond the usual economic objective of maximally increasing the output of goods and services in the shortest possible time. Dudley Seers, in the article presented below, makes a strong case for this less narrowly "economic" view of development. It is not surprising, at least to a political economist, that in the long run such an approach should do more than the conventional approach to promote economic satisfactions. Without wishing to impugn the motives of those who employ conventional econometric models, we would suggest that such models tend to exploit short-run growth potential at the expense of achieving the structural changes needed for longer-run development. The political implications of such models are that the underdeveloped countries are consequently less likely to be able to escape their subordinate position in the world's stratification.

If any "principle of development" can be advanced, it is that people should use their *own* resources to the fullest extent possible, since output produced with other persons' inputs must mostly be paid to *others*. A corollary rule is that development can be best advanced by using the admittedly initially meager resources of the less well endowed, so that the returns from development go more to the many than to the few and the factor endowments of the many are correspondingly raised. This is not a "growth" strategy that maximizes gross national economic product within a limited amount of time but a strategy aiming at changes in the parameters and structures of production.[64]

[64] This strategy is not necessarily a "left" strategy or a "right" one, since the basic principles of self-reliance can find support at any point along the ideological spectrum, though it is "ideological" in the sense of attaching more value to some economic, social, and political stratifications than to others. What it is not is a "liberal" strategy in the classical sense of relying on competition among persons as presently endowed. The strategy resembles in a number of respects, without accepting the conventional Marxian world view, the development perspective of the present regime in Communist China. The development

The rationale for this strategy is not as "uneconomic" as it may first appear. Because of a preoccupation with "bottlenecks" on the input side of production, too little attention is paid to the constraints on output resulting from insufficient effective demand for outputs or to the distortion of production that a limited demand encourages—for example, luxury housing and first-class hotels. Clearly it would be foolish to raise the purchasing power of the many if there were no concomitant increase in the available supply of goods and services, because price inflation would wipe out any gains in purchasing power in such a situation. But just as demand does not necessarily create its own supply, neither does supply create its own demand. Moreover, producing those goods and services which are "profitable" under present conditions—that is, those meeting existing demand—will satisfy primarily the needs of the few and not the underendowed many. This appreciation supports a strategy that deliberately aims at using and upgrading the factor endowments of the majority. Raising incomes is, of course, one way of raising factor endowments with respect to, say, capital or education. But the main emphasis in development strategy should be on increasing the *productive capability* of persons and groups by increasing their factors of production. Income would then flow to those who had strengthened claims on it in terms of their productivity.[65]

"Growth" calculus dictates that those resources which are already most productive be employed, whereas the calculus of "development" suggests that resources commonly need to be employed in order to become more productive. This "reversed" sequence applies, of course, principally to human resources. That labor unemployment raises political and social problems has become widely recognized in recent years as unemployment has burgeoned in most underdeveloped countries.[66] What is too little appreciated is that the separation of economic from political and social considerations in conventional analysis underestimates the importance of providing employment opportunities, because not all costs are weighed at the same time. Dorner in his contribution on pages 129–134 provides a more integrated perspective on this and related problems.[67] Which and whose resources are em-

---

strategy it resembles most is that of the Tanzanian regime under Julius Nyerere. This is best articulated in "The Arusha Declaration" of February 5, 1967, reprinted along with other statements on development strategy by Nyerere in *Ujamaa: Essays on Socialism* (Oxford University Press, 1968).

[65] This sequence is relative rather than absolute, and income transfers could have the effect of raising productive capacity. We would call attention to the recent report, *Poverty in India,* prepared by the Indian School of Political Economy at Poona with support from the Ford Foundation. It found that 40 to 50 percent of the Indian population have incomes too low to afford a minimally adequate diet. Economic "growth" has not improved the situation, since the living standards of the poorest sectors have actually declined over the previous decade, while the fruits of growth have gone disproportionately to the richer sectors. The "merely poor" have stayed where they were. The report urges a massive rural works program—providing more

irrigation, roads, afforestation, and land improvement—which would guarantee all Indians a minimum acceptable income. This could be financed by a 15 percent cut in consumption expenditure by the top 5 percent of the population and a 7.5 percent cut for the next 5 percent. Such transfers of income would not directly raise GNP, but by improving nutritional levels and infrastructure, productive potential could be considerably increased. Moreover, the transfer would in effect raise demand, since its composition would shift somewhat from imported goods to domestically produced commodities, thereby also improving the Indian balances of payments position. The report is published in *Economic and Political Weekly* (Bombay), January 2 and 9, 1971.

[66] See the article by Dudley Seers presented in Part III, pages 365–382.

[67] Such a perspective is being offered by more and more economists, such as Seers (see pages 123–129 below), Guy Hunter, Folke Dovring, and Philip Raup. Hunter has written

ployed will make a considerable difference in subsequent time periods, and this effect must be weighed.

Emphasis on the utilization of all available resources and on the mobilization of otherwise unused resources is surely not a new idea. The point we would stress is that such utilization and mobilization should not be treated as a function of physical capital or a consequence of capital formation. We would assign priority in development efforts to human and natural resources. These together can produce capital, a derived factor of production, which in turn can make labor or the exploitation of natural resources more productive. There are possibilities for substituting some of one factor for some of another, but this also shifts the pattern of distribution of outputs. In his article below, John Gurley examines the relationship among economic factors of production in a useful way. The conclusion that human resources are the key factor, we would endorse.[68]

One reason for proposing this view of labor vis-à-vis capital as a factor of production is the analytical point made by Theodore Morgan, that no clear distinction can be made between consumption and investment as is conventionally done in economics. He suggests that some forms of expenditure, those upgrading the health, knowledge, and security of individuals, are *both* consumption and investment. A strategy reducing "social" expenditures in favor of "economic" ones, building up economic infrastructure at the cost of social and human infrastructure, is not likely to promote development as much as a strategy more attuned to the multiple effect of expenditures on education, medical services, housing, and social security. "Most people and organizations are working well within their production capacities. The critical problem of raising production seems often that of diminishing the gap: of enabling and persuading them to work more productively." [69]

Productivity is certainly affected by the incentives people have to produce more. In an analysis of various productivity studies, Harvey Leibenstein found that more gains were to be achieved from better motivation and organization than from improvements in resource allocation per se among alternative uses.[70] Indeed, W. Arthur Lewis, who is often cited by advocates of accelerated capital formation to justify their position, suggests limits to this. An attempt to accelerate the pace of development by devoting (or diverting) a larger share of increased output to savings and capital investment, rather than to consumption, will only "defeat itself," he says, because it will give rise to political unrest and also because "output cannot

---

that "even to speak of rapid [economic] growth is futile unless some way can be found to use these enormous and half-wasted [unemployed] human resources" (*Modernizing Peasant Societies*, p. 13). In his consideration of "Underemployment in Traditional Agriculture," Dovring argues that in conventional economic analysis, rate of return calculations on the resources *used* generally ignore the losses a community sustains by not using *all* of its labor force. *Economic Development and Cultural Change* (January 1967), pp. 163–173.

[68] We find support for this conclusion in the econometric analysis by Anne O. Krueger of "Factor Endowments and Per Capita Income Differences Among Countries," *Eco-*

nomic Journal (September 1968), pp. 641–659. It is discussed in Part IV.

[69] See Morgan, "Investment *versus* Economic Growth," *Economic Development and Cultural Change* (April 1969), pp. 392–424. Morgan takes what we consider to be a properly broad view of what constitutes "capital" and includes that which raises the intrinsic productivity of labor, rather than only nonhuman material capital formation. Some "consumption," he argues, is also "investment."

[70] "Allocative Efficiency versus 'X Efficiency,'" *American Economic Review* (June 1966), pp. 392–415. Criticisms have been made of this article, but none, in our opinion, that disprove his central contention.

be increased without increasing consumption . . . growth requires incentives." [71]

Contrary to the political economy of development, the conventional approach calls for a "big push" in development through maximally squeezing out savings for capital investment.[72] The burden of the "big squeeze," whether Stalinist or bourgeois nationalist, falls largely on the many and seldom on the few. Both indirect taxation, which is more significant than direct taxation in underdeveloped countries, and inflation as principal means of financing development expenditures cut into the living standards of the poor more than the wealthy. The political economy of development, being oriented more toward production than consumption, offers no basis for consumptionist policies per se. But neither does it support the conventional counsels of "austerity" as a *sine qua non* for development.[73] Capital formation is a consequence of opportunities and incentives, and these are more likely to follow from policies that raise the factor endowments of the many (and hence their income) than from policies that restrict the welfare gains of the many and lower their effective demand.

Productivity and equity are not contradictory goals, as is suggested by defenders of income inequality, who argue that the rich save a larger share of their income and thus contribute more to investment, and hence to economic growth. If capital is no longer seen as the "independent variable" governing development, this argument fails. The proposition that these goals can and should be dealt with sequentially is faulted by the logic of political economy; one cannot simply raise productivity first under conditions of inequality, and then promote equity afterwards. Achieving growth of output with the factors of the few will *reinforce further* their power position within society, making it all the more difficult to effect anything more than a token transfer of income and resources from them to the many. As is seen from the Pakistan experience discussed below, to those who contribute the factors of production "it shall be given."

The former head of the Pakistan planning commission, Mahbub ul Haq, has himself testified in retrospect on this matter. He says:

We have a number of case studies by now which show how illusory it was to hope that the fruits of growth could be redistributed without reorganizing the pattern of production and investment first. Many fast-growing economies in Latin America illustrate this point. In my own country, Pakistan, the very institutions we created for promoting faster growth and capital accumulation later frustrated all our attempts for better distribution and greater social justice. I am afraid that the evidence is unmistakable and the conclusion inescapable: divorce between production and distribution policies is false and dangerous. The distribution policies must be built into the very pattern and organization of production.[74]

[71] "A Review of Economic Development," *American Economic Review* (May 1965), pp. 1–16; see esp. p. 3.

[72] Not all economists see physical capital as the "leading factor" in economic development. See, for example, Nicholas Kaldor, *Essays on Economic Stability and Growth* (1960), esp. pp. 233–238; and A. K. Cairncross, *Factors in Economic Development* (1962), and "Capital Formation in the Take-Off," in W. W. Rostow (ed.), *The Economics of Take-Off into Sustained Growth* (1963); also P. T. Bauer and E. S. Yamey, *The Economics of Underdeveloped Countries* (1957), esp. p. 127.

[73] The Protestant ethic offers more guidance in its emphasis on productive work than in its preference for restricted consumption. The elite advising "austerity," whether it is a domestic or foreign elite, is generally urging the majority to do as it says rather than as it does. In any case, saving and investment out of profits earned from capital involve different sacrifices than those following from arduous labor.

[74] "Employment in the 1970's: A New Perspective," *International Development Review,* December 1971, p. 12. Huq attributes the planner's error to the assumption that "income distribution policies could be divorced from

The critical questions, then, in development policy are: *whose* resources shall be used to achieve increases in output, and *how* can resource endowments for the many be increased?

In this context, foreign economic development assistance takes on special salience. One might well conclude in political economy terms that, in general, less aid was preferred to more aid. Even grants of goods, services, or credit, which presumably require no economic repayment, involve some compensation in terms of political resources—perhaps in legitimacy, status, information, or support given to the donor country. Loans certainly involve some transfer of resources abroad, and many underdeveloped countries are now facing insupportable burdens of debt repayment. Foreign investment is undertaken, indeed, with the expectation that there will be a significant "export" of resources as a return on the investment.

What must be said, however, is that the costs must be weighed against any probable benefits, and the latter should not be discounted *a priori*. Foreign public aid or private investment utilized with a view to achieving increments in output for their own sake are less likely to provide a net margin of benefits to the underdeveloped country. On the other hand, aid and investment can sometimes provide an impetus for development that cannot be generated from the supply or structure of domestic resources. Those forms of aid and even investment which have the effect of changing economic, social, or political structures in more productive ways, particularly by helping elicit and utilize previously unexploited resources, can play an important role.[75] Indeed, it may happen that the only resources available for raising the factor endowments of the many come from outside in the form of aid or investment.

The specific ways in which economic factors should be used within a strategy for development are unfortunately so contingent upon situational variables that no "modal" or "optimal" strategy can be presented. Also, at present, for lack of research that is supradisciplinary and policy oriented, the empirical basis for tendering a set of *ceteris paribus* or configurational propositions does not exist. What can be suggested about development strategy as a consequence of the foregoing analysis would be the importance of agricultural and educational development for the whole process.

For a number of years, the mistaken identification of development with "modernization" or "Westernization" led persons to focus on industrialization as the basic economic strategy. From a developmental perspective, efforts to diversify an economy, to establish more processing linkages in order to raise the value added to final products, and to employ more of a country's resources in new ways—all are appropriate goals. But the emphasis on maximizing growth of output and profitability in the short run has led usually to capital-intensive industries, often largely dependent on imported inputs, which manufacture import-substituting products to meet the demands of the elite. A relatively small proportion of the population have

growth policies and could be added later to obtain whatever distribution we desired . . . once production has been so organized as to leave a fairly large number of people unemployed, it becomes almost impossible to redistribute incomes to those who are not even participating in the production stream. . . . Once you have increased your GNP by producing more luxury housing and cars, it is not easy to convert them into low cost housing or bus transport." Ibid., pp. 11–12.

[75] For an insightful consideration of this subject, see Mikesell, *The Economics of Foreign Aid*. His approach is different from our political economy approach, but he arrives at many of the same conclusions about development that we do.

become involved in these enterprises, few linkages have been established, and the result is "enclave" development. On the grounds of foreign exchange saving through import substitution, subsidies have often been introduced (and seldom reduced). In many cases, such industrialization has become a political as well as an economic barrier to further economic development.[76]

Our purpose here is not to explore the relationship of agricultural development to other aspects of the development process.[77] Rather it is to point to the developmental implications of structural changes in the agricultural sector. Since the large majority of persons in underdeveloped countries live in rural areas and make their livelihood from agriculture, the task of raising the factor endowments and productivity of the many must necessarily marshal significant efforts to improve agriculture. The preferred strategy would be not one that promotes large-scale, mechanized farming, but rather one that, however difficult the task, engages the "modal" farmer or peasant and raises his levels of productivity and income. "Unimodal" or "incremental" development strategy should maximally engage a country's human and natural resources and over time lead to an involvement of the greatest feasible share of these in the production process.[78] In Gurley's terms, this would be building on other than the best available resources, but the alternative is to cut off a large share of potentially productive resources, perhaps indefinitely. Development, in contrast to growth, strategy has regard for these, in human as well as production terms.

We shall consider specifically the political economy of land reform in Part III. This is in many circumstances a key element in agricultural development, raising the factor endowment of the majority of cultivators by redistributing land in their favor. What makes this much more than an economic problem is that such redistribution alters not only the allocation of wealth but of status and authority as well. Many strategic considerations are involved in planning and carrying out land reform so as to achieve the objective not of just reallocating land but of raising the productivity of the many. These are, we think, best understood in political economy terms.

The significance of education, seen from the perspective of the political economy of development, is its contribution to social and political as well as economic development. The information that education imparts can under many conditions contribute to increased economic productivity—through technical skills, knowledge of opportunities, ability to communicate, and capacity for self-education.[79] But

[76] See the insightful critique of development strategy in Pakistan by Hyman P. Minsky, "Passage to Pakistan," *Trans-Action* (February 1970), pp. 27–31. See also Albert O. Hirschman, "The Political Economy of Import-Substituting Industrialization in Latin America," *Quarterly Journal of Economics* (February 1968), pp. 1–32; and Ruth Young, *op. cit.* (n. 30 above).

[77] For such a consideration, see the contributions by Herman Southworth and Bruce F. Johnston, John W. Mellor, and others to the volume edited by Southworth and Johnston, *Agricultural Development and Economic Growth;* also Guy Hunter, *Modernizing Peasant Societies,* and *The Administration of Agricultural Development* (1970).

[78] For a statement on such a "unimodal" (as contrasted to a "bimodal") strategy, see Bruce F. Johnston and John Cownie, "The Seed-Fertilizer Revolution and Labor Force Absorption," *American Economic Review* (September 1969), pp. 569–582. See also Minsky's statement on "incremental" development, *op. cit.,* p. 31; and Donald K. Freebairn, "The Dichotomy of Prosperity and Poverty in Mexican Agriculture," *Land Economics* (February 1969), pp. 31–42.

[79] For an instructive quantitative study of "Education's Role in Development," see the article by Alexander L. Peaslee reprinted below in Part III.

it also enables more people to satisfy status criteria, to qualify for more esteem and deference than if they were illiterate or uneducated, and it improves people's facility for participating in the authoritative processes of decision-making. Economic calculations of the "rate of return" on educational investments in human capital are misleading; only economic benefits are set against the economic costs involved, yet the social and political benefits can be much the greater. Some social and political costs there may be, but one does not find among countries that qualify as making progress toward social or political development any that have not extended their educational system. In particular, education—not necessarily formal education or the highest academic level—is important for raising productivity in the rural or agricultural sectors.

This is not to suggest that education should be indefinitely expanded as part of any development strategy. With a concern for the increased factor endowments that education provides there is a concomitant concern that these be put to productive use. Thus, policies on *employment* need to be worked out concomitantly with educational policies. In Part III, we consider the political economy of education and employment. Here our purpose is to suggest the key contribution made to development by education, with its transmission of information through schooling and its related acquisition of knowledge through research. The ramifications of the spread of information are great indeed.[80]

Political Factors.

Given the nature of politics, almost any resource can become a political factor to the extent that it relates to the exercise or attainment of authority. One might infer from this that the best development strategy would be one that maximally politicizes factors and centralizes authority, but this would be incorrect. Politicization does not constitute or assure political development any more than monetization guarantees economic development. Neither should centralization be equated with development. Political market integration results from the establishment of exchange relationships between and among persons possessing authority and other political resources; it does not require centralized control of all resources. Under many conditions, decentralization will be more productive for meeting people's needs than will concentration of authority at the center.[81]

The political environment of development is the critical factor governing this strategic choice of whether to concentrate or to disperse authority. The very idea of decentralization implies that there is some structuring of political interaction such that authority can be delegated to individuals or groups. This means that au-

[80] We reach a conclusion similar to that of Cyril E. Black, though by political economy rather than historical analysis. In *The Dynamics of Modernization: A Study in Comparative History* (1966), Black finds information or knowledge to be the most salient variable apart from leadership for altering traditional relations in more productive ways.

[81] Hunter says of peasant societies, "Where every scrap of local knowledge and initiative is needed, the task of finding and supporting every hopeful sign of growth is critical. . . .

To find, support, link and expand these initiatives involves giving to the local area a degree of trust, a delegation of both financial and policy-making power [i.e., authority] which is still appallingly difficult to extract from the centre. . . . Delegation is not a modern invention: it happened in States far less developed than those of [contemporary] Africa; it is centralization which is modern and, in the circumstances of peasant countries, disastrous" (*Modernizing Peasant Societies,* p. 205).

thority must have been established or created as a resource, backed by flows of legitimacy, coercion, money, and information, so that it can be decentralized. When the scope and amount of authority within a society are limited by the absence or inadequacy of political and administrative structures, development strategy needs to be concerned with what is called nation-building. This problem is foremost in Africa, as analyzed by Aristide Zolberg in his article below, but it arises wherever a country has a weak political center. There efforts must revolve around politicization and centralization, though the latter does not mean necessarily authoritarian rule. Rather, both processes involve the spread of participation in politics within the framework of a national community.

When authority is more available, other developmental problems come to the fore, modifying the aims of development strategy. When central governments are more extensively linked to the public, the aggregate growth in the productivity of politics may be impeded in a different way. Monopolization of authority by vested interests, shown in the article by Talukder Maniruzzaman on Pakistani politics, can have consequences similar to those of monopolies in an economic market with both production and distribution being restricted. Under such conditions, it is difficult and perhaps impossible to get policies adopted that will raise the factor endowments of the majority, and thus in such cases, the political equivalent of an antitrust policy would become a central element of development strategy, requiring an increase in participation by those sectors otherwise excluded from the making of policy.

Instead of having authority monopolized by some particular sector or sectors, there may be continual competition among power contenders, as Charles Anderson suggests is the prevailing political situation in Latin America, where authority is often successively acquired and lost by different sectors. The consequence of this is that most available political resources are expended to gain or maintain authority, with few resources left over to be devoted to increasing the "purchasing power" of the many, even if some persons well-endowed with political resources wished to do this. Achievement of political stability per se would not necessarily increase aggregate productivity, since the stability could result simply from subsequent monopolization of authority. Although it may appear paradoxical, the principal "remedy" for instability is increased popular participation in the political process. The continual shifting of authority is encouraged when not enough persons are involved in politics with enough resources to make a lasting agreement on aims and policies.[82] Our point is that once the task of political market integration has been gotten under way, efforts need to be directed toward raising the political factor endowments of the majority so that they participate more fully in politics, counteracting the restrictions on political productivity that stem from elite monopolization or rapid rotation of authority.

At the local or micropolitical level, there is more monopolization than rotation of authority, and this is a major structural feature of the political environment of development. The pattern of patron-client relations which James Scott delineates in his article presented below is prominent in Southeast Asia, but it is also found

[82] See Eldon Kenworthy's model of "dual political currencies" for explaining this alternation, presented in "Coalitions in the Political Development of Latin America," in Sven Groennings, E. W. Kelley, and Michael Leis-erson (eds.), *The Study of Coalition Behavior* (1970), pp. 110 ff. This model amplifies some of the analytical points made by Charles W. Anderson in *Politics and Economic Change in Latin America* (1970).

in localities throughout the Third World.[83] The developmental consequences of clientelist political structures are mixed. Political market integration is served by this pattern, but the effect of local patron monopolies is to limit the growth of factor endowments for the many. These structures cannot be wished away. Their inertial effect on development efforts needs to be comprehended in terms of resource aggregation and exchange, and to be made more productive, where possible, for the clients vis-à-vis the rest of society.

Given the prevailing political environment, it would appear that the effect of "politics" on development would be marginal at best and more probably negative. One might expect that the less "politics" involved in development efforts, the better for development. It is widely observed that development efforts of the past decade or two have benefited primarily the better-endowed sectors and even left the poorest sectors worse off than before.[84] Political economists, whether Marxian or non-Marxian, recognize that the state, as it operates, benefits disproportionately the possessors of factors of production, economic, social, and political. Actions by the state in underdeveloped countries to redistribute incomes are likely in substance to work to the advantage of the few rather than the many.[85]

[83] Empirical work in Latin America and Africa has suggested the utility of clientelist models to John Duncan Powell and René Lemarchand, respectively. See Powell, "Peasant Society and Clientelist Politics," *American Political Science Review* (June 1970), pp. 411–425; and Lemarchand, "Political Clientelism and Ethnicity in Tropical Africa," to be published in the same journal in March 1972. See also Scott, "Corruption, Machine Politics and Political Change," *ibid.* (December 1969), pp. 1142–1158. Such relations are not restricted to the Third World but persist in various forms in more developed countries. See, for example, Sidney Tarrow, *Peasant Communism in Southern Italy* (1967).

[84] See the report on *Poverty in India,* cited in n. 65 above. Numerous citations of this can be found in Myrdal, *Asian Drama.* See also Hunter, *The Administration of Agricultural Development,* p. 24, where he notes the tendency for "the bigger and more powerful farmers to benefit most from the development effort." The evidence from India is most dramatic, but there is little to suggest that the situation there is much different from that found in other underdeveloped countries. See e.g., René Dumont, *False Start in Africa* (1966).

[85] See the discussions from the International Economic Association symposium on *The Distribution of National Income,* esp. pp. 323 and 359. There was general agreement that government redistributive measures in underdeveloped countries operate more often to the detriment of the poorer classes than to their benefit. Clear support for this can be seen from the folowing table, which analyzes the *allocations* for different categories of housing in Indian development plans, 1951 to 1969, and the *actual expenditures:*

Program	Allocation	Utilization	Column 3 as % of Column 2
AMOUNT IN MILLION RUPEES			
1	2	3	4
Middle income group housing	445	454	102
Rental housing for central government employees	209	209	100
Integrated subsidized housing for industrial workers and economically weaker sectors	865	671	78
Low income group housing	952	718	75
Slum clearance and improvement	514	343	67
Land acquisition and development	508	285	56
Village (rural) housing	276	119	43
Subsidized housing for plantation workers	14	5	36
Total	3,783	2,804	74

Source: ECAFE, "Finance of Housing and Urban Development in India," a paper contributed to the Interregional Seminar on Finance and Urban Development, 25 May to 10 June 1970, Copenhagen (rows reordered). The first two categories, covering about 5% of the population, receive about a quarter of expenditures; three-quarters of the population have less than 5% of the expenditure.

Recognition of this dynamic, however, should not lead one to prefer apolitical development strategies. Development through secular changes over time in market integration and factor endowments is possible; the economic resources of the many can be enhanced through worker and peasant organizations; their status can be enhanced through education, which can also provide information that enables the many to become more active and effective politically. However, even these changes can probably only come about with state support. In the absence of state intervention in economic, social, and political exchange, the advantages of the better-endowed will continue to accumulate. The advertised neutrality of *laissez faire* turns out to favor the few. At the least, the state must protect the efforts of the many on their own behalf from being snuffed out by the few, whose superior resources would permit them to do this if the state were truly neutral. To achieve positive results, the state would have to act to offset the cumulative effects of previous unequal exchanges so as to encourage exchanges that are more mutually beneficial.

Such a reorientation can only come as a consequence of political resource mobilization and expenditure—either by the many or by some members of the few on behalf of the many. The use or threat of violence, work stoppages, tax strikes, self-education, and other means may be used by underendowed sectors to put pressure on the elite to provide more favorable policies. With organization to aggregate resources, and leadership to wield them, a different orientation may be forced on the state. In the event of great power among the many and intransigence among the few, the many may seize authority and make the state serve their interests directly. Whether authority can be effectively bargained for or whether it can be expropriated depends on situational factors. What needs to be recognized is the significance of the state as a structure and of politics as a process for redistributing resources in *some* direction, whether this is a developmental one or not.

Despite whatever philosophical justifications one can make for doing away with the institutions of the state, as long as inequality of resources persists, the state offers the best opportunity, even if equivocal, for the many to improve their situation. In this context, the establishment and modification of political and administrative infrastructure takes on considerable developmental importance, providing for the aggregation and allocation of political resources, more for the benefit of the many or the few, depending on the way in which resource flows are structured. We shall give consideration in Part III to the ways in which political and administrative infrastructure affect aggregate political productivity in underdeveloped countries. What concern us here are the more general lines of development strategy.

Two basic approaches to development can be characterized, one as being more "political" and the other as more "administrative." The latter relies primarily on the efficient allocation of available resources and corresponds in many ways to a "growth" strategy, and the former, on the other hand, involves essentially the mobilization of resources and activity and is thus more "developmental" in effect. Development strategy that is more elite based and elite oriented generally tends to be more administrative in its approach. Any strategy oriented more toward the many than the few must be more political inasmuch as it involves mobilizing their resources to bring about change in the economic, social, and political stratifications.[86]

[86] For a study of administrative versus political orientations, see Warren F. Ilchman, "Productivity, Administrative Reform and Anti-Politics: Dilemmas for Developing States," in Braibanti, *Political and Administrative Development*, pp. 472–526.

The primacy of more "political" development strategies can be seen from the limitations inherent in an administrative approach. Unless the majority are mobilized and well-endowed, or unless administrators are highly and quite altruistically motivated, there is little incentive or need for the latter to work energetically and equitably for developmental objectives. Public servants serve the public very poorly as a rule when that public is poor, illiterate, unenfranchised politically, and lacking prestige. Hunter, who considers the distinction between political and administrative strategies with respect to rural development, writes:

> It is useless to think only of stable, skilled, paternal administration of rural development; it must have a political base. And even administration backed by local participation is not enough. In many countries, particularly in Asia, changes in the local power structure are needed before administration, even with local committees or associations, can develop local potential—and changes in local power mean political changes.[87]

Such change "can only be generated by a politics which goes to the mass of farmers and enables them to exert political power, by votes and with protection from reprisals," he adds.[88]

There are pitfalls in a "politicized" development strategy. The political process and its institutions can be dominated by the more privileged sectors, even with democratic elections required. Replacing traditional leaders with party politicians may make little difference as far as the interests of the many are concerned. But, as Hunter suggests, a more participatory system at least "offers a way for oppressed but potentially progressive forces to break through." [89] In the absence of participatory politics, the prospects for changing economic, social, and political stratifications are even bleaker than with mobilization and participation.[90]

Politics may move in favor of the better-endowed or the less well endowed, depending on the issues and the leadership involved. The vision that leaders have of a good society (i.e., one which they regard as most productive) shapes their choices of sources to which they turn for resources and the way in which they expend the resources at their disposal. Some sectors provide a regime with the bulk of its resources, and they, together with perhaps a few other sectors that are fortunate to be favored by the regime, receive most of the benefits from policy.[91] Judgments about what makes for a more productive society and which sectors ought to benefit most from government action are bound to vary. Perhaps one of the most illuminat-

---

[87] *Modernizing Peasant Societies*, p. 230. Hunter suggests also a strategy of rural development relying on private sector entrepreneurship. That is tenable in a strictly economic sense, but its social and political implications, given the existing inequality of resource endowments, already make it less acceptable from a political economy view as strategy by itself. This is not to say that such entrepreneurship should not complement more political or administrative strategies. See pp. 216 ff.

[88] *Ibid.*, p. 231.

[89] *Ibid.*, p. 232.

[90] We acknowledge the problem with "politicized" development strategies which Huntington formulates in terms of the "balance" between mobilization and institutionalization. *Political Order in Changing Societies, passim.* His perspective on institutionalization emphasizes the containment of non-elite energies toward improving their own lot possibly even at the direct expense of the elite. Such a course of events could prove unproductive for all, in which case it holds no developmental promise for the many. But we would be less inclined than Huntington to abjure such a tension or disruption in society in order to maintain "stability" per se, since this makes no *a priori* contribution to increased aggregate productivity.

[91] In *The Political Economy of Change*, we suggested that sectors be identified in terms of whether they were in the "core combination" of sectors linked closely with the regime or in the "ideological bias" of the regime's leaders. The other analytical categories of sectors are "stability" and "extra-stability" groups and "unmobilized sectors." See pp. 42–47.

ing analyses of the role and consequence of leadership preferences is Aaron Segal's article presented below, comparing the strategies of rural development adopted by regimes in Kenya, Tanzania, and Uganda. Striking differences are noted, but all can be better comprehended and evaluated, we think, within the political economy model of sectors, resources, and exchange.

Even if a leadership wishes to alter the prevailing stratifications, there are bound to be limitations placed upon it by its own vulnerability to already powerful sectors within the society. We see from Charles Anderson's account below of development policies of regimes in Costa Rica, El Salvador, and Guatemala how strategies there had to be tailored to the political parameters unless these could be successfully altered by radical political action. Overstepping them can lead (and in one case did lead) to political bankruptcy. There is little virtue in "prudence" per se, but the consequences of "imprudence" are wasted resources, often from those sectors which can least afford the loss. Any reformer or revolutionary who is successful has taken the polity's parameters of power into account when reckoning a course of action. Calculated risks may be justifiable, but recklessness is not, since other people's well-being is involved.

Changing the political parameters within a society, whether by reformist or revolutionary means, requires political entrepreneurship.[92] Exploiting existing opportunities for political profit means that the pattern of benefits from politics is not altered much. But mobilizing resources previously unmobilized and constructing political and administrative organizations to marshal and channel resources involves entrepreneurial insights and dedication. We have in Jose Abueva's account of the political career of Philippine president Ramon Magsaysay an unusual example of entrepreneurship. Magsaysay's "enterprising" campaign and exercise of authority provide examples of the innovation and initiative, as well as the necessary resources involved in such entrepreneurial efforts to transform a society in economic, social, and political terms.

Whether Magsaysay could have been successful in his enterprise had he not died prematurely, we cannot say. No thorough transformation of the Philippines was effected; the "production possibilities" of the country were not permanently moved to a higher level than before.[93] The mobilizing tactics, the egalitarian policy aims, and the populistic leadership showed promise of drawing new resources into the political market and structuring them so as to raise the society's aggregate productivity. That the enterprise did not have more effect on the Philippines can be attributed perhaps more than anything else to its "personalist" strategy. Abueva's emphasis on the missing element of *organization* supports our model of development and stresses the need for establishing resource flows—or modifying them in more beneficial ways—so that productivity gains are institutionalized. Otherwise, the advantages of the less well endowed are easily mitigated in political competition.

Our statement of "the political economy of development" has had to be some-

---

[92] An excellent new case study of political entrepreneurship is by Wayne A. Cornelius, Jr., "Nation-Building, Participation, and Distribution: The Politics of Social Reform under Cárdenas," in Gabriel A. Almond and Scott C. Flanagan (eds.), *Developmental Episodes in Comparative Politics: Crisis, Choice, and Change* (forthcoming). This is discussed in Part IV below.

[93] It is reported, not surprisingly in the Philippine context, that the principal improvements in "production possibilities" were for his family, which has come to dominate Zambales province economically and politically. This was not necessarily Magsaysay's doing, but it illustrates the dynamic working against progressive change unless there is significant popular mobilization achieved.

what general and abstract, despite our own disavowal of such work as a general rule. Our strictures have indeed been a brake on our exposition and conceptualization, and a salutory brake, we think. We have been trying to improve comprehension of many people, practitioners and scholars alike, to see as a whole the "process of development," and especially trying to correct what we think are faults in the prevailing view. This requires intellectual work transcending particular situations; at the same time, we have not wanted to take leave of such situations and have borne in mind the empirical observations and conclusions such as those presented by numerous authors below. The contributions that follow provide, we think, substantive and theoretical support for the model and the approach we have presented, even if the authors do not always formulate their analysis in explicit political economy terms.

The various principles of development derived from a political economy analysis offer, we believe, some practical guidance for development strategies and policies, especially as they correct for present parochial misconceptions of the development process that derive from disciplinarily or culturally limited frameworks. Perhaps we cannot totally escape such limitations ourselves, but we think this framework represents a considerable advance. Our work here has been more conceptual and theoretical, but we appreciate the need for more empirical work. The following authors make significant contributions in this direction. It is one in which we are directing our own efforts and which we hope others will choose to join.[94]

[94] After going to press we discovered a new book which makes many of the same points we do and to which we would like to refer readers: *Development Reconsidered: Bridging the Gap Between Government and People* (1972). The authors, Edgar Owens and Robert Shaw, evolved their "revisionist" views on development based on their experiences, respectively, as an officer in the U.S. Agency for International Development and a staff member of the World Bank. They present a straightforword, empirically substantiated argument which closely parallels our more deductively extrapolated analysis. They show repeatedly the central importance of *market integration, factor endowments, organization* and *entrepreneurship,* giving full weight to political and social factors as well as economic ones. Readers who wish more empirical examples and data than we have provided in support of the framework presented here are invited to consider the evidence which Owens and Shaw educe.

Their book has also called to our attention an article by Keith Marsden that previously escaped our notice: "Towards a Synthesis of Economic Growth and Social Justice," *International Labour Review* (November 1969), pp. 389–418. Marsden compares three strategies, "crash modernization," "dual development," and "progressive modernization," the latter corresponding to the strategy of "building on the rest" which we espouse in this book. The author presents historical and contemporary comparative data which produce his conclusion (and ours) that "For too long it has been assumed that economic growth and social justice are incompatible in developing countries. The evidence is accumulating that they can, and should, be mutually reinforcing."

•

Reconsidering
the Economics of
Development

•

IN RECENT YEARS, dissatisfaction and even disagreement have been increasingly expressed with the conventional economic analysis applied to problems of development. The premier place assigned to capital among the factors of economic production is being challenged, as is the attempt to explain or alter development patterns through the use of econometric models. "Revisionist" approaches to the economics of development have sought not to dismiss the terms and principles conventionally used in economic analysis, but rather to extend the scope of analysis, especially to give human factors more weight and to incorporate noneconomic variables.

The statement by Dudley Seers draws on many years of personal experience as a student and practitioner of development economics. Thus, his "apostasy" deserves special consideration. His treatment of international development policy, along with the analysis by Timothy and Leslie Nulty of Pakistan's experience, will serve to raise vital issues that we in our analysis above have not elaborated on because of limitations of space. We concur with the concerns they raise about the role of external assistance in the development process to date. Peter Dorner's suggestions for reorienting economic analysis to deal with agricultural development policy (part of the article presented in Part I) amplify the arguments advanced by Seers. (Dorner also introduces consideration of three of the four policy areas treated in Part III.)

The need for revision of conventional economic theories of development is probably nowhere better demonstrated than in the case of Pakistan, as analyzed by the Nultys. For at least a decade, Pakistan was given as an example of "successful" development based on accelerated capital formation and rapid industrialization. The defects in this strategy when considered in social and political terms, and ultimately in economic terms, are now reasonably apparent. The case of Pakistan makes the features of conventional economic development theory stand out in sharp relief, but it differs from other Third World cases more in degree than in kind.[1]

The article by John Gurley poses an alternative to what the Nultys, paraphrasing Keynes, call "the busy bee route to development." Instead of "building on the best," as is done in capitalist development, a country can build on the common, if not the worst, resources it has. This latter strategy of broad-based development is one preferred by the present Chinese leadership. Though central to Maoist politics and

[1] For readers interested in the case of Pakistan and the failure there of conventional economic advice, we recommend Hyman Minsky's article, "Passage to Pakistan," *Trans-Action,* February 1970, pp. 27–31.

122

ideology, it is not inseparable from these. It represents a different approach for allocating resources over a longer time period to raise aggregate productivity, in the social and political as well as the economic spheres. With the renewed access to China and revived interest in its progress under Mao Tse-Tung, this alternative development strategy will and should receive more consideration overseas.

THE MEANING OF DEVELOPMENT

DUDLEY SEERS

Institute of Development Studies
University of Sussex

The challenges of any period depend on the tasks that face those living in it. I believe we have misconceived the nature of the main challenge of the second half of the twentieth century. This has been seen as achieving an increase in the national incomes of the "developing" countries, formalized in the target of 5 percent growth rates set for the first development decade.

Why do we concentrate on the national income in this way? It is of course convenient. Politicians find a single comprehensive measure useful, especially one that is at least a year out-of-date. Economists are provided with a variable which can be quantified and movements which can be analyzed into changes in sectoral output, factor shares or categories of expenditure, making model-building feasible. While it is very slipshod for us to confuse development with economic development and economic development with economic growth, it is nevertheless very understandable. We can after all fall back on the supposition that increases in national income, if they are faster than the population growth, sooner or later lead to the solution of social and political problems.

But the experience of the past decade makes this belief look rather naive. Social problems and political upheavals have emerged in countries at all stages of development. Moreover, we can see that these afflict countries with rapidly rising per capita incomes as well as those with stagnant economies. In fact, it looks as if economic growth may not merely fail to solve social and political difficulties; certain types of growth can actually cause them.

Now that the complexity of development problems is becoming increasingly obvious, this continued addiction to the use of a single aggregative yardstick in the face of the evidence takes on a rather different appearance. It begins to look like a preference for avoiding the real problems of development.

The starting point in discussing the challenges we now face is to brush aside the web of fantasy we have woven around "development" and decide more precisely what we mean by it. "Development" is inevitably a normative term and we must ask ourselves what are the necessary conditions for a universally acceptable aim—the realization of the potential of human personality.

If we ask what is an *absolute* necessity for this, one answer is obvious—enough food. Below certain levels of nutrition, a

From *International Development Review* (December 1969), pp. 2–6. Reprinted by permission. This article (originally entitled "Challenges to Development Theories and Strategies") is the Presidential Address by Dudley Seers at the Society for International Development 11th World Congress in New Delhi, November 1969. The text here presented is somewhat condensed; the full text is available from the Institute of Development Studies, University of Sussex, Brighton, England.

man lacks not merely bodily energy and good health but even interest in much besides food. He cannot rise significantly above an animal existence. Recent studies show that undernourishment of children leads to permanent impairment of both their physical and their mental capacities.

Since to be able to buy food is a matter of income, the criterion can be expressed in terms of income levels. This enables it to take account also of certain other minimum requirements. People will never spend all their money and energy on food, however poor they are. To be enough to feed a man, his income has also to cover basic needs of clothing, footwear and shelter, but the utility of money clearly declines sharply as these needs are satisfied.

Another basic necessity, in the sense of something without which personality cannot develop, is a job. This does not just mean employment; it can include studying, working on a family farm or keeping house. But to play none of these accepted roles—i.e., to be chronically unemployed, dependent on another person's productive capacity, even for food—is incompatible with self-respect, especially for somebody who has been spending years at school, perhaps at university, preparing for an active role.

It is true, of course, that both poverty and unemployment are associated in various ways with per capita income. If per capita incomes are falling, absolute poverty can hardly be reduced much, nor can unemployment (except in the very short run and exceptional circumstances). But certainly increases in per capita income are far from enough, as the experiences of petroleum economies show, to achieve either of these objectives. In fact, a rise in per capita income, as we very well know, can be accompanied by, can even cause, growing unemployment.[1]

The direct link between per capita income and the numbers living in poverty is income distribution. It is a truism that poverty will be eliminated much more rapidly if any given rate of economic growth is accompanied by a declining concentration of incomes. Equality should however be considered an objective in its own right, the third element in development. Inequalities to be found now in the world, especially (but not only) outside the industrial countries, are objectionable by any reli-

gious or ethical standards. The social barriers and inhibitions of an unequal society distort the personalities of those with high incomes no less than of those who are poor. Trivial differences of accent, language, dress, customs, etc., acquire an absurd importance and contempt is engendered for those who lack social graces, especially country dwellers. Perhaps even more important, since race is usually highly correlated with income, economic inequality lies at the heart of racial tensions.

The questions to ask about a country's development are therefore: What has been happening to poverty? What has been happening to unemployment? What has been happening to inequality? If all three of these have declined from high levels, then beyond doubt this has been a period of development for the country concerned. If one or two of these central problems have been growing worse, especially if all three have, it would be strange to call the result "development," even if per capita income doubled.[2]

PROBLEMS OF MEASUREMENT

The challenges for the remainder of this century arise out of the analysis above. The first is how to find measures of development to replace the national income, or, more precisely, to enable the national income to be given its true, somewhat limited, significance, as a measure of development potential. (A big increase in the national income at least makes it easier in the future to achieve a reduction in poverty, if appropriate policies are adopted.)

There are two points to make here. The first is that the national income figures published for most "developing" countries have very little meaning. This is partly because of lack of data, especially on farm output, but also because, when income distributions are so unequal, prices have very little meaning as weights in "real" income comparisons.

Secondly, the lack of data on poverty, unemployment and inequality reflects the priorities of statistical offices rather than the difficulties of data collection.

The conceptual problems of these measures do not seem to be more formidable than those of the national income. We have just grown accustomed to ignoring the latter. But there are also practical problems. All the measures require information about supplementary incomes, age-and-sex composition of receiving units, etc., additional to that obtained from statistics which are prepared as a by-product of administration, at least in countries where only a small proportion of income receivers pay direct taxes.[3] It is also hard to measure even overt unemployment where unemployment registration does not exist or covers only part of the labor force. But again we must not be diverted by such technical problems from attempting the reassessment which really matters.[4]

THE INTERNAL CONSISTENCY OF
THE DEVELOPMENT PROCESS

The second set of challenges to the social scientists, politicians and administrators in the decades ahead is to find paths of development which enable progress to be made on all these criteria. Since development is far from being achieved at present, the need is not, as is generally imagined, to accelerate economic growth—which could even be dangerous—but to change the nature of the development process.

A major question is whether the criteria are mutually consistent. The answer is that in many respects development on one of the criteria implies, or helps bring about, or is even a necessary condition for, development on one or more of the others.

To reduce unemployment is to remove one of the main causes of poverty and inequality. Moreover, a reduction in inequality will of course reduce poverty, *ceteris paribus*.

These propositions beg many questions, however. The reduction of unemployment means in part finding techniques which are labor-intensive, with the least damage to the expansion of production. This is of course a discussion to which many have contributed, notably A. K. Sen.

There is a well-known, indeed classical, argument that inequality is necessary to generate savings and incentives and thus to promote economic growth—which, as we have seen, can be taken as an indicator of some types of development potential. I find the argument that the need for savings justifies inequality unconvincing in the Third World today. Savings propensities are after all very low precisely in countries

with highly unequal distributions; the industrial countries with less concentration of income have, by contrast, much higher savings propensities. Savings are of course also affected by the absolute level of incomes, but the explanation must also lie in the high consumption levels of the rich, designed to maintain the standards so important in an unequal society.

Moreover, the rich in most countries tend to have extremely high propensities, not merely to spend, but to spend on goods and services with a high foreign exchange content, and, for countries suffering from an acute foreign exchange bottleneck, this is a major obstacle to development. It is true that import demand can be held in check (as in India) by administrative controls, but this leads to the elaboration of a bureaucratic apparatus which is expensive, especially in terms of valuable organizing ability, and which in some countries becomes riddled with corruption. In any case, in a highly unequal society, personal savings often flow abroad or go into luxury housing and other investment projects of low or zero priority for development.

The argument that only inequality can provide the incentives that are necessary is also obviously of limited validity in a country where there are barriers of race or class to advancement. Still, we cannot dismiss it out of hand. The needs for private entrepreneurial talent vary according to the circumstances of different economies, but there are very few where this need is small. Countries relying on growing exports of manufactures, as many are, depend heavily on the emergence of businessmen with the drive to penetrate foreign markets. All countries depend in some degree on the appearance of progressive farmers. Will these emerge without financial rewards on a scale that will make nonsense of an egalitarian policy? Are rising profits of companies, especially foreign companies, an inevitable feature of growth in many countries? Or are we exaggerating the importance of financial incentives? Can other, non-financial rewards partially take their place? Can social incentives be developed to a point where people will take on such tasks with little or no individual reward (as the governments of China and Cuba are trying to prove)? This is one of the great issues to be decided, and the

1970's will throw a good deal of light on the answer.

The compatibility of equality and rising output and employment has recently become doubtful for an additional set of reasons. Can the people who are professionally necessary be kept in the country if they can earn only a small fraction of what they could earn elsewhere? Yet what are the costs in terms of human welfare and even efficiency if they are prevented from leaving?

On the other hand, there are equally serious reasons for questioning the compatibility of inequality and economic growth. Can a structure of local industry be created to correspond to the structure of demand that arises in a highly inequitable society (leaving aside the question of whether it *should* be created)? Will production rise rapidly if the proportion of the labor force too badly nourished for full manual and mental work is only sinking slowly? Can the government obtain the co-operation of the population in wage restraint, and in many other ways that are necessary for development, if there is visible evidence of great wealth which is being transmitted from generation to generation, so that the wage earner sees his children and his children's children doomed indefinitely to subordinate positions? Can it mobilize the energies of the total population and break down social customs which obstruct development, especially in rural areas?

I do not pretend to know the answers to this complex of questions, which point to a set of "internal contradictions" in the development process far more severe than those to which Marx drew attention. What is more, the economic and political objectives are linked closely together. An economic system with large numbers of undernourished and unemployed at the bottom end of a long social ladder, especially if they are racially distinguishable, can never provide a firm basis for political rights or for civic order. Those with high incomes from profits or salaries are not merely slow to tackle the great social problems of poverty and unemployment; they will inevitably try to find ways of maintaining privilege, resorting (as dozens of historical examples show) to political violence rather than give it up. Conversely, those without jobs or adequate incomes will sooner or later try to obtain them through a regime which would not allow organized opposition. Judging from present trends in the climate of opinion, especially among the young, it is very doubtful whether inequalities on anything like the present scale could co-exist with political liberties in the 1970's or 1980's. Yet it is hard to envisage how inequality can be reduced without setting in motion, from one direction or another, forces that reduce political liberty.

There are administrative limits to the main weapon against inequality, direct taxation, apart altogether from any conflict with incentives. Inequality cannot really be reduced so long as property ownership is heavily concentrated. So conversion of incomes from large holdings of property into life pensions (as in Cuba) or bond interest (as in Chile) or their reduction through death duties (as in Britain) are likely to be more effective than taxation, though they may be beyond the bounds of the politically feasible in many countries.

But a great deal can be done even without attacking property ownership. Practically every decision taken by government officials has implications for the degree of equality—to lend to big farmers or small, to set prices of public corporations at levels that tax or subsidize rich consumers, to build roads for private motor cars or for goods vehicles, to put the best equipment in rural or urban schools. It would not be a bad thing to put up in every civil service office a sign: "Will it reduce inequality?" Secondly, if the administrative and political organization is motivated and trained to report tax evasion, corruption etc., all sorts of egalitarian policies, including capital taxation, become more feasible. (Where such a spirit is weak, one can hardly expect rapid development in the sense I have used the word here.)

Lastly, a reduction in equality is very hard, if not impossible, so long as a country is dependent on a major power and shows the influence of its consumption tastes and salary levels. So is a reduction in unemployment, because one of the marks of dependence is reliance on the technology of the countries which play a dominant role in the national life, and this may well be inappropriate to local problems. On the other hand, a country that leaves its social problems unsolved is unlikely to be strong enough to achieve or maintain genuine independence; it may not even survive as a political unit.

ENDS AND MEANS

When political liberty is considered as an end, its importance, though high, is secondary so long as a substantial fraction of the people are undernourished and unemployed. But it appears in quite a different light as a means. Societies lacking open opposition have shown themselves extremely inflexible in meeting the challenge of changing circumstances, whether one considers the continuation by Germany of a war for months after it was already lost, or the stubbornness of Communist regimes in clinging to unsuccessful agricultural policies. Moreover, as Soviet experience shows, there is no guarantee that political liberties will reappear as economic problems are eased.

Higher educational levels are ends in themselves, but education is also a means. Economists have, somewhat belatedly, come to see it as a source of development; but they treat it narrowly as a factor in the growth of national income, relating stocks of manpower with certain qualifications (e.g., university degrees) to national income levels.

But if development is not just or even mainly an increase in the national income, education takes on an entirely different aspect. We need to go a long way beyond the Harbison approach, valuable though this has been. What are important are not the "man years" at school but the methods of selection and the *content* of education. Inequality can be reduced (and also economic efficiency increased) if secondary and higher education are made *genuinely* available to those with the lowest incomes (belonging to minority races), which means of course that special methods of selection must be found. Secondly, by easing shortages of high-level manpower, education can reduce the need for high salaries for those with scarce professional skills. In that case, however, the whole structure of education needs reconsideration; education will hardly fulfill this function if it produces on the one hand a few distinguished academic scholars who, as in Britain, think of themselves as superior to the rest of the population and on the other a mass of people with the wrong qualifications.

The third function of education, and this applies also to adult education and the content of radio and TV programs, is to pre-pare professional classes conscious of the realities of development, both the internal realities and the realities of the world scene, with such an understanding of their historical origins that they see what needs to be done and voluntarily accept the sacrifices implied. Many of the obstacles to policies which would reduce poverty and unemployment have their origin in attitudes to manual work, especially in the countryside, to imported consumer goods, to foreign technologies, etc. Since each generation is in some degree a copy of the preceding one, through parental influences, such attitudes can hardly be changed except by a conscious educational policy, broadly defined.

Finally, one policy area which looks different if one discards the aggregative approach is population. Conventionally, population growth is seen simply as a subtraction from the increase in the national income; the closer the growth rates of population and income, the slower the rise in *per capita* income. This line of argument is fundamentally somewhat suspect because it assumes that population and income are independent of each other. But the real case for an active population policy is simply that, so long as the labor force is growing fast, it is almost impossible to relieve unemployment and poverty, since a plentiful supply of labor keeps the wages of the unskilled, apart perhaps from a privileged modern sector, near levels of barest subsistence. Moreover, the growing pressure of population on the budget makes it very difficult to expand educational and other social services. An additional argument, on the above criteria, is that this growing pressure increases the need for foreign aid and thus postpones the attainment of genuine independence.

INTERNATIONAL POLICY

It is misleading to talk about "development" when we consider the world scene, on the criteria suggested above. One cannot really say that there has been development for the world as a whole, when the benefits of technical progress have accrued to minorities which were already relatively rich, whether we are speaking of rich minorities within nations or the minority of nations which are rich. To me, this word is particularly misleading for the period since the war, especially the "development decade" when the growth of economic inequality and unemployment must have actually accelerated. (I am alarmed at the phrase, a "second development decade." Another "development decade" like the 1960's with unemployment rates and inequality rising by further large steps, would be politically and economically disastrous, whatever the pace of economic growth!)

Certainly in some respects, as I have said, a basis has been laid in many countries for possible development in the future. But there has not been any basic improvement in international institutions. It is true that there are now opportunities for poor countries at least to talk to the rich, but one cannot speak of international order; the international institutions lack the power to impose solutions. . . . Nor has much been done to open the markets of industrial countries to imports of manufactures, the only real possibility of export expansion for the Third World as a whole.

There is no fiscal system for the world. This may perhaps be foreshadowed by 1 percent aid targets, but these targets are in fact ignored and aid programs remain at very low levels. As Gunnar Myrdal warned us many years ago, the establishment of the national welfare state has turned the attention of the public in the rich countries inwards, making them less interested in the welfare of the world as a whole. The aid that does exist often plays an important economic role, but, like immigration and trade policies, it is very largely motivated by the self-interest of donors, sometimes by very short-term commercial and political interests. This often in effect leads them to support, or even help install, governments which oppose the redistribution of income and in other ways block development.

Many countries have in fact slipped further under the influence of one or another of the big powers. This itself hinders development. Independence is not merely one of the aims of development; it is also one of the means. It is a force for mobilizing popular support and the force is blunted if a government is obviously far from independent.

Yet clearly there is a basic inconsistency. Can a world system be created which will accommodate nationalism while providing a truly international and much more equitable economic and political order? And can this be done just by cerebration and

logical clarity, or does it require the poorer countries of the world to organize themselves, perhaps by continent, to use what cards they possess to bring it about? How can nationalism be reconciled on the other hand with the strong tribal and regional forces which are emerging? What form of decentralization do these imply?

Such are the challenges we now face. The role of the practitioner, the politician or the civil servant is the extremely difficult one of finding a politically and administratively feasible path of development in a grossly unequal world. They can be helped by the theorist if he refrains from trying to adapt uncritically models and measures designed in and for industrial countries, where priorities are very different, but helps instead to develop policies, national and international, to mitigate the great social problems of the Third World.

By so doing, indeed, he may incidentally provide the social scientists in the rich countries with food for thought. After all, poverty and unemployment are not so starkly obvious in the North Atlantic area, compared to the conditions before the last war (and this helps explain the reduced interest of their social scientists in these problems until quite recently). Although economic inequality diminished too up to about 1950, it now seems to be growing again and to be accompanied by increasingly severe inequality between races in multi-racial societies. But above all, the aim must be to change international attitudes so that it becomes impossible for the political leaders and social scientists of Europe and North America to continue overlooking and aggravating, often inadvertently, the obscene inequalities that disfigure the world.

1. Thus in Trinidad the growth in per capita income averaged more than 5 percent a year during the whole period 1953 to 1968, while overt unemployment showed a steady increase to more than 10 percent of the labor force.

2. Of course, the fulfilment of human potential requires much that cannot be specified in purely economic terms. I cannot spell out all the other requirements, but it would be very unbalanced if I did not mention them at all. They include adequate educational levels, freedom of speech, and citizenship of a nation that is truly independent, both economically and politically, in the sense that the views of other governments do not largely

predetermine his own government's decisions.

3. Technical problems of measuring distribution are discussed in an unpublished paper, "On the possibility of measuring personal distribution of income," by Professor Dich of Aarhaus.

4. I cannot explore here the measurement of the educational and political elements in development. In as far as the former is covered by the formal educational system, a technique for showing the changing profile over time has been developed by Richard Jolly. (See A. R. Jolly, *Planning Education for African Development,* East African Publishing House, Nairobi, 1969.) Measurement of the extent to which the political aims have been achieved is of course much more difficult; possible clues include the number of prisoners held for political or quasi-political reasons; the social and racial composition of parliament, business boards, senior public administrative grades, etc., and also of those enjoying secondary and university education; the incidence of petty theft; rates of suicide and alcoholism.

Clues on the degree of national independence include the extent to which the country votes in the same way as a great power at the United Nations, the existence of foreign military bases and overflying rights, the ratio of aid from the largest donor to total foreign exchange receipts, etc. Indirect indicators are the proportion of assets, especially subsoil assets, owned by foreigners, the extent to which one trading partner dominates the pattern of trade, and the proportion of the supply of capital (or intermediate goods) which is imported.

NEEDED REDIRECTIONS IN ECONOMIC ANALYSIS FOR AGRICULTURAL DEVELOPMENT POLICY: II

PETER DORNER
University of Wisconsin

Given the rapid population growth of the developing countries, the large proportion in agriculture, and the continuing growth of absolute numbers dependent upon agriculture [9], it is surprising to see how little analytical attention has been given to the need for creating employment and improved income-earning opportunities in rural areas. There is a vague hope that programs designed to increase production will result in agricultural development irrespective of the short-run employment and distributional consequences of such programs. However, experience over the past decade indicates that the questions of increased agricultural production and a more equitable distribution of the fruits of that production must be viewed as parts of the same process. Policies designed to cope with one of these to the exclusion of the other have not succeeded.

These two aspects of development (increased production and a more equitable distribution) are sometimes viewed as being totally independent [3]. The first is seen as the key to development while the second is considered a peripheral problem of welfare or social justice. Some even assume that economists have the recommendations for increased efficiency in production, but that the problem of a more equitable distribution is a political or cultural matter [17].

In most of the nonindustrialized countries a majority of the people depend on the land for employment; jobs in manufacturing are growing much less rapidly than manufacturing output; and the number of people dependent on farming for a livelihood is increasing. To achieve the benefits that may accrue from what Owen has called "farm-financed social welfare" requires that opportunities—even subsistence opportunities—be provided [27, p. 61; 28].

Policies that emphasize modernization

From *American Journal of Agricultural Economics* (February 1971), pp. 11–15. Reprinted by permission.

and increase production from the commercial farm sector without explicit attention to the creation of employment opportunities will yield increased output of certain farm commodities and growing labor productivity for a part of the farm labor force. But they tend to widen the income disparities and throw the burden of adjustment on the disadvantaged who join the ranks of the landless, become migrant seasonal workers, continue to crowd into existing small farm areas, move out to rapidly shrinking frontiers, or join the underemployed in the cities. There is no evidence that the increased volume of commodities moving through commercial channels as a result of increased production creates sufficient jobs for workers displaced by modernization or for the continuing new additions to the rural labor force.

Poverty (the massive poverty among the majority of people in the less-developed countries) is not only or primarily a welfare and humanitarian problem. It is a problem that has direct and important implications for increased productivity. Supply *does not* create its own demand under conditions of a highly skewed income distribution. To focus primarily on production widens the income gap between the rich and poor. It is impossible in many circumstances of development to separate the issues of production and distribution, since distributional measures may be the key to achieving increases in production. And the trickle-down theory of distribution has never worked, especially under conditions of concentrated economic and political power.[1]

Why are policies not formulated to accommodate both of these requirements— increased production and increased employment with a more equitable distribution? The distributional questions, of course, raise many tough issues. Accordingly, and regretfully, policy recommendations of professional analysts using highly sophisticated models usually ignore employment and distributional aspects. Recommendations are too often based on private or on project decision-making criteria rather than those appropriate to the interests of the entire nation. Some redirections in economic analysis are required. Three concepts in such a redirection (and examples of assumptions that frequently preclude their explicit inclusion in analyses) are highlighted in the following sections.

CREATION OF SECURE OPPORTUNITIES ON THE LAND

The "war on hunger" position tends to assume that if there are hungry people, food should be produced by the cheapest, most efficient means possible. Yet frequently, and especially when viewed from the private interest of an individual firm, this course of action includes displacing people with machines. And professional analysts, viewing the problem with decision-making criteria appropriate to the private firm while ignoring the possible lack of correspondence between private and social costs and benefits, can reach conclusions such as the following: "One reason for the high cost [of corn in Guatemala] is the amount of hand labor required. Hence, my desire to try out the corn picker" [29, p. 716]. However, this may not be a solution at all once the need for employment creation is taken into account. Even if means could be found to tax away or otherwise confiscate the increased production ". . . a nation cannot put most of itself on the dole, even if money and food are available for distribution" [26, p. 224].

Land must be viewed as a vehicle for human development as well as a resource for food production. As Raup has put it, "Wherever there is surplus agricultural labor and shortage of working capital, the task of the tenure system is to put people to work" [33, p. 274].

It has become an article of faith, at least among many professionals from the industrial countries, that mechanization (mechanical technology and automation generally) always creates as many jobs as it destroys, sometimes more. According to this faith, there may indeed be some short-run problems of labor displacement and some structural unemployment. But given time, the new technology creates demand for labor in many areas of the economy through its various linkages, and eventually unemployment will rise to a higher level.

This assumption may be justified in a highly industrialized nation. But does the same assumption apply to a country that does not produce its own technology? In the United States, for example, the mechanical cotton picker displaced workers by the tens of thousands [5]. Many of the workers displaced (though certainly not all) and especially the sons of these workers did find employment among the vast complex of industries interrelated with the production, sale, and servicing of cotton pickers—steel, rubber, oil, machinery manufacture, transport, farm implement sales and service etc. But what about Nicaragua, which imports cotton pickers from the United States? Most of the vast complex of industries linked with the cotton picker does not exist in Nicaragua; it remains in the manufacturing country.[2]

The entrepreneur of a large farm enterprise may find the importation of labor-displacing machines highly profitable due to a variety of circumstances, many of them related to government policies: overhauled exchange rates, subsidized credit, rising minimum wages and fringe benefits, etc. Reasoning from analogy, U.S. and European experience of farm enlargement and mechanization is sometimes cited to support this type of development. But such an analogy is inappropriate for the widely different situation with respect to factor proportions and *real* factor costs in non-industrial societies (in contrast to existing factor prices which are often controlled and distorted by some of the above policies) [11].

The cotton picker case illustrates the general principle involved; it does not argue against all modern, imported technology. Much depends on what the machines will be used for. In an agriculture with an overabundant and growing labor supply, it is unlikely that one can make a logical case for importation of labor-saving machinery if the problem is viewed from the standpoint of national policy rather than profit maximization of the firm [19]. If the agricultural sector is to make its most effective contribution to economic development, it must not only improve labor productivity for a select group but must also expand employment opportunities [20, 40].

Mechanical power and equipment might sometimes be justified in terms of increased yields due to better tillage or timeliness of operations. But there is sufficient experience of countries where such needed machine services were provided to an agriculture otherwise based on labor-intensive production practices.

On the basis of his model of rural outmigration and urban unemployment, Todaro concludes:

Perhaps the most significant policy implication emerging from the model is the great difficulty of substantially reducing the size of the urban traditional sector without a concentrated effort at making rural life more attractive [40, p. 147].

But how is rural life to be made more attractive? Presumably public investments in rural education and health services would help; and funds used to accommodate rural migrants in the cities might be diverted to rural areas. Yet such services cannot be extended rapidly because of both capital and professional manpower shortages. Higher minimum wages for farm workers could be counterproductive so long as investment decisions in the farm sector are made by private entrepreneurs. A higher minimum wage might lead to a shift to labor-extensive enterprises or to an acceleration of machine substitution for labor.

Even with low wages there is strong incentive on large farms to mechanize and simplify labor supervision. It is almost impossible to find farms of, say 1,000 hectares in rice or cotton that are planted, tended, and harvested mainly by hand labor. These farms either mechanize or operate with a sharecropper system. To get at the crux of the matter, "making rural life more attractive" in most cases means providing the farm family with a *secure opportunity on the land*. Land tenure arrangements and size of holdings must be included as variables in the analysis. But the basic assumptions underlying production and distribution theories take these as "givens." [3]

DEVELOPMENT OF HUMAN ABILITIES
AND CAPACITIES

Another reason why the employment issue gets so little attention is that in the less developed countries, the most abundant potential resource usually is labor—*potential* because training and work experience are needed to transform raw labor power into the manpower resource (with skills, experience, and discipline required for development). An abundance of people does not necessarily rule out labor shortages in selected occupations. The scarcest resource generally is capital. Given the abundance of people, there has been a tendency to ignore the need for investment in and development of the labor potential. Instead of viewing land as a vehicle for employing people and for developing the skills and experience required of the rural labor force, land has been viewed primarily as a resource to be efficiently combined with scarce capital so as to maximize agricultural output.

T. W. Schultz has written a good deal on the issue of investment in human capital [34], but he places primary emphasis on formal schooling. I do not deny this need, but formal schooling is not the only and not always the most significant dimension of education. Furthermore, many poor countries have not yet been able to supply even elementary schooling for large numbers of their people. Under these circumstances, economic activity should be designed to produce educational effects. Productive work can offer experience and discipline as valid as that gained in the classroom. It is different, to be sure, and neither kind of education is alone sufficient. Work experience can be directed and enriched by learning obtainable only from school situations; schoolroom education can be enhanced by work experience.

The manner in which increased production is achieved, and the number of people who participate and reap some benefits from the experience, may be as important as the production increase itself. One gets a different perspective regarding the role of the land if (in addition to its accepted function in the production of farm products) it is viewed as a vehicle both for creating economic opportunities and upgrading the human skills and capacities required for their exploitation [8, p. 12].

Man is a resource to be used (along with land and capital) as well as the user of the resources. An individual plays a dual role —he is both the user and the used, the interested and the object of interest, the exploiter and the exploited.

In a society where economic and political power are widely shared, there is a continuous attempt to modify institutional structures and norms in order to keep this process of "using others" mutually beneficial. Procedures are designed so that individuals and groups, in pursuing their private interests, are not injuring (preferably, are furthering) the interests of other individuals and groups. When mutuality in the process breaks down and conflicts intensify, zones of discretionary behavior of the individuals and groups involved must be redefined in order to reestablish mutuality in the processes of associated living.

The common formulation in resource allocation-efficiency models is to view man as labor power—as the object of use. This view, far from being value-neutral, accepts the status quo power positions and ownership patterns of land and capital. In fact it places the weight of authority of "scientific analysis" in the camp of present owners. Under conditions of vast and increasing inequality, policy prescriptions based on such efficiency models are consistent with the poor man's view of the world: "Them what has, gets."

INCLUSION OF INCOME DISTRIBUTION AS A VARIABLE IN ANALYSES

Economic literature tends to deemphasize the income distribution consequences of the development process. Since land tenure arrangements are most directly associated with the creation of and access to income-earning opportunities and their distribution, these arrangements receive only passing mention in the economic literature on agricultural development policies.

If the task of development is conceptualized to include income distribution as an endogenous variable, some of the economists' most powerful ideas and tools lose some of their analytical leverage. For example, marginal analysis and the accompanying planning, programming, and budgeting tools implicitly assume certain nonchanging structural parameters. Yet once an elaborate and somewhat arbitrary measurement emerges, as from benefit-cost analysis, a strong faith is placed on it. The unstated assumptions remain unstated and are frequently ignored. The higher the benefit-cost ratio, the "better" the project.

However, the results of these calculations are directly conditioned by the pattern of income distribution.[4] Investments in the increased production of chickens and beans rather than airlines and television sets might give a good benefit-cost ratio if the pattern of income distribution were changed. Poor people, lacking the money votes, cannot register their needs or desires through the market mechanism. But change the income distribution and you change the benefit-cost ratios of various projects and in turn alter investment priorities.[5]

Assumptions like those described in these examples allow certain strategic developmental questions to fall between the analytical slats: productive employment for the growing rural labor force; creation of opportunities for the development of human abilities and capacities; and ownership distribution of land and other resources. An agricultural economist, using a farm management approach, may ignore the displacement of workers or their need to find viable opportunities on the land. He is concerned with profit maximization from the resources available to the firm. Even an agricultural economist dealing with farm policy for the agricultural sector could ignore these questions on the assumption (well founded or not) that industrial and other nonagricultural activities are available for the absorption of excess rural labor. Nor does a macroeconomic approach assure that these strategic questions will be addressed in the analysis. While Keynes may have shown a deliberate disregard for the supply side of investments (and focused only on their demand-creating consequences) [23], post-Keynesian development economists seem to have overemphasized the supply consequences.

There is indeed an implicit assumption that somewhere policies are being implemented to maintain full employment and that when a laborer moves from one job to another it always results in increased productivity. But these are unwarranted assumptions in most cases of less-developed countries. Indeed, these assumptions point to some of the critical problems of development.[6]

1. *The Economist* makes the following comments on FAO's "Indicative World Plan": "As long as incomes are so unevenly distributed within the developing countries themselves, and so little inroad is made with their traumatic unemployment problems, the people who are starving will not have the money to buy the food, even if it is there. This is where the planners of Asia, Africa, and South America would like FAO guidance, but so far they only get alarming figures and some general advice" [15, p. 75].

2. The problem is compounded if, as Singer has pointed out, the investments and the production processes are actually controlled by foreigners. "The main secondary multiplier effects, which the textbooks tell us to expect from investment, took place not where the investment was physically or geographically located but (to the extent that the results of

these investments returned directly home) they took place where the investments came from. I would suggest that if the proper economic test of investment is the multiplier effect in the form of cumulative additions to income, employment, capital, technical knowledge, and growth of external economies, then a good deal of the investment in underdeveloped countries which we used to consider as 'foreign' should in fact be considered as domestic investment on the part of the industrial countries" [37, p. 475].

3. "Distribution theory today concerns itself, in essence, with tracing out the effects of various policies in distributing economic fruits among persons who own or otherwise command control over resources. . . . In current theory, distribution of ownership or other control of resources among people is 'given.' . . . In terms of the dynamics of economic development, however, the real problem of distribution is: 'How does ownership or other control over resources come to be distributed in the manner it is?' . . . The question is not, for example, whether a landlord and a tenant each received the appropriate return for the resources he controls; but rather, is it appropriate, from the standpoint of the economic development of the country in question, for the landlord and the tenant to have these particular proportions of the nation's resources under his control" [24, pp. 729–730].

4. "Cost-benefit analysis as generally understood is only a technique for taking decisions with a framework which has to be decided upon in advance and which involves a wide range of considerations, many of them of a political or social character" [32, p. 685].

5. Hirschman speaks of the centrality of side-effects in judging investment projects. "The quest for a unique ranking device probably accounts for the hostility of economists toward side-effect and secondary benefits. Yet this quest is clearly futile. How could it be expected that it is possible to rank development projects along a single scale by amalgamating all their varied dimensions into a single index when far simpler, everyday choices require the use of individual or collective judgment in the weighing of alternative objectives and in the trade-off between them? There is much to be said, it is true, for facilitating decision making by reducing the many aspects of a project to a few crucial characteristics, one of which would of course be the rate of return. It is one thing to permit, in this way, the decision maker to use informed judgment in making critical choices and trade-offs; it is quite another, however, for the technician to aim at dispensing with such judgment altogether" [18, pp. 162 and 179].

6. ". . . [the] process of labor transfer is

typically viewed analytically as a one-stage phenomenon, that is, a worker migrates from a low productivity urban industrial job. The question is rarely asked whether or not the typical unskilled rural migrant can indeed find higher-paying regular urban employment. The empirical fact of widespread and chronic urban unemployment and underemployment attests to the implausibility of such a simple view of the migration process" [40, p. 139].

[References listed on pp. 44–46 above.]

PAKISTAN: AN APPRAISAL OF DEVELOPMENT STRATEGY

TIMOTHY AND LESLIE NULTY

Ruskin College, Oxford

Along with many other causes of the 1960s, that of development aid and advice from the rich one-third to the poor two-thirds of mankind, has been overtaken by considerable doubt and disillusionment. Quite apart from the vagaries of intellectual fashion, there are many sound and sometimes unpleasant reasons for the increasing discontent with the aid policies of the recent past.

In any discussion concerning the future direction of development effort, and especially the rich countries' share of it, Pakistan is a particularly useful case to examine. This is not only because it is so large (sixth in population in the world), so poor (nearly at the bottom of the international income ladder with $50–60 annual national per capita income), and has received such a large share of the aid cake (since 1963, between $400 and 500 million per annum), but also because its recent history highlights so clearly many of the crucial issues which are disturbing students of development. These issues can be grouped under two general headings: (1) what sort of "economic development" has taken place (in Pakistan) over the last decade and a half, how much of it has there been, and where does the economy appear to be heading? and (2) what has been and what should be the role played by foreign aid, advice and advisors?

One undoubtedly important aspect of economic development is measured by the growth of per capita national product. It is important because it is an indication of the total material resources available to the economy and, as such, it is one measure of the *potential* welfare that could be enjoyed by the country. The ultimate aim of what is generally called development is, after all, an increase in total welfare. We do know, however, that "welfare" does not always come in forms that are readily measured by the national accounts. In rich industrial countries the relationship between increasing welfare and increasing GNP has become an extremely complicated and difficult issue, largely because increasing affluence is accompanied by the diminishing marginal utility of consuming the sorts of goods and services that are measured in the Gross National Product. Such questions as whether to cut down a forest to supply a paper factory (which increases GNP considerably) or to leave it standing as a contribution to a generally healthy and enjoyable environment (which makes little measurable addition to GNP) have become critically important. In extremely poor countries, however, this sort of problem is less pressing; the need for a straightforward increase in material consumption is too obvious and too great. Thus, in poor countries, GNP and especially the growth in GNP over time, is useful as an initial indicator of the economy's potential welfare.

However, using GNP data to assess

Reprinted by permission of authors. An earlier version of this paper appeared in *Trans-Action* (February 1971). Some sections have been omitted.

Pakistan's recent economic progress poses serious difficulties. Quite apart from the inherent problems of assessing a national product of which one-half never appears on the market and much of the other half can only be guessed at, anyone with an intimate knowledge of Pakistan's statistics knows perfectly well that arbitrary evaluation has sometimes played a deliberate part in their compilation.[1] One serious problem is the extent to which statistics for Pakistan as a whole obscure (and have sometimes been intentionally used to obscure) discrepancies in the development of the two provinces—a crucial and highly sensitive political issue.[2] In addition, it has been argued that the usual index number problems involved in attempting to measure "real" growth are made especially awkward in Pakistan, where the price system has been so distorted by government policies that production in many industries could be thought to be negligible or even negative value-added, if measured by more realistic prices.[3] All of these have led to an over-statement of aggregate GNP for all of Pakistan.

Nevertheless, it is difficult to deny that some growth of the sort measured by GNP data has taken place in Pakistan. Apart from the GNP data themselves, circumstantial evidence can be sought in the physical output of certain key commodities. Although the first ten years of Pakistan's independence were years of uncertain growth, output per capita did not actually decline—and in certain sectors continued to rise. Since 1960 the increase in the physical output of key commodities has so far outpaced even the highest estimated rate of population growth (3.2% for the period 1959/60 to 1968/69) that it is quite clear that the per capita supply of such goods from Pakistan's own production, is now considerably higher than it was 20 years ago. Table 1 gives a few illustrations.

The potential welfare contained in this growth of the per capita national product has two aspects. The first is current welfare, represented by the level of consumption enjoyed by the entire population. Second is the welfare (consumption level) that can be expected in the future as a result of decisions made now.

Before we can assess what increase in welfare (present and future) has actually been achieved in the course of economic growth, we must know how the national product has been used. Thus, taking current welfare first, we must also ask why GNP has grown and who has benefited. Later we must also consider what is the likely pattern of future development of national product and welfare as a consequence of the level and distribution of present GNP.

TABLE 1

PAKISTAN: AVERAGE ANNUAL COMPOUND GROWTH RATES OF DOMESTIC PRODUCTION OF SELECTED GOODS, 1960/61–1967/68

Foodgrains	4.2%
Cotton Yarn	6.0%
Fertilizer	6.8%
Cement	3.0%
Electricity	19.9%
Total Manufacturing Output	11.2%
Gross National Product (GNP)	5.4%

SOURCE: Pakistan Central Statistical Office (C.S.O.) Statistical Bulletins.

Considerable evidence seems to show that the distribution of income, never very equal in Pakistan, has become steadily more unequal over the last twenty years. Investigations by ourselves and others [4] suggest that the vast majority (about 75–80%) of the people of Pakistan are now no better off than they were twenty years ago. A large number, something like 15–20%, may actually be poorer in real terms, and this is in spite of the fact that total real output per capita is supposed to have increased by 25% during this period.

This increased inequality can be seen in several dimensions. The gap between the prosperity of the two provinces has steadily increased. The position of East Pakistan, with 55% of the population of the whole nation, has worsened over the years: in 1951/52 the average per capita income in East Pakistan was 85% of that in West Pakistan but by 1967/68 the ratio had fallen to 62%. Within each province the rural population (roughly 90% of the total in the East and 75% in the West) has lost ground compared to the urban sector and in both provinces and in all sectors the wealthiest classes have greatly improved their position relative to everyone else. (See Table 2.)

TABLE 2

PAKISTAN: AVERAGE ANNUAL INCOME PER CAPITA BY SECTOR AND REGION, SELECTED
YEARS, 1951/52–1967/68 (RUPEES PER HEAD IN 1959–60 CONSTANT PRICES)

A. TOTAL INCOME PER CAPITA

Province	1951/52	1955/56	1959/60	1963/64	1967/68
East	292	269	282	310	312
West	342	363	376	428	501
East as % West	85%	74%	75%	72%	62%

B. RURAL AND URBAN INCOME PER CAPITA

Province	1951	1961	1967/68	% Increase 1951–1967/68
East: rural	198	199	187	−9.0%
urban	2,482	2,402	2,768	+11.5%
West: rural	243	232	270	+11.1%
urban	966	971	1,292	+13.4%

C. INCOME PER WORKER EMPLOYED IN AGRICULTURE

Province	1951/52	1955/56	1959/60	1961/62	1964/65	1965/66	1966/67	1967/68
East	714	724	688	589	652	630	585 *	620 *
West	903	990	971	858	891	911	892	881

* estimates

D. REAL WAGES OF PRODUCTION WORKERS IN MANUFACTURING

Province	1954	1955	1957	1958	1959/60	1962/63	1963/64	1964/65	1965/66	1966/67
East	1,023	903	935	957	949	986	996	n.a.	n.a.	n.a.
West	1,104	1,041	1,040	1,066	1,071	977	995	1,047	1,082	989

DEFINITIONS, NOTES, SOURCES

A. Gross Provincial Product ÷ Total Provincial Population. Source: U.S.A.I.D. Statistical Fact Book for Pakistan, Dec., 1968.

B. Agricultural value added ÷ rural population and non-agricultural value added ÷ urban population. While not all agricultural income is earned in the rural sector, nor is all non-agricultural income earned in the urban sector, this data can be used as rough approximations of income distributed between sectors especially since in many instances of data classification in Pakistan statistics urban areas are defined to include villages with populations of 5,000 and sometimes as little as 2,500 inhabitants. The comparatively large figures for the urban sector of East Pakistan can be explained by the very small size of the urban population in that province. Source: computed by L. and T. E. Nulty from data from government sources on sectoral value added in gross provincial product plus provincial population estimates.

C. Average income from agriculture per working member of the agricultural population. Source: computed by T. E. Nulty from data from government sources.

D. Money wages of production workers in manufacturing industry deflated by cost of living index. Source: computed by T. E. Nulty from censuses of Manufacturing Industry and Pakistan C.S.O. Cost-of-living index. After 1963/64 there is no C.M.I. Data for East Pakistan.

The trend towards increasing income inequality is shown also in the National Household Surveys of Income and Expenditure, although they cover only a short period (three years) and in spite of the fact that like all such sample surveys based on voluntary replies to a questionnaire, they understate the income share accruing to the richest classes. (See Table 3.) [5]

TABLE 3

SHARE OF TOTAL INCOME ACCRUING TO DIFFERENCE INCOME
CLASSES AND SECTORS, EAST AND WEST PAKISTAN,
1963/64 AND 1966/67

	1963/64			1966/67		
	Bottom 10%	Top 5%	Top 1%	Bottom 10%	Top 5%	Top 1%
East Pakistan:						
Rural	5.5	9.5	2.0	5.0	10.0	3.0
Urban	5.0	21.0	8.0	4.5	20.0	9.0
Both Sectors	5.5	10.0	3.5	4.5	10.0	3.5
West Pakistan:						
Rural	5.5	10.0	4.0	5.5	13.5	6.0
Urban	5.0	10.0	5.0	5.0	22.5	7.0
Both Sectors	5.0	10.0	4.2	5.0	17.0	6.2

SOURCE: Computed by T. E. Nulty from National Sample Surveys of Household Income and Expenditure, Pakistan Central Statistical Office.[6]

The conclusion that living standards for the mass of the population have been stagnant while incomes for the top few percent have been increasing rapidly, both in absolute and proportionate terms, is strengthened by evidence that the share of the national income owing to profits in the modern sector has been growing steadily. Table 4 shows industrial profits increasing from 2.3% of GNP in 1954 to 5.7% in 1966/67.[7] Of course this is bound to be a natural concomitant of development in any "free" market economy where the modern sector grows faster than the average; however, since two-thirds of the profits in large-scale manufacturing (along with the profits of 80% of the financial institutions in Pakistan) are directly controlled by 20 or 30 families—a fact generally acknowledged, even by the government—these data do provide reinforcement for the view that resources have been steadily and increasingly concentrated in the hands of the wealthiest groups.

TABLE 4

GROSS PROFITS AFTER INDIRECT TAXES IN LARGE-SCALE MANUFACTURING AS PERCENT
OF GNP (AT CURRENT PRICES), ALL PAKISTAN, 1954–1966/67

	1954	1955	1957	1958	59/60	62/63	63/64	64/65	65/66	66/67
Profits in mill. rupees	510	560	800	940	1,020	1,900	2,190	2,470	2,930	3,290
Profits as % of GNP	2.3	2.6	3.0	3.3	3.2	4.9	5.3	5.4	5.9	5.7

SOURCE: Pakistan C.S.O. Statistical Bulletins (National Accounts data) and C.S.O. Censuses of Manufacturing Industries (various years).

NOTE: Large-scale manufacturing industries are defined as all establishments employing at least 20 workers and using power.

The inequalities we have been illustrating have been defended and justified as a deliberate and necessary part of development policy by Pakistani economists and by foreign advisors, on the grounds that they will lead to faster growth and greater future welfare. Dr. Mahbub ul Haq, until recently the Chief Economist of the Pakistan Central Planning Commission, quoted J. M. Keynes on the development of Western capitalist economies in support of his view:

In fact, it was precisely the inequality of the distribution of wealth which made possible those vast accumulations of fixed wealth and of capital improvements which distinguished that age from all others. . . . If the rich had spent their new wealth on their own enjoyments the world would long ago have found such a regime intolerable. But like bees they saved and accumulated not less to the advantage of the whole community because they themselves held narrower ends in prospect.[8]

Mahbub ul Haq himself writes:

What is important and intellectually honest is to admit frankly that the heart of the growth problem lies in maximising the creation of this surplus. Either the capitalist sector should be allowed to perform the role, or, if this is found inefficient because of the nature of the capitalist sector in a particular country or is distasteful politically, the State should undertake it. It would be wrong to dub the consequent emergence of surplus value as "exploitation": its justification is economic growth.[9]

The underdeveloped countries of today cannot be too fussy about . . . ownership of "surplus value." Nor with the "revolution of rising expectations" are they allowed much political time to be fastidious about the means they choose to get rapid growth.[10]

The view of Gustav Papanek, formerly with the Harvard Development Advisory Service mission to the Pakistan Central Planning Commission, was the same:

The problem of inequality exists but its importance must be put in perspective. First of all the inequalities in income contribute to the growth of the economy which makes possible a real improvement for the lower income groups.[11]

Dr. Haq, the Pakistan government, and most Western economists and advisors have successfully advocated that public policy should aim at fostering the same process in Pakistan as that described by Keynes for nineteenth century Britain. On the one hand this was to be done by increasing the share of national income which went to the wealthy (on the grounds that they would be able to save a large proportion of it) and on the other hand by creating powerful incentives for the rich to invest their savings by guarantees of very high returns to invested capital. (Returns have normally been around 50% per annum and have frequently exceeded 100%.)

An extreme form of this view of development was expressed in conversation by an eminent American advisor to the Pakistan government who acknowledged that one reason why state enterprises appeared to be unprofitable was corruption at the top whereby managers skimmed off much of the profits. He then proceeded to defend this on the grounds that being rich, the corrupt managers had a high propensity to save and invest the stolen funds, whereas if the profits were turned over to the government a larger proportion of them would be dissipated in wages and other current expenditure. High level corruption was thus cited as a positive contribution to economic growth.

Has the approach taken by the Pakistan government, with the whole-hearted encouragement of virtually all foreign agencies, been successful even on its own terms? Have the foundations for rapid self-sustained growth, leading to increased welfare for everyone in the future, actually been laid? Certainly the government has carried out the two parts of its program. The distribution of income, as we have described, has been deliberately, heavily and increasingly biased in favor of the wealthy minority. The greater part of Pakistan's increased income has gone to the upper 20% of the population and most of it to a tiny and rich clique at the very top. What evidence is there that this group has "not spent their new wealth on their own enjoyments . . . but like bees . . . saved and accumulated"?

Everything has been done to encourage the rich to invest their wealth: tax holidays for industrial investments, tariff barriers against foreign competition, a highly favorable exchange rate for imported raw materials and equipment, subsidized prices for publicly owned power and low and stable wages, not to mention the complete subjection of any serious labor or political movement that might have challenged the distribution of income aimed at by the government. All this should have encouraged high rates of domestic savings.

How have Pakistan's capitalists responded to this policy? Certainly the consensus in the foreign establishment is that they have admirably fulfilled their intended role. This is clearly the central thesis of Gustav Papanek's book, cited earlier. Although the book was published before the urban riots of 1968/69, one would have expected the events of that winter and spring to have raised doubts and questions in the minds of foreign observers. In many cases this did occur, temporarily. However, the assessment of Pakistan's progress published in the Pearson Commission report in the Fall of 1969, after the "new" military regime had been installed, essentially affirms and justifies Pakistan's chosen strategy.[12]

In the very earliest days of Pakistan's development it is possible that the emerging class of capitalists did save and reinvest a fairly high proportion of its growing income. In those early days their economic and social position was not yet secure; there was rivalry and suspicion from the older landowning and professional civil service elite which controlled the government, and there was little foreign aid and no domestic capital market to supply them with funds to supplement their own savings. These conditions rapidly changed however: lines of communication, common interests and co-operation with other sections of the elite classes were quickly developed and, under the Ayub regime, firmly cemented. The distinctions and barriers within the ruling classes began rapidly to disappear.

Moreover, borrowing from overseas and especially foreign aid, increased enormously. Government agencies were set up to channel aid and domestic funds into the private sector on very favorable financial terms. As the boards of directors of these agencies were composed of high civil servants and the leading industrialists, it is not surprising that almost all of the funds went to the small group of wealthy and favored entrepreneurs who had managed to get to the top and who were represented on the boards. In addition, a large

banking network was built up by the same group, each major industrial family having its own bank and/or insurance company. Virtually all loans and advances by the banking system went to these families at rates of interest far below what was, or would have been, a free market rate, had the supply of finance not been so thoroughly monopolized.[13]

Thus it has become possible for the small class of dominant capitalists to finance investment from outside sources on very advantageous terms without resorting to savings out of their own income. No statistically significant trend can be established for the share of private domestic saving in GNP, as seen from Table 5. With more and more of the nation's income going to the rich there ought to have been a clearly observable upward trend *if* the rich had been using their income to save and accumulate like the bees they were supposed to resemble.[14]

If we look at the data on private domestic savings, we note that in 1966/67, these accounted for 5.9% of GNP. In the same year, gross profits in large-scale industry amounted to Rs. 3290 million, or 5.7% of GNP. If the captains of industry actually saved the high proportion of their profits usually attributed to them (75% is frequently given) this would imply that savings by other sectors amounted to only 1.5% of GNP. Given that these other sectors have accounted for over 70% of GNP, and given what we know about investment which actually took place in sectors other than large-scale manufacturing, this proposition concerning savings out of manufacturing profits is highly suspicious. The conclusion that appears to come out of this is that on the whole the rich have not used their own rapidly increasing incomes to finance their investments to anything like the extent commonly asserted.

What then have the rich done with their share of the pie? Although they may not have saved like the prodigious bees that were supposed to be their model, the wealthy class of Pakistan has certainly performed remarkable feats of consumption, a fact immediately obvious to any casual visitor. We have already mentioned luxury housing (which probably accounts for at least 10% of measured private investment). In addition, imports of automobiles were five times as great in 1964/65 as they were before Ayub came to power in 1958 and they have not stopped growing since. The same is true of Hasselblad cameras, Akai tape decks and private airplanes. In addition, a considerable proportion of the surplus which has not been consumed has been exported to foreign havens.

TABLE 5

CONTRIBUTIONS TO SAVINGS AND INVESTMENT IN PAKISTAN, 1949/50–1967/68
(MILLION RUPEES UNLESS OTHERWISE NOTED)

	Investment					Saving			
Years *	Public	Private	Total	Private as % of Total	Govern- ment	As % of GNP	Private	As % of GNP	Net Inflow of Foreign Resources **	As % of GNP
1950/51	327	543	870	62	−260 †	−.9	1,285	5.9	−155 †	−.7
1955/56	757	710	1,467	48	266	.9	671	2.8	529	2.1
1959/60	1,553	1,269	2,922	44	688	2.1	1,072	3.2	1,062	2.9
1963/64	3,753	2,978	6,731	45	875	2.0	3,327	7.6	2,495	5.6
1966/67	4,166	3,875	8,041	48	1,491	2.5	3,405	5.9	2,973	4.9

SOURCE: Computed by T. E. Nulty from C.S.O. Statistical Bulletins, Government Budgets and other government sources.
* In order to smooth out short term fluctuations, the figures given for each year are three-year averages centered at the stated year (i.e., 1955/56 = average of 1954/55, 1955/56, 1956/57). Because of rounding errors and averaging, the sums of the three "savings" items do not equal "total investment" exactly.
** Including foreign aid.   † Indicates net outflow from Pakistan.

Although not financed by entrepreneurs out of their own income, we have seen that private investment has nevertheless grown at a steady rate (albeit not as dramatically as one might have expected, given the resources that have been directed toward the entrepreneurial class). If, then, it could be established that the investment which has taken place up to now has actually laid a firm foundation for future growth, then an argument could be made that, regardless of how it has been achieved, who has paid the cost and who received the benefits, the net effect of the last twenty years is that a positive and a major step on the road to development has been taken. Such a view would be very much in line with the thinking of those who made and supported Pakistan's development strategy.

However, such a conclusion is unfortunately open to doubt. Rather the indications are that the step that has been taken leads directly to the kind of economic cul-de-sac that has become such a depressingly familiar pattern in Latin America and elsewhere: inefficient industries producing inappropriate goods behind high protective tariffs for monopoly prices.

Some observers, supporting the official position, have argued that in Pakistan this is not the case. They contend that there has been sufficient diversification into investment goods and into industries where Pakistan has a comparative advantage so that the usual pattern of stagnation following an initial burst of industrialization based on highly protected consumer goods industries designed to provide locally what was formerly imported, will not take place.[15] This optimistic view has been challenged by other observers [16] and the statistical methods and empirical evidence used by the "optimists" to support their case are open to serious question. But leaving aside for the moment the question of "product mix," there is no shortage of other reasons to be wary of these sanguine predictions.

Many industries in Pakistan are run very much below plant capacity, contrary to what one would expect in an economy where capital is supposed to be one of the scarcest resources. Such a state of affairs continues to exist, however, largely because capital has intentionally been made artificially cheap by foreign aid and an overvalued exchange rate. The licensing policy for imports and other forms of market protection for many industrial products result in high rates of return being earned even on inefficiently invested capital.

One common influence contributing to an inefficient industrial structure is the practice of over-invoicing capital goods imports as a way of avoiding restrictions on the export of capital. Once a Pakistani buyer has obtained an import license for a certain consignment of goods he comes to an agreement with the overseas supplier to inflate the invoice, with a certain share of the excess being anonymously deposited in a numbered bank account overseas by the supplier on behalf of the buyer. After the 1958 military regime came to power, Ayub Khan declared a temporary amnesty to anyone who repatriated capital that had been illegally exported. $96 million were turned in. This was only the top of the iceberg and yet this amount represents abouts 7% of total export earnings for the five years previous to the amnesty.

Over-invoicing also runs counter to development needs by distorting the factors influencing investment decisions. A powerful industrialist can be reasonably certain of being able to establish a sufficiently strong monopolistic position and to obtain enough protection from foreign competition to be able to produce almost anything at a profit. To take just one example, the sole spark-plug factory in Pakistan as a result of a total ban on imports of spark plugs, is able to break even when operating at only one-ninth of installed capacity. In these circumstances the decision as to what sort of factory to build becomes partly dependent on which supplier offers the best deal on the invoicing of equipment; it is much less related to the question of which sort of factory would be most profitable either to the individual entrepreneur in terms of local market conditions, or to the nation in general. This practice and its consequences are not restricted only to American aid-financed imports: they are quite general.

To go back now to the question of the industrial structure established by the chosen development strategy, the policy of keeping capital cheap, along with the high level of protection and the unequal distribution of income has led to consumer goods industries receiving a much higher share of investment resources than is desirable in an economy that is supposed to be aiming at rapid self-sustained growth. In Pakistan intermediate and capital goods industries have been more difficult to establish profitably, because sophisticated foreign imports are available to those able to obtain licenses permitting them to import such machines (at prices lower than those warranted by market demand). In context the returns to investing in the assembly of foreign components, using sophisticated imported machinery, are relatively high, especially when the final goods are aimed at the middle and upper class market which, as we have seen, has been getting increasing shares of the growing national economy.

We would like to give just one example of how a policy measure, which might appear at the outset as a rational attempt to relax existing constraints on growth, is seen after its implementation to be yet another means of assuring the perpetuation of the status quo. In underdeveloped economies one of the most over-riding considerations of economic policy is how best to allocate extremely scarce key resources. In Pakistan, foreign exchange is one of the economy's scarcest resources and the government is faced with the need to ration foreign exchange while at the same time desiring to assure that it is spent on imports essential for development. The strategy chosen has been to keep the price of imports down (through over-valuation of the rupee) as an inducement to domestic investment. Demand and supply for foreign exchange are equated through a licensing system by which the government can ensure that foreign exchange is spent on desirable goods. Thus before claims to foreign exchange can be obtained it is necessary for the importer to obtain a license for the particular goods he requires. Because foreign exchange is in short supply, licenses are restricted in number and inevitably are subject to black market bidding in the form of bribery and personal influence on relevant authorities.

In the Pakistan context the operation of bribery and personal influence inevitably assures the success of the richest and most influential. On the one hand they can always outbid competitors because of their greater financial resources and on the other hand their political and social standing makes them less vulnerable to prosecution for their illegal acts. This creates barriers to entry for small businessmen and hinders the diversification of industry by restricting the growth of complex backward and forward linkages. In addition, since the rationing system for the issue of licenses was calculated to allot to each license holder enough imported raw materials to permit a certain given proportion of his installed capacity to be utilized, there was an inducement for entrepreneurs to choose techniques which used relatively large amounts of imported capital and raw materials and to install much more capacity than necessary in an attempt to monopolize output of the particular commodity. The cost of the resulting unutilized capacity was easily covered by the high rate of tariff protection and the monopoly position of the producer. Although the import licensing system has now been run down to some extent, giving rather more scope to competitive bargaining, the damage is already done. The monopolistic structure of industry is now entrenched and the original beneficiaries of government policy are now strong enough to maintain their own barriers to further competition; dismantling the original policy cannot easily reverse this situation.

If we could establish that the errors of the past were at least vulnerable to forces for change, the problems would not appear so intractable. But now, however, the lucky few who made it to the top during the initial period of expansion have acquired a powerful vested interest in the existing economic structure from which they have benefited so handsomely, but which is neither efficient nor suited to rapid future growth. In order to protect this vested interest they are forced to extend and solidify their control of the political system, joining forces with the two other ruling groups, the landowners and the senior civil service and army. The rich are thus likely to become more powerful and considerably richer while the poor proliferate and military government follows military government in an atmosphere of economic stagnation.

This vicious circle, with its many Latin American precedents, is perpetuated by the fact that although discontent may be widespread and may occasionally break out in random acts of violence or superficial changes in the political superstructure all real socioeconomic interests which might have acted as countervailing forces have been undermined from the very beginning

by the development policy that has been pursued. This policy, in its effort to provide every incentive and safeguard for the entrepreneurial class upon which it placed its faith as the driving force of development, has succeeded in creating a small class of wealthy privileged monopolists who are now in a virtually unassailable position—freed by that very policy from the pressures of business competition, organised labor movement or political opposition, and with no strong interest in efficiency, change or even, necessarily, in development itself.

With this general background, how are we to evaluate the role of the Western foreign aid and advisory effort? Most advisors and aid administrators see themselves as technocrats (in many cases sincerely dedicated to the cause of economic development) whose job it is to help determine and implement that allocation of the available resources which will most effectively promote economic and social development. As such they produce a great many worthy papers arguing cogently against stepping into this or that economic pitfall.

In Pakistan various aid and advisory agencies have frequently campaigned for such unexceptionable and even progressive causes as lower guaranteed prices for foodgrains in the face of recent surpluses, more rigorous and objective appraisal of development projects, more rational management of foreign exchange, land reform, educational reform and so forth and so on. It is therefore understandable that they react indignantly to suggestions that they have contributed to the difficulties, inefficiencies and anomalies which in many cases they have actively worked against.

The point is that good intentions and worthy papers, even when presented to cabinet ministers, do not measure the real impact that foreign agencies, advisors and aid have made. What we must try to assess is the extent to which foreign involvement has served to support and maintain an economic structure, antipathetic to development, which, once established, generates its own self-perpetuating indigenous lines of development.

There is a built-in influence in the relations between advisors and host governments that assures that the advisors will concentrate their efforts on those policy problems least in conflict with vested interests in the host country and that are most likely to evoke a positive response from the host government. Advisory groups working independent of aid-giving governments often refer to this as "pragmatism." But inevitably this relationship leads to emphasis on policies quickly and easily reflected in GNP data and relative neglect of policies with perhaps longer gestation periods or with less easily measurable impact such as education or land reform.[17]

Western economic advice in Pakistan has concentrated on switching the emphasis of economic policy from what is considered to be the cumbersome inefficiency of direct controls toward the package of indirect controls relying on the market mechanism and market incentives: i.e. the standard tool kit of Western policy makers. Attention is focussed on taxation, credit and so on, as levers for exploiting the presumed efficiency of the market mechanism as an allocative and decision-making device. As already mentioned, there has also been a great deal of emphasis on policies deliberately intended to redistribute income in favor of profits in the modern sector on the grounds that this will lead to increased savings and investment, hence faster growth of GNP and ultimately higher income for everyone.

Quite apart from the objections which can be made *on principle* to such an approach, it is rarely understood by the advisory groups themselves that they must make very strong assumptions concerning the (at least potential) competitiveness and profit-maximizing nature of the market, and the size and resilience of the market structure in relation to public policy measures, for this approach to be even internally consistent. If these assumptions do not hold, the approach readily leads to self-contradiction.

As we have seen, if the economy is not very large and not very competitive, redistributing income in favor of oligopolistic profits may simply enhance the concentration of economic power, reduce the likelihood of new entrants and generally reduce competitiveness even further. It does not necessarily lead to higher rates of savings and investment. Cheap government credit to industry is likely to be pre-empted by established oligopolists who may simply substitute these funds for their own savings.

Even freeing the exchange rate (as was done for part of Pakistan's external transactions via the bonus voucher system) does not necessarily have the intended effect. Established oligopolists, with their superior financial resources, can simply bid up the price of foreign exchange sufficiently to close out real or potential competitors and then pass this on through the prices of their protected, monopolized output.

Eventually it is perfectly possible for a small group of oligopolists to become so powerful that they are virtually unassailable both economically and ultimately politically as well. When this happens (and we would argue that it has virtually happened in Pakistan) there is great danger that the country will find itself in the kind of cul-de-sac which has become so depressingly familiar elsewhere in the world: inefficient industries producing inappropriate goods behind high protective tariffs for monopoly prices.

The model followed by the favored few reverts to that of the high-living, low-saving latifundista rather than the self-denying, high-saving dynamic capitalist of Protestant ethic folklore, which provided the original rationale for the policy package we have outlined. In Pakistan, as in many other countries, it is difficult, then, to avoid the conclusion that the foreign establishment has underwritten and contributed to a socio-economic system and a development strategy which has produced a monopolistic economic structure which is neither efficient, dynamic nor equitable.

---

1. The fact that public expenditure on defense is included in GNP is often cited as one way in which statistical measures may give an incorrect estimate of economic growth (cf. Hyman P. Minsky, "Passage to Pakistan," *Transaction,* February, 1970). However, we do not think this problem was very important during the first twenty years of Pakistan's existence, partly because it affects the national accounts of most other countries in the same way and partly because in Pakistan it has been a low and stable proportion of GNP, averaging around 3.5 percent per annum between 1958 and 1968. Since the end of 1968, however, as a result of increasing political unrest the military budget has probably grown significantly and may now account for a much more important share of total GNP.

2. Whenever possible official statistics are published as national averages, since 1963/64 most major macroeconomic data have not

been available on a provincial basis at all. Protection from the critical scrutiny to which important published statistics are subjected, has permitted a certain amount of deliberate fudging of such important magnitudes as the size of East Pakistan's rice crop. Such magnitudes have always played an important part in the internal political jockeying between Eastern and Western factions within the Pakistan government and therefore the final numbers which are made official (again, most often as aggregate, All-Pakistan figures) often owe a good deal to the pressures of political maneuvering.

3. See A. R. Khan in Discussion in E. A. G. Robinson and M. Kidron, eds., *Economic Development in South Asia*, International Economic Association, Proceedings of a Conference held at Kandy, Ceylon, June, 1969 (London: Macmillan, 1970), p. 66.

4. On this question, see Khadija Haq, "A measurement of inequality of urban personal income distribution in Pakistan," *Pakistan Development Review* (hereafter *PDR*), Winter, 1964; Asbjorn Bergan, "Personal income distribution and personal saving in Pakistan," *PDR*, Summer, 1967; A. R. Khan, "What has been happening to real wages in Pakistan," *PDR*, Autumn, 1967; and S. R. Bose, "Trend of real income of the rural poor in East Pakistan," *PDR*, Autumn, 1968.

5. Although in computing Table 3 the raw data have been adjusted in order to take some account of under-reporting of the highest income groups, it is not possible to make a complete correction. On correction problems, see Bergan, *op. cit.* Thus Table 3 should be read as a rough sketch which probably understates the degree of inequality. The important point is that a definite change in income distribution does appear to have occurred even over so short a period of time as the three years separating the two household sample surveys.

6. It should be noted that this table is computed in terms of average per capita income for each household income class. Often data of this sort are presented in terms of household income, but since household income and household size may be correlated differently in different counrties, international comparisons are best made in terms of average per capita income. Every effort has been made to render the data from the two surveys comparable. The adjustments have been made in such a way as to make it likely that the increase in inequality indicated in Table 3 is a conservative estimate.

7. These are reasonably firm estimates based on the Censuses of Manufacturing Industry.

8. From J. M. Keynes, *Economic Consequences of the Peace*, cited by Mahbub ul Haq

in *Strategy of Economic Planning* (London: Oxford University Press, 1963), p. 2.

9. *Ibid.*

10. *Ibid.*

11. Gustav F. Papenek, *Pakistan's Development: Social Goals and Private Incentives* (Cambridge, Mass.: Harvard University Press, 1967), p. 242.

12. The same can be said of W. Falcon and J. J. Stern, "Growth and Development in Pakistan, 1966–1969," Harvard University Center for International Affairs, Occasional Paper, No. 23, April, 1970. In this monograph the biased income distribution is recognised as being possibly somewhat inefficient because it creates social unrest, but it is not criticized for being a positive hindrance to economic growth, hence, future welfare.

13. In 1959 the Credit Enquiry Commission estimated that 222 families received 60 percent of all bank credit. Since 1960–61, between two-thirds and three-quarters of all loans made by private banks have been made to (at most) .0008 of the population, or less than 1,000 households in a nation of over 100 million people. In order to cover these loans, the banks have built up an extensive and rapidly growing network of local branches but their strong monopolistic position has enabled them to keep interest rates paid on bank deposits very low.

14. The statistical evidence for this is strengthened when it is recognized that the official data on "private savings" includes savings which are expended on private luxury house building (which has been considerable) and investment by state-run firms (including railways, power companies, fertilizer plants, etc.) out of their current income. The latter is not considered "government savings" because it does not appear in government accounts; it does appear in the investment data, however, because these are derived from actual sales and availability of investment goods.

15. Gustav F. Papanek, *op. cit.*; Lester B. Pearson, et al., *Partners in Development* (section on Pakistan); Stephen R. Lewis, Jr., *Economic Policy and Industrialisation in Pakistan;* S. R. Lewis, Jr. and Ronald Soligo, "Growth and structural change in Pakistan's manufacturing industry," *PDR*, Spring, 1965, pp. 94–139.

16. G. C. Winston and A. MacEwan, "A note on the use classification of four-digit industries . . . ," *PDR*, Winter, 1966, pp. 592–597; A. R. Khan, "Import substitution, export expansion and consumption liberalisation," *PDR*, Summer, 1963, pp. 29–65; and K. B. Griffin, "Financing development plans in Pakistan," *PDR*, Winter, 1965, pp. 601–630, to name only a few.

17. Another aspect of foreign advisory services which make them attractive to host gov-

ernments is that they provide essential expertise without being able (even if they so wished) to exercise any of the political leverage which normally goes with being indispensable. In many underdeveloped countries today the government is at odds with its own intellectual class. In many of these countries, those citizens who possess skills needed by the government tend to be precisely the young, energetic, highly educated, and often radical (by the standards of the incumbent regime) intellectuals who are in conflict with existing authority. For governments to turn to their own "Young Turks" for essential expertise has serious political implications. Advisory agencies provide a safe way of side-stepping this problem.

In addition, should it transpire that policies or events go awry, the advisors can serve as convenient (if temporary) scapegoats for the entrenched regime, thus diverting attention from failure and helping to protect the government from the political consequences.

CAPITALIST AND MAOIST ECONOMIC DEVELOPMENT

JOHN G. GURLEY

Stanford University

While capitalist and Maoist processes of economic development have several elements in common, the differences between the two approaches are nevertheless many and profound. It is certainly not evident that one approach or the other is always superior, in regard either to means or to ends. What is evident, however, is that most studies by American economists of Chinese economic development are based on the assumption of capitalist superiority, and so China has been dealt with as though it were simply an underdeveloped United States—an economy that "should" develop along capitalist lines and that "should" forget all that damn foolishness about Marxism, Mao's thought, Great Leaps, and Cultural Revolutions and just get on with the job of investing the savings efficiently.

This almost complete and unthinking acceptance by American economists of the view that there is no development like capitalist development has resulted in studies of China that lack insight and are generally unsatisfactory. Later on, I shall briefly examine some of these weaknesses and then suggest the types of economic studies that might be undertaken if China's development efforts are to be given serious intellectual consideration. The main portion of this paper, however, is a comparison of capitalist and Maoist development processes.

SOME COMMON ELEMENTS

There is a core of economic development theory concerned with ways of increasing a country's national product that would probably be accepted by both the capitalist and Maoist sides. This common core starts by recognizing that national output consists of goods and services that are consumed (consumption) and goods that are accumulated (investment). The consumption of national output may be done by individuals, business firms, and governments; and the consumption items are generally food, clothing, housing services, household operation, and such things. The accumulation of national output—real investment or capital formation—is added to the country's capital stock, to its houses and business structures, its tools and machinery, its highways, its inventories and livestock, and its military equipment. Such capital formation may be undertaken by either the private or public sectors of the economy.

Current investment yields the plant and

From *Bulletin of Concerned Asian Scholars* (April–July 1970), pp. 34–50. Reprinted by permission. Some sections have been omitted.

equipment and other capital goods that can be used to produce larger amounts of output in subsequent years. That is, as the capital stock builds up, a country becomes increasingly capable of enlarging the production of its goods and services. On the other hand, if national output is almost totally consumed year after year, the productive capabilities of the nation will remain depressed; consumption will continue to eat up output that might have taken the form of productive machinery, tools, and similar things.

The output capabilities of a nation, however, depend on more than the size of its capital stock. They also are affected by the size of the labor force and by the amount of available land and natural resources. A nation's capacity to produce, in other words, depends on the amount of "inputs" it has—on its capital stock, labor supply, and land. An increase in any of these factors of production will generally raise a country's output potential.

Since the amount of land is more or less fixed, the variable inputs are capital and labor. Inasmuch as output will generally grow with an increase of either, it would seem to be unimportant which one is emphasized. However, the growth of output is generally not considered as important an economic goal as is the growth of output *per capita*—that is, total output divided by the population. . . . [I]n the absence of other considerations an increase in output per capita can be achieved only if the percentage growth of the capital stock or of land outstrips that of the labor supply. Since, as I have said, it is usually difficult to do very much about the stock of land, the growth of output per capita depends heavily on relatively large rates of investment—on the capital stock growing faster than the labor supply. This process is called "capital deepening" because it leads to the availability of more capital per worker; and so to more output per worker.

However, output per capita may be raised not only by capital deepening but also by improvements in the *quality* of the capital stock or of the labor supply. Technical advances, achieved by inventions and innovations, will raise the quality of a given capital stock and so permit the labor supply to produce more. Capital need not grow in total amount, to raise output per capita, if it "grows" in quality.

The quality of the labor force can also be raised—by improvements in health, by job training programs, by more formal education, and by better living conditions in general. The same number of workers can produce more, even with the same capital goods, if their quality is improved —if there has been investment in the nation's human capital. In addition, the growth of output per capita may come about because of improvements in organization and management techniques—better ways of combining the factors of production and more effective ways of inspiring the labor force to greater efforts. Finally, even in the absence of increases in the quality of inputs, and even though each input grows by an equal percentage, output per capita may still rise owing to economies of scale—to inputs becoming more productive when they are combined in larger and larger amounts.

Thus, if an economy wishes to increase its output per capita, the most promising avenues to success are large investment programs to build up the capital stock rapidly, expenditures for research and development for the purpose of stimulating fast technological advances, investment in human capital by way of health, education, and in-training programs, and efforts to improve organization and management methods. These expansionary policies may then call forth economies of scale and hence additional gains in output.

CAPITALIST ECONOMIC DEVELOPMENT

Within the above framework, the theory of capitalism, as originally developed by Adam Smith almost 200 years ago, generally holds that an economy can develop most rapidly if each and every person, whether he is an entrepreneur, a worker, or a consumer, pursues his own self-interest in competitive markets, without undue interference from government. Progress is best promoted, not by government, but by entrepreneurs owning the material means of production, whose activities, guided by the profit motive, reflect consumers' demands for the various goods and services. Labor productivity is enhanced by material incentives and the division of labor (specialization); economic progress is made within an environment of law and order, harmony of interests and stability.

The goal of economic development, according to capitalist theory, can best be attained by the above means, and the goal itself can best be measured by the national output. There is a heavy emphasis in capitalist development, as there now is throughout most of the world, on raising the level of national output, on producing "things" in ever-increasing amounts.[1] Implicit in discussions of this goal is the view that man is mainly an input, a factor of production, a means to an end. The end is usually not the development of human beings but the development of output.[2]

The practice of capitalism has not, of course, met the ideal specification of it, and the practice itself has changed markedly over time. In practice, many markets have been more monopolistic than competitive, government has interfered in numerous and extensive ways in competitive market processes in pursuit of greater equity in income distribution, higher employment of labor, and better allocation of economic resources. Capitalism of the individualist, competitive type has given way in many parts of the industrial capitalist world to a state welfare capitalism, in which government plays a larger role and private entrepreneurs and consumers somewhat smaller ones than envisaged by Adam Smith and his disciples. Despite these departures from the ideal model of capitalism, I think it is fair to say that the main driving force of the capitalist system remains private entrepreneurs who own the means of production, and that competition among them is still widespread.

There is no doubt that capitalist development, whatever importance its departures from the Smithian model have had, has been highly successful in raising living standards for large numbers of people. It has been relatively efficient in using factors of production in ways best designed to maximize the output that consumers by and large have demanded. And it has encouraged new ways of doing things—innovative activity and technological advances.

At the same time, however, capitalist development has almost always been uneven in several crucial ways—in its alternating periods of boom and bust; in enriching some people thousands of times more than others; in developing production facilities with much more care than it has devoted to the welfare of human beings and their environment; in fostering lopsided development, both in terms of

geographical location within the country and, especially in low-income countries, in terms of a narrow range of outputs, such as in one or two crop economies.

The lopsided character of capitalist development has been evident historically in those nations that today have advanced industrial economies, but it is especially evident at the present time in the underdeveloped countries (with their mixture of feudal and capitalist features) that are tied in to the international capitalist system— that is, those countries that, by being receptive to free enterprise and foreign capital, regardless of whether they are also receptive to freedom, are in the "Free World."

Most of these poor countries are either making no progress at all or they are developing in lopsided ways, within the international capitalist system, as satellites to the advanced capitalist countries. . . . The economic development of these poor capitalist countries is lopsided in many other ways, too. A few cities in each of these countries with their airports, hotels, nightclubs, and light industries, are often built up to the point where they resemble the most modern metropolises in advanced industrial countries—but the rural areas, comprising most of the country and containing most of the people, are largely untouched by modernization.

In most of these countries, industry, culture, entertainment, education, and wealth are highly concentrated in urban centers. A traveller to most of the poor "Free World" countries, by flying to the main cities, can land in the middle of the twentieth century, but by going thirty miles from there in any direction he will be back in the Middle Ages. Education is usually for the elite and stresses the superiority of the educated over the uneducated, the superiority of urban over rural life, of mental work over manual labor. The burden of economic development, which is essentially a restraint on consumption, is shared most inequitably among the people; the differences between rich and poor are staggering, because they are nothing less than the differences between unbelievable luxury and just plain starvation.

While some of these characteristics are not peculiar to the poor countries tied in to the international capitalist system—they can be found in the Soviet socialist bloc, too—and while some are related more to feudalism than to capitalism, much of the lopsided development nevertheless is intimately connected with the profit motive. The key link between the two is the fact that it is almost always most profitable, from a private business point of view, to build on the best. Thus, a businessman locates a new factory in an urban center by existing ones, rather than out in the hinterlands, in order to gain access to supplies, a skilled labor force, and high-income consumers; to maximize profits, he hires the best, most qualified workers; a banker extends loans to those who are already successful; an educational system devotes its best efforts to the superior students, and universities, imbued with the private-business ethic of "efficiency," offer education to those best prepared, most able; promoters locate cultural centers amidst urbanites best able to appreciate and pay for them; the most profitable business firms attract the best workers and have easiest access to loanable funds; satellite capitalist countries, in the interests of efficiency and comparative advantage, are induced to specialize in cocoa or peanuts or coffee—to build on what they have always done best.

This pursuit of efficiency and private profits through building on the best has led in some areas to impressive aggregate growth rates, but almost everywhere in the international capitalist world it has favored only a relatively few at the expense of the many, and, in poor capitalist countries, it has left most in stagnant backwaters. Capitalist development, even when most successful, is always a trickle-down development.

MAOIST ECONOMIC DEVELOPMENT

The Maoists' disagreement with the capitalist view of economic development is profound. Their emphases, values, and aspirations are quite different from those of capitalist economists. To begin with, Maoist economic development occurs within the context of central planning, public ownership of industries, and agricultural cooperatives or communes. While decision-making is decentralized to some extent, decisions regarding investment vs. consumption, foreign trade, allocation of material inputs and some labor supply,

prices of goods and factors—these and more are essentially in the hands of the State. The profit motive is officially discouraged from assuming an important role in the allocation of resources, and material incentives, while still prevalent, are downgraded.

But perhaps the most striking difference between the capitalist and Maoist views is in regard to goals. Maoists believe that, while a principal aim of nations should be to raise the level of material welfare of the population, this should be done only within the context of the development of human beings and of encouraging them to realize fully their manifold creative powers. And it should be done only on an egalitarian basis—that is, on the basis that development is not worth much unless everyone rises together; no one is to be left behind—either economically or culturally. Indeed, Maoists believe that rapid economic development is not likely to occur *unless* everyone rises together. Development as a trickle-down process is therefore rejected by Maoists, and so they reject any strong emphasis on profit motives and efficiency criteria that lead to lopsided growth. Their emphasis, in short, is on man rather than on "things."

Emphasis on Man

In Maoist eyes, economic development can best be attained by giving prominence to man.[3] "In building up the . . . country, we—unlike the modern revisionists who one-sidedly stress the material factor, mechanization and modernization—pay chief attention to the revolutionization of man's thinking and through this command, guide and promote the work of mechanization and modernization."[4] The Maoists' stress on this point most sharply distinguishes their thinking on the subject of economic development from that of capitalist economists. . . . [The latter] have recently stressed the importance for economic growth of "investment in human capital"—that is, investment in general education, job training, and better health. It has been claimed that expenditures in these directions have had a large "payoff" in terms of output growth. The Maoists' emphasis, however, is quite different. First of all, while they recognize the key role played by education and health in the production process, their emphasis is heavily on the transformation of ideas, the making of the Communist man.

Ideology, of course, may be considered as part of education in the broadest sense, but it is surely not the part that capitalist economists have in mind when they evaluate education's contribution to economic growth. Moreover, ideological training does not include the acquisition of particular skills, or the training of specialists—as education and job training in capitalist countries tend to do. The Maoists believe that economic development can best be promoted by breaking down specialization, by dismantling bureaucracies, and by undermining the other centralizing and divisive tendencies that give rise to experts, technicians, authorities, and bureaucrats remote from or manipulating "the masses." Finally, Maoists seem perfectly willing to pursue the goal of transforming man even though it is temporarily at the expense of some economic growth.[5] Indeed, it is clear that Maoists will not accept economic development, however rapid, if it is based on the capitalist principles of sharp division of labor and sharp (unsavory, selfish) practices.

The Making of Communist Man

The proletarian world view,[6] which Maoists believe must replace that of the bourgeoisie, stresses that only through struggle can progress be made; that selflessness and unity of purpose will release a huge reservoir of enthusiasm, energy, and creativeness; that active participation by "the masses" in decision-making will provide them with the knowledge to channel their energy most productively; and that the elimination of specialization will not only increase workers' and peasants' willingness to work hard for the various goals of society but will also increase their ability to do this by adding to their knowledge and awareness of the world around them. . . .

Maoist Ideology and Economic Development

In many ways, then, Maoist ideology rejects the capitalist principle of building on the best, even though the principle cannot help but be followed to some extent in any effort at economic development. However, the Maoist departures from the principle are the important thing. While capitalism, in their view, strives one-sidedly for efficiency in producing goods, Maoism,

while also seeking some high degree of efficiency, at the same time, in numerous ways, builds on "the worst." Experts are pushed aside in favor of decision-making by "the masses"; new industries are established in rural areas; the educational system favors the disadvantaged; expertise (and hence work proficiency in a narrow sense) is discouraged; new products are domestically produced rather than being imported "more efficiently"; the growth of cities as centers of industrial and cultural life is discouraged; steel, for a time, is made by "everyone" instead of by only the much more efficient steel industry.

Maoists build on the worst, not, of course, because they take great delight in lowering economic efficiency, but rather to involve everyone in the development process, to pursue development without leaving a single person behind, to achieve a balanced growth rather than a lopsided one. If Maoism were only that, we could simply state that, while Maoist development may be much more equitable than capitalist efforts, it is surely less efficient and thus less rapid; efficiency is being sacrificed to some extent for equity. But that would miss the more important aspects of Maoist ideology, which holds that the resources devoted to bringing everyone into the socialist development process— the effort spent on building on "the worst" —will eventually pay off not only in economic ways by enormously raising labor productivity but, more important, by creating a society of truly free men, who respond intelligently to the world around them, and who are happy.[7]

U.S. STUDIES OF
CHINESE ECONOMIC DEVELOPMENT

The sharp contrast between the economic development views of capitalist economists and those of the Chinese Communists cannot be denied; their two worlds are quite different. The difference is not mainly between being Chinese and being American, although that is surely part of it, but rather between being Maoists in a Marxist-Leninist tradition and being present-day followers of the economics first fashioned by Adam Smith and later reformed by J. M. Keynes. Whatever the ignorance and misunderstanding on the Chinese side regarding the doctrines of capitalist economics, it is clear that many Western economic experts on China have shown little interest in and almost no understanding of Maoist economic development. . . .

[Economic research on China suffers from an ailment common to most of economics—a narrow empiricism—and it has been usually colored by very strong political biases against China.] The picture that is presented by these studies as a whole is one in which China, while making some progress for a time in certain areas, is just barely holding on to economic life. It is a picture of a China always close to famine, making little headway while the rest of the world moves ahead, being involved in irrational economic policies, and offering little reason for hope that the lives of her people will be improved. . . .

The truth is that China over the past two decades has made very remarkable economic advances (though not steadily) on almost all fronts. The basic, overriding economic fact about China is that for twenty years she has fed, clothed, and housed everyone, has kept them healthy, and has educated most. Millions have *not* starved; sidewalks and streets have *not* been covered with multitudes of sleeping, begging, hungry, and illiterate human beings; millions are *not* disease-ridden. To find such deplorable conditions, one does not look to China these days but rather to India, Pakistan, and almost anywhere else in the underdeveloped world. These facts are so basic, so fundamentally important, that they completely dominate China's economic picture, even if one grants all of the erratic and irrational policies alleged by her numerous critics. The Chinese— all of them—now have what is in effect an insurance policy against pestilence, famine, and other disasters. In this respect, China has outperformed every underdeveloped country in the world; and, even with respect to the richest one, it would not be far-fetched to claim that there has been less malnutrition due to maldistribution of food in China over the past twenty years than there has been in the United States.[8]

If this comes close to the truth, the reason lies not in China's grain output far surpassing her population growth—for it has not—but rather in the development of institutions to distribute food evenly among the population. It is also true that China has just had six consecutive bumper grain crops (wheat and rice) which have enabled her to reduce wheat imports and greatly increase rice exports. On top of this, there have been large gains in the supplies of eggs, vegetables, fruits, poultry, fish, and meat. In fact, China today exports more food than she imports. . . .

In education, there has been a major breakthrough. All urban children and a great majority of rural children have attended primary schools, and enrollments in secondary schools and in higher education are large, in proportion to the population, compared with pre-Communist days. If "school" is extended in meaning to include part-time, part-study education, spare-time education, and study groups organized by the communes, factories, street organizations, the army—then there are schools everywhere in China; then China may be said to be just one great big school.

China's gains in the medical and public health fields are perhaps the most impressive of all. The gains are attested to by many recent visitors to China. For example, a Canadian doctor a few years ago visited medical colleges, hospitals, and research institutes, and everywhere he found good equipment, high medical standards, excellent medical care; almost all comparable to Canadian standards.[9] A member of the U.S. Public Health Service, a few years ago, stated that "the prevention and control of many infections and parasitic diseases which have ravaged [China] for generations" was a "most startling accomplishment." He noted, too, that "the improvement of general environmental sanitation and the practice of personal hygiene, both in the cities and in the rural areas, was also phenomenal." [10]

While all these gains were being made, the Chinese have devoted an unusually large amount of resources to industrial output. China's industrial production has risen on the average by at least 11 per cent per year since 1950, which is an exceptionally high growth rate for an underdeveloped country. And industrial progress is not likely to be retarded in the future by any lack of natural resources, for China is richly endowed and is right now one of the four top producers in the world of coal, iron ore, mercury, tin, tungsten, magnesite, salt, and antimony.

The failure of many economic experts

on China to tell the story of her economic development accurately and fully is bad enough. But even worse, I think, has been the general failure to deal with China on her own terms, within the framework of her own goals and methods for attaining those goals, or even to recognize the possible validity of those goals. Communist China is certainly not a paradise, but it is now engaged in perhaps the most interesting economic and social experiment ever attempted, in which tremendous efforts are being made to achieve an egalitarian development, an industrial development without dehumanization, one that involves everyone and affects everyone. . . .

SOME SUGGESTIONS AND CONCLUSIONS

. . . It is a hopeful sign that many young economists are now breaking away from the stultifying atmosphere of present-day "neo-classical" economics and are trying to refashion the discipline into political economy—as it once was—so as to take account of the actual world and not the world of highly abstract models, scholastic debates, and artificial assumptions—all designed to justify the existing state of things and to accept, without question, the rather narrow materialistic goals of capitalist society. . . .

I mentioned earlier, when discussing the core of development theory that would probably be accepted by both the capitalist and Maoist sides, that economic growth can be attained by increasing the amounts of labor, capital goods, and land used in production, by improving the quality of these factors of production, by combining them in more efficient ways and inspiring labor to greater efforts, and by taking advantage of economies of scale.

Maoism undoubtedly affects every one of these ingredients of economic growth, and often in ways quite different from the capitalist impact. For example, it is likely that Maoist ideology discourages consumption and encourages saving and investment, and so promotes the growth of the capital stock; and does this by preventing the rise of a high-consuming "middle class," by fostering the Maoist virtues of plain and simple living and devoting one's life to helping others rather than to accumulating "pots and pans."

As another example, it is possible that Maoist economic development, by deemphasizing labor specialization and reliance on experts and technicians, reduces the quality of the labor force and so slows the rate of economic growth. On the other hand, as Adam Smith once suggested, labor specialization, while increasing productivity in some narrow sense, is often at the expense of the worker's general intelligence and understanding. "The man whose whole life is spent in performing a few simple operations . . . generally becomes as stupid and ignorant as it is possible for a human creature to become." [11] A major aim of the Maoist is to transform man from this alienated state to a fully aware and participating member of society.[12] . . . [A] Maoist economy may generate more useful information than a specialist one and so lead to greater creativity and productivity. When each person is a narrow specialist, communication among such people is not highly meaningful—your highly specialized knowledge means little to me in my work. When, on the other hand, each person has basic knowledge about many lines of activity, the experiences of one person enrich the potentialities of many others.

1. This is always a main point. However, two other goals of producing the "right" composition of goods and achieving an "equitable" distribution of income are often stipulated. A few of the better books on capitalist development are: Charles Kindleberger, *Economic Development;* Henry Bruton, *Principles of Development Economics;* Gerald Meier, *Leading Issues in Economic Development;* Albert Hirschman, *The Strategy of Economic Development;* and W. Arthur Lewis, *The Theory of Economic Growth.*

2. In recent years, capitalist economists have paid increasing attention to "investment in human capital." (See, for example, Gary Becker, *Human Capital.*) Although this might seem to represent a basic change in their concept of man in the development process, actually it does not. "Investment in human capital" means that economic resources are invested for the purpose of raising the educational, health, and skill levels of labor, not as an end in itself, but as a means of increasing the productivity of labor. Thus, economists are concerned with the "payoff" to investment in human capital, this payoff being the profit that can be made from such an expenditure. Indeed, the very term "human capital" indicates what these economists have in mind: man is another capital good, an input in the

productive engine that grinds out commodities; if one invests in man, he may become more productive and return a handsome profit to the investor—whether the investor is the State, a private capitalist, or the laborer himself. Thus, the peroccupation of capitalist economics is still with man as a means and not as an end.

3. This has been expressed by Maoists in many ways. As Mao Tse-tung has put it: "of all things in the world, people are the most precious" ("The Bankruptcy of the Idealist Conception of History," in *Selected Works of Mao Tse-tung*, Vol. IV, p. 454). The *Peking Review* adds: "Whatever we do, we give prominence to the factor of man and put man at the centre" (Nov. 11, 1966, pp. 19–20).

4. Mao Tse-tung, quoted in *Peking Review,* Nov. 11, 1966, pp. 19–20.

5. For 3,000 years the Chinese have paid much more attention to human relations than to conquering nature. Mao Tse-tung, as a Chinese *and* as a Marxist, cannot help but follow in this tradition. But, as a Chinese, he wishes to make China powerful in the eyes of the world, and, as a Marxist, through socialism. The world views power in terms of GNP and nuclear weapons, not in terms of perfection of human relations. So Mao has to go both directions at the same time, and the two goals often conflict with one another, at least in the short run.

6. Mao Tse-tung follows Marxism-Leninism in adopting the world outlook of dialectical materialism, which is a philosophy of human and natural change and interaction. Changes in society, for example, according to Mao, are not due chiefly to external causes but instead to internal ones—to the internal contradictions between the productive forces and the relations of production, between classes, etc. There is internal contradiction in every single thing, and it is the development of the contradiction that gives rise to changes—eventually to qualitative changes. External causes by themselves could explain only changes in quantity or scale, but they could not explain qualitative or "leap" changes. "The development of things should be seen as their internal and necessary self-movement, while each thing in its movement is interrelated with and interacts on the things around it." See Mao Tse-tung, "On Contradiction," *Selected Works,* Vol. 1, p. 313.

7. This emphasis on man was expressed by Marx in many ways, including the following: "A critique of religion leads to the doctrine that the highest being for man is man himself, hence to the categorical imperative to overthrow all relationships in which man is humbled, enslaved, abandoned, despised." See Marx's essay, "Zur Kritik der Hegelschen Rechtsphilosophie," in Marx and Engels, *Der Historische Materialismus: Die Fruhschriften* (Leipzig: Alfred Kroner Verlag, 1932), I, 272.

8. Much of the material in this paragraph was suggested by John Despres, but he is not responsible for my interpretations of his remarks.

9. G. Leslie Willcox, "Observations on Medical Practices," *Bulletin of the Atomic Scientists,* June, 1966, p. 52. See also William Y. Chen, "Medicine and Public Health," in *Sciences in Communist China,* pp. 384, 397–99.

10. Chen, *op. cit.*

11. Adam Smith, *The Wealth of Nations,* Book V, Ch. I, Part III.

12. See the essay by Mark Selden, "People's War and the Transformation of Peasant Society: China and Vietnam," to appear in Edward Friedman and Mark Selden (eds.), *America's Asia,* Pantheon, 1970.

The Political
Environment of
Development

•

ANY ANALYSIS OF development problems and possibilities entails detailed consideration of the particular political environment in which developmental efforts are to
take place. When it comes to shaping policies, the environment must be analyzed in
terms of the composition and configuration of sectors, themselves having differing
resource positions, propensities, capabilities, and interests. When it comes to gaining an appreciation of the process of development, however, it is helpful to generalize somewhat about the features that characterize politics in Africa, Asia, and
Latin America. For this purpose, we find the following works useful.

The political environment in African states is generally marked by a relatively
low level of institutionalization, that is, a lower degree of economic, social, and
political market integration and a lesser extent of various kinds of infrastructure.
In his essay below, Aristide Zolberg examines the implications of having a weak
"center" vis-à-vis "peripheral" economic, social, and political markets, and the
reciprocal relationship between having a paucity of legitimacy and a greater salience
of force.[1] We note also Zolberg's argument for an existential perspective—a *cinéma
vérité* approach to analysis—in place of the prevailing efforts at explanation through
abstraction and conceptualization.

Political conditions in Asia are more varied than in Africa, and generalizations
are less fruitful. Having considered above the recent experience with development
policies in Pakistan, we present Talukder Maniruzzaman's article on politics in
Pakistan prior to Ayub Khan's take-over in 1958. Its focus on group politics helps
to explicate the role and resources of sectors and particularly the differential relationships of sectors to the regime, that is, political stratification. Of further interest
is how little difference the period of military rule made in Pakistani politics; the
same sectors are still dominant or disadvantaged today. The persistence of factor
endowments is a fact of political life barring significant redistributive measures. In
political as well as economic features, the case of Pakistan differs more in degree
than kind from experiences elsewhere in Asia and the Third World.

Charles Anderson's chapter on the Latin American political system (from his
book, *Politics and Economic Change in Latin America*) draws many useful generalizations about politics in that area.[2] In particular, his examination of power capa-

---

[1] For a more extended treatment of some
of these issues, we would refer the reader to
Zolberg's book, *Creating Political Order: The
Party-States of West Africa* (1966).

[2] We had originally decided to restrict our
selections to articles, but on this subject, we
found nothing so instructive as this chapter.

bilities and their impact on political outcomes is important for an understanding of development problems, there or elsewhere. The interaction of legitimacy and force as political resources is instructively analyzed, as is the delineation and assessment of various political sectors. The idea of a political *process* is elaborated in such a way that one can better comprehend the dynamic between inputs and outputs at the political center.

In contrast to these views of politics at the national (macro) level, and complementing them, we have James Scott's analysis of the political process at the local (micro) level, which in the Third World is primarily rural politics. The geographical references are to Southeast Asia, but the analytical framework relates as validly to micro politics in Africa and Latin America.[3] Scott demonstrates the employment of the full range of political resources—goods and services, status, legitimacy, information, authority, and force—and puts them into a model of exchange and resource management.

Scott considers the effects of different degrees of market integration and points to different bases for the transformation of existing patterns of politics so as to make them more productive for the majority. It is possible that the productivity of the political system can be raised for the many particularly through the structure of elections, which can raise their endowments of political resources by conferring on them individually some small share of authority. The value of this, to be sure, is affected by many factors. Scott discusses these and many other considerations in this piece, which we would note is an edited version of a much longer paper.

An analysis of contemporary urban politics, from the viewpoint of the poorly endowed sectors, by Joan Nelson calls into question some of the prevailing theories about the political environment in Third World countries. In addressing empirically the attitudes and behavior of the urban poor, she deals with questions of resources, satisfactions, and propensities for action in a way that aids in the estimation of effects of alternative developmental policies. In particular she undercuts the rationale for (nonmilitary) "pacification" programs for the poor. The propensities and capabilities of other urban sectors for disruption are found to be considerably greater, which raises different and no less urgent issues.

Although these works focus on different areas of the Third World, the analysis in each is useful for examining politics in other areas. When questions of power and purpose are considered, the factors of political production prove to be as universal as the factors of economic production. The quantities and qualities of the factors vary from one situation to another, but their potential contribution to their respective processes does not. Thus in analyzing the political environment of development, while there are quantitative and qualitative differences in particular situations, the framework of analytical terms can be held constant.

[3] For references to work on patron-client relations in these other areas, see n. 83 on p. 117 above.

THE STRUCTURE OF POLITICAL CONFLICT IN THE
NEW STATES OF TROPICAL AFRICA

ARISTIDE R. ZOLBERG

University of Chicago

INTRODUCTION

Having assumed the burden of understanding political life in two-and-a-half dozen unruly countries, political scientists who study the new states of tropical Africa must leap with assurance where angels fear to tread.[1] We have borrowed, adapted, or invented an array of frameworks designed to guide perceptions of disparate events, and Africa is now uniformly viewed through the best lenses of contemporary comparative politics with a focus on political modernization, development and integration.

Unfortunately, it appears that when we rely exclusively on these tools in order to accomplish our task, the aspects of political life which we, as well as non-specialists, see most clearly with the naked eye of informed common sense, remain beyond the range of our scientific vision. In our pursuit of scientific progress, we have learned to discern such forms as regular patterns of behavior which constitute structures and institutions; but the most salient characteristic of political life in Africa is that it constitutes an almost institutionless arena with conflict and disorder as its most prominent features.

In recent years, almost every new African state has experienced more or less successful military or civilian coups, insurrections, mutinies, severe riots, and significant political assassinations. Some of them appear to be permanently on the brink of disintegration into several new political units. With little regard for the comfort of social scientists, the incidence of conflict and disorder appears unrelated to such variables as type of colonial experience, size, number of parties, absolute level or rate of economic and social development, as well as to the overall characteristics of regimes. The downfall of what was widely regarded as the continent's most promising democracy in January, 1966, was followed in February by the demise of what many thought to be the continent's harshest authoritarian regime. Furthermore, recent events in Nigeria, Ghana, and elsewhere indicate that military regimes are as fragile as their civilian predecessors.

Given the presence of almost every "gap" ever imagined by scholars concerned with development and modernization, and in the absence of the requisites most commonly posited for the maintenance of a political system, there is little place for countries such as these in the conceptual universe of political science. Yet, more often than not, these countries do persist. Hence, we have little choice but either to play an academic ostrich game or come to grips with their reality.

In order to deal in an orderly manner with such disorderly countries, we must alter our vision. Our normal focus on institutions and their concomitant processes resembles the focus of the untrained eye on the enclosed surface, or figure, of an image. The naive observer sees interstices as "shapeless parts of the underlying ground. He pays no attention to them, and finds it difficult and unnatural to do so."[2] Like trained painters, however, we much force ourselves to reverse the spontaneous figure-ground effect in order to perceive "interstices," shapes which initially do not appear worthy of our attention, but are in fact fundamental to put perception of the surface under observation. To understand political life in Africa, instead of viewing political disturbances as the shapeless ground surrounding institutions and processes which define the regimes of the new states, we must try to view them as characteristic processes which themselves constitute an important aspect of the regime in certain types of political systems.[3]

From *American Political Science Review* (March 1968), pp. 70–87. Reprinted by permission. Some sections have been omitted.

AFRICAN POLITICAL SYSTEMS
AND THEIR ENVIRONMENT

On the whole, African countries are distinguished from other Third World clusters by extremely weak national centers, a periphery which consists of societies until recently self-contained, and levels of economic and social development approaching the lowest limits of international statistical distributions.[4] They continue to reflect the fact that their origins stem from a recent European scramble for portions of an international system or sub-system constituted by interacting tribal societies. Although the French, British, Belgian, Portuguese or German nets were sometimes cast over an area dominated by a single society or by a group of societies with similar characteristics, this was usually not the case at all. Within the administrative nets which later became states there were only a few decades ago a varying number of more or less disparate societies, each with a distinct political system, and with widely different intersocietal relationships.

Although the new political units provided a territorial mold within which social, economic, political, and cultural changes that accompanied colonization occurred, we are becoming increasingly aware that these processes, although related, did not necessarily vary "rhythmically," i.e., at the same rate,[5] and that the rates of change varied not only between countries but also between regions of the same country. If we conceive the original African societies as sets of values, norms, and structures, it is evident that they survived to a significant extent everywhere, even where their existence was not legally recognized as in the most extreme cases of direct rule. Furthermore, the new set of values, norms, and structure, which constituted an incipient national center, did not necessarily grow at the expense of the older ones, as if it were a constant-sum game in which the more a country becomes "modern" the less it remains "traditional."

Although many individuals left the country for the new towns, they did not necessarily leave one society to enter a new one; instead, the behavior of a given individual tended to be governed by norms from both sets which defined his multiple roles and even mixed to define a particular role. Because the new center had nowhere expanded sufficiently at the time of independence, we cannot characterize what is contained within these countries today as a single society in the normally accepted sociological sense of the word, with its connotation of a relatively integrated system of values, norms, and structures. But since the new African states in reality do provide territorial containers for two sets of values, norms, and structures, the "new" and the "residual," with the latter itself usually subdivided into distinct sub-sets, it is useful to think of these sets as forming a particular type of *unintegrated* society which can be called "syncretic." [6]

The syncretic character of contemporary African societies tends to be reflected in every sphere of social activity, including the political. If we seek to identify their political systems by asking how values are authoritatively allocated within these societies, it is evident that in every case the most visible structures and institutions with which political scientists normally deal, such as executive and legislative bodies, political parties and groups, the apparatus of territorial administration, the judiciary, and even the institutions of local government provided by law, deal with only a portion of the total allocative activity, and that the remainder must therefore be allocated by other means, by other structures. This is fairly obvious where some functional division of labor between "modern" and "traditional" institutions was provided for initially as part of the constitutional settlement at the time of independence, but it is equally the case where traditional political structures have no recognized legal or political standing, or even where they have been formally abolished, as in Guinea or Mali.[7]

Without denying important variations in the degree of institutionalization of national centers in different countries, it is suggested that from the present vantage point, even the most prominent variations in political arrangements at the time of independence must be viewed as superficial features of the political system since they were never firmly institutionalized. An examination of political parties, the best studied feature of the African scene, reveals such a wide gap between the organization model from which the leaders derived their inspiration and their capacity to implement such schemes, that the very use by observers of the word "party" to characterize such structures involves a dangerous reification.

These comments may be extended to include constitutional arrangements, which in the absence of anchorage in supporting norms and institutions had little reality beyond their physical existence as a set of written symbols deposited in a government archive; about the civil service, in which the usual bureaucratic norms are so rare that it is perhaps better to speak of "government employees" as a categoric group; of "trade unions," which are more by way of congeries of urban employed and unemployed intermittently mobilized for a temporary purpose, such as a street demonstration; and even of "the Army," which far from being a model of hierarchical organization, tends to be an assemblage of armed men who may or may not obey their officers. It is generally evident that the operations of even the most "modern" institutions in Africa are governed by values and norms that stem from both the "new" and the "residual" sets.

The societal environment shared by all the new African states thus imposes severe limits upon the range within which significant variations of regimes can take place. Whether we define political integration in terms of the existence of a political formula which bridges the gap between the elite and the masses, or in terms of linkages between the values, norms, and structures that constitute the political system, it is clear that the level of political integration was, at the time of the founding, very low throughout Africa.

Hence, although we can refer to the existence of "states" and "regimes" in Africa, we must be careful not to infer from these labels that their governments necessarily have authority over the entire country, any more than we can safely infer from the persistence of these countries as sovereign entities proof of the operations of endogenous factors such as a sense of community and the ability of authorities to enforce cohesion against people's will. Persistence may only reflect the initial inertia which keeps instruments of government inherited from the colonial period going, as well as the inertia of claimants which assures in most cases that all the problems will not reach the center simultaneously; it

may reflect also the absence of effective external challenges and even to a certain extent the protection provided by the contemporary international system which more often than not guarantees the existence of even the weakest of sovereign states born out of the decolonization of tropical Africa.

Under these generally shared circumstances, it is not surprising that the founding fathers of most African states behaved very much in the same way in order to achieve the dual goal of modernizing as rapidly as possible while maintaining themselves in office. Like any other government, they had to cope with the problem of managing the flow of demands while at the same time eliciting sufficient support. They could obtain support in exchange for the satisfaction of demands (distribution); they could enhance support on the basis of the internalization by a sufficiently large proportion of the population of a belief in their right to rule (socialization, legitimacy); they could suppress demands by negative reinforcement, while at the same time punishing non-support (coercion and force). In the face of overwhelming problems stemming from the syncretic character of the society they relied increasingly on the latter techniques, thus contributing substantially to the escalation of political conflict.

Initially, the founding fathers of African states benefited from the sudden creation of a multitude of new political offices, from the departure of a number of colonial officials, from the expansion of administrative and state-directed economic activity which had begun during the latter years of welfare-state colonialism, as well as from a prevalent sense that they had earned the right to rule through their leadership of protest movements and that they were the legitimate successors of colonial officials. On these foundations, many were able to construct adequate political machines based primarily on the distribution of benefits to individual and group claimants, in the form of shifting coalitions appearing either as a "multi-party system" or, more commonly, as a "unified" party.

In the light of the politicians' inability to maintain themselves in office for very long (except in a very few cases) and of the lurid revelations of their corruption and ineptitude which made headlines after their downfall, it is easy to forget that many of them were initially quite successful in developing symbols and organizations which could be used to channel support and to establish the legitimacy of their claim to rule in the eyes of their countrymen. Beyond this, they also benefited from the sort of inertia already referred to, whereby those individuals who were aware of the existence of country-wide political institutions simply accepted them as a continuation of what they were already used to, the colonial order, but with a welcome populist flavor. The inheritance of instruments of force (police, gendarmerie, small armies), usually among the more professionalized bodies and often under the continued supervision of European officers, provided a certain backing in case the political process failed.

THE SHIFT FROM POWER TO FORCE

The shift to a new phase of political activity is related to two sets of mutually reinforcing factors, stemming from the interaction of the rulers with the syncretic society in which they operated. First, there was a growing gap between the leaders' ideological aspirations and their capacity to implement the policies these aspirations entailed. Whether or not it is appropriate to speak of a "revolution of rising expectations" throughout the continent, there is little doubt that such a revolution has occurred among those responsible for government, in the form of a commitment to rapid modernization.

The most obvious examples here are the "mobilizing" states, such as Ghana (until 1966), Mali, or Guinea, in which this commitment was defined in a very specific manner to include the transformation of the syncretic society into a homogeneous society by eliminating the "residual" set of values, norms, and structures and institutionalizing the new set according to ideological directives; the creation of an all-pervasive state apparatus, including both an all-encompassing mass party which could function as a controlling organization in the Leninist sense and as an aggregative organization, and an effective Africanized bureaucracy; and a planned economy geared to the achievement of very high increase in the rate of total output, as well as economic self-sufficiency in which the State plays the dominant role. Whether or

not they espoused "socialism" in this form, most other African leaders shared these aspirations, albeit in some modified form.

Since African countries are farther behind with respect to most of these goals than any other set of countries in the world, however, the result is that governments with the lowest load capability have assumed the heaviest burdens. But in the process of trying to raise the capability of their governments to achieve these goals, African rulers frittered away their small initial political capital of legitimacy, distributive capacity, inertia and coercion by investing it in non-essential undertakings, much as many of them did in the economic sector. A major source of the vulnerability of African regimes thus stems from adherence to self-imposed ideological directives.

Secondly, even if properly allocated this capital was seldom adequate to deal with political difficulties stemming from the very character of the syncretic society, the circumstances of decolonization, and the characteristics of the new institutions themselves. This was most obvious in the case of the Congo, where challenges stemming from every direction occurred simultaneously and most dramatically within a few weeks after independence. Although elsewhere the challenges have been less extreme and have usually been spaced over a few years, while the countervailing power and force at the disposal of the government was somewhat greater, their cumulative impact has not necessarily been much less severe.

Everywhere, African governments have been faced with some or all of the consequences of the politicization of residual cleavages which occurred in the course of the rapid extension of political participation prior to independence; and of an inflationary spiral of demands stemming from the very groups whose support is most crucial for the operations of government. Since these processes are often discussed in the literature, only their major features will be noted here.

The Politicization of Primordial Ties [8]

Pre-existing distinctions between groups in Africa were usually supplemented by others stemming from the uneven impact of European-generated change. Often, by the time of independence, one tribe or group of tribes had become more urban, more educated, more Christian and richer than others in the country. Hence, at the mass level, old and new cleavages tend to be consistent rather than cross-cutting; camps are clear-cut and individuals can engage wholeheartedly in the disputes that occur; almost any issue can precipitate a severe conflict; the history of conflict itself tends to make the next occurrence more severe; with few intervening layers of community organization, even localized conflicts rapidly reach the center.

These conflicts tend to be particularly severe where there is an asymmetry between the old and the new stratification system within a single society or between complementary societies, as when for some reason serfs become more educated than their masters or when their greater number becomes a source of political power at the time universal suffrage is introduced.

At the level of the modernizing leadership, recruitment is usually uneven, but nevertheless open to a certain extent to the various groups in the country; common life-experiences insure a certain degree of solidarity which provides off-setting cross-cutting affiliations; and ethnic ties make an important contribution to national integration by preventing the formation of the sharp elite-mass gap that is common in peasant societies. But there is always a very great strain on the solidarity of the modernizing leadership because, regardless of their ideological orientation, political entrepreneurs who seek to establish or maintain a following must necessarily rely on primordial ties to distinguish between "us" and "them."

When it appeared that the shape of the polity was being settled rapidly, perhaps once and for all, a multitude of groups began to press their legitimate claims for the protection of their way of life, for a redefinition of the relationship between their own peripheral society and the center, and for a more satisfactory distribution of benefits. Many latent disputes were revived and flowed into the new arena provided by central institutions.

Hence it is not surprising that even in countries where one party seemed to be solidly established the leadership felt that their country was less integrated than ever before. Where several ethnic-regional movements vied for power, and especially where participation was extended very suddenly,

the consequences of these cleavages and ensuing conflicts upon the center were even more disturbing.[9]

In general, almost any difference between two groups can become politically significant, even if from the point of view of the ethnographer the two groups belong to the same cultural classification. Although each of the oppositions tends to involve but a small proportion of the total population, because of the very nature of the groups involved, many permutations are possible and contagion can set in. Suitable institutional arrangements, such as various forms of territorial federalism, proportional or communal representation, and institutional quotas, are not easily designed in situations where primordial identities are as numerous and fluid as they are in most of the countries under consideration.

The Inflation of Demands

The second major source of challenge involves three crucial categories of individuals: civilian employees of government, men in uniform, and youths. Government employees, who include not only professional civil servants but also a large number of low-level, unskilled clerical personnel and manual workers employed in the operation of the governmental infrastructure (railways, harbors, road maintenance, and public work generally), usually constitute a very large proportion of those gainfully employed outside of agriculture. Promotions were initially rapid because of Africanization and the expansion of government agencies; and many programs of economic development have had as their major consequence a reallocation of national revenue to the benefit of the managers, including both government employees and politicians; and government employees often constitute in terms of income and prestige the most privileged group in the society, after the politicians themselves.

Yet, these same factors have contributed to a process of acute relative deprivation. Because of their very occupation and training, government employees have internalized to a greater extent than most others the style of life of their European predecessors; they feel that on the grounds of native ability and training they are qualified to rule rather than merely to execute policies; rapid promotions only lead to higher aspirations among those who have already been promoted and among those left behind, while the rate of governmental expansion tapers off soon after independence.

During the colonial period, government employees who vented their grievances against their employer were "good nationalists"; as they continue to do so after independence, they are a "selfish privileged class." The deterioration in the relationship between government employees and the politicians is relatively independent of the ideological orientation of the regime itself: in most of French-speaking Africa, government employees are "leftists" in relation to whatever the government's orientation happens to be at a given time; but in Ghana, under Nkrumah, civil servants constituted a sort of "rightist" opposition to the regime. Since personnel expenditures constitute as much as two-thirds or more of the government's annual expenditures, any demands that require translation into resource allocation tend to create a major financial crisis.

The grievance orientation toward government extends also to those employed in the private sector, since even in countries that are not nominally "socialist," étatisme prevails; the private industrial or commercial sector is closely regulated since major firms usually operate on the basis of government guarantees concerning manpower costs. So much of the workers' real income takes the form of benefits rather than money wages (family allocations, housing, etc.) that any sort of collective bargaining usually involves a modification of rules governing labor and leads to a showdown between the government and the unions.

Finally, a similar process prevails among cash-crop farmers, for example, since marketing operations are managed or at least closely regulated by government. Demands in this sector are therefore necessarily and automatically "political," and governments are even viewed as responsible for controlling the fluctuations of world markets for tropical commodities, over which most of them have but a very limited leverage.

Men in uniform tend to act very much like other government employees. In the absence of institutionalized values and norms which transform men in uniform into a military establishment and a police force, officers and men are ruled by the norms that prevail among other groups;

hence what has been said above applies to them as well. Furthermore, they rapidly find out that by virtue of their organizational characteristics and their control of certain instruments of force, they are indeed the best organized trade union in the country. As I shall point out below, this is not the only factor which has led the military to intervene in African politics; but it has helped set the mood for certain types of interventions and for the general relationship between the military and civilian politicians.[10]

As Lucian Pye has noted, "The non-Western political process is characterized by sharp differences in the political orientation of the generations," primarily because of a "lack of continuity in the circumstances under which people are recruited to politics." [11] In most African countries, it was easy for a particular age-cohort to move from relatively modest positions in the occupational structure to the highest positions in both the polity and the economy. Within a single decade, clerks and elementary school teachers became Presidents, cabinet ministers, members of party executives, directors of large trading establishments, etc. But for the next generations, whose expectations are based on the experience of their predecessors, conditions have fundamentally changed. First of all, the uppermost positions have already been filled by relatively young men who see no precise time limit to their tenure. Secondly, men with some education and occupational qualifications have rapidly become much less scarce because of the huge growth of secondary and higher education during the post-World War II decade. Thus, there has been a manifold increase in supply while the demand has abruptly decreased.

The result is that newer generations face an insurmountable glut which frustrates their aspirations, with very few opportunities for movement into alternative spheres of activity.[12] Hence, the intergenerational gap within the political sphere can be noticed in almost every other institutional sphere, including especially the civil service and the military. It is exacerbated by the fact that the newer generations are usually in fact better trained and more highly qualified than their predecessors and hence have a very legitimate claim to take their place.

In concluding this brief review of the

consequences of the politicization of residual cleavages and of the inflationary spiral of demands voiced by crucial groups in the society, it is important to note that the two processes are seldom insulated from each other. Government employees, soldiers, or young men in the towns are *also* members of ethnic groups; yet, these several affiliations do not constitute the sort of web of group affiliation characteristic of "pluralist" societies. Hence, the two processes reinforce each other to produce recurrent, serious, and complex conflicts, which easily penetrate into the political arena because of the weakness of aggregative structures. But even if they do not immediately result in an increase in demands or in a withdrawal of support, they constitute serious disturbances from the point of view of governments engaged in building a nation since by their very existence they provide evidence that this goal has not been achieved.

The added weight contributed by these processes to the burdens of government is relatively independent of the wisdom or devotion of particular political leaders, factors which will not be considered here. The difficulties of government in syncretic societies are so great, however, that the marginal consequences of human error, of weakness, and of sheer roguery—whose incidence among African politicians may be assumed to be about the same as among equivalent men elsewhere—are vastly magnified.

For example, corruption among government officials, which probably did not interfere with the industrial take-off of European countries or the United States (and perhaps even facilitated it), can have very damaging consequences where it diverts a large proportion of very scarce, non-expanding resources, away from the public domain into the pockets of a non-productive bureaucratic bourgeoisie. Impatience and arbitrary actions, which elsewhere may only lead to the discrediting of a public figure and to personal tragedy, can become sparks which ignite a major conflict.

Within a few years the two types of challenges discussed above strained the restricted distributive potential of the new governments and rapidly undermined the limited legitimacy of the founders. The center's weakness, hitherto hidden from sight, was unmercifully exposed, as when the value of the currency issued by a national banking system is drastically reduced when the credit pyramid, itself based on the productivity of the economy, collapses.[13]

In the new situation, demands are expressed more vociferously; depositors knock down the gatekeepers and seek to invade the vault. Parsons has suggested that the system's response can be twofold: "First, an increasingly stringent scale of priorities of what can and cannot be done will be set up; second, increasingly severe negative sanctions for non-compliance with collective decisions will be imposed." [14] Political power, normally based on the overall social structure, gives way to force.

Although no African rulers ever abandoned completely their reliance on the techniques of machine politics to maintain themselves in office, illustrations of a trend toward the use of force abound and constitute by now a monotonous recitation of unpleasant but familiar facts of African political life: intimidation, exile, detention, or assassination of political opponents; modification of the electoral system to make competition either impossible or at least very costly to those who attempt to engage in it; reduction of the independence of the judiciary or creation side-by-side with it of dependable political courts; redefinition of loyalty into unquestioning obedience and sycophancy; use of the military, of the police, and of political thugs to bulldoze dissidents into passivity, and passives into demonstrative supporters; creation of additional quasi-military or quasi-police bodies to offset the questionable loyalty of the existing ones. Although coups which result in changes of government have attracted the most attention, the most frequent coups in Africa have probably been those initiated by an incumbent government against threatening individuals or groups (real or alleged), and those launched by rulers or dominant factions against their associates.

Beyond its immediate unfortunate consequences for the individuals affected, the shift from power to force as a technique of government has serious long-term consequences for political life more generally in that it serves as the prelude to antigovernment coups and revolutions, in the following manner:

(a) In the process of shifting from power to force, governments tend to become over-confident in their ability to reduce the disturbing flow of demands by dealing harshly with their source. They become afraid that any concession might be interpreted as weakness and open up a Pandora's box of claims. Hence, less change occurs altogether. Governments become less adept at discriminating among danger signals and tend to deal with even the smallest disturbances by expending a great deal of force.[15] But since the capital of force is small it becomes rapidly used up in relatively unnecessary undertakings, thus increasing the government's vulnerability to more serious threats.

(b) When a shift from power to force occurs, it is accompanied by a change in the relative market value of existing structures. In the case of the new African states, the relative value of political parties and of civilian administrative agencies has undergone a sort of deflation, while the value of the police, of the military, and of *any* organization capable of exercising force, even by the sheer manipulation of large numbers of people in demonstrations and civil disobedience actions, has been vastly increased.

(c) Although the shift to force represents an attempt to overcome deteriorating legitimacy and inadequate power, paradoxically it enhances the problem of the legitimacy of the rulers in the eyes of those to whom the implementation of force must necessarily be entrusted. As Parsons has indicated: "Most important, whatever the physical technology involved, a critical factor in socially effective force is always the social organization through which it is implemented. There is always some degree of dependence on the loyalties of the relevant personnel to the elements of the social structure ostensibly controlling them." [16] Attempts to balance one instrument of force which is thought to be unreliable by creating another merely modifies the problem of control of force by political means, but does not eliminate it. In fact, resort to this technique may exacerbate the very problem it seeks to overcome by antagonizing individuals identified with the relevant institution.

(d) When individuals and groups are deprived of the right and opportunity of exercising power to express their demands, they have no choice but to submit to force or use it themselves to express their demands. But when the government's capital of force is discovered to be limited, the latter alternative tends to be frequently chosen. Furthermore, since authority is personalized and the government is committed to a rigid course, specific demands tend to be translated into demands for a general change of rulers.

It is within the context of this inter-relationship between governments who rely on force and the remainder of the society that the growing frequency of military and civilian coups, successful or unsuccessful; of mutinies, large-scale and prolonged urban strikes or rural disturbances; of near-civil wars, insurrections, and revolutionary-minded movements, must be understood.

THE COUP AS A POLITICAL INSTITUTION

The coup can be viewed as an institutionalized pattern of African politics on statistical grounds since in recent years it has become the modal form of governmental and regime change.[17] More significantly, however, the coup is a normal consequence of the showdown between a government and its opponents who use force against each other in a situation where the force at the disposal of the government is very limited. This condition, which is met in most African countries, is most important because it distinguishes the conflict situation that tends to lead to a coup from others which tend to develop into some form of internal war as the result of extensive mobilization of support by both sides. In Africa, the government usually falls too soon for this to occur; there is some evidence that governments even prefer dissolving themselves to fighting. Coups determine who will rule, at least temporarily, but do not in themselves affect the fundamental character of the society or of its political system. The scope of the conflict is limited in relation to the society as a whole. Coups may be accompanied by some brutality but seldom entail more strategic forms of violence. . . .

FORCE AS AN INSTRUMENT
OF MAJOR POLITICAL CHANGE

Both the ins and the outs in Africa have also attempted to use force in order to achieve more fundamental changes including the modification of political communities, the alteration of important aspects of the stratification system, and the transformation of regimes (in Easton's sense of "regularized method for ordering political relationships"). These attempts may be initiated by the original founders, by new governments resulting from successful coups, or by alternative elites who seek to construct a competing system of authority while the government they oppose is still in place. Since these attempts usually involve the mobilization of extensive support, they tend to lead to an enlargement of the scope of conflict and may entail more strategic forms of violence. Except in a few specific situations [discussed in the original article], force fails to bring about major political change in Africa. In particular, political revolutions are unlikely to succeed because they entail prerequisites which are absent from the syncretic societies of contemporary Africa. . . .

CONCLUSIONS

Seeking to overcome the parochialism of area studies and the intellectual irrelevance of raw empiricism, many scholars dealing with the politics of new states have hit upon the device of bringing the foreground of the contemporary scene into sharp focus, extracting it from context, and blowing up the recorded image for leisurely contemplation. The background tends to be reduced to an indistinct blur called "tradition," which is discarded because it yields little interesting information. But vastly blown-up stills of political development, modernization, or integration obtained in this manner tend to make these processes appear similar regardless of what is being developed, modernized, or integrated.

One wonders, however, whether the similarities genuinely stem from the phenomena observed or whether they are artifacts arising from the manipulation of the recorded images; whether the information on which many current generalizations are based pertains to the reality the image sought to capture, or whether it pertains mainly to the characteristics of the lens and of the film used to record it.

Surely, as we begin to explore an unknown world, we must master the techniques of cinéma-vérité, using hand-held cameras that are a more direct extension of the observer's eye, suitable for obtaining intimate moving pictures of the varying patterns subsumed under the terms political development, modernization or integration. Understanding of these processes will be achieved, not by reducing them prematurely to a common denominator, but by seeking to preserve their singularity and then comparing their manifestations in different settings.

The characteristics of political life in all the new states can easily be subsumed under relatively few general headings. However useful such efforts may be in clearing the ground, however, we must remember that the same headings will refer to very different things where, for example, national communities are being carved out of a more universal one and the stratification system is defined by an opposition between urban elites that control land and peasant masses, as against situations where many small societies devoid of this sharp differentiation are being amalgamated into arbitrarily defined larger wholes under the aegis of an open stratum of recently educated men drawn more or less evenly from the component societies that constitute the country.

The situation in most of tropical Africa is so extreme that studies focused primarily on incipient central institutions almost necessarily exaggerate their importance in relation to the society as a whole.[18] Hence, I have tried in this essay to provide some balance by considering politics in the more general context of African societies and by focusing on conflict as a major element of political life. This is not to say that no institutionalization is taking place, but rather that until such processes reach a certain level—as yet unspecified—force and violence are likely to remain salient features of political action.[19] Since various factors insure the persistence of most of the new territorial units even if political institutionalization does not occur at a very high rate, we must make a place for conflict in our conceptual apparatus. Although the incidence of certain manifestations of conflict may be relatively random, political conflict is not a random process but derives a discernible structure from the characteristics of the society itself, as do other patterns of political life. Much more precision can be achieved than in this essay by operationalizing independent and dependent variables in a manner to obtain elements from which a comparative typology can be constructed.

From this point of view, it is clear that a small number of countries, e.g., the Ivory Coast and Ghana, stand out from the rest of the pack and are on the verge of reaching a threshold of societal development which may be labeled "incipient modernity." These are exceptional in the contemporary African scene, and are likely to become even more exceptional in the predictable future as the spillover effects of incipient modernization become infused into every sphere of social life, including the political.

At the other extreme, there is a fairly large group of countries, such as the Central African Republic or Upper Volta, which are among the least developed countries in the entire world. Unfortunately, they are likely to remain at the bottom for a long time, since it has become increasingly evident that the die was cast several decades ago in the sense that wherever there was *some* potential for relatively rapid modernization, it was brought out during the colonial period.

In between are countries with some potential but with a complex of problems which has so far prevented it from emerging. Some of these will join the first group, while the others will, unfortunately, join the second. It is not necessary to view politics as merely epiphenomenal to suggest that the general characteristics of the social structure, and especially the nature of primordial solidarities combined with gross differences in degree of modernization, impose limits within which variations of regime can occur.

Although the relationship between political conflict and political development has not been explicitly examined in this essay, this does not imply that I view the functions of conflict in a society as wholly negative. Integration into a free society does not entail the total elimination of conflict from political life, but rather its containment within acceptable limits as indicated by a shift from force to power and authority.[20]

How that is achieved remains a central problem of the social sciences which far transcends the parochial concerns of particular disciplines or of sub-fields within each. One thing is clear, however: Progress in this direction requires an acceptance of the premise itself—the institutionalization at the cultural level of a belief that conflict is a potentially manageable aspect of society, rather than the persistence of wishful thinking about its permanent disappearance expressed in the form of ideologies or scientific theories.

1. The category "new states of tropical Africa" excludes Liberia and Ethiopia.

2. Rudolf Arnheim, *Art and Visual Perception: A Psychology of the Creative Eye* (Berkeley and Los Angeles: University of California Press, 1965), p. 230.

3. Notions concerning the political system apparent in this paper are inspired by the works of David Easton, but clearly lack the intellectual rigor of *A Systems Analysis of Political Life* (New York: John Wiley and Sons, 1965).

4. For the concepts used see Edward Shils, "Centre and Periphery," in *The Logic of Personal Knowledge—Essays in Honor of Michael Polanyi* (London: Routledge & Kegan Paul, 1961), pp. 117–130. See also n. 18, below.

5. See the discussion in C. S. Whitaker, Jr., "A Dysrhythmic Process of Political Change," *World Politics,* 19 (January, 1967), 190–217.

6. The problem with which I am dealing here is akin to that of the "plural society" conceptualized by M. G. Smith in *The Plural Society in the British West Indies* (Berkeley and Los Angeles: University of California Press, 1965). The word "syncretic" distinguishes the present societies from the "plural," which is a particular type involving superordination between components. I prefer it to the more passive "heterogeneous," because "syncretic" connotes that a process of amalgamation and integration is being attempted.

7. For a further development of this point, see my book *Creating Political Order: The Party-States of West Africa* (Chicago: Rand McNally, 1966), chap. V. My reasoning here is deductive; but empirical evidence from micro-political studies of Ghana by David Brokensha and Ernst Benjamin, of Mali by Nicholas Hopkins, and of Tanzania by Henry Bienen, confirm the validity of the assumption.

8. For a general treatment of this topic, see Clifford Geertz, "The Integrative Revolution," in Clifford Geertz (ed.), *Old Societies and New States* (New York: The Free Press of Glencoe, 1963), pp. 105–157. Although every serious monograph on African politics has also dealt with the subject, it is unfortunate that no effort has been made to refine for Africa the comparative analysis of the phenomenon along the lines suggested by Geertz.

9. I have attempted to deal with this question in *One-Party Government in the Ivory*

Coast (Princeton: Princeton University Press, 1964), pp. 47, 77, 128–134.

10. The most useful recent surveys of African military establishments are presented in the publications of the Institute of Strategic Studies, London. See in particular, M. J. V. Bell, "Army and Nation in Sub-Saharan Africa," *Adelphi Papers,* No. 21 (August, 1965); and David Wood, "The Armed Forces of African States," *Adelphi Papers,* No. 27 (April, 1966). For an earlier essay, see James S. Coleman and Belmont Bryce, Jr., "The Role of the Military in Sub-Saharan Africa," in John J. Johnson (ed.), *The Role of the Military in Underdeveloped Countries* (Princeton: Princeton University Press, 1962), pp. 359–405.

11. Lucian Pye, "The Non-Western Political Process," in H. Eckstein and D. Apter (eds.), *Comparative Politics* (New York: The Free Press of Glencoe, 1963), p. 660.

12. On patterns of recruitment of new elites and their consequences see Remi Clignet and Philip Foster, *The Fortunate Few* (Evanston: Northwestern University Press, 1966).

13. The analogy is drawn from Talcott Parsons, "Some Reflections on the Place of Force in Social Process," in Harry Eckstein (ed.), *Internal War* (New York: The Free Press of Glencoe, 1964), pp. 59–64. A similar analysis is provided by Martin Kilson in *Political Change in a West African State: A Study of the Modernization Process in Sierra Leone* (Cambridge: Harvard University Press, 1966), with emphasis on the initial growth of "reciprocity" and the eventual inadequacy of this political technique.

14. Parsons, *op. cit.,* p. 64.

15. This proposition is related to Apter's suggestion that there is "an inverse relationship between information and coercion in a system." See David E. Apter, *The Politics of Modernization* (Chicago: University of Chicago Press, 1965), p. 40.

16. Parsons, *op. cit.,* p. 66.

17. It is difficult to analyze the patterns of coups because it is impossible to identify the components of the universe with which one must deal. If incumbent rulers are to be believed, attempted coups against the government are extremely frequent in almost every African country; but what appear to be anti-government plots may in fact be only government-initiated purges.

18. For example, the most recently compiled *Selected Economic Data for the Less Developed Countries,* published by the Agency for International Development in June, 1967 (data from 1965 and 1966), shows that Africa (not including the United Arab Republic and the Union of South Africa) is the lowest ranking of four areas (Africa, East Asia, Latin America, Near East/South Asia) on total GNP, Annual Growth of GNP, electric power per capita, life expectancy, people per physician, literacy, pupils as percent of population. It was tied with one other area for bottom place on several other indicators, and ranked relatively high only on acres of agricultural land available per capita.

19. An approach to the study of institutionalization and integration is suggested in my paper, "Patterns of Integration," in *The Journal of Modern African Studies* (1968), pp. 449–467.

20. This view is inspired by Ralf Dahrendorf, *Class and Class Conflict in Industrial Society* (Stanford: Stanford University Press, 1959), especially p. 318. See also my general argument in *Creating Political Order: The Party-States of West Africa, op. cit.*

GROUP INTERESTS IN PAKISTAN POLITICS, 1947–1958

TALUKDER MANIRUZZAMAN
Rajshahi University, Bangla Desh

Recent American literature on political science is replete with studies with the "interest-group" focus as "the key to the systematic understanding of political systems anywhere."[1] Following Arthur F. Bentley's "attempt to fashion a tool" in his

From *Pacific Affairs* (Summer 1966), pp. 83–98. Reprinted by permission. Some sections have been omitted.

book *The Process of Government,* first published in 1908, recent writers like David B. Truman, Earl Latham and others have tried to explain the governmental process as the interactions of contending groups.[2] The classic formulation of the theory came in Latham's words: "The legislature referees the group struggle, ratifies the victories of successful coalitions, and records the terms of surrenders, compromises, and conquests in the form of statutes. . . . Public policy is actually the equilibrium in the group struggle at any given moment and it represents the balance which the contending factions of our groups constantly strive to weigh in their favor." [3]

The limitations of group theory even for the study of the American political system, where group processes are more visible than in any other system, have already been pointed out by many political scientists. As Oliver Garceau says, case-studies of particular policy-formations show that "the interplay of forces pictured in these is strikingly more complex than that produced by studies focussed on the parallelogram of interest pressures." [4] La Palombara, while trying to apply group-theory to the Italian political system, found this "simplistic theory" of limited value. He came to the conclusion that (1) "except at a level of abstractions that renders it both useless and dangerous for empirical research, a general theory does not exist; and (2) it is necessary to examine some middle-range propositions about interest groups in order to ascertain if the interest-group focus has any utility at all for the construction of a general theory of politics." [5]

Whether a general theory of politics on the basis of interplay of interest-groups can be constructed or not, the "group" concept is a valuable tool which helps the political analyst go beyond formal institutions to locate the real sources of power. In any society, economically powerful groups come to acquire political power and political and economic power generally tend to be coterminous.[6] Dispersion of political power thus becomes possible only when there is wide dispersion of economic power.

In West Pakistan two economically powerful groups were the landlords and the business group. Political power came to be concentrated in these two groups. In East Pakistan, with the abolition of landlordism after the passage of the East Bengal Land Acquisition Act in 1951 and because of the absence of a strong business group, power came into the hands of the professional middle class. The power struggle in Pakistan accordingly took place between the business-landlord combination of the West and the professional middle-class group in East Pakistan.

[Prior to land reform in the East,] 75 per cent of the land, including all the biggest *Zamindari* holdings, belonged to the Hindu rajas, some of them possessing as much as 750,000 acres of land.[7] They were mostly absentee landlords with residences in Calcutta. The Muslim League Assembly Party in East Pakistan was drawn from the Muslim middle class and the Assembly passed the East Pakistan Estate Acquisition and Tenancy Bill in 1950 in the face of strong opposition from the Hindu Congress Party and fixed the ceiling of land at 33 acres per head.[8] [Enforcement was delayed] "because certain reactionary elements again came into play behind the scenes and sought to keep East Pakistan's progressive legislation a dead letter." [9] [But] East Pakistan by 1956–57 came to be freed from the feudal grip.

The situation was entirely different in West Pakistan. . . . Taking the whole of West Pakistan into consideration, about 0.1 percent of the total landowners, that is, about six thousand people, owned land to the extent of five hundred acres or more.[10] [Their holdings made up 15 percent of the total acreage in West Pakistan, the same amount as was owned by the 64.5 percent of owners with *five* acres or less.]

Because of their economic dependence on the landlords, tenants in West Pakistan were at the beck and call of the *Zamindars.*[11] The result was that elections became a meaningless formalism, the tenants voting at the bidding of their landlords. The West Pakistan Assembly became the cockpit of rival landlord groups and one observer rightly suggested that the "key to Pakistan politics is to be found in a little official publication for restricted circulation by the Government of India before 1914 and entitled *The Landed Families of the Punjab.*" [12]

In the provincial elections in 1951 in the former Punjab about 80 percent of the members elected were landlords. In the Sind elections in 1953 not a single *Hari* (landless peasant) was elected and about 90 percent of the members of the Sind Assembly came from large landowning families. Out of a total of 40 members from West Pakistan in the (Second) Constituent Assembly, the landlord group comprises 28 members.[13] Such dominance by the landlords in West Pakistan as well as in central politics prevented any real progress in land reforms in West Pakistan. . . .

Thus the landlords in West Pakistan successfully prevented all attempts to end feudalism until October 1958. But their role in Pakistan's politics was much broader than the mere preservation of their lands. First, because of the differing systems of land tenure, any partnership between East and West Pakistani politicians became precarious. . . . As the rival groups were more or less in agreement in retaining their landed interest, politics in West Pakistan became more a cynical pursuit of sheer power than a way of implementing social and economic policies for the transformation of the country. The entire political process at the Center and in East Pakistan was thereby affected and the political debate was deflected from economic issues to non-economic ones like the Islamic state and electoral controversies. . . .

As for business groups, at the time of independence Pakistan had only a few industries and about half of those were controlled by Hindus, the government, or by foreigners. The contribution of industry to the total national income was barely 1 percent in 1947. By 1959 industry's contribution to a much larger national income was over 6 percent. Industrial assets had increased ninefold and value added was more than tenfold. Private firms owned by Muslims controlled two-thirds of these new industries.[14]

The Government of Pakistan from the start offered various concessions to persons desirous of setting up new industries. It acquired land through the Land Acquisition Act for prospective industrialists at prices far below market rates and gave various types of tax concessions to new industrialists. The concessions were continued up to 1958.[15] Besides these government concessions "almost any industrialist

was guaranteed a profit, for imports offered little competition, domestic production was inadequate, and those able to import machinery were subsidized by undervalued foreign exchange." [16] In Government patronage, the prospect of high profits, and the sudden increase in economic opportunity brought into existence "a new, able, ruthless group of industrial entrepreneurs." [17] By 1956 these "robber barons" became powerful enough to influence government policy and even to bring about the fall of a Cabinet unresponsive to their pressure. [Here the author details business pressure group politics. Eds.]

In addition to the business interests, another important middle class group was the refugees from India. There were about eight million refugees in West Pakistan and one million in East Pakistan. There were at least twenty main refugee organizations in Karachi, three in Lahore, two in Peshawar, two in Hyderabad, one in Rawalpindi and three in East Pakistan.[18]

The government's policy was to settle agricultural refugees on evacuee land [left behind by Hindus who moved or fled to India] and urban refugees in the cities by the allotment of evacuee houses, shops and factories.[19] [However, evacuee land was mostly rented to refugees or taken over by local influential landlords in collusion with evacuee property officials.] In spite of [the law which gave proprietary rights to refugees], the recovery of the evacuee property proved difficult. The local landlords influenced the evacuee officials who declared the land held by the "locals" as nonevacuee.[20]

The vested interests scored a more direct victory in the case of urban evacuee property. The refugee leaders complained that 50 to 65 percent of evacuee shops and factories were usurped by the "locals." The industrialists (including the refugee industrialists) demanded that the evacuee property be auctioned and the proceeds given to the Refugee Compensation Pools. . . . [The law concerning this, passed in March, 1958] stipulated that the urban properties would be disposed of at "the prevailing market value" and that refugee claimants would get preference over other bidders.[21] As "the prevailing market value" would be highly inflated it was clear that the urban evacuee property would go into hands of the rich rather than the poor refugees. Thus again, the landlords and the industrialists were powerful enough to frustrate administrative policy and influence legislation to grab much of the evacuee property at the cost of the poorly organized refugees.

The influence of workers' and peasant groups was also small in comparison with the well-organized industrial groups. Because Pakistan was just developing her industries, the number of industrial workers was small. Accurate figures about the persons engaged as industrial workers are not available. The I.L.O. report of 1953 gave the figure as three million.[22] According to the *Population Census of Pakistan, 1961,* the non-agricultural labor force constituted 8.49 percent of the population.[23] But despite a steady increase in the number of industrial employees there was no corresponding increase in the membership of trade unions. Though total membership remained more or less the same, the number of unions increased.[24]

The result was a multiplicity of trade unions in each industry. The rivalry among the unions gave employers the opportunity to withhold recognition and deny the workers the right of collective bargaining and the unions in general "failed to achieve wage and welfare gains through collective bargaining, to maintain effective control of plant working conditions, or to discipline members into acceptance of decisions made between leaders and employees.[25] There were three All-Pakistan Labor Federations [which] were far from establishing a countervailing force to industrial power. Their influence on governmental policy was correspondingly weak. This is borne out by the fact that in spite of the anti-labor aspects of the Trade Unions Act of 1926, there was no improvement of the law.

The bulk of the labor force of the country, the agriculturalists, were even less organized.[26] In West Pakistan the domination of the feudal lords in economic and political life was so great that even the Deputy Commissioners and Superintendents of Police had to seek the patronage of feudal landlords to remain at one station.[27] . . . The large scale eviction of tenants by the landlords with the advent of the [Sahib regime] to power in West Pakistan created unrest among the evicted tenants in the former West Punjab. But the tenants could not get organized in the face of the repressive measures adopted by Dr. Khan Sahib's government.[28]

In East Pakistan in the absence of a powerful landlord group, the peasants had greater prospects for developing their organization. But the political parties there concerned themselves more with the urban areas. Only Maulana Bhashani tried to organize the peasants and formed the East Pakistan Peasants' Association. But its function was confined to convening three peasant conferences—at Bogra, Sylhet and Dacca.[29] Maulana Bhashani used these conferences more as a demonstration of popular support for his demand of "provincial autonomy" than for representing peasant interests. . . .

From the discussion above, it is clear that the economically powerful landlords and business groups of West Pakistan had a dominating influence in Pakistan politics during the period 1947–1958. Although the landlords were not formally organized, they could easily get elected to political positions because of their control over the economic life of their tenants. Their influence on the political process was direct. They were part and parcel of the political establishment. The influence of the business group, on the other hand, was indirect. They were formally organized and they put effective pressure on the decision-making authorities from outside the governmental institutions.

The refugees had some representatives in the West Pakistan Assembly as well as in the central legislature. There were also some refugee organizations trying to influence government policy from outside but with only partial success. However, following the revolution in October, 1958, General Ayub's government recovered the illegally-held evacuee property under a Martial Law Regulation and distributed the recovered property among the refugee claimants. The majority of the refugees are now well settled and the refugees no longer exist as a separate interest group.[30]

The workers and peasants were practically unorganized and, until 1958, had virtually no influence on the government. But, under another Martial Law Regulation certain minimum standards of working conditions have been guaranteed. The workers and peasants, however, are still unorganized with little effective voice in the political process.

The landlords and the business groups remain powerful. Ayub's land reform was moderate in nature and did not materially affect the landed interest. The ceiling on land holdings was fixed at 500 acres of irrigated and 1,000 acres of unirrigated land.[31] But most of the land-owning families in West Pakistan distributed their surplus land among their relations and, as the limit of holdings was fixed in respect of individuals and not families, only five or six families were affected.[32] Thus there has been no basic change in the rights and conditions of tenants. Their economic life is still dominated by their landlords, who also control the present West Pakistan Assembly elected under the constitution of 1962.

The business groups have become even better organized. About 74 organizations of trade, commerce and industry are now affiliated with the All-Pakistan Federation of Chambers of Commerce and Industries. The federation is under the domination of a dozen big business houses of West Pakistan. It is the most powerful pressure group operating from outside formal government institutions. Its glossy journals preach the virtues of the free enterprise system. Its powerful lobby still continues to have an effective influence on the economic policy of the government.[33]

1. J. La Palombara, "The Utility and Limitations of Interest-Group Theory in Non-American Field Situations," *Journal of Politics*, Vol. 22, 1960, p. 29.

2. D. B. Truman, *The Governmental Process*. New York: Alfred A. Knopf, 1951; E. Latham, "The Group Basis of Politics: Notes for a Theory," *American Political Science Review*, Vol. 46, 1952, pp. 376–397; G. A. Almond, Rapporteur, "Research Note, A Comparative Study of Interest Groups and the Political Process," *American Political Science Review*, Vol. 52, 1958, pp. 270–282.

3. Latham, *op. cit.*, p. 390.

4. O. Garceau, "Interest Group Theory in Political Research," *The Annals of the American Academy of Political and Social Science*, Vol. 319, 1958, p. 107.

5. La Palombara, *op. cit.*, p. 30.

6. R. M. MacIver, *The Modern State*. London: Oxford University Press (reprint), 1932, pp. 291–301.

7. See F. K. Noon's speech in the Second Constituent Assembly in Feb. 14, 1956 (Second) *Constituent Assembly of Pakistan Debates,* Vol. I, p. 3056.

8. *Dawn* (Karachi), April 20, 1951.

9. Editorial, "The Problem of Problems," *Dawn,* April 20, 1951.

10. F. M. Ayub Khan, *Speeches and Statements.* Karachi: Pakistan Publications, June 1964, p. 50.

11. Masud's Minute of Dissent in the Hari Committee Report, quoted in the Constituent Assembly on Feb. 14, 1956, by Sheikh Mujibur Rahman (Second) *Constituent Assembly of Pakistan Debates,* Vol. I, p. 3060.

12. W. H. Morris-Jones, "Experience of Independence—India and Pakistan," *The Political Quarterly,* Vol. 29, 1958, p. 25.

13. The professional classification of the members of the (Second) Constituent Assembly was as follows:

	West Pakistan	East Pakistan
Landlords	28	0
Lawyers	3	20
Retired officials	5	9
Industry and commerce	4	3
Miscellaneous	0	8

SOURCE: M. Ahmad, *Government and Politics in Pakistan.* Karachi: Pakistan Publishing House, 2nd ed., March 1963, p. 115.

14. G. F. Papanek, "The Development of Entrepreneurship," *The American Economic Review,* LII, 1962, p. 49.

15. See Finance Minister Syed Amjad Ali's budget speech in the National Assembly on Feb. 19, 1957 reported in *Dawn,* February 20, 1957.

16. Papanek, *op. cit.*, p. 50.

17. It is significant that over half of the total private firms owned by the Muslims were controlled by five small "communities" of traditional traders totalling about one-half percent of the population. See Papanek, *op. cit.*, p. 54.

18. These were the main organizations as they were vocal in putting forward refugee demands and tried to influence legislation affecting refugee settlement when they were in the Committee stage.

19. *Report of Economic Appraisal Committee,* November 1952 (Revised February 1953).

20. *Dawn,* September 11, 1958.

21. See the proceedings of the National Assembly, March 12, 1958, reported in *Dawn,* March 13, 1958.

22. *Report of the I.L.O. Labour Survey Mission, 1952–1953.* Karachi: Government of Pakistan, Ministry of Labour, 1958, p. 98.

23. Bulletin No. 5, p. ix.

24. In 1951, 309 unions reported 393,137 members, while in 1957, 621 claimed 357,064. See S. C. Sufrin and S. A. Sarwar, *The Status of Trade Unionism in Pakistan,* Syracuse: Maxwell Graduate School, Syracuse University, 1962, p. 10.

25. *Ibid.,* p. 26. See also I.L.O. Survey, *op. cit.,* p. 98.

26. According to the official census of 1961, the agricultural labor force constituted 24.09 percent of the total population. *Population Census of Pakistan,* 1961, Census, Bulletin No. 5. Karachi: Office of the Census Commissioner, Home Affairs, Division, p. ix.

27. See Maulana Bhashani's statement on

his departure from Karachi after an extensive tour of West Pakistan, *Dawn,* June 11, 1958.

28. See *Dawn,* July 4, July 12, July 21, 1956.

29. *Ibid.,* May 21, 1957, March 4, 1958, September 29, 1958.

30. See editorial, "No More Refugees," *The Pakistan Observer,* Dacca, January 29, 1960.

31. Planning Commission, Government of Pakistan, *Survey of Land Reforms in Pakistan.* Karachi: Government of Pakistan Press, 1962, p. 4.

32. See Abdu Salam, "Of Men and Things," *The Pakistan Observer,* February 18, 1959.

33. See the special report, "Pre-Budget Moves by Big Business: Concession for the Rich," *Pakistan Observer,* June 7, 1964. See also Abu Mahmood, "Political Economy of Patronage," *ibid.,* July 13, 1964.

THE LATIN AMERICAN POLITICAL SYSTEM

CHARLES W. ANDERSON

University of Wisconsin

The problem of winning, consolidating, and maintaining political power is, of course, fundamental to the calculus of political prudence. Even in the most stable of political systems, assessment of the potential consequences of policy choice for future support is basic to the political craft. However, in Latin America, where few leaders can count on a guaranteed tenure in office to work out a strategy of governance, the weighing of potential effects of policy choices on political survival becomes a constant, day-to-day concern. Thus, in assessing the total rationality of development policy-making in Latin America, it becomes essential to devote some attention to the conditions under which political power is won and held in Latin America, and the characteristic ways in which Latin American statesmen cope with the problem of power. . . .

POWER CONTENDERS AND

POWER CAPABILITIES

LATIN AMERICAN POLITICS

The first proposition that must be specified concerning politics in most Latin American nations is that there is imperfect consensus on the nature of the political regime. This in itself is not surprising, nor does it pose an unusual or difficult problem for political analysis, as witness the capacity of Western political science to cope with the problem of imperfect consensus in such nations as France. Nonetheless, the question of regime consensus, or "legitimacy," has attracted a great deal of attention in much current writing on the politics of developing areas. Seymour Martin Lipset specifies political legitimacy as a critical variable in the process of political development.[1] Martin Needler has used the notion of legitimacy as a central concept in a discussion of political instability in Latin America.[2] However, to specify that a particular nation or region has failed to accept one set of institutions or processes as legitimate does not permit one to go much further until the sources and dimensions of that problem, and its particular impact on political life, have been designated and assessed.

To get to the heart of this matter in Latin America, one must shift perspective slightly from the usual development of the argument. Generally, discussions of legitimacy focus on the question of the acceptance of certain political institutions, or a certain locus of authority. In Latin America, however, the problem of legitimacy is very much a part of the political process itself, the way in which individuals and groups mobilize power within their society. For in Latin America, no particular techniques of mobilizing political power, no specific political resources, are deemed more appropriate to political activity than others. No specific sources of political power are legitimate for all contenders for power.

Of course, this is to some extent the case in every society, even those committed most strongly to one source of legitimate power. In the United States, whether we are disciples of C. Wright Mills or not, we recognize that possessors of certain power capabilities, control of legitimate force or economic wealth, for example, make or influence policy, despite the fact that democratic ideology prescribes the aggregation and mobilization of consent as the only legitimate means of structuring power relationships. However, in democratic society, the organization of consent according to prescribed norms is *generally* reinforced by possessors of other power capabilities, and in the long run, democratic processes serve as a sort of "court of last resort" in structuring power relationships. In contrast, in Latin America generally, democratic processes appear as an *alternative* to other means of mobilizing power. However, the point made should be clear, that in suggesting that no power capability is legitimate for all power contenders in Latin America, we are recognizing a difference of degree and not of kind, for the phenomenon applies to some extent in all political systems.

It will be noted that two new terms have been introduced into the discussion. This is not done out of any desire to create a new vocabulary, but to distinguish what is to be said from certain accepted uses of commonplace terms. Hence, a *contender for power* will be defined as any individual or group which seeks to have its demands implemented through state machinery, to control the allocation of values for the society through state machinery, or to make a specific source of power legitimate for the society through the exercise of a power capability. A *power capability* will be defined as a property of a group or individual that enables it to be politically influential, in other words, a political resource. Possession of a power capability is the price of admission to the political arena. Those who possess significant power capabilities will be "taken into account" when political decisions are made. [Here are listed examples of power capabilities and also of power contenders. These are quite consonant with the analysis we propose in terms of "resources" and "sectors"; so to minimize the proliferation of vocabulary, we have, with Professor Anderson's permission, omitted this list.]

Power contenders are also distinguished from power capabilities for another reason. Most conventional analysis of Latin American politics, by equating the two, assumes a unity of "interest" among the holders of a single power capability that is seldom the case.[3] By separating power contenders from power capabilities we avoid saying such things as "the military acts," or "the middle class supports," or "the urban mob or the terrorists are . . ." The use of such gross categories in all contemporary discussion of Latin American politics has led us to accept a rule of thumb theory which we all conventionally employ, but which is both imprecise and inaccurate. Hence, it seems more desirable to postulate a variety of power contenders using or competing for a similar power capability, and a political system that does not legitimate a single power capability, but includes a number of them.

At this point, it would be well to note that Latin American politics cannot be analyzed in terms of nationally self-contained systems. Certainly, foreign power contenders must be included in describing the patterns of alliance and conflict that make and unmake governments in the region. Again, we must distinguish the various power capabilities that serve as tickets of admission for these foreign contenders in the political process—economic assistance, military intervention, ideological influence, and so on. Considerable care must be taken in the units of analysis chosen to describe these foreign contenders. To discuss "United States influence" in Latin America is often quite imprecise when the Department of State, the Agency for International Development, the military, and private firms may be pursuing quite diverse political objectives, in patterns of coalition that include distinct domestic sets of power contenders. Similarly, to use "Communist influence" as a single, undivided unit of analysis is to employ a most blunt and imprecise unit of analysis. In dealing with both foreign and domestic contenders for power, one must bear in mind the coalitional character of Latin American politics. The statement that the United States or the Soviet Union "controls" a certain government or movement certainly distorts an intricate arrangement of political forces in which the foreign contender is one part of the political equation, but seldom plays an exclusive or totally definitive role.

If one insists on the grosser categories of analysis, one is easily driven to such simplistic logical inferences as, "He who controls the army, controls the government." However, control of the army is seldom secure in Latin America. Various contenders within the military establishment are competing for control of the power capability represented by armed force. In their strategy for gaining political power, such contenders may call into play others who have vastly different power capabilities. Thus, even in the more army-ridden states, politics is not irrelevant.

A more precise reflection of what is involved in the general Latin American political process involves not only the various factors within the military, but their relations to holders of various other power capabilities, parties, interest groups, urban mobs, student agitators, economic and bureaucratic elites—the entire spectrum of political forces operating in the society. For in discussing the role of the military in Latin American politics, one quickly comes to recognize that most military regimes are ended by military action, and that such struggles for power do not involve military action alone. Not so many years ago, many serious students of Latin American affairs predicted that as Latin American armies acquired more modern, lethal armaments, military totalitarianism would become more characteristic of the region, for the firepower that guerrillas and civilian mobs could amass would not be equal to tanks and jet bombers. That their prediction was faulty, for military totalitarianism has not greatly increased since the end of World War II in Latin America, would seem to have something to do with the fact that the prediction was based on a logical extension of a faulty initial premise concerning the relevant units of Latin American politics. For the military is not a rigidly united force in Latin America. Rather, military force is one power capability within the society, but control of that power capability is vigorously contested.

No one, of course, would want to hold that one set of propositions could account in detail for the diverse political circumstances of the twenty Latin American nations. Truly, there is no single political system in Latin America, and one is justified in saying that aggregation of consent is incrementally more important and legitimate as a power capability in Costa Rica or Uruguay, and use of military force more significant in Nicaragua or Paraguay. But to say simply that "Costa Rica is democratic" or "Nicaragua is controlled by the military" misses some significant points about the nature of power relationships in these nations. After all, Costa Rica has thrice had recourse to violent means of adjusting power relationships in the twentieth century, and the political strategy of the Somoza family and their heirs in Nicaragua involves a considerable component of manipulation of consent, the relations among economic elites, and other factors as well as sheer control of armed force.

The following set of propositions is not intended to apply only to the Latin American norm, and to exclude such deviant cases as Costa Rica and Paraguay. Rather, it would seem that they are of assistance in understanding the political dynamics of any Latin American nation, and can be adjusted to individual differences by the process of specifying that certain power capabilities are more effective or legitimate in structuring power relations in some countries than in others. (Thus, although we shall not perform the operation, one could construct a continuum for political classification of Latin American nations on the basis of the relative magnitude of effectiveness of various power capabilities in each.)

THE DYNAMICS OF
LATIN AMERICAN POLITICS

The problem of Latin American politics, then, is that of finding some formula for creating agreement between power contenders whose power capabilities are neither comparable (as one measures the relative power of groups in democratic society by reference to votes cast) nor compatible. The political system of Latin America may be described as the pattern by which Latin American statesmen conventionally attempt to cope with this variety of political resources used in their societies and the way in which holders of these diverse power capabilities characteristically interact one with another.

In restructuring our frame of reference to cope with this unfamiliar state of affairs, we might begin by suggesting that the techniques used in advanced Western nations as means of ratifying power relationships more frequently appear in Latin America as means of demonstrating a power capability. The significance of this can best be seen by examining three prominent techniques which we commonly assume are means of ratifying power relationships (that is, of structuring a regime or government) and reflect on where they fit in the Latin American political scheme of things. These would be election, revolution, and military dictatorship.

Elections are not definitive in many parts of Latin America. However, they are conscientiously and consistently held, and just as conscientiously and consistently annulled. Few Latin American nations can demonstrate an unbroken sequence of elected governments over any substantial period of time. In a sense, our real question is not that of why elections are ignored, but why they are held at all given their inconclusive character.

In Latin America, not all elites accept the constitutional norms of election as definitive. In fact, democratic election is really only relevant for those who possess certain specific skills and support, for those who have the capacity to aggregate

consent through political parties and movements and the instruments of mass communication. Insofar as such contenders cannot be ignored by others involved in political life, election, which is the mechanism that tests and confirms their power capability, is part of the political process. But insofar as there are other contenders in the political arena, whose power is not dependent on this kind of popular support, or on popular support at all, elections are but a measure of power and not a means of determining who governs. As a strike may demonstrate the power capability of a labor union, or insurrection that of a military faction, so election tests and demonstrates the power capability of a political party.

Hence, the results of an election are tentative, pending responses by other power contenders. Whether the electorally successful group will be accommodated into the power structure or suppressed depends on subsequent negotiations with other power contenders as well as prior perceptions of the threat posed by the movement. ("Negotiation" may actually occur in the formal sense, but just as frequently inferences are drawn by others from the statements and actions of the new contender's leaders, and political power relations are consequently adjusted.)

Thus, for example, in Venezuela immediately after World War II, the existing government was overthrown in a military coup that involved the collaboration of a new political party, *Acción Democrática*, with certain dissatisfied elements of the armed forces. Shortly thereafter, the candidate of *Acción Democrática*, Rómulo Gallegos, was formally elected to the presidency. Inexperienced at the "inside" operation of the political system of Venezuela, the leaders of the party accepted the election as definitive, and launched a program which was perceived by the military and certain economic elites to threaten their position in the power structure. In 1948, the same military elements which had structured the situation that led to the election itself deposed Gallegos in a military coup.

After ten years of harsh dictatorship, a wiser and more experienced *Acción Democrática* government returned to power, again in an election made possible by military collaboration. This time they were careful and consistent in their reassurances to other power contenders that their place in the political order would not be jeopardized. If one looks at the process of politics in Venezuela, as in many other Latin American nations, in this longer time span, rather than in terms of isolated incidents, what at first seems random and chaotic takes on pattern, a pattern in which election and constitutional procedure play a part, but not an exclusive role in the structuring of power relations.

In terms of the rules of Latin American electoral activity, a party which is perceived by other power contenders to threaten their recognized place in the political system may be consistently suppressed, though it just as consistently is electorally successful, as in the tragic history of APRA of Peru, through the election of 1962. The resources devoted to such suppression may even be said to be a function of the extent of electorally demonstrated power as in the case of *Peronismo* in Argentina. On the other hand, such moderately reformist parties as have come to power in Venezuela since 1958 and Colombia have, upon assuming power, been most explicit in their reassurances to other power contenders, and their accommodation to the power structure has not been recalled.

Not only the "tentative" election, but the "fixed" election can be explained as a demonstration of power capability rather than a technique of ratifying power relationships. While in the short run, the fixed election demonstrates the capacity of a government whose power is primarily based on other power capabilities to run a controlled election, suppress opposition, and mobilize the vote, these results are far from authoritative to those power contenders who, by the nature of their power capabilities, must be committed to constitutional procedures. From their point of view, the results of a fixed election are subject to revision at the first opportunity. However, as in the case of the "tentative" election, such elections may be made more definitive by assurances that the government gives to these contenders, usually promises of a free electoral contest in a short period of time, after the situation is "stabilized."

Similarly, it is conventional to distinguish between "real" revolutions and "typical" revolutions in Latin America. Again,

the "real" revolution, in the Western sense of the term, is a technique of ratifying power relationships, of structuring a new regime. In a "typical" revolution (El Salvador in 1948 and Costa Rica in the same year), the revolutionists did not through their action ratify a new power structure. Rather, they left the political system much as it had been before the "revolution" *although now they were included within it.* In short, they had demonstrated a power capability sufficient to be recognized by other contenders, and had subsequently been successful in their negotiations with other power contenders for the structuring of power relationships. (The "typical revolution" is thus also tentative until such satisfactory negotiations have been established, and this accounts in some important degree for the sequences of instability that have occurred in many Latin American countries, and for many of the revolutions that have failed, as in the case of Guatemala.)

Finally, we generally say that Latin American military dictatorship is to be distinguished from European military totalitarianism. With the possible exception of Perón, political intervention by the military in Latin America does not seem to have the effect of overhauling the power system of the society. Rather, under military governments in Latin America, holders of important power capabilities in the society are assured that their position in the society will not be endangered, and are permitted some participation in the political process. (Certainly, military governments may brutally restrict entrance of other new power contenders into the political arena, and in some nations they are supported by other power contenders for just this reason.) In general, the effect of military coup in Latin America is to add a new power contender to the "inner circle" of political elites, but one whose control is not exclusive or definitive.

THE DEMONSTRATION OF
POWER CAPABILITIES

One may say that the most persistent political phenomenon in Latin America is the effort of contenders for power to demonstrate a power capability sufficient to be recognized by other power contenders, and that the political process consists of manipulation and negotiation among power contenders reciprocally recognizing each other's power capability.

It is apparent that it is often not necessary for a power contender actually to use a power capability, but merely to demonstrate possession of it. For example, in many Latin American nations the military has often proved to be exceedingly inept when actually called upon to use armed force in a combat situation. Thus, Porfirio Díaz's vaunted military power seemed to evaporate when challenged by Madero's ragtag forces in the Revolution of 1910. The fate of Batista's well-equipped Cuban army was similar in 1958. However, except in such "real revolutionary" situations, Latin American armies are seldom called upon to actually use armed force. In the conventional operation of the Latin American political system, it is usually only necessary for the military to demonstrate possession of the capacity of armed violence. In the strategy of the Latin American military coup, it is generally recognized that bloodshed is kept to a minimum, and such as takes place is usually coincidental.

What is at issue is the demonstration and recognition of a *transfer* in the control of the power capability of armed force. This may be accomplished by an announcement of the shift of allegiance of certain critical garrisons, a show of armed force, and the declaration of martial law with a patrol adequate to prevent outbreaks by those who do not understand the manner in which the political system operates, or do not accept the system and consider this an appropriate moment for action. The fact that one of the primary targets in a military coup is control of a radio transmitter so that the insurgents can *inform* interested parties through a manifesto or proclamation that a change in control of power capability has taken place is a pointed demonstration of what is actually going on.

With reference to foreign power contenders, it might be noted that the demonstration, rather than use, of a power capability, is a long-established part of Latin American international affairs. Hence, gunboat diplomacy, "the showing of the flag," certainly pertains to this category of events, as do the subtleties of recognition policy.

Similarly, the "manifestation" or "demonstration" is a common political instrument in Latin America. Seldom is the power it implies actually used (as it was in the *Bogotazo* of 1948 when unrestrained mob violence virtually demolished the heart of the capital of Colombia); rather, the presence of the multitude assembled before the national palace is generally adequate for existing power contenders to recognize and seek to placate or accommodate the new power capability that has emerged in their midst.

Widespread use of manifestation also reflects the imperfections of representation in Latin American politics. Where democratic processes are not totally legitimate, and where institutional processes of representation do not effectively connect decision-makers with all major interests, manifestation substitutes for the more formal processes of structured access available in more fully democratic societies. Therefore, manifestation is frequently, though not exclusively, a technique used to demonstrate a power capability not previously recognized by established contenders. The sanction implicit in the presence of the assembled crowd may be violence, or it may be something far more subtle. This may be appreciated by examining another fascinating technique of demonstrating a power capability in urban Latin America, the general strike.

The *huelga de los brazos caídos*, or general strike, is a recognized part of the political process in Latin America. It was used with great effectiveness as part of a total strategy of deposing an incumbent regime in El Salvador in 1944, Costa Rica in 1948, the Dominican Republic in 1961, and in other nations as well. What is at issue in the general strike is the demonstration of a power capability inhering in the urban population which has not been effectively recognized by other power contenders. This power capability may be described as the disruptive effect of the withdrawal of a number of those specialized, systemic performances on which the complex interdependence of a modern urban community is based.

. . . Threat of nonperformance of a critical social or economic role, implicit or explicit, is a power capability that pertains to a wide variety of power contenders. Hence, the problem of a flight of capital, insofar as it reflects a vote of no confidence in the political regime, is the demonstration of a power capability in this sense, as is the threat or fact of disinvestment by foreign capitalists or entrepreneurs. Although such withdrawals of critical performances are not often designed directly as political strategies, at times they have been precisely such. For example, in 1962, when the reformist Rivera government in El Salvador enacted and enforced a quite thoroughgoing rural labor reform, the landholding elites of the nation threatened to cut down production of basic foodstuffs in retaliation and protest.

Even the use of noninstitutionalized violence and terror is often designed to show possession of a power capability rather than to use it directly for political ends. More true to the Latin American tradition in such matters than the political assassination or widespread destruction of property or life is the symbolic act of terrorism or violence. For example, the theft of an art collection in Caracas in 1962, the kidnapping and release unharmed of a United States officer, the hijacking of ships and aircraft, as components of a rather consistent strategy of the FALN terrorists in Venezuela, were designed to produce the largest dramatic appeal and embarrassment to the regime, without large-scale devastation of property. Although violence in Venezuela in the 1960–64 period often did degenerate into actual destruction of life and property, this seemed to have more to do with the inability of early terrorist leaders to control the forces they had unleashed than any strategic intent to create bloodshed and havoc. . . .

While the Latin American political process is becoming more complex, and such acts of civic disruption and violence are growing more serious and threatening in intent (particularly with the emergence of urban guerrilla warfare as an increasingly prominent phenomenon) in the classic pattern of Latin American political life, such techniques of demonstrating a power capability seem generally accepted as appropriate to the political system. Thus, when such techniques as manifestation, strike, and even violence are used symbolically, that is, as the demonstration and not the use of a power capability, there would seem to be an *a priori* case that the appropriate response of government leaders should be conciliation and bargaining.

However, when use of such techniques actually degenerates into important destruction of life or property, it seems more generally felt that the rules have been transgressed, and that the use of sanctions is called for. Brutal police suppression, with loss of life and widespread arrests, in the face of a student riot, even one that may have culminated in the burning of automobiles or the breaking of windows, may breed an ugly public mood. On the other hand, persistent agitation that actually disrupts the way of life of the society and is not dealt with firmly by constituted authority may lead quickly to agitation for a stronger "no nonsense" government.

The line between "appropriate" and "inappropriate" demonstrations of the capacity to use violence is a fine one, most contingent on the way public opinion chooses to define a particular situation. However, it is clear that many Latin American governments can count the days to their downfall from some initial act of overstepping the bounds of what seems to be accepted as the legitimate use of force in the face of threats of civic disruption. Thus, many Latin American "revolutions" (Guatemala in 1944–45 will do as an example) have as part of their folklore a student demonstration or riot which was vigorously suppressed, and which served as a touchstone of increasing popular discontent against the regime, culminating in a military revolt.

Thus, there is further evidence, which may be tested against a wide variety of situations, for the existence of a Latin American political system, not defined exclusively by constitutional norms, but generally well understood by the contenders. That manifestation and strike and violence have so much to do with the day-to-day operation of the system is in part due to the imperfections of democratic procedures in Latin America, that most contenders for power do not have structured access to the representative system on the basis of an implicit assumption of their power capabilities, but are forced to demonstrate their power capabilities in extrademocratic ways. Yet, the existence of the system does not merely indicate that Latin America is waiting upon the time when democracy will be perfected, for the rules of the game themselves are part of a political heritage which possesses its own legitimacy and persistence. . . .

1. Seymour Martin Lipset, "Some Social Requisites of Democracy: Economic Development and Political Legitimacy," *American Political Science Review,* LII (March 1959), pp. 69–105.

2. Martin Needler, "Putting Latin American Politics in Perspective," *Inter-American Economic Affairs,* XVI (Autumn 1962), pp. 41–50.

3. See, as two examples among many, the "power factors" approach in Harold E. Davis, ed., *Government and Politics in Latin America* (New York: Ronald Press, 1958); and the "middle sector" approach in John J. Johnson, *Political Change in Latin America: The Emergence of the Middle Sectors* (Stanford, Calif.: Stanford University Press, 1958).

PATRON-CLIENT POLITICS AND POLITICAL CHANGE

JAMES C. SCOTT

University of Wisconsin

The analysis presented here is an effort to elaborate the patron-client model of association, developed largely by anthropologists, and to demonstrate its applicability to political action in Southeast Asia. Inasmuch as patron-client structures are not unique to Southeast Asia but are much in evidence particularly in Latin America, in Africa and in the more backward portions of Europe, the analysis may possibly be of more general value in understanding politics in less developed nations. . . .

The need to develop a conceptual structure that would assist in unravelling the large slice of political activity that does not depend solely on [class alignments] or primordial sentiments is readily apparent in Southeast Asia.[1] In the Philippines, for example, class analysis can help us understand the recurrent agrarian movements in Central Luzon (e.g. Sakdalistas and Huks) among desperate tenants and plantation laborers but it is of little help in explaining how Magsaysay succeeded in weaning many rebels away from the Huks, or, more important, in analyzing the normal patterns of political competition between Philippine parties. In Thailand, primordial demands may help us discern the basis of dissident movements in North and Northeast Thailand, but neither primordialism nor class analysis serves to explain the intricate pattern of the personal factions and coalitions

that are at the center of oligarchic Thai politics. The almost perpetual conflict between the central Burman state and its separatist hill peoples and minorities are indeed primordial, communal issues, but communalism is of no use in accounting for the intra-Burman struggles between factions within the Anti-Fascist People's Freedom League (AFPFL) or, later, within the military regime. Ethnicity and class do carry us far in explaining racial hostilities and intra-Chinese conflict in Malaya, but they are less helpful when it comes to intra-Malay politics or to inter-racial cooperation at the top of the Alliance party.[2]

As these examples indicate, when we leave the realm of class conflict or communalism, we are likely to find ourselves in the realm of informal power groups, leadership-centered cliques and factions, and a whole panoply of more or less instrumental ties that characterize much of the political process in Southeast Asia. The structure and dynamics of such seemingly *ad hoc* groupings can, I believe, be best understood from the perspective of patron-client relations. As an informal cluster of a power figure who is in a position to give security, and/or inducements, and his personal followers who, in return for such benefits, contribute their loyalty and personal assistance to the patron's designs, the vertical pattern of patron-client linkages

Reprinted by permission of author. Originally presented at 1970 Annual Meeting of the American Political Science Association, Los Angeles. Some sections have been omitted. Revised version appears in *American Political Science Review* (March 1972), pp. 91–113.

represents an important structural principle of Southeast Asian politics.

The use of patron-client analysis has been until recently the province of anthropologists who found it particularly useful in penetrating behind the often misleading formal arrangements in small local communities where inter-personal power relations were salient. Terms which are related to patron-client structures in the anthropological literature—including "clientelism," "dyadic contract," "personal network," "action-set"—reflect an attempt on the part of anthropologists to come to grips with the fluid mosaic of non-primordial divisions.[3] Informal though such networks are, they are built, maintained, and interact in ways that will allow us to generalize about them.

Although patron-client analysis provides a solid base for comprehending the structure and dynamics of non-primordial cleavages at the local level, its value is not limited to village studies. Nominally modern institutions such as bureaucracies and political parties in Southeast Asia are often thoroughly penetrated by informal patron-client networks that undermine the formal structure of authority. If we are to grasp why a bureaucrat's authority is likely to depend more on his personal following and extra-bureaucratic connections than on his formal post, or why political parties seem more like *ad hoc* assemblages of notables together with their entourages than arenas in which established interests are aggregated, we must rely heavily on patron-client analysis. The dynamics of personal alliance networks are thus as crucial in the day-to-day realities of national institutions as in local politics; the main difference is simply that such networks are more elaborately disguised by formal façades in modern institutions.

In what follows, I attempt to clarify what patron-client ties are, how they affect political life, and how they may be applied to the dynamics of Southeast Asian politics. After (1) defining the nature of the patron-client link and distinguishing it from other social ties, the paper (2) discriminates between different varieties of patron-client bonds and thereby establishes some important dimensions of variation, and (3) examines both the survival and the transformations in patron-client links in Southeast Asia since colonialism and the impact of major social changes such as the growth of markets, the expanded role of the state, and so forth on the content of these ties. . . .

THE NATURE OF PATRON-CLIENT TIES

The Basis and Operation of Personal Exchange

While the actual use of the terms "patron" and "client" is largely confined to the Mediterranean and Latin American areas, comparable relationships can be found in most cultures and are most strikingly present in pre-industrial nations.[4] *The patron-client relationship—an exchange relationship between roles—may be defined as a special case of dyadic (two-person) ties involving a large instrumental friendship in which an individual of higher socio-economic status (patron) uses his own influence and resources to provide protection and/or benefits for a person of lower status (client) who, for his part, reciprocates by offering general support and assistance, including personal services, to the patron.*[5]

In the reciprocity demanded by the relationship each partner provides a service that is valued by the other. Although the balance of benefits may heavily favor the patron, there is nevertheless some reciprocity involved, and it is this quality which, as Powell notes, distinguishes patron-client dyads from relationships of pure coercion or formal authority that also may link individuals of different status.[6] A patron may have some coercive power and he may also hold an official position of authority. But if the force or authority at his command are alone sufficient to ensure the compliance of another, he has no need of patron-client ties which require some reciprocity. Typically, then, the patron operates in a context in which community norms and sanctions and the need for clients require at least a minimum of bargaining and reciprocity; the power imbalance is not so great as to permit a pure command relationship.

Three additional distinguishing features of patron-client links, implied by the definition, merit brief elaboration: their basis in inequality, their face-to-face character, and their diffuse flexibility. All three factors are most apparent in the ties between a high-status landlord and each of his tenants or sharecroppers in a traditional agrarian economy—a relationship that serves, in a sense, as the prototype of patron-client ties.[7]

First, there is an *imbalance in exchange between the two partners which expresses and reflects the disparity in their relative wealth, power [authority] and status.* A client is, in this sense, someone who has entered an unequal exchange relation in which he is unable to reciprocate fully. A debt of obligation binds him to the patron.[8] How does this imbalance in reciprocity arise? It is based, as Peter Blau has shown in his work, *Exchange and Power in Social Life,*[9] on the fact that the patron often is in a position to unilaterally supply goods and services which the potential client and his family need for their survival and well-being. A locally dominant landlord, for example, is frequently the major source of protection, security, employment, of access to arable land or to education, and of food in bad times. Such services could hardly be more vital and hence the demand for them tends to be highly inelastic; that is, an increase in their effective cost will not diminish demand proportionately. Being a monopolist, or at least an oligopolist, for critical needs, the patron is in an ideal position to demand compliance from those who wish to share in these scarce commodities.

Faced with someone who can supply or deprive him of basic wants, the potential client in theory has just four alternatives to becoming the patron's subject.[10] First he may reciprocate with a service that the patron needs badly enough to restore the balance of exchange. In special cases of religious, medical, or martial skills this may be possible, but the resources of the client, given his position in the stratification, are normally inadequate to re-establish an equilibrium. A potential client may also try to secure the needed services elsewhere. If the need for clients is especially great and if there is stiff competition among patron-suppliers, the cost of patron-controlled services will be less.[11] In most agrarian settings, substantial local autonomy tends to favor the growth of local power monopolies by officials or landed gentry. A third possibility is that clients may coerce the patron into providing services. Although the eventuality that his clients might turn on him may prompt a patron to meet at least the minimum normative standards of exchange,[12] the patron's local power and the absence of autonomous organization among his clients make this unlikely. Finally, clients can theoretically do without a patron's services altogether. This alternative is remote, given the patron's control over vital services such as protection, land and employment, that are not lightly abandoned.

Affiliating with a patron is neither a purely coerced decision nor is it the result of unrestricted choice. Exactly where a particular patron-client dyad falls on the continuum depends on the four factors mentioned. If the client has highly valued services to reciprocate with, if he can choose among competing patrons, if force is available to him, or if he can manage without the patron's help, then the balance will be more nearly equal. But if, as is generally the case, the client has few coercive or exchange resources to bring to bear against a monopolist-patron whose services he desperately needs, the dyad is more nearly a coercive one.[13]

The degree of loyalty, compliance, and deference a client gives his patron is a direct function of the degree of imbalance in the exchange relationships—of how dependent the client is on his patron's services. An imbalance thus creates a sense of debt or obligation on the client's part and represents, for the patron, a "'store of value'—social credit that . . . [the patron] can draw on to obtain advantages at a later time."[14] By virtue of his domination of needed services a patron builds up savings of deference and compliance which enhance his status and represent a capacity for mobilizing a group of supporters when he cares to. The larger a patron's clientele and the more dependent they are on him, the greater his latent capacity to organize group action. In the typical agrarian patron-client setting it is this capacity to mobilize a following that is crucial in the competition among patrons for regional preeminence. As Blau describes the general situation, "The high-status members furnish instrumental assistance to the low-status ones in exchange for their respect and compliance, which help the high-status members in their competition for a dominant position in the group."[15]

One could potentially make almost limit-less distinctions among patron-client relationships. The dimensions of variation considered here are selected because they seem particularly relevant to our analytical goal of assessing the central changes in such ties within Southeast Asia. Similar distinctions should be germane to the analysis of other former colonial nations as well.

The Resource Base of Patronage

A potential patron assembles clients on the basis of his ability to assist them. For his investment of assets, the patron expects a return in human resources—in the form of the strength of obligation and the number of clients obligated to him. The resource base or nature of the assets a patron has at his disposal can vary widely. One useful way of distinguishing among resources is according to how directly they are controlled. Patrons may, in this sense, rely on (a) their own knowledge and skills, (b) direct control of personal real property, or (c) indirect control of the property or authority of others (often that of the public). . . .

Resource Base of Clientage

As the other member of a reciprocating pair, the client is called upon to provide assistance and services when the patron requires them. The variation in the nature of such assistance is another means of distinguishing one patron-client dyad from another. Here one might want to differentiate: (1) *labor services and economic support*, as provided by a rent-paying tenant or employee, (2) *military or fighting duties*, such as those performed by members of a bandit group for their chief, and (3) *political services* such as canvassing or otherwise acting as an agent of a politician. Within the "political service" category one may wish to separate electoral services from non-electoral political help.

Balance of Affective and Instrumental Ties

By definition, instrumental ties play a major role in the patron-client dyad. It is nonetheless possible to classify such dyads by the extent to which affective bonds are also involved in the relationship. At one end of this continuum one might place

patron-client bonds which, in addition to their instrumental character, are reinforced by affective links growing, say, from the patron and the client having been schoolmates, coming from the same village, being distant relatives, or simply from mutual love. Comparable affective rewards may also spring from the exchange of *deference* and noblesse oblige between patron and client in a settled agrarian status network —rewards that have value beyond the material exchanges they often involve.[16] At the other end of the spectrum lies a dyadic tie much closer to an almost neutral exchange of goods and services. The more purely coercive the relationship is and the less traditional legitimacy it has, the more likely affective bonds will be minimal. . . .

Balance of Voluntarism and Coercion

There are obvious and important differences in the degree of coercion involved in a patron-client bond. At one end are clients who have virtually no choice but to follow the patron who directly controls their means of subsistence. Here one might place a tenant whose landlord provides his physical security, his land, his implements and seed, in a society where land is scarce and insecurity rife. Nearer the center of this continuum would perhaps be the bonds between independent smallholders who depend on a landlord for the milling and marketing of their crops, for small loans, and for assistance with the police and administration. Such bonds are still based on inequality but the client, because he has some bargaining leverage, is not simply putty in his patron's hands. Finally, let us assume that an electoral system has placed a new resource in clients' hands and has spurred competition among patrons for followings that can swing the election to them. In this case the inequality in bargaining power is further reduced and the client emerges as more nearly an independent political actor whose demands will receive a full hearing from his patron.

Durability Over Time

. . . As patron-client clusters are based ultimately on power relations, they will endure best in a stable setting that preserves existing power positions. A particular patron will thus retain his clients as long as he continues to dominate the supply of services which they need. A patron is also likely to keep his followers if the scope of reciprocity that binds them is greater. That is, the *more* vital needs a patron can meet, such as land, security, influence with the administration, help in arranging mortgages or schooling, and so forth, the greater the tendency for the tie to be invoked frequently and to endure over long periods. Compared with patrons who can provide only legal services, only financial help, or only educational advantages, the *multiplex* bond between patron and client is a solid linkage that serves many needs; it is more of a whole-person tie, and will be called into action often. . . .

SURVIVAL AND DEVELOPMENT

OF PATRON-CLIENT TIES

IN SOUTHEAST ASIA

Conditions of Survival

As units of political structure, patron-client clusters not only typify both local and national politics in Southeast Asia, they are also as characteristic of the area's contemporary politics as of its traditional politics. In . . . my view, most of traditional and contemporary Southeast Asia has met three necessary conditions for the continued vitality of patron-client structures: (1) *the persistence of marked inequalities in the control of wealth, status, and power which have been accepted (until recently) as more or less legitimate;* (2) *the relative absence of firm, impersonal guarantees of physical security, status and position, or wealth,* and (3) *the inability of kinship units to serve as an effective vehicle for personal security or advancement.*

The first condition is more or less self-evident. A client affiliates with a patron by virtue of the patron's superior access to important goods and services. This inequality is an expression of a stratification system which serves as the basis for vertical exchange. Classically in Southeast Asia, the patron has depended more on the local organization of force and access to office as the sinews of his leadership than upon hereditary status or land ownership. Inequalities were thus marked, but elite circulation tended to be comparatively high. With the penetration of colonial government and commercialization of the economy, land ownership made its appearance (especially in the Philippines and Vietnam)

as a major basis of patronage. At the same time access to colonial office replaced to some extent the previously more fluid local power contests as the criterion for local patronage. Although land ownership and bureaucratic office have remained two significant bases of patronship in post-colonial Southeast Asia, they have been joined—and sometimes eclipsed—by office in political parties or military rank, as patronage resources.

If inequities in access to vital goods were alone sufficient to promote the expansion of patron-client ties, such structures would predominate almost everywhere. A second, and more significant, condition of patron-client politics is the absence of institutional guarantees for an individual's security, status, or wealth. Where consensus has produced an institutionalized means of indirect exchange—one that is legally based, uniformly enforced, and effective—impersonal contractual arrangements tend to usurp the place of personal reciprocity. A patron-client dyad, by contrast, is a *personal* security mechanism and is resorted to most often when personal security is often in jeopardy and when impersonal social controls are unreliable. In this context, direct personal ties based on reciprocity substitute for law, shared values, and strong institutions. As Eric Wolf has noted, "The clearest gain from such a [patron-client] relations . . . is in situations where public law cannot guarantee adequate protection against breaches of non-kin contracts." [17]

It is important to recognize the unenviable situation of the typical client in less developed nations. He lives in an environment of scarcity, in which competition for wealth and power is seen as a zero-sum contest in which his losses are another's gain and vice-versa.[18] His very survival is constantly threatened by the caprice of nature and by social forces beyond his control. In such an environment where basic needs are paramount and physical security uncertain, a modicum of protection and insurance can often be gained only by dependence on a superior who undertakes personally to provide for his own clients. Operating with such a slim margin, the client prefers to minimize his losses—at the cost of his independence—rather than to maximize his gains by taking risks he cannot afford. When one's physical security and means of livelihood are problematic and recourse to law is unavailable or unreliable, the social value of a personal defender is maximized.

The growth of strong, institutional orders that reduce the need for personal alliances is a rare occurrence historically—the Roman and Chinese imperial orders being the most notable exceptions—until the 19th and 20th centuries, when modern nation-states developed the technical means to impose their will throughout their territory. Before that, however, the existence of a fair degree of local autonomy was inevitable given the limited power available to most traditional kingdoms. The greater that degree of autonomy, or what might be called the *localization* of power, the more decisive patron-client linkages were likely to be.

In settings as diverse as much of Latin America, feudal Europe, and pre-colonial Southeast Asia, the localization of power was pervasive and gave rise to networks of patron-client bonds. From time to time in Southeast Asia a centralizing kingdom managed to extend its power over wide areas, but seldom for very long or with a uniform system of authority. A typical Southeast Asian kingdom's authority weakened steadily with the distance from the capital city. Beyond the immediate environs of the court, the ruler was normally reduced to choosing which of a number of competing petty chiefs with local power bases he would prefer to back.[19] Such chiefs retained their own personal following; their relationship to the ruler was one of bargaining as well as deference; and they might back a rival claimant to the throne or simply defy demands of the court when they were dissatisfied with their patron's behavior. Thus, the political structure of traditional Southeast Asia favored the growth of patron-client links inasmuch as it was necessary for peasants to accommodate themselves to the continuing reality of autonomous personal authority at the local level.

The third condition under which patron-client bonds remain prominent relates directly to the capacity of such ties to foster cooperation among non-kin. As a mechanism for protection or for advancement, patron-client dyads will flourish when kinship bonds alone become inadequate for these purposes. Although kinship bonds

are seldom completely adequate as structures of protection and advancement even in the simplest societies, they may perform these functions well enough to minimize the need for non-kin structures. . . . However, the scope for non-kin ties in general, and patron-client links in particular, has thus been quite wide throughout the region. . . .

The Transformation of Traditional Patron-Client Ties

The General trend. The typical patron in traditional Southeast Asia was a petty local leader. Unlike the representative of a corporate kin group or a corporate village structure (rare outside Vietnam and Java, respectively), the local patron owed his local leadership to his personal skills, his wealth, and occasionally to his connections with regional leaders—all of which enhanced his capacity to build a personal following. The fortunes of such petty leaders waxed or waned depending on the continuing availability of resources and spoils which served to knit together a following. Perhaps the most striking feature of local patron leadership in Southeast Asia was its fluidity and instability, thereby contributing to a relatively high rate of local elite circulation. In contrast to India, where hereditary office-holding and landholding provided somewhat greater continuity, the typical local leader in Southeast Asia was a "self-made man" who had put together the necessary resources of wealth, force, connections, and status on his own and could probably only promise his son a slight advantage in the next round. The reasons for this oscillation in local power relate to (a) the weakness of the central state, which lacked either the force or durability to sustain and guarantee the continuation of local power elites, and (b) the relative ease with which clients in a slash-and-burn economy could, if dissatisfied, simply move to another area, thus undermining their ex-patron's basis of power.[20]

Patron-client systems have survived—even flourished—in both colonial and post-independence Southeast Asia. There have been important changes, however. New resources for patronage, such as party connections, development programs, nationalized enterprises, and bureaucratic power have been created. Patron-client structures are now more closely linked to the national level with jobs, cash, and petty favors flowing down the network and votes or support flowing upward. In the midst of this, old style patrons still thrive. Highland leaders, for example, still operate in a personal capacity as patron/brokers for their people with lowland leaders. Landowners in the Philippines and elsewhere have used their traditional control of land and the tenants who farm it to win positions of local or regional party leadership. Whatever the particular form they take, patron-client networks still function as the main basis of alliance systems between non-kin throughout Southeast Asia.

The nature of patron-client bonds within Southeast Asia has varied sharply from one period to the next and from one location to another. Different resources have risen or plummeted in value as a basis of patronage depending upon the nature of the political system: the capacity to mobilize an armed following was particularly valuable in the pre-colonial era; access to colonial office was a surer basis of patronage than armed force in the colonial period; and the ability to win electoral contests often became the central resource with the advent of independence. Not only have resource bases proven mercurial over time, but the nature of patron-client ties in the highland, indirectly-ruled areas has remained substantially different from lowland patterns. Amidst this variety and change, it is nevertheless possible to discern a number of secular trends in the character of patron-client bonds. Such trends are far more pronounced in some areas than others, but they do represent directions of change that are important for our analysis.

SECULAR TRENDS IN THE NATURE OF PATRON-CLIENT TIES IN SOUTHEAST ASIA

Quality	Traditional	Contemporary
(1) Duration of bond	More persistent	Less persistent
(2) Scope of exchange	Multiplex	[Increasingly] simplex
(3) Resource base	Local, personal	External links, office-based
(4) Affective/instrumental balance	Higher ratio of affective to instrumental ties	Lower ratio of affective to instrumental ties
(5) Local resource control	More local monopoly	Less local monopoly
(6) Differentiation between clusters	Less differentiation	More differentiation
(7) Density of coverage	Greater density	Less density

(1) In comparison with more bureaucratic empires, patron-client bonds in pre-colonial Southeast Asia were not, as we have pointed out, markedly persistent. With the quickening of social change brought about by the commercialization of the economy and the penetration of the colonial state into local affairs, however, a patron's resource base became even more vulnerable to the actions of outside forces over which he had little or no control. It was an ingenious patron indeed who could survive the depression of the 1930's, the Japanese occupation, and independence with his resources and clientele intact. The major exception to this trend was the colonial period in indirectly ruled areas where colonial military and financial backing of traditional rulers, if anything, brought a stability—or stagnation—to political systems that had been more chaotic. Elsewhere, patron-client links tended to become more fragile and less persistent.

(2) With the differentiation of the economy and its effects on the social structure, the scope of exchange between patron and client tended to narrow somewhat. Where traditional patrons could generally serve as all-purpose protectors, the newer patron's effectiveness tended to be more specialized in areas such as political influence, modern sector employment, or administrative influence. Although patron-client ties remained flexible and personal, the more limited capacities of the patron tended to make the relationship less comprehensive and hence less stable.[21]

(3) The tradition patron for the most part operated with personally controlled local resouces. One effect of the colonial

period—and independence as well—was to increase radically the importance of external resources for local patronage. A following based on purely local office or landholding was seldom sufficient to sustain a patron in a new environment where schools, agricultural services, regional banks, public employment, represented competing sources of patronage. The growing role of outside resources, in most cases, thus led to competition among patrons, each of whom recruited followings with the particular resources at his command.[22] In addition, since those who controlled the new resources were generally office-holders subject to transfers or political changes at the center, the new patrons were less secure than older patrons and probably more inclined to maximize their gains over the short run.

(4) Due both to the weaker and less comprehensive character of the new patron-client ties and to the fact that the new patrons were often from outside the local community, the instrumental nature of the exchange became more prominent. A relationship that had always involved some calculations of advantage lost some of its traditional legitimacy and grew more profane. Patron-client exchanges became more monetized, calculations more explicit, and concern centered more on the rate of return from the relationship rather than its durability. This meant that newer patron-client clusters were likely to have a comparatively large "fair-weather" periphery and a comparatively small core-following.

(5) The breakdown of local patron monopolies follows logically from most of the changes we have already discussed. Where one local landowner or traditional leader had once dominated, he now faced competitors who might be local administrators of state welfare in loan programs, teachers in new secular schools, a local trader or businessman, or the resident manager of a foreign-owned plantation. Factional strife which reflects this competition was most common in villages where socio-economic change and government penetration had been far-reaching, and less common in more traditional areas.[23]

(6) As differentiation occurred within the local societies, they gave rise to patron-client clusters that were distinct. A bureaucrat might have a following primarily within his agency, a businessman among his laborers, and a landowner among his tenants. This process of differentiation among clusters provided the potential basis for durable group interests inasmuch as many clusters now had an institutional distinctiveness.

(7) While the changes we have examined may have assisted the vertical integration of patron-client pyramids, they tended to reduce the universality of coverage. That is, more and more people in the new market towns and cities, on plantations, and on small plots rented from absentee landlords were no longer attached —or very weakly attached—to patrons. These new elements of the population varied greatly in the nature of the interests and their level of organization, but, in any event, fell outside the older patron-client network.

While some long run trends in patron-client ties seem clear, it is difficult to say anything about the balance between voluntarism and coercion over time. On the one hand, changes in the economy have made clients less autonomous and more dependent on patrons for protection against a fall in world prices, for cash advances before the harvest, and so forth. Also contributing to a decline in the client's bargaining position is the imported legal system of property guarantees which allow a wealthy man, if he so chooses, to resist pressures for redistribution that operated in a traditional setting. On the other hand, the breakdown of local patronly monopolies and the exchange resources that electoral systems often place in the hands of clients work in the opposite direction. Given these contradictory tendencies, a tentative conclusion is that patron coerciveness has declined only where extra-local resources *and* competitive elections are common and has elsewhere either increased or remained the same.

In general the tendency has been for patron-client ties to become more instrumental, less comprehensive, and hence less resilient. They still represent diffuse personal bonds of affection when compared to the impersonal, contractual ties of the marketplace, but the direction of change is eroding their more traditional characteristics. Even this supple traditional protective mechanism has had to pay a certain price to survive in the midst of a nation state with a commercialized economy.

The durability and legitimacy of the patron-client tie was best served when all of a client's dependencies were focused on a single patron. But, as Godfrey and Monica Wilson have shown, this situation is less and less likely since the process of modernization tends to create multiple dependencies—each of less intensity—rather than concentrating dependence on one person.[24] The slowly weakening comprehensiveness of the link is, ultimately, what undermines its sanctity and legitimacy for the client.

The dynamics of the transformation. The engine behind the shift in patron-client ties was largely provided by the penetration of the local arena by an intrusive national economy and national political system. This penetration wrought two major changes that transformed patron-client links: (a) during the colonial period, especially, it impaired the effectiveness of local redistributive pressures and (b) particularly after independence it "nationalized" access to patronly resources thus creating new bases of patronage and devaluating old ones.

Traditional peasant societies, operating in an economy of great scarcity where one family's gain is another's loss, have generally developed a variety of social control mechanisms which guarantee a measure of security to each family and temper the centrifugal forces generated by the struggle for subsistence.[25] These mechanisms commonly involve forcing anyone who has accumulated considerable wealth to redistribute a portion of it. A wealthy man is pressed to assume expensive ceremonial offices, to make large religious contributions, to give loans and donations, and so forth. He trades his wealth for prestige and, by so providing for at least the minimum well being of others, he becomes a legitimate patron with a personal entourage of those obligated to him.

The central fact about these redistributive mechanisms, however, is that they operate by virtue of a local power situation. That is, the wealthy man in a peasant village can seldom rely on outside force or law to protect him; instead, his wealth and position are ultimately validated by the legitimacy he acquires in the local community. Unless a wealthy individual can persuade most of the community that his wealth is no threat to them or can win enough personal allies to sustain his position, he is in danger.

Colonialism, however, broke the relative autonomy of the local arena and hence weakened many of the community's redistributive pressures. Supported in effect by the power of the colonial power to enforce its notion of law, the patron could increasingly ignore local levelling pressures. If he lost much of the social approval he previously enjoyed, he had gained an outside ally with the power to guarantee his local position. The colonial power situation thus offered the *older* patron new leverage in the local arena—leverage which was further strengthened by the growing complexity of colonial society. . . . Absentee landlords, the new urban wealthy, and minority communities (who were relatively impervious to local social approval so long as they had colonial backing) were *new* elements in colonial society which could escape patronly obligations. The colonial system thus tended to allow existing patrons greater latitude for exploitation while producing a class of wealthy non-patrons.

If the intrusion of external power could strengthen the hand of an existing patron, it could also create a resource base for the rise of new patrons. The activities of the colonial regime included the hiring, firing, and promotion of public employees, the dispensing of contracts, and the granting of licenses and permits, all of which could be used to create a personal following. With independence, not only did local leaders take over responsibility for all these decisions, but the scope of government activity and regulation was generally expanded into new areas such as community development. The survival or demise of a local patron often depended, as Geertz has shown, on how successful he was in tapping these new bases of power.[26]

Except for the rare local patrons—especially in indirectly ruled areas—who were able to monopolize these external resources, the new situation produced more competition and mobility among patrons. Many potential clients quickly discovered that their needs were best served by a patron who had access to the institutions which controlled the use of these external resources. . . . [This] has occurred in Southeast Asia as the integration of villages into a national economy and political system tended to produce a number of more specialized local patrons who often became factional leaders. . . .

Electoral politics and patron-client ties. Most Southeast Asian states have had functioning electoral systems at one time since their independence. Although only the Philippines retains a parliamentary system, the electoral studies that do exist can tell us much about the effects of party competition on patron-client bonds and, beyond that, highlight some of the unstable features of patron-client democracies.

The dynamics of electoral competition transformed patron-client relations in at least four important ways: (1) it improved the client's bargaining position with a patron by adding to his resources; (2) it promoted the vertical integration of patron-client structures from the hamlet level to the central government; (3) it led to the creation of new patron-client pyramids and the politicization of old ones; and (4) it contributed to the survival of opposition patron-client pyramids at the local level.

First, with popular elections the client gained a new political resource, as the mere giving or withholding of his vote affected the fortunes of aspirants for office. Nor were voters slow to realize that this resource could be turned to good account. Even someone with no other services of value to offer a patron found that the votes of his immediate family were often sufficient to secure the continuing assistance of a local politician. This pattern could be found throughout Southeast Asia in electoral situations but is most striking in the Philippines where most patron-client ties are centered around landholding and elections. The Filipino politician, as Wurfel points out, does favors *individually* rather than collectively because he wishes to create a personal obligation of clientship.[27] The voter, for his part, asks that his patron/politician favor him because of a personal obligation to reciprocate.

In one sense, popular elections can be seen as a re-establishment of the redistributive mechanisms of the traditional setting. Once again a patron's position becomes somewhat more dependent on the social approval of his community—a social approval that is now backed by the power to defeat him or his candidate at the polls. Not able to depend on outright coercion

and faced with competitors, the electoral patron knows he must (unless his local economic power is decisive) generally offer his clients better terms than his rivals if he hopes to maintain his local power.

Secondly, nationwide elections make it necessary for a national party to establish a network of links extending down to the local level. For the most part a party does this by taking advantage of existing patron-client clusters and incorporating them into its structure. The competitive struggle of Indonesian parties to forge such links in Java during the 1950's is apparent in the accounts Feith and Geertz give of electoral campaigns.[28] Both agree that effective campaigning in the village took the form of activating and politicizing pre-existing personal links rather than mass meetings or policy stands.[29]

As elsewhere in Southeast Asia, a party succeeded best at the polls by securing the adhesion of the important local patrons, who would deliver their clients as a matter of course. Working on voters individually or by class affiliation made little sense when most of the electorate was divided into patron-client clusters. The affiliation of patrons was often gained by making them candidates, by promising them jobs or other patronage, or even by cash payments. . . . Since the winning party can generally offer more support to local allies than the opposition, there is likely to be a "bandwagon effect" of local patrons switching allegiance to a probable winner. In addition, the party's need for a powerful local base is likely to lead to a certain localization of power. In return for delivering local votes for its list, the party is likely to give its local patron a wide discretion in administrative and development decisions affecting the locality. Thus many local patrons are able to further entrench themselves as dominant figures.

A third consequence of elections for the patron-client structure is to promote the expansion of patron-client ties and the politicization of existing bonds. Knowing that an electoral victory is important, a local patron with a modest following will probably try to obligate more clients to him in order to strengthen his electoral position. Patrons who had previously been inactive politically would "immediately convert their private power such as control over sharecroppers, debtors, kinsmen, neighbors, etc., into public political power in the form of votes." [30] Given these tendencies, the patron-client structures in a given community are most in evidence immediately before an election, especially a hotly contested one, when the contestants attempt to activate any links that might advance their cause.

A final point about the impact of elections on patron-client structures is that they tend to heighten factionalism and, unless one cohesive party completely dominates, to promote the survival of local opposition factions. In most traditional settings, patron rivalry was largely limited to the local arena so as not to invite external intervention. An electoral system, by contrast, creates rival national or regional parties which need allies at the local level. A weak faction that might previously have been forced to compose its differences with a dominant faction, can now appeal for external support. Many of these external allies are able to provide their local adherents with patronage, cash, or other favors so as to maintain a local foothold. The net effect of electoral competition is thus to exacerbate many of the latent factional differences among patron-client clusters and to occasionally buttress weak patrons whose position would otherwise have disintegrated. . . .

The inflationary character of "patron-client democracy." The introduction of competitive elections in Southeast Asia increased the pressures on regimes for the downward distribution of tangible benefits. In return for votes flowing up the vertical chain of patron-client structures, each patron depended upon the downward distribution of patronage in the form of administrative favors, land grants, public employment, and so on, in order to keep his own pyramid of followers intact. Elections, by themselves, had shifted the balance of exchange somewhat more in favor of the client than it had been. The consequence of this shift in exchange terms was a greater flow of material benefits towards the base of the patron-client network.

The strength of the downward distributive pressures generated by electoral procedures in Southeast Asia depended primarily on four variables which are stated below in contrasting terms.

DISTRIBUTIVE PRESSURES OF ELECTIONS

A. Strongest When	B. Weakest When
(1) Elections determine powerholders	(1) Elections of marginal significance
(2) Weak, unstable regime	(2) Strong, stable regime
(3) Socio-economic change extensive (direct rule, lowland areas)	(3) Socio-economic change less extensive (indirect rule, highland areas)
(4) Traditionalist party	(4) Modernist, secular party

Examples of Strong Distributive Pressure (A): Indonesia (until 1955), Burma (until 1959 at least), the Philippines.
Examples of Weaker Distributive Pressures (B): Thailand, and perhaps Malaysia (until 1967).

Each of the above variables relates to the strength of incentives impelling a party to maximize its clientele and the degree to which that clientele will depend on concrete material incentives rather than ties of affection or deference. The first and obvious requirement for distributive pressures is that elections be important in the selection of an elite. Secondly, a shaky regime or party will be in a less advantageous position to resist client demands than a strong one, since an election is an all or nothing affair and uncertainty over the outcome will raise costs; when the race is close the marginal value of the extra dollar, patronage job, development grant, in recruiting supporters, is all the greater to the party. That is one reason why distributive pressures were greater in 1955 in Indonesia, when an election fraught with uncertainty would determine which parties would form a coalition, than in Malaysia in 1964 when the question was not whether the Alliance would win but whether it would take two thirds of the seats. The third factor concerning social change is based on the fact that patron-client ties in less traditional areas typically require the patron to deliver more in the way of instrumental, material rewards. The maintenance of a loyal patron-client network in a traditional area where deference is strong, will, I assume, cost a party somewhat less in material rewards and favors than a network of the same size in a built-up area where traditional patron-client bonds have eroded. Finally, a neo-traditionalist party such as UMNO in Malaysia can, in part, rely upon the traditional legitimacy of many of its leaders while a party of "new men" such as the PNI in Indonesia or the AFPFL in Burma have to rely more often on highly instrumental ties. Thus a weak party led by "new men" and relying on votes from among an uprooted population is likely to develop a patchwork patron-client structure that is very expensive to maintain. It is indicative of just how much financial backing such structures require, that only a ruling party with access to the public till can generally afford the construction costs.[31]

The distributive pressures experienced by such regimes manifest themselves in familiar ways. Government budgets, and of course deficits, swell quickly with expenditures on education, growing public employment, community development projects, agricultural loans, and so forth. Particularly since votes in Southeast Asia are in the countryside, one would expect that regimes with strong electoral pressures would spend more in the grassroots rural areas than regimes without such pressures. Given such pressures, local expenditure is also arranged as much as possible so that benefits can be distributed individually since that is more in keeping with the nature of patron-client exchange patterns. Even with pork-barrel programs a local party leader will claim personal responsibility for the gift and take a hand in the personal distribution of whatever employment or subcontracting it includes. The capacity of the regime to keep its network intact and win elections depends on its capacity to keep rewards flowing down the network at a constant or even expanding rate.

A regime that is dependent on its partic-

ularistic distributive capacity is also unlikely to solve its financial dilemmas either by structural reform or by tapping new sources of revenue. Most conceivable structural reforms, such as land redistribution, would strike at the resource base of many patrons and are thus unacceptable to parties whose *policy* interests coincide with the desires of its dominant patrons. Such regimes also have a most difficult time raising revenue from internal taxation. A rise in direct taxation would threaten their base of support and, in fact, they are notorious for the under-collection of revenues due them since favors to their clients often take the form of either leaving them off local tax rolls or ignoring debts they owe the government. The Burmese peasants connected to U Nu's faction of the AFPFL, for example, were almost universally in default of agricultural loans they had received as party supporters. They assumed the loan was a gift for clientship and knew that a government dependent on their votes could scarcely press matters.

If this analysis is correct, regimes under intense distributive pressures will characteristically resort to budget deficits, especially in election years, to finance their networks of adherents. Their reliance on heavily instrumental and highly monetized patron-client ties will also make it difficult for them to avoid a running down of foreign exchange reserves to maintain their strength at the polls. The division of expenditures within the budgets of such regimes should also reveal a heavy emphasis on distributive expenses at the local level. Empirical studies of budget distribution, budget deficits, and foreign exchange expenditures over time in parliamentary Burma, Indonesia, and the Philippines, when compared with similar statistics for non-parliamentary periods in these same countries, or, say, with statistics from Thailand and Malaysia should confirm this prediction.

Democractic regimes which must cater to the strong distributive pressures generated by their electoral clientele are thus particularly vulnerable to the vagaries of world prices for primary products on which their budgets depend. As long as the economy expanded and world prices were buoyant, they could afford the costs in public jobs, pork-barrel, and loan programs to solidify and expand their huge patron-client network. But a stagnating economy or declining world prices threatened the entire structure they had pieced together, since it relied so heavily on material inducements and relatively little on affective ties. In this context it may be that the collapse of Korean war-boom prices for primary exports was the crucial blow to democracy in Indonesia and Burma. The Philippines may have narrowly escaped a similar fate by having a longer and more legitimate democratic tradition and by not having suffered as proportionately large a loss in foreign exchange. Malaysia was less vulnerable as she had just become independent and her strong government faced only moderate distributive pressures while the Thai military elite was even less reliant on its distributive performance. The political stability or instability of parliamentary forms in these nations in the late 1950's was thus strongly affected by the strength of distributive pressures fostered by these political systems in the mid 1950's.

1. Two influential anthropologists dealing with primordial bonds are Clifford Geertz, "The Integrative Revolution," in Geertz, ed., *Old Societies and New States* (New York: Free Press, 1963); and Max Gluckman, *Custom and Conflict in Africa* (Oxford: Basil and Blackwell, 1963). A number of political studies of Southeast Asia have dealt with factionalism or patron-client ties. The most outstanding is Carl Landé's *Leaders, Factions, and Parties: the Structure of Philippine Politics*, Monograph No. 6 (New Haven: Yale University—Southeast Asia Studies, 1964). For the Thai political system, Fred Riggs, *Thailand: the Modernization of a Bureaucratic Polity* (Honolulu: East-West Center Press, 1968), and David A. Wilson, *Politics in Thailand* (Ithaca: Cornell University Press, 1965) pursue a similar line of analysis; and for Burma, see Lucian W. Pye, *Politics, Personality, and Nation-Building: Burma's Search for Identity* (New Haven: Yale University Press, 1962). Some notable attempts to do comparable studies outside Southeast Asia are: Colin Leys, *Politicians and Policies: An Essay on Politics in Acholi Uganda 1962–1965* (Nairobi: East Africa Publishing House, 1967); Myron Weiner, *Party-Building in a New Nation: The Indian National Congress* (Chicago: University of Chicago Press, 1967); Paul R. Brass, *Factional Politics in an Indian State* (Berkeley and Los Angeles: University of California Press, 1965); F. G. Bailey, *Politics and Social Change: Orissa in 1959* (Berkeley and Los Angeles: University of California Press, 1963).

2. Class as well as ethnicity is relevant to Malay-Chinese conflict since the different economic structure of each community places them in conflict. Many a rural Malay experiences the Chinese not only as pork-eating infidels but as middlemen, money lenders, shopkeepers, etc.—as the cutting edge of the capitalist penetration of the countryside.

3. See note 5 below for several works using such terms.

4. The reasons for this are elaborated in section IV of the original paper, to be published in the *American Political Science Review*.

5. There is an extensive literature, mostly anthropological, dealing with patron-client bonds which I have relied on in constructing this definition. Some of the most useful include: George M. Foster, "The Dyadic Contract in Tzintzuntzan: Patron-Client Relationship," *American Anthropologist*, 65 (1963), pp. 1280–1294; Eric Wolf, "Kinship, Friendship, and Patron-Client Relations," in M. Banton, ed., *The Social Anthropology of Complex Societies* (New York: Praeger, 1966); J. Campbell, *Honour, Family, and Patronage* (Oxford: Clarendon Press, 1964); John Duncan Powell, "Peasant Society and Clientelist Politics," *American Political Science Review*, LXIV, 2 (June, 1970), and Carl Landé, *op. cit.;* Alex Weingrod, "Patrons, Patronage and Political Parties," *Comparative Studies in Society and History*, 10 (July, 1968), pp. 1142–1158.

6. Powell, *op. cit.*, p. 412.

7. Another comparable model, of course, is the lord-vassal link of high feudalism, except in this relationship the mutual rights and obligations were of an almost formal contractual nature. Most patron-client ties we will discuss involve tacit, even diffuse standards of reciprocity. Cf. Roughton Coulborn, *Feudalism in History*.

8. In most communities this sense of obligation is a strong moral force, backed by informal community sanctions that help bind the client to the patron. A good account of how such feelings of debt reinforce social bonds in the Philippines is Frank Lynch's description of *utang na loob* in *Four Readings in Philippine Values*, Institute of Philippine Culture Papers, No. 2 (Quezon City: Ateneo de Manila Press, 1964).

9. (New York: Wiley, 1964), pp. 21–22. Blau's discussion of unbalanced exchange and the disparities in power and deference such unbalance fosters is directly relevant to the basis of patron-client relationships.

10. These general alternatives are deduced by Blau and are intended to be exhaustive. *Ibid.*, p. 118.

11. Later, we will examine certain conditions under which this may actually occur.

12. There is little doubt that this last re-

sort usually acts as a brake on oppression. The proximate causes for many peasant uprisings in medieval Europe during hard times often involved revocation of small rights granted serfs by their lords—e.g. gleaning rights, use of the commons for pasturage, hunting and fishing privileges, reduction of dues in bad crop years—rights which offered a margin of security. Such revolts, even though they generally failed, served as an object lesson to neighboring patrons. Cf. Fredrich Engels, *The Peasant War in Germany* (New York: International Publishers, 1966); Norman Cohn, *The Pursuit of the Millennium* (New York: Harper, 1961); and E. B. Hobsbawm, *Primitive Rebels* (New York: Norton, 1959).

13. Blau, *op. cit.*, pp. 119–120, makes this point somewhat differently: "The degree of dependence of individuals on a person who supplies valued services is a function of the difference between their value and that of the second best alternative open to them." The patron may, of course, be dependent himself on having a large number of clients, but his dependence upon any *one* client is much less than the dependence of any one client upon him. In this sense the total dependence of patron and client are similar but most all the client's dependence is focused on one individual, whereas the patron's dependence is thinly spread (like that of an insurance company—Blau, p. 137) across many clients. Cf. Godfrey and Monica Wilson, *The Analysis of Social Change: Based on Observations in Central Africa* (Cambridge: Cambridge University Press, 1945), pp. 28, 40.

14. Blau, *op. cit.*, p. 269.

15. *Ibid.*, p. 127. [Sections on the distinctiveness of the "patron" vis-à-vis the "broker" and on patron and clients as distinctive groups have been omitted. Eds.]

16. There is no contradiction, I believe, in holding that a patron-client link originates in a power relationship and also holding that genuine affective ties reinforce that link. Affective ties often help legitimate a relationship that is rooted in inequality. For an argument that, in contrast, begins with the assumption that some cultures engender a psychological need for dependence, see O. Mannoni, *Prospero and Caliban: The Psychology of Colonization* (New York: Praeger, 1964).

17. Eric R. Wolf, "Kinship, Friendship, and Patron-Client Relations in Complex Societies," *op. cit.*, p. 10.

18. In this connection, see my *Political Ideology in Malaysia* (New Haven: Yale University Press, 1968), chap. 6; and for zero-sum conceptions among peasants, George M. Foster, "Peasant Society and the Image of Limited Good," *American Anthropologist*, 65 (April, 1965), 293–315.

19. See, for example, E. R. Leach, "The Frontiers of Burma," *Comparative Studies in Society and History*, III, 1 (1960), pp. 49–68.

20. See, for example, Edmund Leach, *The Political Systems of Highland Burma* (Cambridge: Harvard Univeristy Press, 1954), and J. M. Gullick, *Indigenous Political Systems of Western Malaya*, London School of Economics Monographs on Social Anthropology No. 17 (London: University of London/Athlone Press, 1958).

21. Again, indirectly ruled areas were often exceptions in that local rulers tended to take on new powers under the colonial regime and thus became more comprehensive patrons than in the past.

22. For Malaysia, M. G. Swift, *Malay Peasant Society in Jelebu* (London: University of London, 1965), pp. 158–160, captures this shift in local power. A general treatment of such changes is contained in Ralph W. Nicholas, "Factions: a Comparative Analysis," in M. Banton, ed., *Political Systems and the Distribution of Power*, Association of Applied Social Anthropology Monograph No. 2 (New York: Praeger, 1963), pp. 21–61.

23. In his study of politics in an Indonesian town, Clifford Geertz has shown that the more traditional hamlets were more likely to be united under a particular leader than hamlets which had changed more; *The Social History of an Indonesian Town* (Cambridge: M.I.T. Press, 1965), chap. 6. This finding is corroborated by Feith's study of the 1955 Indonesian elections; Herbert Feith, *The Indonesian Elections of 1955*, Interim Report Series, Modern Indonesia Project (Ithaca: Cornell University, 1961), pp. 28–30. Another comparative study of two Burmese villages also supports this conclusion: cf. Manning Nash, *The Golden Road to Modernity* (New York: Wiley, 1965). In this context, directly-ruled lowland areas tended to develop factional competition among different patrons, while less directly ruled areas (especially highland areas) more frequently retained some unity behind a single patron who remained their broker with the outside world.

24. *The Analysis of Social Change, op. cit.*, pp. 28, 40.

25. For a description of such mechanisms see Clifford Geertz, *Agricultural Involution* (Berkeley and Los Angeles: University of California Press, 1963); George M. Foster, "Peasant Society and the Image of Limited Good," M. G. Swift, *op. cit.*, and Mary R. Hollnsteiner, "Social Control and Filipino Personality," in *Symposium on the Filipino Personality* (Macati: Psychological Association of the Philippines, 1965), p. 24.

26. Geertz shows how local leaders often managed to become agents of the local sugar mills—buying crops, renting land, and recruiting labor and thereby enlarging their power in the community. *Op. cit.*, p. 57.

27. David Wurfel, "The Philippines," in Richard Rose and Arnold Heidenheimer, eds., *Comparative Studies in Political Finance, Journal of Politics,* 25, 4 (November, 1963), pp. 757–773.

28. Herbert Feith, *The Indonesian Elections of 1955;* and Clifford Geertz, *The Social History of an Indonesian Town.*

29. Feith describes the campaign as a "race for a foothold in these villages . . . a foothold involving allegiance of as many as possible of their influential people. Here the first step was to secure the support of those whose authority was accepted by the village prominents." *Op. cit.,* p. 79.

30. Nicholas, "Factions: a Comparative Analysis," *op. cit.,* p. 45.

31. Adrian C. Mayer seems to have this distinction in mind, in his study of an Indian town which compares the "hard" campaign of the Jan Sangh, which relied on durable social ties and tried to prevent defections, and the local Congress Party, which ran a "soft" campaign of short-term links by promising favors and benefits to intermediaries. "The Significance of Quasi-Groups in the Study of Complex Societies," in M. Banton, ed., *The Social Anthropology of Complex Societies,* p. 106.

THE URBAN POOR
Disruption or Political Integration in Third World Cities?
JOAN NELSON
Harvard University and M.I.T.

Most of the nations of Africa and Asia remain predominantly rural and agricultural. However, more than half of the people in most Latin American countries are no longer rural, and a fifth to a third live in cities of 100,000 or more. In Asia and North Africa, Lebanon, the U.A.R., and the Philippines are also substantially urbanized, and Morocco, Syria, Turkey, South Korea, and Taiwan are not far behind. Moreover, virtually everywhere in the developing world, regardless of the extent of urbanization already achieved, cities are growing at rates of 5 to 8 percent annually. That is, they are doubling their populations every ten to fifteen years.[1]

Such rapid growth has far-reaching social, economic, and political repercussions. Rural areas are steadily losing many of their more ambitious young adults. A large and growing share of the cities' population are newcomers to urban life. Exploding physical size and pressure on urban services impinge on long-established urban groups. All of these changes have political effects. Yet to date there has been remarkably little analysis of the political effects of rapid urban growth.

This paper focuses on only one set of effects: the immediate and longer-run political role of migrants to the larger cities, and more generally of the urban poor. It argues that, contrary to widespread speculation by both foreign observers and elites in the countries concerned, neither new migrants nor the urban poor are likely to play a direct destabilizing role. Indeed, historical experience in industrialized nations suggests that the urban poor are not likely to play a significant political role at all. However, there are major demographic, economic, and political contrasts between today's developing nations and Europe and North America in the late

From *World Politics* (April 1970), pp. 393–405. Reprinted by permission. Latter section of article appears separately below. This is augmented by a section from the author's paper on "Urban Growth and Politics in Developing Nations: Prospects for the 1970's," presented to Columbia University Conference on International Economic Development, February 1970.

nineteenth and early twentieth centuries. The differences in context make it possible that the urban poor of Latin America, North Africa, and Asia may come to take a more active part in municipal and national politics than did their historical counterparts.

URBAN GROWTH AND POLITICAL INSTABILITY [2]

Many of the migrants swelling the cities have little or no education and few skills. Moreover, in most developing countries rates of unemployment and particularly underemployment are high and rising. Programs to improve conditions in rural areas are often urged as a means to stem the movements to the cities. But the very processes that promote rural modernization and integration—education, mass media, transportation—also spur the exodus in search of a better life. Labor-intensive techniques in industry are sometimes proposed as a means of absorbing laborers once they reach the cities. But such techniques often imply high unit costs of production, and are unlikely to be adopted on a large scale. In short, the cities face a steady rise in the proportion of their populations that is unskilled, semi-employed, and abysmally poor—marginal to the city's economy and social organization.[3]

From the viewpoint of welfare and economic development, the growth of a large marginal urban population is not necessarily detrimental. Despite insecure jobs and squalid living conditions, most migrants feel that they are better off than they were before coming to the city. The movement to the cities facilitates wider distribution of certain services, particularly schools and clinics. Concern on grounds of welfare therefore is probably misplaced. Rural-to-urban migration also removes redundant labor from agriculture. While productivity in the overloaded service sector is falling in many developing nations, it is still substantially higher than productivity in agriculture.

Though separate data are not available on productivity in intermittent day labor or construction jobs and in low-paid segments of the service sector (vending, loading and carrying, domestic help, petty personal services), these ways of scraping by are probably not less productive than marginal production in agriculture. Moreover,

residence in the city exposes the migrant to modernizing influences, and improves his opportunity to acquire skills, however modest. The major economic disadvantage is the diversion of public funds and energies from more directly and immediate productive uses that is likely to result from pressure for expanded municipal services.

The strongest concern about rapid urban growth and urban underemployment is political rather than economic. A lengthening list of articles asserts that chaos and revolution lurk in the *favelas* of Rio and the alleys of Calcutta.[4] Dire predictions about the political effects of rapid urban growth take two main forms.[5] Some of the prophets focus on the migrants. Uprooted, isolated, disappointed, and frustrated, they are viewed as tinder for any demagogic or extremist spark. Other theorists argue just the opposite: new migrants are politically passive. The threat to political stability lies not with newcomers, but with those deprived and frustrated slum and shanty dwellers who are longer urban residents, or with second generation. These contentions are explored in turn.

The Disruptive Migrants

The theory. In cities growing at annual rates of 5 percent or more, with migration accounting for more than half the increase, migrants come to constitute the bulk of the urban population within a few decades. Moreover, many are very recently arrived: a quarter or more of the population of many major Latin American cities have arrived within the past five years.[6] It is often assumed that many or most of the newcomers have been torn from a tightly structured rural society and plunged into a bewildering, impersonal, and harsh environment with few or no sources of support and guidance. Shock and isolation produce personal disorientation and political anomie. Economic conditions are also an acute disappointment. Frustrated and disillusioned, the migrant is readily persuaded to political violence or extremism.[7]

The evidence. There is virtually no evidence that new migrants are either radical or violence-prone. Direct evidence is hard to find, because it is difficult to separate newcomers from the rest of the population. Myron Weiner examined the Calcutta voting pattern for state assemblymen in

1957 and 1962, and found that districts with heavy concentrations of migrants (not necessarily newcomers) correlated closely with high votes for the Congress Party.[8] Soares and Hamblin, analyzing factors affecting the Chilean presidential elections of 1952, found a negative relation between departments with high proportions of migrants and a high vote for Salvador Allende, the candidate of the radical left.[9] Studies of recent urban violence in the United States have found migrants underrepresented among the rioters.[10] Charles Tilly, studying urban turbulence in nineteenth-century France, finds no consistent relation at all between the frequency of violent conflicts in departments and the rates of increase of the urban population in the cities dominating those departments.[11]

Where the theory goes wrong. Data that shed light on where the theory goes wrong are more plentiful than direct evidence on the political behavior of newcomers to the cities.

(1) Regarding the shock of urban life: many migrants into the great cities come from smaller cities and towns, not from the countryside. Surveys indicate that in Santiago, Chile,[12] and in six Brazilian cities including Rio and Sao Paulo,[13] roughly two-thirds of the migrants were *not* rural in origin. This reflects the well-documented pattern of step-wise migration. In India, higher proportions of migrants come directly from the countryside. Surveys in the mid-1950's found that 50 and 75 percent of the migrants to Delhi [14] and Bombay,[15] respectively, were rural in origin.

Among those migrants who do come from small villages, many have some previous exposure to urban influence. Surveys in squatter settlements in Bogota [16] and Ankara [17] found that two-thirds of the migrants came from less than 100 and less than 120 miles away, respectively. Villages near large cities are often affected by urban influences. Many migrants have also visited city relatives or friends before deciding to move. There are villages where for many years high proportions of the young people have migrated; earlier migrants return on visits to tell prospective migrants what they can expect.

Particularly in Latin America, traditional rural social structure has been eroded in all except the most remote areas.[18] Therefore many of those migrants who are rural in origin do not come from tightly structured social settings. Though rural change and disorganization have little to do with affirmative preparation for urban life, these trends do cast doubt on the assumption that migrants are traumatized by the shattering of deeply ingrained habits and values.

Finally, since most migrants are young adults with better education and training than the average in their places of origin, their capacity and desire to adjust can be presumed to be comparatively high.

(2) Regarding isolation: Newcomers obviously know few people when they arrive in the city. But very high proportions—from 70 to 90 percent—of samples drawn in several Latin American cities [19] report receiving help in settling from family, friends, or employers. In some regions and countries, new arrivals may also find assistance and friends in provincial home-town, tribe, or caste associations.[20]

(3) Regarding economic conditions and migrant's reaction to them: Most migrants find jobs quite quickly. (A Santiago sample: 40 percent within 2 days; [21] a second Santiago sample drawn from squatters only: 47 percent within the first week.[22] A Brazilian sample of the adult population in six cities: 80 percent within a month.[23] Other surveys report similar findings.) [24] Surveys also consistently show lower rates of open unemployment among migrants than among native urbanites.[25] This, however, may reflect age structure: higher proportions of native-born members of the labor force are adolescent or in their early twenties, age groups with higher-than-average unemployment rates.[26]

Migrants are somewhat over-represented in low-level jobs, but the overall patterns of employment are not markedly different from those of urban-born workers.[27] This probably reflects the high proportions of migrants who come from other cities and towns, and who may well be better educated and more highly skilled than the average for the city of destination. The few surveys that compare current jobs (or first job in the city) with jobs before migration show considerable upward mobility.[28]

Migrants' reactions to city housing vary, depending on their previous standards and on the geographic and climatic conditions that largely determine the objective adequacy of low-cost housing and shanty settlements. Germani's working-class samples in Buenos Aires, most of whom came from smaller cities or towns, were quite dissatisfied.[29] But Pearse and Bonilla both stress that *favela* housing in urban Brazil is much like rural housing throughout the nation.[30]

More generally, surveys conducted in settlements ranging from well-established blue-collar neighborhoods in Buenos Aires to squalid shantytowns outside of Baghdad concur: overwhelming proportions of migrants say that their incomes, material possessions, access to services, and opportunities for their children are better in the city.[31]

To summarize: The assumptions that migrants are uprooted and isolated in the city are grossly overdrawn. The assumption that most are disappointed and frustrated by economic conditions is simply wrong. Some migrants undoubtedly are disillusioned, but lack of widespread contacts plus political inexperience and traditional patterns of deference makes it most unlikely that newcomers' frustrations will be translated into destabilizing political action.

The Radical Marginals

The theory. To exorcise the myth of the disruptive migrants is to raise a new specter—that of the radical poor. If migrants feel an initial sense of progress, what happens when their memories of earlier misery fade? If low levels of political awareness, deference to authority, and perhaps political conservatism are part of the rural baggage migrants carry with them, what happens after prolonged urban exposure? As migrants become established urbanites with urban aspirations and attitudes, but still eke out a marginal existence, will not they or their children sooner or later express growing frustration through political radicalism or violence? [32]

The evidence. The theory is hard set to test empirically. Data on length of urban residence are scarce. Adequate indices of radicalism and workable definitions of marginality are difficult to devise. Glaucio Soares states the theory particularly clearly but cites only one piece of evidence: a survey conducted among skilled and unskilled workers in Rio in 1960, showing

that support for the Brazilian Labor Party increased substantially among unskilled workers with longer urban residence, but not among skilled workers.[33]

I have tried to approximate his test using data from the Almond-Verba surveys in Mexico [34] and from Inkeles' surveys in Argentina and Chile.[35] The Mexico data contradict Soares' Rio findings: skilled workers with greater urban experience leaned toward demonstrations and violence as effective political techniques; unskilled workers did not. The Inkeles data look more like Soares' findings, but the index of radicalism is inadequate: replies to questions regarding the need for substantial and rapid social change, with no reference to political means.

Studies of class voting patterns and of participation in urban violence do not distinguish among degrees of urban experience and therefore do not really test the hypothesis. But in the absence of good tests, such studies at least provide data on the political behavior of the urban poor in general. In the Venezuelan presidential elections of 1958 and 1963, there was little support in the poorest districts of Caracas for the Communist ticket in 1958 and the farthest left legal candidate in 1963. In Santiago, Chile, high proportions of the low-rent district vote went to Salvador Allende in 1958, but in 1964 much of this support shifted to Eduardo Frei, a moderate reformist alternative not previously available.[36]

Indian survey data gathered before the 1966 national elections found low-income voters in Bombay, Calcutta, Delhi, and Madras no more or less ready to support extremist parties of the right and left than were more affluent voters.[37] Myron Weiner states that demonstrations in Calcutta are much more likely to involve violence if they are based on the middle class than if they are predominantly working class.[38] Tilly and other students of French history conclude, from formidably detailed police records, that those involved in the repeated Parisian incidents of the nineteenth century were mostly from the skilled, established crafts, "segments of the working class already politically alert, organized, and integrated into the life of the city." [39]

Where the theory goes wrong. Aspirations undoubtedly rise, but they probably do so quite gradually. No studies are available, to my knowledge, on the effects of urban exposure on material and other aspirations. My own attempts to use Inkeles' data for this purpose do show an upward drift in aspirations as urban experience lengthens. Rising aspirations for better jobs, housing, and status are more marked, however, among the skilled than among the unskilled workers. The urban-born are less satisfied with their jobs and self-assessed status.[40]

Sociological studies of working-class norms provide a firmer basis for the hypothesis that aspirations rise slowly. Those at the very bottom are preoccupied with survival. Some may be victims of the apathy Oscar Lewis calls "the culture of poverty." Those a step or two up the ladder set modest targets for themselves: sons of unskilled workers in Queretaro, Mexico, want to be masons, shoemakers, or construction workers.[41] Realism may not only trim targets but may also shape values. Studies of working-class norms in the United States find "getting by" stressed more heavily than "getting ahead." [42]

(1) Turning to achievement: modest occupational progress out of the lowest categories is probably quite widespread. Data on intergenerational occupational mobility in three cities in developing countries—São Paulo, Buenos Aires, and Poona —show a majority of the sons of unskilled workers rising out of this category, and substantial fractions riding into nonmanual occupations.[43] São Paulo may be uniquely dynamic, but the data from Poona probably is not unrepresentative. Moreover, Germani's data from Buenos Aires show that the second generation, with its higher aspirations, is also more likely to move out of the unskilled category.[44]

The much-deplored squatter settlements may provide many urban poor with an additional channel of achievement. Such settlements are not usually the first stop for the incoming migrant, but are more often established by families with longer urban experience. Where squatters are not harassed by the police, and where terrain and initial density of settlement permit, many shantytowns evolve over ten or fifteen years into acceptable working-class neighborhoods.[45] Squatting offers immediate relief from the burden of rent and the threat of eviction, and a long-run prospect of a modicum of comfort and re-

spectability. In many cities in Latin America, North Africa, and Turkey, 10 to 40 percent of the population live in squatter settlements.[46] Not all of these settlements are "self-improving," but for many among the urban poor, squatting is a means of substantial progress.

(2) Regarding frustration: The slow rise of aspirations and the wide incidence of modest progress may explain the otherwise puzzling finding that even among groups reporting that their economic situation has deteriorated in the past few years, overwhelming majorities express optimism about the future [47] and belief that the economic and social system is open to talent and hard work. Surveys in many different countries, asking a variety of questions, concur on this point.[48] Faith in the future may make present hardship less bitter. And general belief in open opportunity prevents conversion of individual misfortune into a sense of social injustice.

(3) Regarding conversion of frustration to disruptive political action: Frustration obviously can be expressed in many ways —withdrawal and defeat, quarrelsome behavior, alcoholism, religion. Political action, whether individual or associational, moderate or extremist, legal or illegal, is only one class of reactions among many. The point is obvious, but it is often overlooked.

Moreover, the urban poor are particularly unlikely to choose aggressive political action to express their grievances. Low status and lack of contacts make them more vulnerable to police force and less likely to get fair treatment in the courts. They are unorganized, their level of political awareness is low, and these conditions are perpetuated by the constant inflow of additional unskilled, poorly educated migrants. Moreover, the causes of poverty, unemployment, and inflation are remote. Wealthier and better-educated people may think in terms of governmental policies and their effect on economic conditions, but the poor and uneducated are less likely to blame the authorities for general economic difficulties.[49] The recent militancy of minority groups among the poor in the United States appears to contradict these generalizations, but that is the product of very different circumstances.

To summarize: The theory of radicalization and the deprivation/frustration/aggression model on which it rests may contain a good deal of truth. The theory itself does not specify the pace of radicalization. But it is usually linked to predictions of political upheaval in the not-too-distant future. This implicit estimate almost surely overstates the rate at which both discontent and political awareness spread among the urban lower classes. Such calculations also imply a high rate of conversion from frustration to radical political action. In fact, the bulk of economic and social frustration is likely to leak into alternative channels, including nonradical political action.

The question of destabilization or radicalization has pre-empted much of the meager attention scholars have given to the study of the political implications of urban growth abroad. Yet if we want to locate the sources of urban turbulence and extremism, the urban lower class is the wrong group to examine. Indeed, most of those scholars primarily interested in civil conflict have focused their attention on other groups, primarily students, organized labor, and the military. If, however, we are interested in the current and potential political role of the urban lower class, preoccupation with instability blinds us to a number of more probable, and equally interesting, patterns of evolution.

In brief, most inquiries into the political role of the urban poor in developing countries have asked the wrong questions. Moreover, most analysis to date has stressed social psychology to the point of ignoring highly relevant political variables. The attitudes of the urban poor, so far as they can be ascertained, are certainly important. But these attitudes are shaped by and interact with the political context in the individual nation and city. The agents and channels of political socialization of the urban poor, and the factors determining the degree and nature of interest in the urban poor on the part of the established political organizations, are topics that deserve much more attention than they have received thus far.

THE MIDDLE CLASSES,
ORGANIZED LABOR,
AND URBAN INSTABILITY [50]

To argue that the swelling urban masses are not likely to be major sources of political instability in the 1970's is not to predict a placid urban scene. The cities will continue to be the strongholds of the opposition, the spawning ground for extremist movements, and the site of non-violent and violent strikes and demonstrations. They are also the home of virtually all institutions of higher education, industrial establishments, and the middle class in general.

The political role of organized labor varies greatly. In some nations it is too small and weak to have any impact. In others all or most union activity is tightly controlled by the government. Where independent, active, and powerful unions exist, their militance and the scope of their concerns vary with the extent and nature of their ties to opposition parties, the amount of in-fighting between and within unions, and the internal structure of various industries. In many countries skilled industrial labor has become a working class elite, enjoying wages and fringe benefits out of line with the general wage structure, and intent upon preserving and improving its privileged position.

These tendencies may be reinforced by labor legislation which is advanced by comparison with legislation in the early stages of industrialization in Europe and North America, by a structure of incentives and exchange rates that encourage capital-intensive and technologically advanced industrial investment, and by the higher welfare standards and political vulnerability of foreign firms which often employ a high proportion of the modern industrial labor force. On the other hand, there is some evidence that more skilled workers are more likely to see a need for radical change. It seems plausible that its activation depends on objective economic and political conditions in individual nations.

The white-collar middle class, however, is more uniformly and predictably a recruiting ground for opposition movements of all kinds, including those that advocate extreme programs or violent methods. Middle-class groups in general are more politically aware, better informed, more conscious of the relevance of politics to their own interests, and more confident of their ability to influence the actions of the government. They are also more likely to be attracted by ideological appeals and explanations than are lower class groups.

. . . [The] true victims of the aspiration-achievement gap are the members of the middle class. It is the clerks, school-teachers, policemen, bank employees, and shop assistants who aspire to a style of life including a varied wardrobe and diet, a conventional house or apartment, a car, a vacation at the beach, a college educa-tion for their children. The wardrobe and diet are more or less within their means. The other elements of a satisfying life, as they define it, are not.

It is hazardous to generalize, and more so to attempt predictions, about so diverse a social category. Moreover, the political traditions, structure, and atmosphere of individual nations and cities will affect the probability of destabilizing action as much or more than the presence of widespread frustration. The over-all efficiency and the specific responses of the national and local governments obviously also are important in damping or exacerbating tensions. But it is nonetheless predictable that parts of the middle classes, plus the closely allied and universally discontented and disrup-tive groups of students and the educated unemployed, will be the sources of much of the instability and extremism which may emerge during the 1970's.

These groups are concentrated in cities. But it is worth noting that the issues which concern them are only in part traceable to the pressures of rapid urbanization. The housing squeeze, a serious cause of dis-content for skilled labor and white-collar groups, is indeed related to rapid urban growth. Hopelessly overcrowded public transportation and public schools undoubt-edly intensify middle-class preferences for owning a car and sending their children to private schools. But they would probably want to do so even if urban conditions were much better than they are.

Students often demonstrate against in-creases in bus fares, but this is hardly their central concern. Other salient issues—open-ings and scholarships in universities, the organization of the universities, opportuni-ties for white-collar and professional em-ployment, taxation levels, foreign private investment and its role in the economy, and national prestige on the international scene—are related indirectly or not at all to urbanization.

To summarize: rapid urbanization un-questionably causes staggering physical, economic, and human problems. Cities are undeniably the locus of political opposi-tion, and often also centers of extremism and violence. Moreover, urban instability may well increase during the 1970's. But the pattern of urbanization without con-comitant industrialization is not the major cause of the instability. Therefore, policies designed to cope with urban problems, whatever their urgency on economic and welfare grounds, will do little to alleviate instability in the cities. That objective must be pursued through other policies and pro-grams directed to improving the relation-ship of education to the economy and to the other issues which move labor, stu-dents, and middle-class groups to political action.

These conclusions suggest a second, per-haps more helpful implication for plan-ning and policy. In a number of countries low-cost urban housing programs, policies for dealing with squatter settlements, and other aspects of urban policy have had a sporadic, stop-start, inconsistent character. This has reflected uncertainty as to how to cope with truly staggering problems, but also has resulted from periodic surges of concern about political instability. Many of the "crash" programs have been ill-con-ceived and poorly executed, thereby wast-ing scarce resources and contributing to cynicism among the poor and defeatism among the affluent. The recognition that the urban poor are unlikely to be politically explosive would help make possible less vacillating policies and a longer time-frame for planning. It is to be hoped that the growing pressure of urban problems is it-self sufficient to sustain an appropriate sense of urgency, without the additional but distorting impetus of fear.

1. In Brazil and Mexico between 1940 and 1950, population in cities of 100,000 or more grew at average annual rates of 5 and 6.7 per-cent respectively. During the 1950's Santo Domingo grew 7.3 percent yearly; Panama City expanded at a rate of 7.9 percent. (United Nations *Compendium of Social Sta-tistics*, 1963, Series K, No. 2, Table 7.) In the 1950's and early 1960's, Bogota's popula-tion rose an average of 6.8 percent a year; Cali's increased at 6.3 percent. Paul T. Schultz, "Population and Labor Force Projec-tions for Colombia, 1964–1974" (Santa Mon-ica, California, RAND, July 10, 1967), p. 12 (mimeo). Between 1941 and 1959 Caracas averaged a 7.4 percent annual growth. Bruce

Herrick, *Urban Migration and Economic Development in Chile* (Cambridge, Mass. 1965), p. 31. In some other parts of Asia and the Near East, rapid urban growth rivals that of Latin America. Korean cities have been growing rapidly since the 1950's: Seoul added 6.6 percent more people each year from 1960 to 1966. Turkey's population centers of 100,000 or more grew 6.7 percent a year from 1955 to 1960; Ankara averaged 6.8 percent annually from 1960 to 1965. (Estimated from figures in the United Nations *Demographic Yearbook,* 1962, 1963, 1967.) In South Asia, urban growth rates are generally lower. Delhi grew 5 percent a year from 1951 to 1961, but greater Bombay expanded at an annual rate of 3.9 percent during that period, and Calcutta's rate was 1.9 percent, reflecting in part the immense size already reached by these two giants. Kingsley Davis and Roy Turner, eds., *India's Urban Future* (Berkeley 1962), 10.

2. For a more detailed discussion of the points in this section, see Joan M. Nelson, *Migrants, Urban Poverty, and Instability in Developing Nations,* Harvard Center for International Affairs, Occasional Paper No. 22 (Cambridge, Mass. 1969).

3. Open unemployment rates of 5 to 10 percent appear repeatedly in surveys of major Latin American and Indian cities. Rates are higher among the unskilled, among young men seeking their first jobs, and in larger cities. Fred Dziadek, "Unemployment in the Less Developed Countries," AID Discussion Paper No. 16 (Washington, June 1967), Appendix A. Urban underemployment must greatly exceed unemployment, but it is extremely difficult to measure. A proxy indicator of the extent of underemployment is productivity in the tertiary or service sector, which drops as the sector is swollen by peddling, domestic service, and other marginal occupations. It has been calculated that in Latin America between 1950 and 1965, while productivity in agriculture grew at 1.8 percent a year and industry, mining, and utilities at 2.5 percent annually, productivity in the service sectors fell, suggesting "a level of underemployment equivalent to 10 percent of the national labor force." Since services absorb much more urban than rural labor, the implied underemployment rate in the cities would far exceed 10 percent. Hollis B. Chenery, "Toward a More Effective Alliance for Progress," AID Discussion Paper No. 13 (Washington 1967), p. 12.

4. See, for example, Barbara Ward, "The Uses of Prosperity," *Saturday Review,* August 29, 1964, pp. 191–92; Frantz Fanon, *The Wretched of the Earth* (London 1965), p. 103.

5. Peter Lupsha's interesting article, "On Theories of Urban Violence," presented at the American Political Science Association meetings in 1968, lists many more theories of the causes of urban violence, including "conspiracy," "riff-raff," "teen-age rebellion," and "police brutality." However, the "recent migrant" and "frustration-aggression" theories discussed here are the two theories that appear most often in discussions of urban problems in the developing nations.

6. Bertram Hutchinson, "The Migrant Population of Urban Brazil," *America Latina,* vi (April–June 1963), pp. 43, 46; Paul T. Schultz, p. 2.

7. Philip Hauser, "The Social, Economic, and Technological Problems of Rapid Urbanization," in Bert F. Hoselitz and Wilbert E. Moore, eds., *Industrialization and Society* (The Hague 1963), pp. 210–11; Glaucio Soares and Robert L. Hamblin, "Socio-economic Variables and Voting for the Radical Left, Chile, 1952," *American Political Science Review,* LXI (December 1967), p. 1055. See also Mancur Olson, "Economic Growth as a Destabilizing Force," *Journal of Economic History,* XXIII (December 1963), p. 534.

8. Myron Weiner, "Urbanization and Political Protest," *Civilisations,* XVII (1967).

9. Soares and Hamblin.

10. National Advisory Commission of Civil Disorders, *Report,* advance edition printed by The *New York Times* Company, 1968, pp. 130–31; Lupsha, p. 7.

11. Charles Tilly, "Urbanization and Political Disturbances in Nineteenth-Century France," presented to the annual meeting of the Society for French Historical Studies (Ann Arbor, April 1966), pp. 7–8 (mimeo).

12. Herrick, pp. 53–103.

13. Hutchinson, pp. 43–44.

14. V. K. R. Rao and P. B. Desai, *Greater Delhi: A Study in Urbanization 1940–1957* (New York 1965), p. 10.

15. D. T. Lakdawala, *Work, Wages, and Well-being in an Indian Metropolis: Economic Surveys of Bombay City* (Bombay 1963), p. 159.

16. William L. Flinn, "Rural-to-Urban Migration: A Colombian Case," Research Publication No. 19 (U. of Wisconsin Land Tenure Center, July 1966), pp. 10, 23.

17. Granville Sewell, "Squatter Settlements in Turkey," unpub. diss. (M.I.T. 1964), p. 304.

18. Marshal Wolfe, "Some Implications of Recent Changes in Urban and Rural Settlement Patterns in Latin America," paper presented at the U.N. World Population Conference (Belgrade, September 1965), p. 25.

19. Gino Germani, "Inquiry into the Social Effects of Urbanization in a Working Class Sector of Greater Buenos Aires," United Nations Economic and Social Council, E/CN.12/URB/10, December 1958, Table 10, p. 26;

Herrick, p. 91; and ECLA, "Urbanization in Latin America: Results of a Field Survey of Living Conditions in an Urban Sector," E/CN.12.622, 1963, 17; Flinn, p. 27; Hutchinson, Table 12, p. 61 (mimeo).

20. William Mangin, "The Role of Regional Associations in the Adaptation of Rural Migrants to Cities in Peru," in Dwight Heath and Richard Adams, eds., *Contemporary Cultures and Societies of Latin America* (New York, 1965), p. 319.

21. Herrick, p. 92.

22. ECLA, "Results of a Field Survey," p. 16.

23. Hutchinson, pp. 67–68.

24. Germani, p. 69, Table 37.

25. Slighton, p. 38; Herrick, p. 84; Weiner, "Urbanization and Political Protest," p. 6; Rao and Desai, p. 341, Table 16-1, and p. 383, Table 17-3; Dantwala, p. 481; R. Mukerjee and B. Singh, *Social Profiles of a Metropolis* (Bombay 1961), p. 116; G. M. Farooq, *The People of Karachi: Economic Characteristics*, Monographs in the Economics of Development No. 15 (Karachi, Pakistan Institute of Development Economics, July 1966), p. 19.

26. Herrick, p. 79; Slighton, p. 37.

27. Germani, p. 51, Table 29; Rao and Desai, p. 373, tables 16–19; Herrick, pp. 86–87, tables 6–9; Lakdawala, p. 466, Table VI-37, columns 7–8; Mukerjee and Singh, pp. 88–89; Rao and Desai, p. 223, tables 12–15.

28. Rao and Desai, pp. 94–95, tables 5-14, 5-15; Herrick, pp. 94–95.

29. Germani, p. 16.

30. Andrew Pearse, "Some Characteristics of Urbanization in the City of Rio de Janeiro," in Philip Hauser, ed., *Urbanization in Latin America* (UNESCO, 1961), p. 196; Frank Bonilla, "Rio's Favelas: The Rural Slum Within the City," American University Field Staff *Reports*, East Coast South America Series, 8:3 (1961), p. 2.

31. Doris Phillips, "Rural-to-Urban Migration in Iraq," *Economic Development and Cultural Change*, VII (July 1959), p. 417; Flinn, pp. 5, 37; Sewell, pp. 109–110.

32. For example, see Glaucio Soares, "The Political Sociology of Uneven Development in Brazil," in Irving L. Horowitz, ed., *Revolution in Brazil* (New York, 1964), pp. 192, 195; also Kingsley Davis and Hilda H. Golden, "Urbanization and the Development of Pre-Industrial Areas," *Economic Development and Cultural Change,* III (1954), pp. 19–20.

33. Soares, p. 192.

34. Gabriel Almond and Sidney Verba, *The Civic Culture* (Princeton, 1963).

35. Large-scale attitudinal surveys of factory workers and control groups were conducted by Alex Inkeles and his associates in Argentina, Chile, Israel, Nigeria, India, and Pakistan, as a basis for a study of the modernizing impact of factory experience on attitudes. I am indeed indebted to Professor Inkeles for permission to use his data.

36. George F. Jones, "Urbanization and Voting Behavior in Venezuela and Chile, 1958–1964," typescript prepared at Stanford University, March 1967, pp. 40–43, pp. 69–72.

37. Indian Institute of Public Opinion, "The Structure of Urban Public Opinion," *Public Opinion Surveys,* XI (February 1966), pp. 15–16.

38. Myron Weiner, "Violence and Politics in Calcutta," *The Journal of Asian Studies,* XX (May 1961), p. 277.

39. Charles Tilly, "A Travers le Chaos des Vivantes Cités," paper presented to the Sixth World Congress of Sociology (Evian-les-Bains, September 1966), pp. 17, 19 (mimeo).

40. Joan Nelson, pp. 45–51.

41. Andrew Whiteford, *Two Cities of Latin America: A Comparative Description of Social Classes* (New York, 1964), p. 120.

42. S. Michael Miller and Frank Reisman, "The Working-Class Sub-culture," *Social Problems,* IX (Summer 1961), pp. 92, 95–96; Herbert J. Gans, *The Urban Villagers* (New York 1962), pp. 219–221, and *passim.*

43. Sources for data in Table I: São Paulo: Bertram Hutchinson's survey data as reported in S. M. Miller, "Comparative Social Mobility," *Current Sociology,* IX (1960), p. 69. Buenos Aires: Gino Germani, "La Mobilidad Social en la Argentina," Publicacion Interna No. 60, Instituto de Sociologica, Facultad de Filosofia y Letras, Universidad de Buenos Aires (mimeo). Poona: N. Y. Sovani, "Occupational Mobility in Poona Between Three Generations," in *Urbanization and Urban India* (Bombay 1966), p. 96. [Table presenting data on occupational mobility in the three cities is omitted here. Eds.]

44. Gino Germani, data developed for but not presented in the study on social mobility cited in n. 43. I am indebted to Professor Germani for permission to use his data.

45. See John Turner, "Uncontrolled Urban Settlement: Problems and Policies," Working paper No. 11 for the Inter-Regional Seminar on Development Policies and Planning in Relation to Urbanization, organized by the United Nations Bureau of Technical Assistance Operations and the Bureau of Social Affairs, October–November 1966, paper numbered 67-44032; Daniel Goldrich and others, "The Political Integration of Lower Class Urban Settlements," prepared for the American Political Science Association meetings, September 1966, p. 4 (mimeo); Flinn, pp. 3–4; William Mangin, "Latin American Squatter Settlements: A Problem and a Solution,"

Latin American Research Review, II (Summer 1967), pp. 74, 75.

46. Estimates place a fifth to a quarter of Lima's population in the early 1960's in squatter settlements; 16 percent of Rio as of 1964; 30 percent of Caracas in the late 1950's (despite construction of immense public housing projects absorbing an additional 18 percent of the city's population); and over a third of Mexico City. Richard M. Morse, "Recent Research on Latin American Urbanization," *Latin American Research Review,* I (1965), 50; John Turner, p. 1. In Turkey, Granville Sewell estimates that squatters comprise a fifth of Istanbul, a third of Ankara, and a third of Adana (pp. 71, 186, 193).

47. Santiago and Lima: Goldrich. Caracas: CENDES print-out. Mexican working class: data drawn from taped data of interviews conducted by Gabriel Almond and Sidney Verba for their study of the "Civic Culture" in Mexico and other countries.

48. Bonilla, p. 11; CENDES print-out; Goldrich, "Politics and the Pobladore," tables 1, 17, and "Demographoc and Socio-economic Background, Social Mobility, and Expectations"; Germani, "Social and Political Consequences," pp. 389–90. Inkeles' survey data demonstrate a similar belief in the hardworking poor man's prospects. See Nelson, p. 61.

49. Based on data from Indian Institute of Public Opinion, *Public Opinion Surveys,* X (March 1965), 21–32. [Table presenting data omitted.]

50. This section is added from a paper, "Urban Growth and Politics in Developing Nations: Prospects for the 1970's," presented by the author to a Columbia University conference on International Economic Development, February 15–21, 1970.

The Process
of Development:
Observations on
Latin America

To GIVE more depth of observation and analysis of the conditions of development, we wanted to present some views of the development process. In surveying the literature, we found more material on Latin America than on other areas which illustrated the dynamics of development. We appreciate that conditions there differ in many respects from those in Africa or Asia, just as conditions certainly differ within Latin America, though to a lesser extent. What we wanted to show were the insights of economists, anthropologists, and political scientists who adopted some of the perspectives advocated in Part I, so that the process of development could be better comprehended as a whole. Without formally employing the political economy of development, the authors demonstrate the analogous conditions of economic, social, and political development in terms of the scope of exchange, factor endowments, organization, and entrepreneurship.

Keith Griffin's article on Latin American development shows how the conditions interact; in particular, an extended scope of exchange without any increase and equalization in factor endowments can restrict increases in aggregate productivity. Market integration in the absence of relative equality in resource endowments can become exploitative, enriching the few and reducing the incentive and ability of the many to increase outputs. Griffin's point that there is already much integration in Latin America is well taken in the context in which he makes it; there is no undisturbed "traditional" social structure isolated from the "modern" sector. Griffin is concerned therefore not so much with increasing integration per se as with changing "the terms of social, political and economic intercourse," that is, with increasing the effective participation of the many, which requires increased factor endowments. He notes that the more privileged sectors are the best organized ones and emphasizes organization as a means for improving the factor endowments of the less privileged many.

The article by Anthony Bottomley addresses the matter of resource scarcity as a cause of underdevelopment, taking the case of Ecuador as an example. He finds there considerable potential for increased productivity because of unutilized resources which with different structuring of incentives—net benefits—could be mobilized. Tapping this potential is not a matter of capital alone or of detailed "planning." In particular, better analysis of development problems is needed whereby cause-and-effect relationships are identified and established, with special attention given to motivational factors. The dangers inherent in continuing present planning practices are appropriately pointed out.

The Vicos experiment in Peru, which Allan Holmberg was instrumental in launching, shows at the micro level how the different resources all figure in the transformation of a community whereby its economic, social, and political productivity for the many is raised. As noted previously, there was little "spread" or "demonstration" effect from the Vicos project, largely because a major shift in authority was required to set other changes in motion under this model of induced or exogenous change. The results of the project showed the beneficial effects of reallocating economic, social, political, informational, and coercive resources.[1]

Development can proceed through spontaneous or endogenous change, as June Nash shows in her study of a Mexican village. In particular, she shows the limited applicability of a dichotomy between "tradition" and "modernity" and how syncretic change can occur, with no simple replacement of the former by the latter. Nash emphasizes the productivity of *organization* with its pooling of resources as well as the catalytic productivity of *entrepreneurship*. We would note that the *ejidos* to which the author refers are community-owned lands returned previously to the people through land reform measures by the national government.

In looking at the process of development in Latin America, we are interested in the progress of the many, both in rural areas and in the cities. Neale Pearson considers the experience of Latin American peasant groups and under what condition these have contributed to development there. First, he shows that not all such groups are organized to operate in the interests of the peasants themselves. Second, there is the question of how productive violence can be on their behalf. An argument for increased peasant participation in political and economic processes is made, with some consideration of their need for increased factor endowment, to be achieved by and large through organization.

Joan Nelson addresses herself to parallel issues with respect to the many in the cities particularly in Latin America but with reference to urban sectors elsewhere in the Third World. She deals with the productivity of status, authority, and legitimacy, stressing the advantages of *organization* for the urban poor.[2] One feature of her paper is a consideration of possible alternative patterns of political integration whereby the less well endowed urban sectors are able to make existing institutions and exchanges more productive through increased political participation. She adds empirical weight, we think, to the approach that we call the political economy of development.

---

[1] We would note that the analytical framework used by Holmberg is that of Harold Lasswell, which treats with "values"—most, but not all, of which are equivalent to "resources" in our framework. Lasswell's frame of reference connotes more the consumption than the production aspect of resources. For more information on the Vicos experiment, see the other articles in the May 1965 issue of *American Behavioral Scientist,* and Holmberg's chapter in R. N. Adams (ed.), *Social Change in Latin America Today* (1960).

[2] Issues which she raises relating to political machines and the participation of the poor are treated at greater length by James C. Scott in "Corruption, Machine Politics, and Political Change," *American Political Science Review* (December 1969), pp. 1142–1158.

REFLECTIONS ON LATIN AMERICAN DEVELOPMENT

KEITH B. GRIFFIN

Magdalen College, Oxford

INTRODUCTION [1]

Fragmented Economies

One of the prominent features of under-developed countries is the fragmented labor and capital markets and the defective functioning of the price system. This in turn has led to a splintering of economic activity into poorly articulated or imperfectly integrated sectors. Thus one finds, for example, that in the least industrialized economies most of the cells in the production matrix of an input-output table are filled with zeros or numbers which are not statistically significant. That is, the volume of trade between sectors is relatively slight.

Equally important, each of the separate sectors of the economy is characterized by distinctive institutions, for example the way in which assets are held, markets are organized, or information conveyed. The response of these institutions to similar stimuli, e.g. a price signal, is quite different, and as a result a given response only can be achieved by introducing a series of discriminatory policy measures in each sector. For example, the injection of capital in the Peruvian highlands may not be sufficient to increase output, since knowledge of improved agricultural techniques also is lacking. On the other hand, additional investment may not be necessary to increase food production in Chile's Central Valley, since all that may be required is a reform of legislation regarding water rights. Finally, increased investment may be both necessary and sufficient to increase energy production in Brazil. Similar examples can easily be found within as well as between countries.

In general, most Latin American nations are split into two major sectors: the rural, agricultural sector, which includes up to 70 per cent of the population, and the considerably smaller urban areas. The former is sub-divided into minifundia—which are largely subsistence farms—and the associated latifundia and plantations. The last named may be owned either by domestic or foreign interests. The urban sector is usually sub-divided into petty services and government (which together include the urban disguised unemployed) and the modern manufacturing and extractive industries, plus the associated transport, banking, and financial services. The modern urban sector frequently includes foreign as well as domestic businesses, and in the relatively more industrialized economies may include some autonomous public-sector corporations.

The apparently respectable rates of development recently enjoyed by the fragmented economies of Latin America [2] are largely illusory. Where growth has occurred it frequently has been due to a rapid expansion of foreign demand for primary exports,[3] e.g. petroleum and iron ore in Venezuela, and the lion's share of the benefits has been captured by foreign interests.

The second major growth sector has been in manufactures. With the possible exception of Brazil, however, much of the industrialization in South America has been largely fortuitous, in the sense that it has not been due primarily to the initiative of native entrepreneurs, but on the contrary has been due either to foreign investment or to government-financed and administered corporations in transport, energy, extractive, or basic manufacturing industries. The manufacturing investments sponsored by private domestic interests are usually located either in small consumer goods industries—for example, textiles, beer, leather goods, and furniture—or are satellite factories to the large foreign and government-managed enterprises. Even these private manufacturing investments were frequently undertaken by immigrants —who no longer are attracted to the re-

From *Oxford Economic Papers* (March 1966), pp. 1–18. Reprinted by permission of the author and the Clarendon Press, Oxford. Some sections have been omitted.

gion in large numbers. Thus the continued rapid expansion of industry is unlikely unless the recent attempts to integrate the Latin American economies are successful.

The final source of growth of GNP has been in the rapid expansion of the "services" sector. This sector, however, is largely a sponge which absorbs the excess population of the rural areas and its "growth" represents virtually no increase in economic welfare. That is, expansion of this sector is a mere reflection of (1) the rapid rate of growth of the population, (2) the increasing inability of the rural sector to provide employment opportunities for the active agricultural labor force, and (3) the pronounced internal migration from rural areas to urban slums. Even if one would not want to follow Marxist national accounting techniques, and consider the services sector wholly unproductive, apparent *increases* in the services sector should be ignored completely in calculating the rate of growth of national income. That is, it would be more realistic to regard the trend rate of increase of output (as apart from employment) in the services sector as zero. If this procedure were followed, Latin American growth rates would be considerably lower than those reported in international statistical sources.[4]

The stagnant agricultural sector has been the principal factor restraining development. Even where there has been a genuine increase in *per capita* national income, however, it has been badly distributed. As we shall argue below, there are reasons to believe that the standard of living of the lowest income groups, i.e. the rural masses, is deteriorating throughout most of the continent.

Thus it would appear, first, that exclusive reliance on the price system is not an acceptable way to allocate resources in fragmented economies of the type we are considering; a series of discriminatory policies would be needed to accelerate growth, and for this reason the active intervention of the state in fostering development is essential. Second, Latin America indeed has enjoyed some increase in its *per capita* income, but (1) this increase has been due largely to factors external to the region, (2) has not been as great as many people believe, and (3) has been badly distributed. Although some economic progress has been achieved, it has been limited to a very few

sectors and as a result social conditions remain deplorable.

Regional Dynamics

Most economists implicitly assume that the growth and development of the rich nations and regions are independent of the stagnation and underdevelopment of the poor nations and regions. Our growth models and development theories, almost without exception, assume that at one point all the nations were more or less underdeveloped. Some of the nations "took off" and developed, leaving the others behind. The problem is to examine the rich nations, try to understand what enabled them to grow, and then adapt the conclusions to the "backward" countries so that they can "catch up." [5]

This, of course, is largely a false picture. The vast majority of today's non-Communist nations participate in a single, integrated, world economic system—and have done so for centuries. This system may be called industrial and mercantile capitalism. A major feature of this system is that the relationships between its various components (nations in the world economy or regions in a national economy) are unequal, and thus the benefits of participating in the system are unequally and inequitably distributed.[6]

The distribution of the fruits of intercourse may be such that in the prejudiced area (a) the level of consumption falls and the region is absolutely worse off, (b) consumption increases once-for-all, but savings and hence the rate of growth of output decline, or (c) only the relative rate of growth declines.

The important point, as Myrdal has stressed,[7] is that in a *laissez-faire* environment, in which unguided market forces determine resource allocation, cumulative movements in income inequalities are likely to be set up. This will occur not only between nations,[8] but also within a customs union [9] as well as between regions of a single nation. The growing inequality in the international distribution of income has received considerable comment. Studies of regional disparities in income within the under-developed countries, in contrast, have been relatively less frequent. Of course, many observers have noted that São Paulo is growing much faster than the north-east of Brazil, for example, but few have become interested in studying the general phenomenon of regional interdependence at either the theoretical or policy-making levels. There has been a proliferation of regional plans from the Cauca Valley in Colombia to the Mesopotamia in Argentina, but their approach essentially has been to consider the region as an *independent* unit and to determine, say, what institutional changes and additional investments would be necessary to increase the region's growth rate by a predetermined amount.

Yet it is quite likely that broader studies of inter-regional relations would indicate that the relative poverty of some areas is due directly to the type of associations experienced with other areas. Furthermore, the study of inter-regional relations—where market forces generally are unhampered by controls or obstacles—could provide useful evidence as to how our (essentially capitalistic) economic system works.

The Case of the Peruvian Sierra

A strong hint that regional interdependence may be an important factor in explaining the poverty of some areas is provided by the case of Peru. It is quite clear that internal migration, trade flows, and capital movements have had *absolute negative effects* on the level of *per capita* consumption and the rate of growth of the poorer region.

Internal migration has resulted in a transfer to the cities of the most ambitious and skilled rural workers. Precisely the most valuable human resources of the countryside are lost to the urban areas, where they may spend up to ten years searching for work in the factories. The government's policy of linking the coast and the Sierra with highways, by facilitating the exodus, has only aggravated the problem.[10]

Even more important than the transfer of labor to the coast has been the transfer of capital. The inter-regional trade figures are eloquent in this respect.

Per capita income on the coast is approximately $520, or roughly 6½ times higher than that of the Sierra. The above table indicates that the Sierra had a surplus of over 50 per cent, in its trade with the coast. This means that its *level of consumption was lower than it would have been had there been no trade*. Orthodox theory would lead one to think that the

export surplus would be compensated on capital account through the accumulation of deposits (and other assets) in the region's banks. These deposits would constitute savings for the region and accelerate its rate of growth.

INTER-REGIONAL TRADE BETWEEN THE PERUVIAN SIERRA AND THE COAST, 1959
(MILLIONS OF SOLES)

	Imports of the Sierra from the Coast	Exports of the Sierra to the Coast
Agricultural products	174	3,002
Minerals	198	459
Industrial products	671	473
Services	233	0
Commerce	476	99
Finance	2	30
Other	89	131
TOTAL	1,843	4,194
Sierra's export surplus	2,351	
	4,194	4,194

SOURCE: Banco Central de Reserva del Peru, cited by Barandiaran, L., "Estrategia de dessarrollo economico en la Sierra Peruana," 1964 (unpublished).

The orthodox presumption, however, is the reverse of the truth. The Sierra's agricultural exporters are latifundistas who live mostly in Lima and deposit their receipts in the capital's banks. Thus the savings of the Sierra are transferred to the coast and as a result *the rate of growth of the Sierra is lower than it would have been in the absence of trade*. Peru's banking system, its land tenure arrangements, and its social institutions are so organized that savings are siphoned from the poorer regions to the rich one. This exploitation of the poor by the rich through the mechanism of inter-regional trade is analogous to the relationship which existed (and in some cases still exists) between the metropole and the colonial territories. In fact, Latin America has been described as a region dominated largely by "colonialisme interieur." [11]

In the case of Peru the consequences of the savings transfer have been disastrous for the rate of growth of the Sierra, as the export surplus represents about 16.8 percent of its gross regional product. This transfer was sufficient to reduce the annual rate of growth of the Sierra by 4 or 5 percent. From the point of view of the coast the capital transfer represents slightly less than 4 percent of its gross regional product, although the contribution to the rate of capital formation on the coast is considerably greater, viz. 14 percent. Hence it appears that inter-regional relations have impeded the development of the Sierra, although it is possible these relations may not have been of crucial significance to the development of the coast.[12]

Evidently the processes of development and underdevelopment are related; they are not independent of one another. It is the manner of integration and the resulting unequal distribution of benefits which in large part may explain the poverty of some nations or regions and the development of others. The predominance of "backwash effects" in some regions probably is closely associated with the degree of concentration of economic and political power.

SOCIAL CONFLICT AND ECONOMIC POWER

Class Conflict and Social Disequilibrium

In the poorer countries of the world one finds that class and group conflicts are much sharper than in the industrial nations. A partial listing of such conflicts might include: agricultural exporters v. industrialists demanding protection; landless laborers v. latifundistas; minifundistas v. monopsonistic middlemen; unemployed urban workers or *Lumpenproletariat* v. high wage union labor.

Within societies characterized by these divisive and enduring coalitions—as opposed to shifting coalitions—it is difficult to achieve a national consensus.[13] Planning in such countries cannot be purely technocratic or indicative but must attempt the much more arduous task of coupling economic expansion with rapid and profound social and institutional transformation. This insistence on the importance of fundamental changes is not merely a question of political preference, but in many cases it is an urgent necessity if the na-

tion is to avoid violent civil discord. Unfortunately, many sociologists (as well as economists) tend to view society as a self-equilibrating model in which chronic disequilibria are a special case. This is particularly true of the Talcott Parsons "structural-functional" school which predominates in the United States and many U.N. agencies. In general, the "equilibrium model" of society is not very useful and should be replaced by a conception of society as a "tension-management system" in which order itself is problematical rather than assumed.[14] In such a context the task of planning cannot be limited to increasing per capita consumption, or even providing for its equitable distribution. It must also foster democratic participation in the decision-making process so that the various groups in the nation associate their own interests with the stability of society as a whole.

Social Dualism: a False Hypothesis

One must be careful, however, not to assume that social tension and a poorly integrated economy imply the presence of a dual society. It is frequently affirmed that colonialism consisted of the superimposition of a European society upon an indigenous social structure, and that the latter *continued its existence essentially undisturbed and unchanged.* The problem of development then is viewed as "integrating" the unchanged, backward, and "traditional" sector into the modern economy. Thus, for example, a group of U.N. economists, sociologists, and political scientists asserts that, "The *social structure* of Latin America has in the past been characterized by a serious lack of integration." [15]

Yet the effect of colonialism was not to isolate but to *destroy* the indigenous social structure and to re-integrate the original population into a capitalist-colonialist [16] system which was and is highly unfavorable to their interests. This system has persisted in Latin America even after 150 years of independence. Referring to Peru, one writer states:

The new landowners introduced a highly commercialized economic system based on the use of money and on competition in the international market, where no market existed before, and they consolidated their power through the encomienda by entail, and later through the hacienda, or plantation estate. By these changes the original population was reduced to a state of social and economic disrespect which persists to the present day.[17]

The degree of "disrespect" to which the original population was reduced is obvious to every tourist who has been to Cuzco and Machu Picchu. "The economic system of the Indians was wiped out by the Spaniards, together with the culture which it supported, . . . but it was not succeeded by an economy of greater productiveness. Indeed, as is evidenced by the numerous terraced hillsides, intensively cultivated before the Conquest and now completely abandoned, productivity declined in many areas." [18]

Hence it appears that any program designed to improve conditions for the underprivileged mass of the population must concentrate not so much on integrating these people into society as on *changing their relationships* with the rest of society.[19] One is not trying to merge two different cultures but to alter the terms in which the separate groups of a single national society engage in social, political, and economic intercourse.

Countervailing Power v. Community Development

It has become quite evident that "planning from above" is impossible and if progress is to occur mass participation in the development process must be encouraged. Such programs, at least in theory, have become increasingly popular. In practice, most of the efforts to mobilize the masses have centered on the rural community or urban residential neighborhood, and the object of the programs has been to assimilate or integrate the community into the national society. . . .

Thus the community development approach to democratic organization assumes not only that non-integrated social groups co-exist, but, furthermore, that there is a "harmony of interests" [20] both *within* the community and *between* the community and other regions of the nation. Our own analysis in the previous sections would seem to indicate that, on the contrary, (a) the society is already integrated—although to the disadvantage of many of its members, (b) the various groups of a community may have sharply differing interests, and (c) there may be serious conflicts

between the interests of one region and those of another. In particular, it would be very ill-advised to assume that the interests of the latifundistas, minifundistas, landless laborers (inquilinos in Chile), seasonal workers (afuerinos), and merchant money-lenders of a rural "community" are identical, or even compatible. In many cases the rural "community" in Latin America is synonymous with the latifundia; agricultural villages are not as predominant as in Asia.

The experience with community or village development programs in Asia— where the U.N. has strongly advocated them—as well as the author's observations in Algeria, show that such projects have not been successful in raising agricultural production, stimulating village industry, extracting savings from the rural sector, or using surplus labor efficiently.[21] Evidently, future policy in this area will have to be based on a different theoretical framework. It would seem that rather than viewing the problem of popular participation in development as one of merging non-integrated societies so that their common interests become apparent, the opposite approach, viz. viewing society as composed of various groups with opposing interests, would be more enlightening.

Such an approach would lead one to search for the *conflicts* underlying the relations between groups, the coalitions and *bargaining* to which they give rise, and the *monopoly* elements pertaining to each group which determine the outcome of the process.[22]

If one looks at Latin American society one finds that each group tries to carve out a monopoly position for itself. Capital markets are tightly controlled by a small minority [23] to which most members of society have scant access, and on the occasions when they *are* granted access they are forced to pay exorbitant rates of interest. It is not uncommon for the monthly rate of interest paid by small borrowers to approach 10 percent, and in Ecuador cases have been found of the Catholic Church charging 200 percent per annum on loans to peasants.[24]

The Marxists have assumed that the financial and industrial monopolists would be firmly opposed—and eventually defeated—by the solidarity of the working class. One finds, however, that it is the more privileged members of the working class—civil servants, professionals (including economists), and skilled industrial laborers—who are best organized. Less than 10 percent of all workers in Chile, for example, are organized, and the percentage in the less industrialized Latin American economies is much lower. The organized groups are anxious to protect their position and restrict entry to their job categories. Their interests differ sharply from those of the unorganized and underprivileged members of society; there is no class solidarity. . . .

Monopoly of the Land and Exploitation of Labor

The rural workers are by far the most numerous and miserable of the prejudiced groups and their relative position has continued to deteriorate.[25] Given (a) the high population-growth rate, (b) the low rate of growth of output and the even smaller increases in food production,[26] and (c) the worsening distribution of income in rural zones, it is quite probable that consumption levels in the lower strata of society are falling.

This deterioration of the economic position of the most vulnerable members of society is due in large part to the lack of bargaining power of these groups. These people are unorganized and dispose of little or no capital or land. Furthermore, they face a monopsonistic labor market.

As Frank has stated, "the key source of the great inequality of bargaining power in the labor market is unquestionably the extensive ownership of land on the part of the few and the absence of or severe limitation in the ownership of land on the part of the many." [27] The fantastic extent to which land has been monopolized in South America is presented in the table below. Unlike most measures—which compare the size distribution of land among landowners—we have tried to estimate the size distribution of land among the active agricultural workers. This should give us a more relevant indication of the extent to which the agricultural producers are able to dominate the labor market, and we find, for example, that in Venezuela roughly one percent of those active in agriculture own nearly 75 percent of the land.

Inequality in the distribution of land (and water) is, of course, reinforced by

an unequal distribution of educational opportunities. This monopolization of the essential complementary elements of production has led to the creation of a vast pool of unskilled, mostly unemployed, and almost unemployable, agricultural labor. The supply of manpower available to the latifundistas (and urban industrialists) is greater, and its price consequently lower, than would occur if the monopoly elements were not present, i.e. if holdings were small and self-employment greater. In addition, concentration of resources "also tends to increase the underutilization of latifundia land [28] and thus reduce the demand for . . . labour. Thus, from both the supply and the demand side, greater concentration depresses the price. . . ." [29]

CONCENTRATION OF LANDHOLDING IN LATIN AMERICA

	% of Active Agricultural Workers Own	% of Land (in Holdings over 1,000 Hectares)	% Agricultural Families without Land or Owners of Less than 5 Hectares
Argentina	1.780	74.9	64.6
Brazil	0.316	50.9	74.9
Chile	0.503	73.2	73.4
Colombia	0.157	26.7	. . . .
Ecuador	0.110	37.4	75.4
Peru	0.098	76.2	. . . .
Uruguay	1.250	56.5	67.9
Venezuela	0.960	74.5	90.6

Source: Barraclough, S., and Flores, E., "Estructura agraria de America Latina," *Informe del curso de capacitacion de profesionales en reforma agraria*, vol. i, pp. 279–80 (Instituto de Economia, Universidad de Chile, 1963). The data refer to various years between 1950 and 1960.

From the point of view of the landowner this system is highly profitable. Case studies in the Ecuadorian Sierra indicate that the average hacienda earns 33 percent gross profit (excluding amortization) on its sales receipts.[30] The reason why the returns are so high is that most factor inputs are provided gratis or nearly so. In the majority of cases labor is provided by "huasipungueros" who work four days a week for the hacienda and, on those days, receive a nominal wage.[31] In addition, the "huasipungueros" are allotted a small plot of land to cultivate. These workers frequently must provide their own houses and hand tools. Additional labor is provided by "yanaperos," who in return for the right to use the hacienda's roads, to collect water for domestic purposes, and to gather firewood, agree to provide several days' work gratis. The "yanapo" or "pago de los pasos" also includes the use by the hacienda of the flocks of the indigenous people to fertilize its fields. Thus even fertilizer is free! . . .

Thus the weak are exploited by the strong, both in the labor market and in the commodity market.[32] The way to redress this exploitation is to increase the bargaining strength of the former relative to the latter, to establish a "countervailing power"[33] by mobilizing political support for the less favored members of society and greatly increasing their command over resources. One will get nowhere assuming there is an inherent convergence of interests among the various groups comprising a rural community.

POLICIES AND A PREDICTION

Ingredients of a Solution

The prejudiced groups in Latin America (a) appear to be poorly integrated into the political power structure of society,[34] (b) are pushed to the margin of the economy as consumers, and (c) are strongly —and unfavorably for them—integrated into the economy as sellers of commodities and their labor. This situation will persist as long as political power, land, and capital are concentrated in the hands of a few families. If one is serious about increasing democratic participation in national development, groups with common interests will have to be organized and these must establish a countervailing power to the long-established vested interests of society.

In some cases relatively "small" changes could have a substantial impact upon the bargaining power and living standards of the rural poor. In Ecuador, for example, the rural population in the Sierra is 1.5 millions. The social and economic position of these people would greatly improve if the government would take two steps: (1) declare all roads, whether on private haciendas or not, open to free public access, and (2) nationalize the "paramos," mountainous regions at the 3,000–4,000 metre level, and allow persons who own less than 15 hectares to gather wood and use the pasture freely. Since the "paramos" are uncultivated wastelands, neither of these measures would directly reduce the hacendado's control over productive resources. Both of them, however, would reduce his monopoly of the land and his consequent control over the labor market. At present, the "huasipunguero" earns roughly $150 per year: 32 percent of this comes from his agricultural activities, 52 percent from livestock and only 16 percent as wages from working on the hacienda—although he spends at least 40 percent of his time there.[35]

Thus the advantage of the proposed minor changes are that they would (1) almost completely liberate the "yanapero" from the necessity of providing labor services gratis; (2) reduce the "huasipunguero's" dependence on the hacienda's grazing lands and thereby liberate the major portion of his income from hacienda control; and (3) increase the bargaining power of the workers in the labor market and hence increase their wages.

Even such simple changes, however, are likely to be strongly resisted by the landowning class, precisely because it would undermine the props upon which their wealth and political power are built. Thus, on the one hand, these measures would be firmly opposed by the dominant political forces; on the other hand, they would not represent a complete solution to the problems of development and social transformation in Latin America. Since partial measures would be largely unsuccessful in achieving the larger objectives and would be bitterly resented anyway, there is little to lose in pressing for more radical and satisfactory solutions.

The essential ingredient in any program of development and social transformation is a fundamental change in agrarian institutions. The expropriation and redistribution of land and the organization of a mixed system of producer co-operatives, family holdings,[36] and state farms should be the basis for all subsequent action in this field.

Tenure reforms, however, are only the first step in the process of social transformation. It is important, therefore, that this step be accomplished swiftly and cheaply. This cannot be done if compensation of the landlords is based upon the commercial value of the expropriated land. Land values in Latin America are much higher than one would guess knowing only the productivity of the soil. This is because the commercial value includes: (1) the value of land as an item of social prestige, and (2) the value of land as a hedge against inflation. The inflation itself, however, is largely caused by the failure of agriculture to expand production and the unwillingness of the upper classes to pay their taxes.[37] (3) Finally, market prices reflect the capitalized value of the right to exploit labor. One does not buy just agricultural land; one buys an entire enterprise, including its monopoly power. Compensation should be based upon the value of the land, exclusive of these three factors, as operated under current techniques of production. Only on this basis, for example, would it be reasonable and just to require the new owners of any family farms that might be created to pay the full purchase price of the land acquired under a reform.

Tenure reforms will have to be supplemented by the creation of agricultural labor unions, the provision of a minimum agricultural wage, and strict legal enforcement. Marketing, storage, and transport facilities also will have to be provided. Perhaps the best way to do so would be through a system of national marketing co-operatives which compete with the existing intermediaries and which guarantee minimum prices. Similar institutions must be responsible for providing credit and other important inputs, e.g. fertilizers. Rural education will have to be expanded and adapted to the new conditions. Finally, once a land reform has ensured that those who work receive the fruits of their efforts, the unemployed should be mobilized in a program of rural public works.[38] Such a program would be the quickest way to provide full employment, increase investments, and transform the countryside —and thereby guarantee that an eventual increase in consumption would be possible.

One would hope that the above policies would be obvious and command general acceptance, yet one notices that even the new and progressive Chilean government have an entirely different conception of "promocion popular." [39] [Note that this refers to the regime of Eduardo Frei (1964–1970). The strategy of his successor Salvador Allende appears more in line with Griffin's proposals. Eds.]

In a major speech President Frei presented his plan for "promocion popular" and announced that a new ministry would be created to execute it.[40] The plan is chiefly concerned with increasing welfare measures and consumption of the low income urban classes. Specifically, the government expects to do such things as pave 29,000 meters of sidewalks and streets; provide water, garbage disposal, and telephone facilities to thousands of urban dwellers; construct 50 social centers and numerous parks and athletic fields, etc.

All of these measures, of course, are defensible; they cater to pressing needs and will help alleviate the misery of an important segment of the population. Still, one must question whether expenditures in this direction represent a good allocation of resources. All of these projects are essentially welfare measures: they increase the consumption of the urban masses, but they do not generate much additional employment, nor do they represent investment which will permanently increase the productive capacity of the economy. . . .

The alternative to increasing urban consumption or investment in infrastructure is to increase directly productive rural investment. It has been conclusively demonstrated—in China and elsewhere—that properly organized labor-intensive rural investments (a) are an excellent way to mobilize the masses for development, (b) are inexpensive, (c) can have a very short gestation period, and (d) provide large returns on capital expenditure. The author has personal experience in Algeria with projects of the type recommended. In the Tizi-Ouzou region, for example, working in poor and eroded soils, the rate of return on investment in the first year was a minimum of 15.6 per cent. Latin America can neglect this experience only at her peril.

A Short-Run Prediction

Yet she probably will neglect it. Historically, the Latin American middle classes have tended to imitate their social and economic superiors and to attempt only to force the latter to allow them to participate in the privilege of power.[41] This coalition then has been able to fragment the lower classes by granting partial concessions which are not distributed evenly. This formula, particularly as applied in Chile, has been successful both in avoiding a social revolution and in maintaining essentially untouched the privileges of the wealthy. Thus the middle class reforms in voting rights, labor legislation, social security, and education were incomplete and fragmentary; they usually were confined only to certain sectors of the urban population and seldom were effectively enforced.[42] Furthermore, in so far as there was a change in the distribution of income, it was the urban middle class and unionized laborers who gained—not at the expense of the rich, but at the expense of the rural masses, *Lumpenproletariat*, and unorganized workers. The increased welfare services were financed, not by higher or more efficient direct taxation of the upper income groups, but, on the contrary, through a combination of inflation and additional indirect taxation.[43]

The "campesino" has been systematically ignored by almost all the progressive parties in Latin America. The latter have chosen to direct themselves to the organized and privileged *elites,* e.g. the unionized industrial workers, students, intellectuals, and bureaucrats.[44] These groups, first, represent a small proportion of the population in most countries, and second, are rarely interested in a profound transformation of society; but instead are concerned primarily with widening their own opportunities for advancement. The programs recommended in this essay are directed to the benefit of the rural masses and are much more radical than the essentially "welfare-state" measures usually sponsored by the urban middle class. Thus experience and logic would lead one to be a little sceptical whether they will be introduced by Latin America's urban-based, middle class parties.

1. In addition to the literature cited, this essay reflects conversations I have had with many foreign and Latin American intellectuals in Chile and Peru. A listing of all those who have been helpful would be lengthy and might lead to invidious comparisons. I would like to express my particular gratitude, however, to A. G. Frank, whose own work and the extensive conversations we had on this topic have greatly influenced my research.

2. As far as one can tell the region as a whole is growing at roughly 4 percent per annum.

3. This is not expected to continue. Projections prepared by the Secretariats of two United Nations agencies and of the General Agreement on Tariffs and Trade (GATT) indicate that Latin American exports to the outside world over the next 20 years will increase at annual rates ranging from less than 2 percent per annum to a high of nearly 4 percent (United States Congress, Committee on Foreign Relations of the United States Senate, *Problems of Latin American Economic Development,* Feb. 1960, p. 9). These export projections should be compared with the 6.5 percent annual rate of growth of imports of the region.

4. Services represent between 35 and 52 percent of GNP in Latin America and, with wide variations, are reported to be growing at about the same rate as the latter. For international comparisons of the relative importance of services in GNP, cf. Chenery, H. B., "Patterns of Industrial Growth," *American Economic Review,* Sept. 1960.

5. Speculations as to the cause of a nation's economic growth have centered on such items as its endowment of natural resources, the "savings coefficient," parental attitudes towards child-care and their effect on the supply of entrepreneurship, "technical change," education, etc. All of these hypotheses include the assumption that the growth of one nation is largely independent of its relations with another.

6. Cf. Balogh, T., *Unequal Partners,* Vol. 1.

7. Cf. Myrdal, G., *Economic Theory and Under-developed Regions.*

8. Cf. Griffin, K., and R. Ffrench-Davis, "Reformulación de algunos aspectos de la teoría del comercio internacional," *Publicaciones Docentes,* No. 6 (Instituto de Economia, Universidad de Chile); Griffin, K., and R. Ffrench-Davis, "El capital extranjero y el desarrollo," *Revista de Economia,* Nos. 83–84 (Santiago).

9. Cf. Griffin, K., "The Potential Benefits of Latin American Integration," *Inter-American Economic Affairs,* Vol. 17, No. 4, Spring 1964.

10. Comisión Ejecutiva Interministerial de Cooperación Popular, El Pueblo lo Hizo, año 1, no. 1, Sept.–Dec. 1964, p. 27.

11. Cf. Dumont, R., *Terres vivants,* ch. 1.

12. That is, the Marxist thesis which affirms that the development of the metropole depends upon the exploitation of the periphery cannot be tested with the limited information available.

13. The U.S. has often been described as a "nation of joiners" in which a large proportion of the population are members of several organizations whose aims duplicate and cut across one another. This has led to a society of shifting coalitions in which class and interest boundaries are softened and blurred. On the other hand, in the underdeveloped countries—and to a lesser extent, in Europe —one does not "join" a class or group, one is "born into" it. This strengthens class consciousness and accentuates divisive tendencies in society. A similar pattern developed in the United States with respect to the Negro minority and led to the "Negro Revolution" we are now witnessing.

14. Cf. Moore, W. E., "Predicting Discontinuities in Social Change," *American Sociological Review*, June 1964, p. 337. For a criticism of the applicability of modern economic theory to the problems of underdevelopment, cf. Seers, D., "The Limitations of the Special Case," *Bulletin of the Oxford University Institute of Economics and Statistics*, May 1963.

15. "Report of the Expert Working Group on Social Aspects of Economic Development in Latin America," *Economic Bulletin for Latin America*, Vol. VI, No. 1, Mar. 1961, p. 56. Emphasis in the original.

16. The common claim that Latin America is "feudal" can be highly misleading. From the beginning of the Spanish conquest the region was incorporated into a world-wide mercantilist system. This was true not only of Mexico and Peru (which exported precious metals) but also of Brazil. Celso Furtado indicates that from the 16th century onward the Brazilian economy was essentially capitalist, being based on specialization and the division of labor (sugar), reliance on foreign markets, and investments in slaves. Cf. Furtado, C., *Formación económica del Brazil*, Fondo de Cultura Económica, México, 1962, pp. 58–59. Translated from the Portuguese (Formacão económica do Brazil) by Demetrio Aguilera Malta.

17. Holmberg, A. R., "Changing Community Attitudes and Values in Peru: A Case Study in Guided Change," *Social Change in Latin America Today*, p. 55.

18. Crist, R. E., "The Indian in Andean America, I," *The American Journal of Economics and Sociology*, Vol. 23, No. 2, Apr. 1964. In spite of the fact that the Inca economy and culture were "wiped out," Crist persists in claiming that the Spaniards "superimposed" the hacienda system upon the Indians.

19. It is not the quantitative aspects of the relationships which interest us here (extent of autoconsumption, value or volume of sales or purchases) but their nature or quality.

20. The assumption of "harmony of interests" is analogous to the doctrine of *laissez faire* in which the welfare of society is believed to be maximized if each individual pursues his private interests. This, as T. Balogh once remarked, is a doctrine designed to make those who *are* comfortable, *feel* comfortable.

21. Cf. U.N., *Community Development and Economic Development*, Part I, *A Study of the Contribution of Rural Community Development Programmes to National Economic Development in Asia and the Far East*.

22. Cf. Silvert, K. H., *The Conflict Society: Reaction and Revolution in Latin America*.

23. The Chilean case has been well documented. Cf. Instituto de Económia, *Formación de capital en las empresas industriales*; Lagos, E., *La concentración del poder económico*; Enos, J., *Entrepreneurship in Chile* (in preparation).

24. Baraona, Rafael, *Rasgos fundamentales de los sistemas de tenencia de la tierra en el Ecuador*, a Report prepared for the Interamerican Committee for Agricultural Development, preliminary version, 1964, pp. 133, 186–7, 267. This is one of a series of reports on land tenure conditions being prepared in seven Latin American countries.

25. U.N., ECLA, *El desarrollo social de América Latina en la post-guerra*, E/CN. 12/660, p. 29.

26. Per capita food production is lower today than it was ten years ago in Argentina, Chile, Colombia, Peru, and Uruguay. Cf. FAO, *The State of Food and Agriculture*, 1964, Annex Table 2B, p. 201.

27. Frank, A. G., "La participación popular en lo relativo a algunos objectivos económicos rurales," p. 32, mimeo, no date.

28. Even in the Argentine Pampa, the most productive and efficiently cultivated region in Latin America, only 48.7 percent of the agricultural land is cultivated. The remainder is in fallow land, natural pastures (41 percent), or woods and brush. On the large "estancias" an even smaller percentage of the land is cultivated. Cf. Domike, Arthur L., *Land Tenure and Agricultural Development in Argentina*, a report prepared for the Interamerican Committee for Agricultural Development, preliminary version, 1965, p. 25.

29. Frank, A. G., *op. cit.*, p. 34.

30. Baraona, R., *op. cit.*, pp. 76, 89, 110, 146, 173, 196.

31. The typical wage is 3 sucres per workday, but this is paid only sporadically. (The sucre/dollar exchange rate is 18.18/1.) Wages are deducted and fines imposed for any infraction of the hacienda's rules, e.g. if the huasipungueros' animals graze on the hacienda's lands. Consequently, money seldom changes hands between the patron and his huasipungueros.

32. For a theoretical discussion of exploitation see Robinson, J., *The Economics of Imperfect Competition,* chs. 18 and 26.

33. Cf. Galbraith, J. K., *American Capitalism, the Concept of Countervailing Power.*

34. U.N., ECLA, *op. cit.,* p. 35, states, ". . . las areas rurales de América Latina . . . permanecicron relativamente segregadas del poder central," and "existen . . . indicios de que las masas rurales no llegaron a constituir, en general, un sector electoral apreciable."

35. Baraona, R., *op. cit.,* p. 320.

36. Many economists from the United States are unduly biased in favor of the family farm system. This certainly is not a general solution to the social problem in Latin America and under some circumstances small, individual holdings may ultimately be prejudicial to the interests of the intended beneficiaries. Crist, R. E., *op. cit.,* p. 140, points out that ". . . at present, whenever the land of a community is divided up among the Indians and given to them in fee simple, it usually comes to be owned within a short time by the local *hacendado,* or landowner, who, with an eye to business, is likely to be the first to favour the breaking up of community holdings and the giving of 'full civil rights' to the Indians!"

37. Conditions in Peru—and much of Latin America—are summarized succinctly by two articles which appeared on the front page of *La Prensa* (Lima) on 18 Feb. 1965. One article reports an invasion of agricultural land in the District of Paca while the other reports that "Solo 25 mil personas pagan sus impuestos."

38. Cf. Balogh, T., "Agriculture and Economic Development," *Oxford Economic Papers,* Feb. 1961.

39. Many of the above recommendations *have* been endorsed by Latin American intellectuals. Cf., for example, Chonchol, J., "El desarrollo de America Latina y la reforma agraria," *Curso de capacitación de profesionales en reforma agraria,* Vol. 1. Mr. Chonchol is the operating head of INDAP (National Institute for Agricultural Development) and one of Frei's major advisers on agricultural affairs.

40. The text of President Frei's speech can be found in *El Mercurio* (Santiago), 11 Dec. 1964.

41. The way by which the middle class was able to force concessions from the aristocracy is explained by ECLA, *op. cit.,* p. 102, as follows: "En la fase ascendente del proceso politico los sectores medios iniciaron su acceso al poder apoyandose por lo general en las masas obreras, y creando, en consecuencia, diversas instituciones cuyo propósito querido o 'manifesto' fue la mejora del *status* social y económico de empleados y obreros. Pero el efecto no declarado o 'latente' de esas instituciones pareceria haber consistido mas bien en la expansión y mejoramiento de las capas medias mismas."

42. *Ibid.,* pp. 113–14.

43. Cf. Sunkel, O., "Change and Frustration in Chile," a paper presented at the Conference on Obstacles to Change in Latin America, Royal Institute of International Affairs, London, Feb. 1965, mimeo, p. 31.

44. Frantz Fanon asserts that this is true in the majority of under-developed regions. Cf. *Los condenados de la tierra,* Fondo de Cultura Económica, 1963, pp. 54, 100. Translated from the French (*Les damnés de la terre*) by Julieta Campos.

PLANNING IN AN UNDERUTILIZATION ECONOMY:
The Case of Ecuador

ANTHONY BOTTOMLEY
University of Bradford

Ecuador has one of the most comprehensive development plans in the world. It runs to some twenty or thirty volumes. A rate of growth in income is set for the years 1964–73. Income elasticities of demand for the various goods and services

From *Social and Economic Studies* (December 1966), pp. 305–313. Reprinted by permission.

which the economy can provide are estimated. This not only gives sector growth rates, but planned expansion in the production of individual items as well. The quantity of additional wheat, for example, which will be demanded and grown during the plan period is projected. The required expansion in the provision of the necessary input items then becomes apparent in terms of land, labor, fertilizer, extension services and so on. The planning board makes estimates of what the direction and extent of government expenditures must be if the private sector is to play its part in fulfilling the goals of the plan. The whole thing is very thorough. It is based upon the best available information. A substantial data-gathering program has been going on for a decade or more. Nevertheless, the plan has its faults.

The Ecuadorian development plan often appears as a smooth, ordered surface resting lightly upon the uneven base of the economy at large. In its thousands upon thousands of words it rarely focuses on the relation between the mechanics of its input-output analysis and the tangled undergrowth of feudal institutions, narrow market structures, inertia and prejudice in which the typical Ecuadorian producer operates. This is not to say that these things are ignored—they are not.

The plan does not merely say that the income elasticity of demand for various kinds of fruit is high, therefore they will be grown as the economy advances. It does agree that not only must the government provide credit, extension services, fertilizer and the like, but that it must also change the land tenure system and/or marketing structure so that the individual peasant will have enough terrain to grow his subsistence as well as an uncertain cash crop, that he will reap sufficient reward after rent has been paid to provide the necessary incentive, and that he will have a road upon which to trundle his produce to market. The planners do realize that the increased production of particular fruits is not only an important consequence of purchasing power arising out of economic growth, but that additional demand generated by farmers when they, too, sell their produce encourages growth elsewhere, rather than the manner of Say's Law.

The difficulty is that they have allocated too much of their time and resources to discovering *by how much* the demand for, say, fruit is likely to expand over the plan period, to *by how much* the provision of input items must increase in consequence, and *to exactly where* the government must invest money so as to facilitate this process. They have not, for example, given sufficient attention to discovering why an underemployed labor force which farms only a fraction of the cultivable land has not expanded its output long, long ago. This is where the curiosity of the economist should be aroused. Unless such a question can be answered, the best laid schemes are almost certain to falter.

What then are the salient features of this economy upon which so detailed a plan will be imposed, and what questions must the planner in such countries ask and answer if their arithmetically ordered objectives are to stand a chance of achievement?

THE UNDERUTILIZATION OF LAND

Table 1 shows that less than 30 per cent of the so-called cultivable land on existing farms of more than 2,500 hectares is used on the tropical Coastal Plain. The figure for the Inter-Andean heights, or Sierra, is lower still (7.5 per cent). The degree of utilization in both regions is inversely correlated with the size of holdings, but Table 1 shows that this inverse relationship is much less pronounced on the Coastal Plain than it is in the valleys of the Sierra. Why is this so? Why is so much land left unused when the typical Ecuadorian is reputed to have a lower calorie intake than his counterpart in the overcrowded Republic of India? [1] A good question, is it not? Failure to find an answer may upset the neat coefficients for growth laid out in the voluminous plan.

This is not to say that the planners have failed to notice such a curious state of affairs. They grew up with it. It preoccupies them greatly. They have a solution to the problem in the shape of land reform. [2] But does this solution arise from a proper consideration of the issues? If large landowners have not found it to be in their interest to rent out more land to an impoverished, underemployed peasantry, then perhaps there is an obstacle to the wider use of land which will still be in evidence even if immense holdings are subdivided.

TABLE 1

INDEX OF THE EXTENT OF LAND EXPLOITATION IN ECUADOR (1964)

Size of Holdings in Hectares	Coastal Plain			Sierra		
	Total Area of "Usable" Land in Hectares	Area Actually Used in Hectares	Index of Land Use	Total Area of "Usable" Land in Hectares	Area Actually Used in Hectares	Index of Land Use
200–499.9	287,200	145,800	50.8%	125,000	54,100	43.3%
500–999.9	171,900	79,800	46.4%	106,900	31,100	29.0%
1,000–2,499.9	230,700	107,200	46.4%	158,000	31,900	20.0%
More than 2,500	415,500	116,000	27.9%	366,400	27,400	7.5%

SOURCE: Government of Ecuador, Junta Nacional de Plantificación y Coordinación Economica. *Reforma a la Estructura de la Tierra y Expansión de la Frontera Agricola* (Quito 1964) Capitulo II. Cuadros III—1, 2, 4, and 5, pp. 26, 28, 32 and 33.

Why, for example, does the Coastal landlord use more of his cultivable terrain than his counterpart in the Sierra, even in spite of the fact that population pressure is much lower there [3] and the opportunities for extensive cultivation considerably less in a jungle area than on the grasslands of the Sierra? Does this hint at some economic force which the planners should recognize? Is it that the inelasticity of produce demand in the isolated valleys of the Sierra brings profitable production to a halt long before all easily cultivable land has been pressed into use? Does the existence of monopolistic landlord power encourage them to keep much good land out of use? If so, why is the margin of cultivation set long before the most miserable standards for national per capita calorie intake have been achieved? Does the landlord on the Coast cultivate more of his land because as an individual, or as a member of an oligopolistic group, he faces the perfectly elastic export market for bananas, cacao, or coffee which the Sierra producer cannot enter? If this is so, why does he not cultivate all of his usable land? Is it the absence of access roads, an insufficiency of peak-season labor supplies, of capital, administrative ability, or what that limits the area under cultivation even where produce demand in an export market is perfectly elastic for the individual producer? [4]

These are the kind of questions which a theoretically trained planner should really ask. The pragmatically tutored Latin American economist [5] plans for improved roads, storage facilities, ready access to markets, and what not. He pushes for land reform, partly for social reasons and partly because he knows that large landowners do not use their holdings to anything like the full. But the point is that he does not do this so much because he has asked and answered the sort of questions which we have raised, but because he calculates arithmetically that such and such a growth rate in a particular region will require a certain amount of credit, so many kilometers of new roads, improved port facilities, and so forth. He also feels that land reform will help generate the necessary incentives to produce and to use these facilities once they have been created. But the result of all this is that his arithmetical plan is vague in spite of its formal precision. It does not arise directly out of solutions to evident problems. If it is carried through, it will doubtless help solve many of these difficulties, but this is insufficient defense. It should be related directly to the answers to the sort of questions we have asked, and not simply provide solutions on a partly accidental basis.

THE UNDERUTILIZATION OF LABOR

A glance at Table 2 will show that rural labor is just as underemployed as land in Ecuador. Why is this? The population is underfed even on the land itself. Does the

TABLE 2

AVERAGE WORKING DAYS PER ECONOMICALLY ACTIVE PERSON IN
ECUADORIAN AGRICULTURAL AND ANIMAL HUSBANDRY (1963)

Region	Available Work-days per Year	Eight-hour Day Equivalents Actually Worked	Percentage Under-employment
Tropical regions (Coastal Plain)	309	226	26.9
Agriculture	300	188	37.3
Animal husbandry	320	304	5.0
Temperate regions (Sierra)	314	232	26.1
Agriculture	300	151	49.7
Animal husbandry	320	304	5.0

SOURCE: Government of Ecuador, Junta Nacional de Plantificación y Coordinación Economica. *Programa de Desarrollo Agropecuario—Metas y Proyecciones* (Quito, 1964), Cuadro 6H.

inadequate calorie intake mean that farmers cultivate as much as their strength allows, precipitating a vicious circle of low levels of production and debilitating malnutrition?[6] Is it that the whole rural population is fully occupied at the sowing and the harvest, and that their off-season underemployment is therefore unavoidable? Perhaps, but [our data] indicate that opportunities exist for growing crops with staggered harvests.[7] Even if this were not possible on the same farm (and it probably is most often possible), it is evident that fuller employment would be attainable if a migratory labor force arose in response to the economic incentives which the wider use of land, coupled with staggered harvests, could doubtless provide.

Why then is labor underemployed? Why is it not used more evenly throughout the year? Why do rural families contribute in increasing numbers to a thoroughly uncalled-for drift to the towns? Do large landowners maintain monopsonistic labor markets, holding down their employment so as to keep wages at a desired level?[8] If they do, why are these wages held so low that the calorie intake which they allow is unlikely to minimize the wage per unit of labor efficiency?[9]

The point is that the chronic underutilization of land in the presence of extreme underemployment does need to be explained, and Ecuadorian planners should have set out to do it. The present situation is one of expectation (probably justified to some extent) that overhead capital provision, institutional reform, and so on will put land and labor to work in a greater measure than before. But the plan should have been solidly based on an examination of the possible reasons why these factors of production are currently underemployed, not dependent on a somewhat haphazard relationship between its largely arithmetically determined provisions and what may in fact prove to be the necessary action.

THE UNDERUTILIZATION OF CAPITAL

Table 3 shows that Ecuadorian factories are used on an average at less than 60 percent of their capacity.[10] Why is this so in a country where capital is supposedly chronically scarce? Again the plan sets forth provision for credit, power, training in certain skills, and the like which further industrial expansion will demand. But it fails to deal directly with the important questions of the underutilization of existing plant and equipment. It notes it certainly, and exhorts managers to greater efficiency, but it does not explain why it occurs, and what must be done if similar wastage of the scarcest of all factors of production is to be avoided in the future. Indeed, one might even claim that it will be unfortunate if the provisions of the plan are successful in creating further capital-wasting factories along present lines.[11]

Let us take the textile industry as an

example of this. Some ninety firms have already crowded into it. The Economic Commission of Latin America has laid down that in textile spinning some 10,000 spindles are the minimum for economic operation, but in Ecuador no more than 1,400 to 2,500 have been installed in existing factories,[12] and even then textile manufacturers as a whole operated at less than 48 percent of capacity in 1961 (see Table 3). The result is high cost, low efficiency production.[13] Meager purchasing power is siphoned off into these heavily protected factories and capital is dissipated.

TABLE 3

PERCENTAGE OF UNUSED CAPACITY IN ECUADORIAN INDUSTRIES

Industrial Activity	Number of Firms in 1961	1959 Inquiry	1961 Inquiry
Food	130	36.5	34.0
Soft drinks	33	37.6	51.9
Tobacco	30	50.0	22.1
Textiles	90	40.0	52.4
Shoes and clothing	36	63.8	47.8
Wood products	24	59.9	57.5
Wood furniture	4	50.0	52.1
Paper and cardboard	7	34.2	59.3
Printing	45	45.4	50.4
Leather products	12	61.5	53.8
Rubber products	12	61.5	53.8
Chemical products	46	53.9	40.2
Petroleum derivatives	2	50.0	a
Non-metallic mineral products	22	32.6	24.1
Metal products	42	43.3	53.9
Miscellaneous	13	44.7	33.1
Average, all industries	b	46.5	43.0

SOURCE: Results of two inquiries made by the Industrial Section of the Junta Nacional de Plantificación y Coordinación Economica, Quito, Ecuador.

NOTE: Full capacity was defined by the managers of the factories concerned. The inquiries came close to covering 100 percent of all producers employing more than six workers.
ᵃ Not available.   ᵇ Not relevant.

Again it seems evident that the planning authorities should supplement their detailed input-output calculations with some inquiry into this problem. They must ask why factories have proliferated when those already in existence worked at considerably less than full capacity. Some of the factories would be able to operate full-time if they had a larger share of this narrow market.[14] Then, too, the planning authorities have pointed to certain indivisibilities in the production process. One large machine which the technology demands may be under-used and could produce more if a particular factory's share of the market were sufficient to merit the installation of more of the smaller machines with which it works.[15] But if this is often so, why have not factory owners tried to gain more of the market, if need be by selling below cost until some of their "too numerous" competitors disappeared?

Sometimes the Government itself intervenes to protect handicraft producers. This has forced plastic shoe manufacturers in Ecuador to operate at less than full capacity.[16] But elsewhere the situation is harder to explain. Is it that some kind of oligopoly exists—that the kinked demand curve analysis applies? This is difficult to envisage where more than, say, ten firms occupy the same field, as is often the case (see Table 3). Perhaps many firms in the same industry fall into non-competing groups. It is always possible to picture a situation in which no one of the twenty-four woodproducts manufacturers competed with any other. But a planning board should question manufacturers in this regard. It should evaluate responses and recommend action on the basis of results. The formal input-output type of plan does not get to the root of the development problem in instances like this.

CONCLUSIONS

Latin American economists get a pragmatic, business-oriented training. Much of their curriculum consists of courses in accountancy and law.[17] They rarely emerge as theoreticians. The Economic Commission for Latin America in Santiago de Chile takes many of those who enter planning boards and gives them a comprehensive training in the sort of input-output techniques which we have described here.

The consequent thoroughness of many Latin American development plans has to be seen to be believed. The problem is that theoretical aspects of economic development take second place.

Foreign economic advisers sense this. They sit over their coffee and remark to one another that the particular plan in question is "all very well in theory, but how will it work in practice?" But the point is that it may not be all very well in theory, and that it is, above all, their function to point out why. Anglo-Saxon economists in particular are generally well grounded in cause and effect. But all too often they seem to go along with arithmetic planners in spite of their unease. They soon enter into the spirit of things—working out still more input-output coefficients, devising fresh statistical enquiries, and so on. They rarely seem to spend the hours, days, weeks, even months in contemplating the existing data which they must if they are to persuade a planning board to ask the right questions. Perhaps the agency for which they work, or the planning board itself, would ask them what they thought they were doing long before they were in a position to reply. Nor is this situation confined to Latin America. Planners elsewhere appear to be similarly mechanical, but often much less thorough.

1. An estimated daily *per capita* average of 1,930 in 1963 (Government of Ecuador, Junta Nacional de Planificación y Coordinación Económica [hereafter referred to as the JNPCE], *Resumen del Plan General de Desarrollo* [Quito, 1963], p. 73) against 2,020 in India (Food 2nd Agriculture Organization, *Production Yearbook*, Vol. 17, 1963 [Rome, 1964], p. 247).

2. See *Resumen*, p. 101.

3. It has been estimated that there are 23.1 hectares of available cultivable land per agricultural family on the Coast, as against only 13.7 in the Sierra (Government of Ecuador, JNPCE, *Reforma a la Estructura de Tenencia de la Tierra y Expansión de la Frontera Agricola* [Quito, 1964], Capitulo I, Cuadro II-17, p. 47).

4. This problem of the underutilization of land is a serious one not only in Ecuador, but throughout Latin America at large (see Economic Commission for Latin America, "An Agricultural Policy to Expedite the Economic Development of Latin America," *Economic Bulletin for Latin America*, Vol. VI, No. 2 [October 1961], p. 4).

5. Organization of American States, General Secretariat, *The Teaching of Economics in Latin America* (Washington: Pan American Union, 1961), *passim*.

6. It has been estimated that the combined effects of malnutrition and ill health (often different sides of the same coin) reduce the typical Ecuadorian worker's output to 48 percent of what has been defined as full capacity, as opposed to 93 percent in the United States. The Ecuadorian percentage comes close to being the lowest among a large number of surveyed developing countries (Hector Correa, *The Economics of Human Resources* [Den Haag, Drukkerij Pasmans, 1962], p. 44).

7. Government of Ecuador, JNPCE, *Desarrollo y Perspectivas de la Económia Ecuatoriann, Libro Primcro* (Quito, 1963), pp. 298–302.

8. Hourly remuneration of rural labor on the Coast is some three or four times that in the Sierra (Economic Commission for Latin America, "The Productivity of Agriculture in Ecuador," *Economic Bulletin for Latin America*, Vol. VI, No. 2 [Oct. 1961], *passim*). Coastal labor is much more mobile and much less subject to the feudal ties which abound in the Sierra. Then too, even with monopsonistic labor markets, wages would be higher on the Coast since the value of labor's marginal product declines less rapidly when produce is sold in an elastic export market.

9. A substantial literature has grown up which purports to show that the lowest wage which labor will accept in poor countries is not necessarily the one which yields the highest return to the employer (see, for example: Harvey Liebenstein, "Underemployment in Backward Economies," *Journal of Political Economy*, Vol. LXVI, No. 3 [April 1957], pp. 91–103; and John E. Moes, "Surplus Labour and the Wage-level: Implications for General Wage Theory," *Indian Economic Review*, Vol. 12 [Aug. 1959], pp. 109–27).

10. A serious underutilization of plant capacity seems to be a widespread problem throughout the underdeveloped world (see Gerald M. Meier, "Export Stimulation, Import Substitution and Latin American Development," *Social and Economic Studies*, Vol. 10, No. 1 [March 1961], p. 62; E. L. Wheelwright, "Reflections on Some Problems of Industrial Development in Malaya," *The Malayan Economic Review*, Vol. VIII, No. 1 [April 1963], p. 74; International Labour Office, *Employment Objectives and Policies: Preparatory Technical Conference* [PTCE/I] [Geneva, 1963], p. 175; and W. B. Reddaway, *The Development of the Indian Economy* [London: George Allen and Unwin Ltd., 1962], *passim*).

11. It has been estimated that the already seriously underemployed Ecuadorian work-

force will increase from 1,704,200 in 1963 to 2,242,700 in 1973 (*Resumen,* Table II-2, p. 32). But investment per worker in under-utilized factories is calculated at US$8,804 as against only US$63 in handicrafts (Ramy Alexander and Frank L. Turner, *The Artisan Community in Ecuador's Modernizing Economy: Supplement No. 2* [Menlo Park: Stanford Research Institute, 1963], p. 19), and about US$600 in agriculture (Economic Commission for Latin America, "Productivity of the Agricultural Sector in Ecuador," p. 72). Moreover, much of capital formation in agriculture can be attained at the cost of some sacrifice of overly abundant leisure, and is not capital at all in the sense that consumption must be sacrificed.

12. Government of Ecuador, JNPCE, Seción Industria, "La Industria Textil" (Quito, 1963), p. 6 (typewritten and in the files of the JNPCE).

13. Ecuadorian per man-hour output in kilograms of cotton yarn is only some 57 percent of what the Economic Commission for Latin America considers standard for the region, and even then the thread is of low quality. In weaving the situation is even worse, with Ecuadorian labor taking nearly twelve times as many man hours as the Commission's estimate of what is standard (*ibid.,* pp. 8 and 11).

14. Ecuadorian manufacturers themselves give the limited market as the principal obstacle to growth in their output (JNPCE, *Plan General . . . , La Industria Fabril,* p. 40). But in many cases this is only true after an industry has become overcrowded. The unexplained overexpansion in existing industries, rather than the narrowness of the market, seems to be the real problem.

15. See *ibid.,* p. 80; JNPCE, "La Industria Textil," p. 20; and JNPCE, Seción Industria, "Acietes y Grasas Comestibles" (Quito, 1963), p. 9 (typewritten and in the files of the JNPCE).

16. *El Comercio* (Quito, September 17, 1966), p. 11.

17. See Organization of American States, *op. cit.,* particularly Appendix II on "Some Representative Examples of Curricula," pp. 90–97.

THE CHANGING VALUES AND INSTITUTIONS OF VICOS, A PERUVIAN COMMUNITY, IN THE CONTEXT OF NATIONAL DEVELOPMENT

ALLAN R. HOLMBERG

Cornell University

More than 50 percent of the world's population is peasantry, the large majority of whom are living in so-called underdeveloped countries or newly emerging nations under natural conditions and social structures that have denied them effective participation in the modernization process. In the context of a modern state, this peasantry plays little or no role in the decision-making process; its members enjoy little access to wealth; they live under conditions of social disrespect; a large majority of them are illiterate, unenlightened, and lacking in modern skills; many are victims of ill health and disease. Characteristic of this sector of the world's population is a deep devotion to magico-religious practice as a means of mitigating the castigations of a harsh and cruel world over which it has little or no control. Such, in fact, were the conditions of life on the Hacienda Vicos.[1]

Operating on the assumption that these conditions of human indignity are not only anachronistic in the modern world but are also a great threat to public and civic order everywhere, Cornell University, in 1952—in collaboration with the Peruvian Indianist Institute—embarked on an ex-

From *American Behavioral Scientist* (March 1965), pp. 3–8. Reprinted by permission of the publisher, Sage Publications, Inc.

perimental program of induced technical and social change which was focused on the problem of transforming one of Peru's most unproductive, highly dependent manor systems into a productive, independent, self-governing community adapted to the reality of the modern Peruvian state.[2]

Up until January, 1952, Vicos was a manor or large estate, situated in a relatively small intermontane valley of Peru, about 250 miles north of the capital city of Lima. Ranging in altitude from about 9,000 to 20,000 feet, Vicos embraced an area of about 40,000 acres [3] and had an enumerated population of 1,703 monolingual Quechua-speaking Indians [4] who had been bound to the land as serfs or peons since early colonial times.

Vicos was a public manor, a type not uncommon in Peru. Title to such properties is frequently held by Public Benefit or Charity Societies which rent them out to the highest bidder at public auction for periods ranging from 5 to 10 years. Each such manor has particular lands, usually the most fertile bottom lands, reserved for commercial exploitation by the successful renter who utilizes, virtually free of charge for several days of each week, the serf-bound labor force, usually one adult member of every family, to cultivate his crops.

The rent from the property paid to the Public Benefit Society is supposed to be used for charitable purposes, such as the support of hospitals and other welfare activities, although this is not always the case. Under the contractual arrangements between the renter and the Public Benefit Society (and sometimes the indigenous population) the former is legally but not always functionally bound to supply, in return for the labor tax paid by his serfs, plots of land (usually upland) of sufficient size to support the family of each inscribed peon.

Manors like Vicos are socially organized along similar lines. At the head of the hierarchy stands the renter or *patron,* frequently absentee, who is always an outsider and non-Indian or Mestizo. He is the maximum authority within the system and all power to indulge or deprive is concentrated in his hands. Under his direction, if absentee, is an administrator, also an outsider and Mestizo, who is responsible to the renter for conducting and managing the day-to-day agricultural or grazing operations of the property. Depending on the size of the manor, the administrator may employ from one to several Mestizo foremen who are responsible for the supervision of the labor force. They report directly to the administrator on such matters as the number of absentee members of the labor force, and the condition of the crops regarding such factors as irrigation, fertilization, and harvest.

Below and apart from this small non-Indian power elite stands the Indian society of peons, the members of which are bound to a soil they do not own and on which they have little security of tenure. The direct link between the labor force and the administration is generally through a number of Indian straw bosses, appointed by the *patron* and responsible for the direct supervision of the labor force in the fields. Each straw boss or *mayoral,* as he was known at Vicos, had under his direction a certain number of *peones* from a particular geographic area of the manor.

In 1952 there were eight straw bosses at Vicos, with a total labor force of about 380 men. In addition to the labor tax paid by the Indian community, its members were obligated to supply other free services to the manor such as those of cooks, grooms, swineherds, watchmen, and servants. The whole system is maintained by the application of sanctions ranging from brute force to the impounding of peon property.

In matters not associated directly with manor operations, the Indian community of Vicos was organized along separate and traditional lines. The principal indigenous decision-making body consisted of a politico-religious hierarchy of some seventeen officials known as *Varas* or *Varayoc,*[5] so named from the custom of carrying a wooden staff as a badge of office. The major functions of this body included settling of disputes over land and animals in the Indian community, the supervision of public works such as the repair of bridges and the community church, the regulation of marriage patterns, and the celebration of religious festivals. The leading official in this hierarchy was the *Alcalde* or mayor who assumed office, after many years of service to the community, by a kind of elective system and who occupied it for only one year. The *Varayoc* were the principal representatives of the Indian community to the outside world.

In 1952 all Vicosinos were virtual subsistence farmers, occupying plots of land ranging in size from less than one half to about five acres. The principal crops raised were maize, potatoes, and other Andean root crops, wheat, barley, rye, broad beans, and quinoa. In addition, most families grazed some livestock (cattle, sheep, goats, and swine) and all families raised small animals like guinea pigs and chickens as a way of supplementing their diets and their incomes. After thousands of years of use and inadequate care, the land had lost its fertility, seeds had degenerated, and the principal crops and animals were stunted and diseased. Per capita output was thus at a very low level, although the exact figure is not known.

In addition, many Vicosinos suffered from malnutrition; [6] most were victims of a host of endemic diseases. Studies in parasitology [7] demonstrated that 80 percent of the population was infected with harmful parasites, and epidemics of such diseases as measles and whooping cough had been frequent over the years. There were, to be sure, native curers employing magico-religious practices and ineffectual herbal remedies to cope with these well-being problems but it can be said that the community had little or no access to modern medicine. The goal of the traditional Vicosino was simply to survive as long as he possibly could, knowing full well that he might be a victim of fate at any moment.

The principal avenue for gaining respect in traditional Vicos society was to grow old and to participate in the politico-religious hierarchy, the top positions of which could be occupied only after many years of faithful service to the community. Wealth was also a source of gaining prestige and recognition but it could not be amassed in any quantity, by native standards, until one's elders had died or until an individual himself had lived frugally and worked very hard for many years. In other words, the principal role to which high rank was attached was that of a hard working, musclebound, virtual subsistence farmer who placed little or no value on other occupations or skills.

Consequently, there was just no place for a rebellious or symbolically creative individual in traditional Vicos society. The manor system was, of course, in large part responsible for this. It needed few skills beyond brawn, and enlightenment could not be tolerated, because the more informed the population, the more it might become a threat to the traditional manor system. Records show [8] that all protest movements at Vicos had been pretty much squelched by a coalition of the landlords, the clergy, and the police.

As a result, over a period of several hundred years the community had remained in static equilibrium and was completely out of step with anything that was occurring in the modern world. The rule at Vicos was conformity to the status quo. It pervaded all institutions and dominated the social process. The peon was subservient to the overlord; the child, to the parents; and both were beaten into submission. Even the supernatural forces were punishing, and the burdens one bore were suffered as naturally ordained by powers beyond one's control.

INTERVENTION FROM WITHOUT

The Cornell Peru Project intervened in this context in 1952 in the role of *patron*. Through a partly fortuitous circumstance —the industrial firm which was renting Vicos on a ten year lease that still had five years to run went bankrupt—we were able to sublease the property and its serfs for a five year period. For a couple of years prior to this time, however, the Peruvian anthropologist, Dr. Mario Vazquez, had conducted a very detailed study of this manor as a social system, as part of a larger comparative study of modernization of peasant societies that the Department of Anthropology at Cornell was conducting in several areas of the world. Thus when the opportunity to rent the *hacienda* arose, we seized upon it to conduct our own experiment in modernization. In its negotiations prior to renting the *hacienda*, Cornell received full support of the Peruvian Government through its Institute of Indigenous Affairs, a semi-autonomous agency of the Ministry of Labor and Indigenous Affairs. In December, 1951, a formal Memorandum of Agreement was drawn up between

Cornell and the Institute of Indigenous Affairs, and the Cornell Peru Project became a reality at Vicos on January 1, 1952.

Several months prior to assuming the responsibilities of the power role at Vicos, a plan of operations was drawn up [9] which was focused on the promotion of human dignity rather than indignity and the formation of institutions at Vicos which would allow for a wide rather than a narrow shaping and sharing of values for all the participants in the social process. The principal goals of this plan thus became the devolution of power to the community, the production and broad sharing of greater wealth, the introduction and diffusion of new and modern skills, the promotion of health and well-being, the enlargement of the status and role structure, and the formulation of a modern system of enlightenment through schools and other media.

In designing our program and a method of strategic intervention, we were very much aware of two, among many, guiding principles stemming from anthropological research: First, innovations are most likely to be accepted in those aspects of culture in which people themselves feel the greatest deprivations; and second, an integrated or contextual approach to value-institutional development is usually more lasting and less conflict-producing than a piecemeal one. Consequently, we established our operational priorities on the basis of the first principle but tried to optimize change in all areas at the same time, realizing, of course, that with scarce resources, all values could not be maximized concurrently. Perhaps a few examples will best illustrate our use of the method of strategic intervention.

Our first entry into more than a research role at Vicos coincided with a failure of the potato harvest of both the *patron* and the serf community due to a blight which had attacked the crop. The poor of the community were literally starving, and even the rich were feeling the pinch. Complaints about the theft of animals and food were rife. At the same time, previous study of the manor had enlightened us about the major gripes of the serfs against the traditional system.

These turned out not to be such things as the major commitment of each head of household to contribute one peon to the labor force for three days of each week, but the obligation of the Indian households to supply the extra, free services to the manor previously mentioned. Since we were in a position of power, it was relatively easy to abolish these services. A decision was made to do so, and volunteers were hired to perform these jobs for pay. Thus an immediate positive reinforcement was supplied to the community in our power relationship with it.

An added incentive to collaborate with the new administration resulted from the fact that we as *patrons* reimbursed the serfs for labor which they had performed under the previous administration but for which they had not been paid for approximately three years. Under the traditional system, each peon was entitled to about three cents per week for the work performed under the labor tax. In some Peruvian manors this is paid in the form of coca leaves, which most adult males chew, but at Vicos it was supposed to have been paid in cash. By deducting the back pay from the cost of the transfer of the manor to our control, we fulfilled earlier commitments, with the money of the previous administration, and received the credit for it.

Through such small but immediately reinforcing interventions, a solid base for positive relations with members of the community was first established. In this regard, of course, we were greatly aided by Dr. Vazquez, who had previously spent almost two years in the community, living with an Indian family, and who personally knew and was trusted by almost every one of its members.

INCREASING AGRICULTURAL PRODUCTIVITY

As mentioned above, one of the most immediate and urgent tasks at Vicos was to do something about its failing economy which, in reality, meant increasing its agricultural productivity. Manors like Vicos are never productive because the renter during his period of tenure puts as little as possible into the operation and exploits the property for as much as he possibly can. The serfs, on the other hand, make no improvements on their lands, or other capital investments, because they have no security of tenure. As a consequence, most such manors are in a very bad state of repair.

Since the Cornell Peru Project possessed funds only for research and not for capital development, the wealth base had to be enlarged by other capital means. It was decided, in consultation with Indian leaders, who were early informed about the goals of the Project, that no major changes would be initiated immediately in the day-to-day operations of the manor. We even retained the former Mestizo administrator, a close friend of the Project Director and Field Director, who agreed to reorient his goals to those of the Project.

The principal resources available to the Project were the labor of the Indian community and the lands which had been formerly farmed by the overlord. By employing this labor to farm these lands by modern methods (the introduction of fertilizer, good seeds, pesticides, proper row spacing, etc.), and by growing marketable food crops, capital was accumulated for enlarging the wealth base. Returns from these lands, instead of being removed from the community, as was the case under the traditional system, were plowed back into the experiment to foment further progress towards our goals.

Profits from the Project's share of the land were not only employed further to improve agricultural productivity but also to construct health and educational facilities, to develop a wider range of skills among the Indian population, and to reconstruct what had been a completely abandoned administrative center of operations. At the same time, new techniques of potato production and other food crops, first demonstrated on Project lands, were introduced to the Indian households which, within a couple of years, gave a sharp boost to the Indian's economy. In short, by 1957 when Cornell's lease on the land expired, a fairly solid economic underpinning for the whole operation had been accomplished.

DEVOLUTION OF POWER

From the very first day of operation, we initiated the process of power devolution. It was decided that it would be impossible to work with the traditional *Varas* as a leadership group, because they were so occupied during their terms of office with religious matters that they would have no time to spend on secular affairs. On the other hand, the former straw bosses, all old and respected men, had had a great deal of direct experience in conducting the affairs of the manor for the *patron*. It was decided not to bypass this group even though we knew that its members had enjoyed the greatest indulgences under the traditional system and, being old, would be less likely to be innovative than younger men. Under prevailing conditions, however, this seemed to be the best alternative to pursue.

As it turned out, it proved to be an effective transitional expedient. Gradually, as success was achieved in the economic field, it became possible to replace (by appointment) the retiring members of this body with younger men more committed to the goals of modernization. For instance, men finishing their military service, an obligation we encouraged them to fulfill, returned home with at least an exposure to other values and institutions in Peruvian society. In pre-Cornell days such returning veterans were forced back in the traditional mold within a few days time, with no opportunity to give expression to any newly found values they may have acquired. Insofar as possible, we tried to incorporate people of this kind into decision-making bodies and tried to provide them opportunities to practice whatever new skills they had acquired.

In the first five years of the Project, not only did age composition of the governing body completely change, but decision-making and other skills had developed to a point where responsibility for running the affairs of the community was largely in indigenous hands. A complete transfer of power took place in 1957, when a council of 10 delegates, and an equal number of sub-delegates, was elected to assume responsibility for community affairs. This council, elected annually, has performed this function ever since.

In the area of well-being it was much more difficult to devise a strategy of intervention that would show immediate and dramatic pay-off. This is a value area, to be sure, in which great deprivation was felt at Vicos, but it is also one in which the cooperation of all participants in the community was necessary in order to make any appreciable impact on it. The major well-being problems at Vicos, even today, stem from public health conditions. All individuals are deeply concerned about their personal well-being but are unwilling to forego other value indulgences to make this a reality for the community as a whole. Nor were the resources available to do so at the time the Project began.

A variety of attempts was made to tackle the most urgent health problems. In collaboration with the Peruvian Ministry of Health and Social Welfare, a mobile clinic was started at Vicos, which made at least one visit to the community each week. Support for this effort came from the community itself in the form of the construction of a small sanitary post at which the sick could be treated. It was hoped to staff this clinic through the Public Health services of Peru, but all attempts to do so were frustrated by lack of budget and responsibly trained personnel.

In Peru, such services seldom extend into rural areas because the preferred values of the medical profession are, as almost everywhere, associated with city life. Consequently, no major public health effort was launched and the community's state of well-being has shown little net gain. What gains have been made stem principally from improved nutrition, but as enlightenment about the germ theory of disease diffuses and the results of modern medicine are clearly demonstrated, through the application of public health measures that take native beliefs into account, we expect a sharp rise in the well-being status of the community to follow.

OPTIMIZING GOALS

Strategies for optimizing Project goals for the respect, affection, and rectitude values, first rested heavily on the examples set by Project personnel. From the very beginning, for example, an equality of salutation was introduced in all dealings with the Vicosinos; they were invited to sit down at the tables with us; there was no segregation allowed at public affairs; Project personnel lived in Indian houses. At the same time, we attempted to protect the constitutional rights of Vicosinos, which had been previously flagrantly violated by the Mestizo world. Abuses by Mestizo authorities and army recruiters were no longer tolerated. The draft status of all Vicosinos

was regularized; they were encouraged to fulfill their legal obligations to the nation.

While not directly intervening in the family, or tampering with religious practice, the indirect effect of optimizing other values on the respect position of the community soon became evident. As Vicosinos mastered modern techniques of potato production, for example, they were approached by their Mestizo compatriots in the surrounding area, seeking advice as to how to improve their crops.

Even the rectitude patterns at Vicos began to change. When we first took control of the manor, rates of theft were extremely high. Every peon farmer, as his crops were maturing, had to keep watchmen in his fields at night. As the Indian economy rose and starvation was eliminated, this practice disappeared completely. Even the parish priest became an enthusiastic supporter of the Project. His services were more in demand, to say nothing of their being much better paid.

A strategy of promoting enlightenment at Vicos was initiated through the adaptations of a traditional manor institution to goals and values of the Project. In most Andean manors run along the lines of Vicos, the peons, after completing their three days labor, must report to the manor house where they receive their work orders for the following week. This session of all peons, straw bosses, and the *patron* is known as the *mando*. We devised a strategy of meeting the day before the *mando* with the *mayorales* or decision-making body and utilizing the *mando* to communicate and discuss the decisions taken. Since the heads of all households were present, the *mando* provided an excellent forum for the communication of news, the discussion of plans, progress towards goals, etc.

A long-run strategy of enlightenment rested on the founding of an educational institution at Vicos that could provide continuity for Project goals, training of leadership dedicated to the process of modernization, and the formulation of a wide range of skills. Through collaboration with the Peruvian Ministry of Education and the Vicos community itself, this became a possibility. Within the period of Cornell's tenure, levels of enlightenment and skill rose sharply and their effects have been substantial throughout the society.

TRANSFER OF TITLE

In 1957, at the time Cornell's lease in Vicos expired, the Project made a recommendation to the Peruvian Government, through its Institute of Indigenous Affairs, to expropriate the property from the holders of the title, the Public Benefit Society of Huaraz, in favor of its indigenous inhabitants. By this time we felt that a fairly solid institutional base, with the goals of modernization that we had originally formulated, had been established in the community. The Peruvian Government acted upon the recommendation and issued a decree of expropriation.

It was at this point that the experiment became especially significant, both in the local area and throughout the nation, for national development. Prior to this time, although considerable favorable national publicity had been given to the Project, little attention had been paid to it by the local power elite, except in terms of thinking that the benefits of the developments that had taken place would eventually revert to the title holders. It was inconceivable in the local area that such a property might be sold back to its indigenous inhabitants. Consequently, local power elites immediately threw every possible legal block in the way of the title reverting to the Indian community. . . .

Fortunately, the Project had strong support in the intellectual community of the capital and among many of Peru's agencies of government. . . . [But even so,] efforts did not bear fruit until almost five years had passed. The reason for this was that not only were the legal blocks of the resistance formidable, but the central government of Peru at this time was an elite government, which, while giving great lip service to the cause of the Vicosinos, was reluctant to take action in their favor. It is a matter of record that many high officials of government were themselves *hacendados,* hesitant to alter the status quo. Consequently, they were able to delay final settlement.

Meanwhile, the Vicosinos, now renting the manor directly, were reluctant to develop Vicos because of the danger of their not being able to enjoy the fruits of their labor. While agricultural production rose through the stimulation of a loan from the Agricultural Bank of Peru, other capital investments were not made because of the fear that the price of property would rise with every investment made.

Finally, . . . after a five year wait following the devolution of power, the community actually became independent in July, 1962. Since that time, Cornell has played largely a research, advisory and consultant role, although the Peruvian National Plan of Integration of the Indigenous Populations has had an official government program of development at Vicos since Cornell relinquished control in 1957.

RESULTS

What can be said in a general way about the results of the Vicos experience so far? In the first place, if one criterion of a modern democratic society is a parity of power and other values among individuals, then vast gains have been made at Vicos during the past decade. Starting from the base of a highly restrictive social system in which almost all power and other value positions were ascribed and very narrowly shared, the Vicosinos have gradually changed that social system for a much more open one in which all value positions can be attained through achievement. This in itself was no mean accomplishment, particularly since it was done by peaceful and persuasive means.

In the second place, the position of the Vicos community itself, vis-à-vis the immediately surrounding area and the nation as a whole, has undergone a profound change. Starting at the bottom of the heap, and employing a strategy of wealth production for the market place and enlightenment for its people, the community of Vicos has climbed to a position of power and respect that can no longer be ignored by the Mestizo world. This is clearly indexed by the large number of equality relationships which now exist at Vicos (and in intercommunity relationships between Vicos and the world outside), where none existed before.

Finally, of what significance is Vicos in the context of national development? Peru is a country with a high degree of unevenness in its development. The highly productive agricultural coast, with off-shore fishing grounds that are among the richest in the world, is moving ahead at a modern and rapid pace. In contrast, the overpopulated sierra, containing major concentrations of indigenous populations, many of whom live under medieval type agricultural organization, such as exists at Vicos, is lagging far behind.

The major lesson of Vicos, for Peru as a whole, is that its serf and suppressed peasant populations, once freed and given encouragement, technical assistance and learning, can pull themselves up by their own bootstraps and become productive citizens of the nations. It is encouraging to see that the present Peruvian Government is taking steps in the right direction. Its programs of land reform and Cooperation Popular may go a long way towards a more peaceful and rapid development of the country as a whole.

1. Vazquez, M. C., "La Antropologia y Nuestro Problema del Indio," *Peru Indigena,* 1952, vol. II, Nos. 5 y 6, pp. 7–157.

2. For a fuller account of the Vicos program, see A. R. Holmberg, "Changing Community Attitudes and Values in Peru," in *Social Change in Latin America Today.* New York: Harper and Bros., 1960, pp. 63–107.

3. Earlier publications on Vicos estimated acreage as much smaller. This figure is correct, based on accurate measurements made by Mr. Gary Vescelius.

4. Alers, J. O., "Population and Development in a Peruvian Community." Ithaca, N.Y.: Cornell University Comparative Studies of Cultural Change, 1964 (mimeo), p. 3.

5. Vazquez, M. C., "The Varayoc System in Vicos." Ithaca, N.Y.: Cornell University Comparative Studies of Cultural Change, 1964 (mimeo).

6. Collazos, Ch. C., *et al.,* "Dietary Surveys in Peru, Chacan and Vicos: Rural Communities in the Peruvian Andes," *J. Amer. Dietetic Assoc.,* 1954, vol. 30, pp. 1222 ff.

7. Payne, E. H., L. Gonzalez M., and E. M. Schleicher, "An Intestinal Parasite Survey in the High Cordilleras of Peru," *Amer. J. Trop. Med. Hyg.,* 1956, vol. 5, No. 4, pp. 696–98.

8. Barnett, C., "Indian Protest Movements in Callejon de Huaylas." Cornell University Ph.D. Dissertation, 1960.

9. Holmberg, A. R., "Proyecto Peru-Cornell en las Ciencias Sociales Aplicadas," *Peru Indigena,* 1952, vol. II, Nos. 5 y 6, pp. 158–66.

SOCIAL RESOURCES OF A LATIN AMERICAN PEASANTRY:
The Case of a Mexican Indian Community

JUNE NASH

New York University

In Latin America, the problem of the integration of rural populations in national life is a crucial issue for both governmental agencies and the social scientist. In order to map the "integrative revolution" [1] which is occurring throughout the world, case studies of the selective absorption of innovation at the local level are of some value in complementing the research into "power domains." [2] This paper is an attempt to document the perception of economic and/or social advantages of innovations in the Maya Indian community of Tzo?ontahal, Chiapas, Mexico, and to show how the Indians have organized their own resources to incorporate these opportunities.

Identification with an Indian subculture has been equated with resistance to economic and political change. This interpretation has led some analysts to point to the Indian population as the reason for the backwardness, poverty, and low literacy of the nation or state of which they are a majority or large minority. The mission sponsored by the International Bank for Reconstruction and Development [3] blames the backwardness of the Guatemalan econ-

From *Social and Economic Studies* (December 1966), pp. 353–367. Reprinted by permission. Some sections have been omitted.

omy on the "Indians whose cultural isolation and defensive attitude, products of the hard experience of four centuries, constitute one of Guatemala's basic national problems." Maclean [4] says that the Indian population of Chiapas constitute . . . "the ballast of collective progress and the major obstacle to the unity of all the sectors of social life."

It is not my aim to acclaim or defend the Indian community; anthropological field work of the past thirty years has established beyond a doubt the industry and resourcefulness of the Indians [5] and the economist Schultz [6] has praised their efficiency in the allocation of their resources. Pictured as the main retardation of the economy by some analysts of Latin American economies, they exemplify the free market tradition.[7]

The problem I raise here is the manner in which bounded social groups perceive alternatives and re-work innovation to fit a local set of givens. Policy makers involved in designing programs for development in Mexico's Indian populations have accepted the premise that Indians can enter into the national society without losing the cultural identification which has been the basis for cultural exclusion or withdrawal.[8] This represents a reversal of an earlier program of incorporation initiated under Cárdenas which, although extolling *indigenismo,* or the Indian heritage, as an ideology, provided welfare programs directed at cultural integration.[9] In order to assess the potential of this doctrine translated into a program of planned change, case materials at the local level are essential.

In presenting the community case material, I shall attempt to assess the social resources in terms of how these have served the Indians in the widening circumstance of their social horizons. These social resources include the patterns of interaction influencing the course of economic change, perception of economic opportunity, resourcefulness in fitting social and technological innovation into a given schedule of production and organization. This is the problem area which Bauer and Yamey [10] point to as significant to development but outside of the domain of economic theory.

Beneath a surface which may appear little affected by changes occurring in the larger society, some Indian communities are mobilizing social resources which may be of crucial importance in effecting integration into the wider society. The model of small-scale change which takes into account the techniques of adaptation and integration of such underdeveloped areas is that of "moving equilibrium." . . . It applies to the corporate Indian communities of Meso-america where the talents of absorbing, reinterpreting, and balancing of opposed forces are implicit in their survival. This paper is an attempt to analyze the social resources which make this kind of change possible in the town of Tzo?ontahal in Chiapas, Mexico.

REGIONAL ECONOMIC AND POLITICAL SETTING

Chiapas is an agricultural state, producing maize as both a subsistence and sale crop. Coffee and sugar are crops grown both on plantations and on small communal land grants and privately-owned plots. Cattle is grazed in large haciendas on the eastern flanks of the highland area, and sheep in the high zones with low soil fertility. Pigs are raised in most communities, more as a storage of value for resale, a kind of "piggy bank," than for profit.

The large coffee plantations located in the western coastal area of Soconusco were developed by German planters in the latter part of the nineteenth century. These plantations were tied to the port city of Tapachula by rail and by telegraphic communications. Indians were recruited as workers from the Chiapas highlands as well as from Huehuetenango in Guatemala. The urban centers of marketing and administration for the highland Indian populations, San Cristóbal de las Casas and Comitán, are not industrially developed, and are unable to absorb the population of the area which has increased 75 percent since the turn of the century. As a result, the population increase has caused either seasonal or permanent movement to the lowland tropical areas in which the large commercial crop enterprises are found.

Although Chiapas was marginal to the revolutionary agrarian movements concentrated in the central plateau of Mexico, the waves of reform affected the Indian and Ladino population of the highlands. [Ladinos are persons of mixed Spanish and Indian ancestry.] In the period of 1930 to 1935, the resistance to nationalization of lands of the German and Ladino *finqueros,* or large commercial crop producers, gave way. The number of *ejidatarios,* or communal land holders, increased from 9,000 in 1930 to 28,000 in 1935 and there was a 202 percent increase in land held by *ejidatarios.*[11] Forms of self-sufficient agriculture were reinforced by *ejido* grants obtained by some communities at different altitudinal levels. With harvests depending on what level the crop was grown, a constant supply of the basic subsistence crop of corn could be acquired by the Indians. Sugar cane, fruits, chile and other crops grown only in hot country could be cultivated on *ejido* plots and were no longer purchased. The initial effects of the *ejido* grant in the 1930's was to arrest the flow of goods and labor into the market. New *ejido* colonies are no longer contiguous to settled villages and the expansion into unsettled territories has made for new migrations of people.

The case material presented here is drawn from the community of Tzo?ontahal, a township of 3,179 living in a nucleated center dominated by an entirely Indian population, with the exception of the Ladino schoolteacher. The town center is adjacent to the Pan-American highway which was constructed in this area in 1953. The town is and has been in a more favorable position in the regional economy than most of the Indian communities. With the addition of over 6,000 hectares (100 by 100 metres) in *ejido* land since 1935, every household has at least two hectares of arable land. The density of population is 3.5 per kilometer compared with 14.1 per kilometer for the state. Pottery handicraft has always provided cash income as far back as there are historical records. Only a minority of the Indians are forced to go to the plantations, and they go temporarily and usually without their women, who remain at home earning money from their pottery production. Tzo?ontahal's favorable economic position has enabled it to resist change, or at least to be more selective about the changes which take place. The town is included in the Instituto Nacional Indigenista (I.N.I.) program for economic and social development in the Tzoltal-Tzotzil

area of Chiapas. The effects of planned change originating from outside the community will be assessed along with the intra-community adjustment.

SELF-DEVELOPMENT IN TZO?ONTAHAL

The case against agrarian peasant communities in development can be paraphrased as follows:

(1) They are tradition bound. Preference is for the old rather than the new, for old technology, old methods of organization.

(2) Leadership positions are occupied by incumbents because of ascribed rather than achieved basis for assignment. Age rather than skill dominates.

(3) Economic motivation is based on consumption ends, which, once satisfied, deprive them of their incentive to produce.

This over-simplified statement seemed to apply to the town of Tzo?ontahal when I first went there to study in 1957. The Indians used the ancient *arada* plough introduced by the Spaniards in the sixteenth century. Fertilizing was haphazard, and the fields were left to fallow or were alternately cropped with wheat and corn in the belief that the wheat helped restore some of the field's nutrients. Their only other tools were the *lum* to cut down weeds, the hoe, and the machete, a "Collins" type imported from Connecticut. About 50 percent of the fields were irrigated by crudely dug ditches fed by mountain streams. In pottery production, the technology was even simpler: with a wooden board on which to rest the pot, a knife for scraping the moulded pot and a smooth stone for polishing the surface, a leather piece to smooth the neck of the vessels, the potter was in business. Capitalization costs did not prevent anyone from becoming a producer in this community. The Indians entered into the market out of consumption necessities. In a series of charts in which I plotted pottery production for two producers, the peaks of production were reached just before the major fiestas of the town and at a time when the people wanted money. The markets of Las Casas and Comitán became so glutted that water jars which sold ordinarily at 2.5 to 3.5 pesos were sold at 1.5 and 2 pesos. A man brought his cattle to market when he needed cash, or when the animals were sick, not when the price was highest. Surplus corn was sold when it was harvested by nearly all except the richest families, not six months later when the price rose by half as much again.

When I returned in 1964 the traditional way of life was apparently unaltered. The sanitary toilet seats which the Instituto Nacional Indigenista attempted to introduce were still displayed outside the co-operative store and used by idlers as seating accommodations. The traditional costume was unaltered, except in the incidence of men wearing the older form of an elongated shirt and high-backed sandals in comparison to those wearing the wrapped and tied white pants with *huarache* type sandals. The tempo of life was unaltered: the policemen appeared at 7 A.M. to take up their duty of sitting on the benches outside the town hall, and the president sat at the table inside with the *sindico,* the judges, and *regidores.* Sundown was marked by a return to these posts. There were two new buildings, a corn grinding mill which was very actively in use, and a public bath house, unused except by visitors and school children herded in by the schoolmaster. Both buildings were built by the Instituto Nacional Indigenista (I.N.I.). The electric wires which had passed over the village to service the sawmill had been tapped to provide electricity in public buildings and cantinas, or bars. "Sleeping" in the *sitio* of one of the co-operative members was a new blue Dodge two-ton truck owned exclusively by the Indians of Tzo?ontahal. These changes were not a matter of new lives for old, flinging out cannibalism and clan systems in the conversion to the dominant Western culture which Margaret Mead describes for New Guinea. This was selective adoption of new items, some acquired from the I.N.I. and used as the Indians perceived their advantage, or more significantly purchased in their own interests.

These were the acquisitions in the six-year period, tolerated or actively sought in this "traditional" community. But more important than the material gains was the solution of major *social-organizational* problems and the development of *entrepreneurial and technical skills* [emphasis added]. These developing social resources are discussed below.

The Co-operative

The notion of a co-operative to mobilize capital had been introduced by I.N.I. in 1937 with the inauguration of a store owned by over one hundred members of the community. In the first years of its existence, the co-operative had some difficulties, primarily in convincing the Indians that when the returns on shares were lower in any year than prior levels, it did not indicate that the agents were stealing the money. . . .

The co-operative store was bought by the Indians of the town from I.N.I. in 1964 after the members had some trouble receiving returns on their shares. There are now 122 members. The policy of admitting anyone in the community who wished to invest has been reversed since the Indians have gained control. Membership is now restricted to these original investors. The profits of the last year's operations were voted to be invested in the purchase of the corn mill which had been introduced by I.N.I. The co-operative store members are thinking of buying a threshing machine and tractor.

Now that the co-operative is independent of the government, one of the stated policies is not to sell a single share to a Ladino or member of another community. "We do not want to give gifts to the Ladinos," says the secretary. He added, "There was a Ladino in Teopisco who wanted to join with 5,000 pesos, but we wouldn't let him in. If you let them in, they would come to dominate the pueblo." The co-operative store does not share profits with the consumers. The 11,380 pesos assets in the year 1965 were reinvested in stock and in the purchase of corn at harvest which is then sold at one and a half times or twice the sale price.

The most enterprising act of the new co-operative has been the purchase of a truck, initiated by the entrepreneur S., whose career is discussed below. The motivation to purchase the truck was a traditional one in Tzo?ontahal—envy of the Ladino secretary, who, with his wife and son, had a monopoly of the traffic carrying pottery, people, and wheat out of the village. The Indians had the example of the neighboring town of Zinacantan where the Indians were successfully operating two trucks. S. went with his brother to the director of the I.N.I. in Las Casas to ask for a co-signee on a mortgage to purchase a Chevrolet truck. According to one informant, they were advised that they would not be able to profit from this venture and that they should buy a tractor with their money. The brothers persisted and went to the Dodge company in the state capital. The company agreed to sell, even to Indians without Ladino co-signers, on the basis of a down payment of 10,000 pesos. The initial payment was raised with thirty Indians putting up the money. Some gave no more than 150 pesos, but, as the instigators of the purchase remarked, "The more members we have, the more power it gives us."

The truck is the focus of the desire for self-improvement, for fighting the Ladino monopoly of the road, for the antagonisms and factional strife and conflict within the community. When they bought the truck, the Indians hired a Ladino in the neighboring town as a chauffeur. One of the conditions of his employment was that he would teach his Indian assistant to drive, which the Ladino tried to avoid doing since he knew it would be the end of his job. But the Indian assistant learned by observation and internalization without practice under supervision, and is now operating the truck with an Indian assistant.

Accounts of the cost and profit of the truck operation indicate a running loss. A new tarpaulin cost 1,200 pesos; there were repairs and bribes to the highway patrol. But the truck was kept in operation because the major share-holders were impressed with the power it gave them. "They" (their ememies, the members of the other co-operative owned by the Ladino along with twenty members of the community) "are afraid of us because of the truck," one said, and one added that it was better than having a *swayohel*, the animal spirit associated with the curers.

Entrepreneurship

Another important social resource which is developing is entrepreneurship. S., the promoter of the last co-operative discussed, had picked up some accounting techniques while he served in the army in Michoacán. He returned to the village because his father walked from Chiapas to Michoacán to tell him he should come back and get

married. When he returned, he kept careful account of his costs and returns from the *milpa*. He realized soon that it wasn't "worth his work" (the Indian has not as yet learned the idiom or the value system which goes into the phrase "worth my time"). He therefore talked a Ladino of Teopisca into lending him 5,000 pesos. He went down to hot country and bought corn when it was scarce in the village, brought it up the hill, sold a little for his needs, but held it until the price went up in the next three months. That year, with his 5,000 investment, he grossed 400,000 pesos. Since then he has been hiring men to work in his *milpa*. At a recent meeting of the co-operative association, S., in defending his investments of the association's funds, showed his carefully kept accounts and held up his pencil saying proudly, "This is my machete! This is my hoe!" The phrasing is an imitation of Ladino rhetoric of the provinces. . . .

S. is now treasurer of the *ejido* commission and of the town. . . . S.'s administration of funds in his public capacity and as accountant for the store, the *ejido* commission, and the truck co-operative, have won him a reputation of honesty and reliability. His knowledge not only of how to manage funds, but also of how to *"manejarlo"* or drive it, and to "make it grow" has indicated an insight into capital operations which makes him a leader in local enterprises. In his present post of shopkeeper, he invests the store's capital in corn bought at harvest. As yet, he has no parallel in the community, but the truck drivers are becoming aware of the possibilities for profit in trade and commercial deals. . . .

Markets

In marketing, the Indians of Tzo?ontahal have neither extended nor gained control over selling and buying operations that have been pursued since before the opening of the Pan-American highway of 1955. The pottery which is produced locally was formerly carried on horseback to the smaller towns within a radius of 50 miles. The pottery was marketed directly by the men of the household which produced the articles, with no specialization in trading by commercial travellers such as had happened in the Zapotec and other areas of

Mexico. With the penetration of the Pan-American highway, the men take the pottery produced in their household by bus or on the trucks to either San Cristóbal or Comitán. This tended to polarize trading operations and dry up the traffic into the small towns not connected by the highway. As a result, the wholesale trade in San Cristóbal and Comitán has become enlarged in the past decade.

The Indians have not taken advantage of the truck to buy pottery wholesale and market it directly in the smaller towns, selling from the truck in the plaza as do some of the wholesale fruit truckers. Another operation which they have failed to profit from is buying the wheat harvest and selling to government warehouses, like some of the Ladino truckers. . . . Lack of capital is the major reason for failure to exploit opportunities.

THE SOCIAL ORGANIZATION
OF NEW ENTERPRISES

In the operation of the new enterprises, trucking, liquor distilling and the expansion of cattle, several patterns have emerged, none of which is completely crystallized.

The most traditional management is found in the case of cattle. Cattle grazing on communal lands is a continuation of activities which are at least as old as the 1915 revolutionary period when informants indicate that most of the cattle was seized by bandits or soldiers. It is "new" only in the size of the holdings, which have expanded from ownership of one or two head per household, primarily useful as draft animals, to herds as large as 200 for the wealthiest man in town.

The increasing herds have stimulated competition for community resources. The control of the grazing and waterhold rights has been exercised through the traditional dual division of the town in an upper and lower section, with rights to pasture allocated on the basis of residence in the upper or lower barrio of the center. An association of cattle owners has developed in each of the sections, and the leaders of each association call together the cattle owners of each side to clean the water holes and repair the troughs. . . .

Liquor distilling has grown in the last ten years from five to forty distillers. The loose syndicate of distillers provides an insurance protection which raises fines for members who are apprehended by federal agents. Security measures are taken to avoid discovery, and the presence of a federal agent is announced in Tzeltal (the Maya language is spoken here) on the loud speaker system of one of the cantinas. One federal agent is on the payroll of the four operating cantina owners, who give him five pesos a week, to avoid legal action on the sale of contraband liquor. Individual distillers pay the tariff of ten pesos, or two liters of liquor a year to the civil officials and to the *ejido* commission, a tariff justified on the basis that they use wood from communally-owned land to process the sugar. The syndicate is a community-wide organization, mobilized in emergencies only. . . .

Structural realignment has been most marked in the case of the truck-owning co-operatives. Membership cuts across the dual division for both the truck-owning co-operatives. The co-operative is the most important factor in local political elections. Until 1950 no political office had been contested. In that year, the first contest with two candidates was based on residence in the upper or lower division. The new truck co-operative organized in 1962 stimulated the contest for political power. Because of the competition between the trucking co-operatives, the president representing one of the trucking co-operatives who was in office from 1962 to 1964 did not issue some of the birth certificates and other local documents needed in order for the new co-operative forming in 1963 to gain operator's licenses and permits.

When the new elections for president took place in 1964, leaders of the new co-operative, backed by the schoolteacher who was gaining *ex officio* power in the community, secured the support of the dominant political party of Mexico, the Partido Revolucionario Institucionalizado. The leading power behind the first co-operative is the Ladino secretary of the town. He promised to secure political backing for one of the barrio residents who was a member of this trucking co-operative if the potential candidate would give him 3,000 pesos. When the candidate failed to gain the elections, he demanded the return of the money, and since this has not been done, he is threatening the life of the secretary. The truck has become both the symbol of power and the basis for the contest for power between the factions within the community.

Entering into competitive areas in which they were formerly excluded, the Indians are encountering opposition from competitors and are the prey of departmental and state government agents. The reduplication of bureaucracies at a state and local level means that they are subject to the double "bite" or *mordida* in order to pursue their enterprises. Operating on minimal capital, they are not able to fulfill all the requirements, or buy all the necessary permits and licenses. Because of monopolization of certain traffic by the larger syndicates of truck owners, they proceed without permits and are often caught.

The strategies the co-operative members have developed in the frequent tangles they have with state police illustrate the combination of traditional and innovative techniques. When caught red-handed, they may respond by playing the stereotyped Indian role: "We don't know anything. We are just poor Indians. How do you expect us to do what the law says?" This is hard for the Ladino authorities to resist, since it feeds their own sense of superiority; but it does not always work. The Indians have devised secondary resources for this. They have put the Department police at each terminal of their usual route between Las Casas and Comitán on a regular monthly *mordida* payroll of 50 pesos each. When trying to extend their operations, they hire a lawyer. A recent coup has been the acquisition of a permit to truck corn to Villa las Rosas, so they can now carry corn from the *ejido* territory which has been recently colonized. The appeal was made on the basis that they are a non-profit co-operative of *ejidatarios*. With the permit, they now undercut the price of their only competitors in the syndicate. Lawyers are beginning to advertise themselves as "Friends of the Indians" and are in some cases specializing in this new patronage which they receive from other communities as well as Tzo?ontahal.

SUMMARY AND CONCLUSIONS

The self-development occurring in Tzo?ontahal may appear paradoxical if we take an external view of the culture. The co-opera-tive association has been adopted as a technique for socializing the risk of making a profit. The truck, although currently an uneconomic operation, is a symbol of power in the struggle for a position in the regional markets and in the intra-community factional strifes. The usual patron-client system is being reversed as the Indian puts the Ladino on his payroll to secure evasion from the law.

To contrast this community as traditional in opposition to modern societies is to ignore the social and economic innovations which they have mastered, and to overrate the achievements of capitalism. In the changes which are occurring the defensive structure of the corporate community is a means by which the Indians are entering into national life not on the lowest rung of the social ladder, but on terms they are setting for themselves. In the new enterprises, the Indians combine old ploys with new strategies. Confronted with legal threats from the outside world, they play the colonial game of defensive ignorance. When this fails, they turn to the professional help of lawyers rather than to the old *caciques* with whom they had formerly maintained patron-client relations. The traditional structural alignment of upper and lower barrios is retained as the basis for organizing the growing cattle herds, but the co-operative provides the flexibility and power needed to launch the new enterprises.

The minimal changes in the material environment and the technology of the peasantry are countered by the development of social resources which should facilitate their integration in the wider society. In operating the new enterprises independently of Ladino control, they are developing entrepreneurial skills and an awareness of the relationship between capital and profit. The restriction of their operations to nonproductive use of capital for profit, such as buying crops at harvest and reselling as the price rises, reveals the limited dynamics of intra-communal development. The town will look to the regional and national networks for fundamental changes in its economy.

The kind of change which is occurring in Tzo?ontahal fits the model of a moving equilibrium. This model makes possible a comparison between communities on a variety of dimensions to indicate what kinds of adjustments are being made to preserve an unchanged exterior design. Resistance to modification of language and clothing continues, along with endogamous marriages contracted by an extended series of exchanges between parents of the couple. These are the boundary-maintaining devices of the community. Continuity in these cultural features is not concomitant with resistance to change in all spheres of activity. A model of change based on the polarized opposition of traditional-modern would fail to take into account the internal adjustments made in control of tensions rising from technical and social innovations.

This kind of change seems to occur in bounded societies. In an open society where many alternatives are available, the painful process of accommodation of the new to a customary pattern would probably not be undertaken if societies followed the usual course of least resistance. The absorption of innovation in Tzo?ontahal illustrates the ability of closed corporate communities to participate in commercial undertakings without undermining the internal cohesion of the group.

1. Clifford Geertz (ed.), *Old Societies and New States* (Toronto: The Free Press, 1963).

2. Richard N. Adams, "Rural Labor," in John J. Johnson (ed.), *Continuity and Change in Latin America* (Stanford, 1964).

3. International Bank for Reconstruction and Development, *The Economic Development of Guatemala* (Washington, D.C., 1951).

4. Roberte Esteños MacLean, "Status socio-cultural de los indios de Mexico" (UNAM RMS), Universidad Nacional Autonóma de Mexico, *Revista Mexicana de Sociologia*, 1960, Vol. 1, pp. 23–37.

5. Oscar Lewis, *Life in a Mexican Village: Tepoztlan Restudied* (Urbana, 1963); Manning Nash, "The Multiple Society in Economic Development: Mexico and Guatemala," *American Anthropologist*, 1957, pp. 825–833, and "The Social Context of Economic Choice in a Small Society," *Man*, 1961, Art. 219, pp. 186–191; Robert Redfield, *The Folk Culture of Yucatán* (University of Chicago Press, 1950); Charles Wagley, "The Peasant," in John J. Johnson (ed.), *Continuity and Change in Latin America* (Stanford, 1964).

6. Theodore Schultz, *Transforming Traditional Agriculture* (Yale University Press, 1964).

7. Sol Tax, "The Indians in the Economy of Guatemala," *Social and Economic Studies*, Vol. 6, No. 3 (1957), pp. 413–424.

8. Julio de la Fuente, *Educación Anthropología y Desarrollo de la Comunidad* (Instituto Nacional Indigenista Mexico, 1964).

9. Carlo Antonio Castro (*Los Hombres Verdaros*, Universidad Veracruzana, Mexico, 1959) records the personal reminiscences of an Oxchuk Indian in a boarding school in Amatenango. The punishment of students for speaking Tzeltal is a poignant reminder of the deculturation taking place in these early pro-Indian programs of change.

10. Peter T. Bauer and Basil S. Yamey, *The Economics of Underdeveloped Countries* (University of Chicago Press, 1957), p. 58.

11. Departamente de Asuntos Agrarios y Colonizados. *Manual de Tramitación Agraria* (Mexico, 1964).

LATIN AMERICAN PEASANT PRESSURE GROUPS AND THE MODERNIZATION PROCESS

NEALE J. PEARSON

Texas Tech University

A high degree of inequality in landownership and political power characterizes most Latin American countries. It is true that in Mexico and Bolivia, bloody revolutions brought about increased distribution of land and political power. It is also true that in parts of Argentina, Brazil, Costa Rica and Uruguay, colonization and settlement pat-

Reprinted by permission of author. An earlier version of this paper appeared in *Journal of International Affairs* (1966), pp. 307–331.

terns have created a rural middle class and a widespread distribution of property ownership in several provinces or regions. But in most parts of these countries and the rest of Latin America, the concentration of landownership in a few hands has contributed to the maintenance of societies resistant to change and plagued by problems such as the following, described by T. Lynn Smith:

(1) a comparatively low average standard of living, although the elite landowning class may live in fantastic luxury; (2) great chasms of class distinctions between the favored few of the upper class and the masses who lack rights to the soil; (3) a comparative absence of vertical social mobility so that this chasm is perpetuated by caste barriers . . . ; (4) a low average intelligence of the population because the high abilities and accomplishments of the few . . . of the upper class are greatly overweighted by the ignorance and illiteracy of the masses; and (5) a population skilled only in the performance under close supervision of a very limited number of manual tasks and lacking completely training and practice in managerial and entrepreneurial work.[1]

Given this situation, it would seem useful to examine the organization of peasant and rural worker groups and the functions which they perform in the modernization process in Latin America. Such organizations have appeared in almost every Latin American country since World War I with the greatest growth coming after World War II. This study will be based primarily on the experience of Argentina, Bolivia, Brazil, Chile, Guatemala, Honduras, Mexico, Peru, Venezuela, and some of the Caribbean islands. . . .

THE FUNCTIONS AND ACTIVITIES
OF PEASANT AND RURAL
WORKER GROUPS

Peasant groups in all of the countries under discussion have performed functions of political socialization, interest articulation, and leadership selection. Patterns of activity, however, vary from country to country and region to region for a variety of reasons—including the conditions under which the organization began, the presence or absence of a literate and socially-organized rural population, the openness of resistance of the political system or sub-system to the group, and the goals and methods of particular leaders.

(1) A first category of organization is the peasant group organized by politicians and/or landowners engaged in land speculation or punitive political action. These groups are not the activities of peasants organizing from below, but rather groups organized by outsiders from above in a patron-client relationship in which low-status clients receive material goods or services or access to land in return for personal services, obligations to work gratuitously or at lower than the normal wage one or more days per week or month, and voting for the candidates of the patron.[2] This type of organization has long been found in Argentina, Brazil, Chile, Guatemala, Honduras, Mexico, Nicaragua, Puerto Rico, and Venezuela. In the 1950's and 1960's, it also appeared in Bolivia and Peru. Several concrete examples may be given.

In Brazil, the *Movimento dos Agricultores sem Terra* (Landless Workers Movement or MASTER) began in 1958 as a genuine protest group of landless agricultural laborers in Encruzilhada do Sul, Rio Grande do Sul. It was, however, taken over by Governor (and later Federal Deputy) Leonel Brizola who used it to mobilize votes for candidates of the Brazilian Labor Party (PTB) and to force landowners to sell land to himself or his friends.[3] In the northeast, the first *Liga Camponesa* (Peasant League) was organized as a mutual benefit burial society in 1954 by tenants on the Galiléia plantation in Vitória de Santo Antão, Pernambuco.

When the owner and his son tried to evict them the tenants were guided to Francisco Julião de Arruda Paula, a landowning lawyer politician elected to the State Assembly as an Alternate Deputy for the Brazilian Socialist Party (PSB). Julião transformed himself from a typical politician with a limited peasant following for whom he provided services into a charismatic leader manipulating modern publicity techniques that brought him a national attention.[4] Ligas were established in many parts of Brazil not only because Julião was able to find and develop leaders of local origin in Goiás, Mato Grosso, Rio Grande do Norte, and Rio de Janeiro but because these leaders affiliated with him were able to provide protection and medical services (doctors, dentists, and ambulances) similar to those furnished by other traditional land-owner politicians. Many of the "peasant leaders" who affiliated themselves with Julião in other states were in fact large land-owners seeking expropriation of the land of political opponents, either as a punitive measure or as a means of acquiring land for themselves.[5]

In Mexico, the governmental party—now known as the PRI—which grew out of the Revolution of 1910 incorporated various peasant organizations into the National Peasant Confederation (CNC) which became part of a supportive clientele network.[6] In Bolivia, although the MNR had a few contacts with a few peasant *sindicatos* in the Department of Cochabamba led by José Rojas of Ucureña before the Revolution of 1952, it spent much time and effort afterwards to organize peasant unions all over the country into a structure capped by the Confederation of Peasant Workers (CTC).

Although Victor Paz Estenssoro was ousted from office by a coup in November 1964, successor governments led by General René Barrientos, Luís Siles Suazo, and General Alfredo Ovando Candia all sought support from the same peasant clientele network, of the CTC. In Venezuela, the Democratic Action Party (AD), "struggling simultaneously to establish a meaningful electoral process and to break the hold of the entrenched, traditional elites on governmental power," began to organize the peasantry during the 1930's and 1940's. After *coup d'état* in 1945 brought AD to power, access to governmental and private land was granted to peasant *sindicatos* organized by the party.[7]

In all three of these nations—plus Guatemala in 1952–1954—agrarian reform functioned as an instrument of patronage and as a developer of future support for the government at the polls.[8]

(2) A second form of peasant organization is the armed militia. Peasants in Bolivia, Brazil, Colombia, Mexico, and Peru have organized paramilitary groups to defend themselves against the arbitrary actions of politicians, landowners, rural judiciary and police (whom landowners often control), and against the destruction of hired or independent thugs who may roam the countryside.

During the "revolutionary" campaigns of 1924–25, which followed the revolt of the *Tenentes* in Brazil, peasants of German, Italian and Polish origin organized armed militias in the southern states.[9] The tradition has not disappeared entirely. In recent years, this writer has seen parades of "hunting" and "shooting" clubs in Rio Grande do Sul which undoubtedly function also as a reminder to state and national civilian and military leaders of the capacity of these *colonos* to organize themselves.

In October–November 1964, the writer observed meetings of armed peasant organizations on former *haciendas* in the Department of La Paz, Bolivia, before and after the fall of President Paz. The preoccupation of these groups with defensive activities decreased the attention which community leaders could give to problems such as schools, irrigation, and improvement of pastures and livestock.

Finally, although the dominant PRI party in Mexico organized the National Peasant Confederation (CNC) to mobilize and channel the aspirations of peasants who previously participated in "guerilla" groups led by Francisco "Pancho" Villa and Emiliano Zapata, the CNC has not always been able to function satisfactorily as a broker for peasant dissatisfaction with the lack of land, water shortages, low prices, and so forth. In 1963–1964, uncoordinated peasant "uprisings" and invasions of public and private lands occurred in Chihuahua, Oaxaca, and several other states. That Gustavo Díaz Ordaz, following his election as President in 1964, gave high priority to these problems can be seen from the following table, which shows his administration second only to that of Lázaro Cárdenas (1934–1940) in the distribution of land, and in the absence of reports in the press since 1964 of continuing land invasions.

(3) Third, peasant unions exist whose function is protection of the interests of their members against landowners, middlemen and government agencies. Such organizations are concerned with such issues as the non-payment of minimum wages, conditions under which the land is farmed, and the prices at which goods are bought and sold. These groups are most numerous and active in Argentina, Brazil, Chile, several Caribbean islands, Honduras, Peru, Uruguay, and Venezuela.[10]

Genuine peasant unions or *sindicatos*

TABLE 1

LAND DISTRIBUTION IN MEXICO BY PRESIDENTIAL TERM, 1932–1968

Years	President	Amount Distributed (1,000 Hectares)	Months in Office	Approx. Annual Rate
1932–1934	Rodríguez	2,095	26	966
1934–1940	Cárdenas	20,073	72	3,345
1940–1946	Avila Camacho	5,378	72	896
1946–1952	Alemán	4,520	72	753
1952–1958	Ruiz Cortines	3,199	72	533
1958–1964	López Mateos	16,004	72	2,667
1964–1968	Díaz Ordaz	12,307	45	3,241

SOURCE: Martin Needler, "Mexico," in *Political Systems of Latin America* (ed. by Martin Needler, New York: Van Nostrand-Reinhold, 2nd ed., 1970), p. 37.

may have been formed with the assistance of outside clergymen, political parties, or government officials—as in the case of Brazil, Chile, Mexico, Peru, and Venezuela —but many have grown sufficiently strong to remain somewhat independent of their founders and to improve the bargaining power of what originally was an unequal patron-client relationship. Probably the most successful examples of this type are the Peasant Confederation of Venezuela (Confederacion Campesina de Venezuela or CCV), the Banana Workers Federation in Honduras, and the Manpower Citizens Association (MPCA) in Guiana.

One must also include in this group the highly-sophisticated organizations created by the Brazilian Catholic Church whose leadership elites and programs vary because they began in states with differing landholding patterns, political traditions, and sources of leadership among the rural population. The foundation of peasant unions by the Church was encouraged by contact with the ideas of such European Catholic social philosophers as Jacques Maritain, Father L. J. Lebret, Emmanuel Mounier, and Teilhard de Chardin. In some instances, *sindicatos* and cooperatives were organized through pre-existing structures such as the Workers Circles (or *Circulos Operários*), especially in Rio de Janeiro and São Paulo. In other cases, new structures were developed.

The model for both was the Rural Assistance Service (Serviço de Assistência Rural or SAR) organized in 1950 by Dom Eugenio Salles de Araujo in Natal, Rio Grande do Norte. SAR's activities include literacy and leadership training programs, and the establishment of *sindicatos* and cooperatives. SAR's literacy programs led to the creation of the Basic Education Movement (Movimento de Educação de Base or MEB), which enlisted the support of university students in a radio literacy campaign. MEB techniques aroused the anger of many Brazilian military officers and civilians because of references to class struggle and its encouragement of new groups. Supported by government funds from 1959 to 1964, MEB has had to depend on the Church for its current programs.

Perhaps the most successful Church effort among rural workers outside of Rio Grande do Norte has been the Rural Orientation Service (*Serviço do Orientação Rural* or SORPE) in the state of Pernambuco.[11] SORPE's advisor, Padre Paulo Crespo, established a Rural Workers' Federation that survived the combined attacks of Julião's *Ligas Camponesas,* infiltration and armed harassment by factions of both the Russian-oriented (PCB) and Chinese-oriented PC do B factions of the Brazilian Communist Party from 1962 to 1964. The federation has been active not only in obtaining increased minimum wages for sugar plantation workers but it can be given credit also for the decree signed by President Castelo Branco in October 1965, establishing the legal right of agricultural tenants to a small plot of land on which to grow subsistence crops—previously only a traditional custom that was often ignored in the early 1960's.

In a third state, Rio Grande do Sul, the

Gaucho Agrarian Front (*Frente Agrária Gaúcha* or FAG) was created under the combined leadership of Catholic and Protestant clergymen, rural schoolteachers, and small proprietors. The FAG maintains a structure parallel to but separate from the *sindicatos* of small farmers and rural workers found in most *municipios* (counties). The FAG also operates regional organizations of varying degrees of effectiveness in the seat of each diocese, and a state headquarters in Pôrto Alegre. Among the most important accomplishments of the Regional Organization in Caxias do Sul and the state leadership of the FAG was payment by the National Department of Agricultural Crop Insurance to small holders for 1964 hail damage and increases in minimum government price-supports for grapes and potatoes raised by small farmers.

(4) Rural *sindicatos* and other peasant groups sometimes act as organizational units for the construction of schools, dams, irrigation systems and other public works. They may also sponsor campaigns for the eradication of illiteracy or of disease. In Bolivia, for example, peasants from thirty unions and communities in the Province of Punata, Department of Cochabamba, constructed a dam and irrigation canal system in 1963–1964 under the direction of Gregório López, a local peasant *cacique* and Alternate MNR Deputy, with the technical assistance of the National Bureau of Rural Development (*Dirección Nacional de Desarrollo Rural*) and the Community Development Program of USAID.[12]

In all of these countries, peasant *sindicatos* have played important roles not only in the acquisition and distribution of land under agrarian reform programs but they have been instrumental also in the provision of technical assistance and loans for the improved farming of newly-distributed land.

(5) A fifth type of peasant organization is the producer cooperative, whose principal activity is an economic one, but which occasionally enters the political arena in order to advance or defend the interest of its members. One outstanding group is the *Cotia Cooperative*, originally founded by eighty-three Japanese-Brazilian potato farmers in the state of São Paulo in 1927. In 1964, the cooperative included over 11,000 members of more than thirty nationalities and operated in Minas Gerais, Paraná, Rio de Janeiro, and São Paulo. The growth of Cotia created enemies; to date, the cooperative has survived the attacks of political and economic rivals.

A second important cooperative is SANCOR, an Argentine dairy organization made up of small dairy farmers generally owning or renting from ten to three hundred acres of land in the provinces of Santa Fé and Córdoba. The cooperative marketed 60 percent of Argentina's production of butter and cassein for domestic and export markets in the mid-sixties. Many SANCOR members also belong to the Argentine Rural Federation (*Federación Rural Argentina*) which represents small and medium-sized family farmers, and is not to be confused with the Rural Society (*Sociedad Rural*) which is the political arm of Argentina's largest ranchers and landowners.

(6) Somewhat related to peasant organizations created as political followings are *sindicatos fantasmas* and *cooperativas falsas* (phantom unions and false cooperatives), found in many countries. In Brazil, the Union of Agricultural Laborers and Workers (*União dos Lavradores e Trabalhadores na Agricultura do Brasil* or ULTAB) a communist-dominated organization, and the Goulart government's Superintendency of Agrarian Reform (SUPRA) created hundreds of paper *sindicatos* of rural workers from 1961 to 1964 in order to out-vote church-sponsored groups in the elections for state and national organizations. Outside of Rio Grande do Sul and São Paulo, it is probably safe to estimate that at least a majority of all agricultural cooperatives in Brazil, regardless of their size, are controlled by one or a few individuals, who use the cooperative structure as a legal device to escape various corporate taxes and regulations or as a means of mobilizing votes and distributing political patronage.

FACTORS AFFECTING THE SUCCESS
OF PEASANT PRESSURE GROUPS

The formation and functioning of small farmer and rural worker pressure groups depend on several interrelated factors.

(1) Patterns of land ownership and land use: There seems to be a definite correlation between the wide distribution of land and the importance of peasant organizations in politics. There is also some correlation with the crops cultivated, processing

undertaken by peasants, and the involvement in national or world markets. Two examples are the grape-growing and wine-producing small farmers in the *colônia* of Rio Grande do Sul, Brazil, and the small dairy farmers of the Argentine pampa region, who through their cooperative organizations can exercise leverage on the market and are not dependent on marketing middlemen. On the other hand, the establishment of minimum government price supports for sugar does not guarantee a minimum daily wage to sugar plantation workers in parts of Argentina, Brazil, and Peru.

(2) A high availability of transportation and communications media within a given region: Peasants in the Department of Cuzco, Peru, for example, may have to walk two or three days to seek the aid of Quechua-speaking Aprista lawyers because of the geographical barriers to communication in the sierra or hacendado control of the means of communication. Organization is obviously difficult under such conditions. In Northeast Brazil, the radius of influence of Francisco Julião's Peasant Leagues could be measured in terms of one day's round-trip travel by car or bus from Recife, Pernambuco, and João Pessoa, Paraíba.

(3) The presence of a literate peasant population. It appears unquestionable, for example, that the success of small farmer pressure groups in southern Brazil and the Santa Fé–Córdoba region of Argentina is in large part due to the ability of peasants to read and write. Literacy makes them less dependent on non-peasants for the articulation and defense of their interests.

(4) The social infrastructure of rural areas, including the presence or absence of formally organized parish church councils, parent-teacher organizations, and recreation groups: The greater the number of these groups, the greater the number of leadership-supplying institutions in the rural sector. For this reason, the disadvantages of the wide dispersion of population in southern Brazil or the pampa region of Argentina are lessened because the small farmers have social institutions and communication networks which draw them into frequent contact with one another. On the other hand, small farmers, day laborers, and sharecroppers in Northeast Brazil who live in towns or in a sugar mill complex and commute daily to their fields, often lack the informal mutual aid gatherings of the *mutirão* (the Brazilian equivalent of the American husking bee) found in the central and southern parts of the country.

(5) The political history, structure, and style of national, state or local politics: The existence of literacy requirements for voting reduces peasant bargaining power just as in the Untied States where literacy, poll tax, or residence requirements reduce the influence of blacks, poor whites, and Mexican-Americans. A second consideration is the relative strength of allies and opponents. In the *colônia* region of Rio Grande do Sul, Brazil, for example, small town businessmen, lawyers, priests, and school teachers are often linked to the peasantry by family ties. Because the rural population is literate and votes, one finds there as many hospitals, hospital beds, and schools, as in the whole Northeast (excluding the facilities found in Recife).

If the leadership chooses to use means regarded as "legitimate" by other groups, opposition is reduced. When the leadership of peasant groups demands or implies a need for changes in the basic structure of society, opposition—especially among large landowners and military officers—is heightened. In many areas, army officers oppose peasant groups out of deference to the political power of landowners, sugar mill operators, or cotton brokers, or because of kinship and business links with these individuals. In these places where local military or police commanders play a minimal role in local politics, such as the *colônia* region of Rio Grande do Sul, Brazil, the situation is different from that found in Paraíba, Pernambuco, or Rio Grande do Norte, where military commanders frequently harass peasant organizations as part of their everyday activity.

(6) The extent of participation by the membership of rural worker and small workers in the decision-making process of the formally-organized groups: the greater the participation of the membership, the more likely it is that a peasant group will be able to withstand outside pressures and the loss of leadership elements at various levels of the organizational structure. One of the greatest weaknesses of the *Ligas Camponeses* of Francisco Julião, the unions dominated by different factions of the Brazilian Communist Party, and the Brizola MASTER group was the restriction of

leadership and policy determination to a small group of non-peasant outsiders. When the leaders of these groups went into exile, were put in jail, or withdrew from the rural sector in 1964, there was practically no one left with leadership experience—even though the membership may have been highly politicized and willing to follow any leaders who might appear. On the other hand, Church-sponsored groups in Brazil emphasized leadership training of the membership from the beginning and this is an important reason for their survival.

In conclusion, it should be noted that the modernization process in most Latin American countries has been based upon the accumulation of capital and resources at the expense of the rural sector—and without consultation of the peasants. It is this writer's opinion that peasant participation in interest groups and development agencies is essential to rural development and the reduction of potential violence. Because traditional *patrones* who provided brokerage services have generally departed for the cities, formal peasant organizations provide important brokerage and other services for the rural area. It therefore seems essential that governments and the Alliance for Progress continue to invest heavily in rural education, domestic peace corps programs (such as Cooperación Popular in Chile and Peru), and in the formal participation of small farmers and rural workers in the planning and implementation of rural development programs.

1. T. Lynn Smith, *Brazil, People and Institutions* (Baton Rouge: Louisiana State University Press, 1963), p. 318.

2. One of the better discussions of this lop-sided arrangement from a political point of view is John Duncan Powell, "Peasant Society and Clientelist Politics," *American Political Science Review*, LXIV, No. 2 (June 1970), pp. 411–425. See also the useful collection of materials in *Peasant Society: A Reader* (Boston: Little, Brown, 1967).

3. See Neale J. Pearson, "Small Farmer and Rural Worker Pressure Groups in Brazil" (unpublished Ph.D. dissertation, the University of Florida, December 1967, available from University Microfilms, Ann Arbor, Michigan, Order N. 68-13, 024), pp. 209–223.

4. Benno Galjart, "Class and 'Following' in Rural Brazil," *America Latina* (Rio de Janeiro) July–September, 1964, pp. 3–24, viewed the Peasant Leagues as a traditional manifestation of reciprocal relations between a leader and potential followers.

5. See Galjart, *op. cit.*, p. 19; Pearson, *op. cit.*, pp. 113–125; and Peter T. White, "Brazil, Oba!," *National Geographic Magazine*, CXXII (September 1962), pp. 314–318, for examples.

6. Leon Vincent Padgett, *The Mexican Political System* (Boston: Houghton, Mifflin, 1966), pp. 110–122.

7. Powell, *op. cit.*, p. 418, and John Duncan Powell, "Venezuela: The Peasant Union Movement," in *Latin American Peasant Movements*, edited by Henry Landsberger (Ithaca: Cornell University Press, 1969), pp. 62–100.

8. For a discussion of Guatemala, see Neale J. Pearson, "Guatemala, The Peasant Union Movement, 1944–1954," in Landsberger, *op. cit.*, pp. 323–373.

9. Emilio Willems, "Brazil," in *The Positive Contributions of Immigrants* (Paris: UNESCO, 1955), p. 139.

10. Excellent treatments of this type of organization in Chile and Peru are to be found in articles by Henry A. Landsberger, Wesley W. Craig, Jr., Julio Cotler and Felipe Protocarrero, in Landsberger, *op. cit.*, pp. 210–296.

11. See Cynthia N. Hewitt, "Brazil: The Peasant Movement of Pernambuco, 1961–1964," in Landsberger, *op. cit.*, pp. 374–398, and Pearson "Small Farmer and Rural Worker Groups," pp. 144–203 for an account of the impact of SAR, SORPE and other church-sponsored groups in the North and Northeast Brazil.

12. Despite the turmoil of Bolivian politics since November 1964, 270 projects involving an estimated one-third of the rural population were organized between August 1965 and May 1966 by peasant community development councils with the aid of Desarrollo Rural and the Community Development Program of USAID headed by David Anderson. Although this writer does not know how many of the projects became fully institutionalized, peasants were contributing over 80 percent of all project costs.

THE URBAN POOR: THEIR CAPACITY
FOR POLITICAL PARTICIPATION

JOAN NELSON

Harvard University and M.I.T.

> The great masses of Chileans have no organization, and without organization no power, and without power no representation in the life of the country.   EDUARDO FREI

Built into the lives of the urban poor are a multitude of factors impeding political mobilization. Industrial labor and workers in large modern service establishments are relatively well-paid and secure, usually unionized, and often politically active. In contrast to this labor elite, the bulk of the urban poor work in occupations that provide few handles for political mobilization. Small artisan and service shops, vending, and domestic service are inherently difficult to organize. Stevedoring and construction are organizable, but the relentless pressure of unskilled job-seekers impedes unionization. Even social and religious organizations are weak among the urban poor. Insecure jobs and rented rooms mean that many move frequently, which probably prevents the growth of interest in and knowledge of local issues, certainly impedes the growth of ties within the neighborhood, and in the past has legally disenfranchised large numbers of the poor. In many cases, ethnic religious cleavages further reduce the potential for collective action.

Moreover, the most urgent needs of the very poor are intensely individual—a day's work, a room, a week's credit, medical aid, someone to fix trouble with the police. Others equally poor and ill-connected usually cannot offer much help. The poor, rural as well as urban, turn for aid to better-established individuals or organizations—landlord, employer, shopkeeper, church, settlement house, regional or caste or tribal association, local fixer, ward boss. The patron-client relations that result may or may not form a stable pattern. They are less likely to do so in an urban setting where there are several possible sources of assistance, and where the best or most accessible source of help for one problem may be less appropriate or available for other problems. Where a stable pattern exists, it may or may not be tied into the broader political system, depending on the interests and connections of the patron(s). Politicized patron-client relations therefore are possible, but not automatic, in an urban setting.

In the cities of the United States during the late nineteenth and early twentieth centuries, both the needs of the urban poor and their ethnic loyalties were used as bases for powerful political machines. But while their votes might elect the candidates of the machine, the urban poor had little or no influence over the city governments they put in office. The nature of their political role—the large-scale institutionalized trading of individual votes for individual favors—precluded any substantial impact on governmental programs and policies. Political integration in this more fundamental sense of influence on governmental actions took place, in the experience of Europe and North America, only as the urban poor were gradually absorbed economically and socially, that is, as they joined the stable and organized working class.

In the cities of today's developing nations, the social and economic characteristics of the urban poor are in many ways similar. Is there then any reason to expect them to play a different or more active or influential political role in Latin America, Africa, and Asia than they played historically in the industrialized nations? Perhaps not. But there are major differences as well as similarities between current and past patterns of urban growth and industrial ex-

From *World Politics* (April 1970), pp. 405–414. Reprinted by permission.

pansion. These contrasts may produce different political results.

First, cities today are growing much more rapidly. Annual growth rates of 5 to 8 percent are common among the cities of the less developed world. In contrast, few major European cities grew more rapidly than 3 or 4 percent a year during any decade on the nineteenth century.[1] North American cities mushroomed rapidly in their early stages but then slowed down, despite heavy immigration as well as internal migration. Today's more rapid growth in the developing world results not from heavier migration into the cities but from lower urban mortality rates, in turn the product of improved public health measures.[2] Moreover, in Europe millions chose to emigrate rather than move to their own growing cities, and in North America the frontier long offered an alternative channel for the restless and ambitious. In the developing countries today, few can emigrate, and only a handful of the nations of Latin America and Africa have extensive arable frontier regions. In most countries there is only one magnet for those who want a better life: the city.

Second, although cities are growing faster, urban jobs are probably multiplying less rapidly than they did in the past. Surely this is true of employment in manufacturing. Even in those few countries where industry is making good progress, employment in manufacturing rarely expands by more than 3 or 4 percent a year.[3] Modern technology is, of course, laborsaving. Moreover, poorly trained and unreliable labor plus legally required social security benefits may mean that labor costs per unit of output are high despite low hourly or daily wages. Development policies such as rapid write-off and other tax concessions and special exchange rates for imported capital equipment reduce the cost of capital compared to labor. From the entrepreneur's standpoint, labor may be relatively costly and capital comparatively cheap even in countries where labor is plentiful and capital scarce.

In short, demographic and economic trends conspire to produce a larger marginal class persisting over a longer period than in the cities of nineteenth- and early twentieth-century Europe and North America. In view of the limited capacity of the urban poor for political action, a large mass of marginals persisting over many decades has no necessary political implications. However, the political climate and structure of today's developing nations differ from those of nineteenth-century Europe and North America in ways that may produce more political activity among the urban poor.

The poor themselves may be better educated and informed, and therefore may have a greater capacity for political action than did their historical counterparts. Because urban mortality rates are much lower, a higher proportion are urban-born. In the cities, free or cheap primary schools are more widely available than they were in the late nineteenth or early twentieth century in Europe and North America. Radio now reaches even the illiterate.

For many of the urban poor, squatting provides a social setting that is more conducive to political integration. Squatting was not unknown in Europe and North America, but is far more extensive in today's developing countries, largely as a result of more rapid urban growth. Widespread squatting almost certainly implies more stable residence patterns. Stephan Thernstrom[4] and other historians interested in United States social history around the turn of the century report incredibly high rates of turnover among the urban poor. Although housing is only part of the picture, it is clear that a man who rents his shelter and loses his job is likely to be evicted, while a man who owns his house and loses his job is likely to cling to his remaining source of security.

Stable residence and home ownership or quasi-ownership encourage collective action for collective neighborhood interests. Studies of squatting settlements often mention neighborhood councils that are more or less active and effective in pressing for legal recognition and extension of city services into the community.[5] Their demands are concrete and often limited: for example, the covering of a former irrigation ditch that endangers neighborhood children. Some goals are startling for their upward-striving character: Alejandro Portes describes a government sponsored community in Santiago, Chile, where the *pobladores* insisted that their monthly payments for their lots and houses be increased to hasten the day when they could claim ownership.[6] Nonetheless the combined demands of many neighborhoods can seriously strain the administrative and financial capacity of responsive city or national governments. From an economic standpoint, therefore, it is important to add that many communities have proved capable of substantial self-help programs, contributing funds and labor for a series of community improvements with or without external support.

In some cities, presumably where squatter's relationship to legal authorities is unclear or insecure, neighborhood councils have also played a quasi-judicial role, adjudicating local disputes regarding boundaries, right of way, and similar issues.[7] Neighborhood councils undoubtedly are providing many of the urban poor with their first experience in limited local self-government.[8] Recognizing this potential, Chile in 1968 passed legislation that grants legal status to the neighborhood councils that had grown up spontaneously in many low income urban areas, gives them a voice in the allocation of the (very limited) annual municipal budgets, authorizes them to borrow from the banks, and empowers them to share in other ways in urban government.

Neighborhood councils in low-income urban areas also offer political parties an organizational channel through which to reach the urban poor on a more sustained, institutionalized basis than periodic campaign tours and speeches. Whether parties take advantage of the opportunity depends largely on the national political context—on the importance of elections, the extent of the franchise, the degree of party competition, the nature of the major parties' ideologies and leadership, and other factors, all of which vary tremendously. However, the political context of urban growth in Latin America, Africa, and Asia appears more likely to encourage responsiveness to or alliances with the urban poor than was the case in the now-industrialized nations in the late nineteenth and early twentieth centuries. The franchise is considerably broader, if only because women are included in the electorate in almost all developing countries. Despite the immense diversity of political systems, ideas about the proper role of government and the scope of governmental responsibility for the welfare of its citizens are everywhere more interventionist than in even the most progressive nations fifty years ago.

In sum, while the urban poor are unlikely to play a major political role in the developing countries, they may well prove more active than were their counterparts in the past experience of the industrialized nations. Urban marginals are likely to be more numerous relative to total urban population. They may also prove somewhat more alert and sophisticated, with greater capacity for political organization. This capacity will probably be matched, in at least some countries, with stronger interest on the part of established political groups in organizing and tapping the political potential of the poor.

POSSIBLE PATTERNS OF POLITICAL INTEGRATION

The suggestions that follow are doubly speculative. Any effort to anticipate the pattern of events as they unfold is necessarily speculative. But even early returns can provide useful clues to eventual outcomes. Hence my second disclaimer: what follows are preliminary hypotheses, supported by general structural considerations but not yet tested against available evidence.

I start from the assumption that in most developing countries, the urban poor are at best weakly integrated politically. This need not mean that they are alienated from the system. It may mean merely that few among them have much interest in politics, or perceive politics as relevant to their interests. They may regard the government as legitimate (or at least not illegitimate) but (probably quite realistically) view politics and politicians cynically, and discount the possibility that they themselves can influence government policies or actions. Political parties, for their part, may give lip service to the needs of the urban poor, and candidates will put in an appearance in slum and squatter areas during political campaigns. One or more parties may make a more serious effort to organize support based on patron-client relations. However, they are unlikely to alter their programs significantly, nor, if they take office, to reflect the needs of the poor in budget priorities. The exchange of individual favors for individual votes falls short of any sustained influence on party priorities or programs.

Sharp ethnic cleavages can change this picture drastically. The easiest and in some cases the only effective way for elite or middle-class leaders in racially divided societies to expand their following is to appeal across class lines to ethnic loyalties. Race or religion transforms legitimacy into a simple, concrete, and highly charged issue and also provides a ready link between legitimacy and bread-and-butter issues such as jobs. Race also provides a basis on which to appeal simultaneously to urban and rural groups whose interests and outlooks might otherwise conflict. In short, race politics operates as a powerful unifying and mobilizing force within racially homogeneous segments of the urban lower class and across class and rural-urban boundaries. However, it may be profoundly disintegrative at the national level, creating or exacerbating tensions as disruptive as and more enduring than those based on class in the absence of race cleavage.

In racially homogeneous societies, class is the more formidable barrier to political integration. In theory, one possible pattern of evolution in such a society might be the formation of class consciousness and class-based political organization. Some analysts of Latin American politics, particularly those with European backgrounds, seem to regard this possibility as not unlikely. Several surveys have attempted to detect the emergence of class consciousness among factory workers or among more marginal groups.[9]

Such a pattern seems to me improbable. The highly individual needs of the very poor plus their distrust and lack of organizational experience militate against collective organization. Kerr and Siegel's theory of isolated masses suggests that shared work experience and conditions of life, coupled with isolation from the broader society, are likely to produce unified and aggressive action.[10] But by these criteria the urban poor in today's developing nations are less likely to develop strong group consciousness than were those of yesterday's European and North American cities. A smaller proportion share the common experience of factory work; more earn a precarious living in constantly shifting day labor, with little opportunity to develop ties with fellow workers or hostility toward a common boss. Fewer live in rented tene-ment rooms in solidly lower-class neighborhoods; more are housed in squatter settlements where they may have as neighbors (though not necessarily friends) aspiring lower-middle-class clerks, policemen, or teachers. Maurice Zeitlin's study of the determination of revolutionary attitudes among Cuban workers suggests that those in occupations in which management and workers are sharply separated and have little contact are most likely to develop radical sentiments.[11] But many marginal occupations such as vending or day labor involve either no management or a constantly changing series of bosses, while domestic service and artisan manufacture are characterized by close and constant though not necessarily cordial relations with employers. Germani suggests that class consciousness in Latin America is also impeded by the constant inflow of rural miciousness in Latin America is also impeded by the constant inflow of rural migrants, diluting the shared experience and attitudes of the more experienced urban poor.[12]

Several alternative patterns seem much more probable than mobilization and organization of the urban poor on a class basis. One possibility is the emergence of a strong urban populist party appealing both to urban marginals and to industrial labor, possibly in alliance with low-level white-collar groups, on a platform stressing employment, public works, housing programs, and other immediate benefits. Such a pattern is more probable where urbanization and industrialization are comparatively extensive but established parties have proved unresponsive not only to urban marginals but also to industrial labor.

A second possibility is a pattern of gradually increased responsiveness to the needs (and votes) of the urban poor on the part of one or more of the established political parties, to the point of a significant revision of party programs and organization. Such a trend would appear most likely where elections are important in the national political system, party competition is substantial, and at least one major party is disposed to seek mass support. Interest in the urban poor may reflect ideology, a calculation of electoral advantage, or a combination of the two. In Italy in the early 1960's the Communist Party recognized the political potential of mass migration from the south into the industrial cities of the north, and made an all-out play for the migrant's votes.[13] The Christian Democrats followed suit, but only after a lag. In Chile, also, the Communists and Socialists were first to try to capture local neighborhood councils in low-income areas of the cities; the Christian Democrats have since made a strong competitive bid. Where middle-class groups face an unyielding traditional elite, they may well seek alliance with the urban poor. In Venezuela, middle-class parties shut out of the political arena after a taste of power in the late 1940's found that they could use the power of the *barrios* to oust Pérez Jiménez in 1958. Thereafter, they competed vigorously for control of local *barrio* organizations and first claim on the loyalties of the *barrio* residents.[14]

If it is the case that the urban poor in many developing countries have more capacity for self-autonomous local organization for limited purposes than did their historical counterparts, the possibility of direct confrontation tactics by organized groups of the urban poor is also greater than it was in the past. A particularly clear-cut and large-scale instance occurred in July, 1968, in Lima, where squatters threatened a march on the Presidential Palace unless the government decreed that they could be issued title to their lots.[15] With the proliferation of local neighborhood councils, mothers' organizations, and similar groups, it is easy to envisage more limited demonstrations along the lines of recent protests by welfare recipients in several cities in the United States. Direct pressure for needed services or immediately relevant policy changes is not necessarily an alternative to the other suggested patterns. It could well occur in combination with them. In dominant-party, single-party, or no-party states, however, petitions and limited local confrontations over specific issues may be the sole channels available, if indeed the authorities will tolerate this degree of pressure from a relatively weak group.

CONCLUSION

Fear of the urban mob is as ancient as cities. Concern about rapid urbanization was widespread in Europe before and during the nineteenth century. But there is little ground for belief that the swelling urban masses of today's developing nations will prove to be politically radical or violent. There is, however, some reason to expect that they may play a more active and influential role than did their historical counterparts.

The important question, then, is how and under what conditions the urban poor are integrated into these political systems. In plural societies, race, religion, or tribe is the pole around which political organization will almost certainly coalesce. In more homogeneous societies, urban political machines may well appear, transforming traditional patron-client relationships into the large-scale institutionalized trading of votes for favors. Neighborhood associations in squatter settlements offer an alternative channel of political integration, with greater potential for influence by the poor on governmental activities. Or populist leaders may seek a coalition between poor urban voters and better-educated working-class groups.

Any pattern of integration that gives the urban poor some significant influence on the allocation of material and human resources will alter the path (and may retard the pace) of economic growth. The political mobilization of the urban poor does, then, challenge the political systems of the developing nations. The challenge, however, is not the containment of extremism or anarchic outbursts, but the evolution of means to respond to concrete and usually moderate demands without the sacrifice of other development objectives.

1. Adna F. Weber, *The Growth of Cities* (New York 1899), chap. 2.

2. Kingsley Davis, "The Urbanization of the Human Population," in *Cities* (New York 1966), pp. 18–19.

3. Economic Commission for Latin America (ECLA), "Structural Changes in Employment within the Context of Latin America's Economic Development," *Economic Bulletin for Latin America*, X (October 1965), p. 166; see also Werner Baer and Michel Herve, "Employment and Industrialization in Developing Countries," *Quarterly Journal of Economics*, LXXX (February 1966).

4. Stephan Thernstrom, "The Case of Boston," *Massachusetts Historical Society* (Autumn 1967), pp. 114–15, and "Working-Class Social Mobility in Industrial America," prepared for delivery at the Anglo-American Colloquium of the Society for Labour History (London, June 23, 1968), pp. 5–6 (mimeo).

5. William   Mangin,   "Latin   American

Squatter Settlements," pp. 69–70; Talton Ray, *The Politics of the Barrios of Venezuela* (Berkeley 1968), *passim*.

6. Alejandro Portes, "Los Grupos Urbanos Marginados: Un Nuevo Intento de Explicación," typescript (Santiago, Chile, June 1969).

7. Kenneth Karst, "Preliminary Report on a Study of the Internal Norms and Sanctions in Ten Barrios of Caracas," talk prepared for a meeting of Latin American Scholars, New York, Autumn 1968 (mimeo).

8. This experience is not necessarily positive. See Daniel Goldrich and others, "The Political Integration of Lower Class Urban Settlements," prepared for the American Political Science Association meetings, September 1966, pp. 10–14 (mimeo).

9. See, for example, Alain Touraine, "Conscience ouvrière et développement economique en Amerique Latine," *Sociologie du Travail*, IX (July 1967), 229–54.

10. Clark Kerr and Abraham Siegel, "The Inter-Industry Propensity to Strike: An International Comparison," in Arthur Kornhauser, Robert Dubin, and Arthur Ross, eds., *Industrial Conflict* (New York 1954).

11. Maurice Zeitlin, *Revolutionary Politics and the Cuban Working Class* (Princeton 1967), chap. 6.

12. Gino Germani, "Social and Political Consequences of Mobility," in Smelser and Lipset, *Social Structure and Mobility in Economic Development* (Chicago 1966), p. 387.

13. Robert C. Fried, "Urbanization and Italian Politics," *Journal of Politics,* XXIX (August 1967), p. 525.

14. Ray, chap. 7.

15. *New York Times,* September 24, 1968.

•

Development Strategy
and Leadership

•

THERE ARE many economic, social, and political strategies that may be employed to further national development. They are bound to differ because of the differences in national conditions and in the preferences of different regimes. What we have tried to do here is present various examples and experiences of development strategies in Africa, Latin America, and Asia.

The East African countries of Tanzania, Uganda, and Kenya offer many bases for comparison, in particular their common political heritage of British colonial rule and their similarities of economic structure. In the article below, Aaron Segal shows the salience of regime preferences, that is, the visions of a "good society" embraced by different leaderships. In each country there is a somewhat different configuration of sectors, that is, a different political stratification, according to the resources each sector possesses and the ideological predisposition of the regime. These differences in strategy can have quite divergent implications for the pattern of development as shown by Segal. Clearly, development is shaped in the final analysis by the political choices made within a society as these interact with the resource constraints and possibilities which each confronts.[1]

A similar comparison of experiences with development strategies is presented by Charles Anderson with reference to the Central American countries of Costa Rica, El Salvador, and Guatemala. His analytical scheme presented above helps to elucidate the events considered here. Anderson gives particular attention to the constraints on development strategy raised by the existing political stratifications in Latin America. The best-endowed sectors, in terms of political resources, are the least likely to favor energetic development efforts. He finds development policy used to enlist support and establish legitimacy for the regime, and at the same time development-oriented regimes proceed "prudently" with concrete policies. It is quite possible that a regime, such as that of Arbenz in Guatemala, will be ousted because of its efforts at development. It is observed that, given the patterns of resource possession and the expectations which sectors have, successor regimes are likely to imitate many of the policies of their predecessors (an observation not confined to the Third World).

We found no similar comparative analysis of development strategies in Asia but found Jose Abueva's article on President Magsaysay's development efforts in the Philippines most instructive. Magsaysay's activity represents one of the most concerted demonstrations of political *entrepreneurship* seen in the Third World

[1] An expanded version of this article appeared subsequently in *Economic Develop-* *ment and Cultural Change* (January 1968), pp. 275–296.

246

in the last twenty years. The many innovations designed to mobilize and allocate political, economic, and social resources deserve consideration for their breadth and orchestration. Magsaysay made a deliberate effort to integrate the many into the Philippine political market. His failure, as Abueva points out in conclusion, lay not in a lack of imagination or political talent but in a lack of success in developing *organization* all the way down to the political grassroots. After the death of Magsaysay in 1957 it was not possible to perpetuate the resource flows he had set in motion, and recent events in the Philippines have shown that the problems with which Magsaysay grappled have not been resolved since then. There are in any case important lessons to be learned for development strategists from the attempts by Magsaysay to "bridge the gap" between the many and the few.

THE POLITICS OF LAND IN EAST AFRICA
AARON SEGAL
Cornell University

Land—two thirds of a million square miles of it—is of more concern to a majority of East Africans than anything else. It is at the heart of politics in Kenya, Tanzania, and Uganda, whose post-independence governments have adopted land policies that reflect aspirations toward some distinctive national goals. The land legislation in these three countries ranges over the entire field of land tenure, public investment, and agricultural development strategy—and the approaches are strikingly different. Each country has in fact embarked on a separate path toward a different objective.

British policy and administration in the three territories fostered three sets of attitudes toward land, but the post-independence policies to which I refer are much more than carryovers from colonial practice. They are distinct innovations which in some respects repudiate the former colonial system, for they reflect the differing visions of the good society held by the dominant political and civil service elites in each country. Each national elite seeks to impose its vision as a matter of public policy in order to give substance to political nationalism. Because more than 90 percent of East Africans live in rural surroundings, the national vision is necessarily a vision of

social change in the rural areas. By the same token, the effort to build different kinds of nations is carried on neither uniquely nor principally in the hurly-burly of urban politics, but, more significantly, in the countryside.

In the abortive federation talks of 1963–64, the three countries agreed that within any scheme of federation they would keep their separate jurisdictions over the sensitive issue of land. Since then, Kenya, Tanzania, and Uganda have further defined their positions on the juridical problem of land tenure, the role of the public sector in agriculture, and agricultural development strategy. Each group of national policies reveals a significant internal rationale. As we shall see, the discussions which preceded the adoption of a policy furnish some useful insights into the thinking of national political elites and the decision-making process, the role of political parties, the civil service, and pressure groups.

TANZANIA: HOMOGENEITY IN THE COUNTRYSIDE

As one of its first major policy moves after independence in 1961, the Tanganyikan Government enacted a law to replace free-

From *Africa Report* (April 1967), pp. 46–50. Reprinted by permission.

hold tenure with leasehold tenure. In principle, land became the property of the state, and existing freehold titles were converted to 99-year leaseholds, removing the possibility that land could be inherited and divided among the surviving members of a family. In so changing the basic premise governing the occupancy and use of land, Tanganyika took the first step toward developing the kind of rural society most recently envisaged by President Julius Nyerere in the Arusha Declaration of February 1967.

The number of landowners and the actual acreage affected by the original legislation was very limited. A handful of non-African farmers in the southern and northern highlands had to have their title-deeds amended, and that contributed to their growing unease for the future. The owners of most of the major sisal and sugar plantations had their 999-year leases converted to a 99-year period. The few Africans who contemplated purchasing land on a freehold basis were effectively discouraged from doing so.

The government's decision to adopt the principle of leasehold tenure was taken with little public discussion and no serious opposition. Aside from the Bahaya, Chagga, and Meru peoples, few Africans in Tanganyika had developed export-based farming operations that involved individual freehold tenure. Non-Africans relied on their friendly relations with the government and its emphasis on cooperation between the private and public sectors to protect their interests. In fact, the decision meshed with colonial policies which had always sought to curtail freehold tenure and the alienation of land by non-Africans.

The law offered some satisfaction to TANU party militants who were calling for Africanization of the civil service and the economy, but more importantly it conformed with TANU election manifestoes setting forth principles of an African socialism based on communal rather than individual land tenure, and economic development without the emergence of African social classes based on the ownership of land. These ideological and political considerations were discussed first by the TANU Central Committee, then considered by the party conference and an interministerial civil service committee, and finally approved by the cabinet for presentation to the National Assembly.

The change from freehold to leasehold tenure has had several important consequences. It effectively discourages African civil servants and businessmen from investing in land, thus narrowing the economic and social base of the African middle class. Secondly, it contributes to intertribal mixing—another of TANU's objectives. The communal land-use habits of many Tanganyikan tribes allow people from friendly tribes to use "their" land. In time, freehold tenure might have interfered with this practice by encouraging tribes to define limits around their traditional areas, thereby stirring intertribal rivalries. Finally, until the Arusha Declaration, the law furnished the government with crucial leverage in negotiating with foreign businesses, for instance by putting muscle into the government's insistence that new investments in sisal must include provisions for cooperative villages and outgrower schemes.

The government's second major policy choice was to concentrate public investment in agriculture in capital-intensive village settlements. It was first made public in the Development Plan (1964–1969) published in June 1964. The decision to opt for villagization resulted from a combination of ideology, party politics, emotional attachments, the advice of foreign technical experts, shortages of manpower and capital, and other factors. It was not a sudden move, but the outcome of several years of frustration in the search for an effective policy. The plan proposed to establish 67 village settlements and by 1980 to have over one million Tanzanians living in these new schemes. At the end of 1966, however, less than ten schemes were proving viable and able to hold their settlers. Without abandoning villagization entirely, the government was looking for a new agricultural development strategy.

Prior to independence, TANU made political capital of local resistance to changes in traditional agricultural practices proposed by expatriate civil servants. The party made a connection between nationalist sentiment and its defense of the traditional way of life, which is characterized by scattered individual homesteads, shifting cultivation, subsistence rather than cash production, and the absence in many areas of organized village life. Once in power, the party and government were committed to rapid improvement in rural standards of living and to demonstrating that Africans were capable of managing their own institutions and generating their own development. This led to an early and eventually disillusioning emphasis on self-help schemes sponsored by the party with government direction. As long as Tanzanian farmers lived in separate homesteads and lacked mechanical implements, the economic returns from self-help remained low in relation to the labor involved.

The original disillusionment with self-help strengthened demands within the party for rapid economic development. One alternative was industrialization, but it would require foreign capital and know-how and have little impact on the rural economy. Meanwhile, the Africanization of agricultural technical services and mounting demands for government expenditures were decimating the inherited colonial practice of encouraging the evolution of individual "progressive" farmers through easy loans and concentrated technical assistance. A means was needed to tap the party and nationalist sentiment in the rural areas in order to mobilize the masses, not merely a handful of individuals, for a deeper kind of social change.

The first tentative experiments in village settlement were organized on the self-help principle in late 1962. By 1964, advice from expatriate experts in the Planning Office and expectations of foreign aid had moved villagization to the center of public-sector investment strategy in the new development plan. Given the characteristics of Tanganyika's rural economy—the islands of economic activity separated and isolated from one another by vast semi-arid tsetse-infested wastelands, and the skilled manpower shortages—it was clear that a policy of working with individual farmers would have limited results. Village settlement offered a means of reconciling party and government through use of the party as a tool of rural development.

Economically, the village settlements are capital-intensive mechanized farms that are managed by expatriate experts until they are ready to be turned over to African cooperators. Socially, they are the first attempt in East Africa deliberately to produce organized multitribal village life on a foundation of modern farming and communal land tenure. Although for geographic reasons a single tribe may be predominant in a given scheme, all of them are open to membership on a voluntary multitribal

basis. Most settlements have at least some members from several tribes, and Swahili is the language of meetings held in all of them.

The first glance at a Tanzanian village settlement and a Kenyan land settlement scheme reveals the essential difference: there are no fences in Tanzania separating individual plots. Tanzanian villages are co-operatively owned and producing villages; Kenyan land settlement schemes are made up of individually owned farms which may or may not market cooperatively. The income of Tanzanian villagers represents equal shares of the total income of the group, with its allocation decided by majority vote of the members; the income of a farmer in a Kenyan settlement scheme depends on his own efforts. Each Tanzanian villager has provided for him a standard home with cement floors, at the insistence of President Nyerere; farmers in Kenyan settlements build their own homes, according to their tastes and means.

The Tanzanian system will eventually lead to major differences in rural income between the inhabitants of government-subsidized villages and everyone else. Villagization is, in fact, an expensive way to change the lives of a few thousand people, while leaving the vast majority untouched. Perhaps recognition of both the expense and the disparity is behind the emphasis on self-help in the Arusha Declaration, which did not mention villagization specifically. These factors apparently weighed in the recent decision to nationalize the banks. In submitting the nationalization bill to the National Assembly in February, Finance Minister Amir Jamal said, "It was clear that, with the best will in the world, foreign banking interests would not have moved as fast as we would wish to move our rural areas. They would have probably taken 50 years. We would wish to cover our rural areas within the next 15 years."

Though the government is apparently seeking a new tactical approach to its rural problems, the overall strategy continues to project a distinctively Tanzanian vision of the good society. Unlike the Kenyan and Ugandan vision of the yeoman peasant-farmer who moves gradually into the cash economy, financing his children's school fees, buying a bicycle, and paying taxes to the local council to improve secondary roads, the Tanzanian elite sees the country dotted with highly organized, communally owned cooperative villages directly linked to the party and government hierarchy. Instead of yeoman farmers, they see party and cooperative members driving tractors, operating sisal decorticators, practicing irrigation farming, living next to one another, speaking and eventually reading Swahili, and encouraging their children to marry across tribal lines. These are visions, not realities—but whether or not the Tanzanian elite succeeds fully in realizing its vision, the result of its efforts will be a society very different from either Kenya's or Uganda's.

UGANDA: THE ROOTS OF DIVERSITY

A prominent factor in every government policy decision involving land in Uganda has been the fragility of the government's political base, the weakness of the political parties, and a consequent need to use land as a political weapon. While the Tanzanian elite has sought to move toward rural social homogeneity, Uganda's problem has been to manipulate overwhelming heterogeneity to extend the government's influence and base of support.

Colonial policies restricting freehold tenure and non-African leasehold plantations combined with the availability of unused arable land in many areas to leave each Uganda tribe free to work out its own land policy. Several Bantu tribes imitated aspects of the basically individual system of Mailo land tenure adopted by the Baganda in 1900. African civil servants were not allowed to maintain active interests in business, but they were and are both able and eager to invest in land.

The independent Uganda Government has consistently shied away from the complicated and sensitive area of land tenure, leaving the diverse inherited systems intact. The Ministry of Justice sought to unify customary and civil law by helping each tribe to produce its own written customary law; but unlike Tanzania, Uganda has made no attempt to produce a nationwide uniform customary law. As landowners or potential landowners, most educated Ugandans favor a modified system of individual land tenure, and they accept differences in income among rural Africans as the desirable consequence of differences in individual initiative and ability. Since there is still enough unused land for everyone,

there are few objections to the concept of individual wealth based on land ownership.

At one time there were pressures for change in land tenure from Baganda clan leaders who lost land in 1900 to the appointed civil servants of the Kingdom of Buganda. The growing property-owning Baganda middle classes resented the hereditary privileges in land consolidated by the 1900 agreement, particularly when the growth of the Kampala urban area and the extension of coffee cultivation led to a rise in land values. But the only intervention by the independent Uganda Government into the question of land tenure came immediately after the attack on the Kabaka's Palace in May 1966, when the government abolished the privileges accorded to certain of the Kingdom's office holders and redistributed their land. This was a gesture to pacify some Baganda at a moment of extreme alienation from the central government. Although it contributed to social reforms in rural Buganda, it does not represent a new system of land tenure.

The government sees no present political or economic benefit in a national land policy, and is highly sensitive to the risk of arousing local sentiment which a discussion of land tenure could provoke. Blessed with an abundance of land (and a superabundance of social systems), Uganda continues to hover somewhat ambiguously between individual and communal tenure. The politicians have ignored the advice of expatriate experts that *de jure* recognition should be given to the widespread *de facto* practice of individual landholding. Government agencies work with individual farmers as though individual tenure existed, and extend them credit on that basis; but unlike the Kenya Government, the Uganda administration has no desire to see peasants clutching pieces of central government paper attesting to individual land ownership.

In mid-1963, the government decided to concentrate its investment in agriculture in group farms. The program got under way in 1964, and today group farms coexist with farms in the private sector, as they do in Kenya. The Ugandan farms are different, however, from both the Kenyan land settlement schemes and the village settlements in Tanzania. The government clears unused land with modern machinery and assists individual farmers by subsidizing tractors and technical services. The farmers do not live in villages, nor are they obliged to produce or market cooperatively (though cooperative marketing is encouraged). Nor does the government select the participants or require them to renounce title to any other land they may hold, as do Kenya and Tanzania. In effect, the government's role is limited to subsidizing an extension of the traditional system.

The decision to invest in group farms was a direct result of the government's search for a means to increase its popularity, broaden its political support, and reward its followers. (Both parties contesting the 1961 elections promised the voters tractors.) After independence, the hostility of the Baganda to the majority Uganda People's Congress (UPC), its organizational weakness, and the real possibility that blocs of voters would shift their allegiance, made it politically imperative for the government to consolidate its support. Uganda's sharp regional differences in income and the government's ethnic and political base in the visibly less developed north called for a policy of resource allocation which would reward government supporters, give the north hope that it was catching up with the wealthier Baganda, and demonstrate on a carrot-and-stick basis to the Baganda and their allies the rewards of siding with the party in power.

The government's choice of economic levers in attaining these goals was limited to coffee and cotton, the principal cash crops grown by the peasantry and marketed by the government at officially established prices. An expansion of coffee cultivation was ruled out by world market conditions and Uganda's quota under the International Coffee Agreement. In any event, Uganda coffee is grown principally by the Baganda and is not well suited to mechanical cultivation. Cotton was thus left as the crop offering both a promising world market and growth characteristics suited to an extension of cultivation in the main political target area, the north.

The government's first attempt to make an economic virtue of political necessity was the free distribution of insecticide for the 1963 cotton crop. The experiment turned out to be disastrously expensive. For political reasons, no control was exercised over who received the insecticide or how it was used. As a result, there was little or no increase in cotton yields per acre; a number of persons received medical treatment after using the insecticide as a wonder drug, and there was a substantial deficit in the Ministry of Agriculture's budget. When an effort was made to sell the insecticide at half the original cost to the government, there were few takers and considerable resentment at the imposition of a charge for something that used to be free.

After the insecticide imbroglio, the government took a fresh look at the opportunities and chose group farming as the approach to its politico-economic problem. Probably as the result of a cabinet decision reached under pressure from Prime Minister Milton Obote, and certainly without public, party, or civil service discussion, a decision was taken to import tractors to clear land for group farms. They were to be strategically located in the north in areas where government supporters were concentrated, and elsewhere in areas where voters might be won over to the majority party.

As it happens, they have not been a political success. Bewildered peasants who overnight became "group farmers" remain unenthusiastic. The Baganda believed from the start that the program was another example of systematic governmental discrimination against them. Why not, they asked, use the money to raise the price of coffee to the grower? Civil servants, both African and expatriate, considered it a sizable mistake, but did their best to organize cooperative marketing.

The picture is not altogether bleak, for the mechanical clearing of virgin land and the use of fertilizers may well produce above-average cotton crops for several years. Yet the fact remains that the introduction of group farms was a short-term political gesture that diverged from but did not substantially alter the prevailing concepts of land use and agricultural development. The participants continue to work their own plots, live in their separate homesteads, speak their tribal languages, and look on the group farm as someone else's responsibility. They are under no obligation to cultivate their new plots or to pay for mechanical services, the government having declined to impose requirements which might affect political loyalties.

The ideal of the sturdy yeoman cash-cropping farmer is solidly implanted in Uganda, along with a receptiveness to temporary migrant labor from nearby Rwanda and Burundi. Official policy encourages progressive farming through agricultural extension services and loans (each of Uganda's eleven districts will have an agricultural training center with a small model farm and intensive short courses for progressive farmers and their wives). Though ideals and practices foster differences in income among farmers, at the same time the government's long-term development goal is to extend cash cropping in the north and reduce the economic and educational gap that separates the prosperous Baganda from everyone else. Since the policy envisages no pronounced change from traditional practice, there is no attempt to produce social homogeneity along Tanzanian lines; the group farms remain unitribal and bilingual, the second language being English.

KENYA: CONSOLIDATION AND RESETTLEMENT

The revised Five Year Development Plan published in 1966 commits the Kenya Government to promote land consolidation and freehold tenure on a nationwide basis. European settlers in the once racially restricted white highlands introduced freehold tenure to that part of Kenya, but it did not spread to other areas until the colonial government adopted land consolidation as part of its counter-insurgency strategy against the Mau-Mau movement in Kikuyuland. Loyal individuals were given outright title to single consolidated plots rather than to the small, fragmented pieces of land they traditionally farmed—and that was enough to begin a revolution in smallholder farming practices.

This system introduced more than ten years ago has proved to be extremely popular. Despite the fees charged for surveying and titling, the government can hardly meet the demand for consolidation and individual title. The less developed tribes now conceive of consolidation and titling as a means of preventing landless Kikuyu and other peoples from encroaching on their territory, while the spread of cash-cropping has made individual title a *sine qua non* of peasant initiative. Only among some elements of the Luo, living in dry country near Lake Victoria and practicing a different agricultural system, has there been outright opposition to land consolidation.

The decision to transform a significant but regionally limited program into a pillar of Kenya's national development policy was the outcome of several factors: the encouraging experience of the original consolidation program, subsequent financing provided by the World Bank, the UK, and other Western sources, and popular wishes expressed outside party channels. Indeed, popular aspirations have been stimulated by the example of Kenya's political and administrative elites, for politicians and civil servants were among the first to consolidate their own lands and buy non-African land on a willing-buyer, willing-seller, freehold basis. President Jomo Kenyatta himself symbolizes the country's new land-owning squirearchy by residing on his prosperous coffee farm near Nairobi, an example thousands hope to emulate. Kenya is undergoing a rural revolution in which the major export crops, particularly the coffee and tea formerly grown largely by non-Africans, are increasingly produced at high quality by African small-holders. Consolidation and individual tenure have in turn made possible new initiatives in the selective application of farm credit and quality controls.

Since independence, there has been no direct opposition at the national level to land consolidation. The opposition Kenya People's Union party, which favors cooperative farming and limits on individual land holdings, criticized the government for making land consolidation its number one priority, but did not question its desirability. Tom Mboya, the Minister of Economic Planning and Development who spearheaded the drive for a national policy, challenged opposition leader Oginga Odinga to explain why, if he did not consider land consolidation a top priority, he had been one of the first Luos to consolidate his own land.

Simplified methods of surveying and registering land, and a major increase in government funds, were called for in the revised development plan of 1966 to enable most of Kenya's high quality land to be consolidated by 1970. Less attention was paid to the suitability of consolidation to pastoral peoples, or to the special agricultural problems of the Luo. Thus, Kenya became probably the first black African state to opt decisively for the Western model of land tenure and to reject the traditional order.

The second dimension of Kenya's land policy is resettlement—the moving of African peasants from marginally productive lands to more fertile acreage acquired from European farmers. Resettlement was initiated on a limited scale before independence, when carefully selected "progressive" African farmers were moved, with the aid of British, West German, and World Bank funds, onto "low-density schemes" with annual target cash incomes of $280 to $700 per person. Growing unrest among the European farmers, a serious economic recession accompanied by large-scale unemployment and landlessness, and the sweeping expectations kindled by the prospect of political independence, dictated a change from this cautious and limited approach.

The pre-independence government elected in June 1963 and headed by Jomo Kenyatta believed that massive and immediate resettlement of Africans on European land was a precondition of political stability. Africans in rural areas had to be given visible tokens of independence if the new state were to have a chance of achieving political order. The British Government agreed, and provided the money for a crash resettlement program. Veteran agricultural officers objected to what they considered the economic waste involved in buying out the European farmers and replacing them with Africans; a Department of Settlement had to be created to carry out the program, for the Ministry of Agriculture refused to be responsible for it. Nevertheless, the major share of Kenya's post-independence public agricultural investment has gone into resettlement schemes in which more than 30,000 African families have been moved onto individual plots on a million acres of formerly European-owned land. Nearly all of the funds—approximately $170,000,000—have come from Britain, and about one-third of the amount has been used to buy out the Europeans.

It is widely believed that resettlement made a critical, perhaps decisive, contribution to Kenya's immediate post-independence stability. Contrary to prevalent belief, however, the Kikuyu were not the major beneficiaries of the policy, though nearly half the resettled families were Kikuyu. Comparable numbers of Kikuyu farm laborers were displaced when members of other tribes were resettled on the European farms where they had been employed. It has been the Kalenjin-speaking peoples and the Kisii who have acquired the most fertile land, as well as the most land in relation to population and needs. These tribes have acquired a significant stake in the present *status quo* and have switched their allegiance to the government, contributing to the isolation of the Luo (who were largely left out of resettlement) and enabling the government more easily to forego Luo support.

The settlement schemes are organized on the basis of individual consolidated plots and voluntary cooperative marketing. The settlers are contractually bound to repay government loans for land purchases, purebred cattle, mechanized plowing, and other services. The ultimate authority of government settlement officials lies in dispossessing recalcitrant settlers, but the government has been extremely chary of using this power, even when loan payments are in serious arrears. The settlers are free to plant and market when and what they choose, and few of them have developed much in the way of cooperative or community spirit. The schemes have varied widely in their output and profitability, and the overall experience of cooperative marketing has been somewhat discouraging.

Political considerations aside, the replacement of large-scale mixed farming with African smallholders appears to have brought few benefits to the economy as a whole. The British Government, weighing its foreign exchange problems against a possible future commitment to buy out European farmers in Rhodesia, has declined to invest in resettlement beyond the first million-acre program. Technical experts agree that Kenya's grazing areas, plantation agriculture, and some of the remaining non-African mixed farms are not suitable for peasant smallholding. The transfer of these large farms intact to Africans who receive government loans has also raised problems, at least over the short term, for few Africans now have the skills and capital to retain the former level of production on the big farms.

Sooner or later, the government faces a policy choice on the future of the existing settlements. It can insist on loan repayments with the ultimate sanction of dispossession, or it can write off part of the loans as bad debts. There is evidence that on individual schemes, a minority of settlers are achieving more than the target incomes; but a minority of comparable size have virtually no monetary incomes, and sometimes work the land on a less than full-time basis. The majority of farmers fail to meet their targets, but still generate some cash income. The government can dispossess the poorer farmers, or allow them to be bought out by the more enterprising settlers, who in any event are likely to be frustrated by the small size of their plots and the danger of renewed fragmentation of land holdings through inheritance.

In effect, the choice is between continuing to subsidize all of the settlers or encouraging the emergence of income and class differences based on ownership of land. The revised development plan has apparently postponed the decision by shifting the emphasis in public investment and agricultural development policy from the settlement schemes to improvement of the African tribal areas. No new major settlement programs are to be initiated, and efforts are to be concentrated instead on increasing output in the existing schemes.

Kenya's vision of the good society is clear. The nation-wide adoption of land consolidation is to produce the legal and psychological basis for greatly expanded government technical services and rural credit to enterprising individual peasant farmers. The fences, improved housing, purebred cattle, and specialized farming which characterize some of Kenya's already consolidated districts are seen by the politicians and civil servants as the key to economic development and political stability. The image of the relatively prosperous, independent, land-owning and individualistic peasant farmer, with a conservative stake in the *status quo* and a progressive investment in improved farming practices, is totally different from Tanzania's values; in its call for discarding much of traditional society, it is distinctively more radical than Uganda's practices.

The question is whether the problems of rapid population growth, mounting desires for wage employment among those completing primary school, and galloping urbanization will prevail politically over the interests of the new agricultural middle class. Kenya's finite scarcity of arable land obliges the most educated tribes to look beyond their own areas for land or employment. These tribes include the people most able to profit by the system of individual enterprise which land consolidation entails, and those most likely to be discontented if their opportunities do not measure up to their desires.

The government may be tempted to deflect their dissatisfaction toward non-Africans or less educated tribes which are not exploiting arable land. For the policy of land consolidation, while implicitly non-tribal, is being carried out in Kenya within a tribal framework. It is caught in a crossfire between those who wish to push it to its logically non-tribal fulfillment, and those who fear that their own people could not compete within a non-tribal society based on individual land ownership.

These problems of land tenure, public investment in agriculture, and rural development strategy are at the heart of East African efforts to achieve political stability. The means and ends embody the politics of culture—the balance between homogeneity and heterogeneity which is to characterize the new national societies.

Tanzania seems to be on the road to becoming a nation of Swahili-speaking cooperative farmers living in multi-tribal villages controlled by the government and party. Uganda appears committed to a nationhood of tribes who live in traditional communities, practice a modified form of individual land tenure, and look to the government for leadership and assistance. Kenya's leaders wish to build a nation of prosperous and individualistic peasant-farmers whose output will permit the emergence of a multi-lingual, multi-tribal urban society supported by a stable and contented rural order. The success or failure of these policies will largely determine whether East Africa can reduce the gap between state and nation and enjoy economic development and political order, or will succumb to pressures that exceed the capacity of the existing systems.

POLITICS AND DEVELOPMENT POLICY
IN CENTRAL AMERICA

CHARLES W. ANDERSON

University of Wisconsin

The formation of economic and social development policies lies close to the heart of the political process throughout Africa, Asia, and Latin America. Many interpret the conflict engendered in the making of such policy as an episode in a universal ideological struggle. Yet the formulation of development policy is not often a purely ideological matter, to be defined in a political vacuum. Rather, the approach to such issues adopted by a political movement is apt to be influenced by the group composition of a movement, by its strategy for winning political influence, and by its position in relation to other groups and movements within the political system of the particular nation.

This study will focus on the development policies formulated by three major political movements which emerged in Central America during the past fifteen years. It will approach such policies as "political instruments" of these movements, as techniques adopted to mobilize and consolidate political influence, just as armed violence, the formation of personal alliances, the organization of political parties, electoral fraud or the holding of honest elections may, in this region, be adopted as instruments in attaining this end. This is not intended to imply that such policies merely represent the "rationalization" of other motives. Certainly, they may represent sincere ideological conviction and commitment on the part of those who formulate them. All that is argued is that something of politics and of the course of economic and social development in Central America may be learned by approaching the subject in this fashion.

In Central America, as in some other parts of the newly developing world, the process of mobilizing and consolidating political power would seem to have a dual character. First, development policy is a political instrument used to "aggregate" interests [1] in support of a leadership group, that is, to attract the support of a large number of important groups within the political system, and to provide them with a sufficiently common sense of political purpose that a viable political movement might be created. But statements of policy intent have a second political function in areas where Western constitutional norms regarding the mobilization of political power are not fully effective. In nations where a small sector of the population (which in Central America would include the army, the Church, the "families" which have traditionally constituted an upper class, etc.) has historically controlled access to the political arena, the admission of a new political movement as a contender for power is to some extent dependent on the assurances which the movement can give to these traditionally dominant groups. The power which these established groups exercise over the future of a new political movement in Central America may be this region's equivalent of the concept of "legitimacy" in the advanced nations. Development policy, while serving to aggregate interests within the political movement, may also be used to establish the acceptability of the movement as a competitor for political power.

An examination of the development policies of three specific Central American political movements will help to illuminate the points made above. The movements chosen, José Figueres' *Liberación Nacional* party in Costa Rica, the *Prudista* movement in El Salvador, and the Castillo Armas administration in Guatemala, are intended to be merely illustrative. The comments that apply to them could equally well be made of a great number of the political movements that have appeared in Latin America since the end of World War II.

From *Midwest Journal of Political Science* (November 1961), pp. 332–350. Reprinted by permission. Some sections have been omitted.

LIBERACIÓN NACIONAL OF COSTA RICA

In 1948, in response to an attempt to annul the elections of that year by the government in power, José Figueres, a hitherto relatively unimportant radical leader, raised an insurrectionist force and waged a successful revolt. For two years, Figueres headed a *junta* government, then voluntarily turned power over to Otilio Ulate, the apparent victor in the disputed election.

During Ulate's presidency, Figueres shaped the coalition of forces which had supported his revolt into a political movement, *Liberación Nacional*. With the support of this party, Figueres won the Costa Rican presidency in 1953, serving in that office until his party was defeated by the "modern conservative," Mario Echandi, in 1958.

Liberación Nacional quite self-consciously represents itself as an ideological movement, seeking to present the Costa Rican electorate with a coherent political doctrine. Next to Peru's *APRA* movement, this party has perhaps given more attention to the construction of a distinctive political philosophy than any other in Latin America, a preoccupation which reflects both the intellectual interests of its founder and the attitudes of the student groups which have from the beginning played a dominant role in its organization. . . .

In giving substance to their conception of the development process, the *Liberacionistas* have stressed programs which have by now become commonplace throughout the newly developing world. Emphasis is placed on the rationalization and nationalization of capital providing agencies, and on programs of technical assistance. Other programs are designed to provide the economic and social infrastructure on which private development efforts depend. Construction of roads and public hydroelectric power facilities, and similar projects directly related to the expansion of productivity, are to be undertaken, as well as projects which have social reform as their primary objective—primarily in the fields of education, social security, and public housing.

The favored instrument of *Liberación Nacional* for achieving its ends is the "autonomous institution" or public corporation. During Figueres' presidency, such in-

stitutions were established in the fields of banking, electric power, social insurance, public housing, tourism, and commodity and production regulation. The *Liberacionistas* defend the use of such public corporations as a form of large-scale productive organization that is more appropriate to the needs of a developing nation than the private corporation. They are "socially inspired," and profit is but one of many tests of their success. They permit "democratic participation" in the development effort. Such public corporations are better equipped than private enterprise to provide large-scale development capital and resources in the developing nations.[2]

Liberación Nacional has given far more conscious attention to the creation of a formal doctrine in development policy matters than most comparable movements in Latin America. Its leaders explicitly regard sophisticated social theory as a weapon in their political arsenal. In order to fully comprehend the development policy of the movement, therefore, one must inquire into the political function served by the doctrine, and the impact of political considerations upon it.

The Costa Rican political process does not encourage political success through the mobilization of a narrow coalition circumscribed by a rigorous ideological position. Rather, within a presidential system where strong executive leadership has been traditional, and electoral means of winning power generally respected, victory is apt to come to that movement which can successfully appeal to many disparate elements in the population. Furthermore, in the Costa Rican political system, where certain upper-middle and upper-class groups have traditionally controlled access to the political realm, a new political movement, emerging outside the conventional arena of the political game, must give evidence that it will not seriously jeopardize the position of any dominant political group.

Liberación Nacional seeks to act as a "modern" political party within the Costa Rican political process. As a hard-campaigning, well organized group, it believes that it will be able to mobilize mass electoral consent far more effectively than the ephemeral, loosely knit factions that have historically dominated Costa Rican politics.

Political doctrine is regarded as a basic instrument of the "modern" political party.

A primary function of this intellectualized version of development policy would seem to be the creation of a "nuclear adherent group" of dedicated party members, who will provide the "modern" party with the organization and campaigning effort necessary to create an effective mass political appeal. For *Liberación Nacional,* this group is largely drawn from the highly politicized, intellectually sophisticated, upwardly mobile elements of the population. Students, younger civil servants and professional men predominate. This group seems drawn by the heroic context in which Figueres has set the development policies of the movement. Seeking a more advantageous social role, these people drawn by the promise of reform and participation in a great undertaking from which they may derive personal benefit.

Development policy, however, must serve other political purposes as well. The dominant sectors of Costa Rican society must be assured that the impending transformation will not jeopardize but enhance their social role. Thus, the *Liberacionista* leaders elaborately and consistently interpret their "welfare state" doctrine so as to indicate that the traditional functions of these dominant groups in commerce, industry and agriculture will be at the forefront of the development enterprise. The state will act, not to diminish their activities, but to invest them with the potential for ever greater enterprise. It will provide credit and technical advice for new undertakings, the stabilization of commodity prices, a trained labor pool, and other services.

Yet the strength of a movement like *Liberación Nacional* is based, in the long run, on its mass electoral appeal. In the developing nations, such an appeal is assumed to rest on a political movement's promise of leadership in the struggle for a better way of life for the mass of the population. Thus *Liberacionista* spokesmen must justify a development policy which stresses the role of the dominant sectors as the most efficacious way of bettering the economic and social condition of the less prosperous groups in the society. Much of *Liberación Nacional's* campaigning has been devoted to establishing the plausibility of this position. In an almost quixotic fashion, *Liberacionista* leaders remain convinced that they can communicate much of the complexity of their position on development issues to

the mass of the Costa Rican people. In Figueres' campaign speeches and in such writings as his *Cartas a un ciudadano,*[3] directed to a mass audience, the effort to communicate a highly sophisticated position on development policy is revealed. Certainly, much of what is said goes over the heads of the listeners or is greatly distorted, but the attempt is a persistent one.

Thus for *Liberación Nacional* the construction of a political doctrine of development policy is not so much a problem in working out the implications of a set of premises concerning the social order as it is a political act calling for the reconciliation of a variety of interests under the aegis of intellectually satisfying constructs, perhaps a crucial political tool in a culture which seems to demand philosophic justification for action.

THE PRUD MOVEMENT IN EL SALVADOR

The political movement which was dominant in El Salvador from 1948 to late 1960 was structured quite differently from *Liberación Nacional.* Rather than being composed of social elements striving for greater access to the political arena, the *PRUD*[4] movement was based on a subtle coalition of the dominant power factors in the society, the army and the "oligarchy,"[5] which sought the cooperation of major elements of the middle sectors and endeavored to base their power on a mass electoral appeal. Furthermore, the political system of El Salvador is distinct from that in Costa Rica. El Salvador lacks a tradition of stability and relatively democratic political procedure. The nation has historically been the scene of frequent resort to violence in effecting political change. The characteristic form of political leadership has been that of the *caudillo,* or "strong man."

The *PRUD* movement grew out of a successful *coup* waged by junior army officers in 1948. On this event, quite characteristic of the conventional means of adjusting power relations in El Salvador, the *PRUD* leaders attempted to superimpose the flavor and tone of a true "social revolution" which promised a better life to the impoverished lower classes of the nation.[6]

The military leaders of the *coup* of 1948 thus attempted to consolidate their power through the creation of a mass electoral appeal, based on the promise of rapid economic and social development. This appeal was to be made effective through the action of a well-organized party, *PRUD*, based on the same core of middle sector activists which was observed in *Liberación Nacional*. As in the case of the Costa Rican party, this group was to be attracted to dedicated partisan activity in part through a statement of development policy phrased in the most idealistic terms.

The *PRUD* movement's efforts to carry out major programs of economic and social development met with a relatively high degree of success. Assuming that the agricultural and mineral potential of this tiny nation would be inadequate to support the desired level of economic development, the movement placed considerable emphasis on industrial growth. Fiscal policies were directed toward the needs of new entrepreneurs. A huge hydroelectric power project was completed. Public works activities, to provide the infrastructure for development, were undertaken. Road construction, water supply facilities, education, and public housing were emphasized.

However, the leaders of the PRUD movement found it essential, while attempting to build mass support for the regime through development policies, to so interpret the revolution as to make it acceptable to the Salvadorian oligarchy. What El Salvador was to realize was essentially a "controlled revolution"; the transformation would be orderly, the position of the oligarchy would not be jeopardized, radical ideas would not influence the movement's program.

For many years the Salvadorian upper classes have been almost obsessively fearful of radical political movements and ideas. This dread dates at least from the Communist-influenced peasant revolts of 1932, which were quelled only when the strongman, Maximiliano Hernández Martínez, rose to power to begin a twelve year period of rule.[7] Developments in neighboring Guatemala during the 1950's under the Arbenz government further served to strengthen this fear of radical activity. It would seem that the *PRUD* leaders were able to sell their moderate social revolution to the oligarchy as the only viable alternative to a more radical outburst of mass discontent. . . .

The *PRUD* prescription for a "controlled revolution" included development policies which would not involve the dislocation of the existing economic order in the name of a new system. Free enterprise and private property were to be regarded as "basic principles" of the Salvadorian economy. Furthermore, *PRUD* would maintain a strong and stable government, which, while generally allowing political freedom, would permit only such opposition as would surely operate within the juridical order that *PRUD* specified.

PRUD's moderate, "controlled" social revolution is thus a development policy designed to accommodate the diverse interests and attitudes of groups which are often found in conflict in other political systems. For twelve years this program brought stability and a measure of progress to historically tumultuous El Salvador.

In October, 1960, a military *coup* brought an end to *Prudista* dominance in El Salvador. To date, the new rulers of the nation have departed but little from the general outlines of *PRUD* policy. However, the conditions under which this *coup* took place reveal chinks in the armor of the *PRUD* solution to the politics of development. Few would deny that the *PRUD* movement has been one of the most successful in Central America in terms of actual development policy accomplishments. But the political aspects of the doctrine of the "controlled revolution" are subject to greater question. The notion that the regime would control opposition activities in terms of its own interpretation of their danger to the constitutional order was, if not a thin disguise for political suppression, at least a great temptation for its employment. Granted that irresponsible opposition activity has retarded Central American political and economic development, the *PRUD* "formula" for stability seems to have been less than an optimum solution to the political requirements of development policy in El Salvador.

In the first years of *PRUD* dominance, freedom of opposition and expression seems, on the whole, to have been quite well respected. However, at least by the time of the presidential election of 1956, opposition was so firmly controlled that the ballot of that year was virtually a parody of democratic procedure. In 1960, when student protest demonstrations were put down with violence and terror, opposition to the regime's political policies became so intense that certain cadres within the military found it advisable to depose the government of the *PRUD* president, José Lemus. However, it seems likely that the basic political coalition, and the development policies established by *PRUD* have become firmly entrenched in the Salvadorian political system, and will continue to be developed by future governments.

THE CASTILLO ARMAS
GOVERNMENT IN GUATEMALA

Nowhere in recent Central American history is the need to understand development policy in the context of the political situation faced by a political movement as evident as in the case of the Carlos Castillo Armas government in Guatemala. The program of this military leader, who overthrew the Communist-influenced regime of Jacobo Arbenz in 1954, and served as President of Guatemala until his assassination in 1957, is only meaningful when viewed in relation to the development of the Guatemalan "Revolution."

Thus, to fully understand Castillo Armas' position in Guatemalan political life, one must return to the political events of 1944. In that year, the long-time strong man of Guatemala, Jorge Ubico, was deposed in a revolt of the students and the junior officers' corps. The overt motive for the revolt was political, a reaction against suppression of opposition in the name of more democratic rule. But reform of Guatemala's virtually feudal economic and social order was an implicit aim of the groups which became politically prominent in 1944.

Guatemalan life is characterized by two great social problems. One is the *patrón-peón* relationship on the great estates which are the basis of the nation's economic life. This relationship falls somewhere between medieval serfdom and debt slavery. A second and related problem is that of the Indian. Sixty percent of Guatemala's population is composed of indigenous groups who retain their own languages and live in poverty, almost completely isolated from the Westernized society of the *Ladino* of Guatemalan or European descent. The distinction between *Ladino* and *Indio* is the basis of an almost unbridgeable caste system within Guatemalan society. Insofar as "conservatism" has, since the Revolution, represented in Guatemala a desire to return to the social patterns that were accepted prior to 1944, it has implied acceptance of this archaic social order.

The approach of those who wished to see the Revolution of 1944 used as an instrument of economic development and social reform was by no means clear-cut. Nationalism, Indianism, broad social revolutionary tenets, *Aprismo,* the inspiration of the Mexican Revolution, fuzzy Marxism, and committed communism, separately or in subtle, half-understood combinations, all sought to represent the "significance" of the Revolution. The prime mission of the first "revolutionary" president, Juan José Arévalo, was merely to find a program within which the claims and counterclaims of the plethora of factions which sought to represent the Revolution could be accommodated. Arévalo's government has been charged with vacillation and the rule of expediency. However, his ability to maintain himself in office with a minimum of suppression for his elected term would seem to be a considerable achievement under the circumstances.

In 1951, after a relatively open election, Arévalo turned power over to a former military officer, Jacobo Arbenz. Arbenz appeared committed to a continuation of the policies instituted by Arévalo. In fact, in view of some of his earlier public statements, one might have suspected that the Revolution would take a more conservative direction under Arbenz.[8]

However, during the Arbenz period, the activities of the small Communist Party which had emerged with the Revolution burgeoned. It came to dominate the Guatemalan labor movement. It won access to the President.[9] The development policies of the Arbenz government reflected the influence of Communist advisers.

By early 1954, opposition to the Arbenz regime had come to focus on two key government policies. One was agrarian reform. The Arbenz government had enacted and was carrying out a policy of expropriation and distribution of some of the land on the great estates. Second, a "worker's militia" was to be formed, substantially under the direction of the Communist Party, as a rival to the power of the regular army.

In June, 1954, Castillo Armas, at the head of an insurrectionist force, entered Guatemala from staging areas in Honduras and El Salvador and overthrew the Arbenz government. His action was formally justified as a response to Communist activities in the Arbenz government

The role which Castillo Armas sought to play as President was one which is increasingly coming to be identified with the younger elements in the Latin American military elite. To these groups, "politics" is the prime evil that prevents their nations from achieving effective economic and social development. These military leaders seek to "rise above" political maneuverings and factional doctrinal squabbles, in the interest of achieving a government that will represent the "national interest." In other words, they seek to promote policies which will be acceptable to the largest numbers of politically significant groups, to steer a moderate course which, if buttressed by a firm, "no nonsense" government, will bring an end to civil strife between the partisans of the Left and the Right. . . .

Many responsible Guatemalans have commented that the actual programmatic achievements of Castillo Armas do not seem to reflect a diminished role for the public sector in development efforts, but rather a logical extension of the course of policy taken under Arévalo and Arbenz prior to 1954. By the Castillo Armas period, the Guatemalan Revolution had to some extent become "institutionalized." The new "spirit" of Guatemalan public life in the post-Ubico years was something to which nearly all sectors of public opinion could assent. Programs begun during the early years of the Revolution were generally continued by later administrations. Furthermore, the needs of an underdeveloped nation are clear and basic. Under whatever ideological aegis, programs of road building, education, etc., are clearly priority projects. When policies of economic development, and not of the redistribution of existing wealth, are at issue, perhaps it makes little difference, in the short run, whether these policies are carried out under the auspices of a government that interprets its role as broadly social revolutionary or generally conservative. The primary objectives on the agenda are apt to be about the same in either case.

In this perspective, the political uses of development policy become predominant concerns. What matters is the conceptual framework within which the basic work of building roads, schools, and dams is cast. For Castillo Armas, the primary endeavor was to find an interpretation of development policy which would create a broad consensus beyond existing factional ideologies. Through adopting a moderate position, carefully expressed as consistent with the aspirations of the Revolution and thoroughly saturated with nationalism, he sought this end. Furthermore, the policy was consistent with the desires of U.S. foreign policy in that period, providing thereby political buttressing for Castillo Armas in the favor of the great power to the north, and in the implicit promise of substantial aid for the development program of the administration.

CONCLUSIONS

Politics is the art of the possible. Latin America differs fundamentally from many of the new nations of Africa and Asia in that the traditional power holders have not withdrawn, but remain a vital part of the political system. The new leaders, the fervent interpreters of the revolution of rising expectations in this area, have a fundamental political choice to make. To make their program effective, they must either destroy their political competitors when their policies come in conflict with the interests of the dominant groups, as seems to be the case in Cuba, or seek to accommodate and reconcile the interests of these dominant groups within their programs.

The three approaches to development policy described above reflect the use of development policy as a political tool—as an instrument of consensus building. These examples are not atypical nor, it would seem, restricted to Central America alone. The remarks that apply to them could fit equally well many of the political movements that have emerged in Latin America in recent years.

At the outset, two distinct political purposes served by development policy were identified. First, such policies are used to "aggregate" consent, to create mass electoral support behind the leadership of a political movement. Generally, the leaders of the new political movements come from outside the traditionally dominant groups in the society. To win political influence, they turn to a virtually untapped source of political power in these societies, the support of the mass majority. To mobilize this support, a core group of dedicated adherents is required. This party nucleus is drawn from the highly politicized middle sectors. Student and professional groups play a significant role. This would seem the primary audience of the sophisticated, often quite idealistic statements on development policy which usually appear early in the movement's life.

However, to gain political influence in Central America, a new movement must do more than win mass support for the program of its leaders. It must reckon with the established power of the dominant groups in the society. The political success of a new movement in the subtle and often sinister game of Central American politics depends to a large extent on its ability to win the acceptance, or at least the neutrality, of these dominant groups. In their evaluation of a new political movement, these established power holders must weigh carefully the adjustments necessary in view of the new political climate in their nations against the threat the new movement poses to their privileged position in the existing order.

No more striking example of the impact of this "legitimatizing" of a new political movement is available than the overthrow of the Arbenz government in Guatemala. As long as the Guatemalan revolution pursued an essentially moderate course, the established groups did not seriously threaten its dominance. But the overthrow of the regime was swift once an agrarian reform policy threatened the position of the landholding groups and the establishment of a "worker's militia" threatened that of the army. It is noteworthy that no other major political movement in Central America has seriously advocated an agrarian reform which would involve division of existing holdings.

Thus, to win and retain political influence, new political movements must reconcile their development policies with the interests of established groups. The doctrinaire calls to action and reform of an earlier day are moderated. Figueres' "welfare state" policy becomes advocacy of a "mixed economy." *PRUD*'s "social revolution" is transformed into the "controlled revolution." Castillo Armas carefully describes a moderate course for Guatemalan development.

The formulas devised to achieve the reconciliation of dominant interests on development policy are remarkably similar. In part, of course, this is because they borrow heavily from the advice and recommendations of economic theorists interested in development questions and economic missions from the advanced nations.[10] The goals of these development policies are increased productivity through inputs of technology and scientific technique, capital, and investment in basic public services. Basically, the state will act to create the infrastructure of development and to direct the allocation of capital resources. Direct productive activities will be left in the hands of private enterprise.

From an economic point of view, such policies may minimize the "costs" inherent in the development effort. In view of the Central American political system, this "formula" may represent the only feasible alternative for a new political movement. But the apparent merits of the moderate approach to development policy must not blind us to the problems that are inherent in it.

The mass support for these new movements was in large part won through the promise of immediate and dramatic results in the struggle for a higher standard of living and a better way of life. To win the support of the middle sectors, so vital in the creation of an effective party organization, the development effort was cast in an heroic mold. Through formal statements of "political doctrine" and through partisan activity, something of the fervor of a holy crusade was brought to the idea of economic and social development.

While the expectation of great undertakings brought mass support and consequently political influence to the leaders of these new movements, the conditions of political survival in these societies required them to moderate their development policy intentions. In this latter task they were, as has been seen, at times remarkably resourceful. Yet their efforts to win acceptability as contenders for power may have jeopardized the popular backing which had originally brought them to play a significant role in political affairs. For gradual achievements and a moderate approach have not succeeded in satisfying the adherent of a movement which has pledged a "social revolution" through development programs. The "utopia" described to stimulate dedicated partisan activity pales when political necessity requires that it be squared with the prevailing "ideology." Among the perpetually restless political activists of Central America, new political formulas are sought which promise more striking results. The Cuban Revolution has appeal for some, but the ferment is in fact much broader.

Nonetheless, the achievements of the political leaders discussed herein are not to be despised. The skill with which they used the political instrument of development policy did bring a modicum of political stability, economic progress and social reform to Central America during the past decade. However, it is apparent that the development policies they devised did not "solve" Central America's politico-economic problems. New conditions and events will require new "formulas" of development policy in this region of rapid and often turbulent change. As they appear, it is essential that they be evaluated not only in terms of their consistency or inconsistency with the ideological commitments of the world's great powers, but also in terms of their ability to cope with the complex environments for which they are proposed.

1. The term is used here in the context developed by Gabriel Almond in Gabriel Almond and James Coleman, *The Politics of the Developing Areas* (Princeton: Princeton University Press, 1960), pp. 38 ff.

2. Figueres, *Address to the Third Stanford University Conference on Latin America*, July, 1951 (mimeo). Copy in possession of *Partido Liberación Nacional*.

3. Figueres, *Cartas a un ciudadano* (San José: Imp. Nacional, 1956), p. 52; *Diario de Costa Rica* (San José), July 16, 1948.

4. Herein, this movement is identified by the initials of the *Partido Revolucionario de Unificación Democrática*. This designation, although convenient, does not really do justice to the nature or composition of the movement. The PRUD was actually the instrument used by the leaders of the movement to stimulate middle sector and mass support for a government structured primarily on the basis of other power factors.

5. According to Salvadorian tradition, some "fourteen families" are said to control the nation's economic life. Actually, the number of groups which should be included is a subject of some dispute. There is some evidence to indicate that about 30 such "clans" control over 50 percent of the national income. *Hispanic American Report*, 6 (December, 1953), p. 13.

6. The tone of "social revolution" carries through virtually all *Prudista* writings. See, for example, José María Lemus, *Mensajes y Discursos* (San Salvador: Imp. Nacional, Vol. 1, 1957, Vol. II, 1958); Óscar Osorio, *Mensaje: 14 Septiembre de 1951* (San Salvador: Imp. Nacional, 1951); Elodoro Ventocilla, *Lemus y la revolución Salvadoreña* (Mexico: Edic. Latinoamerica, 1956); Republica de El Salvador, *El Ejercita, brazo armado del pueblo* (San Salvador: Imp. Nacional, 1949); *Justica social en Salvador* (San Salvador: Imp. Nacional, 1949); *Por qué soy Revolucionario* (San Salvador: Imp. Nacional, 1954?); *Viaje a una Revolución* (San Salvador: Imp. Nacional, 1953); PRUD, *Manual doctrinario de Prudisto* (San Salvador: PRUD, 1952); and the *Plan de gobierno* (San Salvador: PRUD, 1950?).

7. On the events of 1932, see: Jorge Schlesinger, *Revolución Comunista* (Guatemala: Unión Tipográfica Castañeda Avila y Cia, 1946); Joaquim Mendez h., *Los sucesos comunistas en El Salvador* (San Salvador: Funes y Ungo, 1932).

8. See Arbenz's inaugural address, reprinted in *El Imparcial* (Guatemala), March 15, 1951. See also his essays in Estrella de Centroamerica, *Transformación económica de Guatemala* (Guatemala: Tip. Nacional, 1951).

9. The best discussion of the relationship between Arbenz and the Communist Party is found in Ronald Schneider, *Communism in Guatemala: 1944–1954* (New York: Praeger, 1959).

10. See the similarities between the development policies of the movements cited herein and such documents as: United Nations, Technical Assistance Administration, *Proposals for the Further Economic Development of El Salvador* (New York: United Nations, 1954); International Bank for Reconstruction and Development, *The Economic Development of Guatemala* (Washington: The Bank, 1951). Figueres' close association with such noted figures of North American economic thought as John Kenneth Galbraith and A. A. Berle should also be noted.

BRIDGING THE GAP BETWEEN THE ELITE
AND THE PEOPLE IN THE PHILIPPINES

JOSE V. ABUEVA

Graduate School of Public Administration
University of the Philippines

This is an attempt to analyze "the gap between the elite and the people" in the Philippines and the experience in "bridging" that gap during the administration of Ramon Magsaysay (1954–1957).

By definition, the "elite" have decisive influence over the allocation of wealth, prestige, and other values of society. In Harold Lasswell's terms, the elite decide "who gets what, when, how"; the rest are "mass." [1] In this paper I shall stick to the dichotomy of "elite" and "people" suggested by the panel chairman. I shall use "elite" interchangeably with "political leaders," especially, but not exclusively, elective officials at the top of the governmental hierarchy. [2] Occasionally, I shall use the term "aspiring elite" [3] in referring to those who are in, or competing for, elite positions, but who do not generally belong to the social class or groups from which the elite have been traditionally recruited in the country.

I shall assume that the gap between the elite and the people has several dimensions: income and wealth, education, social class and prestige, access to political power, influence, expectations regarding role and behavior, access to social services and community facilities, and mobility of persons, ideas and information. The total gap is thus a combination of objective and subjective factors which is theoretically measurable. However, limitations of data and space prevent an analysis involving all these factors.

Significantly, both political ideology and religion in the Philippines formally aim to "bridge the gap between the elite and the people." "The general welfare," "justice," "liberty," and "democracy" are declared constitutional ideals that are to be pursued within a framework of republicanism and presidential government. [4] The Constitution specifically commits the state to *the pro-motion of social justice to insure the well-being and economic security of all the people. . . .* [5] What "social justice" guarantees, according to the Supreme Court, are "equality of opportunity, equality of political rights, equality before the law, equality between values given and received, and equitable sharing of the social and material goods on the basis of efforts exerted in their production." [6] Catholicism, the preponderant religion, supports the principle of social and economic equality and active citizenship as a fitting condition for the brotherhood of men under Christ. Yet, in the Philippines, as elsewhere, the closing up or the widening of the multidimensional gap between the elite and the people is a complicated process variably influenced by social, economic and political change.

I. MEASURES OF THE GAP

Although my main objective is to present the experience of the Magsaysay administration in trying to bridge the gap between the elite and the people, I believe it is useful to view that experience not only in relation to the gap *then* but also in the perspective of the *present* gap. For nothing depicts the continuing gap so sharply as to indicate its present dimensions, after the Magsaysay administration and succeeding administrations had endeavored to narrow it.

The Elite and the Aspiring Elite

Historically, Filipino political leadership has been tied up with wealth, education and social prestige in the local community or region. The first local officials and the delegates to the Philippine Assembly in 1907 were the nation's local notables, landed gentry and intelligentsia. Property qualifications for suffrage in the early years

From *Philippine Journal of Public Administration* (October 1964), pp. 325–347. Reprinted by permission. Some sections have been omitted.

ensured the dominance of the landed aristocracy. Wealth based on land, and the
education and family social prestige that
went with it, continued to be the most important basis for political power throughout
the first four decades of American rule
(1898–1941), despite widening opportunities for professional education and practice, government service, town politics, and
business.

After the war, some new political personalities rose from the ranks of guerrilla
leaders who turned their personal following and "backpay" into political capital,
and from among successful buy-and-sell operators, professionals (mostly lawyers and
doctors), prominent bureaucrats, and some
dealers in U.S. army surplus goods. But
national political leadership remained, by
and large, in the hands of wealthy landowners, some of whom had branched out
into urban real estate, logging, commerce
and manufacturing. The rising cost of getting elected and keeping in office favored
wealthy politicians, while not a few of
them used their political power to acquire
more wealth.

In general, the political elite may be
characterized as belonging to the upper
socio-economic levels, westernized in education and consumption tastes, residing in
urban areas, predominantly Christian, and
necessarily "transitional" (combining varying degrees of traditionality and modernity)
in their attitudes and behavior. They share
a common ideology which—with their high
incomes, their social status, and their over-
lap with the "economic elite"—makes them
essentially conservative. Among the nation's
highest leaders are members of the "aspiring elite" who came from the ranks of successful professionals, businessmen, and top
administrators; their strength lies in their
support by fellow middle-class members,
urban residents and awakened rural elements who look to them for progressive
ideas and reforms.

Role Expectations and Strains

Like most landlords and employers, the
elite are generally paternalistic in their attitudes towards those in lower stations,
their constituents and the people at large.
As stated earlier, however, their democratic
ideology and religion dispose them, in spite
of their economic interests and because of
competition from aspiring elite personalities, to favor increasing welfare programs
and social services, and occasional reforms.
But this desire is often contradicted by the
elite's reluctance to impose or pay taxes, or
to give substance to public policy through
vigorous implementation. Consequently,
elaborate social justice measures and reforms are often symbolic of outward intentions rather than descriptive of palpable
realities.

Politicians and other upper class persons
are still expected to act as patrons, especially in the rural areas: "to make substantial contributions toward community projects and provide leadership in community
activities; to give advice to their less secure
neighbors and assist them in their dealings
with government officials." [7] In times of
distress or calamity, they are called upon
to open their homes to relatives and tenants
of the lower class. "They act as godparents
and sponsors at the baptisms and weddings
of selected lower-class persons, and by virtue of the alliances thus established they
may feel obliged to assist them in obtaining education and jobs. . . . In return, a
member of the lower class is expected to
show deference to upper class persons and
in particular to his benefactor; to provide
him with small services as cargo handler,
odd-job-man, cook and servant when he
entertains; to vote for his candidate at election time." [8] Frank Lynch suggests that this
two-class system—an economically secure
upper class and an economically insecure
and dependent lower class—is prevalent in
rural areas and small towns.[9]

In Central Luzon, where tenancy coupled with absentee landlordism has always
been high, John J. Carroll observes that
the mutual support between the upper and
lower classes has been breaking down. As
evidence he refers to the chronic agrarian
unrest there which blew up into a full scale
rebellion under Communist leadership from
1946 to 1953, and to the fact that leasehold is gradually being favored over share
tenancy. Moreover, while plantation workers, e.g., in sugar lands of Negros, have
been unionized,[10] in other old provinces
which used to be tenancy areas the breaking up of smaller farms due to inheritance
practices and investments in education have
also created a void in the relationship between the tenants and landlords which politicians have tried to fill.

In the urban areas much of the traditional relationship between the social classes persists, as between a family and its servants, employers and employees, senior and junior executives, political leaders and followers.[11] But many among the new urban (upper) middle class, who are achievement-oriented, now reject or minimize the traditional upper class role expected of them.[12] Those of the (lower) middle class —office and factory workers—tend to unionize rather than to depend entirely, as "clients," on the paternalism of their employer.[13] Carroll also notes "a growing urban proletariat of the unemployed and casually employed, beggars, squatters, and petty criminals. Economically insecure, they rely on the protection of local politicians whom they repay by their votes, or as beggars on the traditional 'generosity' of upper class persons, on the bribery of the police and threats of violence." [14]

Other Indicators of the Gap

Out of a labor force of 10,692,000 in 1962, 5,768,000 (53.9%) were employed in agriculture, 3,535,000 (33%) in "non-agriculture," and 377,000 (3.5%) in "others"; the unemployed were 1,012,000, or roughly 9.5 percent. The per capita national income in the same year was estimated at ₱360.00 (US-$95.00).[15]

Table 1 shows the distribution of families and total family income by income class in February 1962. The concentration of wealth is shown in the following figures: more than 25 percent of the total family income was in the hands of a meager 4 percent of all families; 76.1 percent of all families earned less than ₱2,000, and together they earned only 39 percent of total family income.

Moreover, other data show that the 34 percent of all families who live in urban areas earn 56 percent of total family income, whereas the 66 percent of all families who live in the rural areas earn only 44 percent of total family income. The high concentration of income and wealth in Metropolitan Manila is suggested by the fact that the 8.15 percent of all families who reside there earn as much as 21.65 percent of total family income.

A different view of the concentration of income is suggested by table 2, which shows the distribution of employed persons by major occupation group and by weekly earnings, in May 1956. About 61

TABLE 1

DISTRIBUTION OF FAMILIES AND OF TOTAL FAMILY INCOME BY INCOME CLASS, APRIL 1962

	Philippines	
Income Class	Families	Income
Total (thousands)	4,426	7,981,766
Percent	100.0	100.0
₱10,000 and over	1.4	15.3
₱ 8,000 to ₱9,999	0.7	3.4
₱ 6,000 to ₱7,999	1.9	7.1
₱ 5,000 to ₱5,999	1.8	5.5
₱ 4,000 to ₱4,999	2.4	5.8
₱ 3,000 to ₱3,999	5.0	9.4
₱ 2,500 to ₱2,999	4.1	6.2
₱ 2,000 to ₱2,499	6.7	8.3
₱ 1,500 to ₱1,999	12.0	11.5
₱ 1,000 to ₱1,499	17.8	12.2
₱ 500 to ₱ 999	29.3	12.0
Under ₱500	17.0	3.3

SOURCE: Table 3, "Family Income and Expenditures: April, 1962," *Philippine Statistical Survey of Households Bulletin*, Series No. 14 (Jan., 1964).

percent of all employed persons, who were in the group of "farmers, farm laborers, fishermen and related workers," received a median average weekly earning which was from about one-half, to one-fifth, to one-seventh of the earnings of other much smaller occupation groups.

Despite the restraints upon it, the Philippines is a fairly open society. Opportunities for upward social and economic mobility are being gradually afforded by education, business, the professions, the bureaucracy, politics, the military, and to a lesser extent, the labor unions. On account of the more rapid social, economic and political changes taking place in the urban areas, particularly in Manila, opportunities for improving one's status, and the belief that one can rise through achievement, are much greater there than in rural areas where two-thirds of the population live and work.

The disparity in opportunities between urban and rural areas is, of course, illustrated by discrepancies in health, education and other welfare services and in infrastructure facilities such as roads and power.

TABLE 2

DISTRIBUTION OF EMPLOYED PERSONS BY MAJOR OCCUPATION GROUP AND
WEEKLY EARNINGS OF WAGE AND SALARY WORKERS (MAY 1956)

Occupation Groups	Percent Distribution	Median Average Weekly Earning
Managers, Administrators and Officials	4.1	₱44.30
Professional, Technical and Related Workers	2.4	37.00
Clerical, Office and Related Workers	2.0	28.90
Workers in Operating Transport Occupations	1.9	21.70
Workers in Mine, Quarry and Related Workers	2.0	20.90
Craftsmen, Factory Operatives and Related Workers	13.5	17.40
Manual Workers and Laborers	2.4	16.00
Service and Related Workers	6.4	11.90
Salesmen and Related Workers	5.4	10.20
Farmers, Farm Laborers, Fishermen and Related Workers	60.7	6.70
Occupation not reported	9.0	24.50
	100.0	

SOURCE: Charts III and IV, *Philippine Statistical Survey of Households Bulletin,* Series No. 1,
Vol. 1 (Manila, Jan., 1957), pp. 12 and 13.

Even greater is the gap between the urban elite and middle class on the one hand and the so-called cultural minorities, the Moslems and hill-peoples in tribal areas, on the other, despite the increasing institutional contacts between the latter and the lowland Christians.

Rural Philippines, Early Post-War

Our generalized description of the contemporary elite vis-à-vis the other social strata is also generally true of the Philippines in the early 1950's, which is the focus of our attention. In explanation, it should be stated that, although certain aspects of the gap have been alleviated, the increase in population by at least five millions, the faster economic development and the concentration of wealth in the Manila area, and the fragmentation of farms due to inheritance have tended to "freeze" the stratification of Filipino society.

In the words of a report of the International Bank for Reconstruction and Development: "Real wages in the cities appear to have declined since the mid-fifties, and evidence does not point toward significant increases in the real income of the larger part of the rural population during the same period. Income distribution is probably more uneven by now than a de-

cade ago. The present per capita income of some $130 in 1962 is the average for the whole 30 million population; over 80 percent live in the villages (*barrios*) where average incomes are probably not much more than half the national average." [16]

Now, we need to highlight the conditions in the rural areas that led to social reform and intensified rural development activities during the Magsaysay administration (1954–1957).[17]

The once well-publicized and controversial Hardie Report of 1952 summarized the problems of the *barrio* (the village community) economy that were at the root of rural poverty and agrarian unrest, as follows:

(1) The smallness of farms acts to limit potential gross income. As a national average, the tillable land area per farm is three hectares. Farms containing less than two hectares of tillable land, constituting more than one-half of the total farms, occupy less than one-fifth the tillable land area.

(2) Tenant frequency is high, averaging about 35 percent for the nation as a whole and soaring to nearly 68 percent in those areas where unrest is greatest.

(3) Farm rentals are oppressive. Most tenants pay 50 percent of the gross product

(after planting and harvest costs) as rent.

(4) Net family incomes derived from farm operations are woefully inadequate for a decent standard of living. Farm income from outside sources is insignificant.

(5) Interest paid by tenants on borrowed money is grossly onerous. Rates of 200 percent and even higher are common. The majority of small farmers borrow regularly from year to year.

(6) A lack of adequate and economic storage, marketing and buying facilities forces farmers to sell in a low price market and buy in a high.

(7) Guarantees against ruinous prices are nonexistent.

(8) The development of institutions conducive to the growth and strengthening of democratic tendencies has long been neglected in the rural areas.[18]

Earlier, in 1950, the Bell Report had pointedly described the Filipino farmer as being caught "between two grindstones. On top is the landlord . . . beneath is the deplorably low productivity of the land he works." [19] Aggravating social tension was the rise in the people's material aspirations, as a consequence of increasing contacts with town and city, without an increase in their incomes and in their expectations for amelioration.

On the whole, even the barrios most favored by local politicians received little assistance in the form of roads, drinking water, irrigation, medical services, credit, and agricultural advice. The reasons adduced were inadequate funds, insufficient technical personnel, limited transportation facilities, the disinclination of official to travel in barrios (due, in part, to lack of travel support), inaccessibility of barrios, and shaky peace and order conditions.

Functional literacy, a quality needed for intelligent political participation, was estimated at 44.6 percent,[20] with almost two-fifths of persons 20 years or older not having gone to school at all. Some 76 percent of the rural people did not read newspapers; a majority of them relied principally on the barrio lieutenant (appointive village leader) and neighbors for information, and barely 5 percent regarded the radio as the best local source of news.[21]

Although the barrio people had a group consciousness that expressed itself in mutual help, as in farm work and in building the barrio schoolhouse, they lacked the legal authority to raise funds and the formal organization for regularly making authoritative decisions for the entire community. The failure of the government to meet essential community needs, the breakdown of law and order in many provinces, the abuses of law enforcement agents, the frequent reports of scandalous official corruption in Manila, and the wholesale frauds and terrorism in the 1949 presidential election undermined popular faith in the government.

The spread of the Huk rebellion beyond Central Luzon in 1949 and 1950 was symptomatic of the social, economic, and political gulf between the elite and the masses of the people. The Huks and Communists held sway over most of Central Luzon when night fell, and their Politburo members and agents were operating in Manila!

II. AWARENESS OF THE GAP

The pre-war "social justice program" of Manuel L. Quezon had led to the passage of enlightened laws and the formation of some agencies to govern relations between landlord and tenant, and between employer and employee. The Court of Industrial Relations (1936), which also handled tenancy cases,[22] and the National Land Resettlement Administration (1939) [23] were illustrative. By the end of 1946 the Rice Share Tenancy Act of 1933 [24] (with succeeding amendments) was declared in force throughout the country. The Minimum Wage Law was enacted in 1951.[25] A presidential relief and welfare agency was organized in 1948; [26] in 1949 the Bureau of Public Schools embarked on a nationwide Community Schools Program.[27] In 1952 the Bureau of Agricultural Extension [28] was established, and the Rural Bank Act and the Agricultural Credit and Cooperative Financing Act were passed.[29] The Magna Carta of Labor, replacing compulsory arbitration with collective bargaining, became law in 1953.[30] Mobile rural health units were organized in the Department of Health. As earlier stated, however, most of these measures were largely ineffective because of half-hearted implementation. A few were, of course, still in their infancy.

In 1952 three voluntary agencies concerned with rural reconstruction through community leadership and self-help were organized: the Philippine Rural Reconstruction Movement (PRRM), the Philippine Rural Community Improvement Society (PRUCIS), and the Community Centers of the National Movement for Free Elections (NAMFREL). . . . By 1953, therefore, some government agencies and citizen groups were visibly astir, helping to bring about increasing services to the rural areas and to catalyze community organization and self-help efforts.[31]

What were the forces behind the post-war crescendo of rural development programs and activities? the underlying concern of upper- and middle class, westernized leaders in the urban centers for their lower class, rural fellow-citizens? In my book, *Focus on the Barrio* (1959),[32] I pointed up seven interrelated factors:

(1) the spread of democratic values and the idea of social justice in a changing social structure;

(2) renewed agrarian and political unrest in Central Luzon which threatened the survival of the Republic, at a time when Communism was rampaging in China, Korea and Vietnam;

(3) the egalitarian attitudes born of wartime experiences of rural and urban people who were forced to live and survive together during a crisis (the experience made upper class members intimately familiar with rural conditions);

(4) post-war socio-economic studies of the rural areas, such as the cited Hardie Report, the Rivera-McMillan Report, and the Bell Report—through U.S. aid and technical assistance resulting from the latter, the U.S. Government was able to exert pressure for social and agrarian reform policy and for the improvement of public administration;

(5) and (6) the "experiments" in directed change in rural communities, partly aided by the influx of foreign ideas of "rural reconstruction" and "community development"—to the cited examples of the Community Schools Program, PRRM, PRUCIS, and Community Centers should be added the spread by the United Nations of the concept of "community development" as a national program; and

(7) the unprecedented and successful grass-roots presidential campaign of Ramon Magsaysay in 1953 in which he espoused the uplift of "the common man" as his rallying battle-cry and aroused the masses

to their potential for making and unmaking national politicians.

Contrary to the legend about Magsaysay's having suddenly brought about the elite's concern for the welfare of the barrio people, it is clear that there were many forces simultaneously at work. Yet, as I wrote in my book: "The unprecedented upsurge of official and urban interest in rural improvement cannot be understood apart from Ramon Magsaysay's brief and dramatic public life. Indeed the hallmark of his tenure as President was the Administration's active concern for the welfare of 'the common man' in the more than 19,000 barrios of the country." [33] . . .

Sensitive to the rural problems and the burgeoning rural development activities around him, Magsaysay dramatized the chasm between the living conditions of the elite in the urban areas and those he found in the barrios while campaigning. He introduced the myth of his humble origin, which his image-makers maximized. He invented the so-called "barrio-to-barrio" national campaign—shaking hands in marathon style, wearing a short-sleeve shirt and a native hat, delivering folksy speeches, jumping over ditches and fences, and short-circuiting the local political leaders in the urban centers.

Moreover, he had a nationwide group of middle class political organizers known as the Magsaysay-for-President Movement (MPM), and its women and student counterparts called the WMPM and the SMPM. Yet, as a realistic leader, Magsaysay also used traditional organizations: the Nacionalista Party and the splinter sugar-bloc faction of the Liberal Party that became the Democratic Party. So popular was he as an alternative to the old and ailing Quirino, an *Old Guard politico*, that Magsaysay was able to co-opt professionals and civic leaders connected with the NAMFREL, and to secure the backing of the Catholic Church and the Iglesia ni Kristo.

Magsaysay's colorful and penetrating campaign paid off handsomely. He won by the largest margin in the entire history of Filipino presidential elections, getting 68.9 percent of the votes against Quirino's 31.2 percent. He carried with him 48 of the 52 provinces, 25 of the 28 cities, and 940 of slightly more than a thousand towns. His widespread popularity helped to elect his vice-presidential running mate, Senator Carlos P. Garcia, all the eight NP-DP coalition candidates for the Senate, and 63 of the 100 NP-DP candidates for the House of Representatives. Significantly, also, the turnout of voters was almost 30 percent higher than in 1949.[34] Evidently, Magsaysay had been highly successful in electrifying the rural population and in giving them hope for a better government.

III. BRIDGING THE GAP
UNDER MAGSAYSAY

Lines of Communication

By word and action, Magsaysay constantly pointed to the rural population as the principal beneficiary of his administration. He was literal in implementing his campaign promise "to bring the government closer to the people." Breaking precedent again, he threw open the gates of his office and residence to hundreds of people and personally tried to attend to their particularistic needs. His first executive order created the President's Complaints and Action Committee (PCAC) which made it possible for thousands of people to cut official red tape and obtain the needed action of government agencies by sending a telegram for a mere ten centavos (5 cents).

He made frequent trips to the provinces and barrios and surprise visits to government offices, in which he often made on-the-spot decisions. Thrice, he held Cabinet meetings in the provinces. He often transmitted problems and instructions to his department and bureau heads by telephone. Following his personal example, administrators spent more time in the field. By using the far-flung military extensively, he was able to cut down delays in relaying orders and extending assistance to those in distress.

There were other symbols that made the people readily identify with him. There was the lingering campaign myth about his being the son of poor parents. Then he popularized the native *barong* which he began wearing, unbuttoned at the neck, at his inaugural. He renamed Malacañan Palace *Malacañang,* thus removing its colonial aura. On his orders he was to be addressed simply as *Mr. President,* no longer *His Excellency.* He even dignified the Ilocano *basi* (native wine) by offering it at his receptions for diplomats. The noticeable decrease in official graft and corruption, accentuated by Magsaysay's publication of his personal assets and his ban on official dealings with his family and relatives, was also a popular symbol of his honesty and integrity.

The conviction of two powerful politicians of the Quirino administration impressed the people immensely. These were: former Governor Rafael Lacson of sugar-rich Negros Occidental, for murder and terrorism in the 1951 election; and Oscar Castelo, Quirino's Secretary of Justice and concurrently Secretary of National Defense, as successor to Magsaysay, for complicity in a murder. Theretofore, it seemed improbable that men of their elite stature could be jailed at all.

Skill in utilizing public relations and propaganda was one of Magsaysay's advantages as Secretary of National Defense, as presidential candidate, and as President. Among his assets were, of course, his charismatic personality, his flair for drama, and his instinct for simple symbolism. Moreover, he had gathered around him an able propaganda staff, headed by Press Secretary J. V. Cruz. Sensing how greatly the press and radio had helped him rise to the presidency, Magsaysay continued to nurture, and even pamper, the gentlemen of the mass media. He kept his eyes and ears cocked to them, reacting almost instantly to their suggestions and criticisms. Naturally, this brightened his image of responsiveness to public opinion, which contrasted with that of some presidents. But it also led to wrong decisions and, perhaps, to a subtle distortion of news reporting. It seems that part of the disenchantment that some well-informed people felt with Magsaysay's leadership stemmed from the variance between fact and report.

Social Reform

Like many Filipino political leaders, Magsaysay was not consciously motivated by an articulated theory of social reform. Not being an intellectual, his approach to problems was eminently practical and pragmatic. His singular emphasis upon "uplifting the common man," especially the *tao* in the barrios, was essentially spurred by his compassion for him in his poverty and misfortune. Nevertheless, Magsaysay's leadership and administration became a hardy vehicle for intensified rural services and social reform policies.

Expansion of Rural Programs. To begin with, Magsaysay obtained funds to expand those programs and services in education, health, social welfare, credit, agricultural extension, and resettlement which Congress had already authorized. In addition, he secured legislative authority to float bonds to finance public works and economic development projects. Fulfilling specific election promises, he successfully launched a pre-fabricated schoolhouse program with the help of the army and an artesian wells program with the assistance of the Liberty Wells Association, a civic organization.

Resettlement. In his first year, 1954, Magsaysay replaced the disorganized Land Settlement and Development Corporation with the National Resettlement and Rehabilitation Administration. . . . By June 1956, NARRA had resettled 10,651 families, 5,914 of which came from areas of high tenancy.[35] In fiscal year 1956–57, it served 21,587 settler families in its 16 settlement projects.[36] NARRA provided the settlers with farm implements, work animals, livestock and poultry, seeds, water supply, schools, and subsistence aid. It surveyed and subdivided new land and issued patents. It even helped to organize community associations that undertook self-help projects.

Supplementing the NARRA was the army's EDCOR [37] resettlement project for ex-Huks and retired soldiers; but EDCOR's most important value was its political impact on the anti-Huk campaign. The fact that not more than 1,000 families were resettled (only 246 ex-Huks) and that it cost upwards of ₱10,000 to settle one family, despite the use of army personnel and equipment, limited EDCOR's contribution to colonization per se.[38]

To complement the resettlement program, Magsaysay also secured legislation in 1954 which created the Land Registration Commission and revised outmoded provision on land registration to expedite title issuance.[39] Moreover, he encouraged the U.S.-supported modernization of patent-processing in the Bureau of Lands, which resulted in a tremendous speeding

up of its works. The issuance rate of land patents jumped from 3,500 per year in 1952 to in excess of 46,000 in 1955.[40]

Farmers' Credit and Marketing. Congress expanded the revolving capital of the Agricultural Credit and Cooperative Financing Administration. Under Colonel Osmundo Mondoñedo, the agency's expanded operations during Magsaysay's administration are reflected in the following figures showing increases in: (1) Farmers Cooperative Marketing Associations (FACOMAs) organized, from 22 to 455; (2) membership, from 6,643 to 259,027; (3) geographic coverage, from 11 to 50 provinces and from 110 to 33,758 barrios; (4) authorized capital, from ₱1.3 million to ₱24.9 million; [41] (5) outstanding loans, from ₱4.1 million to ₱91.8 million.[42]

Aside from the economic benefits enjoyed by the farmers, their cooperatives gave them valuable experience in leadership and group action. This tended to undermine the traditional rural elite whose power had been based on credit and land ownership. By their election to FACOMA boards of directors, tenants and small landholders assumed posts that were considered only second in importance to the elective municipal positions.

FACOMA leadership was, in fact, a stepping stone to local politics, and in some places, vice versa. In David Wurfel's judgment: "Cooperatives showed themselves increasingly to be the most important focus of rural reintegration in a democratic pattern. Their ideal structure constituted democratic models for rural communities, but of more immediate national importance they provided the institutional framework for the strengthening of a vertical interest group [in Northern Luzon], tobacco . . . , as a counter to the long powerful sugar bloc." [43]

Land Reform. Because of partisan difficulties and Magsaysay's inexperience and insecurity, his early pronouncements on tenancy and land reform were not matched by timely and resolute legislative leadership. Consequently, the Agricultural Tenancy Act of 1954 was a watered-down version of its original and was not accompanied by a companion law that would have created a Court of Agrarian Relations.

The most formidable force behind this

political development was the resistance of landowning legislators and their allies. Nevertheless, the Act codified and clarified existing tenancy laws, detailed the rights and obligations of landlord and tenant, reduced the interest rates, reduced the creditor's liens on the tenant, and otherwise provided for its practical enforcement.[44] . . .

Magsaysay was deeply committed to land reform, but he was unable to obtain from the landlord-dominated Congress the kind of legislation he had initiated [until September, 1955]. . . . Experience since its passage has lent support to the opinion of Frank Golay that the Act was "unlikely to disturb existing land tenure relationship," because "the original interest of land reform [had] been circumvented by far-reaching congressional changes in administration proposals." [45]

Yet it should be stated that the passage of a land reform bill for the first time, weak though it was, evidenced the force of Magsaysay's popular leadership and the growing sensitivity of the national elite to probable peasant reactions, because it was conspicuous that the peasantry had exerted little direct influence on the legislators.

The effect of the land reform act on the peasantry and peasant unions was described by Frances Starner as follows:

Prior to its enactment, the barrio people, on the whole, had maintained an attitude of extreme skepticism toward government in general. If their morale was higher than it had been for many years, this was largely the result of the improved conditions of peace and order in the barrios and of the greater confidence of the people in the President. There had been little evidence in the past, however, that the government was concerned with improving their social and economic status, and their expectations here were slight. . . . This change in peasant attitudes was reflected in the peasant organizations, which found it almost impossible to resist the growing demands of their members for greater political involvement.[46]

From the perspective of later years, after a stronger land reform act (The Agricultural Land Reform Act) had been passed in 1963, the Land Reform Act of 1955 had been a strategic beachhead for agrarian reformers. . . .

Mobile Agrarian Court. The bill creating a Court of Agrarian Relations was also finally passed in 1955.[47] The Agricultural Tenancy Act of 1954 had merely continued the jurisdiction of the Court of Industrial Relations over tenancy disputes. In this prewar set-up the function had been ineffective, due to lack of funds and the inability of the tenants to support themselves in Manila during litigation, both of which evidenced the overwhelming power and advantage of the landlords over their tenants. Under the leadership of Guillermo Santos, who was promoted from ATC, the mobile and flexible CAR received 2,589 cases in its first year, which was more than the total cases filed with the tenancy division of the Court of Industrial Relations in the previous three years. More important, the CAR disposed of all the cases and some 300 back cases as well. Through vigorous action in the field—aided by less formal procedures, waiver of docket fees, and the policy of resolving doubts in favor of the tenant as embodied in the Land Reform Act of 1955—the CAR gained the tenants' confidence.[48]

Community Development. In addition to rural social services, agrarian reform, and agricultural development, "community development" received considerable impetus during Magsaysay's time. We have noted that when Magsaysay campaigned for the presidency in 1953 various governmental and voluntary agencies were already engaged in projects aimed at changing the barrio people themselves and at improving their livelihood and living conditions. The enthusiasm engendered by Magsaysay's accent on rural development naturally led to heightened, if uncoordinated, rural activity.[49] . . .

After a year's planning, with U.S. and U.N. assistance, Magsaysay abolished an inter-agency Community Development Planning Council and appointed a dedicated young lawyer, Ramon P. Binamira, as Presidential Assistant on Community Development.[50] Early in January 1956, the PACD began training multi-purpose community development workers who were later assigned to the barrios as agents of change: to train barrio leaders and to help them organize their village people for self-help community projects, to stimulate these projects with grants-in-aid and technical advice, and to aid in coordinating rural technical services.

Basically, PACD fieldmen, working with local leaders and government technicians, endeavored to change traditional rural attitudes of resignation and dependence on the government to active self-reliance and community self-help in developing local leadership, increasing food production and family income, improving health and sanitation, and constructing essential public facilities.

The PACD's far-reaching impact began to be felt after Magsaysay's death on March 17, 1957. A scientific measurement of its impact is still under way. Yet, many leaders and students have already attributed to the community development program part of: the noticeable assertiveness of local leaders, the growing rural self-help activities, and the increasingly discriminating judgment of the people in national elections. Because of its eroding effects on the traditional political structure in the villages, the community development program deserves some elaboration.

A significant achievement of the PACD relates to the formation and strengthening of elective barrio councils as the underlying structure of Philippine government. The election of a weak barrio council with merely recommendatory functions was made possible in 1956 by a law authored by Senator Tomas Cabili, a PRRM trustee.[51] Inasmuch as the PACD operated mainly through the barrio councils, it was eager to strengthen them. Thus the PACD helped to draw up a bill which Senator Emmanuel Pelaez, one of Magsaysay's most trusted advisers, initiated in Congress in 1959. Under the Barrio Charter,[52] the rural people, acting through their elective barrio councils, were authorized for the first time to raise contributions, receive a share of the property tax, and undertake projects without prior approval from higher authority. Up until 1964, PACD had assumed responsibility for administering barrio elections all over the country.

By 1963, barrio councils had undertaken 40,814 PACD-aided community development projects, such as pump and gravity irrigation systems, oyster beds, improved seed, poultry and swine, salt ponds, multipurpose centers, and drinking water systems. Some 1,000 kilometers of barrio feeder roads had been constructed.[53] As a rule, the barrio people contributed leadership, labor and materials amounting to at least half of the total costs of the projects. It has been through the barrio people's involvement in identifying their problems, planning and implementing projects, and generally in running their community affairs that the PACD has sought to realize its principal objective of changing values and attitudes. . . .

Economic Growth

In the three years from 1954, which bracketed Magsaysay's administration, the economy continued to expand: the index of physical volume of production increased by 25 percent, agricultural output by 20 percent, mining by 34 percent, and manufacturing by 40 percent. The growth in national income from 1954 to 1958 was substantially higher than the increase in population. . . . In Golay's overall appraisal:

The momentum of the Magsaysay political campaign served to unite the Philippine nation behind the new administration and established conditions favorable to rapid economic progress and social reform. These potentialities for progress were realized to a limited degree. The *élan* evident in the first two years of the administration was noticeably diminished in 1956, and there was increasing disillusionment and bitter political controversy both between Congress and the administration and within the administration.[54]

Political Organization

One of Magsaysay's most obstinate problems as a social reformer, apart from his inability to fully exploit his unbroken mass popularity, was the lack of strong elite support even within the Nacionalista-Democratic coalition. The reason for this lay in the structure of Filipino political organization. In socio-economic composition and in interests, the Nacionalista Party and the Democratic Party were no different from the vanquished Liberal Party.

. . . In a situation where most of the elite in all parties were generally of the same upper-class and conservative orientation, political struggle still centered on personal power considerations. In fact, at times Magsaysay seemed to enjoy more political backing from young Liberals than from the older Nacionalistas.

As Magsaysay confronted the clashing individual and group interests within the coalesced Nacionalista and Democratic parties, he found it necessary and advantageous to preserve his personal aggregation of young professionals, businessmen, and army officers. Moreover, he quietly befriended and shared his patronage with sympathetic Liberals. And, of course, his frequent contacts with the people in Malacañang and out in the provinces kept up his rapport with the masses, which, however, he only partially utilized for political leverage. Indeed, there were talks of forming a third party around Magsaysay.

Historically, peasant unions had suffered from economic, organizational and leadership problems. Their status under Magsaysay was assessed by Starner thus:

While there were apparently no legal guarantees that agrarian unions would continue to enjoy protected status, the positive encouragement and protection accorded them by the Magsaysay administration provided favorable conditions for immediate expansion of their activities. Indeed, the outlook for organized agrarian activity looked fairly bright in 1955, for not only was there reasonable assurance that the unions would enjoy the protection of President Ramon Magsaysay for another six years, but also it seemed likely that they would succeed in consolidating their position substantially during this period. . . . By the fall of 1955, many of the agrarian unions were being pressed by their members into more active cooperation with the President and into increased participation in his program.[55]

Although urban labor unions were generally stronger and better organized than the peasant unions, they had suffered from similar weaknesses. Like the political parties, labor leadership and political activity were highly personalized, with little common ideological content. Neither did labor as a group have a unifying class consciousness. As in the peasant unions, the leaders of labor unions were mostly middle class professionals, usually lawyers, whose ambition was to belong to the new elite group. Nevertheless, labor groups were politically behind Magsaysay. The record of the Department of Labor, under the leadership of Colonel Eleuterio Adevoso, the young former head of the Magsaysay-for-President Movement, showed a marked improvement in the implementation of labor laws, in the number of unions organized, in the volume of cases adjudicated, and

in the amounts therefrom awarded to labor unionists.[56]

One outstanding contribution of Magsaysay to political change was his encouragement of upper- and lower-middle class elements, many of them from outside of the regular parties—the young professionals and businessmen and military men, farmers and labor leaders—to join the government service and to direct their interest to social reforms. Magsaysay co-opted these young leaders into his personal political alliance.

The ensuing years have revealed some consequences of the entry or ascendancy of these new elements in the political system. These new elements have never been systematically studied, but at least their numbers, particularly in local politics, are considerable. Among the newer crop of local leaders are professionals, businessmen, former FACOMA officers, former elected barrio lieutenants, and a few community development officers. Some of Magsaysay's "fair-haired boys" now occupy strategic places in national politics.

IV. CONCLUDING OBSERVATIONS

In conclusion, here are my observations regarding the gap between the elite and the people and the experience in trying to bridge that gap during Magsaysay's time.

(1) Even our imprecise analysis of the gap between the elite and the people suggests striking differentials in incomes, levels of living, education, status, access to information and community facilities. Inasmuch as these differentials also constitute political resources, a differential in the chances of gaining power is also evident. However, the social structure assigns appropriate roles to members of each group and allows for upward socio-economic mobility by lower- and middle class persons. Thus, to the extent that Philippine society is open and that mutual aspirations and expectations are satisfied, aspiring elite are possible and mass alienation and radicalism are prevented.

(2) "Bridging the gap between the elite and the people" has a certain circularity in its dynamics. The redistribution of economic and social opportunities depends upon the effective political participation of the awakened but still weakly organized rural people, in alliance with the aspiring

elite (and liberal elite members) and the urban middle class. Yet, unless the fruits of economic development are increasingly shared by the rural people in particular, they will not be able to free themselves from dependence on the traditional elite, much less articulate and enforce demands for favorable public policy. Population growth and the concentration of wealth and economic growth in urban centers tend to counteract the gains in narrowing the gap.

(3) Popular attitudes toward the President and the ruling party and towards the government that they personify in the public mind are an important dimension of the elite-people gap. On the whole, economic growth under Quirino was probably faster than under Magsaysay, partly because, under Quirino, the country had just gone over the hump of post-war reconstruction. But, the people were strongly against Quirino's administration and strongly favorable to Magsaysay's administration. It seems that when people emotionally identify with a charismatic President and his ameliorative programs, the psychological gap tends to lessen, at least temporarily, the social and economic gap in their relations with the elite. And this phenomenon also seems to obtain as between the local elite and the people.

In the Philippines, where, historically, government has been regarded as a remote, exploitative and repressive institution identified either with a colonial power, as under Spanish rule, or with a grudgingly attentive *cacique* elite, Magsaysay's success in "bringing the government closer to the people" cannot be overestimated. Some urban intellectuals do not fully appreciate this condition.

(4) Rural services and development programs expanded considerably under Magsaysay. His administration introduced new institutional bridges to reach the barrio people, such as the PCAC, the PACD, the Court of Agrarian Relations and the Agricultural Tenancy Commission. As I concluded elsewhere:

Under him the barrio took the limelight and its folks were "dignified" by the personal attention which he, and others through his example, lavished upon them. The ameliorative resources of the State were channeled into the barrio; and although their ultimate effects may have

been negligible or even nil with respect to many particular villages, the flow of public services in their direction was unmistakable.[57]

(5) Despite Magsaysay's penchant for political paternalism and direct action, his administration made progress by introducing or supporting policies and programs aimed to develop the people's self-reliance and initiative, as in the ACCFA and the self-help community organizations of the Bureau of Public Schools and the Bureau of Agricultural Extension. Most significant was the launching of the community development program of the PACD.

In many of these programs, Magsaysay was not the real innovator, nor did he always understand their implications. But his known concern for barrio people and his official support made it possible for several forceful and imaginative leaders, mostly in their early thirties, to develop their programs. The hospitable climate likewise encouraged the growth of modern institutions for improving public administration and economic research. . . .

(6) By far the most important achievement of Magsaysay was in his role as catalyst of political change. As Secretary of National Defense, he successfully led the government's anti-Huk campaign and helped keep the 1951 elections free and honest. For both accomplishments he regained the citizens' faith in their government.

Magsaysay's concern for the welfare of the common man left an indelible impression on all people and politicians. After him, for instance, the political campaign style has never been the same. The people have come to expect to see and hear and personally "appraise" the candidates, who have to stump in the "grass-roots," pledge rural progress, and identify with the rural people to win votes. The influence of Magsaysay's concern for the "common man" and his accent on official honesty permeate the thinking of contemporary politicians and the platforms of both major parties. . . .

Moreover, Magsaysay set in faster motion some forces that undermined the historic dominance of the landholding, conservative elite: the farmers, cooperatives and elective barrio councils; rural services and the beginnings of agrarian reform; and the shortcircuiting of the local elites and the political awakening of the mass voter through direct channels by Magsaysay himself. In the long run, the new middle class leaders, or the aspiring elite, have been and will continue to be the most effective agents of political change. Among the nation's highest leaders now are those who bear the stamp of Magsaysay, his "political heirs" so to speak. . . .

The emerging political combination that has already made irreversible inroads into the traditional political structure consists of the progressive leaders, such as those mentioned above, their urban middle class allies, and the once quiescent masses whose awareness of their power to elect local and national leaders of their choice Magsaysay had excited. Even the traditional landowning politicians have found it vital to court the rural voters to retain their power. The expansion and diversification of the economy has been creating strong, competing pressure groups among the economic elite and certainly between the traditional elite and the aspiring elite. This development should contribute to a political competition increasingly based on policy, even as parties continue to be personality-oriented for many years to come. Other social and technological agents of social change are also contributing to the changing political structure.

But again, this caveat: as long as peasants and laborers are not more economically secure and better organized to support the new national leaders in extracting reforms from the traditional powerholders, the mass leverage needed for sustained success in effecting social and fiscal reforms and promoting economic development will not be fully realized.

1. *Politics: Who Gets What, When, How* (New York: McGraw-Hill Book Co., Inc., 1936).

2. I have used the legislators as the main basis of my concise analysis of the elite. As a group, the 24 nationally-elected senators and the 104 district-elected representatives truly represent the politico-economic elite, because they make up a large part of the national political elite and several of them also belong to the economic elite. I have analyzed the political elite more intensively in my paper, "Social Backgrounds and Recruitment of Legislators and Administrators in a Developing Country: The Philippines," presented at the UNESCO Symposium on Leadership and Authority, Singapore, December 1963.

3. I borrowed the term "aspiring elite" from David Wurfel, "The Bell Report and After: A Study of the Political Problems of Social Reform Stimulated by Foreign Aid" (Ph.D. dissertation, Cornell University, 1959).

4. Preamble to the *Constitution of the Philippines.*

5. *Ibid.,* Art. II, Sec. 5.

6. *Guido vs. Rural Progress Administration,* G.R. No. L-2089, Oct. 21, 1949; 47 O.G. 1848; XV. L.J., 221.

7. Frank Lynch, *Social Class in a Bikol Town* (Chicago, 1959), *passim,* as cited in John J. Carroll, *Changing Patterns of Social Structure in the Philippines, 1896–1963,* UNESCO Research Center, 1963 (preliminary draft), Chap. 11, pp. 3, 4.

8. *Loc. cit.*

9. *Ibid.,* Chap. 11, p. 2.

10. Carroll, *op. cit.,* Chap. 11, p. 4.

11. *Loc. cit.*

12. *Ibid.*

13. *Ibid.*

14. *Ibid.*

15. Program Implementation Agency, *A Prospectus on the Philippine Economy,* Oct., 1963, p. 4.

16. "The Economic Situation and Prospects of the Philippines," Jan. 6, 1964, Chap. 1, Para. 3.

17. Much of the data on rural problems were taken from J. V. Abueva, *Focus on the Barrio* (Manila: U.P. Institute of Public Administration, 1959), pp. 11–31.

18. Robert S. Hardie and Associates, *Philippine Land Tenure Reform: Analysis and Recommendations* (Manila: STEM/MSA, 1952), pp. v–vi.

19. *Report to the President of the United States,* by the Economic Survey Mission to the Philippines, 1950.

20. John E. de Young, *A Pilot Study on Communincation Problems on the Barrio Level* (Quezon City: U.P. Community Development Research Council, 1955), p. 96.

21. *Ibid.,* p. 82.

22. C.A. No. 103, Oct. 29, 1936.

23. C.A. No. 441, June 3, 1939.

24. Act No. 4054, Feb. 27, 1933.

25. R.A. No. 602, April 6, 1951.

26. The Social Welfare Commission, then the President's Action Committee on Social Amelioration.

27. Bureau on Public Schools, *"A Report on the Community School Projects in Public Schools,"* Sept. 2, 1955.

28. R.A. No. 680, April 24, 1952.

29. R.A. No. 720, June 6, 1952; R.A. No. 821, Aug. 14, 1952.

30. R.A. No. 875, June 17, 1953.

31. A summary account of rural develop-

ment activities during the administration of President Quirino and of President Magsaysay is found in Abueva, *op. cit.,* Chap. 4.

32. *Ibid.,* Chap. 2.

33. *Ibid.,* p. 34.

34. Frances Starner, *Magsaysay and the Philippine Peasantry* (Berkeley and Los Angeles: University of California Press, 1961), p. 62.

35. NARRA, *Annual Report* for FY 1956.

36. NARRA, *Annual Report* for FY 1957.

37. Economic Development Corps.

38. Frank H. Golay, *The Philippines: Public Policy and National Economic Development* (Ithaca, N.Y.: Cornell University Press, 1961), p. 284, citing Margaret Ruth Harris Pfanner, "Postwar Land Colonization in the Philippines" (M.S. thesis, Cornell University, 1958), p. 80.

39. R.A. No. 1151, June 17, 1954.

40. Golay, *op. cit.,* p. 283.

41. ACCFA, *Annual Report* for FY 1957.

42. Golay, *op. cit.,* p. 90.

43. Wurfel, *op. cit.,* p. 786.

44. Starner, *op. cit.,* pp. 140–141.

45. Golay, *op. cit.,* p. 275.

46. Starner, *op. cit.,* pp. 198–199.

47. R.A. No. 1267, June 14, 1955, as amended by R.A. No. 1409, Sept. 9, 1955.

48. Golay, *op. cit.,* p. 400.

49. Abueva, *Focus on the Barrio,* Chap. 7.

50. *Executive Order* No. 156, Jan. 9, 1956.

51. R.A. No. 1408, Sept. 9, 1955.

52. R.A. No. 2370, June 20, 1959.

53. Community Development Division, USOM/AID, *op. cit.,* p. 2.

54. Golay, *op. cit.,* p. 95.

55. Starner, *op. cit.,* p. 105.

56. Department of Labor, *Annual Reports* for FY 1956 and 1957.

57. *Focus on the Barrio,* p. 34.

PART III

PROBLEMS
AND POLICIES OF
DEVELOPMENT

Above all, the economist must recognize clearly that political considerations dominate land reform. Always it involves restructuring patterns of wealth, income flow, social status and prestige. These are the raw materials of politics. It is almost a truism that pressures for land reform are predominantly political.   PHILIP M. RAUP [1]

INTRODUCTION

PROBLEMS of development, and the policies designed to cope with them, invariably involve economic, social, and political factors intricately connected, as Philip Raup's statement on land reform suggests.[2] An intelligent understanding of development problems and, even more, an effective set of policy actions require analysis that links the various factors—raw materials—of economic, social, and political production.

The observation that pressures for land reform are predominantly political will surprise few readers, but policy areas such as education and economic policy, which are often presented as relatively "non-political," are similarly thoroughly politicized, as we will indicate below. Benefits are distributed unevenly, and more likely than not in favor of those sectors already well-endowed with economic, social, and political resources; that is, unless there is some intervention to the contrary, mobilizing and employing resources through political processes to achieve some other outcome. As Raup and other authors below will show, "political" pressures are not necessarily undesirable with respect to development, contrary to the view of those who would regard such pressures as invariably un- or counter-productive. In the absence of these, policies will be shaped which utilize primarily the existing endow-

[1] "Land Reform and Agricultural Development," in H. M. Southworth and B. F. Johnston (eds.), *Agricultural Development and Economic Growth* (1967), p. 303.

[2] This statement comes from a section entitled "The Political Economy of Land Reform," which is subdivided appropriately into discussions of transportation and communication, the status of women, nationalism, and the political dimension as these bear on and are affected by land reform.

277

ments of land, labor, and capital and which consequently reward primarily their possessors.

Our purpose in Part III is to present a number of empirical and analytical contributions to the study of the political economy of development. Although the authors represent various disciplinary backgrounds, they all allow for the interaction of other factors in their analyses, giving tangibility to considerations of political economy. None have used our model explicitly, but their encounter with the realities of the Third World has led them to use the terms, categories, and concepts of political economy. In their exposition, they support, extend or modify the framework of analysis we have proposed.

Having offered our view of the political economy of development in the essay introducing Part II, we will do no more in this Part than introduce the various contributions, pointing to the elements of analysis exemplified or elaborated in each work. We have organized this Part around four policy areas of particular relevance to the political economy of development: land reform, education and employment, economic policy, and political and administrative infrastructure. Two are more substantive, dealing with the productive factors of land and information; two are more instrumental, concerning means for effecting changes in market integration or factor endowments.

Readers will find that these areas are not self-contained if viewed in political economy terms; many of the articles suggest how these areas impinge on one another, and some might have been placed in a different section than the one we put them in. There are many worthy pieces we should like to have included here but which we could not use if we were to adhere to our own rule of optimal ignorance, and because of limitations of space. We believe that the pieces presented below offer substantive and analytical perspectives on the political economy of development that demonstrate the validity and utility of the approach.

The
Political Economy
of Land Reform

•

WE WOULD begin by considering the relationship between land reform and development, first, because of the importance, already suggested, of the agricultural sector for economic, social, and political development, and, second, because land reform offers a clear demonstration of the salience of the four elements of development: market integration in its several aspects, increase and equalization of factor endowments for the many, organization of the underendowed, and entrepreneurship to effect economic, social, and political change. These all can contribute to a raising of levels of productivity, though we would add that we do not assume that land reform must necessarily (by definition) raise these levels.[1] In the final analysis, land reform contributes no more to development than the contribution it makes to increased aggregate productivity—the extent to which it enables more people to participate in and benefit from economic, social, and political processes.

This is not a book or even a whole chapter on land reform. We make no attempt to describe land reform as a phenomenon or to trace all of its many connections with the development process.[2] Rather we present several valuable analyses and instructive case studies that help to clarify the political economy of land reform.

The critique of economists' treatment of land reform offered by Philip Raup below could very well have been presented in Part II. His analysis, though starting from "economic" considerations, addresses broader organizational and structural issues associated with land reform. Raup clarifies the consequences of alternative structures of land tenure for productivity, emphasizing the distributional and factor endowment dynamics generally neglected, except with respect to the single factor of physical capital. Indeed, by elaborating the process of "accretionary" capital

[1] We would concur with the view of Peter Dorner and Don Kanel, Director and Associate Director, respectively, of the Land Tenure Center at the University of Wisconsin, that:

There is nothing inherently good or bad, right or wrong about land tenure systems as such. While ideological arguments on the best way of organizing agriculture continue, no tenure system can be adjudged best in the abstract. Any judgments concerning a particular system must take note of the institutional and technological conditions in the society and the stage at which that society lies in the transformation from an agrarian to an industrial economy. Our judgments should also consider what specific groups and individuals in that society are attempting to accomplish.

"The Economic Case for Land Reform," U.S. Agency for International Development, Spring Review of Land Reform, June 1970, p. 3.

[2] Readers wishing a more comprehensive overview of land reform are referred to Doreen Warriner's book, *Land Reform in Principle and Practice* (1969).

formation, in which underemployed resources are mobilized and utilized at the micro level, he improves our understanding of the role of capital in development of the agricultural and also other sectors. In the analysis he suggests the real possibility of periods of development without growth.

Given this broadened perspective on land reform, Raup points to the importance of nonphysical as well as physical forms of infrastructure, noting in particular the significance of human fixed capital formation. Not really by coincidence, his analysis touches upon the other policy areas considered below. One interconnection he considers is the impact of land reform on education through the intervening variable of economic policy; a more widely dispersed pattern of landholding provides a broader tax base, which makes increased educational expenditure politically more feasible, whereas taxes gathered primarily from a few large landowners are not likely to be used to educate the children of the many. Raup notes also that a different land tenure structure is more likely to generate information resources needed to make more realistic economic policies, once farmers' relationship to the bureaucracy is altered through land reform.

One principally "economic" point that Raup makes deserves to be highlighted. In countries where labor is relatively abundant and land relatively scarce—a condition common in underdeveloped countries—the objective should be to maximize output and income per unit of land, not necessarily per unit of labor as most economists trained in Western institutions and theories assume. This consideration has led a number of agricultural economists to find merit in land reform on purely economic grounds apart from any social or political benefits to be derived from it.[3] There are now a number of studies showing a consistent decline in yield per acre from larger landholdings in many countries. This suggests that there may be few or no significant economies of scale in agriculture with respect to inputs of land under many conditions.[4]

A political economist, of course, would not be satisfied with considering only economic factors, but neither would he minimize this finding. It has major implications for increasing levels of food production, aggregate economic income, and (especially from a political economy point of view) employment, at the same time income is distributed more widely and effective economic demand is directed more to domestically produced products. What the recent findings suggest is that political economists need not make apologies for land reform, arguing that economic costs are offset by social and political benefits, since under many circumstances there appear to be definite economic benefits as well.

To be sure, even if one is satisfied that land reform ought to be undertaken in a country, much needs to be known about the conditions under which it is likely (or most likely) to be successful. The analyses by Hung-Chao Tai and, in a later section, by John Montgomery deal, respectively, with some political and administrative conditions for achieving results in land reform. While two general strategies of

[3] See Dorner and Kanel, *op. cit.,* esp. pp. 23–31; and Folke Dovring, "Economic Results of Land Reforms," U.S. Agency for International Development, Spring Review of Land Reform, June 1970; also references given in these papers.

[4] See article by Raup, "Economies and Diseconomies of Large-Scale Agriculture," *American Journal of Agricultural Economics,* December 1969, pp. 1274–1283; also Don Kanel, "Size of Farm and Economic Development," *Indian Journal of Agricultural Economics,* 1967, pp. 26–44.

land reform can be outlined—reform from the bottom up and from the top down—the authors consider principally the effects of the latter. Where the many are well organized and have sufficient resources collectively, they may be able to carry out redistribution of land by themselves, as a consequence of political revolution or as an alternative to it. That this occurs so rarely can be explained in political economy terms; the weakness of the many, even in using violence effectively, stems from their underendowment and lack of organization. Those persons most in need of the benefits of self-initiated land reform are the least capable of initiating it. Therefore, if one does a comparative study of land reform attempts, one invariably examines the efforts of political and/or administrative elites.

Land reform efforts have been most effective where the elite sought to gain the resource of *legitimacy* from the most numerous sectors, according to Tai's study. Corollary motivations were the acquisition of the political currency of *support* and the avoidance of revolutionary *violence*. It is not clear how effective land reform is with respect to the latter or whether the support gained is more valuable than the costs of undertaking land reform (and of losing support from the landed sectors). It does appear, however, that a regime lacking legitimacy in the countryside has sufficient incentive to try to establish itself by, in effect, exchanging land for legitimacy, incurring whatever costs are involved in securing the land for redistribution.

A critical relationship which Tai extracts from his data is whether the regime elite is separated or alienated from the landowning sector or whether it is cooperative and conciliatory toward this sector. This relationship affects the means employed to acquire land as well as the speed and extent of acquisition; it also biases distribution policies toward emphasizing production more than equity, or vice versa. One "variable" which Tai proposes is elite commitment to reform, or "political will." This verges on tautology unless one sees it as a function of political conditions rather than as a purely subjective thing. One would expect more "political will" for reform where this is more profitable politically. Tai finds that land reform was diligently pursued where it could break the power of certain sectors opposed by or opposing the regime: in Iran, Taiwan, Mexico, and Egypt.[5] Land reform could not have been so politically profitable in Colombia, India, Pakistan, and the Philippines, given the regimes there and the composition of their core combination of sectors. "Political will" is thus not simply a matter of courage or conviction but is heavily overlaid with considerations of opportunities, alternatives, and costs. Entrepreneurship by political leaders, described in other words by Tai, is noted as a critical element in successful land reform, though it is not an autonomous one.

Both Tai and Montgomery (whose analysis is discussed later) emphasize the contribution of *organization* to successful land reform. For any degree of elite involvement in promoting land reform, this is more likely to achieve significant results if the peasants or farmers benefiting from it are organized. What this means is that the many are enabled to participate themselves in the land reform

---

[5] For a discussion of the Shah of Iran's political strategy behind his land reform program, see Richard Pfaff, "Disengagement from Traditionalism in Turkey and Iran," *Western Political Quarterly*, March 1963, pp. 79–98.

process. By pooling and directing their resources, however meager on a per capita basis, the many are providing inputs to the process and staking a more secure claim thereby to its outputs. As Samuel Huntington puts it:

> Peasant leagues, peasant associations, peasant cooperatives are necessary to ensure the continued vitality of land reform. Whatever their declared functions, the fact of organization creates a new center of power in the countryside. De Tocqueville's democratic science of association brings a new political resource into rural politics, counterbalancing the social status, economic wealth, and advanced education which had been the principal source of power of the landowning class.[6]

In the absence of peasant organization, reform is achieved only with elite forbearance and good will. If undertaken principally with the resources of the elite, the reform is unlikely to impinge on their interests very much.[7] This reinforces the point made by Montgomery that *how* land reform is undertaken may be more significant than *whether* it is attempted.

Three case studies of land reform are presented, each demonstrating different aspects of political economy. Ronald Clark focuses primarily on those changes worked by land reform in Bolivia which increase possibilities for economic development, though he acknowledges as very important the effects on social mobility and political participation. Bolivia has in the past been used as an example to show the negative economic consequences of land reform, because agricultural production apparently declined in the wake of reform. By examining family incomes and changes in marketing structure and participation, Clark finds that land reform indeed contributed both to extended (and beneficial) market integration and to increased incomes (and factor endowments) of the rural population.[8] He also points to the importance of organization for achieving land reform in Bolivia.

Few have questioned the productivity of land reform in Taiwan, but most analyses have been done primarily in economic terms. Bernard Gallin examines the effect of land reform on social structure, and the effect of changes in social structure on the productivity of local politics. Quite succinctly, he shows the microdynamics

[6] *Political Order in Changing Societies* (1968), pp. 395–396. Huntington obscures the dynamic quality of organization, we think, by referring to it as a "resource." Rather we find it useful to view organization as mobilizing and channeling (or withholding) resources for political advantage. In support of his conclusion about the importance of organization, Huntington cites Charles Erasmus's statement: "Most important to the growth of power among the rural masses is the phenomenon of peasant syndicate organizations which tend to accompany agrarian reform. The formation of these interest groups may well prove to be the most important outcome of many agrarian reform movements." *Ibid.*, p. 396. See also the case studies in Henry Landsberger, *Latin American Peasant Movements* (1969); and Solon Barraclough, "Farmers' Organizations in Planning and Implementing Rural Development," in Raanan Weitz (ed.), *Rural Development in a Changing World* (1971), pp. 364–387.

[7] There usually needs to be at least some peasant inputs for reform to be initiated.

"Short of revolution, rural unrest and *violence* and the *organization* of peasant leagues capable of making effective and coordinated demands on the government usually serve to hasten land reform legislation." Huntington, *op. cit.*, p. 393 (emphasis added).

[8] Clark's conclusions are phrased here in our language, not his. A separate study supporting Clark's findings is Melvin Burke, "Land Reform and Its Effect upon Production and Productivity in the Lake Titicaca Region," *Economic Development and Cultural Change*, April 1970, pp. 410–450. On the Mexican experience, see Folke Dovring, "Land Reform and Productivity: The Mexican Case," University of Wisconsin Land Tenure Center, RP. No. 61 (January 1969); Marnie W. Mueller, "Changing Patterns of Agricultural Output and Productivity in the Private and Land Reform Sectors in Mexico, 1940–1960," *Economic Development and Cultural Change* (January 1970), pp. 252–266; and R. S. Weckstein, "Evaluating Mexican Land Reform," *ibid.* (April 1970), pp. 391–409.

of political resources and exchange at the community level; how land ownership was converted into status and authority before the reform, and how, for example, education was used by former landlords after the reform to acquire these resources, admittedly in lesser measure. Gallin finds the landlord sector, which previously monopolized status and authority in Taiwan communities (especially under the Japanese hegemony), shifting their resources out of local political markets after the reform, leaving a "vacuum" and what he calls "social disorganization." This is a good illustration of development without growth in the social and political spheres, however. Gallin describes the restructuring of social and political resource flows, with the consequence that one finds a new kind of leadership emerging, one drawn from the community more on the basis of talent and public spiritedness than on the basis of putative class membership or economic wealth. While there are costs incurred by communities during a period of disorganization, leadership resources previously foregone on ascriptive grounds can be mobilized to serve community needs. This contributes to augmented social and political productivity as a result of land reform.[9]

The Japanese experience is perhaps the example of land reform most noted for success. Tsutomu Ouchi examines this experience to determine what benefits were in fact achieved and also what problems are raised by this success. The process of land reform in Japan resembles that in Taiwan. Landlords were not all ruined, but they were ultimately "rendered impotent as a social force," to use Ouchi's phrase. In his analysis, he concentrates on economic questions but refers to social and political consequences as well.[10] A conclusion of considerable interest is that the structure of land tenure established by the reform, a structure that mobilized and energized resources over two decades, has itself become a constraint on further gains in productivity, the average farm size now being too small to induce maximum utilization of improved technologies.

Ouchi does not wish to detract from the contribution or centrality of land reform to Japanese development, but he does raise the issue noted at the outset of this introduction—not every land reform structure is necessarily or perpetually productive. Structures may need to be modified over time to be most appropriate in changing conditions. It appears now that further "reform" in Japan in the direction of larger, consolidated holdings is indicated. However, this situation could not have come to pass without an earlier pattern of small, dispersed farms that helped to raise the factor endowments and productivity of the many. Also in undertaking new reforms, the aim of maximizing economic output must be modified to take into account the social and political values still served by the existing tenure pattern.

A further implication of land reform suggested by Ouchi is that it contributes to the maintenance of political stability. This conclusion is much disputed, but it has been accepted by some knowledgeable people.[11] Whether or not possession of land

---

[9] For a more extended analysis, see Gallin's book, *Shin Shing, Taiwan: A Chinese Village in Change* (1966).

[10] Much of Ouchi's detailed exposition on economic matters has been omitted here, readers being referred to the original article in *Developing Economies,* June 1966.

[11] Huntington writes: "In terms of political stability, the costs of land reform are minor and temporary, the gains fundamental and lasting." *Op. cit.,* p. 378. USAID officials Princeton Lyman and Jerome French reach a similar position in their survey of "Political Results of Land Reform," U.S. Agency for International Development, Spring Review of Land Reform, June 1970, pp. 38–39. Indeed, this position on the political effects of land reform has led to criticism of land reform as

makes rural sectors conservative is a matter to be resolved empirically, and the data at hand are not definitive. What would be clear on the basis of our model is that a peasantry endowed with land, and with the other resources derivable from land, would have the wherewithal to contribute to and receive from the political processes in a way that poorly endowed peasants cannot.

It is true that people who find a system reasonably productive for themselves are generally loathe to change it. Such a conservatism, however, need be the consequence not of elite manipulation but rather of a system's ability to satisfy people's needs. This is what development is about. If a peasantry were better endowed through land reform and still denied what it felt to be a fair share of the national political product, it would be in a better position to struggle for a more equitable distribution of resources than if it were impoverished and hence more vulnerable to pressures from other sectors.

The political consequences or outcomes of land reform are not fixed or determined *ex ante*. There are many kinds and degrees of reform. Some reforms can forestall significant changes in the distribution of resources, but others can entrain such changes even if they do not make them directly. Our concern is how land reform could under various conditions enable persons to achieve more abundantly those things they value. Most studies we have seen suggest that land reform frequently makes this possible, provided it is undertaken with appropriate political, economic, and administrative analysis and strategies.

THE CONTRIBUTION OF LAND REFORMS
TO AGRICULTURAL DEVELOPMENT:
AN ANALYTICAL FRAMEWORK

PHILIP M. RAUP
University of Minnesota

INTRODUCTION

The increasing attention to problems of economic development since World War II has been paralleled by a refocusing of attention on barriers to this development that are centered in land tenure structures.

In the past fifteen years we have seen this interest in land reforms expand to cover the world stage. The aftermaths of wars have typically included demands for drastic revisions in economic institutions,

From *Economic Development and Cultural Change* (October 1963), pp. 1–23. Reprinted by permission. Some sections have been omitted.

a policy; e.g. Al McCoy, "Land Reform as Counterrevolution: U.S. Foreign Policy and the Tenant Farmers of Asia," *Bulletin of Concerned Asian Scholars*, 3:1 (Winter-Spring, 1971), 15–49. We see the effects as less certain and refer readers to the engaging debate waged with quantitative methods in *World Politics* over the last several years; see Bruce Russett, "Inequality and Instability: The Relation of Land Tenure to Politics" (April 1964), pp. 442–454; Edward J. Mitchell, "Inequality and Insurgency: A Statistical Study of South Vietnam" (April 1968), pp. 421–438; Jeffery M. Paige, "Inequality and Insurgency in Vietnam: A Re-Analysis" (October 1970), pp. 24–37.

particularly land tenure systems. So the recent flood-tide of interest is not exceptional. What is exceptional is the fact that in many countries the energizing influences of land reform are being given primary attention while the egalitarian motive slips into second place.[1]

This reorientation of interest has thrown in sharp relief the lack of a body of theory to guide economic analysis. There is no shortage of partial theories or of rigidly held dogmas that pass for theory. But there is an acute shortage of comprehensive studies that draw together the experiences of many countries and areas into an articulated framework.

It is conventional in the formulation of studies and plans for economic development to include a reference to the need for land reform. Yet its inclusion in an enumeration of needed steps is sometimes done grudgingly or apologetically. It is often treated as a quasi-economic issue or perhaps not an economic question at all.

This reluctance is difficult to understand. It will be argued in this paper that land reform concerns the formation and reshaping of attitudes and motivations that lie at the roots of economic behavior. Where similar attitudes or influences are involved in theories of saving or investment there are no doubts about the "economic" nature of the issue. It is instructive to speculate on the reasons why these doubts arise when land reform is involved.

A primary reason for hesitancy is the general unwillingness of economists to tamper with broad organizational and structural frameworks within which economic activity occurs. Available theories of economic behavior have emerged from the systematic study of firms and individuals. Built into these theories is a strong tendency to hold the institutional framework stable in order that analysis of the response of firms and individuals to economic stimuli can be reduced to manageable proportions. Formidable complexities arise when economic dynamics are applied to the institutional framework.

This predominantly static nature of most economic theory is generally recognized. In recent decades this recognition has led to the formulation of an impressive body of theory under the general heading of economic dynamics. Dynamics, in this setting, typically means the introduction of time into the analysis—time in which consumer tastes alter, technologies change, and depreciation schedules are revised in the light of experience.

Much current "static" and "dynamic" (time-weighted) economic analysis is practiced within a static institutional framework. One distressing feature of the land reform issue is that it cannot be introduced without questioning the basic structural characteristics of the economy. It compels a dynamic treatment of the total economic framework as an organism subject to change. For some economists the solution has been to invite the sociologists, social psychologists, political scientists, and philosophers to take over. The alternative proposed in this paper is that, as economists, we re-examine our theories and explore the extent to which the land reform issue can be brought within an analytical framework of economic study.

SOME DEFINITIONS

The terms "land tenure," "land reform," and "economic development" have many interpretations. Therefore, we must first identify the sense in which they are used in this paper.

Land tenure is given one interpretation in jurisprudence. It is taken there to mean the full body or "bundle" of rights that spring from the concept of an "estate" in land. The emphasis is on the land, particularly on the proprietary nature of the basic ownership right.

A more useful interpretation of the term includes all rights and relationships that have been created among men to govern their relations with respect to the land. It includes any interest in land, extending to the interest of the creditor who had loaned funds to a land user, and to the laborer who works the land. The emphasis here is on rights and men, rather than on the land as such.[2] This is the concept of land tenure used in this discussion.

Land reform has sometimes meant the expropriation of large land holdings (with or without compensation) and their redistribution to former tenants, serfs, or laborers—nothing more.

In a broader sense, as used in this paper, the concept of land reform refers to the full range of measures that may or should be taken to improve the structure of relations among men with respect to their rights in land. The term can then be paraphrased as "land tenure reform," and is here used to include the following types of reform: [3]

(1) Measures directly involving the tenure under which land is held.

   (a) Promotion of ownership by the operator and the reduction of absentee landlordism.

   (b) Regulation of rental rates and practices, and the enactment of lease protection laws.

   (c) Consolidation into efficient-sized units of strip parcels and scattered holdings.

   (d) Subdivision of large holdings.

   (e) Control of land inheritance to prevent excessive subdivision of holdings, or to discourage the accumulation of large holdings.

   (f) Improvement of land surveys and systems of title registration.

(2) Related measures essential to the success of land tenure improvements.

   (a) Development of an effective agricultural extension service.

   (b) Improvement in commercial and cooperative marketing systems when the structure of land ownership dominates or restricts the market outlets.

   (c) Improvement in the conditions of agricultural labor under tenure systems in which land ownership includes some claim to the services of people living on the land.

   (d) Improvement in the agricultural credit structure when inadequate credit is a barrier to tenure reform.

   (e) Improvement in the arrangements under which land is bought and sold.

   (f) Reform in land tax and fiscal policies.

The imprecision surrounding concepts of land tenure and land reform is compounded when we come to the concept of economic *development*. To some economists the term is largely identified with a reduction of the percentage of a country's labor force engaged in agriculture. Indices of development have been constructed on this base. More adequate uses of the term relate to increases in the ratio of capital to labor inputs, rates of net capital formation, and rises in per capita income. As used in this paper, the term reflects [a] concept of development [that] . . . is free from any implication that "development" is a plateau.[4] It recognizes that a country can develop by promoting the better use of its land and other natural resources, as well as through industrialization. It is thus free of the "industrial fundamentalism" that has characterized much recent discussion and planning for economic growth. [This "fundamentalism" is a leading "denomination" in the "religion of development." Eds.]

BACKGROUND AND SETTING

The basic importance of agriculture to economic growth is often obscured. With transitory exceptions, the food supply is not currently a barrier to further economic growth in the more developed nations. Problems of the food component in labor costs remain, with consequent foreign exchange and terms-of-trade difficulties. But the current good health of the agricultural economies of the more developed nations, coupled with localized problems of agricultural surpluses, have made it difficult to reconstruct the contributions that agriculture can make in the early stages of growth.

This difficulty can be seen most clearly in prescriptions that call for the movement of labor resources out of agriculture. At appropriate stages in the development process this is commendable advice. Its feasibility increases as industry develops and as realistic opportunities emerge for non-farm employment. For many presently underdeveloped countries and regions it is an unrealistic goal. . . .

The setting within which land reforms must be analyzed is provided by recognition that agriculture must provide employment for large populations of underdeveloped countries. But this recognition alone is not enough. In contrast to the "developed country" prescription that labor be moved out of agriculture, an opposed situation has emerged in some regions of Africa, the Middle East, and Latin America. Rapid urbanization in these areas has created large pools of underemployed labor, predominantly in urban places. In terms of realistic development potentials, a goal of moving people solidly into agriculture seems indicated. . . .

The combined effects of improved public

health and medical care, food gifts, and air transport have attracted to the cities populations that are redundant under existing price and market relationships. Thus, the rural areas may not be the scene of the most serious underutilization of human resources, particularly women. Where this prevails, one goal of land reform may appropriately become the expansion of occupational opportunities in agriculture to relieve urban centers of population pressures.

The creation of incentive conditions that will lead to the full utilization of both male and female labor is one precondition for the development of backward areas. This fact is apparently well understood in the U.S.S.R. and in mainland China. But it is seldom stressed in Western literature on economic development. One contribution that land reform can make is to create conditions in which total family labor can be utilized as fully as existing technologies and capital stocks permit.

PROCESSES OF AGRICULTURAL CAPITAL FORMATION—THE PRIVATE SECTOR

The agriculturist's interest in land reforms derives from the desire of rural peoples for the achievement of full operational and managerial potentials. The economist's interest in land reforms focuses sharply on the central issue of capital formation.[5]

A clear understanding of the capital-forming processes that lead to agricultural growth is essential. In the early stages of agricultural development this process is predominantly one of accretionary gains in capital stocks. The investment decisions involved are typically made in small segments, spread over many seasons or gestation periods. The capital formed adds to impressive totals, but the process is characterized by many small, plodding steps. This relationship is obscured by the emphasis on large-scale, dramatic investment programs in much current economic development planning. The image of development projected by a hydroelectric dam or by a steel mill is misleading if applied to agriculture. Capital in farming is rarely concentrated, in a spatial sense, and its formation is heavily weighted by the time dimension. It accumulates by an incremental process that is best described as accretionary.[6]

A nation's livestock herd is a good example. Increases in numbers and quality, slow improvements in feeding levels, better disease protection, and increases in rates of gain are all achievements in which time plays the important role. In early stages of agricultural development in Europe and North America, this gradual accretionary improvement in the livestock herd was a primary capital-forming process. It is still under way in areas shifting from reliance on cash crops to animal agriculture. Accretionary processes are also important in the stock of farm capital represented by buildings, fencing, water supplies, land clearing, ditching, drainage, and other acts of melioration, soil improvement, and conservation. Where tree or bush crops are important the process of accretionary buildup is particularly prominent.

This excursion into history should remind us of the validity of two propositions:

(1) Accretionary forms of agricultural capital formation are the important ones in early developmental phases, and in phases involving a shift from a cash-crop economy to a livestock-feed economy.

(2) The time spans required for effective operation of these accretionary processes are measured not in years but in generations.

This point of view throws a revealing light on Rostow's attempt to explain the processes through which some economies have broken away from a predominantly agricultural base into a take-off stage that has subsequently led to self-sustaining industrial and agricultural development.[7] Preceding this take-off stage and after initial stirrings of economic growth have been manifest, there have typically been long periods of seeming stagnation. New agricultural processes are adopted, the shift to a money economy becomes apparent in rural areas, small but significant capital inputs appear to take place—yet nothing appreciable happens. [This we call development without growth. Eds.]

One reason for this delayed response may be found in the time required for accretionary processes of capital formation to work themselves out. Where capital stocks are biological in nature, the limits within which capital-forming processes can be accelerated are relatively fixed. Agricultural policy for maximum growth in this development phase calls for the creation of patterns of production, consumption, and investment that maximize accretionary processes.

We can now state a major hypothesis that will guide the subsequent discussion: the land tenure system is a major force in maximizing accretionary formation of capital in agriculture and insuring that surpluses above sustenance levels are reinvested in the productive plant. . . . A system of tenure that makes these rights of use and reward specific to the user is a necessary although not a sufficient condition for capital formation to occur. The tenure must also be adequate, in terms of time and scale, to motivate the user to reinvest his surplus.[8]

. . . From the standpoint of capital formation the first important characteristic of the small proprietary or family firm lies in the fact that every act of consumption in the household requires a decision not to invest in the productive enterprise.

Operation within this consumption-investment matrix is calculated in two different units of measurement: (a) the allocation of money income, and (b) the allocation of family labor time. In terms of money income, and where tenure security is at a maximum, the operator can afford to balance the alternatives of maximum return over time from slow maturing enterprises against possibly lower yielding but quick-turnover investments. He can rationally afford to undertake investments whose yield may not reach a maximum in his lifetime. He can also afford to balance appreciation in value of his capital assets against enjoyment of realized periodic income. In short, a maximum incentive situation is created in which the growth of investments can be weighed heavily when balancing them against annual yield.

In the terms of the disposition of family labor, the prospects of long and secure tenure may create a condition in which the maximum incentive is given for the investment of total available labor time in productive undertakings. Much of agricultural capital formation can be explained in this fashion. Livestock care, repair and maintenance of structures, improved water supplies, drainage, soil improving practices, and a variety of similar tasks are often ac-

complished in agriculture at the expense of what might validly be regarded as leisure time. . . .

The generation of new attitudes toward debt and credit is another major contribution that land reforms can make to capital formation. Tabus against debt are characteristic of tradition-bound agrarian societies. The tabu has not prevented debt, but it traces from and tends to preserve attitudes that confine the use of credit to consumption purposes.

The emergence of concepts that relate debt repayment ability to increased output is one important prerequisite for agricultural development. It is in this regard that land reforms, properly conceived and executed, can make decisive contributions. Where land has been received through land reform, the development of payment schedules based on the income-yielding potential of the land can introduce the concept of amortization. More importantly, it can provide a vehicle for supervised production credit under conditions that make supervision acceptable to the farmer.

The development of workable schemes for supervised credit has been a prominent feature of successful land reforms. Without this feature, land reform can become little more than an episodic redistribution of wealth, shorn of the dynamic influence that credit can introduce. New incentives to invest family labor may be of little value if the agriculturist has no new tools and processes with which to work. A secure tenure in land can lead to stagnation if it is not coupled with attitudes and institutions that will make production credit available and encourage farmers to use it. In this sense emphasis upon extension services and credit supervision acquires a dominant position.

These optimum conditions for capital formation in agriculture have been presented in terms of the owner-operated farm firm, but this is not the only tenure arrangement that can create these conditions. It is possible to devise leasing arrangements that will create security of expectations, specific to the operator, and for a period of time enough to encourage long-term investment. In economic theory, the model for this form of lease-hold tenure is typically presented in terms of a cash lease, for a period long enough to encompass at least one cycle of crop rotation or animal production. Leases providing this degree of security are comparatively rare, and they were not characteristic of North America in the nineteenth century. They are conspicuously absent in the underdeveloped countries of today.[9] . . .

PROCESSES OF AGRICULTURAL CAPITAL FORMATION—THE PUBLIC SECTOR

Alfred Marshall, and the generation of economists that he trained, contributed to economic theory the concept of external economies of scale. The concept was crucial to further development of the theory of the firm. It provided the framework needed to accommodate those aspects of economic behavior and development that could not be explained by conventional tools of microanalysis. In a similar vein, the analysis of capital-forming processes in agriculture is incomplete if it is confined to the behavior of firms and individuals in their private role as entrepreneurs.

Recognition of this fact is widespread in recent literature on economic development, and a new terminology has emerged. We speak of social overhead capital, of the economic infrastructure, and of contributions to growth that follow from investments of public capital in activities that would be unprofitable if undertaken by private firms.

The image evoked by this terminology is typically of physical, tangible goods: hospitals, power dams, irrigation systems, port facilities, and (in the majority of countries) the entire road, rail, air, and wire system of transport and communications. Of no less importance are the intangible forms of this public capital represented by systems of public health, education, local government, and community organization. It is for these latter forms of public capital, represented by institutions and organizations, that the land tenure system of a country is of great importance.

Buchanan and Ellis have pointed out that there is little common agreement upon the indicators of economic development among culture-areas of the world except those relating to health and longevity.[10] Had they written today, they might well have added education and the acquisition of new skills. The growing emphasis on capital investments in human beings is one encouraging trend in current discussions of the mainsprings of economic growth. This emphasis is of primary importance to agricultural development. Improving the quality of the labor input through new knowledge and new skills offers one rewarding opportunity for agricultural capital investment. For this reason a major test of the performance of land tenure structures is to be found in the role they play in advancing capital investment in education.

The most serious consequences of weak government, and it typically is weak in underdeveloped regions, result from the poor quality of education, public health, police protection, and roads. Fundamental to this weakness is the lack of local public revenues remaining in the community. Given semi-subsistence income flows and primitive levels of trade, the only feasible base for local taxation is land and natural resources. This introduces us to one of the most serious dimensions of underdevelopment—the inadequacy of land and property tax systems.

Land tenure structures carry the burden of responsibility for this inadequacy. And education is the principal victim. Where the individuals who benefit from education are the children of persons taxed, the identification of costs with benefits is immediate and within the range of comprehension of virtually every taxpayer.

But where the benefits of public capital investments in education are not specific to those bearing the cost, the incentive for this capital formation is weakened. This is the typical situation in areas characterized by high rates of farm tenancy, absentee landlordism, and defective tenures in land. In many countries and areas (not only in underdeveloped countries) this has led to a passive or even negative attitude toward public education.

The basic reasons for these rural underinvestments in education are essentially the same as those connected with investments in land, improvements, and structures. It has not been clear to those required to pay that they will be among the principal beneficiaries. The emphasis upon time is also great in this portion of the analytical framework. Education is a slow-maturing enterprise. Progress is recorded in accretionary gains that are analogous to qualitative improvements in land and livestock herds.

As governments grow in their capacity to govern and as taxpayers mature in their understanding of the benefits of public capital formation, the identification between taxpayer and beneficiary is typically relaxed. Heavy public investments in education and training are supported in developed countries by individuals who cannot conceivably be reckoned among the direct beneficiaries. Where the land tenure structure will support a companion land tax structure, an incentive situation is created within which the almost universal human desire to see one's children prosper can begin to work. Rural education in underdeveloped regions emerges as one form of public capital investment for which taxpayer support can be most readily mobilized.

An increased willingness to support rural education through land taxes is only one value that may be derived from land reforms if they are coordinated with reforms in the tax structure. Alexander Eckstein has pointed out that:

. . . while administratively it may be easier to collect taxes from a small number of landlords than from a numerous peasantry, politically just the reverse may be true. Actually land reform may serve as one of the means by which it becomes politically feasible to transfer the accumulating function from the landlord to the state.[11]

Without parallel reforms in land taxation the operation of land reforms may be condemned to a low level of achievement. The Philippines provide a current example. "Philippine land is usually appraised at about 20 percent of value, taxed at one percent of appraisal value, and payment is collected on an estimated 60 percent of total land taxes due." [12] Should this situation continue it will preclude realization of one of the principal capital-forming opportunities that a land reform can create.

In addition to increased tax revenue, land reforms have typically brought a train of events leading to important secondary benefits to the social overhead capital structure. One clear example is improvement in systems of cadastral survey and land title registry.

The absence of accurate surveys has been a severe handicap to economic development in many underdeveloped countries. Inability to establish a legally defensible title to land restricts the development of mortgage credit.[13] Settlement is inhibited, and wasteful disputes over boundary rights are frequent. . . . It is not customary to include the value of cadastral surveys in computing a nation's wealth. This reflects the "developed country" bias of much economic theory as it concerns definitions of wealth and income. Where these surveys are lacking, they are a prominent measure of a nation's poverty. The costs of overcoming this defect are so high that they must typically be spread over several generations. For these reasons the early construction of survey and land title registry systems is high on the list of prescriptions for agricultural development. A tenure structure that contributes to this goal can exercise an undramatic but long-lasting influence over the course of a nation's growth.[14]

A related form of public capital investment in agriculture concerns the data systems through which agricultural statistics are assembled. Rational economic behavior is a function of the quality of information at hand. The growth of data-collecting systems can be helped or hindered by the nature of the country's land tenure structure and the relations it engenders between rural people and their governments.

The tax structure plays a key role in this regard. Where the tax collector is the primary contact between rural people and government, the suspicion with which he is traditionally regarded extends to all government representatives. An effective agricultural education and extension service finds this an inhospitable climate in which to grow. The collection and interpretation of agricultural data from farm operators becomes an exercise in subjective bias estimation.

In more developed countries, it is possible to place considerable reliance upon self-reporting techniques in agricultural data collection and tax assessment. Where land users have secure possession of their land they can project their long-run interest in the accuracy of reported data. This interest-base is typically lacking in areas of insecure tenures in land, absentee ownership, or layered tenancy. Self-reporting techniques are unreliable and the investment of public capital in better data is stunted or yields a low return.[15]

A fourth form of social overhead capital in agriculture comprises the structure of marketing institutions available at the farm and village level. George Mehren has pointed out that insecure tenure in land, not specific to an individual, plus small and fragmented units may make it difficult to promote effective market or distribution systems in many backward and agrarian systems. "Modern distribution systems do not graft to primitive production units, and vice versa." [16] Small-scale and localized monopoly is the rule with the landlord often performing the related functions of creditor and local market outlet. In this setting, the development of efficient commercial or cooperative marketing and credit facilities should accompany changes in the tenure system.

This list of the forms of social overhead capital in agriculture that are strongly influenced by the land tenure structure might well have included water supply, irrigation, local roads, police protection, accessible civil justice, and community recreation facilities. Enough has been said to emphasize that the cost of providing these services is a heavy burden on the net capital-forming capacity of underdeveloped areas. Land tenure structures can inhibit or promote the assumption of this burden by local people. Where these services must be provided by central government, costs are higher and government loses an essential element of identification with the hopes and aspirations of the people served.

THE SIGNIFICANCE OF LAND REFORMS IN CREATING INCENTIVES FOR INCREASED OUTPUT

The discussion to this point has been focused upon the nature of agricultural capital and the processes of its creation. If we accept the general argument that land tenure structures condition the investment process in agriculture, we must then ask: how many land tenure reforms contribute to the increased agricultural output that is required before there can be any surplus to invest?

We must recognize that one shibboleth of economic thought is a belief in the potential economics of large-scale production. On this point Marxian and non-Marxian economists typically see eye to eye. In Western economic thinking this is paralleled by a preoccupation with output per man hour as an appropriate measure of productive efficiency. These twin articles of faith have strongly influenced conventional economic thinking in Western countries about land reform.

With this in mind, let us examine the course of technological development in the agricultural economies of more developed countries. It will be useful to classify technological development in terms of changes in production techniques that are (a) labor-saving, or (b) output-increasing. . . .

The majority of output-increasing forms of agricultural technology depend on an improvement of the technical skills and management capacity of virtually the entire farm labor force. Fertilizers, chemical weed controls, pesticides, and improved animal feeding practices are examples. The land tenure reform that will best serve these needs is one that will give the maximum incentive for increased output to the largest percentage of the agricultural labor force. Large-scale, heavily mechanized units do not seem suited to this task. Small-scale units, intensively worked by a literate and skilled labor force having a direct interest in high output and good husbandry, are the ones indicated.

If this reasoning holds, the "early" forms of agricultural technology that are symbolized by the tractor as it was used in the United States and the U.S.S.R. do not provide an appropriate model for many underdeveloped countries. A. K. Sen has pinpointed the reason: land is a major factor of production in densely populated countries. The choice among labor-saving and output-increasing technologies is thus quite different than in more developed economies. Mechanization and large-scale units may increase the yield per unit of labor but not the yield per unit of land. Conventional planning for the economic development of backward areas has assumed that any policies focused upon labor-lavish techniques of land use are only transitional. Sen argues that they are destined to remain a more or less permanent prospect for many countries.[17]

The impact of land tenure structures upon the choice of technology is also apparent in irrigation agriculture. Economists have noted a tendency in underdeveloped countries to focus upon large dam and irrigation works while neglecting the development of fertilizer and agricultural chemical industries. In terms of increased food output, capital invested in water supply and irrigation would often yield a greater and a quicker return if devoted to fertilizer production. Why do poor countries continue to build big dams?

A part of the reason is that political leaders can point to tangible results and international credit agencies can rest assured their capital has gone into durable assets. Further explanation can also be found in the land tenure structure. It has been difficult to persuade U.S. tenant farmers to apply fertilizer up to the levels indicated by agronomic research. This difficulty is compounded in underdeveloped countries with a history of insecure rights in land, absentee landlordism, and share tenancy.

In an agricultural economy characterized by several levels of subtenancy the cost of applying fertilizer or a new cultivation technique may fall heavily or entirely upon the tenant. He may understandably be reluctant to add this risk and expense. Traditions with respect to water rights, on the other hand, are often strongly influenced by egalitarian customs of "equal rights." The distribution of rights in water may be more nearly in proportion to the tenant's share in marginal costs. Defective land tenure arrangements thus provide a clue to the reason why "use more fertilizer" campaigns have met with limited success in many underdeveloped regions.

The improvement of product quality offers an additional and significant opportunity for land tenure reforms to affect a nation's agricultural output. Where land reforms have been accompanied by the development of strong producer cooperatives, the producer's pride in his farm could be coupled with market pressures for product quality improvement. Denmark provides an outstanding example.

Difficulties in securing farm products of uniform and high quality from a multitude of small peasant-type producers have led some economists to conclude that the task is impossible in many underdeveloped countries. Attention has shifted to estate and plantation-type units or to variations of large-scale collective-type forms of farm organization.

These centrally directed units can organize masses of unskilled rural labor into reasonably efficient production cadres. In backward areas where managerial talent is scarce, these units economize on management. There are thus strong reasons why

they have tended to emerge early in the histories of agricultural development of a wide variety of countries, including the U.S., India, and the U.S.S.R. Plantations or collective farms conserve scarce managerial skills, permit labor supervision on a mass basis, and make possible the achievement of acceptable levels of product quality and standardization. These are impressive short-run accomplishments.

But these gains have been acquired at a high price in many countries. Plantations and other large-scale units have seldom contributed to the development of quality in the human labor resource. And they have conspicuously failed to promote the development of intensive animal agriculture. By inhibiting the development of widespread networks of agricultural education, extension, credit, and marketing services they have perpetuated an agricultural structure made up of a small, modern sector using high skills, and a large primitive sector of native production.

One body of economic theory in agriculture holds that the question of size of firm and the land tenure system appropriate to its support is predominantly a technical one. This reasoning typically includes an implied assumption of decreasing costs or increasing returns to scale. It is generally invoked to protest land reform programs that threaten to create uneconomically small units.

As our understanding grows of the functioning of economic systems in a variety of cultural settings it is increasingly common to find recognition of the fact that, in Hirschman's phrase: "Minimum economic size is not a technical concept, but is defined in economic terms relative to normal profits and efficient foreign suppliers." [18]

This is a step forward in the application of theory, but it still does not bring us to the central issue. The "economic" size of firm is not only an economic concept—it is a cultural concept as well. It cannot be interpreted without reference to the total setting in which economic activity occurs.

One characteristic of output-increasing technologies in agriculture is that many of the most important ones are divisible—they are technically capable of applications in small "doses." Fertilizers, better seeds, agricultural chemicals, and improved animal feeds and feeding practices are examples. It may be granted that small farms can apply this technology effectively, but it is then often argued that they cannot meet the quality standards demanded in export markets or offered by competing imports.

Where this argument has merit it will often be found to have its roots in a defective land tenure structure.[19] In this sense, land tenure reforms can promote qualitative as well as quantitative improvement in agricultural production and in the human skills and abilities on which increased productivity must ultimately rest.

CONCLUSION

Much discussion surrounding the issue of land reform and economic development is presented with a negative cast. Defects in land tenure appear as an obstacle to development; the issue is resolved when the obstacle is removed.

This paper emphasized the view that land reforms may contribute to economic development, not by removing obstacles but by promoting a new climate of expectations. The stress here is on the creative act of devising a new basis for the identification of reward with effort, of balancing costs against returns.

No attempt has been made to enumerate all of the steps that should be taken. This paper is not a blueprint for the conduct of land tenure improvements. Rather, it is an effort to indicate some major items for consideration in constructing a framework for the economic analysis of the consequence of land reform.

Land reform can be a sterile and debilitating experience if carried out in a narrow setting, without the support of other reforms in systems of education, extension, credit, and taxation. It can build upon or it can dissipate the political strength inherent in programs that can generate high levels of emotion and national effort. Whether or not these potentials are realized depends heavily on the extent to which political and social demands for land reform can be supplemented with economic analysis.

We have argued that accretionary types of capital are typically needed in the agriculture of underdeveloped countries. Capital formation in this setting may depend less on large-scale injections of money capital into agriculture than upon changes in attitudes and the institutional structures they support.

From this point of view, a premium attaches to the land tenure structure that can create incentives for rates of output expansion that will run ahead of consumption and will promote investment of the surplus in superior productive processes.

In some areas, economic development plans call for capital formation along these lines, using a variety of forms of coercion. Inflation, suppressed levels of consumption, mandatory product delivery quotas, artificially low fixed prices, and ultimate threats of physical violence are all in use. This paper reflects the view that production effects are maximized and social dislocations minimized when the agriculturist can be attracted to these same ends through opportunity instead of coercion. The primary task of land tenure policy is to create conditions that permit opportunity motives to operate. No forms of exploitation are so palatable as the ones we impose upon ourselves.

1. Evidence of this refocusing can be read out of the professional literature of the 1950's. The following examples have been selected from the literature in English: UN, Department of Economic Affairs, *Land Reform: Defects in Agrarian Structure as Obstacles to Economic Development* (New York, 1951); Raleigh Barlowe, "Land Reform and Economic Development," *Journal of Farm Economics*, XXXV, No. 2 (May 1953); Erich H. Jacoby, *Inter-Relationship between Agrarian Reform and Agricultural Development*, FAO Agricultural Study No. 26 (Rome, September 1953); Alexander Eckstein, "Land Reform and Economic Development," *World Politics*, III, No. 4 (July 1955); Doreen Warriner, *Land Reform and Economic Development*, National Bank of Egypt, Fiftieth Anniversary Commemoration Lectures (Cairo, 1955); K. H. Parsons, R. J. Penn, and P. M. Raup, eds., *Land Tenure*, Proceedings of the International Conference on Land Tenure and Related Problems in World Agriculture (Madison: University of Wisconsin Press, 1956), pp. 3–22.

2. Past experience has taught me that it is necessary to add that "land tenure" is not "tenancy." Rentals, leaseholds, and tenancy are terms that relate to only a few of the many relationships among men that are encompassed within the concept of "land tenure."

3. The use of this concept of land reform

is discussed in more detail in Philip M. Raup, "Agricultural Taxation and Land Tenure Reform in Underdeveloped Countries," *Papers and Proceedings, Conference on Agricultural Taxation and Economic Development* (Cambridge: Harvard University Press, 1954), pp. 246–55.

4. See Jacob Viner, *International Trade and Economic Development* (Oxford: Oxford University Press, 1953), esp. definition on p. 98 [omitted here].

5. This should not be interpreted as a neglect of the powerful motives for land reforms that rest in desires for social justice, political good health, and reductions in agrarian discontent. The economic consequences of these goals of land reform are far-reaching and lead beyond the boundaries set for this paper.

6. An earlier version of this portion of the argument was presented in "Farm Family Capital Accumulation and Investment Processes," Ch. 9, pp. 163–76, in E. L. Baum, H. G. Diesslin, and Earl O. Heady, eds., *Capital and Credit Needs in a Changing Agriculture* (Ames: Iowa State University Press, 1961).

7. W. W. Rostow, *The Process of Economic Growth* (New York: W. W. Norton, 1952), pp. 12–21. The argument is substantially expanded in his *The Stages of Economic Growth* (Cambridge: Cambridge University Press, 1960); pp. 21–26 are pertinent to the point here under discussion.

8. "Unless the individual can appropriate and distribute the benefits created by his efforts and his property he has no incentive to achieve efficiency in their provision." Anthony Scott, *Natural Resources: The Economics of Conservation* (Toronto: University of Toronto Press, 1955), p. 117.

9. For an illuminating discussion of reasons why both landlords and tenants in underdeveloped areas prefer share tenancy, see Paul J. Klat, "Whither Land Tenure in the Arab World," *Middle East Economic Papers* (Beirut: Economic Research Institute, American University of Beirut, 1955), pp. 52–54.

10. Norman S. Buchanan and Howard S. Ellis, *Approaches to Economic Development* (New York: Twentieth Century Fund, 1955), pp. 8–13.

11. *Op. cit.*, p. 660.

12. Hugh L. Cook, "Land Reform and Development in the Philippines," Ch. IV, pp. 168–80, in Walter Frohlich, ed., *Land Tenure,*

Industrialization, and Social Stability (Marquette University Press, 1961). The quotation is from p. 179. See also James P. Emerson, *Land Reform Progress in the Philippines, 1951–55* (Manila: ICA, U.S. Operations Mission, Philippines, February 1956).

13. This point is emphasized in *Land Mortgage Banks* (Bombay: Reserve Bank of India, 1951), pp. 70–71; and in Carl Iverson, *Monetary Policy in Iraq* (Bagdad: Central Bank of Iraq, 1955).

14. A related argument applies to the early execution of surveys of soil characteristics, land use capabilities, geological formations, and mineral wealth. In these instances, too, the nature of the land tenure system can play a major role in triggering widespread public support for these forms of social capital formation.

15. The difficulties that may arise in this situation are discussed in K. E. Hunt, "Colonial Agriculture Statistics: The Organization of Field Work." Colonial Research Publication No. 22 (London, 1957), mimeo.

16. "Market Organization and Economic Development," *Journal of Farm Economics,* XLI, no. 5 (December 1959), p. 1311.

17. "The Choice of Agricultural Techniques in Underdeveloped Countries," *Economic Development and Cultural Change,* VI, No. 3, Part I (April 1959). Data from a study by Folke Dovring would seem to support this claim. See "The Share of Agriculture in a Growing Population," FAO, *Monthly Bulletin of Agricultural Economics and Statistics,* VIII, 8/9 (August–September 1959).

18. Albert O. Hirschman, *The Strategy of Economic Development* (New Haven: Yale University Press, 1958), pp. 101 ff.

19. Referring to West African cacao producers, a recent FAO publication states: "That absentee ownership has grown markedly in recent years is the view of every experienced agricultural officer. Nor can there be any doubt as to the adverse effects of this development on agricultural efficiency in general and on cacao production in particular. . . . All agricultural officers are of the view that hired laborers or tenants are even more lackadaisical in maintaining productivity, when special effort is required, than owners. This situation poses special difficulties for such hard and exacting tasks as spraying." *Cacao,* Commodity Series Bulletin No. 27 (Rome: FAO, 1955), p. 43.

THE POLITICAL PROCESS OF LAND REFORM: A COMPARATIVE STUDY

HUNG-CHAO TAI

University of Detroit

Current research efforts on land reform seem to concentrate predominantly on its economic implications and consequences.[1] This concentration on economic analysis, often justified by the fact that economic development is one of the most pressing issues of the developing countries, reflects a relative intellectual neglect of the political aspects of land reform. The implications of this neglect are only now appreciated. The political conditions of a given country determine whether or not a meaningful reform program can be introduced in the first place, and, if it is introduced, whether or not it can be effectively implemented.

This paper attempts to analyze the political process of land reform in selected developing countries. It will examine how different political systems, in response to the problems of land tenure, initiate, formulate, and implement reform programs. Throughout this paper attention is focused on the role of the political elite. In the developing countries, in the absence of well-organized associations effectively representing the interests of the peasantry, land reform is a change of the agrarian structure effected primarily from the top. The political elite plays almost an exclusive role in land reform, from its conception to its fruition.

The countries included in this study are the Philippines, Taiwan, India, Pakistan, Iran, the United Arab Republic (a name used herein interchangeably with Egypt), Colombia, and Mexico.

LAND TENURE DEFECTS

In the developing countries land tenure. i.e., the institutional arrangements governing the ownership and utilization of agricultural land, exhibits a number of serious

defects. Foremost among these is the maldistribution of land. On the one hand, an extremely large amount of land is concentrated in the hands of very few people. On the other, an enormous number of farmers share very little and fragmented land. Table 1 presents data on the distribution of farm holdings of the eight countries studied in this paper.

TABLE 1

DISTRIBUTION OF TOTAL NUMBER AND TOTAL AREA OF FARM HOLDINGS, IN PERCENTAGES

Country	Year	Distribution of Number of Farm Holdings (%)	Distribution of Area of Farm Holdings (%)
Colombia	1954	55	3
		45	97
India	1954	39	5
		61	95
Iran	1960	66	18
		34	82
Mexico	1930	68	1
		32	99
Pakistan	1960	43	7
		57	93
Philippines	1948	84	42
		16	58
Taiwan	1952	71	25
		29	75
U.A.R.	1950	53	9
		47	91

Tenancy also presents a serious land problem. Working on tiny plots, tenants pay very high rentals, enjoy no security in regard to occupancy right, and lack free-

From *Civilisations* (1968), pp. 61–79. Reprinted by permission. Because of limitation of space, many source materials and notes were omitted in the original article but will be presented in the author's forthcoming book, *Land Reform and Politics: A Comparative Analysis.*

dom in farm operations. Instances of sub-leasing are frequent, creating a feudalistic system of hierarchical exploitations. In a number of countries there was, for some time, a tendency toward rising incidence of tenancy, reflecting the fact that high rentals induce large landowners to lease rather than to operate their land.[2]

And finally, underutilization of land, partly a consequence of land maldistribution and tenancy, constitutes still another problem. With a pronounced disinterest in farm operations, many large landowners leave a sizeable portion of their land under-cultivated or uncultivated at all. Lacking capital, a sense of security, and innovating attitude, small farmers and tenants have neither the capacity nor the motivation for improvement of land utilization. As a result, agriculture suffers from low *labor* productivity and, excepting for countries with high soil fertility, low *land* productivity.[3]

INITIATION OF REFORM
AND POLITICAL LEGITIMACY

To correct defects of land tenure, the developing countries have introduced numerous measures which they commonly designate as land reform. The precise meaning of the term has, therefore, been subject to different interpretations. For the present purpose, the term refers to redistribution of land holdings, while excluding such measures as agricultural research, extension, credit, marketing and the like. These latter measures, it should be emphatically noted, are indispensable to the increase of agricultural production. Indeed, agricultural policies emphasizing only land redistribution often result in the fall of crop output. But since these measures are not directly related to the tenurial structure, they are analytically separable from the measures seeking to correct tenure defects.

The reform programs of the eight countries under study were initiated under widely divergent circumstances. But the experiences of these countries indicate that there existed certain common and recurrent conditions likely to lead to reform. These include revolutions (as in Mexico and Egypt), rural unrest (ranging from land invasions in Colombia and East Pakistan to large-scale rebellion in the Philippines), deter-

rence to Communism (as in Taiwan and the Philippines), ideological commitment of the ruling elite (e.g., agrarianism and socialism as advocated by Mahatma Gandhi and Jawaharlal Nehru of India, and the adherence of the Chinese Nationalist Party to Dr. Sun Yat-sen's *Three Principles of the People*), the rising population pressure upon the supply of food as felt by all these countries, and international advocacy of land reform (e.g., the repeated endorsement of reform by the United Nations and the Alliance of Progress).

It is suggested, as the first hypothesis of this paper, that in initiating land reform political elites are *decisively* influenced by the consideration to gain political legitimacy, i.e., to strengthen popular support of a new political order or to avert threatened political changes. When political elites perceive the need to gain legitimacy, the conditions likely to lead to reform will become relevant or important; when they fail to perceive such a need, the existence of these conditions may not lead to reform.

It appears that, in introducing their respective reforms, the elites in Mexico, Egypt, India and Pakistan were aiming at eliciting popular support for the newly established regimes. In Mexico, Venustiano Carranza was initially at best lukewarm toward the agrarian issue. But when confronted with serious military challenges of the peasant forces of Emiliano Zapata and Pancho Villa, Carranza issued the January 6, 1915, decree, laying down the foundation for future land reform. He took this action to steal the issue of agrarianism from his opponents, while General Alvaro Obregon under his command secured a military victory. Carranza was then made President of the Republic.[4] In Egypt, the 1952 revolution was brought about by a very small number of "Free Officers" who constituted a tiny group with neither an established image of their own nor sufficient share of power within the military. And yet, they attempted to effect simultaneously two revolutions: a political revolution to topple the monarchy and a social revolution to promote justice for all classes of people.[5] The advocacy of a reform program that was initially aimed at the enormous landholdings of the royal family was intended to serve both purposes.[6]

In India, the Congress Party took no

definite position on the agrarian issue in the early part of the party's history. It was only in the 1920's, when the party sought to convert itself from a small group of intellectual rebels into a mass independence movement, that it began to take an interest in the peasantry. In 1935, the party adopted a resolution seeking to abolish the *zamindari* system, "the system . . . introduced with the advent of the British." [7] In East Pakistan, the reform law introduced in the aftermath of partition, known as the East Bengal State Land Acquisition and Tenancy Act of 1950, was by and large a measure of the new government to legalize what had already taken place: the seizure and occupation of land of the fleeing Hindu *zamindars* by the Moslem peasants. In West Pakistan, the reform initiated by Field Marshal Mohammad Ayub Khan following the 1958 coup represented an effort by the army regime to broaden its base of support. In both East and West Pakistan, the reform proved popular, winning for the new regimes some goodwill of the peasantry.

If the elites discussed thus far sought through reform to gain political legitimacy for the new regimes, the elites in Colombia, Iran, the Philippines and Taiwan initiated reform primarily to avert forceful change of the existing political order. In Colombia, the various land reform laws introduced since 1936 have been in part a response to the persistent rural unrest. But it was not until after the dreadful years of 1946–1958, a period of civil strife known as *la Violencia* in which at least 200,000 people lost their lives, that the national leadership under the banner of the National Front evinced a serious interest in changing the defective tenure structure. Today the Social Agrarian Reform Act of 1961 represents an important part of President Carlos Lleras Restrepo's program of peaceful "national transformation." In Iran, Mohammed Reza Shah Pahlevi resolutely issued the land reform decree of 1962, but only after his throne was nearly lost to Mohammad Mossadeq in 1953. After the Shah witnessed the fall of the monarchy in Egypt in 1952 and in Iraq in 1958, and after his government again faced a serious political and economic crisis in 1960–1961, what the Shah then undertook to do was to reconstitute a new coalition of social forces

supporting the throne; land reform was the instrument for substituting the expected allegiance of the peasant masses for the loyalty of the landed aristocracy.[8]

In the Philippines rural unrest in Central and Southern Luzon dates back to the 1930's. However, it was only when the Hukbalahap (the Communist guerrillas, known as the Huks) rose in rebellion in the 1940's that the government discerned the urgent need for rural reform. And it was Defence Minister Ramon Magsaysay who saw the connection of the Huk rebellion with the land issue. When Magsaysay ran for presidency in 1953, the Nationalist Party, which had nominated him for the position, declared in its platform: "As the best means to combat and eradicate Communism, [we pledge to] effect land reform through legislative and executive action." [9] It was against this background that a number of reform laws were enacted in the 1950's. As these laws were not effectively implemented, and as the Huks have revived their strength, the initiation of another law —the Agricultural Land Reform Code of 1963—was deemed necessary.

In introducing land reform to Taiwan in 1949–1953, the Nationalist Party in effect carried out a pledge—with reference to mainland China—that it had made over a quarter of a century ago. Though the Party has since 1924—when Dr. Sun Yat-sen formulated *The Three Principles of the People* —repeatedly announced its intention to engage in land reform, it failed to take any serious action. In 1949 when it introduced to Taiwan the Rent Reduction program, the Chinese Communists were about to take over completely the Chinese mainland and simultaneously posed, through their underground organization and propaganda activities, an ominous threat to the island's internal security. The reform in Taiwan must be viewed as a move primarily to ward off a Communist effort to penetrate into the rural area.[10]

PROCESS OF PROGRAM FORMULATION

Classification of Political Elites

Once having decided to initiate land reform, political elites must resolve a number of conflicts in the process of formulating programs. The second hypothesis of this paper is that the manner in which political elites resolve these conflicts and the kind of program that they finally introduce are primarily determined by the relation between elites and the landed class. In the context of this paper, elites initiating land reform may be separated from, or cooperate with, the landed class. Separated elites include a non-indigenous type (Taiwan) and a revolutionary type (Mexico, U.A.R.). Cooperative elites consist of a dominant type (India, Iran, and Pakistan) and a conciliatory type (Colombia and the Philippines). These different types of elites may be summarized in Table 2.

TABLE 2

TYPES OF POLITICAL ELITES AND LAND REFORM

Elite's Relation with the Landed Class	Separated		Cooperative	
Types of Elite	Non-indigenous	Revolutionary	Dominant	Conciliatory
Countries	Taiwan	Mexico U.A.R.	Iran Pakistan India	Colombia The Philippines

In Taiwan, it is the Nationalist Party that fathered the idea of land reform; coming from mainland China, it includes no representatives of the local landed gentry. In Mexico and the U.A.R. the landed aristocracy was the very class which the revolutionaries sought to destroy. In all these countries, the separation between the elites and the landed class is evident.

With respect to cooperative elites, it may be said that the dominant elites are politically less dependent upon the landed class than are the conciliatory elites; they generally envisage land reform as an essential part of the modernization process which they lead. Conciliatory elites, on the other hand, often consist of a substantial portion of the representatives of the landed gentry. Taking a conciliatory attitude toward the landed class, they sponsor land reform primarily as a symbolic gesture to pacify rural discontent rather than as a substantive measure to satisfy the demands of the peasantry.

It is significant to note that the consideration of political legitimacy has altered the relationship of the elite and the landed class in both Iran and India. In Iran, the royal family had been the largest landholder of the country before the 1950's. The desire to obtain peasant support for the survival of the threatened monarchy was so overpowering that the Shah had to cut off ties with the biggest landlords of the country, while his reform program leaves his relation with the lesser landlords undisturbed. In India, in leading the independence movement, the Congress Party denounced the *zamindari* system in order to identify the peasantry with its revolutionary cause. Since independence, having felt no urgency to elicit further peasant support, the party leadership has failed to exert its influence seriously on the State governments, which have jurisdiction over land reform, and where the lesser landlords retain considerable strength, to effect a meaningful reform.

In West Pakistan, when Field Marshal Ayub Khan seized power in 1958, he was succeeding a regime that had been under the continuous domination of the landed class. With the strong backing of the army, Ayub Khan enjoyed a measure of political independence that was denied his predecessors. In line with his nation-building effort, he expressed determination to bring about a reform program. However, his program, with generous allowances to the landholders, neither reduced the landlords' political influence much nor precluded their loyalty to the new regime.

In Colombia and the Philippines, there has never been a basic shift of political power as in the three countries just discussed. The landed gentry constitutes one of the vital bases of power upon which the governments must rest, and whose interest the governments must respect. In accepting reform programs, the elites of both countries did not act out of a conviction to seek fundamental alteration of the agrarian structure. Rather they were persuaded of the symbolic value of land reform to relieve rural tensions, tensions that threaten the very interests they try to protect.

Resolution of Conflicts

In formulating a reform program, political elites must resolve conflicts stemming from three kinds of problems. The first is a political problem: how to overcome the almost unanimous opposition of the entrenched landed class. The second relates to complex policy questions: the choice of gradual, selective versus immediate, comprehensive approaches; the establishment of criteria according to which land rights are to be altered; the determination of a financing formula; the selection of beneficiaries. Finally there is the problem of selecting social justice or increased production as the primary objective of land reform. Those who consider the political and social inequality implicit in a defective land tenure system to be the major rural problem would emphasize equity as the primary objective of reform. They would advocate as far as is practicable equal sharing among the farming population of land ownership and agricultural income. In contrast, those who consider poverty the most serious rural problem would emphasize productivity as the primary aim of reform. They argue that in a country with limited per capita arable land and a rising population, equalization of land ownership—no matter how concentrated it is—would only reduce farm holdings to an uneconomical scale and would, therefore accentuate the poverty problem.

How do political elites resolve these three sets of conflicts? For separated elites, it appears, the task of conflict resolution is relatively easy. With the landlord class becoming powerless in the policy process or destroyed in revolution, these elites can freely formulate a program on behalf of the inarticulate peasants. In resolving the policy questions, they tend to adopt measures that can be easily enforced without imposing on themselves excessive financial and administrative burdens. They often act speedily without careful deliberation, preferring executive decrees to legislative enactments as the legal form of their programs. In general they emphasize equity as

the primary reform objective and come to consider the question of raising productivity only after reform has been introduced. The experiences of Taiwan, Mexico, and the U.A.R. substantiate these points.

For cooperative elites, the task of conflict resolution is understandably far more arduous. Most of them have to bargain with the landed class to work out a program that may entail immediate sacrifice to the powerful few, but that may yield no sufficiently meaningful benefits to the intended masses. Thus, these elites become scrupulous in dealing with policy questions. They tend to formulate detailed programs that can be enforced only gradually, benefiting limited numbers of farmers at a time. They stress productivity as the primary objective of reform—in the hope that they can reduce the antagonism of the landed class by offering in the prospect of increased agricultural production while providing limited land to the landless to win their allegiance.

To overcome the opposition of land reform, cooperative elites appear to have two alternatives. One is a gradualistic approach. The elites can persist in a continuous battle for reform within the legislative arena. Obtaining first a land reform bill with whatever provisions are agreeable to the opposition, and seeking to improve the law whenever possible, they may hope that in time a balance of forces in favor of effective reform will emerge, thus helping enact a meaningful law. The legislative history of land reform in Colombia and the Philippines seems to justify this hope.

An alternative to the gradualistic approach lies in the emergence of a dynamic political leader who excludes a recalcitrant parliament from further participation in formulation of the reform program. Such a political leader must combine a commitment to reform with some authoritarian rule. The recent reform laws in West Pakistan and Iran were brought about by such type of political leaders.

CONTENT OF PROGRAMS

Land redistribution, whether it is intended for equalizing farm holdings or for creating a complete owner-farmer system, requires compulsory transfer of land from some to others. In countries where public, royal, or foreign holdings exist, as is the case with the countries under study, it is logical and prudent for political elites to first transfer these holdings. And, as long as they are committed to reform, the elites will find relatively little internal political opposition to the distribution of these types of holdings.

To redistribute private holdings, ot course, constitutes by far the most formidable task for political elites. They must resolve two basic issues. The first relates to the amount of land an owner is permitted to retain. The task is to establish ceilings of retained land which are low enough to enable a large number of peasants to acquire land and high enough to avert excessive division of land and, in places where the landed class is dominant, to make the reform politically acceptable. It appears that, with the landed class removed as a factor in the policy process, separated elites as a rule encourage broad sharing of land own-

ership, thus prescribing low ceilings, and that most of the cooperative elites, who seek to preserve the interests of large or small landlords, tend to establish outright high ceilings or to prescribe low ones with numerous restrictions.

This statement can be substantiated by a comparison of the ceilings of retained land in the eight countries under study. Whether the ceilings of one country are high or low in relation to those of another country can be determined by a comparison of the ratio of the prescribed ceilings to the size of the average farm holdings of the countries concerned. The country with the higher ratio has the comparatively higher ceilings. In order to keep the comparison manageable, in the case of countries with more than one ceiling, only the uppermost and the latest is selected. The pertinent data of the eight countries are presented in Table 3.

TABLE 3

RELATION OF CEILINGS OF RETAINED LAND
TO AVERAGE FARM HOLDINGS

Country	Ceiling of Retained Land		Size of Average Farm Holding		Ratio of Ceiling to Average Farm $\dfrac{(B)}{(D)}$	Rank of Countries, Low to High Ratio
	Amount	Year	Amount	Year		
(A)	(B)	(C)	(D)	(E)	(F)	(G)
Mexico	300 ha.	1942	77.1 ha.	1950	3.89	1
Taiwan	6 chia	1953	1.44 chia	1952	4.51	2
Colombia	200 ha.	1961	25.7 ha.	1954	7.78	3
U.A.R.	100 feddans	1961	6.1 feddans	1950	16.39	4
Iran	150 ha.	1964	4.76 ha.	1960	31.51	5
India	216 acres	1961	6.65 acres	1959–1960	32.48	6
Philippines	75 ha.	1963	2.24 ha.	1948	33.48	7
Pakistan, E.	125 acres	1961	3.1 acres	1960	40.32	8
Pakistan, W.	1,000 acres	1959	6.8 acres	1960	147.05	9

NOTE: *Units of Land:* 1 hectare (ha.) = 2.47109 acres; 1 acre = 0.40468 ha. 1 *chia* (Taiwan) = 0.96992 ha. = 2.39680 acres; 1 feddan (U.A.R.) = 0.42 ha. = 1.038 acres.

Table 3 shows that in countries where elites are separated from the landed class the ratios of the ceilings to the average farm sizes are as a rule low, whereas in countries where elites are cooperating with the landed class such ratios are high. The case of Colombia stands as a major exception. However, an examination of the

Colombian Social Agrarian Reform Act of 1961 would reveal the superficial character of the low ratio. Without requiring automatic expropriation of the land beyond the ceiling, the law's land redistribution provisions can be enforced only in a piecemeal fashion. Where the law is enforced, it is specified that cultivated land be given the lowest priority in redistribution—after the exhaustion of uncultivated and inadequately worked land. The most serious barrier to enforcing the ceiling provision of the law is the financing and compensation formula which makes it practically impossible to redistribute land on any large scale.

The second issue relating to the redistribution of private land is concerned with the problem of financing. The elites must devise a compensation scheme that is beneficial to the landless, acceptable to landlords, and realistic about the government's financial capacity for initial payment. In resolving this issue, separated elites, because they attempt to enlist peasant support, tend to assume a stand favorable to the new owners; whereas cooperative elites, because they are still in varying degrees identified with the landed interests, generally seek to protect the interests of landlords.

In Mexico, land was distributed free among the *ejidatarios* (peasant members of *ejido*, a farming community) with the government paying the original owners an extremely meager amount in bonds.[11] In the U.A.R., the land price was fixed at 70 times the land tax (as compared to 105 to 180 times the land tax in Iran) and payable in bond only. This land price, one author estimates, amounted to only 40 percent of the market value.[12] Farmers purchasing land, who were originally required to pay the equivalent of the full price assessed for compensation, have been paying since 1964 only one-fourth of it, with the government paying the difference. In Taiwan, the land price was assessed at 2.5 times the annual main crop yield of the land and payable in bond and stocks of governmental corporations. The author calculates that this assessed price is 29 to 47 percent below the market value.[13]

In contrast, Colombia, India, Iran, West Pakistan, and the Philippines have adopted financing formulas favorable to the original landowners; they all require farmers to pay the price in full; and they, with the exception of Iran, fail to make adequate appropriation necessary for transfer of a substantial amount of land. The cases of Colombia and the Philippines may be particularly noted. In Colombia, the land price was first set in 1962 at 130 percent of the cadastral value—a formula unfavorable to the original landowners as the cadastral

value was extremely low. In 1963, the formula was revised to allow owners to make self-assessment—for taxation as well as for compensation purposes. In the Philippines, the law, without specifying the basis of land valuation, requires the Land Authority to reach an agreement with the landowners on the purchase price. Payment of compensation is in bond, but the terms are very favorable to the bond holders.

IMPLEMENTATION AND POLITICAL COMMITMENT

Factors affecting the implementation of a given country's land reform program are numerous. They may include the administrative competence and financial capacity the elite commands, the presence or absence of political stability in the country, the extent of landlord resistance, the awareness of the peasantry, and the degree of political commitment to reform. The final hypothesis of this paper is that political commitment to reform—i.e., the willingness and readiness of the political elite to mobilize all available resources to carry out a reform program—is of critical importance. With strong political commitment, a country is likely to implement its program successfully even though some of the other factors are unfavorable. Conversely, without strong political commitment, a country may not implement its program effectively even if some of the other factors are favorable.

Countries with Strong
Political Commitment to Reform
Mexico, Taiwan, the U.A.R., and Iran appear to be the countries which have demonstrated a strong political commitment to land reform. One may say that the strong political commitment in the first three countries is partially due to the type of elite in power. Having removed the obstructive influence of the landlord class from their governments, the elites of these countries can speedily carry out their programs. It should be emphasized, however, that in these three countries the strong political commitment is also due to the emergence in time of individual political leaders—in contrast to elite as a collectivity—who are devoted to the interests of the peasantry and personally identified with the reform effort. The more prominent of these lead-

ers include Lazaro Cardenas of Mexico, General Chen Cheng of Taiwan, and Gamal Abdel Nasser of Egypt. In the case of Iran, where the dominant elite is in power, personal identification by the Shah with the country's reform probably constitutes the most vital political commitment on which the progress of the reform critically depends.

In all these four countries, the need for a vigorous espousal of reform by individual political leaders may be explained by two considerations. As elites in these countries do not include representation of the peasantry, a personal identification with reform by political leaders can create a visible link between the elites and the peasantry, thus demonstrating their serious reform intentions. More importantly political leaders with resolute will, dynamic leadership, and compassion for the peasantry can energize the reform movement, fire it with enthusiasm, and dramatize its results. In doing so, such political leaders can help generate popular support and weaken landlord resistance.

With their political leaders firmly committed to land reform, Mexico, Taiwan, the U.A.R. and Iran could overcome many obstacles to the implementation of their programs. Without the necessary administrative and technical competence to make a pre-reform land survey, both Mexico and Iran, in the incipient phase of their reform, adopted "short-cut" methods. In Mexico campesinos could acquire land from large holdings located within a 7-kilometer radius from the village in which they lived. In Iran the landlord was simply allowed to retain one "village," while all incumbent cultivators obtained the rest of the land they had been working on. To deal with the problem of shortage of public funds, Mexico practically made no payment; in Taiwan the government pioneered the method of partial payment in stocks of public enterprises; in Iran the government was willing to use a substantial portion of the oil income that had been allocated to the Planning Organization.

To cope with the problem of peasant indifference and landlord obstruction, the elites of Mexico and Taiwan tried to institutionalize the peasants into a political force. In Mexico, the integration of the farmers' organization (*Confederación Nacional Campesina*) with the Official Party may be considered one of the principal

reasons why the Mexican reform has been sustained over several decades. In Taiwan, the direct participation in implementation by tenants helped offset landlord resistance. In Egypt and Iran, the elites preferred to dramatize their reform efforts by forcefully confronting themselves with the obstructionists. In both countries, the prompt and stiff punishment by the governments of the rebellious landlords in the initial phase of the reform convinced many landowners of the serious intent of the elites to remove the forces of opposition.[14] Subsequently there was no sustained struggle by landlords against the reforms.

Countries Without Strong
Political Commitment to Reform

In India, Pakistan, Colombia, and the Philippines, a sustained political commitment to land reform is lacking. Though a number of political leaders of these countries have consistently endorsed reform, some have failed to exert any lasting impact on their countries' agrarian policy, while others have yet to demonstrate their devotion to the interest of the peasantry. In India Jawaharlal Nehru helped remove the *zamindari* system and constantly urged further reform, but he never established an image of himself as a man of the peasants. In Pakistan Ayub Khan first came to recognize the necessity of reform when he issued in 1954 a statement entitled "A Short Appreciation of Present and Future Problems of Pakistan." He considered the Egyptian reform a good one and worth imitating. When he came to power in 1958, however, he became preoccupied with the task of restoration of political order and stability, leaving the matter of reform to a commission dominated by rather conservative civil servants. And despite his admiration for the Egyptian reform, the ceiling of retained land for East Pakistan was nearly quadrupled in 1961 (from 33 to 125 acres)—the very year in which the Egyptian ceiling was lowered to half of its original level (from 200 to 100 feddans).

In Colombia, President Carlos Lleras Restrepo has been for some time intimately associated with the country's land reform movement. But, as head of a coalition government under the banner of the National Front, he cannot personally exercise a decisive influence over national policy. As a skilful, pragmatic politician, he can only do what a substantial majority of the ruling groups is willing to support. In the Philippines, Ramon Magsaysay was undoubtedly a strong advocate for reform. Professing "that he would live like Mexico's Cardenas, 'who always stayed with the people to learn their problems and their needs . . . ,'" [15] he was able, during his short Presidential term, to exact from the uncooperative Congress three reform bills. Magsaysay's death in 1957 left much of his program unfinished and, more unfortunately, caused the reform spirit he generated to disappear.

One consequence of the lack of strong political commitment in these four countries is their inadequate mobilization of available resources to carry out their program. It may be said that in terms of man-land ratio, administrative capacity, and financial resources most of these countries enjoy a more favorable position than the four countries discussed earlier. The difference in the extent of implementation between the two groups of countries can be accounted for only by the absence or presence of political commitment.

IMPACT OF LAND REFORM
ON LAND HOLDING PATTERN

In a given country, and within a specified period of time, the proportion of the total farm land that was redistributed and the proportion of the total farm families receiving land indicate the degree of change in landholding patterns brought about by land redistribution. Table 4 presents data on the eight countries under study.

Table 4 reveals the sharp contrast in the results of land redistribution between Iran, Mexico, Taiwan, and the U.A.R., on the one hand; and Colombia, India, Pakistan, and the Philippines, on the other. The reforms in the first group of countries all affected much larger amounts of land and benefited far greater numbers of farm families—thus fulfilling to a greater extent the objective of equity—than the reforms in the second group of countries. In terms of land redistributed or to be redistributed as a percentage of the total farm land, column (E), the lowest of the first group of countries (the U.A.R.) is over twice as large as the highest of the second group (West Pakistan). As to the beneficiaries of reform, as seen in column (H), the proportion of farm families receiving land in the U.A.R. (the country with the lowest proportion among the first group of countries)

is over twice as large as that in India (the country with the highest proportion among the second group of countries).

CONCLUSIONS

The foregoing analysis appears to verify the three hypotheses offered in this paper. In a decisive way, perception of the need of legitimacy prompts political elites to initiate land reform; the relation between the initiating elite and the landed class affects the kind of program presented; and political commitment determines the extent of implementation of a program.

The reform programs of Mexico, Taiwan, the U.A.R., and Iran have been more extensive than the programs of Colombia, India, Pakistan, and the Philippines. The contrasting performance in land reform of these two groups of countries suggests strongly that elites separated from the landed class are apt to respond more effectively to the problems of defective land tenure and to achieve a greater success in resolving them than most of the elites cooperative with the landed class. It further suggests that a dominant elite, one that severed ties with the big landed aristocracy but cooperating with the lesser landlords, can also achieve success in reform if the elite possesses a sympathetic attitude toward the peasantry and a resolute will to carry out its program. This is what the case of Iran has demonstrated.

These findings imply that since initiation of reform by a non-indigenous elite is rare and probably not duplicable, and since a conciliatory elite lacks deep conviction in broad agrarian change, the contest for offering an effective land reform in the future in many of the developing countries will be one between the revolutionary and dominant elites. The test of statesmanship and political skill to which the dominant elite is subject will be particularly severe. For it must be able to put forward a reform program moderate enough to prevent a total alienation of the landed class and, at the same time, sufficiently progressive to avoid the loss of peasant allegiance to the revolutionary forces. . . .

1. See, for example, published works listed in Land Tenure Center, University of Wisconsin, *Agrarian Reform and Land Tenure: A List of Source Materials* (Madison, Wisconsin, 1965); and Hung-chao Tai, *Land Reform in*

TABLE 4
RESULTS OF LAND REDISTRIBUTION

Country	Period	Area of Farm Land Acquired for Redistribution or Actually Redistributed	Total Area of Farm Land	Land Redistributed or to Be Redistributed as a Percentage of Total Farm Land $100 \times \frac{(C)}{(D)}$	Farm Families Acquired Land	Total Farm Families	Farm Families Acquired Land as a Percentage of Total Farm Families $100 \times \frac{(F)}{(G)}$
(A)	(B)	(C)	(D)	(E)	(F)	(G)	(H)
With extensive redistribution							
Iran	1962–1967	14,834 villages	48,592 villages (1960's)	30.53	587,566	3,218,460 (1960)	18.26
	1962–1965	12,875 villages		26.50	455,959		14.17
Mexico	1915–1960	9,807,167 ha.	22,506,766 ha. (1960)	43.57	1,552,926 (1950)	2,918,599 (1950)	53.21
Taiwan	1951–1963	242,550 chia	899,264 chia (1963)	26.97	360,266	824,560 (1963)	43.69
U.A.R.	1952–1964	839,678 feddans	6,122,000 feddans (1964)	13.72	263,862	3,143,000 (1964)	8.40
With limited redistribution							
Colombia	1962–1965	80,483 ha.	24,229,712 ha. (1960)	0.33	35,000	1,193,837 (1960)	2.93
India	1951–1966	9,000,000 acres	329,585,000 acres (1961–1962)	2.73	3,000,000	72,466,000 (1961–1962)	4.14
Pakistan, E.	1950–1960	292,849 acres	21,726,000 acres (1960)	1.35	n.a.	n.a.	n.a.
Pakistan, W.	1959–1962	2,195,304 acres	37,037,000 acres (1960)	5.93	56,906	3,757,000 (1960)	1.52
Philippines	1954–1965	211,661 ha.	7,772,485 ha. (1960)	2.72	n.a.	n.a.	n.a.
	1963–1965	8,701 ha.		0.11			

Colombia, India, Iran, Mexico, Pakistan, the Philippines, Taiwan and the U.A.R.: A Selected Bibliography (Cambridge, Mass.: The Center for Rural Development, 1967).

2. See, for instance, The experiences of Egypt and the Philippines in the years before 1950 in respectively Gabriel S. Saab, The Egyptian Agrarian Reform 1952–1962 (London: Oxford University Press, 1967), p. 12; and Jorge Piron, "Land Tenure and the Cost of Living in Central Luzon," Philippine Studies, IV (September 1956), p. 408.

3. For information on land and agricultural labor productivity of the eight countries under study, see Food and Agriculture Organization of the United Nations (FAO), The State of Food and Agriculture 1963 (Rome 1963), pp. 110, 116.

4. Elyer N. Simpson, The Ejido, Mexico's Way Out (Chapel Hill, N.C.: University of North Carolina Press, 1937), p. 61. See also Frank Tannenbaum, The Mexican Agrarian Revolution (New York: Macmillan Co., 1929), pp. 166–171.

5. Gamal Abdel Nasser, The Philosophy of the Revolution (Buffalo, New York, 1959), p. 36.

6. Ibid., pp. 38–40; and Doreen Warriner, Land Reform and Development in the Middle East; A Study of Egypt, Syria, Iraq, second ed. (London: Oxford University Press, 1962), pp. 12–14.

7. H. D. Malaviya, Land Reforms in India (New Delhi: All India Congress, 1954), p. 59.

8. Samuel P. Huntington, "The Political Modernization of Traditional Monarchies," Daedalus, XVC (Summer 1966), pp. 778–779;

and Hossein Mahdavy, "The Coming Crisis of Iran," Foreign Affairs, XLIV (October 1965), p. 134.

9. Quoted in Frances L. Starner, Magsaysay and the Philippine Peasantry (Berkeley and Los Angeles: University of California Press, 1961), p. 41.

10. See Chen Cheng, Land Reform in Taiwan (Taipei, Taiwan, China: China Publishing Company, 1961), pp. 47–48.

11. See Elyer N. Simpson, The Mexican Agrarian Reform, Problems and Progress (Mexico City: Institute of Current World Affairs, 1933), pp. 106–111; James G. Maddox, "Mexican Land Reform," American Universities Field Staff Reports (July 3, 1957), pp. 11–12; and William H. MacLeish (ed.), Land and Liberty, Agrarian Reform in the Americas (New York 1961), p. 5.

12. Saab, op. cit., p. 24.

13. "Land Reform and National Development: Taiwan," Papers of the Michigan Academy of Science, Arts, and Letters, LI (1966), 310. The following sources of information are consulted in this calculation. Hui-Sun Tang, Land Reform in Free China (Taipei, Taiwan 1953), p. 15, n. 5; and China, Auditing Office, Statistical Bureau, Statistical Analysis of the Chinese Tenancy System, in Chinese (Chung-king, China 1946), pp. 80–81; and Chen, op. cit., pp. 114–115.

14. See respectively Mohammed Neguib, Egypt's Destiny (London: Victor Gollancz Ltd., 1955), pp. 174–175; and John A. Hobbs, "Land Reform in Iran: 'A Revolution from Above,'" Orbis, VII (Fall 1963), p. 625.

15. Starner, op. cit., p. 39.

LAND REFORM AND PEASANT MARKET PARTICIPATION ON THE NORTH HIGHLANDS OF BOLIVIA

RONALD JAMES CLARK

University of Wisconsin

The purpose of this article is to describe and analyze the changes which have taken place on the north highlands of Bolivia since 1952 with regard to the extent to which peasants in this area now participate in markets on a cash basis. The land reform, instituted in August of 1953, was the most important factor in restructuring markets and marketing relations in this area. It will be seen that direct results of the land

From Land Economics (May 1968), pp. 153–172. Reprinted by permission. Some sections have been omitted.

reform have not only been the distribution of opportunities for peasants to earn a cash income and their greater participation in a money economy, but also the creation of a greater number of regional and national markets.[1]

THE SYSTEM OF THE AGRICULTURE ON THE NORTH HIGHLANDS BEFORE 1953

The present study covers 51 pre-reform properties.[2] They ranged in size from 335 to 9,408 hectares, with an estimated 5,400 families living on the properties at the time of the land reform, or a total population of roughly 25,000 people.[3]

Before the land reform the management of most of the farms in this study can be characterized as absentee ownership. On only five of the 51 farms where interviews were made did the landlord live there or remain there for any extended period of time during the year. The usual practice was for the landlord to visit his farms for a few weeks during the periods of planting and harvesting, with possibly one other visit to the farm during the year. All 51 of the landlords in this study had homes in the city of La Paz. Many had non-agricultural businesses and/or professions to which they devoted the greater part of their time. In some cases farming was of secondary economic importance to the owner in terms of his total income. It was not possible to get data on the other economic interests of pre-reform landowners which would allow generalization.

On all these pre-reform farms the day-to-day management of the farm was left in the hands of a paid white or *mestizo* administrator (in no case a peasant or someone of direct peasant extraction) who had to oversee all farm operations on a yearly basis and carry out the orders of the owner. Beneath the administrator there were several positions which were usually filled by peasants through whom the orders of the administrator and landlord were implemented.

The vast majority of the rural population on the north highlands owned no land whatsoever. Peasant families, in order to have access to land, had to work within the rural institutions or tenure relations which long ago had been set up between those who owned land and the peasant families who owned none. Each peasant family was obligated to render personal and farm labor services to the landlord in exchange for the right to use a small parcel of land, primarily to grow crops for family consumption and to raise a few animals. The basic obligation of the peasant family was to work a certain number of days per week on the lands which the landlord had reserved for himself. There was no sharing of the production from the landlord's lands.

On the farms included in this study, this basic family labor obligation ranged from three to 12 man-days of labor per week, and was a function of the quantity and quality of land which the peasant received from the landlord. . . .

In addition to the economic obligations mentioned above there was a set of economic prohibitions which reduced substantially the ability of peasant families to obtain a higher cash income. For example, on most farms the peasant could not sell wood or the grasses that could be made into brooms, even though these came from his plot of land. These were the products of the farm and reserved for the landlord.[4]

Also, in almost all cases, the peasants were restricted in their use of lands for pasture. In five of the study cases there was a limit of five sheep which each family could own, since the landlord wanted to assure proper feeding and care of the oxen and mules which every peasant family had to have to meet the work obligations on the farm. In four cases the families were prohibited altogether from having other than draft animals.[5]

Failure to fulfill both farm and personal service obligations, or failure to abide by the rules within the farm organization, brought fines in money, animals, or agricultural products, or physical punishment and possibly eviction from the farm. No matter how unjust the treatment of the peasants they had no one or no institution outside the farm to which they could take their complaints.

About the only recourse they had was to flee from the farm, usually at night, to try to secure better treatment elsewhere. If they were caught they would be returned to the farm. For all intents and purposes the peasant was a slave, the property of the landlord, for whenever properties were advertised for sale the number of families on the property also was included.

Besides granting access to land, the landlord was expected to meet certain needs of the peasants in order to secure their labor services. For example, he was expected to construct and maintain a church, to provide funds for alcohol and food on the major holidays, and to loan money to individual families for marriages, burials, and health expenses. There were no community obligations placed on the landlord except for the church and community fiesta days. The almost complete absence of educational facilities on the farms studied demonstrates that landlords generally felt no obligation to build and staff a school.

Large landholdings, absentee ownership, and serfdom would be the best general characterization of the system of agriculture and labor exploitation prevalent on the north highlands in Bolivia before 1952. The landlord or his representative had nearly absolute authority within the landholding and acted as the *pater-familias* of the many peasant families. Under this system the landlord realized his income from the exploitation of non-remunerated labor, which had few or no alternatives for other employment or access to land. . . .

The pre-reform landholding structure was, if not wholly then in part, responsible for the fact that the flow of agricultural products to the city and mines was not offset in any way by a return flow of private investment funds for expenditure in the rural sector. Such flows might have generated agricultural development and increases in production of agricultural staples. Instead, without them the agricultural system remained static.[6]

PRE-REFORM MARKETING ON THE
NORTH HIGHLANDS

Before the Bolivian land reform, as now, markets the for agricultural products of the north highlands area were primarily the city of La Paz and the mines. Given the landholding structure at that time it is not surprising that the marketing structure and all large volume, cash sales of agricultural products were dominated by the owners of land, almost to the complete exclusion of the mass of peasants.

At the time of harvest the landlord visited the farm to make sure that he received the agricultural produce that was due him. Once he knew the quantities it was easy to hold the administrator and the peasants accountable for bringing them to La Paz. At the end of the harvest the major products of all the farms on the north highlands were the same: barley, potatoes, *oca* and *papaliza* (both tubers), *cañaqua* and *quinua* (both cereals), and *habas* (broad beans).

The landlord usually entrusted to the administrator the potatoes that were to be dried. Barley, a major crop on the highlands, was sold immediately and directly to the brewery in La Paz, or in a few cases to representatives who came out to the farm. Wool generally was taken directly to La Paz market for sale to the mills, but on some farms the peasant women were obligated to wash, spin, and weave the wool into blankets and rugs to be sold by the landlord. The rest of the produce was stored on the farm or was taken immediately to La Paz for sale or storage. . . .

Once in La Paz agricultural produce was stored and subsequently sold in the store or *aljería* owned by the landlord. These stores or the storehouses on the ground floor, in basements, or in second patios of landlord's houses, were exclusively devoted to the agricultural produce from the owner's farms. All but five of the landlords in this study had *aljerías*. These were managed by the landlord or members of his family and the help used in the stores was brought from the farms. . . .

The production, transportation, and marketing of the landlord's agricultural produce were unremunerated obligations of the peasants. As a result, agricultural production and marketing was nearly costless to the landlord in terms of actual money expenditures and the produce of the landlords seldom entered into local fairs or rural markets in the north highlands region. It was no advantage for the landlords to sell their produce any other way than that described above.

Primarily the result of the land ownership structure and the predominant system of labor exploitation, cash and volume sales of agricultural produce in the north highlands region were dominated by the owners of large landholdings. The bulk of agricultural produce reaching La Paz markets came from the lands which landlords had for their exclusive use. This does not mean that peasant production of agricultural products did not reach La Paz or the mines either directly or through local fairs.

However, the produce of the landlords was more important in supplying both La Paz and the mines.

PEASANT MARKET PARTICIPATION
BEFORE THE LAND REFORM

The Bolivian peasant was given a plot of land where he could build a house, have a garden, and keep some animals in return for rendering stipulated farm labor and personal service obligations to the landlord. He also was allowed small parcels of land and limited pasture rights in certain defined areas of the landholding, including lands lying fallow. The peasants were expected to meet their needs by working these lands after meeting their labor obligations on the lands of the landlord.

As a result, the primary orientation of all peasant families working within this system of agriculture was almost exclusively toward their own subsistence or consumption needs, rather than production for the market. The small quantities of land they were given, as well as the little time they had to work it, precluded their being able to think in terms other than family subsistence requirements. Generally, the only contacts which the peasant families had with markets were through the sale or barter of small amounts of staple commodities, and sale of some meat, eggs, or cheese.

It was usually by means of the frequent, small-scale barter transactions that peasant production of staple commodities entered local fairs and eventually was consumed in small towns, La Paz, or the mines. These transactions, as well as cash purchases, usually took place in the plazas of rural towns, usually cantonal or provincial capitals, and not on the landholdings, for the peasants were completely free to buy or sell wherever they wanted.[7] Usually, peasant families attended only one of these markets once a week or less often, for distances between these fairs were too great for more frequent trips on foot. . . .

In addition to weekly fairs there were annual fairs held in all of the larger cities, especially provincial and departmental capitals, which coincided with religious holidays held in honor of the specific capital. It was at these larger fairs, as well as when the peasant had to go to La Paz to work in the store or house of the landowner, that the peasant family made its major cash purchases. Usually the family had accumulated some cash before these fairs by taking animals, such as sheep or pigs, or agricultural produce to be sold there. With cash they purchased work animals—oxen for plowing, donkeys and mules for transporting agricultural produce—and agricultural implements. These were needed to meet their labor obligations on the landlord's lands and to work their own lands.

The only agricultural products which were available in these fairs from other regions—coffee, rice, fruit, noodles, sugar, etc.—were considered as specialty goods, to be purchased only on certain occasions such as fiestas, etc. A few manufactured goods were purchased infrequently, such as cotton cloth, wool clothing, agricultural implements, kerosene and dyes, mirrors, combs, ribbons, thread, needles, buttons, candles, pots and pans, cookies, soap, beer, soft drinks, cups, plates, nails, etc. Before the land reform there were few purchases by the peasants that could be considered as consumer durable goods such as a radio or sewing machine.

The tenure system, with its peasant farm labor and personal service obligations to the landlord, as well as outright prohibitions as to what the peasant could produce and sell, was the main cause for the low level of his participation in markets on a cash basis. The effect of these obligations was to diminish the opportunities available and capacity of the peasant family to earn a cash income. In the case of some of the obligations, eggs for example, the landlord appropriated for himself the peasant production of these high-value, protein-rich products, which he knew had a good market and which he could sell directly to consumers in his store in La Paz. As a result, the subsistence base of the peasant family, that is, potatoes and cereals, had to be used even to a greater extent to meet the cash expenditures of the peasant family.

It is always difficult to try to reconstruct, after the passage of 14 or more years, the extent to which peasants acquired goods by either barter or cash. It is possible, however, by means of group interviews with the older members of peasant communities, to get a good idea of the more common articles and quantities acquired on a regular basis during one year for a family of five before the land reform.

Table I indicates the extent to which a peasant family of five participated in mar-

TABLE I

ARTICLES, QUANTITIES, AND VALUES OF
MOST COMMONLY ACQUIRED GOODS
AMONG THE BOLIVIAN PEASANTS IN
NORTH HIGHLANDS BEFORE 1953
(1966 PRICES)

Bartered Articles	Quantity	Present Value
Condiments	—	$ .65
Cooking grease	3 lbs.	.60
Noodles, etc.	15 lbs.	1.50
Pots for Cooking	5	1.65
Salt	3 panes	.75
Wool	4 hides with wool	2.70

Total Value of Goods Acquired by Barter During the Year on a Regular Basis $7.85

Purchased Articles	Quantity	Present Value
Alcohol	5 quarts	$ 3.50
Bread	30 pieces	1.25
Cigarettes	5 packages	.50
Coca	10 lbs.	4.20
Dyes	2 lbs.	.25
Hats	2	4.15
Kerosene	26 bottles	1.10
Matches	50 boxes (small)	.85
Pants	1 pair	1.50
Sugar	15 lbs.	1.25
Tocuyo (cloth)	10 yards	4.25

Total Value of Goods Acquired by Cash During the Year $22.80

Total Value of All Goods $30.65

kets before 1953.[8] The total was US$30.65. Of this amount, $7.85 worth of common household consumption items was acquired by bartering agricultural staples for them. Cash purchases of household consumption items were made in the amount of $22.80. There were also infrequent cash purchases of agricultural implements and animals, such as donkeys or oxen, to meet the farm labor obligations. Most of the time these were cash expenditures, made only infrequently as replacements were needed. . . .

Thus, marketing in the pre-reform period can be characterized, on the one hand, by the commercially-oriented, large-volume, direct transactions of the landlords whose production was destined for the urban market of La Paz or the mines, with little return flow of investment goods or funds to the rural sector which could have stimulated development there. On the other hand, the market system was made up of labor exchanges, barter and small cash transactions among the many peasant families in markets located primarily in the provincial and cantonal capitals. Peasant sales were commonly staple goods and barter transactions were more frequent. The most important characteristic of this subsistence-oriented marketing system was that, because of the low income of the peasants, the peasantry was excluded from participation at a higher level in markets and in a money economy and there were relatively few sales of simple manufactured goods.

LAND REFORM AND THE PROCESS OF
MARKETING ADJUSTMENT

After winning election in 1951 the National Revolutionary Movement Party (MNR) was allowed to assume power in 1952 only after a revolt among army units in La Paz forced the incumbent government out of office. The MNR Party began its reform program by nationalizing the three major mining interests and by enfranchising the peasant masses, at the same time creating a national peasant union movement. Peasant unions were necessary to maintain the government in power and to bring about the passage of the Bolivian Land Reform Law of 1953.

The MNR accomplished the creation and unification of a national peasant union movement by not taking the drastic measures of repression (taken by previous governments in other areas) to put down the popular uprisings and invasions of lands which took place in the Cochabamba region in 1952 and after.[9] In this area the government chose to work with a rural peasant movement which was aided by members of mining unions and an urban-based, middle-class intellectual group organized into a political party called the Revolutionary Party of the Left.

In areas where popular manifestations for land reform among the peasants did not occur, which was nearly all the country outside the Cochabamba Valley region, the government sent its agents or members of various mining and urban labor unions to advise peasant leaders about the coming land reform and how they should organize themselves in order to acquire their lands. The new MNR government took these actions after assuming power and continued them after the passage of the Land Reform Law in August 1953.

When peasants were informed about the land reform they were told they would receive the lands they worked and should not work any longer for the landlords under the old system. During this time, regional peasant union leaders, who were receiving support from the government and, in some cases, who were receiving or already possessed arms, were making it difficult for anyone to travel from La Paz and other departmental capitals to rural areas. A result of this situation was that, even before the Land Reform Law was signed in 1953, few landlords or their administrators remained on the farms in the region of the north highlands.

Within the context of this revolutionary situation it would be completely erroneous to reason that *land reform*—the division of large one-owner farms into many small individually worked farms—led to a decline in agricultural production. In the case of Bolivia it would be less incorrect to suggest that a popular revolution which led to universal suffrage, to expropriation of the three larger mining concerns, to the creation of peasant unions and armed militias in the countryside and, finally, to a land reform law, would [be likely to] have immediate repercussions on the agricultural system and possibly the level of agricultural production—especially on the quantities of agricultural produce delivered to urban centers.

To alter tenure relations between the landowning minority and the non-landowning majority required the organization of peasant unions to undercut the power of the landlords and their efforts at counter-revolution. In this context, the [short-run adverse] effects on agricultural production or the movement of agricultural products to the cities should be a secondary but still an important consideration. This was the price of beginning to create a new agricultural system and a new popularly based government.

Seventeen farms in this study were idled largely as a result of the political situation created by the Revolution. The lands of the landlords on these farms were left unworked for varying periods of time, beginning in October 1952 or in 1953 and ranging from two years to the present. Four farms were idle for 2 years, five for 3 years, four for 4 years, two for 5 years, one for 7 years, and one for 14 years. A total of 70 production years were lost. On these farms no subdivision of lands occurred during the periods they were idle; the decline in agricultural production was not a result of the subdivision of large farms into small peasant holdings but occurred for other reasons. . . .

On eight of the 51 farms, lands were subdivided among the peasant families in 1953, usually with the peasant unions playing an important part in the subdivision. The peasant union leaders had interpreted the Revolution and the talk of land reform as meaning that the peasants now had rights to all the lands. The lands were divided among the peasant families (not always evenly), to be worked individually. These are the only cases of large farms which were subdivided immediately after the Revolution of 1952.

In a total of 34 cases out of 51, all cases except the 17 where lands were idled, the lands were worked continually from 1952 to the present. A few were divided immediately among members of the local peasant union while the rest were worked as a unit under sharecropping arrangements or by the peasant union. In the latter case, lands of the landlord were worked as a unit but the total production was divided between the families who worked the lands.

At times the peasant union reserved some of the product for the expenses of the school which the members wanted to construct, or to pay expenses of the peasant union, topographers and agrarian judges which were necessary to begin the land reform process according to the Land Reform Law. On all these 34 farms the peasants say that the same agricultural products were raised and sold after the Revolution as before the Revolution, and in all cases the peasants willingly say that they withheld a part of the products from the landlords' land for their own consumption, but sold the rest.[10]

A decline in production of agricultural goods may have taken place on all these

34 farms where lands were not idled because of several adjustments begun shortly after the land reform. For example, the peasant family was no longer obligated to work a disproportionate amount of time on the landlords' lands. Some may have decided to take some time off. In the first years after the reform, peasants spent much time at local and regional peasant union meetings. This may have been at the expense of working landlords' lands as intensively as before.

The extent to which peasants were unable to work the land of the landlord as "efficiently" (in terms of the exploitation of their own labor), either individually or as a group, as under the agricultural system before 1952, would have reduced agricultural production. Also, the use of natural fertilizers on the landlords' lands may have declined since peasants were not obligated to use them. This was the case especially on those farms where the landlord had sold some or all of his animals, fearing the coming land reform. . . . In the north highlands region all of these were major adjustments and probably affected agricultural production temporarily. This should be expected when land reform is undertaken rapidly during a period of political change.

There is evidence that the Bolivian Government was aware of the above adjustments and tried to take some steps to avert a decrease in agricultural production and a disruption in the flow of agricultural produce to the cities. Peasant unions and inspectors from La Paz were asked to enforce Supreme Decree 03375 of April 30, 1953,[11] which made the peasant unions and their leaders specifically responsible for the harvest (from February through May) during that year, and for the planting and harvesting of lands in the succeeding years. There were 19 cases out of the total of 34 farms that were not idled by the land reform where peasants took the landlords' share of production (50 percent) to the Ministry of Rural Affairs in La Paz for varying periods of time after April 30, 1953. This shows that the Government was trying to use the peasant unions as a channel of communication to assure that no farm lands would be idled. However, because of the political situation as well as confusion and lack of communication during that period, it was surely very difficult to enforce this decree. Also, peasant unions were not equally organized in all areas at that time.

It has been shown that the greater number of farms included in the study continued producing after the land reform and that little of the landlords' lands were left idle for long. In addition to problems of reorganization and adjustment on the farms stemming from the absence of the landlords or their representatives, the other major adjustment which had to be made by the peasants was in marketing a much larger quantity of agricultural produce than previously.

Immediately after the Revolution there remained only a part of the pre-reform marketing structure, that is, the weekly, subsistence-oriented fairs based on the exchange of small quantities of agricultural staples for other consumption items. Landlords did not dare return to their properties in their own or rented trucks in order to bring agricultural produce to the city as they had done before 1952. As a result the large-volume cash sales made directly by the landlords in La Paz or to the mines diminished. The effect of this was that the stores of landlords ceased to function and the major source of supply of agricultural staples to La Paz markets and middlemen was reduced substantially. . . .

As a result of the land reform the full burden of getting agricultural products to urban markets in sufficient quantities became the responsibility of the peasantry and buyers from rural areas and the city. Both were unable to meet the challenge rapidly enough without disrupting the flow of products to the city. This does not mean efforts were not made, for peasants began to come to the city more frequently than previously and men with transportation and others with money combined to go to the countryside to buy products from the peasants, not only in established fairs but also by stopping along the road whenever a peasant appeared who wanted to sell products.

This period of adjustment was necessary to begin the creation of a new marketing system based on the sales of peasants instead of landlords. This was the most important adjustment that had to be made in the post-reform period and was the major reason why agricultural produce marketed in La Paz decreased during the first three to five years after the Revolution of 1952.

It is unfortunate that a decrease in agricultural production is associated with the Bolivian Land Reform in the minds of so many. Such a decrease is not shown in indices of production distributed by the United States Department of Agriculture.[12] Neither has it been possible to find such a decrease officially registered elsewhere. . . . The "apparent" decline in agricultural production after 1952, while true in part, is better explained by marketing adjustments and transportation scarcity, and weather phenomena, with the former by far the more important bottleneck to be overcome during that period.

The peasants, their unions and leaders, as well as local officials and middlemen, responded to the bottleneck in marketing and transportation which had been created by the land reform by creating a large number of new fairs and markets and by rapidly increasing the number of trucks visiting these areas. Most of these new fairs have started out on a very small basis, with only one or two trucks coming once a week to bring buyers from the city of La Paz to deal with the peasants. In 1966 most of the fairs visited during this study had an average of 5 to 9 trucks coming regularly, and many with 10 to 14 trucks. There are a few post-reform fairs with 75 to 150 trucks coming regularly. The agricultural produce sold in the new fairs and in the older ones consists mainly of agricultural staples most of which are destined for the La Paz market. These are the same products which were grown and taken directly to La Paz and sold there by the landlord before the land reform. The cash income which landlords received from the sale of these products is now received by the peasantry. Ex-landlords generally play no part in these newly created fairs on the highlands. . . .

The actions of peasant union leaders were very important for the creation of new fairs. It was these leaders who pushed for the creation of new fairs by submitting the necessary papers at the cantonal and provincial levels for creating new marketing and administrative political centers. These papers were submitted in the name of the peasant union. In these cases the major reasons given for the creation of new fairs were to give a stimulus to the creation of an urban center, to create a new canton, to increase the commerce coming to the area, and to get better prices for agricultural produce than was possible in the established fairs at the cantonal and provincial levels. . . . No matter what the reasons were for the creation of new fairs, the result was the same: each new fair contributed to restructuring the rural marketing system.

Besides the above changes, all the old fairs have increased substantially in importance in recent years. In some provincial capitals, however, especially Achacachi on the north highlands, people familiar with the amount of economic activity concentrated in these centers before the land reform affirm that distributing lands to the peasants has led to economic stagnation at the provincial level.

What they fail to discern is that the economic prosperity these centers realized before the land reform was based on a landholding structure which no longer exists and that, with the distribution of lands, these few centers lost volume to the many new fairs and urban centers that have been or are rapidly being created.[13] By now most of these older centers have recovered their pre-reform economic prosperity, as is seen in the new construction, the greater number of stores and restaurants, and the number of trucks which come to these areas now.

Thus far, one can see that, as a result of redistributing land, the function of selling agricultural produce destined for urban centers redounded to the peasants exclusively, with the buying function passing to the increased number of middlemen coming out from La Paz on trucks to deal with peasants on an individual basis. Increased peasant participation in rural markets was a result of this change.

PEASANT MARKET PARTICIPATION IN
POST-REFORM MARKETING

There are many farms where the peasant families barter little or nothing today. These farms are usually found close to the city of La Paz, especially in the lower regions where vegetable production is profitable for the La Paz market. Generally, most peasant families still barter the same products as before the land reform—agricultural staples in small quantities for the same consumption items as before the land reform. . . .

In an agricultural economy such as that

of the north highlands, where the peasants make most production decisions based on subsistence criteria and where they have not yet been accustomed to keep *or need* ready cash in all of their day to day transactions, bartering has an important function and still is practiced. However, most peasants agree that now they or their wives barter less frequently than before the land reform.

Table II shows that the annual total value of goods purchased for consumption on a regular basis for a family of five is $100.95, or three times more than the pre-1952 value shown in Table I. The quantity bartered now is $5.05 of the total while the regular participation of peasants now in a money economy is over four times what it was before 1952. This has been a direct result of the land reform and the concomitant redistribution of opportunities to earn a cash income in the rural sector.

Tables I and II do not show the entire change that has taken place, for these tables are based only upon the transactions made on a regular or weekly basis in local markets or in La Paz. Besides the above, the peasants also make certain infrequent purchases, such as farm tools, implements, and work animals. These have changed little in terms of quality, quantity, or in that they are acquired largely for cash. The infrequent cash purchases, which are more important now and which almost did not exist before 1952, are the purchases of corrugated metal sheets for roofs; also the purchases of windows, cement, sewing machines, radios, and bicycles. Peasants are just beginnng to purchase kerosene stoves and, more recently, records and record players.

One former large landholding can be cited to give an impression of the type of change one can expect to find on almost any of the landholdings which were expropriated by the land reform, namely, the increasing frequency with which the above products are being purchased. In this case there are approximately 200 families. In 1956 there was 1 house with a metal roof and 1 bicycle; now there are 40 metal roofs and 80 bicycles. In 1952 there were 7 sewing machines; now there are 120. In 1959 there was 1 radio; now there are 100.[14] In most areas of Bolivia this great a change has not yet taken place but in the north highlands region this would not be an exceptional case.

TABLE II

ARTICLES, QUANTITIES, AND VALUES OF MOST COMMONLY ACQUIRED GOODS AMONG THE BOLIVIAN PEASANTS IN THE NORTH HIGHLANDS: 1966 (1966 PRICES)

Bartered Articles	Quantity	Present Value
Condiments	—	$ .65
Pots for cooking	5	1.65
Salt	3 panes	.75
Other food items in small quantities		2.00
Total Value of Goods Acquired by Barter During the Year on a Regular Basis		$5.05

Purchased Articles	Quantity	Present Value
Alcohol	5 quarts	$ 3.50
Soft drinks	20 bottles	1.75
Beer	10 bottles	2.50
Cooking grease	3 lbs.	.60
Cooking oil	3 bottles	1.25
Fruit and vegetables	various (in season)	2.50
Noodles	15 lbs.	1.50
Bread	75 pieces	3.15
Flour (wheat & corn)	50 lbs.	3.40
Rice	35 lbs.	3.00
Sugar	25 lbs.	2.10
Coca	5 lbs.	2.10
Cigarettes	20 packages	2.00
Matches	60 boxes (small)	.95
Kerosene	26 bottles	1.10
Cloth of all kinds	15 yards	7.00
Dyes	—	.50
Shoes	2 pairs	12.50
Suits	1	12.50
Skirts	1	5.00
Sweaters	1	5.50
Pants	1	5.00
Shirts	2	2.00
Hats	2	8.00
Shawls	1	5.00
Soap	10 pieces	1.50
Total Value of Goods Acquired by Cash During the Year		$ 95.90
Total Value of All Goods		$100.95

The above does not include the increased purchases of chairs, tables, beds, plates, knives, forks and spoons, cups, metal pots, etc., as well as the construction of larger houses, many with two stories, which the peasants now have. In terms of material comforts the north highland peasant is much better off than previously. All these commodities have been acquired by cash over the years since the land reform. . . .

CONCLUSION: LAND REFORM AND
ECONOMIC DEVELOPMENT

The significance of the foregoing is how the documented changes relate to increasing possibilities for economic development in Bolivia. It is this relationship, as well as how land reform relates to social mobility and political participation, which is important in determining whether or not land redistribution programs should be initiated in other areas where work relations between landlord and peasant are similar to those which existed in Bolivia before 1952.

In the case of Bolivia the land reform on the north highlands accomplished three things quickly. One, the increased access to land realized by the peasants was equivalent to redistribution of opportunities to earn a cash income. Two, restructuring of the market system began immediately after the redistribution of land, but because it was not accomplished instantaneously, bottlenecks were created and the marketing of agricultural produce in the urban centers fell off. Nevertheless, the process was begun which would eventually lead to the creation of a marketing system in which the peasantry would play a more important role than before 1952. Three, for the first time those who were producing on the land began to spend for consumption items within the rural sector, not just in La Paz or in foreign countries as the landlords had done.

The peasants, most of whom had never before worked their lands as owner-operators, needed time to adjust to this new situation. Perhaps the most important thing the peasant had to accept was that the land reform was a fact and that it would not be undone by a counter-revolution. Two things—a combination of *revolution and land reform* carried out by the government through the peasant unions, and *time*—were necessary to increase the horizons and expectations of the peasantry. This was only to be expected of people who had worked for centuries as serfs on land belonging to others. In particular, time was needed to increase the number of rural families experiencing the new incentives, attitudes and motivations, all of which derived primarily from the development and use of individual managerial talents.

There are indications that what has taken place so far in the rural sector on the north highlands has increased the possibilities for economic development in other sectors of the economy. For example, a greater number of markets with an increased number of peasants participating in them on a cash basis signifies a greater frequency of contact between peasants and buyers from the city. A result of this is that new channels of communication are created. Markets and commercial contacts can be a source of change in attitudes and of expansion of social, political and economic horizons among the peasantry. The expansion of economic horizons leads to new wants, purchases, and consumption patterns. It also acts as a stimulus to the manufacture of commodities for a mass market.

Greater frequency of peasant transactions within the framework of a money economy has increased the extent to which specialization of functions can develop within the rural sector and also between the rural sector and the rest of the economy. When peasant transactions are based largely on barter, opportunities for trade and specialization are reduced considerably, especially in terms of the sales of products of one sector against those of another, and in terms of possibilities for creating regional or national markets for agricultural or manufactured goods. It is in relation to this latter point that considerable change has taken place in Bolivia; national markets for agricultural and non-agricultural products have been created since the land reform.

Development within the agricultural sector has been stimulated by the creation of new markets for agricultural products in precisely those areas where the land reform took place. These small but growing markets for agricultural products are for all kinds of fruits, vegetables, coffee, wheat products (such as bread and noodles), sugar, rice, corn and corn flour, wheat flour, and soft drinks and beer. Admittedly, the per capita consumption of these food products is still low, but the tastes for these products have been created and increased consumption and sales in the future will be more a function of increases in income than new market creation.

The creation of new markets for manufactured goods is even more impressive than that for agricultural products. Widely consumed, locally manufactured goods are plastic and leather shoes, clothing of all kinds, materials, wools and threads, agricultural implements, and the many small items for the home such as doors, windows, beds, tables, chairs, plates, glasses, cups, utensils of all kinds, hand tools, etc. It is the producers of these domestically produced goods who now have access to a wider market than before, assuring to some degree the chances that the domestic production of these goods will continue and grow.

Generally, it can be concluded that the landholding structure and tenure relations which characterized Bolivia before the land reform forced the peasant to produce largely for himself and to consume a minimum of goods not produced on his own lands. This inhibited the development of markets of adequate size for light manufactured goods, domestic or otherwise, which acted as a brake on the development of a manufacturing sector, thus contributing to the slow growth of the country.

In this respect the pre-reform landholding structure was inimical to economic development, for the consumption demands of the relatively few landlords could never have created a market of sufficient size to promote development. However, with the redistribution of land—that is, a redistribution of opportunities to earn a cash income from the land—and the greater participation of the peasantry in a money economy, regional and national markets have been created, which has given and may continue to give a significant impetus to economic development over the coming years.

1. The data used herein were gathered during 1966 by means of individual and group interviews. Group interviews were used to obtain all historical data, particularly peasant family expenditure data before 1953. Table I and historical parts of the text present the most common answers to questions about markets and purchases made by barter and cash before 1953. Table II represents the most common answers of 100 families interviewed individually using an economics questionnaire. Data in Table II were substantiated on a broader regional basis by unstructured interviews with groups in other areas besides where the questionnaire was used.

Interviews were carried out in 51 peasant communities which before 1953 were landholdings held by individual owners. All of these landholdings have been affected by the land reform and most of the land has been distributed to the peasants. The landholdings included in this study are distributed on what is usually considered the north highlands of Bolivia, i.e., primarily the Department of La Paz. This region coincides roughly with the major agricultural supply area which serviced the city of La Paz before the land reform. La Paz still is the most important market for agricultural produce coming from this region.

2. According to the Bolivian Agricultural Census of 1950 (Dirección Nacional de Estadística y Censos, Ministerio de Hacienda, p. 2 *et passim*), of a total of 82,598 private holdings reported for the country as a whole, 7,924, or approximately 9.6 percent, were farms of 200 hectares (one hectare equals 2.46 acres) or more, representing 74 percent of the total area reported. These same farms also reported 62 percent of the land that was being cultivated that year. At the other extreme, there were 50,483 farms, or 61 percent of those reported, which were smaller than 5.0 hectares, representing .28 percent of the total area reported and 8.1 percent of the cultivated lands. The landholding structure in Bolivia before 1952 was one of the more extreme to be found anywhere in Latin America, then or now.

3. If one looks at the pre-reform data only for the Department of La Paz, where this study was carried out, one finds that of the total of 6,221 privately held properties, 1,058, or 17 percent, were farms of 200 hectares or more, representing 96 percent of the total area reported and 81 percent of the land that was under cultivation. In the same Department the number of farms less than 5.0 hectares represented 48 percent of the farms reported in the census but this number had only .09 percent of the total land and only 2.0 percent of the lands under cultivation. From interviews, as well as from data in the National Agrarian Reform Service's archives, it was possible to determine that the total number of holdings which 44 of the 51 different landlords represented in this study was 159 different farms, or a rough average of 4 per owner. Multiple holdings were common and in 1950 land ownership was even more

concentrated in the Department of La Paz than it appears in the 1950 Agricultural Census. . . .

4. It should be added that, whenever possible, the peasant ignored this prohibition using these to earn a bit of extra cash income.

5. The above are the more generally found farm obligations and prohibitions other than labor and personal service obligations. . . . There were other prohibitions of a social nature which maintained and re-enforced the caste-like distinction which had grown up between the peasant or *indio* and the landlord or *blanco*. In many cases peasants were prohibited from speaking Spanish to the landlord, either on the farm or in the city. Similarly, when a peasant came to the city to work in the house or the store of the landlord dressed in ready-made clothing, rather than the coarse homespun goods which they usually produced for themselves, they had to change into the latter. This was especially true if they wore shoes rather than coming barefooted or in the crude sandals which were common. There is no other explanation for this than that which is usually given for the lack of schools on the landholdings: landlords did not want to encourage learning or the adoption of non-peasant dress and language for fear that the farm labor would leave the rural area for the city.

6. This does not mean that there were not some farms with improved animals, pastures, and some agricultural machinery. These cases were so few that, in trying to generalize about the pre-reform agricultural system, they would not be important. . . .

7. In only a very few cases of the 51 farms studied on the north highlands did the landlord sell non-agricultural commodities to the peasant families on his farm. These sales were for cash or credit but were not a way of tying the families to the farm (debt peonage) as was so frequent in Mexico before the land reform there. On about half the farms studied the landlord did sell staple commodities to the peasant families but only when they ran out of their own supplies.

8. Using present values will allow a comparison with the extent and the basis of the peasants' present participation in markets. The author is completely aware that changes in the structure of prices as well as quality of goods between 1950 and the present does not make the two points in time completely comparable but for lack of specific price and quality data in 1950 this is the only way that such a comparison can be made.

9. Richard W. Patch, "Social Implications of the Bolivian Agrarian Reform," Ph.D. dissertation, Cornell University, Ithaca, New York, 1956. See also Patch's chapter, "Bolivia: U.S. Assistance in a Revolutionary Setting," in R. N. Adams, et al., *Social Change in Latin America* (1960).

10. Military evidence bears this out to some extent because the height and weight of recruits into the Bolivian army from some areas have increased since the land reform, indicating either higher levels of calorie consumption or a general improvement in quality of diet, or both, during the last decade. (Ministry of Defense, La Paz, Bolivia.)

11. *Ley de la Reforma Agraria en Bolivia: Leyes Conexas, Decretos, Resoluciones y Circulares,* Servicio Nacional de Reforma Agraria. Departamento de Relaciones Publicas, Supreme Decree 03375, Articles 1 and 2, p. 35. It is necessary to point out that this decree antedates the Agrarian Reform Law of August 1953 by three months, showing once again that farms had been abandoned as a result of the Revolution. Also, the decree is ample recognition of the existence of peasant unions before the Land Reform Law was passed.

12. *Indices of Agricultural Production for the 20 Latin American Countries,* Preliminary 1966, ERS-Foreign 44, Economic Research Service, United States Department of Agriculture, pp. 10–11.

13. Research in the Cochabamba area also shows that this was the major reason for the decline in economic activity in the city of Cochabamba in the years immediately after the land reform. Other data indicate that provincial leaders in Achacachi before the land reform used their influence to deny the creation, and in some cases destroy fairs in other areas, areas where the people wanted their own fair because they thought the taxes they had to pay to officials in Achacachi to sell goods there were too high. Even the merchants in La Paz have, since the land reform, tried to have legislation passed which would control the creation of rural fairs; they were losing business to merchants who would go to the rural areas to see goods.

14. It is fully realized that price changes and increased availability of many of these commodities, especially radios, sewing machines, and metal roofing, would have induced some of the above changes. However, it is the author's opinion that the most important factor determining increased consumption of these articles is the higher level of income realized by the peasant families as a result of the land reform.

LAND REFORM IN TAIWAN:
ITS EFFECT ON RURAL SOCIAL
ORGANIZATION AND LEADERSHIP

BERNARD GALLIN

Michigan State University

INTRODUCTION

The Hokkien village of Hsin Hsing where the writer carried on field research for 16 months in 1957 and 1958, is in Chang-hua Hsien (county) on the west-central coastal plain of Taiwan. It is a wet-rice agricultural village whose population of 650 persons comprises descendants of Chinese who emigrated approximately 170 years ago from Fukien (near Amoy) in southeastern China.

Each of the village's 115 households represents an economic unit as well as a family unit whose members are related through a grandfather or great-grandfather whom they have in common. Such *tsu* [1] groups vary in size. . . . [however,] there is no single, dominant *tsu* to provide leadership for Hsin Hsing's diversified kin groups. In this, it conforms to the prevalent pattern in this area of Taiwan.

Because of the lack of *tsu* leadership, in Hsin Hsing and in similar villages throughout Taiwan, village leadership roles were filled by landlords who had no particular kinship identification with the village as a whole, although they might be related to one segment of the village population. Their main concern with the village was an economic interest based on large landholdings in the immediate area.

In the years before and after World War II, steadily mounting tenancy problems plagued Hsin Hsing village, as well as much of Taiwan and the mainland. As the population expanded on the fixed land supply the problem of land tenure increased. In the densely populated Hsin Hsing area, especially during 1945 to 1949, competition among tenants for rentable land was rife. Exorbitant land rents were not the tenant's main concern. Instead, his greatest worry was whether or not the landlord would permit him to retain the rented land, since the landlord could force the tenant off whenever he wished.

All too often, a good personal relationship (good *kan ch'ing*) with the landlord was the tenant's only possible security. And although there was an economic, social, and educational line between most landlords and their tenants, it is apparent that a good personal relationship often did develop between them. The landlord then often played a paternalistic role toward the tenant and a certain amount of reciprocal obligation was felt by both parties.

If the tenant failed to maintain good relations with his landlord, or if he openly complained about his treatment at the hands of the landlord, he was in grave danger of being thrown off the land and replaced by another tenant. Other tenants or prospective tenants who needed more land would often offer the landlord a higher rent for the land; the competing farmers would attempt to put the tenant in disfavor by informing the landlord of real or fictitious misuse of the land. As a result, tenants in the area feared to agitate openly for land reform.

THE LAND REFORM

Once settled in Taiwan, the Nationalist Government, which was faced with a serious tenancy situation, instituted a land reform program in line with past promises and scattered attempts at reform on the mainland. This program aimed to give the tenant security through contracts which would insure the tenant of his continued right to work the land. Rent was reduced from perhaps 40–60 percent to 37.5 percent of the annual main crop. These provisions were effected by the Provincial Law of 1949 known as the "Regulations Governing the Lease of Private Farm Lands in Taiwan Province"; they were then more

From *Human Organization* (Summer 1963), pp. 109–112. Reprinted by permission.

firmly enforced by the National Act known as the "Farm Rent Reduction Act of 1951."

The landlord class was immediately affected by these measures which were designed to help the tenants. Because the rent reduction cut into profits, around 1951 some landlords chose to sell part of their land. Many others, anticipating a land expropriation law, felt they would do better by selling large portions of their land before such a law became effective.

In 1953, an expropriation law known as "The Land-to-the-Tiller Act" was promulgated and contributed greatly to altering the land situation in Taiwan. This measure affected the status of landlords in the rural areas and helped change the nature of social organization and village leadership. Under this act, the government assumed the authority to expropriate, with compensation, part of the land of the landlords which, in turn, was sold to the tenants, thus creating a new group of owner-farmers. In the Hsin Hsing village area, most landlords could legally retain a maximum of 3 chia (7.2 acres) of paddy land and 6 chia (14.4 acres) of dry land. The expropriated portions of land were sold to the former tenants by the government at a price to be paid in 20 semi-annual installments, usually in kind.

The landlords did not receive cash payments for their expropriated land. Rather, the purchase price fixed by the government was 250 percent of the total annual main crop yield. Of this proportion, 70 percent was paid to the landlord in land bonds and 30 percent in stock shares. These stock shares were in government enterprises such as paper, mining, and cement which had been taken over from the Japanese after the war. The land bonds held by the former landowners are being redeemed in kind, in a series of 20 semi-annual installments. Payment in kind ensures the stable value of bonds in times of inflation. The land bonds are transferrable and can be sold on the open market or used as security in financial matters.

EFFECTS OF THE
LAND REFORM ON LANDLORDS

In general the landlords were neither happy with the expropriation of their land nor satisfied with the manner of compensation. In addition to being unhappy with their monetary losses, they were particularly disturbed by what they considered the disruption of their whole way of life. It had been traditional in China for wealthy businessmen or landlords to buy up land for investment or simply for security and status. To these landlords and especially to many urban capitalists who had followed this pattern, the land reform program made it clear that it was no longer profitable or even safe to invest new capital in agricultural land. For many, the alternative was to shift their excess capital into industrial and commercial activities.[2]

These new investments were made mainly in urban centers but also frequently in smaller market towns of the local area. When money was invested in the small market towns, it usually went into financing various kinds of light industries and small business activities. It meant that the investor often needed to acquire new technical knowledge to keep pace with his new financial interests. In some cases, the landlords or their sons became so involved in business or industrial activities that they gradually sold off portions of the three chia which they had been allowed to retain under the Land Reform Act, and used the money for additional investments. In shifting their economic interests away from the village to the market towns, these landlords usually abandoned their social and political interests in the village.

Many other landlords, however, have maintained their economic investments in the villages. For instance, in the two villages adjacent to Hsin Hsing, a few formerly large landholders continue their activities very much as before. While their holdings were cut significantly by the land reform, they retain at least their maximum three chia of land. In addition, they continue to engage in non-productive financial endeavors such as money-lending at a very high interest rate, thus helping the small farmer meet the ever-present farm-credit problem, which the government or private agencies have not yet solved. Because of their education, some landlords retain positions as minor government officials or teachers and in this way maintain their role in village life.

Many landlords, however, have been unable to adapt to the new economic situation. Some went into business, failed because of inexperience, and lost much of their capital. Often uncertain of the value of the industrial stock shares which had been forced on them in partial compensation for their land, they sold their shares at prices much lower than face value. Such landlords, embittered by the new situation and their inability to cope with it, frequently went on the downgrade socially and economically. Some spent much time and money—which they could no longer afford—drinking and gambling. Their status and prestige greatly declined, and their interests in their villages decreased.

EFFECTS OF LAND REFORM
ON VILLAGE LEADERSHIP

How did these developments affect village leadership? Traditionally, the village landlord has played a major leadership role in his village and surrounding area. During this period of Japanese occupation of the island, such leadership roles were reinforced by the Japanese who preferred to handle village problems through the wealthy landlord class rather than to deal directly with the "peasants." The Hsin Hsing villagers readily recall that the local Japanese police and officials showed respect only for the rich landlords. Consequently, for the villagers to get along successfully with the Japanese, it was necessary for them to work through their landlords. A landlord was usually elected by the villagers to handle local affairs and to represent village interests in dealing with Japanese authorities.

This arrangement was to the landlord's advantage. As the official village leader, he wielded greater power by which he could more easily manipulate the villagers, and even the tax collector and others to his own advantage. Recognition as a leader by his fellow villagers and by the authorities also increased his prestige in the area. Not only was such a landlord the elected village political leader but he often was an informal leader as well—a person who assumed an active part in most of the social and religious affairs of the village. He usually contributed time and money to help make these affairs a success. Such efforts by the landlord helped to build his reputation as a public-spirited person.

Frequently, the landlord assumed the role of mediator in discussions of village or inter-village problems and in disputes between his own villagers or between members of other villages. When the landlord's efforts as a mediator extended beyond his own village, he enhanced his own reputation both in his native village and in other villages in the area, as well as the reputation of his village itself.

These conditions continued after the Restoration into the post-Land Reform period. Today, the landlord class continues in the rural areas and wields power in local grass-roots politics as well as in socioeconomic affairs. In many villages, the recognized leaders are still those who are rich, maintain big landholdings, and have had a fairly good education. Such people are also known to have influence in some government agency. It is still an advantage for a village to have a wealthy representative of the landlord class to deal with the authorities since most of the local government officials are also drawn from the same class.

However, in some areas this picture is changing as a result of the Land Reform program. Village affairs are being profoundly affected as many formerly large landholders and traditional village leaders transfer their economic interests and activities away from the land. When the landlord gives up his major economic interests in an area, it is usually not long before he also loses interest in the village and is unwilling to spend his time and money on social, religious, and political affairs. Because the personal advantage is gone, he is no longer concerned with maintaining his status or leadership role. He may even move his residence out of the village in order to be closer to his new economic interests. When this happens intra- and inter-village problems frequently go unsolved because of the unavailability of the traditionally responsible and respected local leadership.

How have the villagers reacted to this leadership vacuum which developed from the changes in land tenure patterns? In those villages where such a situation has developed, the villagers have reacted in two different ways. The first reaction has been one of apathy, a reluctance to occupy positions of formal village leadership.

For instance, in the 1958 village election, there was no candidate for mayor in six villages of the twenty-two villages in Pu Yen Hsiang (district) in which Hsin Hsing is located. According to the district officials, no one in those villages was willing to spend the time or the money required for the position. The office of the village mayor must be filled by a person who is not bound to his fields or to other work in order to earn a living for his family. He must have ample time to give to the office as well as an interest in being active in village affairs. He must have enough money to meet the expenses of the traditional functions of the office such as entertaining public officials or police visiting the village. He must have enough education and social acumen to handle the many relationships with villagers as well as outsiders with whom he is in frequent contact in his role as village head.

Here it may be noted that the office of mayor no longer requires that an individual have a relatively high degree of education and literacy since today village records and paperwork are handled by a minor official from the District Public Office who acts as village secretary.

In other villages, the reaction to the withdrawal of landlords from participation in village affairs has been for other people to try to fill the position of mayor and general village leader. Usually the elected mayor is the general village leader. In some villages, people who have the basic qualifications for the office as well as a sincere interest in working for the village, have gained the respect of their fellow villagers and have successfully filled the leadership roles. These are usually people whose reputations in the area are on the upswing because they have more land and education and therefore more time to contribute to the community.

On the other hand, there are those villages—and Hsin Hsing appears to be one of several in the area—in which individuals elected to the office of mayor have failed to win respect or acceptance as village leaders. Although they have the qualifications of time and money, and often were the only candidates in the village, the motives of these new leaders are suspect.

The mayor of Hsin Hsing during my stay is perhaps a good example of this. He is a man whom most of the villagers fear but do not respect. They point to his minimal education—*He knows very few characters,* they say.

They say that he has kept more than one wife at a time by taking other men's wives. They feel that he does not really want to work for the village but only wants to increase his own power and status in the area.

In spite of all this, he was elected. The main reasons for his election seem to be that he has enough time and money to carry out at least the superficial functions of the office. Village factionalism proved to be to his benefit and his membership in one of the larger village *tsu* groups provided him with a following that worked hard for his election.

Although this man bears the official title of mayor, he is not really accepted as village head. Today, Hsin Hsing village, like many other communities, appears to be virtually leaderless. Here and in some other villages observed, this has led to a state of village disorganization in meeting many village problems, especially those concerning relations with other villages.

SUMMARY AND CONCLUSIONS

The post-Land Reform period in rural Taiwan is one of social as well as economic transition. Although the landlords still form an important class in the rural areas, the changes taking place may mark the beginning of a decline in the almost exclusive leadership of the landlord or gentry class. There appears to be the beginning of a crack in the traditional social system which had grown out of the unequal distribution of rural wealth and income as a result of the land tenure system. The Land Reform program which has led to many landlords withdrawing their interests from the rural villages appears to be leading to some equalization of social status in rural Taiwan. This makes it possible for new village leaders to become effective.

In the past, and in the present to a lesser degree, there were capable villagers who had no chance to compete with the landlord class for primary village leadership. Perhaps now for the first time, these people will have some opportunity to manifest their leadership abilities. Many traditional attitudes must be cleared away before a more widespread acceptance of these new leaders can be obtained. In addition to actual economic equalization, there must be a more complete social equalization. There must be a change in the attitudes of the villagers themselves regarding leadership and authority, for the villagers have not yet been emancipated from their respect for wealth and power and the use to which these two can be put in manipulating people and politics.

It was evident during my stay in Hsin Hsing that these changes are gradually coming about. It has been shown that respect for a man today is not based solely on his power and wealth. These qualifications are not enough but must be accompanied by a feeling of responsibility on the part of the leader towards the village, an active participation in village affairs and an outward appearance, at least, of not looking down on less fortunate fellows.

The consequences of village social disorganization have not yet been felt. While it appears too soon to tell how successful these new leaders will be in filling village leadership roles, it appears likely that if problems of village disorganization continue as a result of the gradual withdrawal from leadership by the landlord class, the capable villagers among the aspirants for village leadership will of necessity find increasing acceptance among their fellows.

1. A *tsu* is a patrilineal common descent group, commonly referred to in the literature as a clan.
2. For an amplification of this point and a general discussion of the role that traditional Chinese values toward the land play in influencing the direction of change, see my forthcoming, "Chinese Peasant Values Toward the Land," *Proceedings of the 1963 Annual Spring Meeting of the American Ethnological Society,* University of Washington, Seattle.

THE JAPANESE LAND REFORM:
ITS EFFICACY AND LIMITATIONS
TSUTOMU OUCHI
University of Tokyo

I

The land reform which was carried out in Japan between 1916 and 1950 may perhaps be said to have been the most successful of the land reforms carried out in many of the countries of Asia and Africa after the Second World War. The Japanese land reform included the strengthening of the rights of tenant cultivators and the fixing of rents at low sums payable in money (not in kind), but these aspects of reform were essentially secondary in nature and the main content of the reform consisted of the compulsory purchase by the government of the greater part [1] of the land on lease by landlords and its resale to former tenants, thus making the latter into owner-farmers. How thoroughly the conversion of these tenants into owner-farmers

was carried out may be gauged by referring to Figure 1.

The Figure shows that tenant farmers, who before the war had accounted for nearly one-third of the total, accounted for 5% by 1950, while part-owner farmers, who had accounted for 40% of the total before the war, accounted for somewhat more than 30%. On the other side, the owners, who before the war accounted for 30% of the total, now accounted for 62%. The same situation is apparent in the light of the land statistics, and we find that land cultivated in tenancy, which before the war had accounted for nearly 50% of cultivated land, had shrunk by 1950 to around 10%.

In addition, we must note in connection with the Figure that although the land reform itself was completed in 1950, the

From *Developing Economies* (June 1966), pp. 129–150. Reprinted by permission. Some sections have been omitted.

numbers of the owner-farmers have been increasing from that time up to the present day. In 1965 owners exceeded 80% of the total, while tenants accounted for less than 2%. We have land statistics only up to 1955, but in that year the land tenancy rate was 6%, and we may suppose that it is now under 5%. . . .

Figure 1. Proportions of Owners and Tenants, and Changes in the Tenancy Rate.

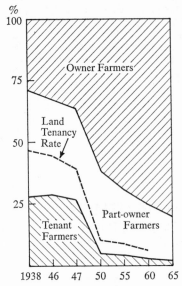

SOURCE: *Nōrinshō Tokeihyo* (Statistics of the Ministry of Agriculture and Forestry).

When the thoroughgoingness of land reform is called in question it is of course insufficient merely to draw attention to the quantitative increase in the numbers of owners or the area of land cultivated by owners as we have done above. Alongside this matter we must at all costs draw attention to the following two facts.

First the liberation of the land in this reform was carried out practically without compensation. [Land was purchased from landlords but at 1945 prices which, because of post-war inflation, amounted to only about 5% of their 1950 value when compensation was actually paid.] . . . some millions of landlords who were entirely dependent on income from leased land were deprived of the basis of their livelihood at a single stroke and lost their

position as members of the upper class in their villages. It is of course true that a certain section of them were also performing the functions of cultivating farmers, and about the time of the land reform there were not a few who took back, legally or illegally, some of the land which they had leased to tenants, thus enlarging their holdings of cultivated land. Further, the landlords and their children had received a fairly high level of education, and not a few entered intellectual occupations while a considerable number used their knowledge to obtain posts in village offices, agricultural co-operatives, etc. It is therefore not the case that all the landlords were ruined but it is true that there were some instances of landlords being reduced to pauperism.

. . . [T]he fact that the liberation of the land had been carried out in a manner which was virtually a form of expropriation did not only mean that it had great significance in rendering the landlords impotent as a social force. From the point of view of the tenant farmers who had received the benefits of the liberation of the land it meant that they were wholly spared the obligation of paying over a long period for the land they had acquired. To this extent it also implied that they were given some margin with which to enlarge productive investment in their own holdings. . . . [T]he fact that the reform was carried out in a manner which was virtually a form of expropriation was of greatest significance, rather than the mere fact of the vast scale of the reform.

Second, as a result of the Japanese land reform the tenancy relations on the small remaining area of land cultivated by tenants were brought thoroughly under control. In the first place, the severest restrictions were placed on the landlord's depriving tenants of their land by revoking tenancy contracts at will or refusing renewals. Such action was possible only when the Village Agricultural Land Committee (later the Agricultural Committee) certified the fulfilment of certain conditions— such as that the landlord had the ability to cultivate the land himself and that the tenant's livelihood would not be embarrassed by his handing back the land—and when the Prefectural Governor had granted permission on the basis of the Committee's certification. Since these conditions were seldom fulfilled in Japanese agriculture, in which the majority of the tenants were running very small holdings, this virtually meant that once a landlord had leased some of his land to a tenant it would be practically next to impossible for him to get it back, even if he should find that he required the land for himself. From the opposite side, it meant that a tenant farmer, although cultivating land under a lease, had to all intents and purposes as secure a hold on the right to cultivate his land as any owner-farmer. . . . Further, in regard to rents, not only was all levying of rents in kind forbidden, but the money rents were fixed by the government at low levels. . . . [Table not shown here shows 1957–1963 rents as low as 3–4% of the total return from the land. Eds.]

In this way, then, the Japanese land reform was carried out with a thoroughness scarcely paralleled in history. As a result of it there was built up in Japan a system of cultivating proprietorship which is also scarcely paralleled in history. The development of Japanese agriculture in the succeeding ten and more years has taken place on the stage provided by these events.

II

What influences were exercised on Japanese rural society and Japanese agriculture by the land reform is a very many-sided question, and it is no simple matter to present an account of the subject which will include all its aspects. Again, as is the case with all social phenomena, the efficacy of the land reform merges with social effects derived from numerous other political and economic trends, and it is no simple matter to delineate clearly the bounds of the efficacy of the land reform.

In the present paper we shall refrain from going deeply into the most important aspect of the land reform, namely, the political efficacy of the land reform, but shall merely put forward the following suggestion. We would suggest that the efficacy of the land reform lay in diverting at a stroke into the direction of a tranquil state the farmers' movement which was already fairly well developed before the war and which burst fiercely into flame after the war. It was of course the case that in terms of slogans the farmers' movement included many demands in its political platform, beginning with such ideas as opposition to war or the democratization of Japan, and extending to demands for better prices for rice and opposition to heavy taxation, but the heart of the farmers' movement always remained the land question. To express it in other words, the farmers' movement was begotten from the explosion of the petty bourgeois demands of the part-owner farmers and tenants vis-à-vis the landlords that they should be allowed to own land, or, failing that, should at least have security of the right of cultivation and low rents. However, those who expressed such views now had their demands more or less completely satisfied by the land reform.

This quieting down of the farmers' movement, however, did not merely bring about peace in rural society. Up to this time the farmers' movement had links in greater or lesser degree with the socialist movement, and since it was the stronghold of the socialist forces in rural society the quietening down of the farmers' movement also meant the collapse of the socialist forces in the country-side. The fact is that since the time of the land reform up to the present the socialist and communist parties have been unable to maintain satisfactory party organizations in the rural areas, and at election times they have been able to do no more than collect a few floating votes. Today the rural areas are still the greatest supporters of the conservative parties, and we may be justified in saying that in a certain sense this is the most important result produced by the land reform. In the case of Japan there is now no room for the use of a tactic which has been employed in China and the countries of Southeast Asia, where socialist parties have pursued the policy of gaining the support of the peasantry by promising them the liberation of the land. We may say that the role which the land reform performed for the ensuring of the stability of the Japanese capitalist order may have been greater than we imagined.[2]

We shall also refrain from a detailed discussion of the sweeping changes in the social structure of the villages and the great changes in the consciousness and behavior of farmers which were caused by the land reform. It is of course true that the power of the landlords in the villages had been gradually declining for some time before the land reform. But in spite of this the presence in the villages of a landlord class living off high rents and distinctly superior in regard to property and education, and, on the other side, the existence of a large number of poor tenant farmers who could have their land taken from them and be reduced to beggary on the following day if once they offended their landlords, were the cause of feudal ideology, emotions, and customary practices remaining deeply rooted in rural society.

The virtual disappearance of the landlords as a result of the land reform was of great efficacy in sweeping away these old social relations. It is certainly true that even today a considerable number of the influential persons in village society, such as the village headman, the members of the village council, and the head of the agricultural co-operative, are drawn from the former landlord "class." Their tenure of these posts, however, is due to their prior education and experience, and is not due to the social position or remaining glory attaching to the status of a landlord.

It need hardly be said that what may be described as the tradition of social living or established custom is scarcely to be changed in so short a time. We may also suppose that there is another side to the question, the fact that the backward system of production itself, which was originally based on production centered on hand tillage by small producers, obstructs the modernization of the farmers' consciousness. Consequently, it is not surprising that feudal ideology and customary practices should have remained in rural society after the land reform, and we would expect that with the change of generations and the advance of agricultural technology such things will naturally fade away.

Yet it would seem to be an undeniable fact that on the whole the modernization and urbanization of the social structure of the village and the consciousness of farmers in the last ten or fifteen years has proceeded at a speed which has astonished all eyes. Many reasons can be given for this—the democratic development of Japan as a whole, the spread of education, increased contacts with the cities, the influence of mass communication, etc.—but it is probable that few would be found to dispute the inclusion of the land reform among the most important causes of it.

For our present purposes, however, let us concentrate our attention on economic questions. In doing so, the points which we must at all costs raise are the two following.

First, the land reform possessed great efficacy in relation to the subsequent development of Japanese agriculture. There are some differences between the development which has taken place in the products of crop husbandry and that which has taken place in the products of animal husbandry, for the former is of a more static character when compared with the explosively rapid growth of the latter. Since 1960, in particular, the products of crop husbandry have been static or show a tendency to decline slightly. As we shall see later, there is an important question here, but leaving it aside for the moment we may note that during this period agricultural production as a whole increased at a fairly rapid rate. The rate of growth is more than 4%, and although it indeed appears low when viewed in relation to the growth rate of the Japanese economy as a whole, which has been growing at an annual average rate of 10% or more since 1955, the fact is that it is exceptionally high when compared with the agricultural growth rates of many other countries.

Further, it is noteworthy that these increases in production have not been brought about by an increase in the agricultural population—by what may be described as "human sea" tactics—but to the accompaniment of a decrease in working population which is unprecedented in Japanese history. The agricultural population has declined throughout the period, and in particular under the high growth rate economy since 1955 agriculture has lost many of its working hands, this being a reflection of the sudden swelling of non-agricultural employment. The approximately sixteen million persons engaged in agriculture in 1950 became fifteen million in 1955, and twelve million in 1960. Since during this period there has been a marked out-migration from agriculture among the lower age groups, a rapid aging of the agricultural population is in progress.

Since these increases in agricultural production took place under such conditions of rapidly declining working population, it is self-evident that these increases in production could have taken place only when background conditions were present which would permit innovation in agricultural technology and a consequent rapid rise in the productivity of labor. In fact, the ten to fifteen years following the land reform were a period in which innovation in agricultural technology advanced at a rate which was almost unprecedented in the history of Japanese agriculture. . . .

When we consider what made possible such innovation in technology, we can of course list a large number of governing conditions. As representative of them we may cite the development of agricultural research itself, the perfection of the technological extension organization centered on the government's Agricultural Improvement Extension Personnel System, the importation of new agricultural chemicals and their manufacture in Japan, the improvement in efficiency and cheapening of the prices of agricultural machinery which accompanied the development of the automobile and machine industries, the spread of education and the development of communications, the sharpening of the labor shortage as an accompaniment to the efflux of labor from agriculture, and the development among farmers of a mentality which seeks the reduction of labor, etc. In considering these in relation to the land reform, however, the following two points must on no account be omitted.

(1) We would first consider a point which we will touch on later, the farmers' desire and ability to invest. As regards the farmers' desire to invest, in a certain sense this was the result of "the magic of ownership," as it has been called since the times of Arthur Young. In more concrete terms, however, it would seem that the facts which were of importance were that tenant farmers, who hitherto had had half of the returns which they had wrested from the land taken from them by their landlords, now came to believe that they could improve their standards of living by their own efforts, and that whereas formerly the greater part of tenant farmers were forced to carry on part-time non-agricultural occupations in order to obtain income with which to defray the expenses of their rents and consequently were unable to devote themselves wholeheartedly to agricultural

TABLE 1
INDEX OF INVESTMENT IN CAPITAL GOODS FOR
AGRICULTURAL PRODUCTION
(1934–1936 = 100)

	Total	Fertilizers	Feeding Stuffs	Agricultural Chemicals	Agricultural Machines and Implements
1951	106.4	79.6	42.9	190.0	212.5
1952	123.9	93.2	58.1	319.1	261.8
1953	151.8	104.7	81.5	505.2	290.3
1954	174.6	112.2	86.1	618.0	293.3
1955	190.1	122.8	94.9	678.8	320.5
1956	197.5	128.3	114.0	824.1	315.5
1957	191.2	136.0	98.9	1,041.7	492.5
1958	199.0	141.2	101.6	1,270.0	544.9
1959	224.1	148.6	119.5	1,479.0	595.1
1960	262.1	157.0	150.0	1,740.0	689.8
1961	276.1	157.9	192.0	2,078.0	975.0
1962	340.2	172.0	252.1	2,641.0	1,000.1
1963	380.5	179.0	312.5	3,278.0	1,139.0
1964	439.0	187.6	372.0	3,835.0	1,385.0

SOURCE: Calculated from the *Agricultural Budget Survey* and the *Rural Price Indices*.

NOTE: The index figures have been arrived at by converting the average investment per household to base-year prices by means of the appropriate price index.

production, it now became possible to some degree for them to do so. To this we must add that of late these effects have markedly weakened, and to this point we shall refer again.

In regard to the ability to invest, we may first point out that the burden of rent had disappeared, and that the incomes of the farmers had been increased to that extent. At the same time, of course, this raised the level of consumption among the farmers, and since it operated as a factor expanding the propensity to consume, it is not the case that all the reduction in rents was put into investment. But even so the enlargement of farmers' investment was very marked, as is shown in Table 1, and it is scarcely to be denied that it was sustained by an enlargement of the farmers' ability to invest of the kind which we have supposed.

(2) Together with these, fixed investment in the land itself, in the form of a marked enlargement of investment in land-improvement schemes, is important. In agriculture, as is well known, practically every innovation in technology must presuppose land-improvement works. For example, such a technique as increased applications of fertilizers will not produce results unless it is accompanied by drainage facilities. However, particularly in the case of an agriculture such as Japan's, which is centered on the cultivation of paddy, matters will not go well when innovation in technology of the "tractorization" type which we have described above is got under way, unless it is accompanied by the provision of agricultural roads, the rationalization of plots, the complete provision of irrigation and drainage facilities, etc.

It goes without saying that since land-improvement schemes involve vast investments and large-scale agricultural engineering works, they can scarcely be got under way without financial assistance from the government. . . .

III

We have already shown that since 1955 agriculture has rapidly lost population within the framework of the high growth-rate economy. Although in itself this reduction in agricultural population is to be welcomed by agriculture, there is no particular reason for it to cause embarrass-

ment. It is of course true that this efflux of population from agriculture is concentrated in the lower age groups and among the more able members of the agricultural population, and consequently it is not the case that it raises no problems for the development of agriculture, since the population left in agriculture is progressively aging. Hitherto, however, rural Japan has been burdened by a vast surplus population, so that on the one hand this has made impossible the enlargement of the size of the individual holding and consequently has stood in the way of the adoption of technology which would raise the productivity of labor, while on the other hand, we may suppose that the decline in the agricultural population is more likely to have provided occasions for the development of agriculture, since the presence of surplus population performed the function of depressing agricultural incomes and the farmers' standard of living.

Figure 2. Trend of Numbers of Farm Households, Numbers of Farm Households in Full-Time Agricultural Employment, and Agricultural Population (1955-100)

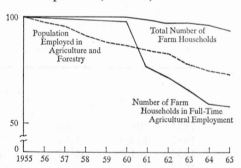

NOTE: The enclosed dates are years in which an Agricultural Census was taken.

SOURCE: Based on the *Labor Survey* and *Statistics of the Ministry of Agriculture and Forestry.*

Nevertheless, as we see from Figure 2, the direction in which the situation is developing is not necessarily a desirable one. . . . By this we mean that this failure of the numbers of farm households to decline will become . . . a serious obstacle standing in the way of those farmers who wish to grow as farmers by enlarging the size of their holdings. This is because they will be required to pay very large prices for land if they try to get possession of land owned by part-time agriculturalists. Again, this obstruction of the enlargement of the holding may also be expected . . . to have the effect of blocking any higher development of technology centered on the full-time agriculturalists, that is, any raising of productivity. . . . [There has been a falling off in the rate of growth of agricultural production and a consequent marked shortage of foodstuffs, resulting in a definite rise in prices.]

Looking back once more at the land reform with these problems directly before us, we find it natural that while it is recognized that the reform was efficacious in the ways we have described, an appreciation of the land reform is now obtained in which it is seen as having begun to lay fetters on Japanese agriculture, rather than liberating it. For if a large number of farmers had not become proprietors, the majority of them might well have forsaken agriculture and left the land [thereby permitting the more productive minority to expand their holdings]. Again, if the farmers were more free to lend and borrow, those farmers who happened to be faced with a shortage of labor would find it easy to lease their land, even if they did not go so far as to sell all or part of it. We have grounds for thinking that if this were done it would provide room for the enlargement of the holdings of full-time farmers by the acquisition of leased land.

As regards the former case, although we may agree that it may have been the case that such a situation existed, it is now far too late to do anything about the matter. Consequently, as a matter of concrete political policies it is the latter which is in question. At present, under the Agricultural Law it is practically impossible for a farmer to get back his land once he has leased it, and the rent which he can draw from the land is kept at a low level. In these circumstances it is natural that farmers who have land to spare are not inclined to lease it, and so one comes to the conclusion that the restrictions imposed by the Agricultural Law should be relaxed and the liquidity of agricultural land increased.

This contention seems to enjoy fairly powerful support, but on the other hand, of course, the opposite opinion is held to some extent—that it would be undesirable because if this were done the results produced by the land reform would crumble away, and it would lead to the reappearance of the old landlord-tenant relations. However, this latter opinion would not seem to be so well founded. The landlord-tenant relations of former days were formed under the conditions of a huge accumulation of surplus population in the villages and fierce competition among prospective tenants, but today these conditions are entirely different. . . .

Viewing the matter in this way, we see clearly that the problem does not consist in the land reform or the system of relations which it produced. It is really meaningless to criticize the land reform on the grounds that it was a mistake to produce a vast number of small proprietors. Since at the time of the land reform the economic and technological conditions for the enlargement of the size of the individual holding did not exist, there was no alternative but to create a large number of small-scale proprietors. Moreover, since the development of agriculture to date is in itself, as we have shown above, one of the results produced by the land reform, to postulate the case of there having been no land reform, or of the land reform having been carried out differently, is really devoid of meaning.

Further, the problem of the present day will not be solved merely by destroying the presuppositions of the land reform and allowing for the expansion of land held in tenancy. In solving this problem a greater priority should be attached to facilitating withdrawal from agriculture as an occupation by providing an environment which will give manufacturing laborers a stable livelihood without need of support from part-time agriculture, accomplishing this by means of the improvement of conditions of employment outside agriculture and by the fullest provision of social security. But considering it as a question of land tenure, it is necessary, on the one hand, to have a policy for the purchase of the land of farmers who are in a position to leave agriculture which will assure them of the most advantageous prices possible, and on the other hand, to have a policy for selling the land to full-time agriculturalists under such conditions that the high price of the land will not be an excessive burden to the running of their holdings. Assuming a two-price system to be unacceptable, it should be made possible for the purchaser to pay for the land by low-interest annual instalment payments over a markedly long period. Without this it will be impossible to press towards a solution of the problem, and these measures will not destroy the results produced by the land reform, but will rather mean that they will be advanced still further.

1. In fact, all land on lease by absentee landlords (landlords not resident in the administrative division [city, town or village] in which the land was situated), and all land in excess of a family holding of 1 hectare (3 hectares in Hokkaido) in possession of resident landlords, was subject to compulsory government purchase.

2. The author has suggested in correspondence that this may be due to several reasons: even part-time farmers want to keep their land in order to provide for their old age or in case they lose their off-farm jobs; possession of land is also a hedge against inflation; and they may hold on to their land speculatively, anticipating still further rises in land prices. This is to say that even "idle" land is "producing" something of value. Eds.

The Political Economy
of Education and
Employment

BECAUSE of its employment and status effects, education is a major instrument for maintaining the status quo, allocating information differentially among the population. At the same time, it is one of the cheapest and most far-reaching means through which a regime can redistribute economic, social, and political income, information being a factor of production in all three markets. Relative to other major redistributive policies, however, education is less punitive to the already well endowed. Land reform and taxation take from one sector and give to another; but educating one sector does not deprive another of the information it already possesses. Enfranchisement of new voters literally debases the value of the vote for those who previously possessed it and raises the possibility of their expropriation if representatives of the new voters achieve public office.

This is to say that education generally entails fewer direct political costs than other developmental policies. However, extending education to new groups may have an outcome somewhat similar to that of enfranchisement; the status value of education for those who possessed it exclusively may decline when their monopoly is broken and they face greater competition for employment, elected office, marriage dowries, or public recognition. Moreover, education is usually paid for out of taxes; and an increase in educational opportunity entails some increase in taxation, the effects of which are likely to be redistributive. Still, compared to other measures, redistribution through education is more relative than absolute, more indirect and long-run; its extension can be risked by an elite with some equanimity. Further, because of education's widespread popularity with the majority in most underdeveloped countries, it offers some short-run and possibly long-run political profit.

"Education," of course, is an omnibus category, including diverse policies: primary and secondary education, university and professional education, technical and vocational instruction, adult literacy, compensatory education for disadvantaged minorities (or majorities), formal and informal instruction through mass media, community development programs, and so forth. What is taught and to whom is a matter affected by political change, but so are matters of the administration, financing, and standards of education and of how it relates to employment. Simply making any choices in these areas involves certain costs to the regime, costs which may or may not be compensated for by certain increases in its political revenue.

When educational opportunity is extended to persons not formerly educated—at all, in that way, or to that level—this raises political problems for any regime. Such persons will expect to have extended to them also the opportunities for employment and social deference which that education implied in the past. What is commonly referred to as "educated unemployment" (or underemployment) is a major threat to regimes in the Third World as persons with educational qualifications and skills find no satisfactory return for what they feel they can contribute to society. Likewise, teaching the landless and tenant farmers to read and do sums creates conflicts with landlords and moneylenders, who can in turn put pressure on the regime. A national secular school system displaces traditional religious schools and downgrades the status of their teachers; the educational association founded to bring about the uplift of a backward sector may become the core of an opposition or revolutionary party; community development and rural extension programs may enrich the already powerful and increase the disparities and tensions in the countryside. Finally, regardless of the conflicts that may arise and the costs they impose on the regime, the financial costs of developing, sustaining, and expanding education in all its modes are high, and these expenditures mean foregone opportunities in other areas. Such lost opportunities, too, have their political economy and developmental significance.

The competitive and bargaining perspective, however, neglects the developmental impact of education, and it is for this that statesmen may be willing to endure the costs. Once again, each educational program—its content, audience, and administration—contributes in a different way and to a different degree to development: to integrating markets to increasing resource endowments of the less endowed, to building infrastructure, and to creating organization in which innovative leadership can take place. The various educational programs and systems can contribute to knitting together the various subsistence markets—economic, social, and political—into a more nationally cohesive market with a wider scope for exchange. This requires a common vocabulary for dealing with purposes (often in teaching a lingua franca), common valuations of resources (often the resource of status becomes stable and convertible nationally through education), and a focal point for continuous exchange between local citizens and the central government.

The contribution of education to infrastructure is part and parcel of the process of market integration. In many respects, the village teacher, the block extension officer, the rural literacy corpsman are the most continuous presence a regime might have in the most isolated parts of a polity. Such a network allows for the mobility and predictability of certain resources to increase, especially the resource of information. Programs such as community development or health education can penetrate the countryside without the costly construction of an alternative civil administration. Not only does this aspect save the regime resources; the presence of the regime in a local schoolteacher reduces the costs for citizens as they treat with the government.

The desire to secure education for their members has been a major factor in the development of organization by underendowed sectors.[1] Often through the pooling of resources in the building of a school, a college, a hostel, or in making representations to the regime, a sense of sector identity and efficacy emerged.

[1] See chapter on "The New Associations" in Thomas Hodgkin, *Nationalism in Colonial Africa* (1957), and Audrey Smock, *Ibo Politics: The Role of Ethnic Unions in Eastern Nigeria* (1970), for examples of this in West Africa.

Through pressing for educational opportunities for their members, sectoral leaders developed positions on other social, economic, and political issues. Some leaders, by virtue of the resources available to their organization to secure educational opportunities, became genuine innovators, capable of unique combinations of resources that increased productivity in achieving their sector's purposes. Such is the case of Gandhi and U Nu.

But the developmental significance of education is mostly in its contribution to an increase in the factor endowments of the many. To the resources a person has by dint of luck or existence, education of most kinds adds the resources of information and, consequently, status, allowing for potentially greater personal productivity. So significant is education felt to be in increasing the economic productivity of persons that economists have come to talk of "human resources" and to estimate, in comparison with other factors, the contribution education makes in improving worker productivity.[2] One analysis suggests that 26 percent of the increase in national income in Japan since the 1870s is attributable to education.[3]

The same dynamic would appear to be true in politics and social exchange. Education permits its possessor both to contribute more to political and social enterprises and to make claims for other resources—authority and status, for instance—which would be difficult to do without such education. How much education and for whom are key political economy issues. Making the ubiquitous but not necessary connection between education and employment, manpower planners assume that by forecasting future needs of skills in an economy, educational processes can be guided to avoid waste and bottlenecks, surpluses or shortages of skills. Such an approach might conserve on economic resources, but it ignores the resource-enhancing function of education for those who exceed the forecasted need. Often a surplus of educated persons, wishing economic resources through employment to mix with their enhanced informational or social resources, can create opportunities for new production. Or apart from quantitative changes, they may upgrade productive activities qualitatively by bringing new skills associated with higher educational levels.[4] By keeping the many resource-poor, manpower planners can keep political and social pressures from building up for change in the status quo, which many regimes will find quite satisfactory. Basic policy questions need to be raised concerning how much education is "enough" and "for what"—for meeting present needs? for achieving broadened productivity? for transforming the social structure or the political system?

Employment is a separate issue from education in many respects. Some people seek education for purposes other than employment, that is, to "consume" information rather than acquire it for other productive purposes. Also, much employment requires only a modicum of education. To provide employment through regime action is a separate issue in the redistributive sense as well: the resources needed must be found somewhere, often from the educational area itself, as when members of one sector—perhaps expatriates—may lose employment to provide it

[2] See, for example, G. S. Becker, *Human Capital: A Theoretical and Empirical Analysis with Special Reference to Education* (1964).

[3] Ryōji Itō, "Education as a Basic Factor in Japan's Economic Growth," *Developing Economies* (1963). See pp. 344–54 in this volume.

[4] See W. A. Lewis on this, *Development Planning: The Essentials of Economic Policy* (1966), cited at the conclusion of Alexander Peaslee's article, which follows. To be sure, the persons displaced by such upgrading can cause political problems, which must be considered along with the economic gains.

for others, similarly educated. Like education, however, policies for employment have their political economy—their costs and benefits. There is also the developmental perspective; expanded employment opportunities utilize more fully the resources of the population, increase its factor endowments, stimulate organizations such as labor unions, and give impetus to the development of entrepreneurial leadership in economic, social, and political affairs.

There is a plethora of works on education, and a poverty of findings. As education is the most protected industry in almost every country, claims are made about its efficacy without the slightest shred of evidence or without considering educational policies in their many dimensions, such as political economy requires. There are exceptions, and we have chosen some of them to illustrate the political economy of education and employment as issues in development.

By comparing for many nations their rates of expansion of education and gross domestic product, Alexander Peaslee is able to suggest that certain percentages of population enrolled in schools of various levels seem critical for economic growth. In particular he points to what appears to be a basic requirement for widespread primary education, distributing basic informational resources throughout the population. The proposed "optimal mix" of educational policies implies that there are certain thresholds to be crossed, certain sequences of educational development to be achieved in order to have the amount and distribution of skills and comprehension which provide the technological and organizational underpinnings of economic growth. Peaslee's analysis provides guidelines for determining "how much" expansion of education is desirable and for which levels, though this relates to the modal case rather than to the fruitful, extraordinary exception.

The increase in factor endowments provided by education and the resulting increase in worker productivity have been the focus for educational economists for almost a decade now. Various estimates have been made, all confirming the proposition that education is usefully regarded as investment and not simply consumption, and as a rather good one at that. Only university education of certain types comes under especially critical judgment.[5] The case of Japan, examined by Ryōji Itō below, supports this view of education as investment and the model Peaslee proposes. Itō finds education a major source of Japan's economic success, especially the early development of primary education. This has served to integrate the status and political markets in Japan and to increase the factor endowments of the many, especially those of commoners and women. Moreover, he advances the position that the level of educational investment is not tied to the already achieved level of economic development.[6] Available economic resources constrain but do not determine the level of educational expenditure, and a larger share of national re-

---

[5] See, for example, Edward F. Denison, *Why Growth Rates Differ* (1967); Theodore W. Schultz, "Investment in Human Capital," *American Economic Review* (1961), pp. 1–17. The judgment on university education in relation to other levels has been argued by Arnold C. Harberger, "Investment in Man versus Investment in Machines: the Case of India," in C. Arnold Anderson and Mary Jean Bowman (eds.), *Education and Economic Development* (1966).

[6] Some recent cross-national studies have taken a contrary position; see Frederic L. Pryor, *Public Expenditure in Communist and Capitalist Nations* (1968), p. 226; and Friedrich Edding and Dieter Berstecher, *International Developments in Educational Expenditures, 1950–65* (1969). We find the quantitative techniques used in these studies unconvincing, with Itō's simple classification more to the point.

sources can be devoted to this purpose with a view to reaping a multidimensional return.

The kind of educational infrastructure, who shall control it, and whose endowments will be increased by education, have been major political issues in China since the Revolution, though they are hardly issues of concern to China alone. Donald Munro's analysis of the conflict between Maoists and others over the issue of egalitarianism versus economic productivity through expertise is relevant to the debate on educational policy throughout the Third World. Munro recounts the struggle over and use of work-study schools and admissions policies to break down the monopoly of status and income enjoyed by urbanites and intellectuals vis-à-vis rural persons and workers. Moreover, he analyzes the debate and eventual policy choice in the conflict between education as a distributor of information and as a component of the ideological infrastructure of the regime. Throughout the analysis, Munro sustains an emphasis on political costs and benefits of these choices.

From a developmental point of view, the basic alternatives of egalitarianism or expertise would each lead in the direction of a more productive polity, but each would be productive more or sooner for some members of the polity than others. The choice of strategy and the fashioning of concrete policy allocations had to be "political," in that they would be determined by the relative amounts and kinds of political resources mobilized and channeled by different factions at any point in time to bias the distributional effects of government action in one direction or another. "Building on the best" would be politically easier than engaging and upgrading resources across the board (land), but in either case, the inputs of political resources (power) would be critical and would shape future patterns of well-being.

The final selection by Dudley Seers is a model of political economy analysis, suggesting what an integrated social science of development would look like. Employment in Trinidad and Tobago, for Seers, is not a manpower problem or an economic problem alone. Increases in the number of jobs created by investment depends on the kind of concessions the regime has offered to foreign industrialists; population growth is related to educational and migration policy; the amount of inflation that is tolerable is a function of the political turmoil that arises because of inflation or unemployment; the possibilities for greater control over the internal and external economy depend on the United States and other foreign powers; the balance of trade may be undone or improved by shifts in the status attributed, positively or negatively, to consumption of imported goods; the bases for social and political conflict may be more or less aggravated by poor economic performance according to the prevailing ideology, the common image of a "good society," and a "proper" distribution of resources within it.

Underlying Seers's analysis is a concern with rising unemployment in Trinidad, but he treats ameliorative policies as though they were not dictated by politics or economics alone. He examines the probable resource position within the country some ten years hence and seeks to discover what present and subsequent choices could make for a preferred future by then and even twenty years hence. Seers's methodology is to incorporate "exogenous" variables and to adopt a time horizon such that "constraints" can be converted into variables. Insofar as the political structure represents a constraint, it too must be considered in terms of how it might be altered to enable the people of the country to enhance their well-being over time; what kind of leadership would be required and with what ideology to cope with the problems of an underdeveloped country, which for the foreseeable future will be severe. Seers shows how limited the options for Trinidad are, but also how any successful strategy would require a political economy perspective.

EDUCATION'S ROLE IN DEVELOPMENT
ALEXANDER L. PEASLEE
Halifax, Nova Scotia

INTRODUCTION

In the last one hundred years significant economic growth has been achieved only in those countries in which a high proportion of the total population is found in primary schools. High enrollments in elementary education do not guarantee growth; other complex factors are obviously involved. But high enrollments appear to be a requisite for significant growth.

As economies industrialize, urbanize, and mature, their requirements for more sophisticated citizens appear to increase. After primary enrollments have become high, in the more economically successful countries the emphasis on education has shifted onward to the secondary and higher education levels.

This paper presents a hypothesis of the relationship of the various levels of education to economic growth and—by implication—to political and social growth. It examines the association of elementary, secondary, and higher education enrollment ratios to total population with economic development. The paper summarizes historical trends in enrollment ratios to total population in what are now the more economically developed nations. The type of educational investment most likely to be conducive to growth in the developing countries is outlined. In conclusion, an optimal educational mix for growth is suggested.

It is necessary to stress that while certain quantitative educational levels are a requisite for economic development, they do not by themselves assure it. Other factors—economic, behavioral, and political—will continue to exert their varying influences.

PRIMARY EDUCATION

A close relationship appears to exist between high primary enrollments as a proportion of the total population and healthy economies. Those countries [1] which in 1920 had more than 10 percent of their population in primary schools were compared with a United Nations listing of nations according to their gross domestic product per capita in 1958. Twenty-five countries had more than 10 percent of their population in primary schools in 1920. In addition, France and Hungary historically had a record of enrollments well above 10 percent, and their temporary decline below that level can be ascribed to low birth rates during World War I. These same 27 countries led the world in per capita output by 1958, with only minor and inexplicable exceptions.[2] The details are presented in Table 1. No country with a population over a million that is not listed in Table 1 had a per capita production in 1958 or 1962 as large as that of the 27 countries.[3]

Thus, we find that among the first 35 countries in per capita gross domestic pro-

From *Economic Development and Cultural Change* (April 1969), pp. 293–318. Reprinted by permission. Some sections have been omitted.

duction in 1958, all but six had a record of over 10 percent of their population in primary schools by 1920 or earlier. The six exceptions attained the 10 percent mark by 1938 (the U.S.S.R., Mexico, Greece) or by around 1948 (Venezuela, Israel), or had hovered around the 10 percent mark for decades (Uruguay).

Of the more than 50 countries that had not reached the "over 10 percent" point, only one—Colombia—had attained by 1958 production above US$300. It ranked 33rd in per capita production. If allowance is made for the 1955 (rather than 1958) data on Bulgaria and Japan's subsequent rapid growth, Colombia appears to rank about 35th. Colombia itself passed the 10 percent primary enrollment mark in 1956.

To sum up, almost all of the nations that achieved high rates of primary enrollment subsequently were among the 34 world leaders in production per capita. The few countries not among the ranking 34 that had high primary enrollment rates were in almost all cases growing impressively and were ahead of their neighbors.[4] No country had achieved significant growth until after 8 to 10 percent of its total population was enrolled in elementary education.[5]

Available data did not permit as detailed an assessment of enrollments in proportion to age groups. A comparison of the country-by-country enrollment statistics with the initial periods of growth in real income per capita indicates that sustained growth generally starts when primary enrollment is in the neighborhood of 30 to 50 percent of the school-aged population (those 5–14, which is the age group generally used in population age data).

The key factors in the association of expanded primary enrollments and subsequent economic growth appear to be:

(1) The "crust of custom" in traditional societies is not broken until a significant segment of a culture has been introduced to a more systematic means of obtaining and disseminating information about the production and distribution of goods. In fact, we might speculate that the tighter the grip of tradition, the longer it takes to break the "crust of custom." This may explain why France reacted more rapidly to enrollment expansion than did Spain. The French in the first part of the nineteenth century had just come through an era of

rationalism which left relatively little "crust of custom" to break, whereas the strongly traditional Spanish culture was a tougher "crust" that took much more time to break. (2) By breaking traditional, inefficient word-of-mouth communication patterns, primary education on a large scale brought a new, more systematically informed set of actors onto the economic stage. (3) This break in the traditional way of doing things, further reinforced by the information obtained in school, contributed to the increased productive efficiency of each person.

This coincides with the conclusions of economists such as Abramovitz, Kendrick, Denison, and Schultz that the tremendous increases in per capita product in the now developed countries derive primarily from a rise in efficiency. Technical knowledge does not take root in a traditional society. It can, and does, establish itself when that society has had many of its members exposed to a more systematic approach toward knowledge, especially knowledge related to production and distribution.

The triggering effect of primary education tends to explain why traditional agriculture has been transformed in some countries and seems immovable in others. The conclusions reached in this paper agree with those reached by an observer in the field, Dr. A. B. Lewis:

General education in the elementary schools is perhaps the best instrument for breaking the fetters of the traditional way of thinking just as it is for teaching the people to read, write and count and interpret cause and effect in nature. The elementary school is the place where one could succeed in destroying superstitions, where first of all one could stimulate ordered thinking and where one could impart knowledge of a new and better life. Agricultural experts find a greater understanding and a greater confidence in their advice amongst people who have had the benefit of good elementary education than amongst people who are ignorant.[6]

SECONDARY EDUCATION

Secondary enrollment ratios to total population are not associated with economic growth until 8 to 10 percent primary enrollment ratio has already been attained. Subsequently, a pattern of secondary school expansion and output increases appears,

Table 1

Percentage of Total Population in Primary Schools, Selected Years,
and Gross Domestic Product Per Capita, 1958, 1962

Country [a]	1920 [b] (Percent)	1938 [b] (Percent)	1948 [b] (Percent)	Gross Domestic Product Per Capita (US Dollars) 1958 [e]	1962 [o]	Energy Potential Rank Among Nations, KWH Per Capita [a]
Argentina	12.4	11.9	13.0	476	—	71
Australia	14.4 [d]	17.1 [g]	15.0 [g]	1,215	1,416	11
Austria	14.7	12.8 [h]	12.2	656	656	47
Belgium	12.5	11.4	8.9	1,093	1,215	25
Bulgaria	11.8	11.8 [h]	12.7	285 [w]	—	72.5
Canada	20.0 [d]	18.2 [i]	16.8 [d]	1,767	1,807	6
Ceylon	8.8 [d]	13.7 [d]	15.3 [d]	122	129	96.5
Chile	10.7	13.2	11.6	352	—	50
China-Taiwan	3.6	8.7	11.7	114	—	80
Cuba	11.5	10.8	11.9 [p]	379	—	98
Czechoslovakia	14.2	11.7 [j]	8.5	543 [w]	—	23
Denmark	14.4	12.6	11.7	975	1,390	105.5
Finland	12.4	10.5	12.0	751	1,047	52
France	9.6	13.0	11.6	1,089	1,300	44.5
Germany	14.9	10.9	12.9 [q]	920	1,349	9
Greece	8.8	13.9	12.1	307	394	74
Hungary	9.5	10.6	12.3 [r]	387 [w]	—	79
Ireland	10.8	15.8	15.0 (12.8 [f])	472	641	44.5
Israel	—	—	9.4 [s]	579	823	—
Italy	10.0	11.7	10.5	493	688	81.5
Japan	14.5	17.3	13.7	285	504	52
Korea	2.5	4.6	13.3	104	—	84
Mexico	8.3	10.1	11.3	288 [o]	356	59
Netherlands	16.3	14.2	11.8	767	1,003	38
New Zealand	18.6	13.8 (11.9 [f])	12.6 (10.8 [f])	1,281	1,316	35
Norway	14.3	12.2	11.6 [t]	1,012	—	12
Philippines	7.9	10.9	13.0	192	—	87.5
Poland	11.8	14.0	14.2	468 [w]	—	7
Puerto Rico	14.8 [d]	15.0	19.2 [d]	581	825	114
Rumania	8.9 [e]	12.5	11.3	320 [w]	—	69
South Africa	8.3	9.1 (18.7 [k])	12.3 (19.0 [k])	385	435	8
Spain	12.5	18.7 [l]	15.1	324	—	43
Sweden	12.0	9.8	8.4	1,309	1,703	41.5
Switzerland	14.0	11.1	9.2	1,338	1,740	64
U.K. ⎰ England & Wales	13.8 [f]	11.0 [f]	12.5 [v]			
U.K. ⎱ Scotland	13.8 [f]	12.4 (11.2 [f])	7.0	1,084	1,288	10
U.K. Northern Ireland	—	15.0	14.1			
U.S.	19.3	14.4	13.0	2,324	2,691	1
U.S.S.R.	3.6 (6.6 [m])	19.9 [i]	15.2 [d]	682 [w]	—	4
Uruguay	8.8	9.7	9.8	450	—	93
Venezuela	3.0 [m]	6.7	10.2	715	901	29

India, for example, has had a secondary enrollment ratio since World War II that compares favorably with many European countries. However, India has not yet attained an 8 to 10 percent primary enrollment ratio, whereas all of the European countries have.

When enrollment ratios at the primary and secondary levels are placed in a time series on a semilogarithmic graph (one for each country) along with gross national product or real income per capita data, a fairly clear pattern emerges. There were 12 cases in which there were obvious sharp increases in secondary enrollment ratios.[7] The average lag until real income per capita climbed rapidly for all cases of secondary enrollment was 11.5 years.

When the trend lines for secondary enrollment ratios on the country graphs are compared with subsequent real income per capita, there is a general tendency for the two to show a good relationship after universal primary education has been attained. As time passes, however, the relationship between secondary ratios and growth becomes less close, and a better correlation appears between university enrollment ratios and subsequent economic growth.

We will have additional comments to make about secondary enrollment ratios after we have looked at the relationship of higher education enrollments and economic growth.

HIGHER EDUCATION

The association of higher education enrollment ratios with subsequent growth in real income per capita (after more or less universal primary education has been established) is impressive. Of the 37 countries for which we have analyzed and graphed data, we find that 21 show a very close relationship between rate of growth of university enrollment ratios and subsequent growth of real income per capita. In seven countries the rate of increase of higher education enrollment ratios has been greater than that for growth in real income per capita. In four countries the data are not complete enough to allow a judgment, although the statistics that are available show no variation from the pattern in other nations. In five countries the prerequisite primary enrollment ratio either has not been attained or was reached so recently that judgment of the relationship of growth and higher education enrollment ratios is not justified. The breakdown for countries is contained in Table 2.

Only one of the four categories of countries listed in Table 2 seems to call for comment. Why did France, Sweden, the

---

[a] Only countries with more than one million population in 1920 are listed, in order to reduce exogenous factors. Years are footnoted if they vary more than two from column heading.

[b] Years vary slightly according to available sources. Primary sources are *Statesman's Yearbooks* for years immediately subsequent to data year.

[c] *Yearbook of National Accounts Statistics, 1962,* United Nations.

[d] Primary and secondary.

[e] 1927–28 enrollment figures as a percentage of 1930 census population.

[f] Average attendance.

[g] Public and private school enrollment, New South Wales, primary and secondary levels.

[h] 1934–35.

[i] 1941–42 primary and secondary.

[j] 1930.

[k] European population only.

[l] 1935.

[m] 1926.

[n] 1945.

[o] *Yearbook of National Accounts Statistics, 1963,* United Nations.

[p] 1945 enrollment as a percentage of 1943 population.

[q] Excluding Baden.

[r] 1954–55.

[s] 1951. 13.52 percent in 1954–55.

[t] 1952–53 enrollment as a percentage of 1950 population.

[u] 1958–59.

[v] 1951, including kindergarten.

[w] 1955. Norton Ginsberg, *Atlas of Economic Development* (Chicago: University of Chicago Press, 1961).

[x] *Ibid.,* p. 58. This is estimated *stock* of energy.

TABLE 2

SUMMARY OF GRAPHS ON HIGHER
EDUCATION ENROLLMENT RATIOS AND
REAL INCOME PER CAPITA GROWTH

---

*Countries in which real income parallels
and follows trend lines of higher education
enrollment ratios:*

Western Europe—Austria, Belgium, Denmark, Finland, Germany, Great Britain, Ireland, the Netherlands, Norway, Switzerland
North America—Canada, Puerto Rico
Southern Europe—Greece, Italy, Spain
Eastern Europe—Czechoslovakia
Asia—Israel
Latin America—Argentina, Mexico
Africa—South Africa
Oceania—New Zealand

---

*Countries in which higher education enrollment ratios during extended periods increased at a greater rate than real income
per capita:*

Western Europe—France, Sweden
North America—the United States
Eastern Europe—Russia
Asia—Japan
Latin America—Venezuela
Oceania—Australia

---

*Countries for which there is insufficient
data, but the pattern shows a parallel between real income and higher education
enrollment ratios:*

Eastern Europe—Bulgaria, Hungary, Poland, Rumania

---

*Countries in which "triggering" primary enrollment ratios have not yet been achieved
or were only recently attained:*

Southern Europe—Portugal
Latin America—Chile, Cuba, Uruguay
Asia—India

United States, Russia, Japan, Venezuela, and Australia have extended periods in which the higher education enrollment ratio increased more rapidly than subsequent growth in real income per capita?

Undoubtedly, part of the answer involves other factors unrelated to education. The United States, for example, showed greater growth in the university enrollment ratio compared to real income per capita during 1910–40. Some of the difference in growth rates can be attributed to the effects of the Great Depression of the early 1930's. We may speculate as to whether the U.S. economy was operating inefficiently during this period in terms of human resources as exemplified by university enrollments. That is, a question is raised as to whether U.S. education was itself inefficient in comparison to other countries, or whether the economy was inefficient in using the human resources provided by formal education. There may well have been a mixture of both.

One other question arises in this connection: was education overexpanded in the U.S., or expanded too rapidly? The answer to either version of the question seems to be "No," for two reasons: (1) the over-all pattern of development in the other countries studied does not suggest that the U.S. during 1910–40 approached either a saturation point or expanded too rapidly; and (2) the U.S. in subsequent years has shown a better rate of economic growth, especially in the 1960's.

From about 1900 to 1930 Japan's higher education enrollment ratio climbed at a faster rate than real income per capita. The rate of climb of the higher education enrollment ratio was steady throughout the period, but the rate of increase of Japan's real income per capita picked up momentum. This may indicate that the increasing volume of university-educated Japanese had a growing influence on the economic growth rate.

In the case of Russia, the higher education enrollment ratio grew more rapidly than real income per capita during 1915–60. One cannot discount the effects of two world wars, which undoubtedly explain part of the difference in rates of growth. But the difference may also emanate partly from inefficiencies in Russian utilization of human resources. There has been considerable evidence of such inefficiencies. For example, the chairman of a regional economic council (*Sovnarkhoz*) complained that most engineers, and particularly the most talented, prefer work in management:

Our plants have far too many engineers and technicians, 1 (one) for every 12–15 workers, whose function is to keep records of fulfillment of norms and plans by the workers. There is a need for a long overdue review of the work of engineering and technical personnel in order to increase their productivity. It would appear necessary to reduce the ratio of engineering and technical personnel to workers from 1 to 12–15 to 1 to 20 or 40 or 50 and to transfer the laid-off engineers to designing bureaus, research departments, experimental shops, laboratories, etc. These services are non-existent in our plants or badly need strengthening and expansion. . . . This we cannot do because the pay of a shop engineer is substantially higher than the pay of an engineer-designer, researcher, or a laboratory specialist. . . .[8]

In the cases of France, Sweden, Venezuela, and Australia, there appears to be a fairly obvious explanation for much of the more rapid increase in university enrollment ratios in comparison with real income growth per capita. The relative step-up in university enrollment rates occurred in recent years and has not yet been reflected adequately in subsequent economic growth. We can expect that these four countries are likely to see increased university enrollment ratios reflected soon in more rapid growth in real income per capita. This, of course, assumes that all other factors relating to growth remain essentially the same.

Whether one uses the data of Kuznets, Clark, Maddison, or the UN,[9] the evidence suggests that, after universal primary education is substantially attained, a higher rate of economic growth per capita results when the secondary level number of pupils is ten or more times the number of higher education students. As time moves on, the proportions should decline to much less than 10 to 1 for the best economic results. In other words, after primary education is well established, emphasis should be placed on secondary enrollments and then gradually shifted toward the tertiary level.

CAUSALITY: EDUCATIONAL CHICKEN OR
ECONOMIC EGG?

It may be asserted that educational enrollments are associated with economic growth only because rising income enables countries to afford the luxury of education. The evidence, however, does not support this. Aside from our earlier conclusion that there was no "triggering" of sustained growth per capita until after from 8 to

10 percent of total population was enrolled in primary schools, there is other evidence. India, Pakistan, and Egypt, for example, achieved very impressive increases in secondary and higher education enrollment ratios during periods in which little or no per capita economic growth was recorded. Obviously, the three countries found resources to expand education even if their income per capita remained level.

We have graphed the educational and economic growth of 37 countries. On 29 of the graphs,[10] periods can be clearly identified in which per capita real income has been level while enrollment at one or more of the three educational levels has been significantly increased. In other words, there are many examples of periods in which income has not risen, but enrollment ratios have been greatly enlarged. In the remaining eight countries it has not been possible to isolate periods of level income and increasing enrollment ratios on the graphs, because either the economic growth was so steady that there were no level periods (Sweden, Mexico, Israel, and Puerto Rico), or the data were not sufficiently complete (Rumania, South Africa, Cuba, and Venezuela).

Still another valid question concerns an assessment as to whether the countries with more resources are able to provide more education. Perhaps this is true, but the historical record suggests that variations in energy resources have not prevented educational growth. The last column in Table 1 lists the ranking world countries in stocks of energy resources.[11] Many countries ranked in the lower half of the list according to energy resources per capita and yet were among the 1958 leaders in per capita production. Among the lower half in energy were Switzerland (3rd in per capita production), Denmark (6th), Puerto Rico (18th), Italy (21st), Argentina (22nd), Uruguay (25th), Hungary (26th), Cuba (28th), Rumania (31st), Greece (32nd), and Bulgaria (34th).

It was not possible, however, to discount completely the influence of resources. What seems more important, though, is the emphasis given to education in the allocation of resources. One might ask what economic conditions made Denmark (universal primary education implemented beginning in 1814), Sweden (universal primary education implemented during 1842–47), Switzerland, and many of the German states attain such a high rate of primary education in the first half of the nineteenth century. It seems doubtful that the economic circumstances were so much—if any—more favorable than they were in countries with lower rates of enrollment, for example, France, the Netherlands, or a few of the German states such as Mecklenberg-Schwerin and Hesse-Cassel.

AN OPTIMUM EDUCATIONAL MIX FOR GROWTH

It is obvious that variations in natural resources, capital formation, behavior patterns, and the host of other factors involved in economic development would create local modifications in any model of an optimum educational mix aimed at maximum growth. Nevertheless, the experience of 37 countries enables us to establish an outline for allocation of resources for education.

The outline would resemble the record of Japan more than that of any other country, although the Swedes, Swiss, Danes, Puerto Ricans, Mexicans, Americans, and Russians (to name a few) all have instructive histories.

In our model, the emphasis at first would be largely on primary education. After the ratio of primary students to total population passed 10 percent, the stress should be moved to secondary education, although enough emphasis on elementary schooling should remain to carry it to the point of universality.

Japan took 27 years to raise its primary ratio from 3.7 percent to 10.7 percent. England and Wales took only fifteen years to move from 4.3 percent to 10.8 percent. Scotland went from 4.97 to 8.97 percent in only five years. Venezuela went from 3.7 to 6.7 percent in five years, and later from 6.8 to 10.2 percent in eight years. Russia went from 3.6 to 10.36 percent in nine years. Puerto Rico moved from 6.04 to 11.49 percent in six years. Chile increased its primary enrollment ratio from 5.0 to 10.55 percent in four years. In all of these cases (except Chile and Puerto Rico, for whom we don't have appropriate real income data), the subsequent economic results were excellent.

There does not appear to be anything in the experience of other nations to rule out ten years as a realistic goal for expansion of primary enrollment to more than 10 percent of total population if that nation is starting from around 2 to 3 percent.

As the 10 percent primary ratio is passed, the emphasis should be turned toward secondary enrollment expansion. The pattern of the economically successful countries has been one that tends to focus on achievement of a ratio of approximately 2 percent of total population in secondary schools before emphasis is shifted to the university level.

Some of the more rapid increases in secondary enrollment ratios have been: the United States—from 1.01 percent to 2.11 percent in ten years; Sweden—from 1.129 to 1.994 percent in three years; Spain—from 0.868 to 2.41 percent in seven years; Norway—from 1.355 to 2.652 percent in three years; Japan—from 0.31 to 1.07 percent in ten years, and from 1.07 to 2.80 percent in ten years; India—from 1.31 to 3.64 percent in ten years; and France—from 0.981 to 2.04 percent in four years.

These figures indicate that it is indeed possible to increase the secondary enrollment ratio very rapidly in a short period. They don't, however, necessarily take into account the quality of education involved. From the standpoint of effect on subsequent economic growth, perhaps the most useful examples above are those of Spain and Japan. Spain's jump from 0.868 to 2.41 percent took place between 1953 and 1960, and to the extent that subsequent results can be judged, it seems to have been associated with later very good economic growth per capita.[12] Japan's 0.31 to 1.07 percent jump occurred between 1900 and 1910, and its leap from 1.07 to 2.80 percent during 1910–20. The results in terms of growth of real income were excellent.

India is not a good example because it did not first acquire a 10-percent-plus ratio in primary education. However, it is instructive to note that a country with as low a per capita income and as vast a population was able to expand its secondary enrollment from 1.31 to 3.64 percent in ten years.

It does not seem unrealistic to expect that a country (if it concentrated its resources and were aware of the economic benefits that could be derived) could expand its secondary enrollment from, say, about 0.5 to 2.0 percent in five years.

As the 2 percent secondary ratio was approached, we would expect the country to turn its attention to an expansion of university-level education. We would expect the country to continue the momentum of expansion of secondary schools in the direction of a 5 percent ratio (such as achieved by New Zealand), but this should not be the area of greatest emphasis or urgency. Expansion of higher education would then be the focal point.

Some of the better records in expanding university enrollment ratios to the total population are: Austria—from 0.264 to 0.608 percent in seven years; Canada—from 0.424 to 0.707 percent in eight years; Greece—from 0.133 to 0.277 percent in eight years; India—from 0.093 to 0.218 percent in ten years (representing an increase in number of students from 335,000 to 940,484); Israel—from 0.134 to 0.642 percent in eleven years; Italy—from 0.095 to 0.181 percent in four years, and from 0.181 to 0.419 percent in eight years; Japan—from 0.47 to 0.68 percent in five years; Puerto Rico—from 0.78 to 1.07 percent in two years; Russia—from 0.347 to 0.888 percent in ten years; Spain—from 0.146 to 0.281 percent in twelve years; the U.S.—from 0.57 to 0.90 percent in ten years; and Venezuela—from 0.090 to 0.253 percent in seven years.

These figures suggest that it would not be unrealistic to expect a country that emphasized higher education to expand enrollment by 100 percent in five years and expand *that* figure by another 100 percent in the following five years.

Thus, for an optimum mix, a policy framework for expansion of enrollment of an economically undeveloped country would begin with ten years' concentration on primary education, which hopefully could bring enrollment up from around 2 or 3 percent of total population to over 10 percent. Then, somewhere in the neighborhood of five years could be spent expanding secondary enrollment from about 0.5 to 2.00 percent. In the final ten years (while expansion was continued for primary and secondary enrollments), the emphasis could be focused on expanding university enrollments from, say, 0.075 to 0.300 percent. As far as education's impact on economic growth is concerned, the record of countries that have achieved development indicates that this type of enrollment expansion would be most conducive to increases in real income per capita.

We can translate this into approximate ratios in the appropriate age groups. In ten years a country should be able to move primary enrollment from around 10 percent of the 5–14 elementary age group to close to 50 percent of that age bracket. In the following five years, an optimum educational mix would suggest expansion of secondary education enrollment from a little above 5 percent to those aged 15–19 to roughly 25 percent. Optimum expansion of university enrollment would vary considerably according to the age structure of each country's population. Generalizing, we can anticipate an increase in ten years from about 1 percent or less of the 20–24 age group to as much as 5 percent.

It is possible to separate 36 countries by categories according to their economic outlook through the late 1960's and into the mid-1970's, as far as enrollment prerequisites for growth are concerned. The usual *caveat* must be inserted to the effect that there are other factors affecting growth per capita, such as political stability and capital formation shifts. But insofar as the important element of education is concerned, the following breakdown appears quite reliable. It is possible to shift a number of the borderline cases by one category, but that appears to be about the limit.

The areas that have *very good* prospects for growth in terms of recent increases and phasing of their enrollments are Finland, France, Ireland, the Netherlands, Norway, Sweden, Canada, Puerto Rico, Spain, Hungary, Rumania, South Africa,[13] Chile, Israel, Japan, Australia, and New Zealand. Of these, the outlook for Norway and Sweden seems particularly bright as far as the human resources input of education is concerned.

The outlook is *good* in Austria, Belgium, Denmark, Germany, the United States, Greece, Italy, Portugal, Poland, Russia, Cuba, Mexico, and Venezuela.

The outlook appears *fair* for Great Britain, Switzerland, Bulgaria, and Czechoslovakia.

Poor is the outlook for India and Uruguay. If, in India, much more emphasis were given to primary education, the outlook would be considerably better. In the case of Uruguay, primary enrollment is still not high, and there subsequently will be need for much greater emphasis at the secondary and higher education levels.

COMPARISON OF FINDINGS WITH OTHER STUDIES

The tentative conclusions of this paper do not conflict with those of Bowman and Anderson, who made a systematic study of the relationships of primary and postprimary enrollments and literacy to economic growth.[14] They found little relationship between 30 and 70 percent literacy of the adult population and economic growth, although there were clear positive correlations below 30 and above 70 percent. In comparing 1930 to 1950 changes in primary enrollments with 1938 to 1955 changes in per capita income, they found very low correlations.

However, their scattergrams and correlations do not test the kind of data presented in this paper. Their comparisons of 1930 enrollments with 1955 GNP measure a 25-year period. This does not measure the association between 8 to 10 percent of total population in primary schools with concurrent initiation of sustained per capita growth. Nor does it measure the average 11.5-year lag from sharp increases in secondary enrollments to subsequent jumps in GNP per capita. And it does not measure the average 8-year lag between higher education jumps in enrollment and subsequent notable climbs in economic growth per capita. . . .

In this paper it has been noted that in the case of countries like India and Egypt, expansion of university education came before there was a broad enough primary base. Bowman and Anderson reached the same conclusion and noted that "some educated elites may even impede developments relative to what could occur without them. . . . There can be wasteful and even dysfunctional investments in education."[15]

A basic criticism of Harbison and Myers[16] is that they failed to look at time-series data, instead simply examining country differences at one point in time. They therefore failed to note the importance for economic growth of various stages of enrollment. Looking at one cross-section they found the highest GNP's per capita associated with the countries that had high university-level enrollment ratios. They did not note that the countries with the best records of economic growth expanded primary education first, secondary education next, and university enrollment last. . . .

In other words, using the pattern of enrollment expansion outlined in this paper, Greece, Spain, and Turkey outpaced almost all of the economically advanced countries. The experience of other countries indicates that the three countries would not have obtained such impressive rates if they had changed their enrollment stress to the extent outlined by Tinbergen and Bos.

The conclusions of W. Arthur Lewis[17] do not fundamentally differ from those of this paper. Lewis's manpower budget calculations are in the same range as our data. He has calculated his on industry-by-industry requirements for a specific country. Our similar conclusions are derived by looking at the record of many countries. For example, he states: "Allowing for some absorption into farming, and for the expansion of non-agricultural employment, a developing economy needs to have at least 50 percent of its children in primary schools, so this is a priority target."[18] That dovetails with the conclusions of this paper.

Lewis also notes some of the factors involved in the development pattern outlined in this paper:

[The economist] can point out that a surplus of educated persons can only be a temporary phenomenon, since any economy can ultimately absorb any number of educated by reducing the premium for education and raising the educational qualifications for jobs. He can stress that a wide educational base is needed to find the best brains, which may make the crucial difference. He may welcome the fact that education raises aspirations, because low aspirations are one of the causes of low achievement.[19]

Lewis says the secondary school has priority over the primary school and the university.[20] This, of course, depends on the stage of development. In numerical terms this is not true of Laos (where the emphasis should be on primary education) or the U.K. (where the emphasis should be on expansion at the university level), but Lewis was obviously describing a country at what might be termed the secondary school expansion stage in economic development.

"Since the continual upgrading of the requirements for jobs is one of the more important reasons why productivity increases, one should always train more skills than current estimates of demand would indicate." [21]

1. Only countries with more than one million population in 1920 were listed, in order to reduce exogenous factors.

2. The U.S.S.R. had only 3.6 percent of its population in primary schools in 1920, but rapid expansion of primary education resulted in achievement of the 10 percent mark by the early 1930's. Japan lagged slightly in per capita production by 1958, but moved up significantly by 1962. Bulgaria's enrollment figures failed to reflect poor attendance and quality. The inefficiency of the Bulgarian system is suggested by its relatively high enrollment ratio during the late nineteenth and early twentieth centuries and a continuing high rate of illiteracy. It is questionable whether Bulgaria should actually be considered among the "over 10 percent" countries. Actually, average attendance figures are even better indicators than enrollment data, but in many cases the statistics are not available. Generally, as primary educational systems are developed, the gap between enrollment and average attendance narrows.

3. Except for Japan in 1958. Japan's lead in elementary education in the Far East was subsequently paralleled by its pre-eminence in production per capita.

4. Per capita gross domestic product in recent years has been, in U.S. dollars:

Country	1953	1958	1962
Ceylon	114	122	129
China-Taiwan	78	97	121
Republic of Korea	77	103	110
The Philippines	90	113	125
Mexico	222	288	356

[Appendix Table: ratios to Population of Primary, Secondary and Tertiary Educational Levels, Enrollment, and Gross Domestic Product per Capita (at factor cost) omitted here; for this data, readers are referred to original article. Eds.]

5. French data indicate that primary enrollment was less than 8 percent when it began to show sustained per capita growth.

6. A. B. Lewis, "El Fomento de Recursos Agricolas," in *El Desarollo Agricola y Economico de la Zona del Mantaro en el Peru* (New York: International Development Services, Inc., December 1954), pp. 1, 145.

7. Belgium, Denmark, Great Britain, the Netherlands, Sweden, Switzerland, Italy (twice), Portugal, Argentina (twice), and Chile.

8. *Spetsiizalizatsiai kooperirovaniie promyshlennosti* [Specialization and cooperation in industry] (Moscow: Gosplanizdat, 1960), p. 183.

9. Simon Kuznets, "Quantitative Aspects of the Economic Growth of Nations. VI. Long-term Trends in Capital Formation Proportions," *Economic Development and Cultural Change*, Vol. 9, No. 1, Part II (July 1961), p. 29. Colin Clark, *The Conditions of Economic Progress* (London: Macmillan, 1960) pp. 88–252. Angus Maddison, *Economic Growth in the West* (New York: Twentieth Century Fund, 1964), p. 231. UN Department of Economic and Social Affairs, *World Economic Survey, 1961* (New York, 1962), p. 90.

10. Australia, Belgium, Denmark, Finland, France, Germany, Great Britain, Ireland, the Netherlands, Norway, Switzerland, Canada, the U.S., Greece, Italy, Portugal, Spain, Bulgaria, Czechoslovakia, Hungary, Poland, Russia, Argentina, Chile, Uruguay, India, Japan, Australia, and New Zealand.

11. A total of 116 countries or areas were rated, including a number with populations less than one million in 1920.

12. International Bank for Reconstruction and Development, *The Economic Development of Spain* (Baltimore: Johns Hopkins Press, 1963), pp. 52–53.

13. Only when the non-European population is totaled *with* the European population in South Africa do we find a development pattern similar to that of other countries. This suggests that education of non-Europeans in South Africa is associated with subsequent growth.

14. Particular reference is made to the chapter "Concerning the Role of Education in Development," by Mary Jean Bowman and C. Arnold Anderson, in Clifford Geertz (ed.), *Old Societies and New States* (New York: Free Press, 1963), pp. 247–79.

15. *Ibid.*, p. 277.

16. Frederick Harbison and Charles A. Myers, *Education, Manpower, and Economic Growth* (New York: McGraw-Hill, 1964).

17. W. Arthur Lewis, *Development Planning* (London: Allen & Unwin, 1966).

18. *Ibid.*, p. 109.

19. *Ibid.*, p. 110.

20. *Ibid.*, p. 232.

21. *Ibid.*, p. 106.

EDUCATION AS A BASIC FACTOR IN JAPAN'S ECONOMIC GROWTH

RYŌJI ITŌ

Ministry of Education, Japan

INTRODUCTION

Japan's modern educational system was established in 1872, only four years after the Meiji Restoration, and the benefits it has bestowed on modern Japan may be considered from various angles. Educational experts in many countries of the world pay special attention to its contribution to the development of the Japanese economy. Their attention has been attracted by the spectacular economic recovery and its subsequent "miraculous" growth of Japan in the period following the close of World War II. It has been said that Japan was able to achieve this, in spite of the loss of a quarter of her material wealth through war, only through the "know-how" and technical skills of the Japanese people which had been gained from the prewar educational system.

Japan is one of the countries which has made swift economic progress in the Twentieth Century. The many factors, political, social and spiritual which have contributed toward a rapid economic growth in these countries have little in common, except that in all cases the educational system has played an important role. In addition, it must not be overlooked that the system developed in these countries was "modern" in content, and designed to vigorously promote vocational and technological skills to meet social needs.

Japan's modern educational system was also devised along these lines and included courses on agriculture, engineering, commerce, medicine and education.

Education in Japan, too, helped to overcome unfavorable social and economic conditions during its "take-off" period. Japan soon outdistanced other Asian countries and has approached the levels of advanced European and American countries. This is in spite of Japan's late arrival in the field, problems of overcrowding, and a poverty of natural resources. One important feature at this stage was the spread of elementary education among the farming communities, which then comprised a very great proportion of the gainfully employed population of the country.

Japanese education, in the early period of the Meiji Era (1872–1885), was more concerned with raising educational levels and modernizing the country's outlook and ways of thinking, rather than trying to attempt to contribute directly toward economic activities, which could be left to a later stage.

The evaluation of the role of education in the economic development of Japan should be attributed to the effort of the people who restricted consumption and invested the money thus saved in education. That the ratio of educational expenditure to national income in Japan was among the highest in the world substantiates this statement.

QUANTITATIVE DEVELOPMENT OF EDUCATION AND ITS RELATION TO ECONOMIC GROWTH

In examining the spread of education and the aims and contents of education, it must be realized that the industrialization of Japan advanced at an extremely rapid pace, outstripping the social development of the community, which had only recently been released from feudal bondage. Consequently the quantitative development of education had to proceed at a much more rapid tempo than that of the more advanced European countries. This must be pointed out as a characteristic feature of modern education in Japan.

Japan's modern history dates from the 1870's, and the educational system of this

From *Developing Economies* (January–June 1963), pp. 37–54. Reprinted by permission of the publisher, the Institute of Developing Economies, Tokyo. Some sections have been omitted.

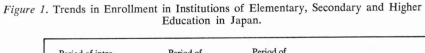

Figure 1. Trends in Enrollment in Institutions of Elementary, Secondary and Higher Education in Japan.

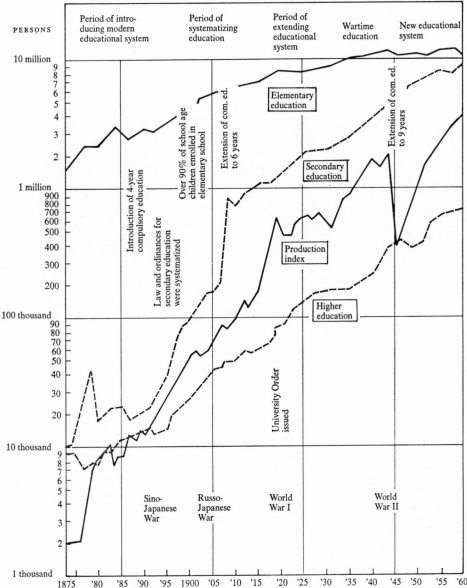

SOURCES: Ministry of Education, *Mombushō Nempō* (Annual Reports of Education), Tokyo, 1876–1960, *passim;* Nihon Tōkei Kenkyūjo, ed., *Nihon Keizai Tokeishū* (Collection of Japanese Economic Statistics), Tokyo, Nohon Hyōronsha, 1958, p. 27; and Economic Planning Agency, *Keizai Yōran* (Handbook of Economy), Tokyo, 1962, pp. 88–89.

period provided an elementary basic education for the nation, and a higher education for the training of its potential leaders.

As light industries were established, centering on the textile industry, and heavy industry began to appear, the system was expanded to include secondary and vocational education, and the education of women made rapid progress. As heavy industry ushered in a period of economic maturity, the system for higher education was expanded by a spread of secondary education. The recent period following the Second World War marked a remarkable increase in the national income, a feature development in heavy and chemical industries, and growth of tertiary industries. In this period post-secondary education and higher education under a new educational system were introduced. The relationship between education and economic development is illustrated graphically in Figure 1, in which enrollments in schools of different types, and manufacturing and mining production indices are correlated.

As stated above, the first stage dealt with universal elementary education and the special training of leaders. This was in line with the following socio-economic policy.

The Meiji Government, intent on modernizing the country rapidly, and at a much later period than the more advanced European countries, had to preserve the independence of the country, yet at the same time introduce modern military, fiscal, and administrative systems, and modern methods of production. This was carried out under the slogans of "Wealth and Military Strength," "Promotion of Industry" and "Development of Culture and Civilization." Thus the educational system was a part of the measures taken by the Government.

In 1872 the "School System," patterned after the European and American school systems and incorporating the ideals of "equality of educational opportunities for all" was promulgated. The "School System" which made education compulsory for children of either sex irrespective of class, was of immense significance in Japan's later industrialization. In 1900, it was prescribed that tuition in public elementary schools would not be charged for in principle, while in 1907 the period of compulsory education was extended from four to six years. In spite of this extension of the period of compulsory education, the percentage of enrollments reached 98 percent in 1907, which meant that practically all school age children were receiving elementary education.

It is worthy of note that six-year compulsory education became a reality after only 30 years of enforcement of the "School System." This was a factor that contributed greatly toward the smooth development of light industries centering on the textile in-

dustry and the establishment of heavy industry. The remarkable speed with which elementary education was consolidated in Japan may be explained by the fact that there were practically no religious, linguistic, national or other social and cultural traditions to hinder the modernization of the country. But more than anything else it was due to the fact that the Government was keenly aware of the part that education could play in developing the country, and made unflagging efforts to this end.

Nor should we lose sight of the fact that in the early stages of the modernization of this country, where the spread of education was not yet sufficient, leaders of the country played a significant role in thought and action. Higher education before the modernization of the country was aimed to produce a class of leaders from the upper strata of society. After the promulgation of the Government Order of Education, higher education was provided for all who had ability and talent as future leaders of the country, irrespective of social origin. Thus the country was able to draw for its talents from a wider range of its people.

TABLE 1

DISTRIBUTION OF STUDENTS ENROLLED IN THE UNIVERSITY OF TOKYO BY SOCIAL ORIGINS (PERCENTAGES)

Year	Peers	Descendants of "Samurai" Class	Commoners	Total
1878	0.6	73.9	25.5	100
1879	0.5	77.7	21.8	100
1880	0.9	73.6	25.5	100
1881	0.0	51.8	48.2	100
1882	0.1	49.1	50.8	100
1883	0.1	52.9	47.0	100
1884	0.2	50.2	49.6	100
1885	0.2	51.7	48.1	100

SOURCE: Ministry of Education, *Mombushō Nempō*, 1872–1885, *passim*.

Table 1 classifies according to social origins the students enrolled in the University of Tokyo, which enjoyed a privileged position as a higher educational institution.

Figures cited in this table show that higher education was open to various classes of society in the transitional period from feudalism to modern society.

Secondary Education

It was in the period from 1895 to 1905 that secondary education was firmly established as an integral part of the nation's education system. This period corresponds to the "growth period" of the Japanese economy. This period saw a gradual growth of industry, a change from cottage industry to factory production, replacement of the old apprenticeship system by new vocational education, and direct adaptation of socio-economic requirements into the public educational system. Thus, as secondary education advanced, Japan's economy entered a period of maturity after 1905.

Increased national income led to an advance in the rate of enrollment in the institutions of higher learning, whereas the spread of higher education was accompanied by an increase in production. Shown in Table 2 are per capita income figures of gainfully employed persons and the number of students enrolled in secondary schools, in 10-year steps. Thus the national income, which followed a slow upward curve from 1895 to 1905, rose sharply between 1915 and 1925. The number of students enrolled in secondary schools made a corresponding advance.

Education of Women

Women's education in Japan lagged behind men's education. Women, previously educated at home, gradually began to receive the same schooling as men, and then not only ordinary cultural education but also vocational and specialized education. This gradual spread of education among women contributed as much as the spread of education among men to the social and economic modernization of the country. It is true that many of the women graduating from schools were tied down to housework instead of becoming career women and that the percentage of women employed in the labor force was much lower than that of men, but there is no denying the fact that women who received higher education helped develop the society and economy of the country through their family life and by encouraging their children to higher learning.

Higher Education

Higher education represents the third stage in the spread of education. The number of students receiving higher education did not begin to increase until about 25 years after the Meiji Restoration. Secondary education was not yet so popular while greater importance was attached to the institutions of higher learning, which though limited in number, were regarded as centers to produce a leading class for the nation. However, in or around 1900, the number of students receiving higher education began to rise. This is explained by an increase in and after 1903 of the number of colleges, which were established to meet the demand for specially trained people due to the industrial development of the country fol-

TABLE 2

INCREASE IN ENROLLMENT IN SECONDARY SCHOOLS AND INCREASE
IN PRODUCTION AND INCOME

Year	Employed Population Per Capita National Income for Gainfully (in Thousands of Yen)	in Secondary Schools No. of Students Enrolled (in Thousands of Persons)	Production Index Mining and Manufacturing (1914 = 100)
1895	45	46	22.8
1905	47	191	52.1
1915	73	1,058	126.0
1925	111	2,069	478.3

SOURCES: Kazushi Ōkawa, ed., *Nihon Keizai no Seichōritsu* [The growth rate of the Japanese economy] (Tokyo, Iwanami, 1956), pp. 72–73 and 162; and Ministry of Education, *Mombushō Nempō*, 1895–1925, *passim*.
NOTE: Currency adjusted to 1960 values.

lowing the Sino-Japanese and Russo-Japanese wars.

A period from 1920 to 1925 saw a rapid increase in both the number of schools of higher learning and students enrolled in them. This indicates that the expansion of the industrial productivity following World War I increased the demand for specially trained people and that a rise in the income of ordinary people provided means for enrollment in schools of higher education. However, the number of students receiving higher education fell between 1927 and 1935, reflecting the worldwide crisis and the resultant depression of the Japanese economy. But with the year 1935 as the turning point, the numbers began to rise rapidly, manifesting Japan's national policies for expansion of production in preparation of military adventures. Then, after World War II the demand for university graduates again rose sharply as a result of a rapid expansion of secondary and tertiary industries, while the number of persons wishing to receive higher education and that of students enrolled in schools of higher education reached unprecedented heights with a remarkable improvement in the living standard of the people.

Shown in Table 3 are the interrelations between the quantitative development of higher education and the economic development of the country by comparing the percentages of students receiving higher education to the total population of corresponding ages with the mining and manufacturing production index and the growth rate of national income. Figures in this table show that, except for the year 1950, increases in the percentage of students against total population of corresponding ages roughly corresponds to that of the production index and the national income growth rate.

Thus, the quantitative development of school education at all levels during the past 90 years since the establishment of

TABLE 3

PERCENTAGES OF STUDENTS ENROLLED IN HIGHER EDUCATIONAL
INSTITUTIONS IN TOTAL NUMBER OF PERSONS IN
CORRESPONDING AGES, COMPARED WITH
ECONOMIC INDICES

Year	Percentages of Students Enrolled in Higher Educational Institutions *	Mining and Manufacturing Production Index (1953 = 100)	Adjusted National Income Index (1953 = 100)
1895	0.3	3.0	20.1
1905	0.9	6.8	23.1
1915	1.0	16.5	37.0
1925	2.5	62.8	60.7
1935	3.0	100.0	100.0
1950	6.2	96.8	93.3
1960	10.2	476.9	225.8
1961	10.2	577.1	266.9

SOURCES: Ministry of Education, *Mombushō Nempō*, 1876–1950, *passim*, and *Gakkō Kihon Chōsa Hōkokusho* [Report on the basic research on schools] (Tokyo, 1955 & 1960), *passim;* Ministry of Health and Welfare, Institute of Population Problems, *Meiji Shonen Ikō Taishō 9-nen ni itaru Danjo Nenreibetsu Jinkā Suikei ni tsuite* [On the estimated male and female population by age groups, from the beginning of the Meiji Era to the ninth year of Taishō] (Tokyo, 1962), pp. 35–36; Economic Planning Agency, Keizai Yōran, pp. 88–89; Tōkei Kenkyūjo ed., *op. cit.*, p. 27; and Prime Minister's Office, Statistics Bureau, *Kokusei Chōsa Hōkokusho* [Report on population census] (Tokyo, 1925–1960), *passim*.
* Includes post-graduate students. The scope of persons in corresponding ages differs according to years.

TABLE 4

PERCENTAGE DISTRIBUTION OF PRODUCTIVE AGE POPULATION,
BY LEVEL OF SCHOOL COMPLETED

Year	Productive Age Population	Receiving No Education	Completed Elementary Education	Completed Secondary Education	Completed Higher Education
1895	100	84.1	15.6	0.2	0.1
1905	100	57.3	41.6	0.9	0.2
1925	100	20.0	74.3	4.9	0.8
1935	100	7.1	82.1	9.2	1.6
1950	100	2.3	78.5	15.8	3.4
1960	100	0.5	63.9	30.1	5.5

SOURCES: Ministry of Education, *Mombushō Nempō*, 1876–1950, *passim;* Ministry of Health and Welfare, Institute of Population Problems, *op. cit.,* pp. 35–36; and Prime Minister's Office, Statistics Bureau, *op. cit., passim.*

NOTES: 1. The productive age population for 1895–1925 includes persons between 15 and 54 years; that for 1935 and after—between 15 and 59 years. Figures up to 1900 are based on the population estimates by age, compiled by the Institute of Population Problems, and other figures on the National Census.

2. As reported in the Annual Report of the Ministry of Education, the number of graduates of elementary and secondary schools, and institutions of higher learning was taken as the basic data. The number of deaths, estimated on the basis of the life-span table compiled by the Institute of Population Problems, was deducted from the cumulative total to obtain the figures in the table.

3. The number of persons who received "no education" represents the difference between the working population and the total of graduates from schools of various levels.

4. Figures for 1960 are based on the National Census.

the modern school education system has led to changes in the percentage distribution of the productive age population by level of school completed. It has provided a highly qualified labor for and contributed greatly toward economic development. Table 4 shows the productive age population has achieved qualitative improvement as seen from the percentage distribution by level of school completed.

QUALITATIVE DEVELOPMENT OF EDUCATION AND ECONOMIC GROWTH

Just as the quantitative development of education has a close relationship to the development of society and the economy, so has its qualitative development, namely the improvement of its aims and contents, a close bearing on the socio-economic development of the country. Many arguments may be advanced on the task and functions of education, but when we view the development of education in a selected country from a historical perspective, we must take it for granted that the purpose

of education is to produce a younger generation in the image of the state or society of the country. To attain this purpose of education, the contents of education are formulated, the curriculums organized, the education system formalized, textbooks and other teaching materials prepared and teachers trained.

In the following we will touch on the development of aims and contents of Japanese education in consideration of the socio-economic growth of the country.

Change in the Aims of Education

In the early years of the Meiji Era the national policy of "Wealth and Military Strength" and "Promotion of Industry" determined the contents of education so that Japan might maintain itself as an independent country by repelling pressure brought to bear on her by foreign powers. During the period in which heavy industries were gradually developed to take the place of light industries after the Sino-Japanese and Russo-Japanese wars, the training of technicians required by industry and the economy was added to the aims of education, extending the social development of the country. In the Taishō Era, tendencies of democracy and liberalism were introduced into education, but as the nation's economy was placed on a wartime footing, ultra-nationalism became the uppermost aim of education. And in the postwar Japan the rights and needs of the individual have become the cornerstone of education.

Subjects and Their Contents

The syllabus to be taught in elementary and secondary education was basically decided in 1886. Later, this was increased in scope and contents enriched in keeping with the development of society and the economy.

Then, on what subjects was emphasis placed in elementary education? Up until 1900 or thereabouts, a large proportion of time was allocated to the teaching of the national language and arithmetic in view of the need for the entire nation to be taught in the basic subjects of the three Rs. Later, as the national economy and character developed, Japanese society began to require the younger generation to be equipped with broader academic and technical attainments.

Changes in the contents of the subjects taught in school may be observed through textbooks, which are the main teaching material. In the early part of the Meiji Era emphasis in the textbooks had been laid on the acquisition of knowledge and techniques. These books, both practical and utilitarian in nature, were in most cases translations of foreign texts, however.

After the Sino-Japanese War (1894–95), improved educational levels were strongly demanded for the unity of the nation, and in 1904, school education was unified on a nationwide scale through the adoption of the Government-compiled textbooks in all the elementary schools throughout the country. This system continued until 1949, when the Government-approval system was re-adopted for textbooks. In the meantime, Government-compiled textbooks were revised four times with the aim of improving and enriching the contents in keeping with the development of society and to unify the nation's awareness of the ethics of loyalty and filial piety.

In the case of a typically Japanese subject "morals," moral virtues dealt with in this subject mostly concerned "diligence," "thrift," and "application to studies." This is interesting in view of the fact that the rapid development of the Japanese economy depended largely on a high rate of national savings, which registered 15–20 percent after 1900. We should not underrate the role played by "morals" in the growth period of the Japanese economy, which discouraged wasteful spending and encouraged saving as a commendable virtue.

In most cases, these virtues were inculcated in the minds of the pupils through historical figures. It is easy to understand why these figures and their acts must have left an indelible imprint on the minds of the school children—Emperor Meiji as laying the foundation for the development of Japan; Ninomiya-Kinjirō as a man who succeeded in life thanks to thrift, perseverence, and devoted application to studies; Uesugi-Yōzan as a feudal lord who succeeded in developing industry in his domain through application of his doctrine that economic development should be supported by strong moral virtues; and Toyotomi-Hideyoshi as an exemplary person who rose to eminence from a low social position.

The words and acts of these historical figures, regarded as examples for the nation to follow, helped the people to acquire the virtue of diligence. More worthy of attention is the fact that historical figures selected as exemplifying the moral virtues did not belong to a particular class but to various classes of the nation. From the standpoint that man is the indispensable factor for economic development, it is of special importance that these examples gave hope and encouragement to the pupils in that they showed that any man could rise in the world depending on his ability and effort, whatever his station in life might be.

The syllabus may be said to have changed in keeping with or in anticipation of social development. If the tempo of social development leaves this behind, investment in education fails to achieve its desired effect and can no longer be a factor to promote the development of society and the economy. In this sense, it may be said that the contents of education in Japan accorded well with the social and economic requirements of the country, particularly during the period of its development. A glance at

Government-compiled textbooks will show how the contents and teaching methods of the subjects other than "morals," such as geography and history, mathematics and science, improved in keeping with the new social and economic requirements of the country.

EDUCATIONAL INVESTMENT

So far we have outlined historically the development of education in this country. In the following we shall examine educational investment in the past 90 years.

Shown in Figure 2-a are shifts in the actual figures of national income and public educational spending in and after 1885. Except for the World War II years, national income followed a steady upward curve, particularly after World War II. . . . Figure 2-b indicates shifts in the proportion of public educational spending to national income. The figure shows that the rate of educational spending has increased from some 2 percent to about 5 percent during the past 75 years, showing the same tendency as the actual amount of educational spending.

As will be seen in Table 5, there are considerable differences in the proportion of public educational spending out of national income among countries where per capita national income is roughly on the same level. Like Spain and Mexico, Japan belongs to a group of countries where annual per capita national income ranges from $200 to $499, but falls within the category of countries where the proportion of public educational spending to national income is more than 5 percent. This presents a sharp contrast to Spain and Mexico, where the proportion is less than 2 percent.

The situation, indicating as it does the traditional policy of attaching importance

TABLE 5

PER CAPITA NATIONAL INCOME AND PROPORTION OF PUBLIC EDUCATIONAL SPENDING
TO NATIONAL INCOME IN VARIOUS COUNTRIES

Rate of Educational Spending to National Income	Per Capita National Income				
	More than $900	$899–$500	$499–$200	$199–$100	Less than $100
More than 5%	U.K. Norway	U.S.S.R. Finland Belgium Netherlands	Japan		
4–5%	U.S.A. Canada	Germany Venezuela		Ceylon Republic of Korea	
3–4%	New Zealand Sweden France	Australia Italy Israel		Philippines	Burma
2–3%			Yugoslavia Chile Turkey Portugal	Peru Thailand	
Less than 2%			Spain Mexico	Ghana	India Pakistan Indonesia

SOURCES: UNESCO, *Basic Facts and Figures* (Paris, 1961), pp. 72–79. U.N., *Report on the World Social Situation* (New York, 1961), p. 71.

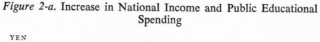

Figure 2-a. Increase in National Income and Public Educational Spending

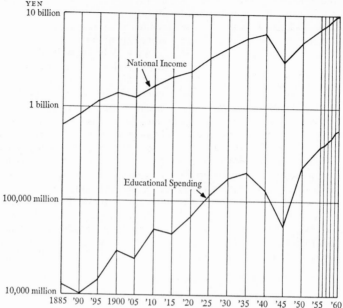

Figure 2-b. Percentage of National Income Spent for Public Education

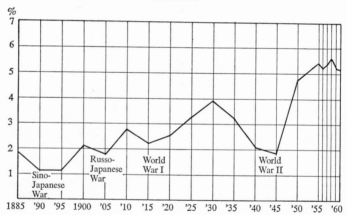

SOURCES: K. Ōkawa, ed. *op. cit.,* p. 161, Economic Planning Agency, *Kokumin Shotoku Hakusho* (National Income Statistics of Japan), Tokyo, 1960, pp. 140–143; Ministry of Education, *Mombushō Nempō,* 1885–1940, *passim; Gakkō Kohon Chōsa Hōkokusho* (Report on the Basic Research on Schools), Tokyo, 1951–1960, *passim;* and *Chihō Kyōikuhi no Chōsa Hōkokusho* (Report on the Research on Education Spending by Local Autonomous Bodies), Tokyo, 1960, *passim.*

to education, is considered to be a main factor contributing to the rapid development of the Japanese economy.

We see to what level of education priority was given in allocating educational in-

vestments from Tables 6-a and 6-b. In the early stage of modern industrialization, emphasis was laid on the spread of elementary education and the training of leaders through higher education. In addition, the

TABLE 6-A

PERCENTAGE DISTRIBUTION OF TOTAL EXPENDITURES FOR NATIONAL,
PUBLIC, AND PRIVATE SCHOOLS, BY SCHOOL LEVEL

Year	Total	Elementary	Secondary	Higher	Teacher Training *
1885	100.0	84.3	2.8	8.3	4.6
1890	100.0	76.9	3.1	10.9	9.1
1895	100.0	77.1	6.1	10.2	6.6
1900	100.0	67.6	16.5	7.0	8.9
1905	100.0	64.6	18.2	10.2	7.0
1910	100.0	68.0	16.5	9.6	5.9
1915	100.0	65.5	17.3	12.0	5.2
1920	100.0	67.6	17.9	10.6	3.9
1925	100.0	61.1	20.1	14.6	4.2
1930	100.0	58.4	20.1	17.8	3.7
1935	100.0	61.9	18.7	16.9	2.5
1940	100.0	55.7	21.8	20.1	2.4
1950	100.0	41.8	46.2	12.0	...
1955	100.0	46.0	42.3	11.7	...
1960	100.0	42.4	44.5	13.1	...

* The expenses for teacher training are included in the expenses for the higher education during the period 1950–1960.

TABLE 6-B

PERCENTAGE DISTRIBUTION OF ENROLLMENT IN NATIONAL, PUBLIC,
AND PRIVATE SCHOOLS, BY SCHOOL LEVEL

Year	Total	Elementary	Secondary	Higher	Teacher Training *
1885	100.0	98.9	0.5	0.4	0.2
1890	100.0	98.6	0.6	0.6	0.2
1895	100.0	98.3	1.1	0.3	0.3
1900	100.0	97.0	2.3	0.3	0.4
1905	100.0	95.8	3.1	0.7	0.4
1910	100.0	95.6	3.4	0.6	0.4
1915	100.0	94.7	4.2	0.7	0.4
1920	100.0	93.8	5.1	0.8	0.3
1925	100.0	90.2	8.0	1.3	0.5
1930	100.0	89.2	8.8	1.5	0.5
1935	100.0	89.3	9.0	1.4	0.3
1940	100.0	86.7	11.3	1.7	0.3
1950	100.0	59.3	38.6	2.1	...
1955	100.0	57.4	39.7	2.9	...
1960	100.0	56.1	40.7	3.2	...

* Enrollment in institutions for teacher training is included in that of institutions for higher education during the period 1950–1960.

training of teachers was promoted systematically and preponderantly under governmental plans. This education policy provided conditions for the development of the Japanese industry from its infancy. Then, consideration was given to the spread of secondary education and education of women, in order to meet the demands of the developing secondary and tertiary industries.

Further special emphasis was given to

higher education during the economic boom following World War I and later, prior to the outbreak of World War II, in order to carry out the Government's "manpower" policy. Today, a remarkable development is observed in the spread of higher education, owing to increased demands for trained personnel in the heavy and chemical industries and in the expanding tertiary industries as well. There is also an additional individual demand due to the general rise in living standards and income. Thus, what we pointed out in discussing the spread of education, is also observed in educational spending.

In considering the distribution of the burden of educational spending among different administrative bodies, it is noted that in the early days, a greater part was borne by municipal, town and village authorities, and then the proportion borne by prefectural and Central Government gradually rose. The proportion borne by the national treasury increased in step with the increased importance of the role of education in the social and economic development of the country, and as the social and economic activities of the nation advanced in scale from a regional to a national basis. Thus, the shifting of the burden from the shoulders of local authorities to the national treasury was carried out in many smooth stages. . . .

[For a discussion of ways to calculate the rate of return to investment in education and the percentage contributed to national income by education, see original article. Eds.]

EGALITARIAN IDEAL AND EDUCATIONAL FACT IN COMMUNIST CHINA

DONALD J. MUNRO

University of Michigan

INTRODUCTION

Twenty years ago the leaders of Communist China faced two problems: how to transform egalitarianism from cardinal ideal into reality, and manpower requirements from modernization blueprint into fact.[1] This study examines the role of the educational system in China's pursuit of these aims. More precisely, it deals (among other things) with the eventual conflict between the two aims that brought in its wake a fundamental dispute over what the manpower requirements are. The study concludes with the judgment that the existence of quality education, necessary to produce high level scientific and technical skills, is impossible without some serious abuse of the egalitarian ideal. The leadership is then left with a choice of minimizing the need for quality education while pushing closer to the ideal; it must then reassess manpower needs. Or it can more and more ignore the utopian social vision. Each of these choices in turn matches a position on the most desirable locus of educational control: the local organization (commune, production brigade, etc.) or the central Ministry of Education. This matter will also be examined.

China's problems are in some ways common to those of most developing nations, and, to some degree, even have counterparts in a country like the United States. The group that was favored by the existing educational institutions in China in 1949 and, in spite of certain corrective measures, for seventeen years thereafter, was the

From *China: Management of a Revolutionary Society*, edited by John M. H. Lindbeck, pp. 256–290. Copyright © 1971 by University of Washington Press. Reprinted by permission. Some sections have been omitted.

same group that is favored in Nigeria, Brazil, France, the U.S.S.R., and the United States: an urban segment, including the leading educationalists, that is separated in a number of ways from the rural citizenry and/or the urban poor. The gaping inequity that an education can perpetuate or ameliorate is between rural and urban areas.

Julius Nyerere has pointed to the problem in Tanzania:

The education now provided is designed for the few who are intellectually stronger than their fellows; it induces among those who succeed a feeling of superiority, and leaves a majority of the others hankering after something they will never obtain. It induces a feeling of inferiority among the majority, and can thus not produce either the egalitarian society we should build nor the attitudes of mind conducive to an egalitarian society. On the contrary, it induced the growth of a class structure in our country.[2]

. . . A recent visitor to Brazil has written:

This obsolete social order maintains itself with the help of an archaic educational system. A good education is reserved for a minute segment of the youthful population, and every attempt is made to recruit the future elite from those circles which are already in power. . . . Instead of expanding the necessary efforts in the field of education, Brazil tries to keep a growing number of young people from obtaining a higher education by making crucial examinations constantly more difficult.[3]

. . . Mao Tse-tung may have taken some time developing the opinion, but it is clear that he now faults the Soviet educational system for perpetuating an elite class. A recent article states:

Under the Soviet educational system, it is obvious that treatment as between the poor and the rich differs vastly and an extreme inequality prevails. On the one hand are the sons and daughters of the bourgeois strata who enjoy every kind of favorable treatment and on the other are the sons and daughters of the workers, peasants and other working people who are discriminated against and always get unfair treatment.[4]

Thus one of China's fundamental problems was and is: How can the educational system be used to help institutionalize the egalitarian ideal of the revolution? Needless to say, we have here a question of values. But the pursuit of this ideal is also a means for achieving the political power necessary to realize other policy ends. Peasant loyalty won through increasing the educational possibilities of their children is an important source of that power.

China's second problem has been determining how best to introduce congruity between educational practices and manpower needs. The problem is related to the previous one. If one lays relatively strong stress on the need for a number of highly trained scientists and technicians, one will be very concerned about quality in students and about providing special schools for the bright (especially college preparatory middle schools). If one is especially concerned with the egalitarian ideal, one may argue against special schools as being elitist and also as being non-essential in terms of manpower needs. One will be less concerned with the quality of schools than with making easy access to schools available to all. Quantity over quality.

. . . In many modernizing states the manpower problem has a special feature: Professional educators assume that the kind of heavy academic burden in the arts and sciences that will ultimately prepare students to enter a college or university is right for many students. Thus a large share of the educational budget may go to ordinary middle schools that turn out too many graduates for the colleges and job market to absorb. Concurrently, educators will be doing far less than they could in the teaching of new, basic level skills that must exist to meet the ever changing problems of the developing economy. . . . The Maoist critique of regular middle schools in China reflected this judgment: "They were turned into preparatory schools for colleges, and their main task was to send students to colleges instead of training up ordinary workers with both socialist conscience and culture."[5]

The debate in China over the relative desirability of a centralized or decentralized school system, which is our third problem, was colored from the start by the Soviet model, which was extremely centralized. In Mao's eyes, the resolution of the debate on the side of decentralization gradually took on signs of urgency because he eventually regarded it as bound up with the issues of egalitarianism and manpower needs. The initial reason for decentralization was largely economic. The argument was that unless decentralization occurred, local areas would wait for the central government to provide money for schools and to send teachers. A poor central government that spends much of its funds on quality education in cities will provide little. Decentralization shifts the financial and training burden to the local areas, releasing untapped physical and motivational resources. From the standpoint of the egalitarian ideal, there is a payoff. More schools blossoming forth mean more places for children of peasant families. In manpower terms, more technicians are educated, and the schools they attend have a curriculum geared to local production needs, unlike those provided by Peking.

A recent Chinese Communist study on the educational revolution in rural China makes the following point: "The poor and lower-middle peasants change their former viewpoint on the schools when they really exercise power over education. The former relationship between the school and the production brigade was: 'I do my teaching, you do your farm work.' When speaking of a school, the poor and lower middle peasants often said, 'your school. . . .' Now they always talk about 'our school.' " [6] The assumption is that only when they talk about "our school" will the schools really begin to serve China's new goals.

Those who share confidence in decentralization have yet to direct their attention to two problems. First, can controls be established to insure that membership in local governing boards will not simply find itself moving into the hands of a new elite? Furthermore, what guarantees are there that local boards will not opt for quality education and special schools (for their own children, or to increase the number of high level technicians locally available)? Second, if local areas not only have self-management but also provide a substantial amount of their own financing, does this mean that poor areas will provide educational facilities inferior to those of prosperous areas, and, thus, that the problem of equity will not be completely solved after all?

The efficacy of the educational system in helping to realize any revolutionary goals since 1949 has been seriously hampered by one brute fact: in the brief twenty-year period, four traumatic shifts in educational policy have occurred. From 1949 until the late fall of 1951 (in some areas, until 1953) many middle schools and institutions of higher learning still followed the Anglo-American model, that is, a liberal arts approach with teachers and students using many English and American texts (translated or in the original). From 1952 until 1958 China emulated the Soviet educational example with a heavy stress on engineering and science, a preference for the specialized and technical college, a stress on the quality of the students rather than on their quantity, the professional ideal, the use of Soviet texts, the highly centralized control over all schools, and a heavy academic burden on students. . . .

Matters crystallized between 1958 and 1961 when Mao, inspired by the Yenan experience, sought to apply to China at peace a model that in part was derived from guerrilla days. This meant combining education and productive labor, a stress on the quantity of students enrolled rather than on their quality, the reduced importance of academic study, the use of locally prepared Chinese texts, and decentralization. After the failure of the Great Leap, from roughly 1961 to 1964 (especially until September, 1962), there was a return to a liberalized version of the Soviet model— one more permissive of reading and discussing previously taboo subjects and foreign writings, which gave more authority to senior teachers in running the school. In 1964 Mao began his attempt once more to control the destiny of the educational system, an attempt that reached its climax during the Cultural Revolution. . . .

CENTRALIZATION OR DECENTRALIZATION

Those who view the educational system as a key instrument for realizing the egalitarian ideal have a preference for decentralization. . . . The group who advocated the reduction of quality control and of standards supervised by the Ministry of Education (through admissions policies, examinations, and uniform curriculum) thought this would make it possible to admit many more students into extant schools and to allow them to go farther up the ladder. And new "irregular" schools (a pejorative term used by professionals) with irregular standards could be opened. Education, including upper level education, would no longer be open only to a select group. Quantity would dominate over quality. In contrast, those whose primary concern has been with quality education in order to train high-level scientific and technical skills and who have not been troubled by the abuse of the egalitarian ideal that this entailed, have advocated centralization.

The question of locus of control is also important in the debate over manpower needs that stems from the "quantity versus quality" dispute. Decentralization is the vehicle for cultivating on a large scale basic level skills geared to local production needs. There will be more students, and a local character can be given to the curriculum. For example, in a chemistry course in an agricultural area, students might study chemistry only as it relates to chemical fertilizers. In fact, national reforms in teaching method and curriculum content in order to make education more functional, were expected to follow from the decentralization. In contrast, when there is a stress on schools that offer a solid grounding in fundamental mathematics and scientific theory (and on middle schools serving a college preparatory function), centralized control is viewed as the most effective guarantee that they will all fill this role.

The centralization/decentralization issue has two dimensions: the relative power balance in school policy between the ministry and the local organization (commune, production brigade, and so on), and the locus of authority within any given institution. Mao has assumed that when local people have substantial control, they can be relied upon to carry out the national policy of placing quantity over quality in admissions and promotion policies, and that they will opt for a curriculum with courses that relate closely to China's production demands. . . .

One dimension of the centralization/decentralization issue concerns whether the ministry or the local district has the dominant voice in deciding on school policy. The Soviet educational system, which was inherited from the czarist era, is highly centralized. During the period of intensive borrowing from the Soviet Union in the 1950's, officials in the Chinese Ministry of Education reinforced the argument for centralization by appeal to the Soviet model. Thus, before and after the period 1958–60,

the ministry determined nationwide policy on school administration and organization, curriculum, textbooks, and teaching method.[7]

It was not until 1958 that Mao began the effective implementation of an educational revolution, a major feature of which was local control. His slogan was "control by the entire party and all the people."[8] The chief instruments for turning slogan into fact were the half-work (farming), half-study schools, most of which were directly managed by the brigade or production team in the communes. The state provided little or no financing and had minimal control over admission policies, teaching plans, course contents, and so forth. One source of the financing was the payment for productive labor done by students, which was used to support the school rather than being given as remuneration to the students. . . .

[Following its establishment in 1952, the Ministry of Education] was intended to provide the machinery whereby uniform control could be exercised over the following matters in all schools of higher learning: admissions requirements (with some exceptions), financial plans, personnel (hiring and transferring teachers), teaching plans, and the establishment of new departments in colleges. In 1958, however, the Ministry of Higher Education was abolished, and its functions were absorbed by the Ministry of Education.

The consequence for decentralization was immediate. . . . Of 227 schools of higher learning, the Ministry of Education and the central specialized ministries were to have authority over 40, and the other 187 were to be returned to local control.[9] At this time, the uniform, nationwide admissions system was replaced by a system whereby each school either established its own admission procedures or entered into some cooperative arrangement with other schools. Local provincial or city conditions would dictate different policies for different places.[10] "Local control" meant not just a significant policy voice for the regional authorities, but more authority for the individual university administration with the aim of encouraging educational creativity and particularity.[11] . . .

The other dimension to the problem concerns the decision making process within schools. Let us speak now about students.

One must always attempt to differentiate representative bodies that exist primarily to enable a leadership group to implement its policies on a large scale from those bodies that exist, among other things, to solicit ideas and to solidify the sense of identification between an organization and its members.

. . . [T]he establishment in 1958 of the Three-in-One groups in charge of running schools and departments was intended, among other things, to solidify the sense of identification between the organization and its members by soliciting their ideas on educational matters. The group in charge of a given department would be composed of Party members, certain teachers, and students; the Party members always were supposed to have the "leading role." The experience of the physics department at Nan-k'ai University is typical of the kind of topic on which student opinion was solicited. Its Three-in-One section (*san chieh-ho hsiao-tsu*) decided on what courses should be offered, the content of those courses, the kinds of teaching materials to be used, and the method of instruction.[12] . . .

An indirect but positive consequence of the decentralization spirit in individual schools might have been the reform of teaching methods in order to develop the students' ability to solve problems in the technical sphere. Essentially, rote memorization was to be terminated as much as possible, and in its stead the active involvement of the student in the learning process was to be substituted. This applied to lower schools and to institutions of higher learning.

Administrative changes that formalized student participation in decisions about course content, examinations, and teaching method were expected to entail an alteration of the classroom teacher-student relationship as well. The work-study model was expected to have an additional favorable effect. However, teacher discipline often broke down as the bounds within which student participation was to be exercised were transgressed.[13] The academic orientation of the reforms was often submerged in generalized attacks on teachers as representatives of the "mental aristocracy," with substantial intimidation and purposeless disrespect. Student leverage was not merely theoretical; the governing body in

a school had the authority to transfer a teacher, and the recommendation of students that a teacher should be transferred carried weight.[14] . . .

Official publications often note that students cannot cease the reflexive response to antecedent blueprint and develop independent judgment unless the traditional domineering posture of the teacher is changed.[15] "Equalize the relation between students and teachers in institutions of higher learning," was one slogan.[16] Problem solving in class, open book examinations, and a host of other techniques were called for. Another aspect of the teaching reform was to reduce the amount of academic work that students must do, both the number of courses required and the amount of material covered in individual courses. The argument is that excessive absorption of facts or memorization of abstract theory does not leave time for students to think things out for themselves or to take part in activities where they can apply what they have absorbed.

The rote approach is traditional in China, and like the heavy academic burden, it is also characteristic of the Soviet model. These faults with the Chinese educational system were recognized early (actually in the 1920's, by Hu Shih and his Society for Chinese Educational Reform). Year after year in Communist China journals echoed the plea to get on with the reforms, and individual universities claimed to have implemented them.[17] But, symbolically, the provincial educational journal *Anhui chiao-yü* (Education in Anhui) still complained in 1966 that teachers are simply not aware of the significance of letting students figure out by themselves the answers to questions posed by the teacher.[18]

The work-study school introduced in 1958 and again in 1964 was designed to embody in its very structure one of Mao's solutions to the dilemma. The close liaison between teaching unit and production unit was believed to insure the rapid transition from theoretical study to concrete application. Learning would not depend on rote memorization. The immediacy of the economic demands of the production unit would inhibit the inclusion in courses of material that was not relevant to production needs. Hence, the mushrooming academic burden on students would be reduced. But the work-study schools were aborted, and the Maoist demand for radical reforms in ordinary schools ran into the cautionary wall of the educational authorities. . . .

After 1960, in individual courses the teacher's position once more became dominant with respect to homework, course examinations, and other details.[19] There was peace in the schools, but no reform of teaching methods. As for the school itself, the Party committee again took over exclusively the decision making function. There is one important qualification to this, however. Old teachers, especially in institutions of higher learning, were given a greater local voice than they had had since the early 1950's. They expressed it through the Committee on College Affairs, which in some cases exercised more authority than the Party committee.

Decentralization, which was aborted in its various dimensions after 1960, had been intended among other things to help resolve the conflict that arose between the egalitarian ideal and actual educational practices. Let us return to this matter.

EGALITARIANISM AND QUALITY EDUCATION

During the period 1952–57, leading educational officials hoped eventually to provide a uniform, common core primary and middle school education of high academic quality for all students. The nationwide uniformity of curriculum content and quality was expected to be conductive to realization of the egalitarian ideal—equalization through a common educational experience. Each student was to develop into the identical type of "all-round man," fully developed in the spheres of general academic knowledge of all kinds—knowledge of production, technology, morality, aesthetics, and physical education.[20] Actually, general academic knowledge of all kinds became the central feature of all-around development during this period. As opponents of the policy were quick to point out, teachers would make no attempt to take account of individual differences in capability or interests.[21] Certain highly placed officials and teachers struggled against excessive homogeneity and favored "teaching according to the student's abilities" (yin ts'ai shih chiao). But to overemphasize individual differences between students made

one liable to the charge of resurrecting the pedagogical principles of John Dewey and Hu Shih.[22] Thus, academic uniformity emerged as the policy in the 1950's.

The conflict between these educational practices entailed by the egalitarian ideal and the actual qualitative differences between students (resulting from differing backgrounds or innate factors), broke to the surface. Institutionally, the conflict showed itself in the increasing appearance of tracks within certain schools separating the backward students from the others, and, in 1962, in the formal maintenance of special schools for more qualified students. But from the broadest perspective, the approach through homogeneity simply did not deal with the essential barrier to egalitarianism in China: the imbalance between rural areas (poor and heavily populated) and the cities (more prosperous and with a fraction of the population). Quite simply, the ministry policy of emphasizing quality education meant that there were too few schools, and in those that existed, the admissions practices and internal standards impeded the mobility of children of peasants and workers.

The term "quality education" refers to a system with at least three characteristics. First, the ordinary schools offer preparation for a higher rung on the educational ladder rather than feeding directly into the manpower pool through providing vocational training (for example, the middle school curriculum is college preparatory). Second, at the middle school and university level there is a stress on basic theory and fundamentals (for example, in mathematics and the sciences) that may have no direct and immediate practical application. Third, there is a certain selectivity in enrollments, and not all who are admitted survive the competition. Quality education by definition posed a threat to the egalitarian ideal. The Maoist response to that threat was to tamper with the procedures that insure superior quality in an educational system, to insist on substantial productive labor for all students (intended to help break the barrier that exists between mental and manual laborers, and between students in ordinary schools and those in work-study schools), and to inject political indoctrination of a special kind in the schools. Purely academic study was downgraded.

Eliminating Quality Control

[Most of this section has been omitted here for reasons of length. Munro reports that efforts in this direction instigated by Mao were largely if not completely thwarted by the educational authorities. Eds.]

In sum, the situation during the early 1960's was generally this. Many middle schools and universities had not institutionalized admissions procedures that would genuinely open their doors to students of peasant background. The examination hurdle remained in most ordinary schools. The elite status of a school was actually measured not in terms of the number of its students of worker or peasant background, but in terms of how many of its graduates were able to go on to more advanced prestigious schools.

Combining Education and Labor

The typical Maoist approach to breaking the status barrier has been to transform the occupants of one position into the other: "Workers and peasants must be intellectualized; intellectuals must be transformed into workers and peasants." [23] In his "Sixty Points on Work Method" of January 31, 1958, Mao laid out the concrete policy direction for realization of this goal. In essence he said that where possible universities and urban middle schools should establish alliances with factories, technical middle schools should try running factories or farms, students in agricultural middle schools should do labor on their own farms and on those of the cooperative as well as send their teachers down to do labor, students in rural village primary and middle schools should do farm labor for the cooperative, and so forth.[24] The educational guideline was pinpointed in the maxim, "education must be combined with productive labor," which was contained in the State Council "Directive Concerning Educational Work" of September 19, 1958. Work-study schools blossomed forth. In ordinary middle schools labor was treated as a standard course.

In addition to the educational value of labor, from a Maoist perspective there are very important economic reasons for combining education and labor, especially in rural areas. It is a way of rapidly spreading education without the state having to bear the financial burden. Students often build their own buildings. And the money they earn through their labor goes to support the school.

In the educational sector, high level opposition to Mao's policies seems to have emerged well before the failure of the Great Leap had become obvious. Lu Ting-i, Lin Feng, Ch'en Tseng-ku, and others are now reported to have criticized many aspects of the educational revolution during 1958 and 1959. At the school level itself, some teachers and students were aghast at the probable lowering of educational standards when ordinary schools were transformed into work-study schools.[25] One report frankly says that when the program was first launched, only 20–25 percent of the students were enthusiastic about it. Student stipends were removed in order to force the students to earn their keep.[26] . . .

The Ministry of Education took formal steps to return to the pre-1957 educational system, eliminating the labor requirement, between July, 1961, and August, 1962. Lu Ting-i played a major role in formulating the new policy. Alliances between factories and schools were terminated, as were many of the 1958 work-study schools.

Since the beginning of Mao's 1958 education revolution, much of the distrust and eventual open conflict over the labor question between him and his opponents has centered on the work-study system. . . . The potential for conflict lay in the fact that the function of the work-study system in society was open to various interpretations. People like Liu Shao-ch'i and Lu Ting-i clearly interpreted the function differently from the way Mao did. Most important, Liu and Lu wanted two completely different educational systems in the country: work-study for future skilled workers, technicians, plant supervisors, and the like, and ordinary schools for other people. That is, they failed to regard the ideological purpose of labor as all important. The idea that labor is essential for the proper political education of the youth leads rather to the Maoist position that eventually there should be one system, not two, with labor for everyone, even if it is not necessarily half labor. . . .

Political Indoctrination

Among other things, political education aims to create in students a selfless attitude that prevents the quest for personal privilege that characterizes the elites. There was a hiatus in political education which lasted from 1953 to the end of 1957. In imitation of the Soviets, by 1956 the only remaining course for many middle school students was a meeting for one hour a week on "The Constitution" for students in the final year. In September, 1957, university Party committees for the first time established "Committees on Education in Socialist Thought," and each department was required to establish a "Section on Education in Socialist Thought." [27] The Maoist approach to political education in the school . . . emphasizes making the lessons concrete and avoiding a theoretical approach where possible. Thus, the teaching is often by model emulation with "selfless" Party cadres (in the late 1950's), PLA men, and old workers or peasants (in the 1960's) doing the instruction rather than academicians. Symbolically, in 1958 at Peking and Tsinghua Universities, the strongest opponents of attempts to strengthen political indoctrination of students came from the heads of "The Offices for Research in Education in Political Theory" (cheng-chih li-lun k'o-chiao yen shih).[28] . . .

Conclusion

After the Great Leap, the labor and political education that were instruments especially designed to realize the egalitarian ideal were reduced or eliminated. They were accused of taking time from academic study. . . . In essence, as the conflict between the egalitarian ideal and the practices needed to insure quality education became manifest, many educators ignored the conflict by ignoring the ideal. If the conflict required an ostrich attitude toward the egalitarian ideal on one side, it required on the other side that Mao Tse-tung reassess China's manpower needs to justify playing down the special concern with quality education.

MANPOWER NEEDS AND THE EGALITARIAN IDEAL

In quantitative terms, the government's attempts to increase rapidly the number of engineers, scientists, and others with high level skills have been successful. After the revolution, education in general received a much larger budget (for example, 1 percent in 1948 versus 7.28 percent in 1956).[29] The number of institutions of higher learning increased significantly between 1949 and 1962: 205 in 1949, 841 in 1960 (including many rapidly organized schools of uncertain quality as a part of the Great Leap), and 400 at the end of 1962 after the disbanding of some Great Leap schools. In 1949 some 117,000 students were in colleges and universities; by September, 1962, there were 820,000.[30]

With the adoption of the policy of emulating the Soviet model, a special stress was placed on engineering colleges and on strengthening natural science departments in comprehensive universities.[31] According to figures compiled by Cheng Chu-yüan, during the period 1949–63, 671,000 students graduated from colleges and universities in the categories of engineering, natural science, agriculture and forestry, and medicine, compared with only 70,000 in the 1928–48 period.[32] . . .

Now the problem. In 1956 the number of Chinese youths in the middle school age bracket (twelve to seventeen years inclusive) was approximately sixty-three million. Of these, only 4,196,000 were in middle school. In 1966, the number in the age bracket was about seventy-three million of whom only fifteen million were in middle school (ten million in ordinary schools and the other five million in specialized schools).[33] Sizable funds were being spent to give ten million youths a middle school education that was essentially college preparatory. The college preparatory curriculum dictated by the ministry and the extreme concern with quality control from the center were both aspects of the Soviet model.

In terms of China's immediate manpower needs there are two related questions: (1) Should there be less college preparatory education and more stress on gearing the curriculum to locally needed agricultural and industrial skills? (2) In spite of the impressive growth since 1949, is the number of students in middle schools (especially in lower middle schools) really enough (or as many as possible)? Mao's own answer to (1) was "yes," to (2) "no." His response was to encourage the liaison of schools with production organizations in 1957–58, which meant decreasing the amount of academic material covered in order to increase time for learning production skills. The work-study schools were established as Mao's answer to the question of whether or not the number of students was really sufficient.[34]

The whole approach rested on decentralization. A local character for the curriculum is more possible under decentralization, and, it is believed, so is a surge in enrollment (through the blossoming of work-study schools that could not previously meet ministry standards). The Maoist answer is dictated in part by his primary commitment to the egalitarian ideal (ordinary middle schools are elitist, catering to a select number of "future mental aristocrats" who look down on manual labor and on work-study schools). But the rationality of his answer must be evaluated on its own terms.

Any extensive evaluation of the above approach to introducing congruity between China's education and manpower needs is beyond the scope of this study. But a few facts are suggestive. First, there is no question about the fact that the ministry policy was turning out large numbers of upper middle school graduates in cities every year who had college hopes that were shattered because they could not be admitted. They were also generally untrained to enter production and were often sent (again untrained) to agricultural areas. Their frustration constituted a serious political problem.

It is perfectly true that keeping the upper middle school youths in school was a means of alleviating the unemployment problem. But equally significant is the fact that the content of their education was largely unrelated to the rural or urban production tasks in which they would have to be employed in the long run. Second, in the USSR, where the Khrushchev reforms were aborted, a serious shortage of blue collar workers and technicians is already being felt, and the projection is for the shortage to increase. The cause lies in an insufficiency of specialized secondary schools. Officials are seriously questioning whether too many engineers are being turned out.[35]

Third, the most impressive evidence in any evaluation is the tested experience of other countries that share significant characteristics with China that have implemented similar policies. Tanzania (formerly Tanganyika) is a case in point. Tanzanian educational policy has differed in one way from the Maoist. The government has purposively impeded the growth of primary education beyond that needed to keep the present level at pace with population rise. Until the economy generates more funds, it prefers to invest in secondary and high level manpower training and agricultural extension. Because the country is so short on highly trained skills, secondary school graduates face no unemployment problem. Thus village "self-help" primary schools have been positively discouraged.[36] The egalitarian ideal in China would not permit this policy of aborting, even temporarily, the universalization of low level education.

But the Tanzanians have been inspired, in part by Maoist models in the late 1950's, to implement two policies that institutionalize the rural perspective.[37] The correctness of the policies has been affirmed by UNESCO and English specialists as well as by the Tanzanians themselves. First, it has been recognized that attitudinal questions regarding rural life are fundamental to any educational changes. This means that a substantial amount of political education of students, teachers, and parents must occur to facilitate their acceptance of (1) changes in the schools, and (2) the desirability of the students' returning to a modernizing rural life. This makes it necessary, among other things, to change the primary school syllabus itself so that it concretely demonstrates to student and teacher what can be done in a transformed countryside. In other words, it is not enough just to maintain schools. This must be accomplished by a battery of procedures (societal, economic, and educational) to help make the agricultural life appear more attractive; otherwise the investment in rural schools will be lost as graduates flock to pools of unemployed in the cities, increasing the imbalance of town and country. And one of these procedures is to correct the improper portrayal of rural life in the previous educational materials prepared by city intellectuals.

Second, the textbooks and curriculum in the traditional Tanzanian schools prepared students for a higher rung on the educational ladder and ultimately supplied them with skills for the British style civil service. It was essential to reverse this trend and to teach in rural schools a subject matter that could be understood and utilized in a rural economy. The identification of these issues as vital in Tanzania and the indications of success of policies put forth to cope with them is serious evidence that certain Maoist educational guidelines are on the right track. . . .

1. Egalitarianism is the core of Mao's revolutionary dream. Two aspects of it must be distinguished. One pertains to distribution of wealth, and here we must speak of modified egalitarianism. As early as 1929 Mao waged ideological struggle in the Red Army against "absolute equalitarianism," saying that it is wrong to seek completely equal distribution of goods (see *On the Rectification of Incorrect Ideas in the Party*). Although he still accepts this position (intellectuals are often accused of the sin of "absolute equalitarianism"), he has favored policies that come closer to absolute equalitarianism than those found in other socialist states. For example, in a factory in Communist China wage differentials exist, but the difference between the highest and lowest paid worker is much smaller than in other Communist countries. He clearly meant it when he said (same reference) that the distribution of goods in the Red Army should be "as equal as possible." A radically more equitable distribution of the wealth has consistently been a principal Maoist aim. The other aspect of the egalitarian ideal is even more important to Mao: breaking down the barriers that separate people from each other (class, type of occupation, region). In China the main barrier today is said to be between elitist "mental aristocrats" who "work with their minds" and others who "work with their hands." The second aspect of egalitarianism (breaking barriers) is especially pronounced in the ancient Confucian vision of an Age of Grand Unity (*ta-t'ung*) in which "all men are brothers" and the barriers of family and clan were not present. Mao used the term *ta-t'ung* to refer to the age of utopian communism (in *On People's Democratic Dictatorship* the term is translated as "world communism"). Socialism has drawn strength in China from this legacy. The communes were the first instrument of social organization intended to realize the egalitarian ideal. Khrushchev accused the Chinese of seeking "equalitarian communism" through the communes (see *The Origin and Development of the Differences between the Leadership of the CPSU and Ourselves* [Peking: Foreign Languages Press, 1963], p. 27). Of course, even the Maoist approach to status egalitarianism permits certain individuals (such as model soldiers, peasants, or workers) to occupy a position above that of the ordinary citizen. The distance between the party member and the citizen is reduced, not eliminated, in Maoism.

2. In his essay, "Education for Self-Reliance," quoted in Colin Legum, "Africa on the Rebound," *Africa Report* (December, 1967), p. 26.

3. Leonard Singer, Toronto Telegram News Service feature, *Ann Arbor News,* January 30, 1969.

4. "Going All Out With a Revisionist Line in Education," *Peking Review,* No. 45 (November 3, 1967), p. 34.

5. "'Indigenous Experts' and the Revolution in Agricultural Education," *Peking Review,* No. 51 (December 21, 1968), p. 4.

6. *"Jen-min jih-pao* [People's Daily, hereafter JMJP] and *Hung ch'i* [Red Flag] Investigation Report on Education Revolution in Countryside," New China News Agency (hereafter NCNA), Sept. 15, 1968, in U.S. Consulate General, Hong Kong, *Survey of China Mainland Press* (hereafter SCMP), September 19, 1968.

7. Leo Orleans, *Professional Manpower and Education in Communist China* (Washington, D.C.: Government Printing Office, 1961), p. 13.

8. *Kung-fei ti hsüeh-hsiao chiao-yü* [School education in Communist China] (Taipei, 1966), p. 55. Note: This work was prepared for internal distribution by a governmental office in Taiwan. Information within is frequently documented. References are made to standard newspapers and journals, regional newspapers, and radio broadcasts. The authors give evidence of relying on other non-public sources as well, e.g., interviews. Evaluation is kept somewhat to a minimum. The work is basically descriptive.

9. *Kung-fei ti hsüeh-hsiao,* pp. 15–16.

10. *Ibid.,* p. 39.

11. Yang Hsiu-feng, "Ch'üan-kuo jen-min tai-piao ta-hui ch'ang-wu wei-yüan-hui chü-hsing k'uo-ta hui-i chien-ch'a cheng-fu kung-tso" [Standing Committee of the National People's Congress arranges expanded meeting to investigate the government's tasks], *Hsin-hua pan-yüeh-k'an* (New China Bi-Monthly), No. 11 (109) (1957), p. 42.

12. *Kuang-ming jih-pao* (hereafter *KMJP*), June 27, 1960. See also *Chiao-yü ko-ming,* p. 5.

13. *Ibid.,* July 19, 1961.

14. Wen Shih, "Ch'ing-nien hsüeh-sheng ju-ho keng-hao ti hsüeh-hsi ho lao-tung" [How youthful students can study and labor even better], *Hsin-hua pan-yüeh-k'an* No. 424, 5 (1959), p. 7.

15. *KMJP,* March 29, 1956, and November 16, 1961.

16. *KMJP,* February 18, 1959.

17. *T'ou-k'ao ta-hsüeh shou-ts'e* [Handbook on reporting for university examinations] (Shanghai: *Wen hui pao,* 1951), pp. 2–4. Ts'ao Chao-lun, "T'i-kao kao-teng chiao-yü ti chih-liang" [Elevate the quality of higher

education], *Hsin-hua pan-yüeh-k'an,* No. 8 (106) (1957), p. 113.

18. Liu Ch'ao-jan, "K'o-t'ang t'i-wen shih ch'i-fa shih ma?" [Is posing questions in class a way of instructing?], *An-hui chiao-yü* (Education in An-hui), No. 2 (1966), p. 25.

19. *KMJP,* July 19, 1961, and August 2, 1961.

20. Tu Ch'ing-hua, "T'an kao-teng kung-yeh-chiao-yü ti fang-chen" [A discussion of the guidelines for industrial education in institutions of higher learning], *Hsin-hua pan-yüeh k'an,* No. 6 (104) (1957), p. 79. See also *KMJP,* September 24, 1955, and *Chiao-yü ko-ming,* p. 2.

21. Chang Yeh-ming, "Ho Chiang Nan-hsiang t'ung-chih shang-ch'üeh chiao-yü fang-chen wen-t'i" [Discussing some questions about educational guidelines with Comrade Chiang Nan-hsiang), *Hsin-hua pan-yüeh-k'an,* No. 3 (101) (1957), p. 77.

22. Ch'en Yu-sung, "Chien-ch'a Hu Shih tsai chiao-yü fang-mien ti fan-tung ying-hsiang ho Hu Shih ssu-hsiang tui-wo ti ying-hsiang" [An examination of Hu Shih's reactionary influence in the educational sector and of the influence of Hu Shih's thought], *Tzu-ch'an-chieh-chi chiao-yü p'i-p'an* [A critique of capitalist education] (Peking, 1955), pp. 193–97. Also, *KMJP,* May 15, 1956.

23. Quoted, among other places, in Ch'en Po-ta, "Tsai Mao Tse-tung t'ung-chih ti ch'i-chih hsia" [Under the banner of Comrade Mao], *Pei-ching ta-hsüeh hsüeh-pao,* No. 3 (1958), p. 21.

24. *Chiao-yü ko-ming,* pp. 4–5. In 1957 the Ministry of Education had directed that a course in the fundamentals of agriculture should be offered in elementary schools, a manual labor course offered in some elementary schools and lower middle schools, and a course in productive labor be given in all middle schools.

25. *Chi-so pan-kung pan-tu ti hsüeh-hsiao* [The half-work, half-study schools in various places], (Peking: Pei-ching jen-min ch'u-pan she, 1958), p. 2.

26. *Ibid.,* p. 3.

27. *KMJP,* August 22, 1957.

28. "Ma-k'o-ssu-chu-i li-lun chiao-hsüeh ti i ko chung-ta wen-t'i" [An important question on education in Marxist theory], *Hsüeh-hsi* [Academic Studies], No. 2 (1958), pp. 17–18.

29. "Hsin-chung-kuo chiao-yü shih-yeh ti fa-chan kai-k'uang" [The general situation in the development of New China's educational enterprise], *Hsin-hua pan-yüeh-k'an,* No. 1 (123) (1958), p. 138.

30. Cheng, *Scientific and Engineering Manpower,* pp. 73 and 84; *Kung-fei ti hsüeh-hsiao,* pp. 36–37; *KMJP,* February 5, 1960.

31. Cheng, *Scientific and Engineering Manpower,* p. 37.

32. *Ibid.,* p. 269.

33. The number of youths in the 12–17 years age bracket is roughly 10 percent of the population. The population according to the 1953 census was 580,000,000. The 1966 population is crudely estimated at 730,000,000. The number of students in middle schools in the 1960's is based in part on figures (and inferences from figures) given the chancellor of Toronto University when he visited China in 1962. See *Kung-fei ti hsüeh-hsiao,* pp. 51 and 55.

34. Work-study schools at the lower middle school level predominated. They were especially common in the fields of agriculture, forestry, fishing, and so forth. Rural children often began to acquire on-the-job skills at the primary level in so-called "Ploughing-study primary schools" (*keng-tu hsiao-hsüeh*).

35. See Ann S. Goodman and Murray Feshbach, *Estimates and Projections of Educational Attainment in the U.S.S.R. 1950–1985* (Washington, D.C.: U.S. Bureau of the Census, 1967). Also see *New York Times,* July 29, 1969.

36. Guy Hunter, *Manpower, Employment, and Education in the Rural Economy of Tanzania* (UNESCO: International Institute for Educational Planning, 1966), p. 37; and George Skorov, *Integration of Education and Economic Planning in Tanzania* (UNESCO: International Institute for Educational Planning, 1966), p. 44.

37. Hunter, *Manpower, Employment, and Education,* pp. 30–33, and Skorov, *Integration of Education,* pp. 60–61.

A STEP TOWARD A POLITICAL ECONOMY
OF DEVELOPMENT:
The Case of Trinidad/Tobago

DUDLEY SEERS

Institute of Development Studies
University of Sussex

We are in great need of a general theory of development, as a guide to policy. In its absence all sorts of strange views flourish, from a belief that a conservative monetary policy is a sufficient condition for development to a trust in wholesale nationalization. Until we make substantial progress towards it, universities in "developing" countries will continue to base their social science syllabuses on those of countries which are "developed."

Many people are, of course, doing work which may eventually be incorporated in such a theory and I do not pretend to make much of a contribution myself; but it is worthwhile pondering the experience and problems of Trinidad. Why Trinidad? One could argue that Trinidad is not sufficiently typical for its experience to throw light on the general problems of development. It is small, with a population of only about a million; it is relatively well off by the standards of the "Third World," with a *per capita* national income of the order of $600 (U.S.) a head; it is a "mineral economy," petroleum accounting for a quarter of the domestic product; and it is highly urbanized. It is true that Jamaica and many other small, mineral, largely urban economies also have relatively high incomes, but these can all be considered in some respects a special category, of limited significance to the problems of the world as a whole.

One answer is that research on the central problems of any "developing" country can throw light on those of them all. Certain characteristics are shared by all countries which are not industrially developed, small or large, rich or poor, exporters of agricultural or mineral products. These include foreign production techniques and consumption habits (we shall go into this further below). Perhaps most the signifi-

cant common feature of such economies now is chronic large-scale unemployment. In Trinidad more than 10 percent of the labor force are out of work (even on a restrictive definition), and those with jobs are far from being fully occupied.

If there is one generalization that can safely be made about the whole of Africa, Asia and Latin America, it is that, though the nature of unemployment and its causes vary from country to country, it has become massive, chronic and dangerous everywhere, in contrast to the industrial countries, in all of which unemployment has been kept at low levels almost continuously since the war.[1] Unemployment is the very mark of backwardness, and any opportunity to study it takes one at once to the heart of the problems of development.

Moreover, there are even advantages in small economies as case studies for anyone seeking a frame of analysis not confined to economic factors. It is much easier to see the interaction of political and economic forces when the scale is small; the total development process is, in a country the size of Brazil, let alone India, much more complex—though it is true, of course, that the problems are in some respects qualitatively different for large economies, especially if their agricultural sector is both big and poor.

A few mineral countries that have had a fast rate of economic growth, like Jamaica or Trinidad, are particularly interesting, because their experience shows beyond doubt that rapid economic growth is not enough to reduce, or even to contain, unemployment. The domestic product of Trinidad has risen at an average of 8 percent a year for at least fourteen years, in real terms, a pace which would be beyond the dreams of the great majority of governments. Yet unemployment has also risen; not nearly

From *Social and Economic Studies* (September 1969), pp. 218–253. Reprinted by permission. Some sections have been omitted.

so large a proportion of the labor force was unemployed in the early 1950's. We are therefore forced to look more deeply than national income trends to explain what has happened, and we shall find that we have to search beyond economics for possible solutions to the problem of unemployment. In fact a relatively developed economy like Trinidad is in some ways particularly interesting, because its experience is a warning to others at an earlier stage along the same path.

RECENT CHANGES IN OUTPUT
AND EMPLOYMENT IN TRINIDAD

The starting point is Trinidad's strange recent economic history. Despite the petroleum boom which has been continuing since the war, and which surged forward once more recently, the number "unem-

ployed" in 1967 was 35,000 or 10 percent of the labor force.[2] Among those aged under 25, the percentage was twice as high. In addition, more than 70,000, or another 20 percent of the labor force, had worked for less than 32 hours in the week before enumeration (26,000 for less than 16 hours). Exporters of agricultural products, especially sugar, were trying to cut down on staff in order to increase their competitiveness, and two of the major petroleum producers had announced plans to dismiss substantial numbers of employees. The main clues to this strange pattern of development can be found in Table 1.

The employment figures are derived from samples and should be considered approximate, especially for 1955. Since they are however largely confirmed by other surveys, they establish the failure of employment to rise as rapidly as the labor force during this period.

TABLE 1

EMPLOYMENT AND PRODUCTION BY SECTOR, 1955 AND 1966

	Numbers with Jobs ('000)		Gross Domestic Product ($m at Current Factor Cost) [a]	
	Nov. 1955	June–Dec. 1966	1955	1966
Agriculture (including forestry and fishing)	75	63	84	104
Mining (including refining)	55	57	139	314
Manufacturing			60	248
Construction and Utilities	21	36	29	82
Commerce and Distribution	33	50	64	250
Transport	17	22	15	78
Services	49	73	76	206
Ownership of Dwellings	. . .	. . .	11	47
Total	250	301	478	1,329
Unemployed [b]	17	35		
Labor force	267	335		

SOURCES: *Employment:* Labour Force Survey for 1955, cited by Jack Harewood in "A Comparison of Labour Force Data in Trinidad and Tobago, 1946 to 1964" in *Trinidad and Tobago Research Papers No. 2, 1965. Continuous Sample Survey of Population,* Publication No. 9, LF 1–6. *Production: The National Income of Trinidad and Tobago, 1952–1962* and *The National Income of Trinidad and Tobago, 1963–6.*
[a] All prices are in Trinidad dollars, 4.80 of which equal £1.   [b] For definition, see note 2.

The first point to note is that the increase in the labor force was not especially rapid. It grew by 25 percent, or about 2 percent a year. The population aged over

15 was in fact increasing at a faster pace, by nearly 3 percent a year, but the labor participation rate declined from 63 percent to 57 percent, the decline being particu-

larly marked among young people and self-employed.[3] What is particularly striking is the contrast between the pace at which employment rose and the rise in the domestic product. This is true even when one allows for price changes. The real domestic product at least doubled. This implies that productivity has been climbing sharply, by about 6 percent a year in real terms, in fact, taking the economy as a whole.

The most serious disappointments, so far as the creation of employment is concerned, has undoubtedly been the manufacturing sector. Even allowing for some decline in the mining sector (petroleum production can usually be expanded without increasing employment), the rise in manufacturing employment was very small. Yet output in this sector was certainly not stagnant: the growth in real terms cannot have been much less than threefold.

One explanation of this sluggishness of employment is that wages rose rapidly. Rates of wages increased by about 5 percent a year from 1954 to 1960, soared by 25 percent in 1961, when public sector wages jumped 39 percent, and then continued to rise by about 10 percent a year until 1965.[4] Altogether wage rates more than doubled between 1954 and 1965. This had three consequences. Firstly, although it may have helped reduce the participation rates (see above), because some in poorly paid jobs dropped out of the labor force when the incomes of their households rose, it also meant that others preferred to wait for well-paid work than take such jobs, especially jobs in agriculture. Secondly, the government could employ fewer people out of the expenditure of a given amount of revenue than it would otherwise have done. Thirdly, mechanization in the private sector was stimulated; comparable figures for the whole period are not available but private fixed-capital formation, excluding the petroleum sector, rose from $49 million in 1955 to $125 million in 1961.[5] . . .

Such a fast rise in investment, unaccompanied by a significant rise in employment in manufacturing, naturally raises questions about the industrial development policy of the government. This policy was intended essentially to encourage foreign private investment with various types of subsidy. The government offers "tax holidays" of up to ten years. It also allows accelerated depreciation allowances against taxable income;[6] since these can be taken at the end of a "tax holiday," the effective "holiday" may be thirteen or fourteen years. It eliminates customs duty on imports not only of materials but also of plant and equipment, and provides protection to new industries. It makes available sites, loans and (in a few cases) technical aid. By December, 1967, a total of $214 million had been invested in the 146 establishments helped in one way or another by the Industrial Development Corporation. But they were employing fewer than 8,000 people, i.e. over $25,000 had been invested per employee.[7]

This type of "incentive" policy does not have a great impact on employment even when "indirect" effects are taken into account. Since their need for labor is small, new factories have not even contributed much employment through the spending of wages and salaries; and they appear to buy few intermediate products from the rest of the economy. They have contributed little to government employment through tax revenue because of the concessions they receive. On the credit side, mention must be made of the rise in exports of manufactures. As we shall see, this is relevant in any discussion of the employment effect of a sector's expansion, but it is of limited consequence if—as seems to be the case— much of the foreign exchange so gained flows out again in profits and in payments for imported parts and materials.[8]

On such matters we are, however, almost completely in the dark, because few data have been collected from firms enjoying tax privileges—not enough apparently even to evaluate past decisions on concessions or to check whether the firms which benefited from them had honored the undertakings made when these were granted. Even income tax data on the manufacturing sector are meager and out-of-date.

Yet the big rise in output of manufacturing (and of other sectors) did permit the domestic product to rise rather more quickly than the import bill. Excluding imports of crude oil for refining, total payments for goods and services fell in relation to the domestic product from 54 percent in 1955 to 31 percent in 1966. On the other hand, largely because of the way in which foreign capital was attracted into the country, the other side of this coin was that payments of profits and interest climbed sharply, much more quickly than capital inflows. In 1955, "factor payments" on external account equalled "capital inflows" (to business and government) at $35 million; by 1966 the factor payments were $100 million and capital inflows $56 million.

Trinidad is still in fact highly dependent on exports, to meet debt service obligations and to pay for necessary imports. This means it is still dependent on petroleum; the petroleum sector was in 1966 responsible for 60 percent of exports (even after deducting the value of imported crude oil) and accounted for nearly one-quarter of the domestic product, as against nearly 30 percent in 1954. Petroleum exports and the domestic product had both risen by around 10 percent a year from 1954 to 1962. When the rise in the former tapered off between 1962 and 1965, economic growth slowed down to about 3 percent a year.

In 1965 a renewed rise in petroleum output occurred, due to the reactivation by the Texaco Company of Guaguayare field, and this was apparently accompanied by renewed economic growth. So Trinidad's prosperity is still highly precarious after more than a decade of subsidized industrial development. The recent revival of economic progress depended mainly on the decision of a single foreign company to reactivate one of its oil fields, which in turn was partly a matter of geological chance.

A SIMPLE FRAMEWORK FOR ECONOMIC ANALYSIS OF AN EXPORTER OF PRIMARY PRODUCTS [pp. 223–232 in original; omitted here because of length]

THE POLITICAL CONSTRAINTS ON EMPLOYMENT POLICY IN TRINIDAD

I have only in a very superficial sense "explained" chronic and growing unemployment. This is like "explaining" the spread of undernourishment in terms of declining caloric levels. The real question is why no effective policies are adopted to stop it. It would be incorrect, and in any case logically superfluous, to assume that governments are unconcerned. So the question becomes: Why do they find the elimination of unemployment so difficult? After all, in industrial countries too (as shown by the experience of the 1930's), automatic

mechanisms for fully employing the labor forces are also weak; nevertheless, since the war, as I mentioned at the beginning, unemployment in these countries has been kept down, partly by deliberate policies, to levels very much lower than in Trinidad, in fact to about 3 percent to 5 percent of the labor force. One way of finding the real reasons for unemployment in Trinidad is first to look at the prospects that face the government, next to construct a hypothetical full employment economy, and then to ask what political restraints would prevent the government achieving it in the next few years.

Prospects for the Mid-1790's

First it is necessary to be more specific about the short-term future of Trinidad, starting with the variables which can, over the period we are considering, be considered "exogenous." One basic fact is that the population of working age is rising at a rate of some 18,000 a year, reflecting the high fertility of the 1950's. Assuming that net migration is unimportant, and that the labor participation rate will not change sharply, the labor force will grow by at least 10,000 a year, i.e. by 3 percent. . . .

It looks therefore, taking everything into account, including the "adverse" underlying trends discussed in the previous section, as if employment will not grow fast enough to check, let alone reverse, the rise in unemployment, unless there is either a sharp rise in petroleum exports or a sharp fall in the import coefficient. Yet a rise in petroleum exports would of course weaken the resistance of both the companies and the government to wage increases, which could —as in the past—absorb much of the increased revenue. A fall in the import coefficient raises difficulties which will be discussed below. There is one possible safety valve, emigration. However, even although entry into the United States has been made easier, visas can only be readily obtained by those with skills needed in the United States (e.g. in the professions and teaching), apart from those going to join close relatives. These skills are expensive to create, and they are already in short supply in Trinidad.

The irrationality of this solution does not prevent its being frequently put forward (though there is not much that the government can do to promote it). Yet to look on a reduction in the labor force as desirable is really very odd. There is, after all, a lot of work to be done—feeding, housing and clothing the population. It is true that emigration would reduce these needs, but not *pro tanto*. From a common-sense viewpoint, a reserve of labor, especially of labor with skills, is a potential asset. Moreover, those who emigrate have cost a great deal to feed, clothe and educate. It is also strange if productivity increases are considered inherently undesirable, as they appear to be to many people.

There is something fundamentally wrong in the political situation if such attitudes are widespread. Just as an individual's evasion of the real issues in his life suggests the need for deep psycho-analysis, so the widespread support for these pseudo-solutions confirms my view that we must look for some explanation of structural unemployment outside the purely economic (or demographic), and go beyond economic measures if it is to be eliminated.

Hypothetical Solutions: a Possible Pattern of Full Employment

In order to probe more deeply for the reasons why solutions are not adopted or even seriously proposed, let us pose a hypothetical question: what would happen if they *were* adopted, i.e. if the government took steps to mobilize the country's human resources within the near future, by which is meant (say) five years? The human reserves of Trinidad are considerable. Since the labor force will grow by some 16 percent in those five years, and at most 70 percent of it is currently being used (allowing for underemployment as well as unemployment), over 60 percent more labor will be available in five years' time than is being used today. Actually even a 60 percent increase in the use of labor would not entirely eliminate unemployment, because, as it dwindled, the labor participation rate would rise with, e.g. more mothers deciding to take jobs, and so also would the population of working age, with immigration from the Eastern Caribbean.[9] Moreover, there is certainly some underemployment among those "working" for more than 32 hours a week.[10] We could assume, for the purposes of this paper, that the hypothetical full employment situation would still leave some slack. A 50 percent rise in the use of labor over five years should

nevertheless be possible; this would reduce overt unemployment very considerably.

We must now try to imagine the economy operating at (in this sense) full employment in (say) 1974. It would be a very big job to work out a full set of projections, allowing for inter-sector transactions, but the general shape of a hypothetical full employment economy is clear. The manufacturing sector would be larger, but its employment could hardly be expected to rise by 50 percent. There would not be sufficient numbers of technicians, managers or engineers, and it is difficult to see how large enough quantities of capital could be mobilized in time. A good part would need to be attracted from abroad, and to induce foreign capital to create more labor-intensive industries at a much lower price in terms of tax concessions would require expertise in industrial policy on a scale not at present available. Indeed the very attempt to expand the economy so quickly under government initiative would discourage foreign capital.

Commercial services (transport, finance and distribution) could hardly employ many more people without big rises having occurred in income in other sectors. There is certainly spare agricultural land but the difficulties currently being experienced with the scheme for settlement on Crown Lands indicate the organizational problems which would be encountered in a big expansion of this sector. Construction—slum clearance, road-building, etc.—must therefore be the core of any policy of rapid elimination of unemployment (as many governments have found in the past).

Yet this could not be sufficient. Many of the unemployed have received a good deal of education (although little or no technical instruction); among those who have completed primary education, but not reached school certificate standard, unemployment is close to 20 percent.[11] These expect office jobs of one kind or another and would not accept at all readily manual work, especially in the countryside, even assuming they were capable of it. (Attitudes on this question may be correlated with racial origin.) Increased output in construction, and in other sectors which produce goods, would of course create white-collar jobs, both directly and indirectly through increased use of services; but simply in order to eliminate this type of unemployment, government services would have to rise as well. Other special measures might have to be taken to eliminate special types of unemployment.

Although it would be a somewhat fanciful description of the pattern of resource use which would emerge to call it "optimal," we can conclude that the problem of unemployment is *physically* soluble. One is tempted by Keynes's glittering aphorism: *what is physically possible is financially possible.* But is this so? The constraint that comes immediately to mind is foreign payments. Suppose, to give us a very rough idea of the magnitude of the problem, we assume that there would be only a small rise in productivity, and that personal incomes would rise by the extent of the increase in employment, with somewhat greater increases in imports of consumer goods and in imports of materials for making such goods, and that the imports of capital goods would rise at least as fast, then the demand for imports would be more than 50 percent higher, i.e. more than $200 million above current levels. In fact it would rise more than this, because of the difficulty of expanding certain types of domestic production, especially of foodstuffs. Yet actual imports could not rise by nearly as much, on the assumptions made, and inferences drawn, above.[12]

It is not hard to visualize what would happen, especially with three decades of Latin American experience to study. The first sign of the strains involved in lowering the import coefficient would be a crisis over central bank policy. The expansion of economic activity would be halted by tighter limits on credit, especially on government borrowing, as the sinking exchange reserves approached conventional minima. It is true that the central bank could be ordered to ignore these limits. In that case, another devaluation of the exchange rate would not be long delayed. Because the supply of exports is not very price-elastic,[13] the devaluation would have to be substantial, and there would be a big rise in internal prices. Purchases, especially of imports, would rise sharply, while capital imports would fall (indeed the export of capital would be encouraged), aggravating the foreign exchange crisis and halting the program of expansion.

Latin American experience shows that it is precisely in small economies (with their greater dependence on foreign trade) that inflation can easily become particularly violent—compare the experience of Uruguay or Paraguay since the war with that of Brazil, for example.

Hypothetical Solutions:
Three Possible Strategies

There are a number of policies which, on paper, could force down the import coefficient sufficiently without causing an acute foreign exchange crisis. I shall look briefly at three strategies in turn (with the diffidence due from a British economist working well outside his own field, in terms of both geography and discipline).

Fiscal Virtue. The foreign exchange crisis and inflation might be avoided, if tax increases were big enough. But here we begin to face the fundamental problems of lowering the import coefficient. In the first place, taxes could not be increased without some of the burden being borne by reduced savings and by lowered purchases of locally produced goods and services; so the rise in tax rates would have to be very big indeed. Unless the rise in *net* foreign exchange receipts (allowing for the increase in profits of foreign firms) is much greater than now seems possible, revenues would have to rise more than $200 million, i.e. almost to double. Such an increase in taxes could hardly be achieved without hurting the wage-earner and stimulating demands for higher wages, which would aggravate the problem of providing employment. Moreover, it would be very hard, even if the tax increases were designed to fall with particular severity on luxury consumption, to avoid affecting employment, partly because domestic servants would be dismissed, but also because the plants for making inessential consumer goods would dismiss labor.

But, on top of these economic effects, a program of this kind would cause a political crisis. What would really be happening would be a reduction in the real incomes of the majority of the population in order to make it possible to provide jobs for a minority. Would many of those affected look on this as the necessary price to pay for political stability—indeed perhaps as to the price to be paid to enjoy rising real incomes in the future? Would they be encouraged by the press to do so? In any case, would a foreign exchange crisis really be avoided? The political tension would hardly encourage an inflow of capital, which might well move abroad. (The "loss of confidence" following the 1966 Finance Act is a small indication of what could happen.) For any particular government, there is not a great deal of room to maneuver on questions such as taxation—if it wants to continue to govern.

One variant of this theoretical route to full employment would be to raise taxes on traditional exports, which means petroleum in the case of Trinidad. It is by no means certain that the most appropriate rates of taxes have been found in countries such as Trinidad, which depend on exports of primary products (or even looked for in most of them). In some such as Trinidad itself, the rate of taxes on company profits in general is applied, whereas it is far from obvious that the same tax rates should apply throughout all sectors.[14]

It would, however, be very rash to conclude that tax rates on exports could be raised by enough to solve this problem, without harming their expansion. For one thing, considerable expertise on the petroleum industry would be needed to judge what would be the optimal policy in this sector, and to decide what prices should be allowed for intracompany transactions on declarations of income. The result of a tax rise might well be a fall in revenue, rather than an increase. Moreover, due to the traditions of company autonomy, the government could not compel companies to maintain their output at existing levels without causing a major political crisis. Where big companies are involved, this inevitably becomes a crisis between governments too.

Controlled Inflation. The Government might suppress the import coefficient through the use of import and exchange controls instead of taxation. One difficulty is that the industrial structure that has recently emerged limits the scope of such controls: because foreign firms have been permitted, even encouraged, to establish a number of plants which do little more than assemble imported components, it is hard to check the rise in the import bill without adding to unemployment.

But the basic difficulties are more fundamental and intractable. Casting an eye on the experience of the more developed Latin American economies, one can see the consequences of the operation of a tight system of controls. The mass of excess purchasing power, which washes against the walls erected around it, places great strains on administrative capacity. Among other things, it stimulates corruption and smuggling. Could these be avoided in an island which is by no means geographically remote from its neighbors?

In addition, the prices of domestically produced goods, especially foodstuffs, rise. Price controls could of course be used to suppress this, at the cost of burdening the administration still more, but, when excess demand is very large, it is impossible to stop "black markets" emerging. Indeed, general price rises become inevitable, leading to wage increases, and further price rises. Would it be politically possible to push on towards full employment in these circumstances?

The Cuban System. The questions raised on the two former strategies point to another: could structural problems be drastically resolved by adopting central planning and comprehensive controls, including extensive nationalization, higher taxation, wage stabilization, mobilizing youth for work in the countryside, and by breaking away politically from the United States— what one can conveniently summarize as the "Cuban solution"? The response to the word "Cuba" is usually emotional rather than technical. Actually, however, whether such a solution is desirable is not really relevant. Although the Cuban Government did cut down heavy structural unemployment within three years of the revolution of 1959,[15] it is questionable whether this option will be open to Trinidad in the early 1970's, because a Cuban type of regime requires certain preconditions.

In the first place, a really revolutionary government needs to inherit an export industry, the sales of which can be maintained despite the loss of traditional markets. The *marketing* problem would be more severe for a petroleum exporter than for a sugar exporter (the Soviet Union absorbs the bulk of Cuba's sugar exports, but itself exports petroleum); moreover, it would be harder to *produce* (and refine) petroleum than sugar, without foreign technical personnel—and it is not easy to hire the necessary personnel, except through governments which would exact a political price of some kind.

Secondly, a regime in the Western Hemisphere that would be labelled "Communist" needs to be able to rely not merely on technical support but on considerable financial (and political) help from outside to neutralize financial (and political) pressure, which could include pressures on neighboring countries, and even those on Europe, to break off trade. Its establishment could even lead to military intervention. United States' attitudes to systems of the Cuban type are well-known, and resolutions of the Organization of American States are clear and strong, even if not precise, on this point. The smaller the country, the more essential such help would be. Would Trinidad be able to rely on massive assistance of this type?

Finally, but most important, it is hard to imagine a Cuban system without a political organization permeating the bureaucracy, to ensure that controls are operated without corruption and to induce the public to accept the sacrifices required. An organization of this type and on this scale emerges gradually during an armed struggle with both nationalist and social objectives, involving a large section of the population judging from historical experience (e.g., Soviet Union and China, as well as Cuba), and *only during such a struggle.* It is worth noting, parenthetically, that one country which underwent a social revolution without any of these pre-conditions being satisfied, Bolivia in 1952, lapsed into a prolonged economic, social and political crisis, which still continues. Even though the pre-conditions *were* largely fulfilled in Cuba, it has had to face considerable economic difficulties itself in the past decade.

Possible Results of Further
Increases in Unemployment

The outcome of this discussion is that neither the unaided working of economic forces nor any action by the Trinidad government is likely to reduce unemployment very much in the early 1970's. Indeed, a further increase seems on balance probable. Does this mean political disaster, in some sense? One could make out a case for believing that crime and political disturbances would grow among the young men who have little hope of work, and perhaps after a while with little interest in it, especially in a country where there is

evident correlation between skin color and income. Indeed if violent crime is a signal of pre-revolutionary "disequilibrium,"[16] the symptoms are already noticeable. Thus "serious crimes reported to the police" more than doubled in the seven years between 1960 and 1967, a growth rate of more than 10 percent a year, with "felonious wounding" quadrupling in this period.[17] It would be reasonable to expect that with unemployment at the present levels, or higher, economic setbacks could easily develop into political crises.

However, economists naturally tend to link political change too closely with economic trends. Many societies—Jamaica for one—are surviving much greater unemployment without disruption. It would be, moreover, possible to stimulate employment without a sharp reduction in imports (e.g. by public works), especially if petroleum revenues rose once more. There are also, of course, other social evils, and political stability depends on what is done about housing, nutrition, etc.

At some point in the growth of unemployment, however, the government might feel it had no option but to adopt "inflationary" financial policies. The immediate result would not at first be very serious—there are all sorts of "buffers" to stop inflation running away, such as inventories and legal or conventional limits on rises in prices, fees, etc. In fact, a moderate boost in expenditure could be for a time survived quite easily, especially if it were accompanied by higher taxation and IMF drawings, and by some tightening of controls.

In many Latin American countries, however, these developments have led to price rises which have aggravated political tensions [18] to the point where a government came to power with the objective of returning to a system which was at least partially "open" economically, though somewhat repressive politically—what might be called the Dominican system.[19] But such a system also has preconditions, including a large and politically active military establishment, and a foreign country prepared to intervene politically and in other ways on its behalf. In any case a strategy of this type acts as a means of suppressing the symptoms, rather than of curing the disease, though it can survive for many years, even decades, where the preconditions are satisfied.

The point of this section is not, however, to predict the future state of Trinidad;[20] it is to bring out the *non-economic* factors which make a plausible economic solution hard to implement. We have seen that these include the rate of population increase, an educational system which has created a labor force difficult to mobilize, the administrative capacity of the public service, especially in mineral and industrial policy, which limits the possible range of measures, as do the power of trade unions and the position of foreign companies, the last being traceable to the influence of foreign governments. Underlying many of these obstacles is a set of tastes and attitudes, largely imported from abroad, which means that a large section of the population would rather, in the last resort, face a continuation of chronic unemployment than a reduction in their consumption of imports.

While Trinidad has been used as a case study, and the balance of emphasis might differ elsewhere (for example, in countries dependent on exports of sugar and other agricultural products), the extended framework of analysis, in political as well as economic dimensions, seems suitable for any country which exports primary products and is dependent on foreign capital. With some changes, it would be useful in other countries as well—in fact it would not be entirely inappropriate for Britain! Inadequate and irrelevant educational qualifications, and lack of interest in the jobs of social priority, are familiar everywhere. So are the administrative and political difficulties of either raising taxes considerably or of running a policy of "controlled inflation." Finally, in all, apart from the United States and the Soviet Union, the development path is affected by external influences from one source or another, ranging from advice and diplomatic pressure to conditional aid and military coercion. However, each country faces a different set of political contraints, and a great deal can be learned—as is evident, perhaps, even from the brief references given above—by comparing experience with different development paths.[21]

A SCENARIO FOR A VIABLE TRINIDADIAN
ECONOMY IN THE 1980's

The conclusion of the above analysis is that it is very hard to construct even hypothetically a Trinidad that would be fully viable, both politically and economically, capable of using the whole labor force, let alone in any sense equitable, in the early 1970's. Can we envisage it for the 1980's? At first sight it seems even more hopeless peering into the remote and dark future. Any projection of petroleum exports might prove very far out. Yet some attempt needs to be made. The decisions taken in the next few years, especially in population policies, education and land use, will very largely determine the society of the 1980's. Still, my purpose here is not to prepare a perspective plan, which would of course be entirely beyond the resources of a single individual: it is to show the effect of relaxing the political constraints which have to be taken as given for the short-run future. For this purpose, a rough sketch is sufficient, referring to, say, fifteen years hence (which turns out to be 1984), and showing what the shape of a viable system would be.

It is particularly hard to envisage the political system of the Western Hemisphere in the mid-1980's, which will still be an external constraint. The political future depends in part on developments inside the United States. For this very reason, the main need is to create a politico-economic system in Trinidad with more room to maneuver, with the capacity to follow any of the three paths indicated above (or any variant on them) according to the needs of the time, whatever the attitudes of other countries.[22]

We are not entirely in the dark about 1984. For example, we know that the rise in the labor force will be levelling off, because of the declining birth rate since 1960. This will itself make economic problems, and therefore political problems, look less insoluble. However, the population of working age will be much bigger—we know this too, since it has already been born (apart from migrants). It will be nearly 70 percent larger than today, and so—unless there is a big shift in the labor participation rate—will be the labor force, which will in fact be close to half-a-million.

We also know that productivity will be much higher. If recent trends continue, it would be about two and a half times today's level; then (on the basis of earlier identities) either exports would need to be nearly four times[23] as high or the import coefficient not much higher than one-quarter of its present level, or some combination of the two (if we ignore net capital flows as relatively unimportant) for large-scale unemployment to be avoided.

It is possible to imagine exports four times the present level and the import coefficient unchanged, but this is not compatible with the requirement of room to maneuver, which implies a more diversified economy with a much lower import coefficient—in concrete terms, not only a larger but also a more integrated manufacturing sector, with firms buying basic textiles and metals from each other more frequently, instead of from abroad, and also much lower imports of consumer goods relative to personal incomes. Yet it would be very hard to imagine, for a country the size of Trinidad, an import coefficient below 15 percent in the 1980's, i.e. less than half of current levels. So a large part of the adjustment must take the form of higher exports.

This must include higher exports of petroleum and its products.[24] It is hard to imagine exports consisting *largely* of manufactures—i.e. the Hong Kong system—if one considers the late entry of Trinidad into export markets, and the very long way it would have to go in lowering wage costs to more competitive standards, especially since wages would inevitably rise rapidly during a decade or so of fast productivity increase. But the aim of room to maneuver implies the need to export more industrial products as well. Markets for manufactures would have to be wider than those of Trinidad, indeed wider than CARIFTA—whether they cover the Caribbean (including at least some of the Latin republics), or Latin America, or the Western Hemisphere.[25]

Even a significantly higher level of industrial exports may be hard to achieve unless local influence on policy is strong, with much of the capital coming from local sources, whether private or government. A big international manufacturing firm is unlikely to show the same determination to develop exports from Trinidad, especially into countries where others of its subsidiaries are operating, as would a local company or even a "mixed" enterprise, which might have started as a subsidiary of a foreign firm but acquired local capital. Secondly, to envisage a balance in foreign payments in such a situation is hard, unless a substantial fraction of manufacturing

profits are being reinvested locally. Thirdly, it is difficult to imagine that less inappropriate techniques would be used, if the industrial sector were still predominantly in foreign hands. Moreover, while foreign capital may well still have an important role to play, it would come from a variety of sources, if Trinidad is to have political room to maneuver.

But perhaps the most important change compared with the present would be that the stock of professional manpower would no longer be inadequate. A large industrial sector of the kind mentioned would require considerable numbers of qualified Trinidadians, especially since it is assumed that foreign-owned subsidiaries would account for a much smaller fraction of the industrial organization. The government would itself be employing a group of experts to formulate and execute industrial policy. (Its services might be made available to help other members of CARIFTA too.) They would be knowledgeable about the sources of technique and capital available in the world, as well as about the terms on which these could best be obtained.

The higher positions in the petroleum sector would presumably be filled almost entirely by local personnel. But in addition policies on petroleum can only be drawn up if the government has a technical team of geologists, economists, engineers and cost accountants, capable of advising it on petroleum production and prices. This does not imply that the industry will be nationalized; all sorts of arrangements are possible, as can be seen already in various parts of the world, e.g. companies extracting oil for a fee, mixed companies with government participation, foreign companies operating under regulation. But if companies are still operating in this sector, as I shall assume, the government will need to be able to estimate how they would respond to various levels of taxation and to various prices for exports (and for imports of crude). The official team would have built up an informed view of their whole world-wide operations and of the world market for petroleum, and therefore it would be capable of judging the bargaining positions of company representatives.

Other sectors would also require very much higher levels of local expertise, if they are to play the roles allotted to them.

Agriculture, for example, will have to look after virtually all the food needs of the country, as well as contributing to exports. This implies farms run by skilled peasant proprietors or managers, backed by strong marketing, purchasing and financial organizations, and these in turn mean a very much more highly qualified staff in the Ministry of Agriculture.

The government would hardly be maintaining a sufficiently high level of activity without some controls on the use of foreign exchange. How extensive these would need to be is very hard to foresee. But that is really not the point. Even if the government is not running a policy of controlled inflation, it needs staff trained in modern decision-making processes, and capable of administering controls as necessity arises.

On the shape of the productive structure, the role of foreign trade, and the administrative and professional requirements, the outline of the only plausible scenario for a truly viable system in the 1980's is thus in rough terms fairly obvious. It is however far from easy to envisage an income distribution that fits this picture.

Within wages, the problem is not insoluble. While productivity would be much higher than today, it need not differ so widely from one sector to another, nor need wages. Of course the petroleum industry would still be highly productive and be able therefore to pay high wages; it is also highly vulnerable to union pressures. Yet what the country needs, if the leading sectors are to cease to exercise an upward pull on wages in other sectors, is obvious: a unified labor market with wages related to the job rather than to the profitability of the industry.

The real problem is the relation between wages and other incomes. On the one hand, an industrial structure of the size sketched above is easier to imagine if income is less concentrated in a few hands at the upper end of the scale. The Government would need at least the passive support of many wage-earners for its incomes policy. Wider public support would be helpful in case it had to adopt an independent economic policy, which might well be resisted not merely externally but internally as well, and it is more likely to get this backing if inequalities are not conspicuous. The price structure would also need to rein-force the greater equality in distribution, since imports would have to be held in check by indirect taxes on luxuries.

Yet the need for a large professional corps points in the opposite direction. It is true that emigration may be less easy or less attractive in the 1980's, but a large professional class could hardly be kept in the country without levels of living close to those obtainable elsewhere, which will be very high by then, especially by Trinidadian standards. Moreover, the play of internal market forces would also tend to produce high salaries. If industry were substantially in local hands, profits would be high too. These could be reduced by taxes, but lower net profits (or lower relative salaries) would hardly be compatible with the need for much greater local private capital. Farm incomes would also have to be relatively high to keep people in agriculture, possibly very high for larger landowners (as in the United States).

The reconciliation between these different needs would be less difficult if Trinidad were not part of a world economy, with high salaries paid in leading industrial countries. As it is, the basic inconsistency over income distribution is so severe that it puts in doubt the possibility of viability even in the 1980's.

Some of the scenario indicated above is special to Trinidad. In other cases, it might be more or less difficult to envisage political viability in the 1980's. For those where the birth rate has not already fallen below 30 per thousand, it will be particularly hard to envisage a degree of viability in 1984 and a later date might be indicated for this sort of exercise. In nearly all countries, however, professionally competent groups will be required in the leading sectors, whichever they are. The need for this will also conflict elsewhere with the need for income policies and for diversification of the economy. The dilemma over income distribution is therefore a widespread one; it appears indeed (though in a somewhat different form) in industrial countries such as Britain too.

CHANGES NECESSARY IN TRINIDAD
IN THE MEANTIME

Changing Planning

The main issue for a responsible government is whether it can use the time at its disposal to create a more viable economy. To do so it needs to reduce the political constraints revealed by the discussion in [an earlier] section. This indicates two changes in the approach to planning: a lengthening of the period covered, and (therefore) less emphasis on economics.

The need for much less economics in planning does not depend on the precise scenario of the previous section. While one might question the importance of room to maneuver in the 1980's (on the grounds that a stable international system might conceivably have been created by then, which would have shifted decision-making to a higher level), there is no doubt that the government needs to prepare for it in order to open up long-term options. Achieving a higher degree of flexibility depends not merely on diversification of the economy, but also on internal political changes and on finding appropriate foreign policies.

This does not imply that shorter, primarily economic, plans are useless. They are still needed to provide a framework for policy decisions in the immediate future. But since greater economic viability (including full employment) can only be achieved in the longer term, a plan for the next five years, say, in Trinidad needs to be seen primarily, not as a means of reaching short-period goals, but as a set of steps towards a set of longer-term and more attractive objectives.

Here we run into another political constraint, that the interests of governments are short-term. Most politicians discount the future heavily, thinking mainly of the time until the next election. Indeed they are nearly all overwhelmed by the pressing problems of day-to-day business. So longer-term goals are not very interesting. Since the removal of constraints depends on them, this is a serious problem, but I can only note its existence here. (I return at the end of this paper to questions which it raises.)

The content of policy in the 1970's is implied by the "scenario" suggested above. It can only be sketched here very briefly and unsystematically. One implied requirement is to continue and reinforce the policy of limiting the increase in population, if the working population is to level off during the 1980's, and thus the outlook in 1984 to be basically optimistic.

Making Industrialization More Selective

Turning to productive sectors, a critical one for policy in the 1970's is manufacturing, because there is no hope of creating a viable economic structure unless this sector is developed in a much more selective way. In the first place, some criteria need to be worked out on the degree of capital-intensity appropriate for different industries, bearing in mind their export potential (since export industries need to be highly competitive). Secondly, assessments are required of the profit potential in different lines of production. Tax concessions (or protection) are very expensive when they are superfluous; where they are needed, very careful thought should be given to what sort of "incentives" are suitable in particular cases. For example, in some cases extra deductions might be allowed against taxable income for each person employed, or per £ of exports, rather than allowing income to escape taxes whatever the level of employment. Indeed, because it is hard to ensure that firms honor undertakings, subsidies should, where possible, be automatically linked to performance. Achieving the pattern indicated may also require that the government itself creates some industries in the 1970's, instead of subsidizing foreign capital to do so.[26]

Creating a Professional Corps

The scenario brought out the needs for professional manpower in each major sector in 1984. This corps needs to be built up rapidly, not merely because of the high levels that will be required in the 1980's, but also because they are badly needed for policy formation *in the meantime*. The cost of creating it would be very high but, to take the petroleum sector alone, millions of pounds a year are involved in government decisions on the "prices" at which a company values the main grades of exports in its tax declaration.[27] Some experienced Trinidadians could be attracted back from jobs overseas for industrial jobs, but the main need is to train recruits. The training program should include individually tailored journeys abroad, especially to countries such as Japan and Italy, where wage levels are closer to those in Trinidad. (This would also help reduce the dependence on one or two countries for industrial capital.)

Modifying Consumer Attitudes

The hypothetical economy of 1984 shows a changed pattern of consumption. This could be achieved by creating a bureaucratic system of controls on imports and exchange transactions and by taxation, as we have seen, but there is a much easier method of achieving a considerable part of the same purpose, and this is to prevent the formation of tastes for imports. At present there are many and heavy pressures on people to buy imports—consumer credit facilities, personal overdrafts or consumer loans by commercial banks, and advertisements promoting imported goods.[28] It is strange for the media of communication in a country like Trinidad, suffering from chronic unemployment, to be urging people to buy imports (or to travel to Europe), especially where there are local products of similar types available. These advertisements not merely divert purchasing power abroad, they create tastes which restrict, as we have seen, the policy decisions of the government.

It would be better, at least in the first instance, to discourage such inducements than to prohibit them. Regulations could, as is the general practice in industrial countries (though for different motives), require minimum initial payments and maximum periods in consumer credit agreements. Importing agents and retailers need no longer be allowed by the income tax department to charge advertising outlays which promote imports as deductions from taxable income; in effect, the government subsidizes the goods advertised when it allows such deductions. It may be necessary to compensate newspapers or broadcasting companies for the consequent loss of revenue, but this is a relatively minor economic cost.[29]

Restructuring Wages

Another requirement is to start reducing the gap between, on the one hand, wages in the leading sectors, petroleum and manufacturing, and those paid in the others for similar types of work. This could be done by giving the Industrial Court directives which would put a brake on the former, while letting the latter catch up. This raises obvious political problems but the political climate for such a policy could be improved by social measures designed to improve the facilities available for members of trade unions (for example, beach facilities), by educational reforms designed to make it easier for their children to advance, and by reducing hours of work.

Perhaps more important is the general policy of the government. What would be difficult to achieve (or even justify) would be restraints on the wages of petroleum workers which simply allowed bigger profits to be remitted overseas. Such restraints would be more acceptable if the public could have confidence that the government's experts were making a bargain on tax rates, invoice prices, etc., that left the companies with the lowest profits compatible with whatever rate of expansion of exports was part of the government's long-term strategy. Then clearly any wage rise could only be paid for by a reduction in government expenditures and thus less employment.

Altering the Perception of Problems by Education

The main emphasis in preparing for a viable future must be on education. One reason for this is obvious, to create the professional skills required.[30] The need to build a high level of employment, given the productivity and income levels already customary in Trinidad, let alone those which will be found in the future, implies that there will be no place in the 1980's for the uneducated or even the primary-school leaver; yet children are still leaving school seriously under-equipped for the tasks of the future.

But education also has another function. It could become the main way of creating public awareness of the fundamental problems of Trinidad and what they imply, and thus of easing the internal political constraints. Only when the public takes a longer view will it be possible (and even necessary) for politicians to interest themselves at all deeply in longer-term plans. This is not the place to go into the content of educational policy in detail, but the importance of a widespread and deep understanding of the country's position suggests that at all levels of education, and especially secondary, a heavy emphasis should be placed on West Indian history, and on a geography that brings out the political and economic position of Trinidad in the Western Hemisphere (and thus of course in the world), and that other subjects should be impregnated with this approach.

It may be argued that teachers cannot be the main agent of changing a society of which they are a part. This implies the need to emphasize these subjects, and indeed the significance and nature of development, in teacher-training. But there is a limit to what can be achieved by teacher-training colleges (though this has by no means been reached yet) just as there is a limit to the impact a university education can have, even after reform, on a student. Reconstruction of the educational system has to begin lower down the educational ladder. One possible solution would be to set up special schools to create leaders capable of resisting the offers of jobs overseas, and prepared to put a lower value on a car-owning, urban life. One or two elite secondary schools could be set up inculcating discipline and emphasizing technical subjects. The products of such schools could provide in due course recruits to the specialist corps in the petroleum, manufacturing and agricultural sectors discussed above and also to a civil service capable of operating objectively and efficiently as extensive a system of controls as is necessary. If this elite were recruited from all social classes (by means that give the wage-earner's child a fair chance) and if it were taught that salaries needed to be moderate in relation to wages, then the central inconsistency in the scenario of the 1980's would be a good deal less severe.

Reducing External Pressures

Finally, we come to the external constraints which limit the freedom of economic action. It would be helpful if the officials of foreign businesses operating in Trinidad, especially in the petroleum sector, had a better understanding of the economic and political dangers implicit in the present precarious situation, which are ultimately dangers for them too. If they understood why unemployment tends to grow, their attitude on many policy questions would be affected. They might well conclude that, because of the need to protect existing investments, they ought to search much more vigorously for more labor-intensive techniques, and that they should not oppose high tax rates, or controls, as strenuously as in a fundamentally viable economy.

There is a limit, nevertheless, to the sacrifice one can expect a company to make voluntarily. The ultimate constraint is the attitude of governments of countries where such companies are based, especially the United States. While the position of governments will naturally take account of the interests of their companies, they will take account of other considerations too. After the experience with Cuba, State Department officials can have little doubt that a political breach over the treatment of foreign companies (*inter alia*) may prove vastly more expensive than any loss of property income.

Of course, we must not forget that the policies of the governments of industrial countries are limited by their own internal political constraints. The day may come when foreign investments are bought out and handed over by donor governments as a form of aid, but that day is as yet remote. The possible long-term benefits of such a policy would seem very imponderable to a Secretary of State, say, compared to the obvious political costs in the short run. There are, however, foreign policy planning groups in the governments of industrial countries which do look further ahead. One of the typical weaknesses in the diplomacy of a "developing" country is that it makes no effort to influence the attitudes of such departments, with which in fact it may have no contact whatsoever.

A prime aim of the external policy of a country in Trinidad's position should be to make sure that some section of the State Department fully grasps its fundamental economic and political problems, so that this element is not lost sight of in policy formulation.[31] Diplomats who have an ideological bias in favor of a non-discriminatory policy, both in trade and towards foreign companies, need to be helped to realize that, although there are several possible long-run strategies for making Trinidad viable, this is not one of them. One method of achieving this understanding would be to hold seminars and conferences for officials of foreign governments, including those of some European countries.[32] A long-range perspective plan for Trinidad, embellished with projections and exposing the alternatives open, would provide a good starting point for such a discussion.

It is becoming increasingly obvious that what is really needed is an economic strategy for the region as a whole. For this purpose, the "region" could be interpreted as the English-speaking Caribbean in the first place, but in the end a much more viable planning unit would be the Caribbean area, perhaps including Central America. If the political situation in South America continues to deteriorate (precisely because of growing urban unemployment, among other reasons), a buffer zone in the Caribbean might in due course hold some appeal for the State Department, with far-reaching implications for its policies towards countries in that zone, and therefore for their viability. It may fall to countries like Trinidad, which have yet to define their role in the political system of the Western Hemisphere, to play a leading part in its creation.

Wider Implications

Since the diagnosis is more or less appropriate, in general, for "underdeveloped" countries, it would not be surprising if the same were true of prescriptions. Nearly every country needs a long-term strategy to overcome its employment problems without incurring, in some sense, political disaster. The mixture will vary, of course. In mineral exports, an optimal tax rate on foreign countries in the export sector is an urgent priority, and thus so is the need to build up their own expertise for negotiating with foreign companies, hiring such expertise in the meantime; the establishment of an international body to assist such countries with information, and perhaps advice, would not seem politically impractical. In countries with large and backward agricultural sectors, especially bigger ones, a heavier emphasis is needed on the development of the agricultural potential to prevent a food deficit emerging as employment grows.

Nearly every such country needs to build up expertise in the industrial sector—one of the characteristics of backwardness is the lack of it. A selective use of "incentives" is for many a major priority. Indeed an international agreement to eliminate, or at least limit, these concessions would be a great step forward. All countries also require measures designed to control or balance forces which reinforce preferences for imported goods, and an income policy; in many, the need to slow down population growth is even more acute than in Trinidad.

In no country can a viable system be created unless education is used not only to create skill, but also to build up a social climate which would make it easier to wean the public away from inappropriate consumption habits, production techniques, income structures and attitudes to manual or rural work.

Trinidad, by itself, will not be able to change external constraints very much. But, in combination, such countries could do a great deal to convince the small group of rich countries that the continuation of existing trends must lead to political crises that will in the end be, in various ways, expensive. It is true, of course, that events provide more convincing tutorials than logical argument, and perhaps the most that can be aimed at is to help the diplomatic departments of rich countries draw conclusions from what happens more quickly than they have up to now.

This section seems sufficiently general in its applicability to provide an outline of the development strategy indicated by a political economy designed for the present era, concentrating on the vital problem of unemployment.

METHODOLOGY

We have travelled a long way from the economic framework. Looking back, it is clear that if we had stopped at a purely economic analysis, we would have failed to reach the causes of chronic unemployment, which lie deeply imbedded in the social structure, and we would have been limited to only superficial and ineffective solutions. Full employment ultimately depends on apparently remote issues such as the syllabuses of teacher-training colleges and how diplomats do their jobs. This raises more fundamental issues of methodology. The way in which an economist approaches a problem is to construct, explicitly or otherwise, a model with parts classified in a way which has become conventional. Certain features are labelled "constants," and other "variables," the latter falling into various classes—"exogenous variables" (e.g. export prices), "endogenous variables" (for example, the demand for food) and "policy instruments," such as levels of government spending and tax rates.

Undoubtedly systematic model building has been helpful in clearing up some confusions. But, in doing so, it has also caused others. In the first place, the more sophisticated a model is, the more it encourages those who use it to believe that they have analyzed—or even solved—some problem, when they have merely used the variables in the model, usually the sort of variables to which economists have conventionally confined their attention. In the case of Trinidad, it was necessary to introduce other elements—constraints such as the power of trade unions, the social prestige of different types of work and of different forms of consumption, and the quality of administration, as well as additional "exogenous variables," such as the policies of foreign companies and foreign governments. I may well have been very wrong in the roles I have assigned to these factors, but one cannot deny their place in any discussion, political or academic, of employment policy.[33] Indeed such constraints are always assumed, implicitly. (Nobody is much interested in the possibility, say, of whether wages could be halved.) The point is that they are not specified.

But to ignore what are considered "noneconomic" influences is not the only or the most serious weaknesses in the conventional use of models. More fundamental is the failure to consider sufficiently deeply how factors should be classified *for the purpose in hand*. Whether "constraints" ought to be classified as such depends almost entirely on the length of time that is covered by the analysis. Even "natural resources" vary if one is talking of a period of more than a few years—the value of a country's soil, subsoil resources and territorial waters changes, not merely with geological surveys but with technical developments in extraction and processing. The other "constants" I have mentioned are much more variable, including the political constraints, which are usually treated as constant by not being specified— they are included in *ceteris paribus*. This is not just a matter of semantics. The unemployment problem looks insoluble in Trinidad and many other countries so long as one searches for optimal values of the manipulable "variables." The start of the road to a solution is to realize that these variables cannot be altered significantly until certain "constants" have been manipulated.

But two basic questions follow from the above. The first is: whose values are implicit in the analysis? Perhaps unemployment is really not in itself such an evil, compared to, say, lack of consumer choice. I have bypassed this problem here by arguing that growing unemployment will lead to a serious political situation (possibly after a period of "totalitarian" government), which one could—very precisely— call, in some sense, "chaotic." This may well be a false premise and in any case, anyone could argue that certain types of "chaos" would be preferable to the present situation, especially if chaos is viewed as a necessary prelude to an improved social structure sometime in the future. I shall not pursue this question here—I have already strayed too far into the field of the political scientist—except to say that it requires a great act of faith (or a strange definition of progress) to believe that the end result must necessarily be an improvement.

The second could be put, cryptically, like this: what are the constraints on removing the constraints? I have concluded, in brief, that although, in the case of Trinidad at least, there is little hope of achieving a viable full employment society in the mid-1970's, one could imagine it in the 1980's provided that the income distribution puzzle is solved (not merely intellectually but practically) and certain policies are followed in the meantime. But what mechanism will cause these policies to be followed? I have suggested that there is no empirical evidence of an automatic correcting mechanism in the field of economics. Does such a mechanism exist if we take account of politics too? The prospects are not very hopeful. I have already drawn attention to the contrast between the length of life of governments and the length of time before structural reforms would bring results.

Public support for long-term policies would require a high degree of understanding, and of flexibility in attitudes. Indeed the crux of the problem is that the *perception* of basic issues seems too distorted to permit the right policies to be carried out. (In this, of course, Trinidad is very far from unique.) There are even political difficulties in carrying out educational reforms which would lead to a more widespread understanding of the country's problems, in some future period. Would the growing social problems due to chronic unemployment lead to the emergence (or strengthening) of political leaders with enough foresight, energy and capacity to tackle the development problems of a country (as distinct from the adoption of "development plans")? I am frankly sceptical, because I do not see this happening in any country, and in many the consequence of growing social tension is the emergence of leaders characterized by ruthlessness rather than long-sighted sagacity.

It is on paper possible—what one might describe as the Machiavellian solution—that political leaders would surreptitiously put long-term policies into effect, while pretending that basic problems are soluble in a few years. This seems to me perhaps even more implausible. It assumes first that the process of selection and formation of political leaders will produce men supplied not merely with this capacity for dissimulation but with, in addition, a deep understanding of the country's political problems (or the ability to acquire it), on top of all the other skills necessary to acquire and maintain political power. Are these qualities even mutually consistent? Is it plausible that anyone so rational would be able to make the type of popular appeal necessary to stay in power? Does not a politician really have to believe, quite genuinely, that unemployment can be cured soon and without much sacrifice, if his speeches are to have sufficient popular appeal?

I do not know whether it is legitimate to talk of a country "learning" from experience, in the sense of acquiring better mechanisms of adjustment. But this is really what I am asking about. Is a process conceivable through which countries in the position of Trinidad would adjust policy sufficiently to avoid political developments that might well in the end make such adjustments more difficult? When analysis is extended and economics becomes political economy, new possibilities of solution appear at first, but on deeper analysis these possibilities dwindle—apparently to zero; the future seems fully determined already. As perhaps it is.

1. See Alec Nove, "The Explosive Model," *Journal of Development Studies*, Vol. 3, No. 1; also C. R. Frank, Jr., "Urban Unemployment and Economic Growth in Africa," *Oxford Economic Papers*, Vol. 20, No. 2, July 1968.

2. LF 1-6 and 2-2 (CSO). The definition of "unemployment" is somewhat narrow—it covers those who wanted work and had sought it in the week previous to the week of enumeration, or had volunteered specific reasons for not doing so (illness, being laid off or not knowing of openings). On a broader definition—including all those who had sought work within the previous three months —the number was 54,000 and the unemployment rate nearly 15 percent. If one included all those who would be available for work, supposing there were any chance of it, the proportion would of course be higher still. On the other hand, some of those seeking work might, in fact, not accept work that was available, even if it corresponded to their qualifications, if the wage were less than they might be able to get for the same job in (say) the petroleum sector. This is a not unimportant point where the labor market is as imperfect as it is in Trinidad.

3. See Harewood, 1965, *op. cit.* (source for table data). His analysis is of those with jobs rather than of the labor force, but this would not materially affect the conclusions. The labor participation rate has apparently stopped falling and possibly rose slightly in 1967.

4. This index is based on minimum wage rates paid by a sample of non-agricultural establishments (excluding very small ones) to certain categories of manual workers on time rates.

5. *National Income of Trinidad and Tobago, 1952 to 1962.*

6. These rose from $3 million in 1954 to $38 million in 1961. The figure for 1961 is an understatement; firms which were in any case exempt from income tax would not claim these allowances.

7. Industrial Development Corporation, *Annual Report for 1967*. For factories under construction at the end of 1967, the investment per employee was slightly lower, but for factories "in the planning stage," it was nearly $50,000 (though the rise partly reflects price inflation). Further information is available in the memorandum submitted to the Tripartite Conference on Unemployment, July, 1968.

8. In the memorandum cited (and elsewhere) the Corporation has claimed that exactly [only] one additional job is created in other parts of the economy for each additional person employed in manufacturing whatever the branch of industry concerned.

9. The new Immigration Bill introduced in 1968 will, however, when enacted, reduce the possibility of such movement.

10. Because of the conventions used here, the elimination of underemployment would appear as a sharp rise in productivity.

11. *Labour Force Survey*, LF 2-2 (CSO).

12. In fact even industrial countries face

more serious foreign exchange problems than Keynes realized, when they raise employment sharply.

13. Even the elasticity of demand for imports is lower than it would be if Trinidad industry were less dependent on imported inputs.

14. It is true that there are in addition royalty payments. Nevertheless, the need to keep the general rate high enough to capture a significant share of petroleum profits means rather high rates in manufacturing, and thus could be considered indirectly responsible for the generous tax exemptions.

15. By mid-1962, three and a half years after the fall of Batista, the total of wholly and partly unemployed had apparently shrunk to about 215,000 compared to over 600,000 on the eve of the revolution—respectively about 10 percent and 30 percent of the labor force. Official data quoted in *Cuba: The Economic and Social Revolution,* edited by the author, Chapel Hill, 1963.

16. See Chalmers Johnson, *Revolutionary Change,* Boston, 1966.

17. *Annual Statistical Digest,* 1967.

18. This should not be read to imply that political tensions can be contained more easily if "orthodox" financial policies are followed in such countries (Guatemala is one object lesson which springs immediately to mind).

19. Argentina (since 1955) and Brazil (in more recent years) have formally somewhat similar politico-economic systems—as had Cuba up to 1959.

20. The above analysis would suggest in the 1970's rather frequent changes in government policies, accompanied by mild price inflation.

21. If a criticism can be levied at social science teaching in the West Indies, it is that insufficient attention seems to be paid to the experience of Latin America, especially to countries such as Venezuela and Cuba.

22. The Prime Minister of Canada recently remarked, when interviewed by the BBC on his country's policies, that "if" a country has only 15 percent to 20 percent of independence, it needs to use that percentage to the full. (*The Listener,* 10th January, 1969.)

23. I am assuming fixed prices here.

24. A key question for the long term is whether the rise in petroleum exports will level off before population growth slows down to (say) 1 percent.

25. If integration proceeds to the point where political power is centralized, then the points made below would still apply, but at a regional rather than national level.

26. Long-run strategies are discussed at greater length in "Economics of Development in Small Countries with Special Reference to the Caribbean," by William Demas.

27. *The Report of the Commission of Enquiry into the Oil Industry of Trinidad and Tobago, 1963–64,* recommended the establishment of a "strong central government body for the unified planning, coordination and control of oil industry affairs." It also proposed that "some of the existing policies with respect to classification and treatment of such items as intangible drilling costs, dryhole costs, casing costs, geological and geophysical expenses, depreciation, etc., as well as the rate of processing fees charged for foreign crude oil should be re-examined." I have gone into these questions in greater detail in "Big Companies and Small Countries," *Kyklos,* 1963, Fasc. 4.

28. These encouragements to import have been criticized by Demas, *op. cit.,* p. 114.

29. It is perhaps worth noting that the British Government does not compensate commercial television companies for preventing them advertising cigarettes.

30. *The Draft Plan for Educational Development, 1968–83,* seems however to have been prepared without an economic framework (or even up-to-date demographic projections).

31. Needless to say this implies that Trinidad's own officials understand these problems themselves, indicating the need for training courses for the civil service (especially external affairs staff).

32. It is perhaps true that the Old World was brought in to redress the balance of the New!

33. It is true that my analysis starts with an economic framework, and proceeds to move outward into other fields from then, rather than attempting a "total" analysis from the outset. It is therefore still heavily "economic." This may be due simply to the fact that I start as an economist, but it can be defended on two other grounds. In the first place, part of the object is to induce professional colleagues to abandon an indefensibly narrow approach. But in addition, it is usually better to go as far as one can along well-charted routes.

The Political Economy
of Economic Policy

•

ONE of the justifications sometimes given for abstracting economic analysis from its political context is that this simplification of factors allows for greater rigor of analysis, albeit at the cost of greater realism. Insofar as this enables economists to make better predictions of policy outcomes, it can be justified; but as some of the contributions in this section show, such analysis, by eliminating situational or institutional factors, fails all too often to provide predictions or instruments whereby desired conditions can be achieved. The juxtaposition of rigor and realism is usually spurious. Some economists can achieve a measure of both by incorporating political factors in their analysis of economic policy. Below we present analyses by such economists, who go beyond the limits of their discipline and deserve to be regarded as political economists.

Economic policy, despite its nomenclature, is thoroughly and unavoidably political. Some sectors benefit more than others from particular policies, and others indeed suffer loss as a consequence. The state cannot be considered a neutral bystander. Even where it is not making and enforcing policy, by abstaining from using its resources to alter the outcome of "free market" forces, it is acquiescing in and tacitly approving those outcomes dictated by superior economic power. By enforcing contracts or property rights with state resources (ultimately, coercion), it is promoting commerce or economic stability but also in a real sense, the status quo. These things may contribute to economic productivity but not equally for all. Any economic policies altering the status quo are also basically political.

Development policy in particular must take political factors into account. As noted in the introduction to this Part, these do not necessarily detract from development efforts, since under various circumstances, they may press the regime into making changes in the structure of economic activity, which otherwise gives advantage essentially to the already well-endowed sectors. Purely economic choices, which aim at economizing in the use of land, labor, and capital, take the existing structure of economic activity and factor endowments as given. Development, however, requires change in this structure. Structural change, by redirecting resource flows, cannot help but be political because of its implications for the resource position of different sectors. We therefore appreciate the intellectual contributions of economists who address these structural considerations inherent in development efforts. It would seem to us that economic analysis of development issues which neglects political considerations is not very "rigorous."

The articles by Tom Davis and Hans Schmitt show clearly the political foundations of economic policy. What is "rational" about price stability in Chile or en-

383

couraging foreign investment in Indonesia? Who benefits from the "efficient" use of economic resources in these countries? Should one automatically endorse increments to the level of national product without looking at their distribution? Understandably, foreign interests or sectors value price stability, foreign investment opportunities, and free trade policies in underdeveloped countries. And certain sectors in these countries benefit from such policies, but not all sectors.

One cannot sanction a particular policy just because it is "economically beneficial." One needs to know, beneficial for whom? and how will it affect resource endowments in subsequent time periods? May not a short-run gain for certain sectors turn into a long-term liability for other sectors if, for example, the latter are frozen out of productive lines of economic activity? The Nultys' examination in Part II of industrialization policy in Pakistan showed dramatically how this could happen.[1] One cannot set as a criterion for acceptable economic policy that it benefit everybody (or disadvantage nobody), but one ought to analyze the distribution of benefits and costs accruing from it in order to be clear as to its ramifications over time. One cannot understand the selection of policies and their outcomes without such an analysis, let alone begin to alter them in a desired direction.

In his article, Davis examines the conventional economic explanations of Chilean inflation in terms of "controls" that interfered with the "market" or in terms of deficit financing or bank credit. By looking at what political forces were behind the controls or deficits or credit, he formulates a more credible explanation of economic events. By setting aside the simple "economic" explanation, he reclaims the possibility that under some circumstances and for some purposes, controls could be used to dampen inflation.[2] But economic policies alone will not work. There is no solution to Chilean inflation without forging an alliance of sufficiently powerful sectors in whose interest it is to have price stability. This conclusion gets at the political economy of economic policy.

"Orthodox" economic policies prescribed by the International Monetary Fund, criticized by Davis in the case of Chile, are examined in greater detail by Eprime Eshag and Rosemary Thorp in their study of postwar Argentina. Theirs is a long study with considerable historical detail, which we have had to omit, focusing rather on the authors' critique of "orthodox" economic policy and their model of "inflationary deflation." [3] Eshag and Thorp find two basic faults with the standard IMF prescriptions. First, these neglect structural problems—the need for transformation of economic structures, changing the level, distribution, and use of productive factors. Fiscal and monetary policies employed in an orthodox fashion are generally inadequate for these tasks; market forces cannot generate durable growth in production when the price system is keyed to a markedly unequal distribution of wealth.

---

[1] See pages 134–145 above; also Hyman Minsky, "Passage to Pakistan," *Transaction* (February 1970).

[2] Even if one were to believe that certain policy instruments were generally preferred, such as the free market mechanism for allocation, one would still entertain the possibility that they are inappropriate under certain circumstances. See C. E. Lindblom, "Policy Analysis," *American Economic Review* (June 1958), pp. 298–312.

[3] Readers are referred to the February 1965

issue of the *Bulletin of the Oxford University Institute of Economics and Statistics* for the full account. A similar and supporting case study has been done by Rosemary Thorp on "Inflation and Orthodox Economic Policy in Peru," *ibid.,* August 1967, pp. 185–210. See also Tom Davis's excellent article, "Changing Conceptions of the Development Problem: The Chilean Example," *Economic Development and Cultural Change* (October 1965), pp. 21–32.

Second, these prescriptions exclude political interests and pressures from consideration. Though these can defeat the implementation of orthodox economic policies, conventional economists pass off political factors as a matter of "will"; these policies are regarded as "medicine" which it only requires "courage" to take; the prescriptions are confidently regarded as correct, and it is the "patient's fault" if he doesn't or can't take them. As we have suggested, the correctness of economic policies is not as objective a matter as it is often supposed to be. The distribution of benefits is a matter of legitimate "political" concern, thus a political economy framework of analysis is to be preferred.

A leading issue in developmental political economy is the role of foreign capital and investment. In the case of Indonesian economic policy during the 1950s, Hans Schmitt shows that it was not necessarily "irrational" to expel foreign economic interests, and that it could conceivably spur development in that country. Investment choices should not be seen as purely individual ones, unrelated to the structure of political power in a nation. Schmitt makes the crucial point that additions to capital stock enhance the power of those who control it. Thus, incentive to save is a function not so much of the prevailing rate of economic interest as of interest defined more broadly in political terms. Who has an "interest" in seeing capital accumulated? Those persons who will benefit from it. What if the capital accumulators are foreigners and not the political elite? Why should the latter promote capital formation that enhances the power of others than themselves? As Schmitt makes clear, the debate in Indonesia over "fiscal orthodoxy" turned on broader issues of economic and political interest and autonomy. One thing to be said for displacing foreign interests was that it gave the elite a financial stake in capital accumulation. More generally, Schmitt argues that Indonesia's economic problems were due primarily not to individual failings of its leadership under Sukarno but more to a "particularly unfortunate social structure" that derived from and reinforced national economic and political structures.[4]

Economic stagnation can be very costly politically, but so can a growth-oriented economic strategy that does not assure large sectors of the population that they have some satisfactory place in the emerging economy/society/polity. Such considerations are explored analytically by Uma Lele and John Mellor in their essay on the political economy of employment-oriented development.[5] They give further evidence that

[4] A similar conclusion is reached by Eprime Eshag and P. J. Richards in "A Comparison of Economic Development in Ghana and the Ivory Coast Since 1960," *Bulletin of the Oxford University Institute of Economics and Statistics*, November 1967, pp. 353–372. They find that the "failure" of Nkrumah's economic policies in Ghana, compared with Houphouet-Boigny's policies in the Ivory Coast, can be related more basically to differences in the structures of the two economies than to faults of the former leader. They suggest, and we would agree, that such faults exacerbated a deteriorating situation in Ghana, but even a more virtuous and sagacious leader could hardly have looked good under Nkrumah's circumstances. We have calculated that for 1965—the year Ghana's balance of payments collapsed with adverse effects on budgetary balance, price stability, and employment—if Ghana had received 1968 prices for its 1965 volume of exports, even with an all-time high level of imports that year, it would have had a $40 million surplus in its balance of trade instead of a $93 million deficit. External shifts such as this made it absolutely imperative for Ghana to restructure and diversify its economy and thereby reduce its dependence on cocoa. Unfortunately, though the strategy for development was laudable, its execution was deplorable. This matter is dealt with in N. T. Uphoff, *Ghana's Experience in Using Foreign Aid for Development* (Berkeley: Institute of International Studies, 1970).

[5] This essay could have been placed in the previous section along with Seers's piece on policy pertaining to employment. The authors' conclusions rest upon several propositions about technological change in agriculture. These are examined in the context of a

purely "economic" policies are not politically neutral. Any particular policy or development strategy benefits some sectors more than others. Politically, one can choose a different path of development than that prescribed by capital-oriented economists, a path apparently being sought now by Indira Gandhi in India. The analysis by Lele and Mellor relates economic policies to the employment issues raised in the previous section. It addresses the problem of *whose* resources will be used by development policies, and therefore who will benefit therefrom. The authors advise using the resources of the unemployed in rural public works programs, a policy made more feasible by recent advances in agricultural technology.

Employment-creating policies, however, require vigorous top-level leadership. Without it, economic policies will continue to employ primarily the resources of the already well endowed—or will use the resources of the poorly endowed on terms benefiting the latter very little since they have so little bargaining power. The authors' comments on the role of foreign aid are well taken; the aid of donors is needed more than their advice, given the orthodoxy of such advice. Aid should be used by Third World countries principally as it enables them to bring more of their own resources into productive employment. Targets of increased national product per se offer misleading criteria for the use of foreign aid, since little employment need be generated according to such criteria, with only narrowly based increases in productive capacity.[6]

The political economy of development emphasizes structural and distributional issues in economic policy choices. All such choices are ultimately political, altering or reinforcing the productive structure that exists, with all its ramifications for the level and allocation of welfare in society. Anticipating and evaluating such changes and distributions should and can be done in political economy terms.

---

mathematical growth model by Mellor and Lele, "A Labor Supply Theory of Economic Development," Occasional Paper No. 43, Department of Agricultural Economics, Cornell University, June 1971 (mimeo).

[6] Without committing him to our formulations, we would note with appreciation Raymond Mikesell's book, *The Economics of Foreign Aid* (1968). This work addresses development problems in structural terms and maps out a useful but limited role for foreign aid.

EIGHT DECADES OF INFLATION IN CHILE, 1879–1959
A POLITICAL INTERPRETATION

TOM E. DAVIS
Cornell University

Most of us will agree, however, that rapid inflation in any country does serious economic harm by making routine saving highly unprofitable to the saver, by distorting the allocation of investment, by creating a privately profitable but socially wasteful area of activity for middlemen of various species, and in other ways.   JACOB VINER [1]

From *Journal of Political Economy* (August 1963), pp. 389–397. Reprinted by permission.

Continuous galloping inflation is found in some underdeveloped countries; Chile is perhaps the most extreme example. There can be no doubt that it retards growth (through lowering the allocative efficiency of the economy and discouraging savings) even if acute depressive reactions can be avoided.

GOTTFRIED HABERLER [2]

The gross national product of Chile may well be a fifth to a fourth below what one would expect from the fine collection of resources at its disposal were it not for its chronic inflation and malallocations in resources that have occurred as a consequence of the direct controls that Chile has employed.

THEODORE W. SCHULTZ [3]

A BRIEF SURVEY OF
MONETARY DEVELOPMENTS: 1879–1959

The Chilean inflation has a very long history, dating from 1879. The first period of it ended with the creation in 1925 of the Central Bank in accordance with the recommendations of the Kemmerer Mission. The increase in the money supply during this period was a result of loans primarily from the banking system to the government, not for the purpose of meeting government deficits—the budget was generally in balance—but rather for the purpose of making loans by the intermediation of the agricultural mortgage banks to the dominant agricultural interests, which in turn controlled the government. The government even borrowed abroad for this same purpose. It was an amazing period of virtually undisguised use of political power by conservative governments in their own narrowly conceived, short-run, economic self-interest,[4] and it set a precedent for the behavior of the Radical party in the subsequent era.[5]

The inflation was never without its opponents; not infrequently the opposition cut across party lines. In 1895 the opposition succeeded in persuading the government to return to the gold standard, although all that was really required to halt the inflation was to eliminate (incremental) government borrowing from the banking system and to allow a bank or two to go bankrupt rather than to permit additional issue of bank notes.

The conversion was a failure. The gold value of the paper peso was set at 18d. at a time when the exchange rate (the price of pesos in terms of sterling) was in the vicinity of 6d. The result was a rush to convert

pesos into sterling, a deflation within the country, business failures, and unemployment. By 1898, the country had returned to the lesser evil of inconvertible paper money and inflation. This era closed with a turbulent period of protest coming primarily from the "radical" political groupings that brought Alessandri into power in 1920 with a promise of monetary reform.

In 1925 the Kemmerer Mission set up a central bank controlled, at least in theory, by the bankers and safely out of the hands of the government, and restored the gold standard with the gold equivalent of the paper peso equal to (the gold equivalent of) 6d.[6] Convertibility lasted until 1931 and was followed by an inflation that has persisted to the present time. The Central Bank throughout this period was called upon to finance the government deficit. The government, which passed in 1938 into Radical hands, was no longer interested in serving the interest of the *agricultores,* but, instead, the deficits were increased in its attempts to improve the relative position of the *empleados* and provide job opportunities in the public sector for the now dominant "middle classes."

It was soon evident that the Kemmerer Mission had not taken the Central Bank out of the hands of the government. What it had done was force the government to share power with the private bankers and some of the principal non-government borrowers. As a result, the government could not increase its borrowing at the expense of the private sector but had to allow the private sector to increase its borrowing *pari passu* with the public sector. Additional inflationary pressure resulted from the fact that during World War II the Central Bank was accumulating foreign exchange. To acquire the foreign exchange it was necessary, given the situation described above, to expand the money supply still further. Nevertheless, the inflation up to the end of the Radical period (1952) was constrained within limits that appeared reasonable in the light of what was to follow.

By 1952 the industrial sector had lost most of its dynamism in spite of its continued receipt of an inflation "subsidy" in the form of loans at essentially negative (real) rates of interest. (The rate of inflation exceeded the money rate of interest.) Previously, inflation had not infrequently been alleged to have promoted capital formation in Chile. Referring to the period before and during World War II, P. T. Ellsworth writes that "financing industrial developments to a large extent by credit expansion has imposed forced saving on the Chilean people. . . . Chile's industrial development has doubtless progressed more rapidly than would otherwise have been possible." [7] This viewpoint increasingly lost its appeal during the period to the end of 1955, when capital formation virtually ceased despite the fact that the "subsidies" represented by bank loans grew progressively greater as the inflation accelerated.[8] Apparently the fact principally responsible for explaining the stagnation of the industrial sector after the rapid growth it experienced before and during World War II was a drastic fall in the anticipated return on investment, even after allowing for the (increasing) subsidy implied by the policy of accelerated monetary expansion.

When the inflation reached an annual rate of 80 percent in 1955, the Klein-Saks Mission was called in and an anti-inflationary program was effected. This program raised two fundamental questions: Was an anti-inflation program possible without either an increase in unemployment (as a result of withdrawing the inflation "subsidy") or a considerable reduction in real wages? And, if not, were either augmented unemployment or a reduction in real wages politically feasible?

Klein-Saks was employed by a government that depended on right-wing political support. The Mission clearly had to restrict the rate of increase of the money supply by eliminating the government deficit or by forcing the banks to reduce credit to the private sector by an amount equal to the finance they provided to the government. The government deficit could be eliminated either by reducing expenditure (which meant cutting the real wages of public employees, the subsidies on imported foodstuffs, or public capital formation), or by increasing taxation. Klein-Saks eliminated the subsidies on imported foodstuffs and industrial raw materials and cut public capital formation. They made an initial cut into real wages by limiting the wage increase in 1956 to 50 percent while the price level rose by 80 percent in 1955, but thereafter no further encroachment on real wages was attempted and, in 1958, the wage adjustment actually exceeded the increase in the price level of the previous year. Nevertheless, the initial wage cut, the ending of subsidies on "essential" food, the elimination of public capital formation (with resulting unemployment in construction), and the failure to insist on increased taxation earned Klein-Saks the enmity of the Left without obtaining the continuing support of the Right. All parties fought the 1958 election in opposition to Klein-Saks, which left the country in July, 1958, several months before the election.[9]

One fact became rather evident during the Klein-Saks period. At least some of the larger firms in the industrial sector were apparently dependent upon the inflation "subsidy," given the prevailing level of real wages. In 1956 and 1957, there was substantial unemployment in the industrial sector, particularly in construction, shoes, and textiles (which had had the advantage of subsidized raw cotton).[10] The available evidence would appear to indicate that retail sales held up substantially better than individual production.[11]

Whether this apparent inventory liquidation would have ended ultimately and production would have regained its 1955 levels despite the maintenance of the anti-inflationary policy is a moot question. The forces opposing the policy carried the day, and 1958 and 1959 were characterized by marked inflation (in the vicinity of 35 percent per annum), an upturn in employment (at least in the large firms), and economic activity in general.[12]

ALTERNATIVE EXPLANATIONS OF
INFLATIONARY EXPERIENCE

During the past eight decades Chile clearly has not been able to bring the inflation successfully under control for any extended period of time. Successive governments have simply been unable either to eliminate their dependence upon the Central Bank or to force the Central Bank to reduce credit to the private sector by the amount of the increment extended to the government. It is impossible to halt inflation more than temporarily without restricting the increase in the supply of money within the limits set approximately by the growth of total output.

Various explanations have been advanced to explain the persistence of inflation since the Great Depression. One stream of thought holds that "the choice between inflation and taxation is largely political. Governments are driven to inflation when they think the political difficulties of raising resources in this way are less than the political difficulties in the way of raising the same sum in taxes." [13] The failure of successive governments to act decisively against inflation is thus attributed to the "political tie," that is, to the failure of governments to come into power with an overwhelming mandate. In Chile, the "tie" might be interpreted as follows: the conservatives have the power to block increased direct taxation; the radicals and the Left have sufficient power to block any attempt to reduce the real wages of government employees and organized labor permanently; the position of the private sector (or at least the larger firms) in the Central Bank gives it sufficient power to insist that loans to (the larger firms in) the private sector expand *pari passu* with those to the government.[14]

Logically, the next step is to explain the persistence of the "tie" among the political groups that find a common "second best" in the levying of the "inflation tax," or alternatively to explain the continuing failure of groups sorely damaged by inflation to participate more effectively in the political power struggle. There must be many such individuals, and they must contribute significantly to gross national product if inflation is as devastating as is generally alleged (see prefatory statements).

Greater monetary stability presumably would benefit the following groups: the export industries (because the permitted increase in the price of foreign exchange usually fails to keep up with the rise in domestic factor prices); the smaller firms in

important and reasonably competitive industries such as food processing, textiles, leather products, and wood products, which firms obtain direct access to bank credit only at a positive real interest rate; and finally the unorganized laborer and the self-employed person in small-scale industry and agriculture who bear a disproportionate burden of the generally regressive "inflation tax."

The explanation for the failure of these groups to constitute a political force proportional to their numbers or to the fraction of total output contributed by their efforts is rather obvious. These are the foreign and the migrant, the unorganized and the unlettered, the distant (from the capital) and the remote (from urban centers). A government that would attempt to rely upon such a fragmented base for support in implementing a stabilization program, and thereby alienate the "middle sectors," would immediately be threatened by the totalitarian extremes.

Competing explanations of the Chilean inflation are myriad. Five common views can be briefly stated: (1) inflation persists as a result of ignorance of the basic principles of monetary theory; that is, Chileans, despite their long acquaintance with rising prices, continue either to ignore the basic relationship between the expansion of the money supply and a rising price level or to believe that inflation stimulates capital formation and economic growth; [15] (2) the "bankers" are responsible for the failure of the Central Bank to curb loans to the private sector by the amount of expansion in favor of the treasury; [16] (3) the wage-price spiral is sustained by the annual, compulsory wage adjustments with "cost-push" inflation as the result; [17] (4) inflation has its origins in the structure of agricultural land holdings; [18] and (5) the instability of the dominant export industries is chiefly responsible for the inflation.[19]

Some evidence can be cited in support of each of these views. (1) Some writing on inflation would appear to ignore the basic quantity-theory equation and support the "commercial credit theory of banking"; and recently a minister of finance, of some considerable reputation in international financial fields, argued that a large expansion of the money supply was not inflationary because it was for "productive purposes." More pointedly, a former finance minister has argued before the national association of manufacturers that inflation contributed to capital formation because, lacking credit, a farmer would have to slaughter his calf, while if he had credit, he could maintain the calf and add to his herd.

Similarly, it is true (2) that loans from the private banking system to the private sector during certain periods have grown more rapidly than the total money supply;[20] (3) that the greatest expansion of the money supply and increases in prices do occur in the first six months of the year immediately following the wage increases;[21] (4) that the growth of agricultural production has not always kept pace with population, let alone income,[22] and that this phenomenon is frequently attributed to the prevailing land tenure system; and (5) that government deficits are frequently incurred during periods of falling export prices, and that the Central Bank is frequently called upon to accumulate exchange during periods of high export prices.

Nevertheless, none of the five arguments is very convincing; for it would be the grossest exaggeration to suggest (1) that the majority of those responsible for monetary policy deny or ignore the fact that inflation cannot be halted without limiting the expansion of the money supply, or believes that "productive credit" is not inflationary, or that inflation promotes economic growth.[23] Likewise, (2) it would appear unwarranted to hold the "bankers" responsible when the government can modify the Central Bank statutes, and when the evidence clearly shows that the banks suffer during inflation and benefit as a result of anti-inflationary policies.[24] (3) The "chicken-egg" aspect of the wage-price spiral would appear to make it idle speculation to ask which came first (though it is not idle to ask whether the real wage rate after the imposition of the annual readjustment exceeds the rate compatible with reasonable full employment in the system and to argue that it is politically difficult for the Central Bank not to accede to monetary expansion as an alternative to unemployment). (4) The agricultural land-tenure argument would appear to ignore the fact that agricultural prices have not risen substantially relative to other components of the price index and hence can hardly have been primarily responsible for continuing upward pressure on wage rates.[25]

And finally (5) the instability of exports fails to explain why the government cannot adopt a scheme to stabilize its income or why the Central Bank cannot offset foreign exchange accumulation by reducing its loans to the private sector or the government.

In short, none of these arguments by itself appears to be conclusive, although the "political tie" appears to cast considerable light on the recent history of inflation in Chile. The fact remains, however, that many Latin countries where the "political tie" is much less obvious have nevertheless experienced inflation, for example, Venezuela (under Perez Jimenez), Paraguay, and possibly Bolivia.[26]

CAN INFLATION IN CHILE BE "INSTITUTIONALIZED"?

As a result of the persistence of inflation in Chile, it has frequently been suggested that the government attempt to "institutionalize" inflation.

A chronic inflation can be institutionalized and once this has been done the inflation will be virtually neutral in its effects on the allocation of resources. . . . All could go well with flexible product and factor prices and flexible exchange rates and with interest rates attuned to the declining value of money. What would occur then may be represented as a special tax on money and near money. However, when there is such inflation the government feels *compelled to act* and when it does, it undertakes measures which impair the flexibility of prices and which restrict trade. Resource malallocations soon emerge and, as in the case of Chile, they have become exceedingly important.[27]

The principal opposition in Chile that causes governments to feel "compelled to act" comes from the business sector, which objects to paying more for its loans, necessary imports, power, and transportation and fears reduced "protection" (as a result of the long-run elasticity of the supply of foreign exchange). Consequently, the view prevails in Chile generally, but especially within the ranks of the principal borrowers, that the "monopolistic" banking system would, with free interest rates, use its power to maximize "profits" regardless of the impact on aggregate economic activity.[28] To protect the general public from the unemployment that might result from this present-day "usury," it is argued that controls on interest rates are essential.

Thus, despite the fact that the government could presumably place its debt with the Central Bank, and continue to collect the "inflation tax" with higher interest rates, it has acceded to the demand for controls on the interest rate. This policy has persisted despite the fact that the government's control over the directorate of the Central Bank is virtually complete. Presumably the persistence of this policy is simply another reflection of the fact that the larger units in the industrial and commercial sector have become dependent upon the "inflation" subsidy to a degree that Radical, Independent, and Right governments have all felt compelled to recognize and accept. In short, the same forces that cause successive governments to find inflation a convenient way to raise resources impede the governments from adopting those measures that would reduce the "welfare" costs of inflation.

FOCAL POINT OF CURRENT DEBATE ON
LATIN AMERICAN MONETARY POLICY

Many countries in Latin America besides Chile have experienced serious balance-of-payments difficulties over the last several years and have had to appeal to the United States or the International Bank or Monetary Fund for assistance. Increasingly the requirement for this assistance has come to be stated as "obtaining a clean bill of health from the I.M.F." The I.M.F. only awards these "clean bills of health" to countries that have promised to undertake an anti-inflationary program, and usually also to accept an I.M.F. advisor on monetary policy. The I.M.F. position is that the government must reduce the rate of expansion of the money supply with all deliberate speed. The manner in which this reduction in the rate of expansion of the money supply is achieved is not generally a matter in which the I.M.F. chooses to intervene; it is held to lie primarily within the competence of the respective governments.

The position of the I.M.F. is completely understandable. The I.M.F. is being asked for assistance to surmount balance-of-payments problems; this is the business of the I.M.F., so to speak. Such balance-of-payments difficulties cannot be eliminated (in the absence of a freely fluctuating exchange rate) without reducing and virtually eliminating domestic inflation. To do this the rate of expansion of the money supply must be permanently reduced.

The governments in Peru and Argentina as well as Chile have chosen to reduce the rate of expansion of the money supply essentially by reducing real wages. This lowers the real-wage bill of the public sector and permits the private sector to reduce its dependence on the inflation "subsidy." Frequently public investment has also been cut. At least theoretically, there is no overriding reason why government expenditure must necessarily be cut by a reduction in real wages. Presumably, government revenues could be augmented by increased taxation or the government might obtain foreign loans.

Nevertheless, the fact that the governments implementing their obligations to the I.M.F. have tended to react in this way has led to the charge that the I.M.F. requires policies that restrict public capital formation and economic growth and lower real wages. Such policies are alleged to encourage trends toward the political extremes. One possible implication is that if these are the concomitants of the execution of an anti-inflationary policy, the best interests of the United States—which fully supports the I.M.F. and thereby enhances the power of the I.M.F.—are not served by such a policy. Thus, the I.M.F. currently serves as the focal point for the current debate on monetary policy in Latin America.

A widely prescribed alternative is to undertake those measures that would attempt to re-establish a vigorous rate of growth. In that context, an anti-inflationary program would not necessarily imply either a reduction in public capital formation or a reduction in real wages. Opinion differs as to the components of such a program. One standard program for stimulating the rate of economic growth calls for large-scale foreign assistance in the form of direct loans to governments coupled with a thoroughgoing revision of the taxation system, the educational system and the structure of landholding.

The question is whether such a program, which might lay the foundation for future monetary stability by broadening the political base, can succeed in an inflationary environment, and whether, if an anti-inflationary program is pursued concomitantly, a "democratic" government can effect the joint program. The I.M.F. takes an optimistic view of the tenacity of "democratic" governments and a pessimistic view of promoting growth-cum-inflation. The "democratic" politicians in many Latin American countries are less optimistic about their basic strength and, consequently, are virtually compelled to accept the proposition that the "take-off" and continuing inflation are not totally incompatible. One ventures to suggest that the roots of the disagreement relate at least as much to political as to economic analysis.

1. "Stability and Progress: The Poorer Countries' Problem," in Douglas Hague (ed.), *Stability and Progress in the World Economy* (London: Macmillan & Co., 1958), pp. 47–48.

2. "The Quest for Stability: The Monetary Factors," in Hague (ed.), *op. cit.*, p. 171.

3. *The Economic Test in Latin America* (Ithaca, N.Y.: School of Industrial and Labor Relations, Cornell University, 1956), pp. 26–27.

4. See F. W. Fetter, *Monetary Inflation in Chile* (Princeton, N.J.: Princeton University Press, 1931), *passim*. Similarly, according to Robert Triffin, "the issue of paper money and the depreciation of the currency became at times a conscious policy, forced upon the authorities by the pressure of debtors' and exporters' interest. This was conspicuously true of Chile in the period 1898–1907" ("Central Banking and Monetary Management in Latin America," in S. E. Harris [ed.], *Economic Problems of Latin America* [New York: Mc-Graw-Hill Book Co., 1944], p. 95).

5. "The inflation of 1939–42," P. T. Ellsworth asserts, "reflects the dominant position in the government of groups benefited by inflation or favoring it for ideological reasons. The former consisted, in this period, primarily of the smaller producers, the latter, of Popular Front political leaders and bureaucrats who strongly favored the industrialization of the country. Naturally, they received the backing of business in general" (*Chile, an Economy in Transition* [New York: Macmillan Co., 1945], p. 114).

6. The great increase in export earnings and import tariffs accounted for the fact that the price of foreign exchange was no higher in 1925 than it had been in 1895, despite a considerable domestic inflation.

7. *Op. cit.*, p. 122.

8. This occurred despite unusually favorable world copper prices.

9. For a comprehensive discussion of the Klein-Saks period in Chile see David Felix, "Structural Imbalances, Social Conflict and Inflation," *Economic Development and Cultural Change*, Vol. VIII, No. 2 (January, 1960); see also the final report of the Klein-Saks Mission to the President, "El Programa de estabilización de la economía chilena y el trabajo de la Misión Klein-Saks" (Santiago, 1958).

10. Data collected by the Sociedad de Fomento Fabril show employment falling from 107.7 (1956 = 100) in December, 1955, to 96.5 in December, 1956, and finally to 88.4 in December, 1957. A substantial degree of unemployment is reflected also in the unemployment surveys made by the Instituto de Economia de la Universidad de Chile. See "El Programa . . . de la Misión Klein-Saks," pp. 244 and 246.

11. *Ibid.* Note, however, that the data collected by the Servicio Nacional de Estadistica are less conclusive than those presented by the Sociedad de Fomento Fabril. One possible interpretation is that the reduced rate of inflation made inventories less profitable and that, consequently, they were substantially cut.

12. At the end of 1959 the Liberal-Conservative government made a new attempt at price stabilization complete with an airplane announcing over loud speakers the "fair prices" of certain agricultural products, e.g., potatoes. The government's cost-of-living index showed an increase for the year 1960 of only 5 percent despite the fact that the money supply rose by more than 20 percent. If correct, this would imply a marked decrease in the velocity of circulation of money. However, the incumbent President, as Minister of Finance in 1949, achieved the similar feat of holding the increase in the price index to 5 percent while increasing the money supply 17 percent; the figures were exactly reversed the following year when a new minister held the office.

The Liberal-Conservative anti-inflationary program consisted of a postponement of any wage increase for the year 1960 until the final few days of the year when 15 percent was awarded, which was to be in effect during the entire year of 1961. (This would imply a reduction of about one-third, as compared to real wages in January, 1959.) The government's program was subjected to electoral review in March, 1961. The results were not encouraging and the anti-inflationary policy has subsequently been abandoned. In combination with the Klein-Saks experience, this suggests that in a stagnant economy, an anti-inflationary policy that attempts to maintain real wages runs afoul of the industrialists, and policy that attempts to reduce real wages, of the political Middle and Left.

13. W. Arthur Lewis, *The Theory of Economic Growth* (London: George Allen and Unwin, 1955), p. 219; see also p. 406.

14. No government has had the strength to attempt to recast the composition of the governing body of the Central Bank. Furthermore, recent experience suggests that, even if this were done, unemployment is the result of monetary restraint in the absence of a real-wage cut and a reduction in the public expenditure program. The fact that the Right preferred some inflation when they had undisputed political power and the Radicals did not move to end inflation has led a leading Socialist senator to declare that only a Socialist government can end inflation in Chile. In the interim, however, the Socialists have opposed both the recent anti-inflationary programs, on the grounds that a reduction of real wages was involved, that public capital formation suffered, and that unemployment resulted. A Socialist anti-inflationary program would presumably put the burden of eliminating the deficit on a program of increased taxation.

15. See John Deaver, "El Dinero y la inflación" (Santiago, Chile, 1957). (Mimeographed.)

16. See Sergio Vergara V., "Professor Bailey and the Creation of Money" (unpublished manuscript). This view is there attributed to Bailey.

17. Instituto de Economía, *Desarrollo económico de la economía chilena, 1940–55* (Santiago: Editorial Universitaria, 1956), chap. iii.

18. Nicholas Kaldor, "El Crecimiento económico y el problema de la inflación," *Trimestre Económico*, January–March, 1960, pp. 92–121.

19. See "Some Aspects of the Acceleration of the Inflationary Process in Chile," *Economic Bulletin for Latin America*, I, No. 1 (January, 1956), 45–53.

20. M. J. Bailey, "The Creation of New Money in Chile, 1943–56" (Santiago, Chile, 1957). (Mimeographed.)

21. See issues of the *Boletin Mensual del Banco Central de Chile* for postwar years.

22. Marto A. Ballesteros and Tom E. Davis, "The Growth of Output and Employment in Basic Sectors of the Chilean Economy: 1908–57," *Economic Development and Cul-*

tural Change, XI, No. 2 (January, 1963), 152–76.

23. Consider the representative sample of views contained in Anibal Pinto S. C., *Inflacion* (Santiago: Editorial del Pacifico, 1955).

24. See study by Pedro Jeitanovic in *Estudios Económicos* (Santiago: Universidad Católica de Chile, 1961).

25. See the indexes of the components of the cost-of-living index in issues of the *Boletin Mensual del Banco Central de Chile* in postwar years.

26. Of course, it is not necessary that the same explanation account for all countries at one time any more than the same explanation need account for the phenomenon in the same country over time. However, it might be argued that the so-called authoritarian governments manage to maintain their authority not by pursuing "strong" or independent (in this case, anti-inflationary) policies but rather by espousing those policies that would have emerged as a result of the "free play" of the democratic process (were it functioning); this suggests that the "do-nothing" domestic policy of the dictator is merely a reflection of the fact that dictators come to power in situations characterized by the "political tie" and that "do-nothing" policies (inflation) represent the common "second best." To the extent that either authoritarian or "democratic" governments, facing a stagnant economy, are forced by circumstances to "try something," they usually attempt to increase public capital formation. Only when inflation threatens to get out of hand are they compelled to cut back. Monetary policy thus oscillates (when it does not vacillate). Governments in growing economies suffer neither from the limitations on alternative forms of action nor from the pressures to "do something."

27. T. W. Schultz, "Latin American Economic Policy Lessons," *American Economic Review: Papers and Proceedings*, XLVI (May, 1956), 428. (Italics mine.)

28. The failure of nominal interest rates to fall in 1960 with a sharp decline in the rate of inflation has led to renewed insistence on this point. While ample amounts of excess reserves have not been a characteristic of the banking system during this period, it is true that rediscounts have been substantially cut and that the banks have made little effort to encourage time deposits.

ECONOMIC AND SOCIAL CONSEQUENCES OF ORTHODOX ECONOMIC POLICIES IN ARGENTINA IN THE POST-WAR YEARS

EPRIME ESHAG AND ROSEMARY THORP

Oxford University and University of California, Berkeley

INTRODUCTION: THE SCOPE OF THE STUDY

The history of the Argentine economy over the last hundred years or so can conveniently be divided into three periods. The first covers the latter part of the 19th century and continues up to the onset of the Great Depression of the 1930's. During this period Argentina experienced a rapid rate of development aided by foreign capital and manpower and largely within the context of a *laissez-faire* economic philosophy. The emergent structure of production being export oriented, however, the country was highly vulnerable to fluctuations in foreign demand for its exports, which consisted almost exclusively of primary products.

The second period covers the two decades 1930 to 1948—the Great Depression, World War II and the three post-war years. It is characterized by ever-increasing government intervention in the economy and may properly be labelled the period of government control and direction—the antithesis of the first phase of development. Government intervention, which at first was no more than a reaction to the steep decline in foreign exchange earnings and in public revenue due to the onset of the Depression, was towards the end of the period transformed into a deliberate policy of import substitution and industrialization.

The critical problem facing the authorities during most of this period was that of adapting the economy to the severe contraction in the volume of exports and imports experienced during the Depression and the War. A study of the economic developments of these years clearly indicates that the problem was solved chiefly through industrialization promoted by government measures and through public intervention in domestic and foreign transactions. As a result, Argentina was able, with a considerably reduced level of foreign trade, to expand total production and employment and to raise the level of personal consumption, after the middle of the 1930s, at a reasonable rate of about 3 percent per annum without encountering serious problems of internal or external disequilibrium.

The third period, 1949 to 1963, opened with a deterioration in the terms of trade and with serious balance of payments difficulties. It was largely with a view to resolving these difficulties that the authorities initially introduced measures aimed at restraining domestic demand and providing price incentives to the export sector of the economy. The shift of emphasis from governmental intervention and controls to a reliance on the operation of the price mechanism and on demand restriction continued throughout the period, culminating in the IMF Stablilization Programs implemented over the years 1959 to 1963. The new approach, which has for the sake of brevity been labelled "orthodox economic policy," in a sense represented a reversion to the *laissez-faire* philosophy followed in the first period.

The purpose of this study is to examine the nature of the problems encountered by Argentina in the third period and the adequacy of the measures taken by the authorities in attempting to solve them; we are particularly concerned with the five years (1959 to 1963) covered by the IMF Stabilization Programs. The paper starts, therefore, by describing briefly the major problems facing the country at the end of the Second World War and by tracing the main economic and political developments which led to the inauguration of the IMF Stabilization Program early in 1959 (section I).

In section II the social and economic

From *Bulletin of the Oxford University Institute of Economics and Statistics* (February 1965), pp. 3–5, 39–43. Reprinted by permission. Sections II and III have been omitted.

consequences of the implementation of the IMF policy are analyzed in some detail. The study shows that the policy in question, which was inspired by the *laissez-faire* doctrine, is in great part responsible for the critical condition of the country since 1958, which can broadly be characterized as general stagnation punctuated by oscillations in production. With a growing population and labor force, stagnation in production has resulted in a fall in per capita income and a steady rise in urban unemployment. At the same time the country has suffered from a rapid rate of price inflation and from periodic crises in the balance of payments. There can be little doubt that these developments have contributed to the social disturbances and political upheavals experienced in this period.

It may be asked why the *laissez-faire* philosophy, which had operated reasonably well in the first stage of the country's development, could not be successfully applied in the post-World War II period. The reason for this lies simply in the fundamental changes that had taken place between the two periods in both the external and internal situations. Externally, the world demand for primary products in the 1950s was not expanding at the rate experienced before the Great Depression, especially up to the First World War. More important, however, were the structural changes that had taken place within the country during the second stage of its development—1930 to 1948. In particular, the emergence of a big and well-organized urban labor force, accustomed to a high and rising standard of living, had made the deflationary implications of the orthodox measures highly inappropriate to the country. The experience of Argentina clearly lends little support to the view expressed by some economists and policy makers, that classical economic theory and the policies based on it possess universal validity.

The paper concludes by examining critically . . . the main postulates underlying the orthodox economic policy and by presenting a simplified model of the operation of that policy in Argentina under the IMF Stabilization Program. . . . [Because sections I and II are quite long and detailed, they are omitted below, thereby focusing attention on the conclusions drawn by the authors. Readers interested in the history and economic data of this period are referred to the *Bulletin of the Oxford University Institute of Economics and Statistics*, February 1965, pp. 5–39. Eds.]

CONCLUDING NOTE ON THE ORTHODOX ECONOMIC POLICY

It may be useful in conclusion to abstract from the detailed analysis presented in this study and to consider its subject matter from a more general point of view. To do this, it is proposed first to restate briefly the basic postulates underlying the orthodox policy, and then to present a simplified model which helps to explain how the measures based on that policy worked in Argentina.

Basic Postulates of the Orthodox Policy

The orthodox economic policy as practiced by the IMF in Argentina is based on three fundamental postulates, hypotheses, or more accurately, dogmas, expressly stated or tacitly assumed. According to the *first postulate*, the free operation of market forces generally produces a socially desirable pattern of investment, production and trade. The *second postulate*, which is derived from the "Quantity Theory of Money," is that internal and external disequilibrium—price inflations and balance of payments deficits—are caused by excessive domestic demand, often generated by an increase in the supply of money due to budget deficits and easy credit conditions. The *third postulate* expresses the belief that market forces, unhampered by governmental intervention and undisturbed by price inflation, will generate a "durable" growth in production and employment free of balance of payments difficulties.

Although we are here concerned primarily with the validity of the second postulate, a few brief comments on the other two postulates may not be out of order.[1] Regarding the first one, some case, though not wholly convincing, might be made in welfare economics for allowing market forces to operate freely in the industrial countries of the West where the disparities of wealth and income between different classes of the community have to some extent been ironed out. Whatever the merits of this case, it clearly has little relevance to the underdeveloped and developing countries of the world. In these countries, the picture of income and wealth distribution is such that market forces, unhampered by governmental intervention, will generally lead to a pattern of investment, production and expenditure which satisfies only a small minority of the population. Few observers would consider this a desirable result from the social and political point of view in the second half of the twentieth century.[2]

On the third postulate of the orthodox philosophy it is necessary only to point out that the experience of many countries in this century, in particular during the Great Depression of the 1930's, clearly demonstrates that the free operation of market forces, stable prices, and balanced budgets are neither necessary nor sufficient conditions for the growth of production and employment.

Equally questionable is the validity of the second hypothesis on inflation and balance of payments deficits. As many economic studies of internal and external disequilibria in the post-war years have shown, these problems are not always caused by domestic demand pressures on productive capacity.[3] Such factors as a relatively steep rise in wage rates in relation to labor productivity, a deterioration in the terms of trade, bottlenecks, low elasticities of supply especially in the food sector, and harvest failures, can, in certain conditions produce serious problems of internal and external imbalance. In these cases a policy of restricting the growth of aggregate demand [rather than of effecting structural changes in the economy] would only curb production without necessarily restoring equilibrium. This is precisely what happened in Argentina as a result of a faulty diagnosis of the situation based on the second postulate.

The Role of Environmental Factors

The operation of any economic measures in a country is strongly influenced by the institutional factors and by the political and economic conditions found in it. For developing countries like Argentina, the more important of these factors include: deficiencies in administrative machinery, especially in the fiscal machinery for the collection of internal taxes; the power of a large and well organized urban labor force with high aspirations directed at improving its standard of living and therefore unwilling

to submit to a reduction in real wages without intensive struggle; conditions of monopoly or very imperfect competition prevailing in the private manufacturing sector; and finally a very slow and sluggish response of investment to price signals especially in the rural sector of the economy. There is little doubt that a failure to attach adequate weight to these conditions partly explains the reckless application of orthodox measures in Argentina.

In view of the heavy reliance of the orthodox policy on the operation of market forces it is worth explaining further the question of response to price signals. Serious doubts have always existed in the minds of practical economists on the validity of the old text-book assumption that market forces are generally effective in producing tolerably quick results in the economy. These doubts apply to some extent even to industrial countries where capital and labor resources are more mobile and business men have better information on markets. This explains the continuation of backward or depressed conditions in some regions and industries of industrial countries for long periods of time—sometimes decades—side by side with prosperous areas and expanding sectors of the economy. It also justifies in the eyes of some governments the introduction of special schemes and plans aimed at alleviating this state of backwardness and depression.

What reduces the efficacy of price signals in many developing countries is not, however, only a relatively slower mobility of factors of production and an imperfect knowledge about market conditions. No less important is the lack of confidence in the duration of price signals on the part of the public whose views are colored by past experience of instability. In countries where governments, responsible ministers and policies are liable to frequent changes, it is unlikely that any price incentives provided by governmental measures would produce a quick and significant response in fixed business investment with a long amortization period.

This lack of certainty as to future market conditions was no doubt an important factor in the failure of the price incentive measures taken in Argentina to stimulate agricultural activity. Experience in the past had shown that these measures could be modified or rescinded by the authorities, or that their effect could be nullified by a general rise in wages and in non-agricultural prices.

A Model of Inflationary Deflation

The following is a simple picture of the operation of the orthodox measures in Argentina as it emerges from this study. It reflects more specifically the developments of the first and the last two years of the IMF Stabilization Programs—1959 and 1962–1963—when the impact of the orthodox measures was not temporarily neutralized by the massive influx of foreign capital.

Broadly, the first basic postulate of the orthodox policy necessitated action along the following lines: a removal of price controls and elimination of producer and consumer subsidies; the institution of a multilateral trade system free of export taxes and protective tariffs; the devaluation of the currency to a rate reflecting market conditions and the maintenance of a free exchange market.

The second postulate was responsible for the restrictive fiscal and monetary policies. Important measures taken under this heading were: a reduction in the volume of public expenditure through the dismissal of redundant workers, the curtailment of public works and other measures; increases in taxation—direct and indirect—and in the prices charged by state-owned enterprises; limitations on government borrowing from the Central Bank, and restrictions of commercial banks' credit. In addition, credit restrictions and direct government action in the public sector were used to restrain wage increases.

The immediate effect of the devaluation, in spite of the deflationary measures that accompanied it, was to raise the price of all tradable goods. Since food is an important export, this, together with the reduction of subsidies and the rise in indirect taxes and in public enterprise charges, led to a violent rise in the cost of living, which inevitably provoked widespread demands for wage increases. In view of the power of organized labor, these were usually granted after some delay marked by strikes. Wage rises were passed on to consumers in the form of higher prices by suppliers of goods and services, generally operating under conditions of imperfect competition. The additional price rises in due course pro-

voked more wage increases leading to further price rises. Thus was initiated the wage-price spiral of inflation. Money wages could not, however, keep pace with prices and there was a fall in the real earning rates of labor. The devaluation had also the effect of redistributing income in favor of the rural sector and reducing the share of national income devoted to consumption.

The rise in money wages and in prices was reflected in an increase in the level of public expenditure, even in the periods when the *volume* of government outlays was reduced. This rise in expenditure was not matched by the growth of public revenue, and the result was a progressive increase in the size of the budget deficit. Revenue suffered not only from the deficiencies in the tax collection machinery, but also from the elimination of export taxes and the prevailing conditions of tight credit and economic recession mentioned below.[4] Attempts to reduce the deficit through additional measures similar to those mentioned above were frustrated by the continuing wage-price spiral of inflation.

The increase in the supply of money, being constrained by the limitations on borrowing from the Central Bank and other measures of credit restriction, could not keep pace with the general rise in prices. Consequently, there was a steady reduction in the liquidity of the economy reflected in a fall in the real value of the stock of money in relation to the volume of expenditure. This had an adverse effect on private investment, especially on dwelling construction. Moreover, it was largely responsible for the condition of "mutual default" obtaining between the Government and the public, the former failing to honor its obligations to its suppliers and employees and the latter failing to pay taxes.

The contraction in the *volume* of public expenditure and of private investment which was accompanied by a fall in real labor earnings and private consumption, was primarily responsible for a decline in the volume of aggregate demand and in the level of economic activity. A similar effect on demand was produced by the redistribution of income in favor of agriculture, reflected in an improvement in the internal terms of trade of that sector relative to the manufacturing sector. Economic recession was accompanied by a stagnation or fall in employment and a rise in urban unemployment, the latter problem being aggravated by the natural growth of the labor force and the shift of population to urban areas. These developments were largely responsible for the labor discontent and political instability which characterized the period under review, and which in turn further inhibited private investment.

Externally, the policy of encouraging the export sector through price incentives had, for the reasons noted above, no significant effect on agricultural activity and production. Surpluses on the current account of the balance of payments were attained partly through a decline in domestic consumption of meat and partly through a fall in imports resulting from the economic recession. Similarly, the establishment of a free exchange market had done little towards rationalizing foreign transactions, but had introduced an easy channel for the flight of capital and a source of instability in the external equilibrium.

Some of the phenomena which resulted from the application of the orthodox policy are not easily explicable in terms of the "Quantity Theory of Money." There was price inflation accompanied by a fall in the *volume* of aggregate demand, a rise in the size of the budget deficit accompanied by a fall in the *volume* of public expenditure, and a steady growth in the supply of money accompanied by a shortage of money and tight credit conditions. What appears so paradoxical from an orthodox point of view, however, is easily explained in terms of the Keynesian approach to general equilibrium utilized in this study.

1. For a detailed criticism of some of the orthodox economic ideas, see Gunnar Myrdal, *Economic Theory and Underdeveloped Regions,* London (1957).

2. For a detailed and instructive discussion of the operation of the price system in developing countries, see Thomas Balogh, *The Economics of Poverty,* London (1966), *passim.*

3. See, for example, United Nations, *World Economic Survey,* 1957 and 1958.

4. It should be remembered that starting from a position of budget deficit as in Argentina even an equal rate of growth in public revenue and expenditure would have resulted in an increase in the size of the budget deficit.

FOREIGN CAPITAL AND SOCIAL CONFLICT IN INDONESIA, 1950–1958

HANS O. SCHMITT

International Monetary Fund

In December of 1957, after eight years of social and political turmoil following independence, Indonesia expelled Dutch economic interests from the dominant position they had retained from the colonial era. This action climaxed a trend toward economic stagnation which was in striking contrast to the hopes of rapid economic growth held by many Indonesians. The question posed in this essay is this: was there perhaps some connection between survival of foreign economic dominance on the one hand, and political turmoil and economic stagnation on the other?

THE ECONOMIC STRUCTURE

The incentives that make people save and invest for economic growth have as yet found no single and consistent explanation in economic theory. One aspect that is sometimes overlooked is that additions to the capital stock concurrently enhance the power of those who control it, and thereby

From *Economic Development and Cultural Change* (April 1962), pp. 284–292. Reprinted by permission. The last section of the article has been omitted.

induce them to forego consumption. Those who do not share in the control of capital have not the same incentive to save. They may still make provision for contingencies, such as old age and accident, but for the economy as a whole, such savings are likely to be offset by expenditures when the contingencies occur. On balance, therefore, the interests of the "propertyless" lie with maximum consumption. Aggregate savings can in consequence be maximized only to the extent that income payments to the "propertyless" are minimized.

The balance of power between those who do, and those who do not, control the capital stock may therefore be decisive in placing limits on the rate of accumulation. In Joan Robinson's terminology, it sets the "inflation barrier" beyond which further reductions in real wages are successfully resisted.[1] The rate of growth will be maximized when one group is firmly in control, and sees its power enhanced by further accumulation. Until very recently, no Indonesian group has been quite in this position. According to one estimate, before the Second World War only 19 percent of non-agricultural capital was owned by indigenous Indonesians, while 52 percent was held by Dutch interests.[2]

Agriculture is the only area in which Indonesian ownership of resources has been at all substantial, and the larger part of the Indonesian population are in fact peasant small-holders. As W. A. Lewis has pointed out, however, peasant societies "may be happy and prosperous," but are not likely to show rapid accumulation of capital.[3] The reasons for this, he argues, can be found in the fact that in societies where power and prestige are based on land holdings, ambition expresses itself chiefly in additions to real estate rather than to capital, with capital expansion often opposed as a threat to the vested interests of the landowners.

It is at any rate clear that in traditional Indonesian peasant society, capital accumulation has been slow and technical innovation rare, so much so that one Dutch scholar felt justified in assigning "limited needs" and an "aversion to capital" to "Oriental mentality" as inherent traits.[4] He does not seem to appreciate adequately the inhibiting effect of Dutch colonial policy, however. At its best it was designed only to preserve a "happy and prosperous" peas-antry—by indirect rule through traditional chiefs and by the prohibition of sale of land to aliens—while at the same time making any escape from traditional society by Indonesians very difficult indeed.

Under Dutch rule in Indonesia there existed three distinct social strata.[5] The indigenous population constituted the lowest layer; the Western managerial personnel in government, business, and the army, the highest. An intermediate position was occupied by the Chinese who largely controlled the collecting and distributing trades, acting as middlemen between the Western and the indigenous sectors of society. Social advancement from one of the three layers to another was all but impossible.

Nonetheless, not quite all Indonesians were peasants, even under Dutch rule. A small proletariat of wage laborers—about 500,000 by Communist count[6]—worked on the plantations, in the mines, in the factories, and in transport within the "Western" sector. The traditional aristocracy survived in the lower categories of the civil service which remained open to them, and a vestigial business group of pre-colonial origin was also able to maintain itself.[7] For a stagnant society to be transformed into a dynamic one, these groups would have had to acquire a vested interest in capital accumulation. It was precisely this development that foreign dominance in the non-agricultural sector effectively blocked.[8] Unfortunately, when Indonesia attained her independence in December 1949, the economic structure was not changed significantly. The non-agricultural groups, who assumed responsibility for the government, remained narrowly wedged between the traditionalist peasantry on one side, and the Western business community on the other.

The balance of power between economic sectors, however, was changed by the political revolution. Toward the peasantry, the new rulers lacked the weight of power that their colonial predecessors had enjoyed.[9] At the same time, they did not identify their interests with the growth of capital, either. It would seem that whenever indigenous capital is restricted—by market forces or by government policy—from reaching proportions competitive with foreign enterprise, opportunism if not fatalism and resignation in economic activity are the natural consequences in any society in any part of the world. The development of a "capitalist spirit" cannot reasonably be expected under such circumstances. Even "business enterprise" will be consumption-oriented, as indeed it was.[10]

The economic consequences were virtually inexorable. In 1939 the proportion of national income accounted for in the modern sector was 32 percent; by 1952 it had dropped to 24 percent, with the trend continuing in succeeding years. One of the contributory causes was a shift in the burden of taxation between sectors, until in 1952 taxes claimed 29 percent of the income per gainfully employed in the modern sector, as compared with only 5 percent in the agrarian. The end result has been, if one can trust the figures, a level of disposable income in 1952 of Rp. 3,000 per person gainfully employed in the agrarian sphere, compared with only Rp. 2,650 in the modern sector.[11] . . .

POLITICAL REPERCUSSIONS

Both the political and the economic dilemmas of the Indonesian leadership had the same root in the precarious position they occupied between the peasantry and foreign business interests. At the political apex stood a relatively small group often referred to as the intelligentsia, consisting largely of those Indonesians who had been permitted to benefit from Dutch education during the colonial period.[12] Their control over the mass of the population in the countryside was loose, as has already been pointed out. But, though the peasantry was difficult to govern, it was not sufficiently well organized for effective participation in political decision-making, either.

Politics, therefore, reflected primarily the interests of non-agrarian population groups, more particularly of the bureaucracy, the trading interests, and the working classes. These groups can perhaps be described as occupying positions of "intermediate" leadership between the intellectual elite and the peasantry.[13] The bureaucracy was especially strong in Java, enjoying the position which a still somewhat feudal social structure accorded them. Trading groups for their part held a higher status outside Java, where a more commercial orientation had prevailed from early times. The labor movement, concentrated in the cities, held the balance of power between them.

Against this background, three determinants of political developments in post-independence Indonesia can be isolated: (1) the continuing dominance of foreign capital; (2) the division of indigenous society into several ethnic groups; and (3) the different social positions of economic classes within different ethnic groups. Other sources of political division—and alliance —in national politics could of course be listed, among them religious, cultural, and personality conflicts. These did not, however, affect public policy to the same extent; in fact, on balance they tended to accommodate themselves to the three factors isolated here. In combination, these factors produced a logical sequence of events that led directly to the expulsion of Dutch business interests.

Three stages of development can be identified. In the first, we find an initial clash between the Dutch business community in Indonesia and the Indonesian political leadership. The Dutch attempted to minimize the economic impact of Indonesian political independence by retaining control of the central bank and by allowing Dutch enterprises to operate in an environment of maximum *laissez faire*. The Indonesians, for their part, thought that they could acquire some share in the economic management of their country, not yet by expropriation, but by financing the entry of new Indonesian firms into markets controlled by the Dutch. A beginning was made in the import sector.[14] Control of the nation's credit system was thought essential for the success of such a program, so the central bank was nationalized.

The nationalization of the central bank aroused little controversy within the Indonesian camp. To be sure, the sort of program it was supposed to back tended to overcrowd markets and relax financial discipline—thoroughly adverse consequences from the point of view of economic development. But it had the short-run virtue of satisfying most hostile impulses toward foreign enterprise, while at the same time leaving people free to cooperate with foreign management if they wanted to. Financial policy therefore did not as yet provide an issue to divide the political elite. Political competition continued for the time being to reflect individual ambitions for position, with no consistent divisions along social or economic lines. In fact, no such lines seemed as yet to divide society at large either, at least as long as the Korean Boom sustained incomes for all.

But as soon as incomes dwindled with the end of the Korean War, the financial "offensive" against Dutch interests began to have serious domestic repercussions. These repercussions initiated the second stage of development. Without a reduction in government expenditures, dwindling receipts from foreign trade threatened to touch off severe inflation. The reaction was composed of three factors.

(1) Fiscal retrenchment would have required cutbacks in the support given to young enterprises. Consequently, what first seemed to be an academic debate on the merits and demerits of fiscal orthodoxy, soon split the leadership sharply between those who preferred foreign dominance to monetary chaos and those who would jeopardize financial stability to rid the economy of Dutch control.[15]

(2) In the struggle for power between the two groups, both sides turned to the intermediate economic classes for support. This might have seemed difficult for the financial conservatives. A program of relaxing pressure against foreign interests, while imposing austerity elsewhere, could not have held much intrinsic appeal with the Indonesian public. Financial retrenchment did, however, favor at least one of the intermediate groups, the trading interests, especially those outside Java. Combined with fixed exchange rates, domestic inflation threatened the incomes of indigenous exporters in the Outer Regions, where the bulk of exports originate. Dwindling real incomes there caused increased resentment toward populous Java, where most of the nation's imports were being absorbed.

(3) The gains to Java were unevenly distributed, however. The overvalued exchange rate benefited importers—bureaucrats who controlled exchange allocations and their friends—but did not reduce costs for trading interests outside the import sector, to whom imports were resold at high and rising prices. Price controls added further irritation. Trading groups outside Java therefore won political allies among their less powerful counterparts within Java. In combination, the trading interests provided the core of indigenous support needed to put force behind the demand for retrenchment at the top.

What backing the anti-inflationary party could muster still fell short of gaining them control of the government. Their strength merely sufficed to reduce the political base of the government parties to a precarious minimum. Progressive inflation followed, exacerbating social conflict and political instability. A showdown between exporting and importing regions was delayed as long as politicians looked to general elections for a decision in their rivalry for power. The third stage of development begins with the elections of 1955. When these elections turned out merely to reflect the pattern of conflict, without deciding its issues, the representatives of the exporting regions increasingly turned to extra-parliamentary means for defending their interests.[16] Some of them, in fact, in March of 1958, went so far as to proclaim a rival government in Sumatra, with scattered support elsewhere.

To counteract the tendency toward political disintegration, the government parties appealed more and more "recklessly" to nationalist sentiment in the pursuit of the "unfinished" revolution against imperialism. Their chief battle cry was against the continuing Dutch presence in West Irian, a fact used so effectively in inciting popular sentiment against Dutch business enterprises in Indonesia, that businessmen made representations in Holland favoring territorial concessions. However, while agitations within Indonesia intensified with the deepening of social strife, Indonesian efforts in the United Nations to force Holland to negotiate continued each year to end in failure. In reprisal, in December 1957 labor unions took the initiative in a forcible expulsion of Dutch economic interests from the capital. In a matter of a few days, the movement had spread across the whole country.

For a while it seemed the government had lost its power to direct events. The opposition thought to take advantage of this fact when it proclaimed its rival government in early 1958. The timing of the rebellion made its instigators seem more than ever to give aid to foreign interests. It was in some part for this reason that they lost much of the domestic support on which they had counted. The central government did not fall, but on the contrary launched a vigorous military campaign to restore its authority. Nonetheless, the rebels retained enough support to make active guerrilla warfare seem irrepressible, for a while, especially in Sumatra and Sulawesi.

IMPLICATIONS FOR THEORY

The great deterrent to expropriation of Dutch capital had always been the dislocation it would cause—at least in the short run—in the management of the Indonesian economy. When expropriation came, the price had to be paid. In 1958 the governor of the Bank Indonesia reported that "shipping space was in short supply, marketing channels to Holland had to be shifted to other countries, and there was an exodus of Dutch technicians engaged in the production sector." [17] Foreign exchange losses were particularly severe as a recession in export markets and—perhaps most important—the Sumatra and Sulawesi rebellions coincided with the Dutch exodus. Their combined impact reduced exchange receipts of the central government by 34 percent below their 1957 levels.[18] In response, imports were cut by 36 percent.[19] Even so, it was only the beginning of war reparations payments by Japan that prevented further declines in exchange reserves.[20]

For the maintenance of a reasonable degree of monetary stability, it was absolutely essential that the government deficit be cut to offset the drop in the flow of goods. Such a reduction in expenditures was unfortunately impossible—primarily because of the staggering cost of fighting the rebel guerillas. The government's cash deficit in 1958 increased by Rp. 5,025 million over its 1957 figure, to an all-time high of Rp. 10,858 million. The whole of the increase went to finance increases in expenditures for security—they rose by Rp. 6,064 million.[21] The money supply consequently rose by Rp. 10,453 million, or by 34 percent, in 1958.[22] Combined with import cuts, and an uncertain political future, inflation made orderly business management seem irrational. By early 1959, deterioration had gone so far that President Soekarno warned of an approaching "abyss of annihilation." [23]

It is tempting to use this result as evidence for "mismanagement" or "irresponsibility" on the part of the Indonesian government. Somewhat less sharply, perhaps, D. S. Paauw argues that the government "has placed too much emphasis upon essentially revolutionary goals—'sweeping away the vestiges of colonialism'—and too little upon national integration." [24] One can, on the other hand, detect a certain rationality in the behavior of the Indonesian leadership. The course of events looks very much like a simple cumulative process away from an unstable equilibrium. No stable equilibrium may have been possible within the economic structure.

In countries where the control of the capital stock and the direction of public affairs are held by a single elite group, development is stimulated by the fact that the political elite identifies its interests with the expansion of capital. It is primarily this expansion which enhances elite power at home and abroad; politics will therefore be made to serve economic development. In countries where the expansion of capital will in the first instance benefit foreign managerial groups, the indigenous political elite—in spite of protestations to the contrary on grounds of general welfare—will on balance be opposed to it.[25]

Opposition to economic development will in all likelihood be accompanied by a high degree of political instability. Barred from economic careers, members of the political elite find no stable channels for the consolidation and extension of such power as they may individually aspire to, but are restricted to internecine strife in their ambitions for advancement in politics alone. Such strife will tend to crystallize around personalities rather than broad social issues at first, with alignments changing kaleidoscopically and unpredictably. Insofar as consistent lines of demarcation develop among the contestants in politics, such lines will probably divide, as in Indonesia, those who are willing to live with the economic structure that obtains, from those who will insist on the need to prepare for its early destruction.[26] A showdown between the two opposing groups may be delayed. The "radicals" will have to be aware that the expulsion of foreign managerial and financial resources will cause serious economic dislocation. The "moderates," for their part, may come to realize the usefulness of political threats against established interests in winning favors and concessions from them.

The transition from stalemate to showdown may then be described as follows. As the political elite becomes increasingly divided within itself, more and more population groups will tend to lose faith in its leadership. The elite will then be faced with two alternatives: either it makes common cause with foreign interests to maintain itself against the indigenous population; or its attempts to divert the blame for economic deterioration exclusively to foreign interests, ascribing its own internal conflicts to often fictitious foreign subversion, and attempting to lead a movement of popular revolution against foreign control of the economy. The more precarious elite authority becomes, the more necessary one or the other alternative will seem, and the more irreconcilable will be the conflict between rival elite groups. The showdown will come when political strife has reached the breaking point, threatening the country with political disintegration and economic ruin.

We see, therefore, that Indonesia's present plight may not be due primarily to individual failings, but that it seems rather to have been the logical consequence of a particularly unfortunate social structure. Similar results are therefore threatened whenever an imperial power transfers political authority to a former colony without concurrently ceding economic power as well. In the process of disintegration, a new and more propitious economic order may emerge from the shambles of the old. From the point of view of economic development, a new order should unite in power those groups most dissatisfied with traditional arrangements in the agrarian sector, with those whose interests are most clearly identified with an expansion of the modern sector. In the absence of a strong indigenous managerial class, such requirements point to the industrial worker and to the "dispossessed" among the rural population. In conditions of social chaos, when old authorities are discredited, these new aspirants have every opportunity for success. . . .

1. Joan Robinson, *The Accumulation of Capital* (London: Macmillan, 1958), pp. 48 ff.

2. L. A. Mills and associates, *The New World of Southeast Asia* (Minneapolis: The University of Minnesota Press, 1949), p. 352.

3. W. A. Lewis, "Economic Development with Unlimited Supplies of Labor," *Manchester School* (May 1954), p. 175.

4. J. H. Boeke, *Economics and Economic Policy of Dual Societies* (New York: Institute of Pacific Relations, 1953), pp. 40 ff.

5. W. F. Wertheim, "Changes in Indonesia's Social Stratification," *Pacific Affairs* (March 1955), p. 41; and *Indonesian Society in Transition: A Study of Social Change* (Bandung and The Hague: W. van Hoeve, 1956), pp. 135 ff.

6. D. N. Aidit, *Indonesian Society and the Indonesian Revolution* (Djakarta: Jajasan Pembaruan, 1958), p. 61.

7. On the pre-colonial Indonesian trading class, see J. C. van Leur, *Indonesian Trade and Society: Essays in Asian Social and Economic History* (Bandung and The Hague, W. van Hoeve, 1955), p. 191.

8. Even Boeke writes of the Indonesian who finds himself hindered in reaping the rewards of his labor and in developing his paltry little business by the competition of the much more powerful and efficient Western enterprise" (*op. cit.*, p. 215).

9. "The present ruling class is hardly able to wield command over the agrarian masses" (Wertheim, *op. cit.*, p. 52).

10. A. H. Ballendux, *Bijdrage tot de Kennis van de Credietverlening aan de "Indonesische Middenstand"* (The Hague: printed doctoral dissertation, 1951), pp. 79 ff.

11. D. S. Paauw, *Financing Economic Development: The Indonesian Case* (Glencoe: The Free Press, 1960), pp. 205 ff.

12. See, for example, L. H. Palmier, "Aspects of Indonesia's Social Structure," *Pacific Affairs* (June 1955); and J. H. Mysberg, "The Indonesian Elite," *Far Eastern Survey* (March 1957).

13. The importance of "intermediate groups" between the elite and the "masses" is emphasized in G. J. Pauker, "The Role of Political Organization in Indonesia," *Far Eastern Survey* (September 1958). Though examples of intermediate organizations feature economic groupings prominently, the systematic discussion totally omits economic interest as a possible source of division. The distinction between bureaucrats, tradesmen, and labor is most sharply drawn in J. M. van der Kroef, "Economic Origins of Indonesian Nationalism," in P. Talbot, ed., *South Asia in the World Today* (Chicago: University of Chicago Press, 1950).

14. For detailed expositions of these policies, see N. G. Amstutz, "The Development of Indigenous Importers in Indonesia" (unpublished Ph.D. dissertation, Fletcher School of Law and Diplomacy, 1958); and J. O. Sutter, *Indonesianisasi: Politics in a Changing Economy, 1940–1955* (Ithaca: Cornell University Southeast Asia Program, 1959).

15. See H. Feith, *The Wilopo Cabinet, 1952–1953: A Turning Point in Post-Revolutionary Indonesia* (Ithaca: Cornell University Modern Indonesia Project, 1958), for a variant interpretation.

16. The elections showed the Masjumi Par-

ty, which had consistently advocated financial retrenchment, strong among trading interests and dominant outside Java, and the Nationalist Party, which had been chiefly responsible for the government's inflationary policies, strong among the bureaucracy and dominant in Java. See H. Feith, *The Indonesian Elections of 1955* (Ithaca: Cornell University Modern Indonesia Project, 1957).

17. Bank Indonesia, *Report for the Year 1957–1958* (Djakarta, July 1958), p. 128.

18. Bank Indonesia, *Report for the Year 1958–1959* (Djakarta, July 1959), p. 145. Evidence suggests that smuggling by dissidents may have accounted for two-thirds of the drop in reported exports by volume.

19. *Ibid.*, p. 151.

20. *Ibid.*, p. 133.

21. *Ibid.*, pp. 97 ff.

22. *Ibid.*, p. 86.

23. W. A. Hanna, *Bung Karno's Indonesia* (New York: American Universities Field Staff, 1960), pp. 13, 57–59.

24. Paauw, *op. cit.*, p. xx.

25. Referring to "the Government and the national leaders" in Indonesia, Soedjatmoko writes: "It is among these circles that there is a lack of desire and determination to proceed with economic development." See Soedjatmoko, *Economic Development as a Cultural Problem* (Ithaca: Cornell University Modern Indonesia Project, 1958), p. 8.

26. Examples of a similar rift include Egypt (Nasser versus Farouk), Araq (Kassem versus Nuri as Said), Iran (Mossadegh versus the Shah), the Belgian Congo (Lumumba versus Tshombe), and Cuba (Castro versus Batista).

THE POLITICAL ECONOMY OF EMPLOYMENT-ORIENTED DEVELOPMENT

UMA J. LELE AND JOHN W. MELLOR

International Bank for Reconstruction and Development, and Cornell University

I

Unemployment and maldistribution of wealth are now at center stage in the drama of economic development. Prime Minister Indira Gandhi's sweeping election victory, based on *Garibi Hatao*—down with poverty—is to be consummated through greatly increased employment of the poor. Throughout the developing world population growth has added immensely to the army of unemployed while economic policies have failed to increase incomes rapidly and have raised employment even less. Unfortunately, however, increased employment exacerbates the equally explosive problem of inflation. As the poor are employed and spend their incomes on food and other consumer goods, prices tend to rise. Most governments then sacrifice employment of the poor to restrain the price increases resented by the urban middle classes.

Here is the dilemma of the employment problem and it is this which gives special relevance to the "green revolution." The new agricultural technologies can provide the food needed to complement increased employment. Concurrently, as agricultural production increases, the employment-generated purchasing power of the poor can prevent the fall in prices which would dull incentives to peasant agriculturalists. Likewise, the greater purchasing power of agriculturalists provides demand for increased output from the industrial sector.

The utopian promise is in sharp contrast to widely reported realities of the "green revolution." All too often income inequity and unemployment have been dramatically highlighted by the new high-yield varieties of grain. As compared to smaller

Occasional Paper No. 42, Department of Agricultural Economics, Cornell University, USAID-Employment and Income Distribution Project, June, 1971. Reprinted by permission of authors. Published in *International Affairs*, January 1972, pp. 20–32.

cultivators, the larger farmers can better afford the risks of innovation and they wield more political power over the developmental agencies which provide access to credit and the crucial purchased inputs such as fertilizer, seed and pesticides. More striking, the chasm separating the kulak cultivator from the landless laborer is drastically widened as yields per acre rise dramatically, and employment increases little.

Introduction of labor-intensive irrigation and multiple cropping may reduce the *rate of increase* of disparities but the disparities remain and grow until additional action is taken. For laborers to receive the benefit of even these secondary effects, the political environment must be favorable and economic policy astute. The benefits for the poor do not rise automatically from the system as they do for the rich. An additional danger from the system is that the increased profitability of farming tempts landowners to resume cultivation of their tenancies and thereby convert poor tenants into destitute laborers.

If the extraordinary promise of the emerging agricultural technologies is to be realized, drastic change in policies towards employment and industrialization will be needed.

II

Past failure to generate rapid increase in employment can be largely explained in terms of the ascendant theories of economic growth and consequent policies of capital-intensive production and import substitution. Such development strategy was prompted by emphasis on structuring the economy towards heavy capital goods production and reinforced by assumption of low growth potential for exports. The domestic capital goods sector was to be built at an early stage of development to force immediate savings and investment and to refrain from long-run reliance on imports. At the extreme one first produced not food, not fertilizer, not fertilizer factories, but the industries which produce fertilizer factories.

It was also believed that minimization of employment and thereby of consumption in the short run would conserve resources so that they could be ploughed back into further expansion of the manufacturing sector. The conclusions that follow from such assumptions may be stated succinctly but simplistically as follows: The lower rate of growth of employment and consumption in the short run, the higher their levels in the long run. It is a bourgeois approach, for it is the poor who die in the short run.

Contrary to the theory, the practice of capital-intensive industrial expansion has resulted in relatively low rates of savings. This is because the complexity of these industries caused low profits and even losses. Ironically, the prophecies of low growth potential for exports have been fulfilled precisely because the policies followed were based on that initial assumption. Clearly, the low-income countries have little immediate comparative advantage over their high-income counterparts in export of capital-intensive products. India's highly sophisticated Second and Third Five-Year Plans are classic examples of these various assumptions, strategies and consequences. The Philippines and much of Latin America are less precise but still conforming illustrations.

Unfortunately, though the hopes of the investment and capital-goods orientation were belied, it is unlikely that an orientation toward employment, consumer goods and trade would have been generally successful without a technological breakthrough in agriculture. If India in the 1950's and 1960's had expanded nonfarm employment at the otherwise feasible rate of 7 percent per year, the added expenditure on food of the newly employed laborers would have driven up real agricultural prices by roughly 10 percent per year. Not only would the economic base for growth in employment have been cut off, but the situation would have been politically unacceptable as well. World supplies of food were not available on the massive scale needed to back employment-oriented growth strategies in the developing world as a whole, even though individual small countries such as South Korea, Hong Kong and Singapore have been successful in matching employment growth with imported food.

III

Precisely because development policies of the past two decades have been consistent with the old reality of stagnant agriculture, so the new reality of technological break-through in agriculture requires a new strategy. Accelerated growth in food production provides striking opportunities for reversal of the low employment, "basic industry" approach. Such a change has far-reaching implications not only to the industrial structure, but to the choice of production technique, the domestic savings rate, the scale of industrial organization and the level and composition of trade. Further, because of its distributional bias towards the rural elite, technological change in the agricultural sector may itself be turned into an engine for growth in industrial employment.

The upper-income rural people who receive the primary benefit of the new yield-increasing agricultural technologies already eat well. Consequently, they market the bulk of their additional production and thereby support growth in nonfarm employment. This contrasts to traditional means of increasing agricultural production through labor-intensive methods of land reclamation and more careful crop husbandry. Thus, in India of the 1950's food grain marketings increased little faster than production; by the late 1960's, the new technologies had caused food grain marketings to grow about 60 percent faster than production.

Unfortunately, the potential for increasing employment provided by larger food marketings may easily be lost by inappropriate supporting policies. If increased domestic food production is used only to replace food aid, no significant increase in nonagricultural employment will occur. If the food is exported instead of being consumed domestically, growth of employment will depend on the manner in which the foreign exchange is used. In most Latin American countries the pattern has been one of investment abroad or increased imports of consumer goods for upper-income classes, instead of alleviating the domestic employment problem. If the foreign exchange is used for import of capital goods, so as to expand the domestic industrial sector, employment will increase. How much employment increases will, of course, depend on the technology of industrial development. The tendency has been to fritter away the potential on capital-intensive industries. Mexico seems to be a classic case of the agricultural breakthroughs adding

to rural income disparities but not being used to accelerate growth of industrial employment. Taiwan and Japan illustrate particularly successful use of agricultural progress to increase employment.

If food imports cannot be reduced or exports increased, the politically powerful landed classes will press for price supports and government purchases to maintain high agricultural prices. What policymakers often fail to realize is that an employment-oriented policy increases demand for food and thereby maintains agricultural prices without other action. It is thus obvious that the landed classes will receive a pay-off from technological change no matter what the strategy for maintaining prices, i.e., whether prices are maintained by increased exports, reduced imports, building of stocks or increased employment. Laborers will, however, benefit only from increased employment. The best strategy is obviously the latter. Unfortunately, the landowning classes, with their desire for expediency in delivery of benefits, do not support the employment option.

The rapidly rising income of prosperous landowners and peasants also offers a large and growing tax base for the support of employment programs. Even prior to the "green revolution" the landed interests were undertaxed. Latin America is notorious in this respect and in India upper-income rural people pay only about one-third as much in taxes as urban people in the same income bracket.

The landed interests evade the taxes which could support employment programs and maintain high agricultural prices despite the poverty of the masses. It is these tendencies, founded on greed and ignorance, which turn the green revolution red, not the underlying nature of the new agricultural technologies.

IV

Sharp acceleration in the agricultural growth rate places the immediate burden of employment expansion on programs for rural public works. Fortunately, increased demand for purchased supplies such as fertilizer and increased marketings of food, both of which accompany the agricultural breakthrough, greatly increase the rate of return to labor-intensive rural public works such as roads, landleveling, irrigation schemes, and rural electrification. Some of the increased food production may thus be used to feed an expanded rural labor force which in turn facilitates further increases in agricultural production. In addition, adroit handling of productive public works may allow tapping of local tax bases that are not available for distant central government purposes.

A disturbingly high degree of scepticism exists among bureaucrats regarding the effectiveness of such investment. They believe, with some reason, that resources allocated to rural public works will disappear in the coffers of local politicians and enlarge the scale of political patronage. Their views are also influenced by the failure of many such schemes in the pre-"green revolution" environment of largely subsistence agriculture in which there was little economic incentive for villagers to support such schemes.

The increased employment and income consequent to agriculture-led growth cause a much more than proportionate increase in the demand for fruits, vegetables and livestock products. These in turn use large quantities of both production and processing labor. As long as the basic food grains sector is stagnant, however, its effect on both labor supply and output demand prohibits an increase in the production of these types of agricultural commodities. In the case of livestock products, grain shortages also raise the costs of production. A rough estimate for India shows that the "green revolution" and its ancillary effects are consistent with an increase in milk production alone which could provide a 50 percent increase in annual employment and income to the 15 million landless labor families. These secondary potentials in agriculture require substantial public investment in new forms of research, education, credit and market development.

While one set of policies expands rural employment, care must be taken not to allow other policies to throw additional laborers on the market. Tenants must be protected from eviction by avaricious landowners. Small farmers must be assisted by reducing the risks of innovation and increasing the availability of credit and production supplies. Laborers must not be capriciously displaced by machinery. Mechanization is a particularly complex issue in which bad policy may destroy many jobs,

while a selective effort may actually increase production and total employment through reduced costs of transportation, improved methods of water distribution, and the breaking of labor bottlenecks.

Manufacturing and service industries must be the principal long-run source of expanded employment. Rapidly rising incomes of agriculturalists can facilitate accelerated growth in industrial employment through increased demand and greater savings and investment. It may be necessary to reinforce these tendencies with a redistribution of income and additional investment incentives.

Economists have for too long been the jesters who rationalized the desires of the rich to keep their money by stating that growth requires investment and saving and that the rich save more than the poor. In many countries the rich not only save little, but the pattern of their consumption is loaded towards imports and capital-intensive types of domestic production. A higher proportion of wealth in lower-income hands would in many countries direct consumption towards products providing more local jobs, and raise savings and investment rates in newly profitable local industries as well. Latin America is replete with countries needing redistribution of income in order to foster a more employment-oriented industrial structure. It is no accident that the high growth rate countries such as Taiwan, South Korea and Japan have much broader distribution of income than lower growth rate countries such as the Philippines.

Rapid expansion of small-scale industries, both directly in the production of consumer goods and ancillary to larger-scale firms, offers one of the most effective means for employment expansion. Products such as sewing machines, bicycles, transistor radios, agricultural implements and other small tools and machinery have considerable potential for being manufactured in whole or in part in small-scale industries that make many more jobs per unit of capital than do the large-scale industries introduced under modern import displacement schemes of development.

In addition, in absence of an organized capital market and of investment-oriented price and fiscal policies in the agricultural sector, small industries provide an efficient way of fostering and mobilizing small savings in the agricultural sector. Development of medium and small industries may also bypass the route of the rural-urban dichotomy followed by most industrialized nations of today and the social, political and environmental consequences of that route. Development of small-scale industries requires large public investment in power and transport and attention to many special problems of credit, relations with large-scale industry, and access to export markets, supplies of raw materials and machinery.

All the employment measures delineated here are initially more profitable and progress more rapid where agriculture is already prospering most. Consequently, explosive widening of regional income disparities is one of the most intractable consequences of the "green revolution." It is the poorer class in the backward regions who suffer the greatest inequity in economic development.

Unfortunately, the politics of regionalism reinforce an already difficult economic problem by restricting free transfer of food to these regions and of surplus labor away from them, thus seriously hampering a regional balance in development. The limited cost-benefit calculations conventionally used in the allocation of investible funds by planners and aid-giving agencies further reinforce regional imbalances. A fresh view must be taken of the problems of interregional resource allocation with a much longer run multiplier effect of investments in mind. The economic disparities between the two wings in Pakistan have vividly brought home the stark effects of narrow cost-benefit analysis.

v

In the past, massive foreign aid in the face of a stagnant agriculture has pushed low income countries towards capital-intensive industries in which they have the least comparative advantage. This has meant high-cost production, relatively low rates of return, and consequent poor capacity for repayment of loans. The aid-giving agencies have also encouraged low-income countries to adopt the technology of high-income countries, suited to different proportions of capital and labor.

Success in the agricultural sector has provided a new impetus for development of agricultural technologies which cater to the different physical conditions prevailing in low-income countries. A similar effort must be launched in other sectors of the economy to evolve technologies suited to the economic condition of abundant labor. Foreign aid can play a significant role in developing the necessary scientific infrastructure. To do so will require that program development and appraisal make less use of foreign consultants and their technological biases and more use of the rising research and development capabilities of the aid-receiving nations.

Carefully used, in conjunction with a buoyant agricultural sector, foreign aid may supply the capital to complement labor-using industries. This may lead to low-cost production, high profits and increasing capital formation. The contrast of this approach with the capital-intensive one may explain why foreign aid has been so effective in some countries such as Taiwan and South Korea and so ineffective in others.

Since the agricultural breakthroughs have been significant mainly in foodcrops, shortage of other agricultural raw materials, such as cotton and oilseeds, are now likely to be serious constraints on employment expansion. Foreign aid could play a particularly significant role in identifying and supplying these commodities in the short run and in providing technological assistance to increase their production in the long run.

The form of aid thus needs to be complementary to the form of the development process. Where the agricultural sector moves rapidly there may be a need for foreign aid in the form of capital goods and foreign exchange. If the agricultural sector is stagnant, however, and hence inhibits the growth of employment, foreign aid may emphasize development of the technological infrastructure for fostering the seed-fertilizer revolution. While these longer-term policies are being implemented, food aid can be used for expanding employment in balance with growth in capital. East Pakistan is particularly in need of the latter strategy.

The development of a labor-intensive industrial sector also has significant implications for expansion of trade. Demand will expand rapidly for many types of imported raw materials and capital goods to combine with labor. The immediate need for foreign exchange is often viewed by planners as unfortunate. However, what is not recognized is that development of a growing domestic market for labor-intensive industrial products may prepare the way for eventual export. The experience of Japan and Taiwan and more recently of India demonstrates the large potential for exports of labor-intensive goods, not only to other low-income countries, but also to advanced industrial nations where labor has become increasingly dear. Success in exports may even allow supplement of domestic agricultural production with food imports to sustain a somewhat faster growth of employment than would otherwise be possible. Commercial food imports by Communist China appear to have allowed a much more employment-oriented approach than that followed by the Soviet Union. India could profitably develop rice imports from Thailand for the same purpose.

In the long run, expansion of trade is to be preferred to aid as trade encourages specialization in those types of commodities which use more of labor relative to capital. However, foreign aid can play a particularly useful role during the interim period when demand for imports of capital and raw materials outstrips the long-run export capability.

VI

The developmental approach outlined above provides a positive alternative to the capital-intensive, import-displacing, low-employment growth pattern followed by many low-income countries. At the theoretical level, our approach emphasizes a consumer-goods orientation. We contend that this would accelerate growth of employment, savings and exports. We have shown how release of the food constraint is a *sine qua non* for such an approach. Several factors play a crucial role in determining whether the potentials offered by technological breakthrough in agriculture are fully exploited.

First, although the magnitude and the momentum of the agricultural revolution may be disputed, the revolution is a *fait accompli* in the important sense that the concept of agricultural development has been drastically changed. However, if the myriad scientific, administrative, institutional and political intricacies of the "green revolution" are not attended diligently the revolution may halt.

Second, both to accelerate growth in agricultural production and broaden distribution of benefits, effective policies are needed to extend the "green revolution" to small farmers, to prevent displacement of tenants, to confine farm mechanization to the few socially desirable functions and to expand rural employment through diversification of agriculture and development of productive rural public works programs.

Third, success in agriculture provides opportunity for a fresh look at industrialization policies. Governments of many countries are geared to the ideology of large, public sector, capital-intensive enterprises and are often neither willing nor equipped administratively to cater to the needs of a more atomistic employment-oriented type of industrial development. Public sector investment need not be deemphasized, but it may need to be redirected. New industrial policies may need to be coupled with encouragement to private investment and discouragement to import-oriented conspicuous consumption by high-income groups.

Fourth, export markets must be sought more zealously. Industrialized countries have often followed a policy of too much rhetoric and too little action on the question of allowing imports of competitive products from low-income countries. On the other hand, the onus often lies with the low-income countries' lack of initiative, poor quality standards, and delays in deliveries of goods. Improved agricultural and employment conditions should give impetus to the reform of export and import policies.

Fifth, a strong argument must be made for accelerating the flow of aid to low-income countries. American aid in particular has dwindled to appallingly low levels while the poor countries are lectured for not sharing the income of their faster growing regions with their laggard ones. The agricultural breakthroughs, in which foreign assistance may claim a significant credit, provide new potential for self-sustained growth in low-income countries. Our analysis emphasizes the need for a careful examination of the manner in which growth is fostered through aid and a clear need for a short-run increase in aid while growth of agricultural production is accelerating.

To maintain a high growth rate in food production and to foster employment-oriented industrialization obviously requires policies in low-income countries that go beyond the tokenism of socialist slogans and symbolic nationalizations. It also requires more from the high-income countries than pious lectures about free trade and bootstrap development.

The Political Economy
of Political and
Administrative
Infrastructure

EDUCATION, land reform, monetary, fiscal, trade, and investment policies can upgrade the factor endowments of sectors of a population in such ways as to make for a more productive polity. For any policy to succeed, however, acquiring and distributing resources as intended, prior investments by the regime or by sectors in political and administrative infrastructure are in order. This category includes public administration systems, local government, courts, the military, political parties, interest organizations, ideology, communications networks, schools, a legal system, a constitution, and so forth. Like "economic policy," political and administrative infrastructure is a rubric encompassing certain instruments that affect substantive distributions of resources. The class of instruments we are concerned with here are certain structures, or patterns of resource exchange and flow. Without them the costs of making and enforcing public choices would be too high and, consequently, fewer, less developmental choices would be made.

As we suggested in Part II, infrastructure should be construed broadly to include political, social, and administrative processes and institutions as well as economic. In all four categories of infrastructure, resources are saved from current consumption and expended (invested) with the objective of establishing a pattern of resource exchange or a channel for the flow of resources that will conserve on the cost of policy. Their maintenance constitutes an overhead cost, justified in terms of the external economies they effect for a wide range of policies.

Political and administrative infrastructure can promote or facilitate exchange between regime and sectors, and among sectors, in a number of ways. It helps each determine more accurately prevailing "prices" or rates of exchange for resources; it can increase the convertibility of resources, one to another, by raising the predictability of exchange or by accelerating the mobility with which resources are exchanged and used. The more quickly resources are exchanged, the less the "turn around" time for their utilization, the greater their velocity, and the greater the number of purposes that can be potentially fulfilled. Further, by aggregating resources, it may be more possible to achieve certain goals; thus, infrastructure can provide "power" for converting inputs into outputs, just as electric power serves a critical purpose in industrial production, and its transmission lines are regarded as infrastructure.

So far we have treated infrastructure as a generic category. But the contribution

411

to development, if any, varies with the kind we are talking about and the context in which it exists. Some particular infrastructure can hardly benefit everyone in a community or nation; access to the advantages of its external economies is likely to be uneven, if only because one must have resources in order to derive benefits from the exchange which it facilitates. Our concern is what it does for what we call aggregate productivity, the total amount of well-being within the community or nation when the gains of some or many sectors have been discounted by the costs they and others incur thereby. How much net benefit, if any, results from structuring or restructuring resource flows is something estimated *ex ante* before the investment but can only be known empirically once established.

We do not regard infrastructure as by definition productive or developmental. Assessments of the productivity of infrastructure must be situational and they will be subject to dispute. Infrastructure does not benefit or cost all persons equally, so its establishment is in a fundamental sense "political," as will be judgments about its productivity. While aggregate productivity might increase as a consequence of regularizing commercial relationships through establishment of a court system and legal structure, some sectors might well find their ability to benefit from their resources diminished thereby, for example, moneylenders or speculators in foodstuffs. The problem in analysis is to weigh such sectors' loss against other sectors' gain from the infrastructure. We appreciate all the problems of comparing utility (or disutility) interpersonally which welfare economists have grappled with. But these do not obviate the need for making such assessments.[1]

What should be focused on from a developmental perspective are what the infrastructure does to integrate markets, economic, social, or political, by making exchanges and linkages easier or cheaper, and what impact it has on the factor endowments of various sectors. Of special interest in terms of aggregate productivity is what previously unutilized (or underutilized) resources may be brought into production or exchange. These are matters to be studied, not just in terms of whether a certain kind of infrastructure generally contributes to productivity, but rather how it may be patterned in particular situations to be more productive in terms of the developmental goals espoused by the regime or other political actors. The continuing debate over centralization versus decentralization in administrative infrastructure, considered above with respect to education in China, is best understood and resolved in these terms.

What is required in the way of political and administrative infrastructure depends, of course, on the objectives of political actors, their resource needs, the extent to which they can rely on a nation's natural infrastructure (i.e., that not created by deliberate actions, such as a common language or contiguous states), and previous infrastructure investment. One of the basic strategic questions with respect to infrastructure is the extent to which a regime will rely more on political or more on administrative infrastructure.[2] What "mix" of structures will best promote its purposes? Or what "mix" within structures, since we would not make clearly typological distinctions.

What we commonly think of as "political" infrastructure—parties, interest

---

[1] We will consider the assessment of productivity in Part IV.

[2] This question is nicely addressed by James Heaphey in "The Organization of Egypt: Inadequacies of a Nonpolitical Model for Nation-Building," *World Politics* (January 1966), pp. 177–193.

groups, elections, for example—are more involved in the mobilization of resources and in a relatively voluntary manner, based on promises, bargaining, or ideological appeals; "administrative" infrastructures, on the other hand—civil service, army, police—are more involved in the allocation of resources, backed by the power of the state. The distinctions are gross, but to make more specific distinctions would be arbitrary; many "administrative" activities mobilize resources, and some "political" activities are distributive or coercive (even with official sanction). We are dealing here with a general category which includes actual structures or patterns of resource flow; it serves no purpose to elaborate sub-categories, since these would not illuminate the productivity of certain infrastructure in specific situations.

In this section we consider political and administrative infrastructure of various sorts and in several contexts. Generally the focus is on such infrastructure in rural areas inasmuch as we are concerned particularly with the developmental linkages that can be established through infrastructure between the center and periphery. The analysis by Douglas Ashford of strategies for rural mobilization in North Africa stresses the interaction between increased agricultural production and various linkages between the rural sectors and the regime. Of special interest are the various modes and combinations of infrastructure employed in Morocco, Algeria, and Tunisia. Each regime combined administrative and political structures differently, one basically revamping colonial administrative institutions, another establishing cooperatives, and the third building parallel structures with the regime political party. Ashford points out the deficiencies in each of the approaches and the consequences for the regimes of selective mobilization of rural people. We find the analysis well put in political economy terms—the constraints, purposes, and possibilities in each case, how infrastructure is developed, modified, and even discarded in the search for creating more productive links and integrated markets. From a developmental perspective also, the issue he raises of how farmers' political participation becomes more salient as their economic production increases is of major significance. As Ashford intimates, this process needs to be much better understood.

Infrastructure that has been created for one purpose, such as a nationalist party to achieve independence, cannot always be transformed to serve another purpose, such as the mobilization of effort for development goals. The political landscape of the Third World is littered with ineffective remnants of infrastructure of an earlier era, especially that which was once effective in tapping the citizens' resource of legitimacy. Political parties in many areas are moribund—they have too little invested in them, they are too closely associated with the administrative infrastructure, too wont to extract resources without providing any service. A conspicuous exception is the TANU party in Tanzania. As Norman Miller points out below, TANU has developed a network of relationships that embrace virtually the entire nation, down to the remotest village and family. TANU may be as efficient a system of resource exchange as any Third World regime has devised. This is not to say that the TANU record is entirely encouraging; as Miller suggests, there are opposition and apathy as well. As an integrator of markets, linking center and periphery, TANU has been outstanding, as it has been in acquiring legitimacy and support for the regime; how much long-term effect it will have in improving the factor endowments of the many, an avowed aim of the party, is however still somewhat problematic.

Local government is the infrastructure which most consistently combines "political" and "administrative" activities, mobilizing and allocating resources with varying degrees of voluntarism or compulsion. One basic consideration is articulated by Philip Raup in the first part of his article below: the local power structure, usually based on landownership, is likely to dominate local government structures. The problem of land reform that concerns him cannot be addressed effectively without taking this into account so that there is some substitute source of power, be it farmers' organizations, central government agents, or some combination of the two. One novel idea is that state farms or collectives, of the sort instituted in the Soviet Union, be viewed not so much in terms of their economic as of their political productivity, as functional equivalents of local government and administration.

The question before us is how local government/administration can be made more productive in terms of developmental objectives. In this regard, Raup examines the issue of decentralization versus centralization, citing experiences in the U.S. and the U.K. and concluding in favor of pluralistic structures under various circumstances. In general he also finds merit in a multiple-path approach to development administration, avoiding concentration of responsibility or power so as to make administration more innovative and responsive to its rural constituency, again drawing inferences from the U.S. experience.

Raup's other considerations depart completely from this experience, however; he suggests that cooperatives might be organized more as political than as economic structures, and that the military may under certain circumstances substitute for inarticulate and weak rural interest groups. It is this kind of intellectual flexibility shown by Raup, a willingness to entertain possibilities or relationships that defy the presumed "essence" of things, which marks political economy. Such imagination is not a matter of speculation but an outgrowth of the search for achieving greater aggregate productivity, this being the criterion by which one judges any such innovation.

The issue of centralization vis-à-vis decentralization is examined empirically by John D. Montgomery with respect to land reform efforts, drawing on several dozen country studies. Testing a number of variables against objective outcomes of land reform, he finds that the factor most closely associated with success, in terms of raising the factor endowments of the rural population, is the degree to which the resource of *authority* was devolved to local levels of decision-making in administration of the reform. The ideology of the regime, the reason for undertaking land reform, the degree of inequality in land holdings, and the size of the rural sector—none of these variables appear as powerful in affecting outcomes as the mode of administration adopted: "how" the reform is attempted.

Montgomery concedes that the data, the only extensive ones available, are crude, but the analysis is ingenious, and the inferences to be drawn from the recurrent association of developmental benefits and devolvement are powerful indeed. Political economy accounts for this dynamic quite straightforwardly. The benefits of a process go primarily to those whose factors of production are used. It should not be surprising that use of local resources (and their augmentation through devolvement of authority) should yield more benefits to the local population. This, however, is a general finding, to be considered but not necessarily adopted completely in specific situations.

One of the most ubiquitous issues in administration in underdeveloped countries is that known as "corruption." We would agree with Joseph Nye in his definition of corruption and in his position that it is not at all confined to underdeveloped countries. It is likely to be more of an issue there because of the greater relative cost of corruption in many circumstances and the greater impunity with which well-endowed persons can employ public resources for private ends. However, the issue should not be dealt with by definition, and we, like some others in development administration, would entertain the possibility that corruption can be beneficial for development.

Nye's analysis of the costs and benefits of corruption is one we would commend highly in terms of its form. For him, corruption is a category of real activities, not a concept, and under various conditions these may yield more resources of value to society than they cost it, even if the distribution of costs and benefit is, as usual, uneven. The issue is an empirical one, which Nye elucidates through use of a cost-benefit matrix for different kinds, degrees, and levels of corruption. In developmental terms, some kinds, degrees, and levels of corruption may be beneficial on balance in certain circumstances. Also, corruption may enhance the efficiency of administrative infrastructure in that it increases the predictability of exchange and the mobility of resources.

What all of these authors do is avoid simplifying or solving their problems by definition, by correlating essences of culture, behavior, or structure; rather, they address themselves to possibilities and permutations that could enhance the benefits people derive from their economic, social, and political interaction. We would underscore the appeals made by each of the authors in their conclusions, for more real-world research to ascertain how and under what conditions political and administrative infrastructure—the investment strategies and the tactical policies associated with it—can be made most productive from an aggregate point of view. This is a task political economists welcome.

THE POLITICS OF RURAL MOBILIZATION
IN NORTH AFRICA

DOUGLAS E. ASHFORD
Cornell University

Among the problems confronting the developing countries, rural reform has received increasing attention from a variety of social scientists. There are several reasons for this new emphasis. In the past decade most of the struggles for independence have ended and the newly formed nations are beginning to focus on the complex issues of political integration and economic growth. Few areas reflect this change as dramatically as the Maghreb. A common historical and cultural experience has yielded three sharply contrasting approaches to development. The reassertion of tradi-

From *Journal of Modern African Studies* (Spring 1969), pp. 187–202. Reprinted by permission of author and of publisher, Cambridge University Press.

tional power in Morocco leans towards a liberal policy for economic and social change. The revolutionary government of Algeria searches for order following a decade of profound upheaval. The single-party régime of Tunisia continues in its intriguing way to blend state control with individual initiative.

Confronted with such diversity, the student of contemporary affairs is hard pressed to find a common thread for his analysis. One alternative is to focus on those common aspects of Maghrebi development that might be subjected to more rigorous comparison than political life as a whole. The analyst can make a virtue of diversity by treating the political system as a constraint on the more specific problems that face each government in very much the same form.[1]

One such problem that calls for additional study is the mobilization and integration into the political system of a large rural population. Like most of the less-developed countries, the Maghrebi nations find two-thirds or more of the populace removed from political life and unable to play a constructive role in economic life. In all three Maghrebi nations, agricultural production appears to be lagging behind population increases,[2] while all three import thousands of tons of grain. We might consider, therefore, how the three governments may be expected to deal with this major handicap to their economic growth.

For purposes of discussion, I should like to consider the problem of rural mobilization as an organizational one. There has been a continuing theoretical controversy on the relationship of specialization and control in complex organizations.[3] Very simply, the hypothesis is that the more complex the tasks of an organization, the more must control be diffused throughout its structure. Thus, we would expect that stricter hierarchical control would prevail in an organization having very specific purposes and relatively little specialization among its members. An army used to be an example of a simple organization, although the increasingly scientific character of warfare and the elusiveness of the goals of warfare with weapons of total destruction has created more complex pressures. A university is clearly an example of a complex organization. The relationships among its members, including students, faculty, and administrators, are ambiguous. The university needs to reconcile the conflicting purposes of preserving established knowledge and maintaining academic standards, while also pursuing new inquiries and responding to new social problems. There is seldom a clear point of control and it is probably true that strict supervision would destroy the organization.

Complex organizations tend, therefore, to be guided more by internally generated tensions than by socially or politically defined goals. They also tend to be less hierarchical and to depend on the full participation of their members. The question to be asked next is: in what respect is the rural mobilization of a developing country comparable to the operation of a simple or complex organization? Though I have not yet tried to formulate an exhaustive analysis, my general feeling is that the process of rural mobilization comes much closer to the problems of operating a complex organization than to those of a simple one. The members of a farming community or an agricultural co-operative have a degree of control over their action far in excess of that one might expect in a simple organization. As we have learned in the United States, Russia, and Algeria, the producer of food can disrupt the system simply by not delivering his output to the market. Because it is fairly easy to produce and conceal enough to care for one's family, political and social controls imposed from without are ineffectual. The history of agrarian movements is replete with evidence on the equalitarian nature of rural life.

Rural mobilization involves more complex relationships among farmers and non-farmers as well as more specialization. The difficulties of creating a more productive and more efficient agricultural sector are not simply increasing investment and introducing more efficient methods. Rural mobilization raises new problems of linking farmers to new markets, new credit sources, and new political and administrative authorities. The delicacy of this process is suggested by the total control retained by the cultivator well into the advanced stages of agricultural organization. Only the individual cultivator can judge how weather, germination, growth, and maturation affect his crops. New seeds, new fertilizers, and new techniques may create opportunities for expanded production, but even highly commercialized agriculture defies strict, hierarchical supervision. The organizational complexity of rural development is derived, then, from the farmers' increasing dependence on other activities in the society and, especially in African countries, from the increasing dependence of the society on agricultural output in order to feed growing populations and to support the early stages of industrialization.

How does all this relate to the Maghreb? The North African countries are, above all, agricultural societies. If some agreement can be reached on the organizational problems confronting the North African farmer, we might be able to make some valuable suggestions on how agricultural modernization is likely to come about. In Algeria, Morocco, and Tunisia we have some well-defined strategies for bringing the farmer into the political life of the nation and for making him a better producer in order to meet economic needs.

These two external goals are interdependent, in two main ways. First, the more effective producer is going to exercise more political influence. Given the rapid change in the political environment of the past two decades, it seems reasonable to expect that the Maghrebi farmer will become politically sensitive more rapidly than the nineteenth-century American farmer who was energetically carving out the frontier while the coastal, industrial regions took form. Secondly, the farmer may become a better producer because he is politically activated. If there is some knowledge of his organizational setting, it is possible for the system to respond to his political pressure in ways that encourage him to become more productive. The possibility of making such a response varies, of course, with political systems and their capacity for change. What should be the political strategy to maximize the organizational effectiveness of agriculture? Before turning to this question, I think we should give some attention to the setting in which the North African farmer now finds himself.

ALGERIA'S RADICAL RE-ORGANIZATION

The organizational aspects of an intensified rural mobilization are probably most clear in the case of Algeria. In the summer of 1962 the Ben Bella Government found itself presented with a *fait accompli,* in which 2,300 farms that belonged to some 22,000 *colons* abruptly changed hands during the French exodus from Algeria. These farms included a million hectares of the best land in the country and were those which had been most highly developed. They produced about a third of the grain, a quarter of the wine, and half the vegetable crops of Algeria. The holdings placed under *autogestion* or "workers' control" are estimated to be 2.8 million hectares, or nearly half the 7 million hectares of cultivated land in Algeria.[4] With such a massive transfer of land ownership, the major problem of the Algerian Government has been to recover some leverage over the rural sector.

The first attempts were made by Ben Bella in March 1963, when decrees were issued outlining the organizational structure of the co-operative farms and standards for paying members. Each farm was to have a Director and committee responsible to the newly established *Office national des réformes agraires* (O.N.R.A.), placed under the Ministry of Agriculture. O.N.R.A. was to operate through 90 *Centres coopératifs de la réforme agraire* (C.O.R.A.), which were in fact the old French-organized *Sociétés agricoles de prévoyance* (S.A.P.) from the post-war period. Like the old S.A.P., the C.O.R.A. structure was to provide credit, machinery, fertilizers, and marketing channels for the commercialized agricultural sector. However, conditions were much too turbulent in the post-revolutionary period to enable the ideal structure to become reality.

Under pressure from the Moroccan–Algerian border dispute and from internal dissension in the Kabylie, Ben Bella decided to nationalize all French holdings in October 1963. Late that month the first *Congrès des 'fellahs'* took place in Algiers, representing some 150,000 agricultural workers on 2,300 farms, which once produced nearly two-thirds of Algeria's total agricultural produce. The congress was something less than a success for the Government. The farmers had already shown their reluctance to deliver grain to the Government, which had great difficulty in meeting its obligations. Proposals by the Government for additional assistance from the co-operatives were countered by proposals for tax relief and subsidies to support the seasonal workers, who were largely unaffected by the land seizure. One is tempted to conclude that the agricultural revolution of Algeria produced a rural *bourgeoisie*, if not a squirearchy, that had little intention of altering its interests to meet national needs.[5]

Despite Ben Bella's patriotic pleas, agriculture in Algeria steadily deteriorated. Production in 1963 was one-fifth less than in 1959. Of the roughly 7,000 tractors in Algeria, nearly one-third were broken down and no parts were available. The co-operatives were reluctant to sell their grain to the government cereals office and the administrative machinery was distrusted and cumbersome. The disorganization was so severe that Algeria came close to a major famine, averted in large part by emergency shipments of wheat from the United States. The continued decline of Ben Bella's Government is now part of history and in June 1965 a new régime was established under Colonel Houari Boumediène, whose organizational talents had been well demonstrated during the revolution.

Although President Boumediène moved cautiously, he made considerable progress in bringing the agricultural sector within the framework of government. *Autogestion* was a major topic in the meetings of the Council of the Republic in November 1965. Shortly afterwards, *El-Moujahid* noted the "total absence of the party in the direction and control" of *autogestion,* adding that "the problems at the root of the agricultural economy had never been tackled." [6] When Chérif Belkacem began the reorganization of the *Front de libération nationale* (F.L.N.), one of his two assistants was assigned the task of integrating state organizations into the new party structure. By early 1966 the Government was ready to speak out more sharply on the failures of rural mobilization. In May, Kaid Ahmed, the Minister of Finance, noted that agriculture had once provided 5 million dinars per year to the Algerian treasury, and that it has paid only 2 million dinars in the three years from 1962 to 1965 (1 dinar equals 1 new franc).

The moves to reintegrate agriculture were accompanied with some essential reforms in other institutions. Fiscal reforms of late 1965 promised to improve tax collection. The new *Banque de crédit* and *Banque nationale d'Algérie*, established early in 1966, created opportunities for loans for state enterprises. The new credit agencies were intended to strengthen the more viable co-ops and to overcome the moribund bureaucracy of the O.N.R.A. machinery. In June 1966 a new civil service law sought to restore the confidence of the professional administrator, who had long felt overshadowed by military power. Following intensive F.L.N. discussions through the summer of 1966, the decision was made to strengthen local party organization and to hold communal elections in February 1967.

These changes, plus the effort to revive the F.L.N. and restore effective provincial and municipal government, provided the organizational infrastructure for a new agricultural policy. These preparations were not made without serious tension among political leaders, especially trade unionists like Ali Mahsas and Bachir Boumaza, who had hoped that *autogestion* might provide a means for the unions to preserve political influence. This tactic was eliminated in June 1966, when Mouloud Oumeziane, secretary-general of the *Union générale des travailleurs algériens* (U.G.T.A.) announced his support for *autogestion* reforms.[7] By the end of the year both Mahsas and Boumaza had left the country to become part of a growing, but largely ineffectual, opposition-in-exile.

After these careful preparations during the spring and summer of 1966, the Algerian Government began to reveal a series of measures. In August 1966 Belkacem announced that the income of the farms would be limited and the surplus placed in a National Fund for Agrarian Reform. When Ali Yaha succeeded Mahsas as Minister of Agriculture in October, he announced that special measures were being taken to assist some 550,000 farmers excluded from *autogestion* whose holdings were less than 50 hectares. Later that month it was also made known that the highly controversial new agrarian reform law would be delayed until mid-1967 and that the *Office national de la commercialisation* (O.N.A.C.O.) would have a monopoly of all agricultural imports except tea, coffee, and sugar as well as of all agricultural exports. This left O.N.R.A. reduced to the more manageable concerns of agricultural production methods and rural facilities. Perhaps most symbolic of change was Boumediène's appearance at the rich

Boufarik co-operative in the Metidja plain, where he outlined his plans to require each unit to keep its own accounts and design its own plan under government supervision. Salaries were discontinued, but a new schedule for profit-sharing and allowances was put into effect.[8]

The restructuring of Algerian agriculture involved a wide variety of organizational reforms that had not been anticipated in the early period of independence. Revolutionary fervor was not enough to sustain agricultural production under the simple O.N.R.A. hierarchy. Departmental offices for agriculture were formed early in 1967 and the farm units were soon after obliged to sell their products to the marketing co-operative societies, *Coopératives de la réforme agraire* (C.O.R.A.). The new policy of shared responsibility was symbolized by Boumediène's visit to the Menzel Chonhada co-operative in June 1968. The workers received 1,000 dinars for 1967, but a third of their shares were obligatorily invested in the societies. For the season 572 co-operatives, about a third of the total, are reported to have operated at a profit.[9] The more localized and better co-ordinated structure made O.N.R.A. an anachronism and the agency was liquidated in February 1968.

The Algerian response is of special interest because it suggests that the benefits of massive rural mobilization may be lost through mismanagement at the local level and ineffective central government. Even so, Algeria has a great advantage over Morocco and Tunisia because the political tensions among the farmers, large and small, are on the way towards a solution. Algeria's organizational innovation in five years exceeds efforts in Morocco and Tunisia over ten years.

There remain, of course, major problems of how the 600,000 landless will be integrated into the new society, not to mention that portion of the million rural families untouched by *autogestion*. Paradoxically, there have been fewest benefits for the overpopulated, impoverished mountain villages where the *fellagha* found refuge and sustenance during the revolution. But for the marginal farmer operating under hopeless conditions there is probably no alternative but gradual assimilation into a new agricultural economy in areas of the country open to efficient exploitation. Politically speaking, however, Algeria has already made significant institutional reforms and substantial progress in areas of rural mobilization that are only now being explored in other parts of North Africa.

MOROCCO'S CAUTIOUS APPROACH TO RURAL MOBILIZATION

The organizational problems of Tunisia and Morocco are so different from those of Algeria that they almost defy comparison. While Algeria was confronted with an agricultural sector already incorporating many characteristics of complex organizational activity, the question confronting the other two nations is how to accomplish the initial mobilization of rural energies without impairing agriculture. The profound revolutionary upheaval of Algeria was a special condition that radically altered the structure of authority; Morocco and Tunisia have experienced the more commonly encountered situation of a régime seeking a way to increase participation and productivity without substantially altering the pattern of power in the society at large. If the organizational framework does no more, it alerts us to the very fundamental power conflicts that may follow as an external hierarchy seeks to extend its control to more specialized forms of activity.

Morocco is perhaps the more useful starting-point of the two because the traditional power of the monarchy has, if anything, been reinforced over the past four years and by its nature tends to stress hierarchical relationships in political life. While I am not particularly concerned here with the decline of party activity in Moroccan politics, it should be noted that the Government of August 1964 consisted primarily of trusted civil servants, military officers, and families closely allied with the monarchy. Control became even more pronounced, of course, in June 1965 when Hassan II invoked article 35 of the Constitution in order to assume emergency powers. The general hypothesis suggests that as the hierarchy becomes increasingly rigid and overt it will find increasing difficulty in operating the complex organization of rural development. The experience of Morocco provides a general confirmation of this hypothesis.

The history of rural mobilization is a series of truncated, sometimes impulsive, attempts to bring the farmer quickly and painlessly into the national political system.

The constraints on such attempts are probably more severe than in Algeria and Tunisia. With 1.6 million rural families, Morocco has a higher proportion of rural population than the other Maghreb nations. In addition to over half a million landless households, there are about 900,000 families with less than four hectares. About 3,500 families own 65 percent of the cultivated land; [10] and possibly half of these are of foreign nationality. The over-all pattern of land distribution is, then, the least equitable of any North African country. For these reasons, one may also consider the problem of rural reform more pressing as well as more closely tied into the existing power structure than in the rest of the Maghreb.

An alternative for a political system that finds the complex organization difficult to operate is to break the problem into a series of more easily supervised projects. This is essentially the Moroccan strategy, though it has suffered severe reverses. In the 1964 and 1965 cabinets Mahjoubi Ahardane was Minister of Agriculture, in part to assure the King of tribal support marshalled by the minister. The ministry, however, has not played an active role in rural development since 1960, when its field organization was divided between the *Office national d'irrigation* (O.N.I.) and the *Office national de la modernisation rurale* (O.N.M.R.).

These two agencies absorbed most of the rural infrastructure left to Morocco by France in the form of the *Secteurs de modernisation du paysannat* (S.M.P.). In one of several ill-planned crash efforts to mobilize the rural sector, the remnants of the S.M.P. were divided between O.N.I., which was to concentrate on irrigated agriculture, and O.N.M.R., which was to work in areas of dry-farming. Large sums were expended on both organizations, with very little careful planning. Available estimates are that the two agencies had a deficit of 9 million old francs early in 1965, when they were again merged to form the *Office de mise en valeur agricole* (O.M.V.A.).[11]

Efforts to initiate more fundamental forms of organizational activity to attack Morocco's agricultural problems are, of course, barred so long as the régime works within present constraints. There are several grassroots organizations, such as the rural *commune*, that might be mobilized if the basic obstacles could be removed. Some weak efforts were made in late 1964,

when the Government announced plans to repurchase 500,000 hectares of French-owned land, which was being cultivated under strict governmental supervision. About 250,000 hectares had been transferred by the autumn of 1965.[12] A co-operative statute was passed in December 1964, following the lines of similar Tunisian legislation, but no information is available on any efforts to create self-regulating, self-sustaining, rural organizations. As under the Tunisian law, the co-operative farmers can become owners in ten years if payments are made regularly to the Government and the land is not divided.

The problems of rural mobilization in Morocco began to receive serious attention when the 1966 I.B.RD. report severely criticized the Government for its waste and procrastination in agriculture. The report emphatically stated that the first task of Moroccan agriculture should be to raise production to meet the population increase of about 3 percent a year. The I.B.R.D. team recommended that Morocco should concentrate on the productive and irrigated zones and that the cumbersome central offices for rural assistance should be replaced with effective regional authorities.[13] The candid views of the I.B.R.D. had a decisive effect on the Moroccan Government. The Ministry of Agriculture was thoroughly reorganized late in 1966. O.M.V.A. was dissolved in October of that year and its activities restored to the ministry. The central agency to administer recovered colonial land, *Centre de gestion des exploitations agricoles* (C.G.E.A.), was dismantled and its activities given to provincial authorities. Thus, the costly and useless deadlock at the center gave way to a new organization for rural development.

The key structure in the decentralization of Moroccan agriculture were the eight regional offices to improve and to expand irrigated production. Each regional authority is cleared by the Minister, but includes representatives of other ministries and of *Promotion nationale*, the provincial Governor, the regional president of the Chamber of Agriculture, the president of the Provincial Assembly, and the office director. Operations at the regional level are largely in the hands of the Governor and the office director, working with provincial representatives of ministries, *communes*, and agencies supporting agriculture.

The seven offices are to concentrate on

cultivating more effectively the 380,000 hectares of irrigated land, some of which has gone unexploited over the past decade, and to increase irrigated land to a million hectares. The affected regions are the Rif, the Sebou valley, Tafilalet, Ouarzazate, Haouz, Tadla, the Sousse valley, and La-rache. The first two are pilot projects that have received F.A.O. and U.N. Special Fund support for several years.[14] While ministerial rivalries can still impede rural development, the Moroccan Government has acquired a new organization for agriculture under a trusted servant of the King, M'Hamed Bargach.

The contrast with Algerian experience is instructive. Until severely criticized from outside, the traditional authority was unable or unwilling to take the initiative in rural reorganization. The concentration on more profitable areas of cultivation will no doubt reinforce the large landholders, who already dominate agriculture in several of the areas marked for concentrated assistance. Though some efforts have been made to start co-operatives with C.G.E.A. land, the advantage remains with the wealthy élite closely aligned with the King. French farmers still provide about two-thirds of the country's agricultural exports or 15 percent of all exports.

Thus the more complex organization in Morocco has moved, like the Algerian structure for rural development, to favor the privileged, but without the preliminary massive transfer of holdings and reorientation of political life seen in Algeria. The Moroccan solution contains compromises with vested interests and old authority. The major task of the Moroccan Government will be to guard the new organization against the abuses of an élite untouched by revolutionary fervor and unaccustomed to national sacrifice.

TUNISIA'S ORGANIZATIONAL TOUR DE FORCE

The rural mobilization of Tunisia is strongly influenced by the fact that the single-party state is itself a régime intent on mobilizing all the energies of the Tunisian people. From an organizational viewpoint, a central question has been and remains how far such a mobilization can go before inducing or imposing modifications on the strongly hierarchical structure of the Government. The essential difference between the forms of hierarchical control exercised in Mo-

rocco and Tunisia is that political energies in Tunisia are energetically and inescapably focused on the reconstruction of Tunisian society as a whole. President Bourguiba and the Socialist Destourian Party are firmly committed to a major program of social reconstruction, much of it implying increased participation in political life and more social and economic opportunity for all Tunisians.

Bourguiba turned to the problems of rural reform very early in his rule. During 1956 and 1957 laws were decreed placing *habous* land under government control and establishing the way for individual ownership of collective tribal land. The Government also undertook to repurchase French-owned land very early. By 1958 over 300,000 hectares had been bought by the *Office des terres dominales,* mostly from land-owning companies in France. The land was used to establish the Medjerda Valley and Enfida projects and was not directly distributed for co-operative farming organizations. Much of this activity coincided with other political goals of the régime, but it also gave the Government some experience and interest in the problems of rural mobilization.

Since Tunisia has only about half the area of cultivable land of either Morocco or Algeria, the Tunisian Government was less involved with foreign settlers or *colons.* A total of 800,000 hectares was owned by foreigners, about half in the form of wheat holdings in the north farmed individually by some 2,000 Frenchmen, and the other half in large corporate estates in the center and south.

Bourguiba is known for his gradualist tactics, and there is every reason to believe that land reform would have proceeded in the established pattern had it not been for pressures created by rapid change in Algeria. Agreement was reached to buy 100,000 hectares of *colon* land in 1960, and another agreement was made in 1963 for the purchase of an additional 170,000 hectares.[15] When negotiations dragged, in 1964, the President decided to nationalize the remaining 500,000 hectares of French-held land.

The move towards co-operatives came slowly but steadily, once the party was persuaded that some form of social justice and rapid growth was essential if party hegemony was to be preserved. Under the vigorous leadership of Ahmed Ben Salah,

Secretary of State for Plans and Finance, a director of co-operation was appointed in mid-1962. Under his supervision, *Unions régionales de coopératives* (U.R.C.) were established for each province during 1963.

The concept of rural mobilization embodied in the co-operative societies was derived from the basic formula for party organization: a carefully constructed hierarchy firmly attached to the central government and laced with reliable party officials. Nevertheless, substantial decentralization was accomplished by making the U.R.C. the working center for all types of co-operatives in each province, including consumer, credit, production, and agricultural societies. All worked within a single legal and financial structure and under the provincial committee of co-ordination, composed of party figures, technicians, and high civil servants.

The U.R.C. is comparable to the more recently established regional councils in Morocco. Beneath the U.R.C. are *Unions régionales de développement* (U.R.D.), which group the various types of co-operatives specified in the regional plan. The Tunisian approach to rural mobilization should, therefore, be seen as one component in a centrally conceived strategy to extend co-operative structures to all forms of economic activity: agricultural, commercial and industrial. In this respect, it is more ambitious than either the Moroccan or the Algerian effort. The combination of co-operative societies varies with the socio-economic needs and potential of each province.

The implementation of these plans is carried out with the formidable support of the single-party organization and of the well co-ordinated bureaucracy. The agricultural producers' co-operatives are a major element in this plan, representing three-quarters of the 1,500 producers' co-operatives in 1968.[16] In the citrus, olive, and date regions of the center and south, the major rural innovation has been obligatory membership in marketing societies and service co-operatives which supervise cultivation, provide supplies, hire out machinery, and so on. In the arid regions of the extreme south and the interior, *coopératives de mise en valeur* are being formed as irrigated perimeters are developed around tube wells.

With typical Tunisian pragmatism, rural mobilization is adjusted to the agriculture of each major area. The producers' co-operatives in the north are generally based on a large *colon* farm combined with surrounding parcels of individually held land. By the end of 1964, 97 societies had been formed to cultivate 112,000 hectares of wheat land.[17] About 200,000 hectares were scheduled for co-operative exploitation in the north, but difficulties in staffing new societies have reduced the rate of formation. In the center and south some 280,000 hectares have been brought under service and multi-purpose types of co-operatives, with some 600,000 hectares destined for similar use in the future.

The party and Government have moved forcefully to convert Tunisian agriculture to co-operative organizations, some feel too forcefully. The Sahel, for example, has long been a stronghold of the party, but the strong measures taken to bring the olive farmers into co-operatives caused sufficient discontent to produce open rebellion in one town, M'Saken.[18] But some 5 million of the 9 million trees in the region are estimated to be too weak and old to justify cultivation. A massive program of pruning and replacement has been started through the service co-operatives. The farmer has no choice but to comply, although he retains an individual title to his land.

In visits to the co-operative societies over the summer of 1965 it appeared that in the north they are operated, much as under *autogestion* in Algeria, by the full-time employees of the departed French farmer. Officials were quite frank in admitting that the members tended to become day-laborers with very little involvement in the management of the society. The Government has given some thought to devising an incentive payment scheme, in hopes of raising the morale and motivation of the more energetic members. There have also been some misgivings over the merger of privately owned farms with the co-operatives. The suggestion has been made to enable Tunisian farmers with holdings of 50 hectares or more to recover such land.

The ambitious plans to create a major co-operative sector in the economy have been modified. When the I.B.R.D. gave the Tunisian Government a $15 million loan in 1967 for equipping producers' co-operatives it appeared that many lacked trained supervision and were not using new funds carefully. To achieve better co-ordination the Ministry of Agriculture was added to Ben Salah's "super-ministry." An understanding was reached with the World Bank to consolidate progress on existing production societies. In short, the Government has made a substantial commitment to co-operatives, but is experiencing difficulties in achieving the kind of involvement needed to make them viable, self-managing units.

Though the evidence is scattered, the organizational hypothesis suggests that the Tunisian Government has stressed patterns of control at the price of individual participation in the co-operatives. How far this has occurred because of the political demands of the one-party régime and how far because of sheer shortages of skilled personnel is difficult to determine. The uncertainties of rural mobilization effort have already begun to have repercussions at the upper levels of Tunisian politics. In late 1965 Hedi Nouira, the able director of the *Banque centrale de Tunisie*, expressed his reservations on development plans and progress in the official party organ, *L'Action*.[19] His plea for more conservative fiscal policy and greater emphasis on returns on investment were replied to by Ben Salah a month later. In January 1967 the widely respected Ahmed Mestiri, Minister of Defence, resigned over the forcefulness of Ben Salah's policy and embarrassed the single-party régime by airing his views in public. These incidents, together with reports of retrenchment in other areas of socially controversial policy, suggest that the government may indeed be apprehensive lest its policy of social mobilization carry it further than its economic resources and political limitations permit.[20]

RURAL MOBILIZATION AS A POLITICAL ISSUE

The organizational consequences of rural mobilization vary greatly with the character of the agricultural sector and with the political conditions of the initial effort to increase agricultural productivity. Programs limited to subsistence agriculture are not likely to have political repercussions, within either the new organizations or the political system. Perhaps the one common point of all three attempts at rural mobilization is the agreement, reluctantly perhaps in the case of Morocco, that emphasis must be placed on improving the most modern, commercialized sectors.

The economic reasons for such a strategy are persuasive, but may also enhance the political repercussions of such mobilization efforts. In Morocco this means reinforcing a rural aristocracy closely linked to the palace. In Tunisia this means the public admission by the party that it is not infallible and may distort the country's capacity for any change to organize political support. In Algeria this means resurrecting the F.L.N. as the political framework to link the privileged farm units to the Government, while neglecting areas and people in less productive regions who made severe sacrifices for the revolution. In all three cases the political system must now prepare to deal with the needs and pressures of rural organizations aware of their priority in development plans and of their importance in the future growth of the economies.

As suggested in the introduction, the politics of agriculture tend to take on increasing importance as the farmer becomes more productive. Each political system has its own organizational preferences for new rural activities, setting limits and defining procedures for the exercise of power by the rural sector. Until very recently the dispersed and sporadic efforts of the Moroccan monarchy have virtually precluded political pressures from new rural organizations. Current policies suggest that every effort is being made to minimize the chances of such pressures arising. The extent to which the hierarchical qualities of the monarchy have retarded the emergence of a large modern agricultural sector is difficult to measure, but the programs and policies governing the Moroccan farmer's progress have been slow to take form.

Tunisia is in an intermediate position. The large program to create viable rural organizations is now extended to roughly 10 percent of the rural population and the *Perspective décennale* (1962–71) made the co-operative sector a distinct part of Tunisia's economic structure. The plan now appears to have been too ambitious, and the President's decision to soft-pedal rural mobilization suggests that he may indeed postpone the most important product of new rural organizations, the involvement and motivation of the individual to produce more. The extent to which such a withdrawal is influenced by the limitations of the single-party régime is, of course, a matter for speculation. The fact that the forced draft mobilization of the rural population has produced political pressures, however, does not seem to me to be open to speculation.

The rural mobilization of Algeria has taken place with the maximum organizational complexity, largely because it preceded the formation of a viable government. The *autogestion* mechanism has been used to exercise leverage on government, and the modern sector of the rural economy is irretrievably in the hands of the farmers. The skill of the Boumediène Government will be tested as it seeks to provide coherence and control for the rural organization without impairing its productivity. The Government has made some remarkable steps toward establishing procedures and policies compatible with the needs of the complex organizational structure already existing at the local level. One of the rewards of the bitter struggle for independence may indeed turn out to be the first successful transformation of the Arab world of a neglected and impotent rural society into a viable, energetic, farming organization.

1. There have, of course, been a number of books over the years on such problems as administration, finance, public health, and so forth, but only recently has more attention been given to their political aspects. In a sense, policy studies of developing countries seem to be just beginning. I have tried to put the cumulative effects of series of such policy problems in the perspective of political change in *National Development and Local Reform* (Princeton, 1967).

2. There seems to be little doubt that food production *per capita* in North Africa has declined in the past twenty years. See Pierre Marthelot, "Les Implications humaines de l'irrigation moderne en Afrique du Nord," in *Annuaire d'Afrique du Nord* (Paris), 1962, pp. 126–54; also André Tiano, *La Politique économique et financière du Maroc indépendant* (Paris, 1963). A very good bibliography on agriculture in North Africa is "Situation et perspectives de l'agriculture au Maghreb," in *Maghreb* (Paris), XVIII, 1966, pp. 28–48. For general figures on land distribution and ownership see Paul Moati, "Le Développement de l'agriculture des trois pays d'Afrique du Nord," in *Revue française de l'agriculture* (Paris), XIII, Summer 1966, pp. 23–26; and Hervé Sicard, "Problèmes fonciers au Maghreb," in *L'Afrique et l'Asie* (Paris), 742, 1965, pp. 23–27.

3. For general discussion, see Peter M. Blau and W. Richard Scott, *Formal Organizations* (San Francisco, 1962); Amitai Etzioni, *Complex Organizations* (New York, 1961); and Herbert A. Simon, *Administrative Behavior* (New York, 2nd edn. 1957).

4. Jean Teillac, *Autogestion en Algérie* (Paris, 1965), p. 18. See also the first five chapters of François Perroux (ed.), *Problèmes de l'Algérie indépendante* (Paris, 1963), and David Lewis Porter, "The Role of Workers' Self-Management in Algerian Political Development" (unpublished doctoral dissertation, Columbia University, 1968).

5. This conclusion is reached in an excellent report by George Lazaref, "L'Autogestion agricole en Algérie" (1964, mimeo), p. 21. Curiously, much the same conclusion is reached about Tunisia following her rural mobilization efforts by J. Ben Brahem, "Le 'socialisme' destourien," in *Le Monde* (Paris), 31 May 1966.

6. *El-Moujahid* (Algiers), 3 December 1965, as quoted in *Maghreb*, XIII, 1966, p. 19. An account of Ben Bellist policy is found in the F.L.N. publication, *Comprendre l'autogestion* (Algiers, 1963). See also M. Parodi, "L'autogestion des exploitations agricoles modernes an Algérie," in *Annuaire d'Afrique du Nord*, 1963, pp. 61–84, and Hamid Temmar, "Le Choix des organes de l'autogestion dans l'Algérie de l'ouest," in *Revue algérienne des sciences juridiques, politiques et economiques* (Algiers), IV, December 1964, pp. 7–36.

7. *Le Monde,* 26–27 June 1966.

8. *Le Monde,* 5 and 18 October 1966. For additional comment on the difficulties of more comprehensive reform, see Pierre Bourdieu, "Une Révolution dans une révolution," in *Esprit* (Paris), January 1961, pp. 25–40.

9. *Maghreb,* XXVIII, 1968, p. 11.

10. The Moroccan agrarian reform problem received broad treatment in Jean Dresch (ed.), *Réforme agraire au Maghreb* (Paris, 1963). See also Tiano, *op. cit.,* and Pierre Marthelot, "Histoire et réalité de la modernisation du monde rural au Maroc," in *Tiers Monde* (Paris), II, 6, 1961, pp. 144–64.

11. A. Chenebaux, "Maroc 1963," in *L'Afrique et l'Asie,* LXX, 1965, p. 43.

12. *New York Times,* 27 September 1966.

13. International Bank for Reconstruction and Development, *The Economic Development of Morocco* (Baltimore, 1966), pp. 94–105.

14. *Maghreb,* XXIV, 1967, pp. 36–38.

15. Henry Younès, "L'Expérience tunisienne," in *Développement et civilisations* (Paris), XXII, June 1965, pp. 28–34.

16. *The Economist* (London), 19 October 1968, p. 57.

17. D. E. Ashford, "Organization of Cooperatives and the Structure of Power in Tunisia," in *Journal of Developing Areas* (Macomb, Ill.), 1, 3, April 1967, pp. 317–32. My

figures differ slightly from those of Pierre Bicabe, "Le Développement du mouvement coopératif dans l'agriculture," in *Le Monde,* 31 May 1966.

18. *Jeune Afrique* (Paris), 3 January 1965.

19. See J. Ben Brahem, "Les Difficultés économiques de la Tunisie," in *Le Monde,* 7 and 8 January 1966.

20. See the analysis of party disassociation from planning programs in Charles F. Gallagher, "Family Planning in Tunisia," in *American University Field Service Reports* (New York), North African Series, XII, 2, 1966. Tunisian agriculture has also been handicapped with three consecutive years of inadequate rainfall.

THE RURAL AFRICAN PARTY: POLITICAL PARTICIPATION IN TANZANIA

NORMAN N. MILLER

Michigan State University

INTRODUCTION

. . . Participation, it may be argued, is the problem *par excellence* for leaders of the new nations. The building of a state, both in terms of economic development and in the creation of a national consciousness, depends upon some type of participation by the citizens. If the citizen population is dispersed throughout the state in remote homesteads and hamlets, as many African populations are, then the problem becomes one of linkage between the government and the remote populace. To gain participation, new political structures must be built at the rural level, and old institutions must be changed to fit into national goals. Rebellious attitudes by the people must be neutralized and consensus, or at least some support of the national goals, must be gained. It is necessary that rural people be brought into the government's plan, that they accept the government's general viewpoint and that they provide the will and the manpower to change the status quo. In essence, peasant energy must be expended, muscles used, and attitudes altered if government goals are to be met.

The concept of mass participation presupposes a population shift from a disinterested mass to a participating citizenry. People must accept ideas of individual worth, loyal opposition, and electoral equality. In many new states stimulus for such participation comes from the ruling elite who see participation as a means to insure political stability. In essence, political participation, a degree of political integration, and some economic growth are the price the ruling elite must pay to gain the political stability in heterogeneous societies that will insure their own survival.

Participation, to be meaningful, must be within institutions that have channels of redress to the national level, and, simultaneously, have the capability of bringing about grass-root improvement. In one respect the process is essentially the building of new institutions at the grass-roots level. Mundane changes such as the development of agriculture, the encouragement of land reform, the creation of welfare and extension services, and the building of rural schools, roads, and clinics are necessary for orderly political growth. Participation in rural institutions such as the political party, the local administration, the local councils, the marketing cooperatives, and the local voluntary associations may be either voluntary or coercive. The essential fact is that participation, that is, involvement, occurs.[1]

Because the codes, rules and ideology of mass, single-party systems reach the village

From *American Political Science Review* (June 1970), pp. 548–571. Reprinted by permission. Some sections have been omitted.

areas more slowly than do the tangible personalizations of party authority, a situation of potential misuse of power exists where rural party organizations operate. Peasants are aware of face-to-face confrontations by a familiar figure who has gained a party position; they are unaware of the precepts and regulations that the national party has laid down for the village level functionaries. Consequently, political victimization is most pronounced at the very grass-root level that national leaders are attempting to integrate politically. Moreover, by its nature the rural party is a multi-faceted organization that is acceptable to the peasants because its leaders provide services that in more structured societies are carried out by specific agencies and contracts. Functions such as family arbitration, police investigation and criminal adjudication are mixed with the more classical party activities of representation and the dispensing of patronage. . . .

In summary, the argument is this: two overriding characteristics of rural parties are potential political abuse and a multi-faceted nature. These are in essence countervailing forces. Multi-faceted activities promote individual party participation. Abusive party authority tends to cause the individual to withdraw from party participation. When this occurs, political participation in the broader sense is also nullified; this is because the rural party is one of the few institutions that have communication links between the various upper levels of government and the people. Under these countervailing pressures, the individual pursues one of three courses of action: (1) participation in party activity, (2) nonparticipation, (3) active resistance to party activity.

The continuance in one of these three patterns depends on the satisfaction the individual receives on a wide range of issues of direct interest to him. Intervening factors, such as the individual's expectations, personal links with party leaders in decision-making positions, the actual process by which a conflict situation is resolved, and the time needed to reconcile an issue, will all affect the process of issue satisfaction. They will in turn affect the individual's party participation. Constant pressures exist for the individual to participate. Pressures are exercised directly by local party officials, or indirectly by the propagandizing national leaders. How these processes work may be seen with an analysis of a particular rural party situation.

CASE FOR ANALYSIS: TANZANIA

The Rural Party

One of the most impressive efforts to create a party structure that would avoid the local abuse of authority phenomena while integrating the nation politically and mobilizing the people economically has been led by Julius Nyerere of Tanzania. The Tanganyika African National Union (TANU),[2] the legal single party, has been particularly successful in penetrating the village areas and establishing viable rural branches in some 7,200 locales. Compared to other African states this is an important accomplishment. In most nations rural parties are election-year phenomena; they become viable organizations only to serve the campaign, nomination, and election functions. TANU's rural organizations operate throughout the year, engaging in many official and semi-official activities which are often geared to aiding the government's local development schemes. The party's rural component is doubly impressive when the obstacles are known. Tanzania is an economically poor nation, generally devoid of mineral wealth, and divided into 120 different ethnic groups.

TANU was founded July 7, 1954, as a nationalist independence movement, evolving in part from the earlier Tanganyika African Association. Although at the outset several of the founders of TANU, including Julius Nyerere, wished to keep the party a compact, elite organization for more concerted action, it gradually took on the dimensions of a mass movement. Since independence in 1961, the party has had the quality of an all-encompassing union, open to any citizen and extending to all sections of the society. At the present time TANU is the single legal party in Tanzania.

Although reorganization and experimentation is constantly going on, the party is basically organized into four tiers below the national headquarters: the regional, district, rural (or local), and cell levels. General policy is set through the National Executive Committee in the capital, interpreted by the regional offices and implemented through the district and rural branches. The district branch is generally coterminous with the 61 administrative districts in Tanzania, and will have within it anywhere from 20 to 300 rural party branches, depending on district size and population.

The rural branch usually serves an area designated for local government tax purposes as a village.[3] Incorporated within each rural branch are the TANU Youth League (TYL), the women's organization (UWT), and in many areas, the TANU elders.[4] Each of these affiliates has an administrative counterpart at the national, regional, and district levels. The party cell structure is organized below the rural party branch. Cells are made up of 10 homesteads; each family head has specific duties, such as chairman, vice chairman, or the officer in charge of education, agricultural, medical, security, roads and paths, and forests. The cells are organized for education and economic mobilization, but in many areas they carry out security and police functions.[5]

Rural party organizations have several intrinsic characteristics. They are institutional nerve endings of the national party structure. They are the local institutions by which the people are brought into the national political system and through which the commands of the governing elite are channeled. At the rural level, the government and party functions are largely fused. TANU is the coordinating organization responsible for a wide range of nation-building activities.[6] While keeping its identity, the party has extended its influence and personnel into most rural organizations, including the more important local administration and semi-governmental marketing cooperatives. The rural party is by nature an authoritative mechanism, operated by local influentials who are able to manage the allocation of scarce resources. In most areas the party is composed of poorly paid enthusiasts who hold other jobs as farmers, drivers, carpenters, and store keepers. Their political actions are only loosely controlled by the higher-level district officials.

Such rural party leaders are able to remain in power for at least three reasons. First, they offer the peasant, who may be in domestic or legal difficulty, the possibility of representing him at higher levels of authority. Second, the party leader is privy to information outside the village area

by virtue of his contacts with the party organization. He can, therefore, provide the peasant with specific information, as well as an interpretation of new events. Third, the party leader often controls, or has influence over, the allocation of local jobs and other scarce resources. Such mundane matters as the dispensing of medicines, free transportation, or honorific ceremonial duties, fall within the political arena dictated by a rural party leader.

A key organizational aim of the national party headquarters has been to gain mass involvement in political affairs. To this end a full ideological campaign has been in operation for amplification by the rural branches. From several points of view the results are impressive. Mass participation has occurred in voting, local government councils, marketing cooperatives, and self-help activities. There is general support for party rallies, party slogans, and local mobilization efforts, all of which are usually couched in terms of African socialism.

As a coherent ideology, however, African socialism as yet has little meaning in the rural areas. The attending pronouncements on Pan-Africanism are poorly understood and the running anti-imperialism critique is reacted to more on a specific issue basis than as a part of an on-going ideology. Within the ideology there has been an emphasis on national culture and on the historical uniqueness of Tanzania. African Socialism is referred to by national leaders as the rationale for governmental control of economic institutions. Such statements have meaning in the rural areas only in terms of job opportunities, salaries, and commodity prices. In sum, the parochial nature of the rural party precludes at the present time acceptance or understanding of a unifying national ideology. The ingredients of such parochialism can be seen graphically in the day-to-day activities of a rural party.

The Rural Party's Multi-faceted Activities

The types of activities carried out by rural party branches fall broadly into five classes. First, family and marital mediation is commonplace and includes giving assistance in divorce cases, arbitrating husband-wife disputes, fining wife deserters, and intervening when family heads cannot resolve a problem. Second, village administrative activities are carried out in the writing of reports on local projects, arranging self-help schemes, ordering building materials, and the like. Third, a welfare activity is exemplified in making public announcements, delivering public complaints, and aiding in specific problems such as sanitation or health. Fourth, a form of police activity is seen in protecting private property, warning troublemakers, investigating, and sending individuals to court. Fifth, the party serves as social critic in chastising unpatriotic behavior, in condemning certain acts, or in encouraging compliance in such matters as school attendance and tax payment. Concrete examples of these activities are seen in forty messages transmitted *to,* and received *from,* a typical rural party (Table 1).

TABLE 1

A RURAL PARTY'S COMMUNICATIONS

Content of Incoming Messages	*Result* *
1. Old woman asks TANU's help in getting divorce certificate	Referred to local court
2. Bar owner reports quarrel and requests investigation	No action
3. Woman complains of husband's mistreatment	Letter sent to husband ordering him to improve his behavior
4. Farmer requests vote for local representative to district council be secret and that a box in a private room be used	Party promises to study the request
5. Old man confesses, after a hearing, that he failed to tend his sick wife, who has since recovered and left him	Party fines man 40 shillings and instructs him to pay his wife an additional 5 shillings; wife agrees to return home
6. Local government officer requests forms be completed which give composition of village development committee	Forms completed
7. Village medical officer complains of "great water shortage" at clinic and asks for help	Public water brigade formed
8. Young woman complains a man (named) has repeatedly accosted her in her hut	Party chairman warns man to improve his behavior
9. Farmer complains someone has set his hut on fire, and requests an investigation	Found to be caused by a field fire out of control
10. Teacher complains five children (named) are not attending primary school	Party chairman warns parents
11. Local government officer requests party chairman inspect an individual's house who is suspected of practicing witchcraft, and to look for specific medicines and poisons	Chairman investigates with three other party leaders; suspect banished, but order later rescinded
12. Shopkeeper asks party chairman to remind farmer of debt for kerosene and cloth	Farmer ordered to pay
13. Old woman writes to party chairman: "I am sending my bed on top of the bus and do not trust the bus driver. Please see the bed is put off at the house of Hamud Shams."	Problems given to TANU Youth League
14. Local government officer notes that all teachers are encouraged to stand for local election	Notice posted
15. Farmer writes: "This letter is to say Salaam (Peace) . . . Salaam, that is all."	No action
16. Local government officer gives procedure for elections, and stresses need for peaceful voting	Announcement made

Content of Incoming Messages	*Result* *
17. Divorced woman agrees to stop "misbehavior" in the maize fields, and begs party's forgiveness	No comment
18. Farmer informs TANU that his case against a named individual, and his dog, has been settled without trial. Farmer was bitten on ear while "resting" on beer-hall floor	10 shilling settlement
19. Beer-making license requested for local farmer from local government official	Granted
20. Announcement of TANU parade to open new dispensary	Announcement posted
21. Women is accused by TANU in theft of 89 shillings (12.70)	Referred to court
23. Gift to be given people when new dispensary is officially opened	Large clock presented by party official
24. Village beer sale hours are weekends 3–7 P.M. only	Posted
25. Legal action threatened those who failed to take part in self-help project to repair road	No action taken
26. Agenda announced for next party meeting to include local bus problems, building grass roof for school, and new clinic annex	Agenda sent to 20 party leaders
27. Man given receipt for his bicycle, confiscated when Youth League caught him riding without brakes	Claims he needs no brakes; action deferred
28. Two men charged in court for failing to work on community self-help scheme	Released by agreement with party leaders
29. Complaint sent to district headquarters that local bus runs infrequently, passes many who wish to ride, is too small, and is very dirty	No action
30. Youth League ordered to stop threatening violence	Request acknowledged
31. Chairman seeks job for villager in local government administration	No action
32. Announcement made that party leaders and Village Development Committee (VDC) members must have proof of paid-up tax	Circulated and posted
33. Public notice is made that the new TANU office is open	Posted
34. Man who harvested and ate another man's crops is charged and sent for trial	Trial results not known
35. Divorced woman told 100 shilling bride-price must be returned to her former husband	Woman refers party leader to her father who received the money
36. Complaint to the cooperative union that crop prices are far too low	Complaint not acknowledged
37. Public collections for independence day celebrations will be one shilling per man	Announced
38. Citizens ordered to bring tools, rope, poles, and grass to build new clinic annex, or pay one shilling fine	Building completed
39. Man who used abusive language against TANU secretary is charged in local court	Paid 10 shillings fine
40. Letter to all citizens: "Warning, keep the peace during independence-day celebrations"	Circulated and posted

SOURCE: Random sample of correspondence files, Usagari TANU branch, Tabora District, Tanzania, for period January, 1964 to January, 1966.
* Messages written by party chairman or secretary, on behalf of the party.

The party activities reflected in the messages are varied and far-reaching. They tell us a good deal about TANU and allow for several points of analysis. First, it is obvious that TANU leaders perform nearly all authoritative acts that can be initiated within the limits of the rural political system. The party itself becomes a catch-all organization, its leaders acting as counselors, guides, father-confessors, investigators, and judges. The leaders reprimand and chastise, cajole and announce. They become personally involved in the full range of personal problems. Love quarrels, family feuds, and house-burnings are within their domain. Moral issues and money issues are common concerns. In terms of conflict resolution, party leaders provide a "safety valve" for community tensions by allowing individuals to transfer problems and complaints to them. Direct personal confrontations in many cases are thereby avoided.

Second, there are few guidelines to the leaders' legitimate areas of operation. In reality the party operates in all sectors in which the local chairman or other leaders wish to become involved. Formal authority channels are not recognized, and a leader will delve into administrative or legal matters if he feels he has a sympathetic audience. Nor is there a clear-cut pattern of when an individual will take a problem to a party official in lieu of a former traditional headman, although customary law disputes usually begin with mediation by the traditional headman.[7] Authority is constantly being tested as party leaders try to win support and either succeed or are rebuffed. Other village leaders in more traditional positions such as former chiefs or headmen hesitate to test their long-established authority for fear that new conditions may have undermined their authority. Instead, they spend a great deal of effort in simply negating the party leaders who are attempting to take initiative.

Third, the messages give an indication of the rural people's attitude to the party. TANU is viewed much like a parental authority. Individuals send greetings to the party, beg the party's forgiveness, and wish to stay on good terms with party leaders. There is little questioning of higher authority and usually there is compliance with a direct order. Such attitudes undoubtedly spring from fear of what the party leaders can do as public prosecutors,

and as public informants. The authoritative nature of the traditional political system conditioned such attitudes.[8] The backing the government now gives the rural party allows the modern leader unlimited possibilities to exercise influence. The leader's role is increasingly proliferated.

Fourth, the party performs general police functions such as investigations, arrests, formal court charges, trials, fines, confinements, and property confiscations. The opportunity for party activities of this nature exists because in most rural areas there are no police or formal trial structures immediately available. Trials are held by the party because the approximately 600 primary, or local, courts are spread so thinly over Tanzania that it is a major undertaking to use them. The party fills the void as the most authoritative organization operating in immediate contact with the people.

In dealing directly with the people, party leaders are occasionally coercive. The messages substantiate this, particularly if a dichotomy is drawn between messages which reflect voluntary behavior, and those reflecting that which has been forced by party leaders. From this point of view, nineteen of the forty messages may be considered coercive or enforcing. Another six cases are mildly enforcing. On the other hand, fifteen cases deal with situations where coercion is not involved.[9] As the messages indicate, TANU Youth League members carry out most of the police functions, and much of the coercion comes through this organization.

Fifth, rural party activities are supportive of broader government modernization goals in the sense that they generally enhance village solidarity, help to settle disputes, promote cohesion, build consensus, and aid communications. Activities which would have the *opposite* effects could be argued to negate modernization programs. Assessed in these terms witchcraft allegations, unwarranted party threats, or unfair arrests which cause withdrawal from self-help schemes would be included. Only four of the messages fall into these categories, suggesting that the party is usually a positive modernizing agent.[10]

Potential Abuse of Party Authority

Misuse of party authority occurs because most peasants are not aware of the limits national party leaders have placed on local leaders. In part this is because such regulations have been in effect a relatively short time. In the traditional political system, and the colonial system, the general limits on the main authority—the local chief—were known because they had evolved over time. Historically, there was little chance of flagrant abuse of powers because checks on the chief existed in the form of withdrawal from the chiefdom, or if necessary, violent dethronement by armed attack or assassination. In the modern period, the only recourse for the individual who becomes disenchanted with the local political process is to oppose the process or to withdraw from it. The latter is in essence non-participation. In a political sense it is usually caused by alienation from local party leaders who have committed some abuse of power which has directly affected the individual.

It is important to note that when a rural party leader abuses his powers, it is an abuse of the national party regulations set down and defined by national leaders. It is in the application of party policy at the district and village level that individual misconduct occurs and rights are abused.[11] The criticisms leveled at rural leaders by national officials are broadly of four types [treatment of Asian traders, financial irresponsibility, use of coercion to get participation, and misconduct for personal gain—some actual instances shown in Table 2].

TABLE 2

INCIDENTS INVOLVING MISUSE OF PARTY AUTHORITY

Incident	Result
1. Rural party leader intimidates local court magistrate by insisting he find an individual guilty who allegedly spoke against the party	Magistrate requests guidance from District court officials and incident is referred to higher authority
2. Man is either murdered or commits suicide (hanged). Rural party officials force family to bury body without inquest or police report	Rumor reaches police post, inquest ordered, rural leaders criticized
3. Rural branch holds "court" and fines individuals who do not cooperate with the party	Rural leaders reprimanded by district party officials
4. Rural chairman holds second job as bus driver. On several occasions he halts bus and collects license fees from passing bicyclists, but fails to turn in money to local government clerk	Police investigation requested
5. Leaders of Muslim welfare society claim party leaders used discriminatory tactics and abuse Islam followers in public meetings	Complaint sent to district party office; no action
6. Rural chairman controls rental of TANU-owned tractor. He charges exorbitant fees to some farmers, and allows his father, brother and father-in-law to use tractor without charge	Complaint to district party office causes tractor to be sent to another village
7. Agriculture extension worker threatened with beating for allegedly telling farmers not to join TANU or pay party fees	District party officer hears of threat, warns local branch, and complains to Agriculture department
8. Rural party chairman conducts membership campaign by forcing all farmers who wish to ride local buses or enter clinic to buy party membership card	Chairman relieved of duties and incident referred to as an abuse of powers
9. Meeting at headman's house to resolve husband-wife dispute is broken up by party chairman. He dismisses husband and forces wife to return to his home where he allegedly accosts her	Chairman relieved of duties by district TANU officials and criticized for using party name as his authority; local court case brought by irate husband

Incident	*Result*
10. Asian store owner complains of mistreatment by party leaders who demand contributions, impose store hours, and force road work	Complaint sent to regional party office; no action
11. Hospital staff complains of impromptu "investigation" by local party officials who threaten staff for being "inefficient, drunken, and mistreating patients"	District party officer promises to investigate problem
12. Prosperous bee-keeping cooperative accuses party of controlling their marketing procedures and of engaging in profiteering	After two-year delay regional office settles issue in favor of cooperative
13. Rural office demands and receives credit from local merchant for $478; refuses to settle account	Merchant complains to regional party office; no action
14. Five village-level local government employees (ADEO's) forced out of jobs by the party and "TANU men" put in their places	Administration complains to regional party headquarters of unfair pressure which undermines efficiency; no corrective action taken
15. Audit of rural branch shows cash shortage, no control of membership cards, no cash box, and loss of President's picture	Rural chairman warned to discharge duties in accord with regulations

SOURCE: Survey of eight rural party organizations in Tabora District, Tanzania. Data based on interviews with party leaders, local government officers, district administrators, and a survey of administrative files of Tabora District Administration 1964–66, 1968. The cases are not reflective of specific individuals or leadership positions.

FORMS OF PARTY PARTICIPATION

Findings on the behavior of individuals in rural party situations suggest that participation in the party takes one of three forms.

Active Participation

Under these conditions the individual is actively involved in the party process. He accepts most of the party rules as they are interpreted to him, helps enforce such rules, and generally does so on a voluntary basis. His compliance with the system indicates his general support of the political process, although he may differ on specific issues directly affecting him. His continued support of the party will depend on the satisfaction he gets from his party activities, and the decisions made on his behalf by party officials.

The extent of active participation, the reasons for taking part in party activities, and questions related to the process of active participation may be seen in survey data concerning rural party leaders and randomly selected farmers collected in three widely separated districts.[12]

Satisfaction with Party

Participation in the party may also be seen in terms of a *satisfaction expected* [13] and *satisfaction received* ratio.[14] The responses to the question "What does the party do for the people?" indicate a general satisfaction with the party. Only 1.3 percent reported negative attitudes. The findings also support the general thesis that the party is a multi-faceted organization that engages in a wide range of activities.

The question "whom do you go to when you have a political problem?" also gives an indication of the satisfaction with the party. Over 70 percent of the respondents stated that they took their problems either to the chairman of the party cell (42%) or to the chairman of the village party branch (19%). Some 10 percent stated they would take their political problem to a local government officer. Less than 2 percent stated they would seek satisfaction on a political problem from a traditional leader (headman, subchief). About 22 percent failed to answer the question. The findings indicate an overall satisfaction with the party as an agent for settling disputes and problems.

TABLE 3

WHAT DOES THE PARTY DO FOR THE PEOPLE?

Percent

29	Party leads economic development projects
18	Party is the government; administers, maintains law and order, governs the people
14	Party unifies the people, promotes cooperation, ends colonialism
12	Party is the representative of the people, voice of the people, interpreter of government policy, voice of the government
12	Party is an educator. Party teaches political ideas, agricultural methods, health and welfare improvements
1	Party is a negative influence
14	Other
100	

NOTE: N = 434.

The figures, however, probably underestimate the importance of the family head and the traditional leader in the settlement of problems. My observations indicate that people go to the political party with problems that have been already judged—perhaps unsatisfactorily—by family heads. The same people may have gone to a traditional leader for interpretation and mediation. However, the only "proper" channels of settlement would be through the party, the government agents or the courts; traditional leaders are officially out of power. Our interviews indicate that peasants are aware of political realities, but the figures fail to reflect the *de facto* power of traditional authorities.[15]

Party Membership

Active party participation is indicated in questions concerning party membership. About 92 percent claim to be members of the party (at one time), and about 61 percent state they joined when first asked. Some 16 percent admitted to waiting for several months to join. Over a third of the respondents said they actively volunteered for party membership and another 25 percent said they joined because they were approached directly by a party official. Most members claim to have joined the party prior to independence (1961), and nearly 40 percent claim to have joined the party in the early years of its activity (1954–57).[16]

When asked why they joined the party, over half of the respondents said to "fight for independence" or to "get rid of the colonials." Some 10 percent joined because they saw the party as an organization to help build national unity and to develop the country economically. Some 8 percent reported they joined TANU under somewhat coercive conditions.

Other indicators of basic support and participation in the party activities are reflected in the nearly 50 percent of the respondents who knew the name of the leading political party leader in the district (Area Commissioner). Only slightly fewer knew the provincial political party leader (Regional Commissioner). In response to the opinion question: "Do you agree or disagree that political matters should be left to government officials and village people should not become involved?" a total of 87 percent of the respondents disagreed. The finding indicates a strong feeling among farmers that they at least "should" be involved in local political affairs.

The extent of party activity is also seen in what the respondents believe to be the purpose of the party cell system (10-house cells). Officially, the purpose is to educate farmers to new agricultural techniques, to bring together the 10-house *families* for cooperative purposes, and to provide a local cell chairman for the settlements of disputes. Villagers, however, ascribe far wider purposes to the party cell system. [See Table 4.]

Non-participation

In addition to our basic assumption that individual abuse causes withdrawal of support from the party, non-participation can occur for at least three other reasons. First, if individuals perceive that the party leaders cannot make authoritative decisions that resolve local conflicts, a shift to stronger authority figures such as traditional leaders or administrative leaders will occur. Second, unwanted party decrees or excessive demands can cause a group of individuals to pay lip service to the party, and at the same time, to withdraw from it. This is

TABLE 4

WHAT IS THE PURPOSE OF THE 10-HOUSE
PARTY CELL?

Percent	
12	To provide police functions, to detect criminals, to observe newcomers, to report suspicious activities, to prevent crime
8	To settle disputes and to judge cases
8	To collect taxes
11	To promote cooperation in communal work
15	To bring about economic progress in agriculture
15	To disseminate news and propaganda
10	To aid government administration
3	To aid the party
9	Doesn't know
9	Other/omitted
100	

NOTE: N = 434.

often done by villagers supporting a non-local, alien individual as a party chairman, and using him as a buffer against the unwanted decrees from the district party office. When the lack of participation is noted by higher officials, it is the tribally alien party chairman who is criticized, not the individual farmer. In essence the alien leader lacks kinship ties and other levers to effectively gain local support.

Third, the individual's realization that rural party officials do not have an economic base to their authority, such as controlling land usage, dictating job opportunities, allocating free transportation, and the like, will cause farmers to shift their support to leaders in the local administration or the marketing cooperative who do have economic influence. Shifting allegiances are particularly likely to occur if the administrative grid in a given district is weak. The strength of the local administration varies graphically throughout Tanzania. . . .

Dissatisfaction with party as an agent and partner of the national government is seen in responses to the question "What has the government done for the people of this village?" Over 40 percent of the respondents stated the government had done nothing for the village. Another 10 percent didn't know of any contribution, or refused to answer the question. Other responses include specific contributions as "provided tools and material goods" (10%), "provided administrative help" (7%), "financed an agricultural or construction project" (14%), "financed an education project" (8%), or "provided freedom and independence" (3%). Only 3 percent said the government had done a great deal for the village, or gave details of several contributions.

A further indication of dissatisfaction that would lead to an individual's failure to participate in party activities is seen in the responses to the question "Do you agree or disagree that government matters and politics are so complicated that the average man cannot really understand what is going on?" Nearly 75 percent of the sample agreed with this statement, 18 percent disagreed, and 2 percent were uncertain. The remainder did not answer the question. Overall, the findings indicate a widespread dissatisfaction with the "outside party" and the "outside government." This finding also lends credence to the suggestion that peasants see the government as remote, disinterested, and ineffectual within their village. . . . Seen in this perspective, it is understandable that mild dissatisfaction with the party—and non-participation in its activities—would be in line with the larger dissatisfaction with one's life style. For most individuals, such a situation usually leads more to apathy, disinterest and acceptance of the status quo. In extreme cases of dissatisfaction, active resistance to the party could also result.

Active Resistance

Under these conditions either coercion by party leaders has caused withdrawal from party activities and the individual is actively resisting party leaders, or an organization outside the party sphere has brought pressure on the individual to oppose party activities. The party rules and codes are broken and an attempt is made either to destroy the rural party organization, or to unseat its leaders. Rural party leaders in turn may react by lashing out against the individuals involved, or by calling on higher party authority. When knowledge of anti-party resistance reaches the district or regional party authorities, prompt action is usually taken, either in the form of investigation and rebuke, or when necessary, containment by the police or the field force.

Resistance to party leaders may be mixed with general resistance to government activities. Such a situation usually springs from one of two sources. First, resistance to a specific demand or decree; in essence a collective refusal to follow party leadership for a specific reason which can easily become generalized to a refusal to follow party leadership on any issue. Second, resistance may spring from historical animosity. Groups that were at one time out of the party, such as former chiefs, Muslim organizations, or labor groups, are currently included in the broad party structure. Old antagonisms and old rivalries, however, create factions within the party which on the local level can lead to overt resistance to the existing leadership.

. . . Most cases of resistance are directed at the local leadership. There is little indication that organized wide-scale disenchantment exists with the national party organization, as was the case in Ghana in the latter years of the CPP. Cases usually erupt spontaneously, are resolved, and generally have no implications beyond the village area. Leaders of the dissident groups generally find no support for continued active resistance and they slip back into an on-going pattern of non-participation in party activities.

FACTORS AFFECTING
PARTY PARTICIPATION

In addition to the forms of party activity, four other questions must be analyzed for an understanding of rural party participation. First, what is the context of political life in which rural party participation takes place; second, what are the processes by which issues are resolved for the individual by party authorities; third, what are the links between village and national party organizations that affect peasant participation; and fourth, what are the broader implications for national leaders concerning the political participation of rural peoples.

Context of Political Life

A rural society is often a pedestrian society. There are limited means of transport, the peasant is largely immobilized, and movement to the outside is a major undertaking. The distance a man can easily walk to have a dispute settled or to gain assistance from a higher authority is the effective boundary of village political systems. For most rural individuals the world is in essence a microcosm with the village as the center. Attitudes toward movement are dictated by the relative magnetism of the home village versus the attraction of the outside world. . . .

The most important structures operating within this political context are the rural party and party cells, the village council (Village Development Committee), the marketing cooperatives, and voluntary associations such as parent-teacher groups, welfare societies, dance groups, and in some areas, secret societies. If the village serves as communications center for outlying areas, it may also include a primary court, and a local government divisional headquarters. Other local structures often involved in political activities include the local stores and markets, primary schools, tea houses, beer-shops, dispensaries, and mosques or mission stations.

The relationship between these structures at the rural level is characterized by overlapping leadership, a great deal of economic interaction, and communication linkages based on the informal village network, and rumor diffusion. The Village Development Committees (VDC) usually have 20 members who represent sections of the dispersed village area, as well as specific positions (teacher, dispenser); the party chairman is the VDC chairman, and members of the VDC are likely to include the leaders of the marketing cooperative, the local administration, and other organizations. Meetings are open to any individual with complaints or problems. Rural party functionaries are usually members of other social and economic structures and business tends to be transacted informally. Roles tend to be fused. This is not the case for relationships between the party and other organizations at the district, regional and national level. These relations are formalized by written contract and letter, although overlapping leadership exists among the national elite.

Process of Issue Satisfaction

The various survey findings give a picture of what issues are taken to the party. In fact, any potential conflict situation can become a party issue. There are no hard rules, and no precedents are followed except for the interests of the peasant who initiates the incident. He, as noted, will take the issue where he has the best chance of satisfaction. This is conditioned by his view of who is the most authoritative figure in his political arena—and, of these individuals, who would receive his request with the greatest sympathy. It is in part the peasant's view of the relative balance of power between a few local influentials.

Since traditional authorities have been severely curtailed in their legal exercise of power, and since government administrators often lack legitimacy in the village areas, the most potentially useful leaders for the peasant are often party functionaries. However, the peasant is usually the initiator of the resolution process and the arena he chooses will depend on where he believes he can get the greatest satisfaction. He may demand, for example, that both traditional and administrative authorities have some voice when party officials are judging his case. Essentially then, party participation is based on how satisfied the individual peasant continues to be with a number of issues taken to the party. The peasant is in fact a political chameleon. The situation can change with the issue at stake. . . .

Links Between Village and National Party

The Tanzania party structure is organized to incorporate the village party officials under the administrative direction of a district branch which is usually headquartered in one of the sixty-one district capitals. The effective linkage between the village and the outside world is in this district-village connection. Although communications from the national and regional offices supposedly filter down to the village through the district offices, the district-village tie is the weakest link in the party structure. Communications are often non-existent, and requests are often misunderstood or unheeded. Guidelines from the district headquarters on how village leaders should deal with various problems are followed at the whim of the local leader. The immobilized

and remote nature of the country creates a situation in which party authority is essentially "Land Rover" authority. District officials come to the village, confer with local leaders, settle problems, and depart. The circuit-riding nature of the system in fact only offers temporary solutions to village problems. . . .

Implications for the National Government

Political participation in the rural party is the implicit goal of TANU. To gain the continued participation of the peasant is the overriding problem facing national leaders. One of the key problems is that the party at the rural level is suffering the throes of general economic disenchantment following the high hopes of the nationalistic period. In spite of peasant expectation, little has changed in their essential routine. The economic life of the people has not been greatly altered and most of the lofty expectations of the pre-independence period are unrealized.

The party has been forced to shift from a nationalist protest organization to an agency for the mobilization of human and natural resources. Its new role is creative and positive. It is a role which in some respects is a contradiction of the earlier goals which were to bring about the destruction and downfall of the colonial regime. Those individuals who led the nationalist protest had personal qualities which could arouse mass dissent. Although these nationalist leaders have remained in important offices they do not necessarily have the talents nor the personal inclinations to provide the more mundane form of administrative leadership necessary for building a state.

Even those leaders who do combine administrative talents with some form of charismatic ability, face continued problems of peasant apathy toward the party, unpaid membership, and cynicism toward the government. As noted, links between the district and rural branches are difficult to maintain. Representation of the individual peasant's problems is on an *ad hoc* basis. The two-way highway that Julius Nyerere envisioned by which the goals and plans of the government reached the village and by which the problems and wishes of the people reached the government, is often simply not operative. The government's recruitment of rural leaders encounters basic problems of an individual's status, his traditional basis of legitimacy, and his kinship obligations. In many ethnic groups, there are strong pressures not to assume leadership for fear of alienating neighbors or of gaining undue economic advantages. In other areas there is little understanding of what a party leadership position entails.

Perhaps the most important problem concerning the political participation of peasants lies in how the central government consciously plans for such participation. There is a tendency for officials, particularly those in ministries dealing with resource planning, to either implicitly or explicitly oppose political participation in specific geographic areas. This is because resources are allocated on a priority basis for economic development. Political participation without accompanying economic change is considered unwise, particularly if political stability of the geographic area is in question.

However, this form of Machiavellian banishment of inaccessible, semi-desert or exceptionally backward areas, mainly on a rationale of economic priority, may in fact be more politically dangerous than the cost-benefit thinking anticipates. Political participation is necessary for the entire population. If national leaders attempt to create "holding areas" where rural institutions are not encouraged, the inhabitants of these areas are politically alienated as well as economically depressed. This process does not, however, exclude peasants from travelling to see strikingly better human conditions in the privileged areas. Nor does this form of planning prohibit migration out of the rural sectors to the overcrowded, socially-deprived urban areas.

When such exposure does take place, the individual is in fact in the larger political arena. His disenchantment with the events in his home region and his knowledge of better conditions elsewhere make him a potential dissident and agitator. It may be argued that the difficulties this individual can cause the central government would be eliminated if he had opportunities to participate locally in political institutions which are engaged in economic development. If rural political institutions are to survive, they must be created universally. No amount of Machiavellian banishment and isolation, no amount of government refusal to plan for a depressed region will

keep agitation from beginning. Once begun, it is impossible to predict the speed at which agitation can lead to collective, destructive political action.[17]

In spite of the difficulties in gaining party participation, there are other strong reasons why national leaders persist in promoting such involvement. First, the party has a potential capability of economic mobilization. It serves as a catalyst of several local interests and, if supported, can be effective in reducing the conflicts brought about by rapid economic change. The rural political party is at the cutting edge of the national plans for agricultural development; its leaders can stimulate support for these plans and gain their acceptance among the local populace. Second, if there is no participation in the rural party, checks and balances on party leaders will not exist. The party apparatus has been constructed but, if it is not used and supported by the people, it can be misused by self-seeking local leaders who gain support from the remote higher party levels.

A further reason for the national leaders to encourage local participation is to facilitate the building of local institutions such as the cooperative societies and voluntary welfare associations. Like the party, these rural institutions introduce specific innovations that may benefit the peasant. Other reasons for participation exist. Party leaders at the local level are often alien to the village in which they are working. Acceptance of alien party leaders will eventually mean the acceptance of local leaders in other positions. The process aids in the breaking down of ethnocentrism and the establishment of new forms of legitimacy. The local party, by encouraging peasant participation, is forcing the individual into a broader political system and exposing him to institutional structures that can represent larger numbers of people, and more effectively introduce modernizing innovations for the village.

Perhaps the most convincing argument for national leaders to promote and channel local participation is that political involvement by the peasant in some form has always occurred. Traditional political systems stimulated political participation in several forms as indicated by the constant intrigue and subversion that occurred within and between chieftains. Individuals have participated and will participate politically over what affects them directly: their purse, their dignity, their job, their food, their status, or their future. What is new is the individual's participation in a broader system of values and in new institutional forms. As events move along in a new nation like Tanzania, it may be that peasant participation on a broader scale cannot be avoided.[18]

1. For further discussion of the concept of participation and its importance in political science, see Lester W. Milbrath, *Political Participation* (Chicago: Rand McNally, 1965); and Aristide R. Zolberg, *Creating Political Order* (Chicago: Rand McNally, 1966).

2. Since the union of Tanganyika and Zanzibar in April, 1964, the United Republic of Tanzania has kept two autonomous political parties, the Afro-Shirazi Party on Zanzibar and TANU on the mainland. For the most important literature on TANU, see Henry Bienen, *Tanzania: Party Transformation and Economic Development* (Princeton: Princeton University Press, 1967). See also George Bennett, "An Outline History of TANU," *Makerere Journal* (No. 7, 1963), pp. 15–32; and Harvey Glickman, "One Party System in Tanganyika," *The Annals,* 358 (March, 1965), 136–149. For party activity on Zanzibar see Michael F. Lofchie, "Zanzibar," in James S. Coleman and Carl Rosberg, Jr. (eds.), *Political Parties and National Integration in Tropical Africa* (Berkeley and Los Angeles: University of California Press, 1964), pp. 482–511. For literature on the administration and its relation to the party, see William Tordoff, *Government and Politics in Tanzania* (Nairobi: East Africa Publishing House, 1967); and Stanley Dryden, *Local Administration in Tanzania* (Nairobi: East African Publishing House, 1968).

3. In Tanzania, the term *village* generally means a wide area of dispersed homesteads. There are few concentrated villages such as those found in the West.

4. The TANU Youth League is usually the most important of the rural affiliates because it serves as a village police force. In most areas members have the right of arrest. They also serve as messengers, official escorts, and general party functionaries. Most TYL are between ages 18 and 35 and as a group may carry on commercial ventures such as operating a local bar or sponsoring sport or ceremonial activities. In some areas the youth groups have been subject to criticism from party leaders for becoming overzealous, taking the law into their own hands, holding illegal trials and occasionally forcing younger boys to drill with imitation rifles. Changes since the Arusha Declaration (1967) have included

other, more politically oriented youth movements such as the Green Guards.

5. The administrative organization of the party is more complex than this brief statement suggests. For example, in some districts there are interim branch offices between the district and local branches. In other areas the village development committee (VDC), which ostensibly is a part of the local government apparatus, is often one and the same as the rural party branch. The officers, by government decree, are the same. In the early months of 1970 some village branches were reportedly to be consolidated into new TANU local branch offices which would be coterminous with district council wards. A new TANU constitution in 1965 reorganized the party structure in terms of the working and executive committees, and the annual conference of delegates at each level. Party leaders were empowered to summon witnesses, take evidence, and call for documents. A commission of inquiry was also established which gave citizens a means of airing their grievances against wielders of party and government authority. The commission received some 1,627 complaints in 1966–67, some 439 were rejected as out of its jurisdiction, 114 were investigated, 54 were found justified, and 443 were under consideration at the end of 1967. See: *Tanzania, Permanent Commissions on Inquiry: Annual Report, 1966–67* (Dar es Salaam: Government Printer, 1968). Also see a review article on this unique constitutional entity by Robert Martin, *Journal of Modern African Studies,* VII (April, 1969), 178–183.

6. With the Arusha Declaration, the party has been charged with implementing the teachings of African Socialism and self-reliance. The party was declared the supreme government institution in Tanzania during the 14th TANU Conference (June, 1969), with the government its instrument in implementing policies. (*East African Standard,* June 9, 1969). See *Tanzania, The Arusha Declaration* (Dar es Salaam: Government Printer, 1967). Also see Julius K. Nyerere, *Freedom and Socialism* (London: Oxford University Press, 1968), and *Ujamaa: Essays on Socialism* (London: Oxford University Press, 1968).

7. Although traditional chiefs, sub-chiefs, and headmen were officially removed from power in 1963, many were able to retain influence by taking party or administrative jobs. Other traditional leaders relied on their religious-magical, ritual, and customary law functions to retain local influence. A headman usually presided over what is now designated as a village. See Norman N. Miller, "Political Survival of Traditional Leadership," *Journal of Modern African Studies,* VI (July, 1968), 183–201.

8. Based mainly on the institution of chief-

tancy, the traditional political system in its purest form would be equated with pre-European administration (Tanzania, 1890). Remnants from the traditional system persist into the present period. Both German and British administrators relied on chiefs for indirect rule, and although chiefs were often appointed, in lieu of hereditary claimants, their local authority was considerable in terms of law, tax collections, and ritual. *Ibid.*, pp. 188–196.

9. Those messages classified as indicating coercive pressure were 3, 5, 6, 8, 10, 11, 13, 18, 21, 22, 24, 25, 27, 28, 30, 34, 35, 38, 39; mildly coercive: 15, 17, 20, 32, 37, 40; non-coercive: all others.

10. Messages 11, 28, 30, 39.

11. The Permanent Commission of Inquiry was established essentially to hear such abuse. *Tanzania, The Permanent Commission, op. cit.*

12. For details of the sample survey, see the Appendix [in original article, pp. 570–571].

13. Regarding satisfaction expected, an important parenthetical question is what is the rural party's ability to actually satisfy expectations. In most areas the local party leaders are increasingly able to control resources. The party has been declared the supreme governing body of the nation and the national party propaganda gives local leaders and cell chairman continuous support and legitimacy. The result is party control over such basic resources as new jobs, local wages, access to some schooling, appointment to honorific positions, access to important meetings, free transportation, and the like.

14. Other approaches to analyzing participation such as formal-informal, and leader-follower typologies or the comparing of relative degrees of commitment to various roles, are considered less appropriate for an African rural party setting.

15. Indicating the problem of getting totally candid responses from farmers on government matters. There is good reason to believe farmers are guarded in an interview situation and are less critical of the government in an interview than they are in their day-to-day exchanges.

16. Observations indicate the figures are high; farmers are inclined to falsely claim membership or to claim current membership if annual dues were paid in any one year.

17. See Samuel Huntington, "Political Development and Political Decay," *World Politics,* XVII (April, 1965), 386–430.

18. Goran Hyden, *Political Development in Rural Tanzania* (Nairobi: East African Publishing House, 1969), based on research in the Bukoba area, is directly related to the above findings. . . .

SOME INTERRELATIONSHIPS BETWEEN PUBLIC ADMINISTRATION AND AGRICULTURAL DEVELOPMENT

PHILIP M. RAUP

University of Minnesota

PROPRIETARY AND FAMILIAL ROOTS OF AGRARIAN POWER STRUCTURES

It is increasingly true of developed countries that possession of political and economic power is not dependent on ownership of property. Progressive differentiation of economic functions, the universality of achievement-based criteria for personal advancement, and protection of personal and social rights through stable government all combine to substitute intangible for tangible rights in the individual's value system.[1]

There is the resulting danger that public administration advisers in underdeveloped countries will assume the existence of a developed country's power structure at local levels. This parallels in the public sector the tendency for management advisers in the private sector to assume that

From *Public Policy, 1967,* edited by John D. Montgomery and Albert O. Hirschman, pp. 29–58. Copyright © 1967 by the President and Fellows of Harvard College. Reprinted by permission. Some sections have been omitted.

labor is the scarce resource, and efficiency is properly measured in output per man hour. These twin misreadings of the relative importance of men and land in underdeveloped countries are at the root of many of the failures of technical assistance and development aid efforts.

Throughout most of the underdeveloped world, political power structures are land-based and family-focused. Land is the primary source of new wealth. Where a subsistence is the dominant form of personal income, the control of land is the preeminent demonstration of political power. This control is often achieved through group action. It may not involve private property in a European sense, but it is almost always exercised through a power structure in which family ties dominate. . . .

Where land reform has been attempted, or is planned, a major cost is the destruction of old farm management control structures. If a former landowning class is removed, the greatest threat to agricultural production comes from the vacuum in managerial direction that may result. This is widely understood, but action based on this understanding is typically inadequate. It is difficult to cite any land reform efforts that have included a vigorous program of farm-management training for those who received land.

This shortcoming in development administration planning for the private sector may be less serious than the lack of any realization of parallel managerial gaps in the public sector. Realization of potential gains from a thoroughgoing land reform may call for development of a new generation of farm managers. It will almost surely call for erection of new structures of local government or drastic reform of old structures.

In this respect the many efforts around the world to introduce communal, cooperative, or collective types of farm organization can be viewed in a new light. It may well be that large-scale, collective-type farms have their greatest value as proxy forms of local government, rather than efficient forms of farm production organization. The average size of a collective farm in U.S.S.R. in 1963 was 32,-470 acres, approximately the size of the average rural civil township in Iowa or Minnesota; the average Soviet state farm

was the size of half a Minnesota county.

In many functional respects, the Soviet collective farm is the minor civil division of local government. It has been responsible for road building within the farm area, and it administers local distribution of electric power. Health, sanitation, and welfare programs are also administered through collective and state farm offices. It is at least arguable that the cumbersome inefficiency of the collective farm as a production organization is partially offset by its relative efficiency as a unit of local government.

The appeal of the large farm is apparent in other dimensions of government. Central credit agencies have often viewed the large farm or collective as a "better risk," mainly because it is seen as a substitute for nonexistent or ineffective local administration of development credit. A similar preference has often dictated choice of units for the allocation of better seeds or scarce fertilizers. This aspect of the presumed efficiency of the large farm may have little to do with its performance as a production organization, rather, it may instead be a reflection of the weakness of local government.

Whether efficient or not, the Soviet collective farm filled the rural government vacuum left by the destruction of the prerevolutionary land tenure system. This type of vacuum, which has contributed to the failure of many attempts at agrarian structural reform in developing countries, provides a key lesson for rural development administration: Because reform on the scale needed to release rural development potentials is almost certain to destroy rural political power structures centered on a few land-owning families, it will do little good to provide credit, fertilizers, or farm advisers for new land owners without parallel attention to the reconstruction of local government. In many developing countries local government reform deserves top priority in rural development plans.

SOME PROBLEMS OF
ADMINISTRATIVE STRUCTURE

An almost universal fact in underdeveloped rural areas is that public administration is weak. This may be because it is overburdened, but, more commonly, it is due to domination by a local elite. The local elite may be of a low order, for example, leadership may devolve upon the only one in the village who can read or write,[2] a member of the local "wealthy" class, or a local satrap who owes his position to support or tolerance by local religious leaders or a local landed elite.

In the majority of the developing countries, the chief—albeit low-level—local bureaucrat is typically dominated by the Ministry of the Interior. This is particularly true in Asia. Under colonial regimes, the motives for improved public administration were revenue collection, and maintenance of law and order, commonly functions of Interior Ministers. This set a tone for local government that is still dominant, even where independence is well into its second decade. The effective local (district) administrative officer in India, for example, is still called the "collector," meaning collector of revenue. In Ceylon, he is bluntly the "revenue officer." In Thailand (with no history of colonial status) the same functions are performed by appointed governors of the provinces (*changwats*). In all of these countries employees of central Ministries of Interior or Finance function as local government; these employees are not responsible to the local populations.

The above pattern is less widespread in Africa, but still prominent. Where colonial powers were strong enough to impose their system of administration on a region, the "Asiatic pattern" of a strong focus on the Ministry of the Interior has been repeated. The consequence of this pattern of local administrative structure is that in underdeveloped countries the Ministry of the Interior is typically one of the most conservative ministries; if there is a unit of government that resists reform and must be bypassed if development is to take place, it is traditionally the Ministry of the Interior. It is significant that the Minister of the Interior is, in most Asian countries, primarily responsible for matters concerning land, a responsibility traditionally associated with land revenue collection and local police protection.

It is particularly difficult for agricultural technical advisers trained in the United States to appreciate this situation. The U.S. Department of the Interior, which is their reference point, did superintend distribution of the public domain and still does play a major role in management of public lands, reclamation and drainage, mineral land policy, and recreational and water resource development. But the U.S. Department of the Interior does not maintain registers of land titles, does not dominate tax assessment or cadastral surveying, does not collect land taxes, and it does not administer the FBI or a secret police. . . .

In contrast, the U.S. Department of Agriculture has been strongly research-oriented, with parallel action programs that penetrate into every rural community. With the exception of the Post Office Department, no other department of the United States government has an organization that is so far-reaching. Four agencies of the Department of Agriculture reach into virtually every county: the Extension Service, the Agricultural Stabilization and Conservation Service, the Soil Conservation Service, and the Farmers' Home Administration. In addition, the Forest Service and the Rural Electrification Service reach almost as many counties. The emphasis in these agencies is on discovery of new knowledge and its dissemination, and on action programs to promote change. This focus has dominated the agricultural policies of the federal government for over a century.

The role of the U.S. Department of Agriculture is distinctly at variance with the traditional status of Ministries of Agriculture in most developing countries. Agriculture is still a "low caste" ministry in most of these governmental structures. It is often confined to low-order inspection and regulatory functions, or preoccupied with the production problems of an export sector. If research has been undertaken, it has rarely concerned food staples or subsistence crops. As a result, there are few instances in underdeveloped countries where well-developed systems of local agricultural offices of the central government can provide reference points and quality standards for local bureaucracy.

More important, there are few local "signal stations" to pass information up the channel of command when agricultural development programs are going badly. Hierarchies of control exist, but they were designed primarily to pass orders down, not to transmit grass-roots information up. In a number of land reform programs, attempts to solve this problem at the local level have involved the use of farm tenancy committees (in Japan or Taiwan); cultivation committees (in Ceylon); or Courts of Agrarian Relations (in the Philippines). . . .

The rapid execution of land reform in Pakistan provides an example of how the hierarchic type of structure can be by-passed. This achievement was possible primarily because of the system of survey and land title registration promoted by the British. Local land records facilitated a "crash-type" action program. Although land reform was executed in six months, it was a small-scale operation in absolute terms, involving only two percent of the land. (Ayub Khan was only interested in curbing the powers of the largest land owners, who were threatening to break the government.) Its weakness was that it did not have continuing contact with the farmers. Without tenancy courts or local tenancy committees on the Japanese or Chinese (Taiwan) model, it is doubtful whether subsequent attempts at tenancy control can succeed.[3]

While execution of the Pakistan land reform is praiseworthy, the administrative structure does not permit effective follow-through. In the Philippines, on the other hand, commendable pioneering efforts have been undertaken to set up mobile tenancy courts and to provide accessible justice to tenants in rural areas, but the lack of a uniform system of land survey and title records has been a prominent barrier to efforts to carry out land reform or to improve the status of tenants. [This lack is a legacy of American colonial rule, which differed from French, British, and other patterns.] After fifteen years of vigorous agitation for land ownership and tenancy reform, the government of the Philippines still does not know who the tenants are. For this deficiency the structure of local government administration is primarily to blame.[4]

CENTRALIZED VS. DECENTRALIZED PROGRAMS: A LESSON IN POLITICAL COST-BENEFIT ANALYSIS

The key to good public administration lies in the quality of the men and women who are the administrators. Although quality of personnel and training is central to problems of development administration, emphasis must also be placed on the form of the administrative structure, for it plays a crucial role in fixing the limits within which individual judgment can be exercised. And to a decisive degree, the nature of the structure influences the extent to which governments are responsive to local needs.

Where the articulation that links systems of central, provincial, or local government has grown slowly over generations, there has been opportunity to adapt and to compromise. When this occurs it is appropriate to observe that good men can make a bad system work tolerably well. But when good men are scarce, and when internal governmental structures are new, or undergoing rapid change, the characteristics of the structural framework take on added importance.

Developing countries can gain valuable perspective on some of the costs and benefits associated with centralized and decentralized forms of governmental structure from experiences of the United Kingdom and the United States in the past decade. The examples chosen illustrate principles of crucial importance to developing countries where costs of administrative failure are high, and benefits come slowly. [Detailed consideration of the Crichel Down affair in the U.K., and the Billie Sol Estes case in the U.S., is omitted here. Eds.]

These experiences of the United States and United Kingdom illustrate the political costs of decentralization in administration, and the bureaucratic costs of hierarchic or centrally controlled systems. Where responsibility is clear-cut, and power-structure relations clearly understood, then failure at the bottom threatens to produce failure at the top. There is great pressure on top administration, and ultimately on top political authority, to cover up, deny, or depreciate the existence of any defects down the line of command. A reading of the intensities of these pressures can be had from the histories of the Catholic Church, the French Army, or the Communist Party of the U.S.S.R.

Where the power structure is less hierarchic, where responsibility is diffuse, where sometimes duplicative agencies of government are competing in the same local community, there may be lower levels of political risk involved. Failure at the bureaucratic bottom can be treated as an episode but not necessarily as evidence of rottenness at the core. The top political authority can join in the cry for a house-cleaning without necessarily exhibiting an intolerable level of hypocrisy.

But the political cost of decentralization and delegation of bureaucratic authority can be high. If abuse is great in a decentralized system, the difficulty of making any improvements by administrative reforms may exceed the capacity of the administrative structure. The linkage among levels of authority may not stand the strain of a reform administration. What might become an efficient, decentralized bureaucracy with adequate powers can turn instead into a political jungle inhabited by warring tribes.

The desirability of decentralization, a weak hierarchy of command, duplicative efforts, and substantial involvement of those regulated in the acts of regulation seem to add up to the prescription for dangerous political living to be distilled from the Crichel Down and Estes cases. It may not be the most efficient prescription from the standpoint of bureaucratic control, but it does seem to be the least cost combination in terms of political losses.

What can developing countries learn from these examples? That the rewards of administrative decentralization are great if the system can stand the political heat of occasional failure. That this political risk can be hedged most successfully by promoting control from within by duplicate agencies, and control from without by local political interest groups. If local political interest groups are weak or non-competing, as in the Billie Sol Estes case, the door is opened for administrative abuse. Even the highest levels of bureaucratic professionalism, as in the United Kingdom, cannot ensure against an occasional failure. And the shock of that failure is greatest in a unitary command hierarchy. It was men who were on trial in west Texas; it was the system that was on trial at Crichel Down.[5]

THE MERIT OF PLURALISTIC STRUCTURES

In analyzing the structure of hierarchic systems it is important to distinguish between two aspects. On the one hand, there may be sharp functional differentiation among agencies: Public Works may exist in a world apart from the Finance Ministry; Agriculture may be separate from the Ministry of Land Settlement or Colonization; Interior may administer the Civil Guard, and be virtually at war with the Army. Inter-agency conflict at the local level results in a form of suppressed warfare, with resolution of the conflict only possible at the level of top command. On the other hand, there may be widely varying degrees of decentralization and delegation within functional agencies. The typical structure in developing countries is one in which local representatives of central agencies are custodial rather than managerial in nature.

Where there is sharp functional separation among agencies, with local representatives confined to custodial roles, the structure discourages or renders impossible any "multiple-path" approach to political and economic development. Within an agency, all eggs tend to get put in one basket. Thus, if a development project is attempted, it represents a major commitment of scarce resources. More important, it represents a major investment of political capital in that the political status of agency leadership is heavily dependent on success or failure of the project. Therefore, in an action program set in motion in this type of hierarchic system, project success in the short run takes primacy over project effectiveness in the long run, which tends to be self-defeating. But this phenomenon is not confined solely to hierarchical systems. It can be argued that some of the early urban renewal and redevelopment projects in the United States exhibited this tendency.[6]

These drawbacks demonstrate the wisdom of retaining a multiple-path approach to the achievement of complex goals. A parallel flexibility is demanded in administrative structure, but unfortunately in many cases a bureaucracy that is given this degree of freedom may ultimately use its freedom for self-serving ends. Discouraging experiences of this type in the past have resulted in rules of bureaucratic behavior designed to prevent local administrators from exercising any options. They are given clear-cut instructions with a focus on single projects. This reduces the possibility of learning by making mistakes, and it reduces the total frequency of learning experiences.

There is accumulating evidence that the most rapid progress is made when administrators can keep their options open. There is more than one path to development, even in the most underdeveloped rural community. A number of different approaches should be tried. Given the rigid social structure of traditional society, there is typically a very small residue of local administrative experience gained from trial and error in the past. Thus, no opportunity exists to pursue the multiple paths to development that have proved their worth in the economic sector.[7]

One reason for the success of the agricultural advisory service developed under the county agent system in the United States is the fact that the agents have been responsible for a number of different types of programs. They are pluralistic bureaucrats in that they have a number of options available in approaching any one farmer's problem. They combine access to technical information with training in management counseling, organizational planning, adult education, and the art of persuasion.

It may be of equal importance to note that the county agent in the United States has several bosses. He is typically hired by elected county officials but has his principal professional contacts with state Agricultural Extension Service officers whose approval carries weight in determining promotions. His employment security is largely dependent on federal government funds. These provide a part, and in poorer countries a large part, of his salary and ensure the adequacy of his retirement pension. He can afford a freedom of action that is denied the typical local bureaucrat. It is a hazard of his profession and also a source of his strength that he is answerable to more than one master.

The possibility of a probing approach on several fronts can also explain the bureaucratic history and administrative growth of several of the national action programs that have developed in American agriculture. The Farmers' Home Administration of the 1960's is a vastly different organization from the Farm Security Administration of the 1930's when measured in terms of its conceptual framework or its administrative dimension. The Soil Conservation Service has evolved through a succession of major administrative forms to emerge with a bureaucratic framework and a concept of its mission in the 1960's that would have been unthinkable in the 1930's.

These evolutionary changes have come about because options were available, even within the command hierarchy of sharply focused action programs. The options could be left open by responsible political authorities because of the existence of control groups or outside interest groups that could perform a policing function if the bureaucrats showed a tendency toward an unreasonable degree of empire-building and self-perpetuating activities.

This is not to deny the existence of motives for self-perpetuation in either the Farmers' Home Administration or the Soil Conservation Service, for these two agencies are highly susceptible to empire-building. However, they have still managed a bureaucratic evolution that provides notable evidence of capacity for change within an administrative structure that might easily have yielded rigidity instead of adaptability.

It is this capacity for bureaucratic evolution that is so often lacking in public administration at the local level in developing countries. Local administrators, operating under authoritarian regimes, have little opportunity to learn from failure; moreover, they have insufficient authority to make changes in scale or direction while projects are still under way. Their options are not open. Responsible political leaders do not feel they can open the options, even if valid, to administrators at local levels because of the great risk that power will be abused.

One major way in which risk of administrative abuse at the local level can be reduced is by the growth of local interest groups which serve a political purpose but remain outside the formal framework of the political system. Until this occurs, there seems little likelihood that the needed flexibility can be introduced into local public administration. Farmers' associations, breeding and crop improvement associations, irrigation or water users' associations, village improvement societies, and, in many communities, religious and ethnic groups can all police bureaucracy at the local level. It is in this sense that they can restrain the bureaucracy from usurping political functions while freeing it to engage in its administrative tasks.[8] Where these interest groups are absent there have been prominent failures in the implementation of agricultural policies. Myron Weiner points to this deficiency as a major reason for the failure of Indian efforts to promote cooperative farming.[9]

Land reform efforts since 1945 demonstrate that the most vigorously prosecuted reforms were those carried out in the presence of control groups outside the bureaucracy. These outside monitors have been occupying powers, military governments, or major aid-dispensing groups. They have also been internal pressure groups, typified by the Federacion Campesina in Venezuela,[10] the Sindicatos in Bolivia,[11] the Peasant Leagues in the northeast of Brazil,[12] or the Farm Tenancy Committees in Taiwan.[13]

In a pluralistic system, this policing function can also be performed by competition among sister agencies of government. The Finnish land reform after 1945, for example, undoubtedly benefited from competition among ministries responsible for agriculture, forestry, and refugee settlement. But most importantly, this policing function in the administration of postwar land reforms has been performed by the military.

THE MILITARY AS A SUBSTITUTE FOR
LOCAL INTEREST GROUPS

There is wide variation in the status of the military in developing countries. In some, the army must be regarded as part of an "established bureaucracy" that has usurped political power and is more or less self-perpetuating. This appears to be a valid analysis of the navy in pre-World War II Japan, and currently of the armies of Thailand, Ethiopia, Spain, and several countries in Latin America.

In other countries, the army is less closely identified with the established bureaucracy. It may even properly be regarded as an "outside" group. This is particularly likely to be the case if the army throws up a corps of junior officers who represent middle-class or "well-to-do peasant" sectors, with accompanying attitudes of approval of or sympathetic tolerance for, property ownership, education, political stability, sound currencies, and law and order. If cadres are made up of peasant sons, with officers drawn from peasant and middle-class ranks, armies can evolve into "outside control groups," preventing entrenched

bureaucracies from asserting near absolute political power.

With this possibility in mind it may be revealing to study the history of the role of the military in execution of programs of land reform. Were military sympathies primarily with the peasantry and only operationally with the bureaucracy? This seems to have been the case in Egypt after the revolution of 1952 and throughout the subsequent execution of the land reform program, or until 1961. Doreen Warriner has noted the dedication to land reform that was the only common goal uniting the young officers who supported first Naguib and later Nasser.[14] The Egyptian officer corps included a liberal sprinkling of sons of middle to well-to-do peasant families. In this sense, they represented the only effective "farmer interest group" in the country at the time. As events developed, the interest group proved durable to the extent that it served as an external group in policing the bureaucracy executing the land reform program.

There is evidence that a similar pattern is emerging in Iran where a number of key officials in the land reform program are army officers in civilian dress. Whether or not the army represents a "middle-class ethic" in a Persian settling is unclear. What is clear is that the Shah has chosen to rely upon the army to supplement the bureaucracy in implementing an action program to which he has attached a high priority.

There are similar reports from Nepal. The army has been delegated a prominent role in attempts to execute land reform programs, though perhaps more from a desire to inhibit open peasant rebellion than from any internal motivation growing out of identification of army aims with peasant aims. The army has been injected into the civil administrative structure at the local level in the unfamiliar role of agent of change and reform.

When peasants occupied lands of some of the large haciendas in the Sierra of Peru, beginning in 1961–62, the Peruvian government did not send in the army. It was widely believed that if the army had been dispatched it would have joined the peasants or at least would have refused to fire upon them. Many of the soldiers in the Peruvian Army were of Indian stock, and it was believed that their loyalties were to the peasants rather than to law and order and the haciendados. The government sent instead the *policia* from the cities to eject the peasants from the haciendas. Officers of the urban *policia* were drawn largely from old Spanish, or mestizo, stock, and represented the aristocratic, anti-peasant tradition. They, unlike the army, were clearly a part of the establishment.

These observations suggest a hypothesis: Where a self-perpetuating bureaucracy is in control and there are no effective local political pressure groups, armies may provide operationally effective substitutes. This is possible if the army is to some important degree outside the bureaucratic establishment. If the military has followed a systematic pattern of peasant recruitment and officer training from within the ranks, this can yield an officer corps basically oriented toward a peasant, middle-class value system. José Nun suggests that such a course of events has resulted in what he has termed a peculiarly Latin American institution: the "middle-class military coup." [15]

The hypothesis advanced here also suggests that the role of the military as a substitute for political interest groups in the control of bureaucratic structures may not be limited to Latin America alone. Where freedom is needed for local operational decisions on an action front, the bureaucracy often cannot be trusted. In the European and North American tradition, this problem was resolved by the emergence of peasant associations, trade and guild-like interest groups, and other rudimentary but essentially political congregations that could police the bureaucracy. Where time pressure or the institutional inheritance precludes this possibility in developing countries today, there is some evidence which suggests that the military has been providing a substitute.

The recent history of land reform movements demonstrates that where there has been some success at land reform in a transitional society, it has often been associated with an active participant role by the local military. Where land reform programs have failed or have made very modest progress, local political pressure groups are absent. It might also be added to the latter observation that no locally effective substitute in the form of army leadership with peasant and middle-class aspirations was available. This appears to have been the case in India. It is not clear whether

the prominent role of the army in the execution of the Pakistan land reform under the leadership of Ayub Khan supports this thesis or not, for it was a modest land reform, aimed only at an elite group that threatened to topple the Khan regime, and it did not bite deep into the landed holdings of the "middle elite." More documentation is needed before it is possible to ascertain the motives and the sympathies of the army in this case.

The danger in this solution to the problem of deficient local political interest groups is obvious. While bureaucracies may perpetuate their control by bureaucratic means, a reform-minded military is almost certain to enjoy its taste of power and can perpetuate its control by force and terror. The long history of military dominance in Latin America and recent events in Africa and Southeast Asia can be read as a warning of the high cost of delay in reform of local public administration. While the military may perform a useful function as an alternative source of administrative skills, there is no clear prescription for removing armies from power once they have assumed it.

SUGGESTED PRIORITIES IN NEEDED RESEARCH

The arguments of this paper point to some needed research in administrative problems of agricultural development. The burden of the argument is that the area of critical weakness is in local aspects of administration. Given the nature of agricultural production, administrative tasks both of farming and of government cannot be concentrated or centralized as they sometimes can be in industry. Good administration for agricultural development must be spatially dispersed, with a large measure of functional authority devolved upon local administrators. . . .

With these factors in mind, two priority areas for research in rural public administration can be indicated. The first concerns the development of local institutions that can provide an alternative to the military administrator and that can build on latent or existing peasant understanding and support. The evidence from developing countries suggests that the most promising institution with which to begin is the cooperative, but not the cooperative as it has been commonly understood.

The organizational form of the European or North American cooperative has evolved through the provision of credit and production requirements to commercial agriculture, or through the promotion of product marketing. The administrative norms are properly taken from the private business sector. Success is measured by the tests of business success.

But, cooperatives in newly developing countries are not exclusively and often not even primarily involved in factor supply or product marketing. They are instead performing a role as proxy local governments, with the collective farms of soviet-type economies or the cooperatives of Eastern Europe as special cases. Their proper norms for management must come from the public sector. Analysis of their criteria for good management decision-making should proceed on the lines of public administration analysis. Operations research, inventory and storage management, or input-output analysis are not proper tools for this analysis.

What are the proper tools? It is here that a reallocation is needed in the traditional division of labor among professional disciplines. In Europe and North America the burden of research in problems of cooperatives has been carried by the agricultural colleges. It is distressingly true that when their experts have gone to developing countries as advisers on cooperatives they have often had little to offer. The reason does not lie primarily in differences in level of development, or degree of commercialization, or "marketization" of agricultural sectors. The difference lies in the fact that cooperatives in developing countries are needed pre-eminently as units of government, not as farm marketing or supply agencies. They are primarily political and not economic institutions.

If this view is valid, it suggests that political scientists and public administration experts should turn their attention to the study of cooperatives in developing countries. Some work along these lines has been done in the area of comprehensive planning, notably in Israel. But the rural cooperative as an institution of local government administration is virtually untouched in the literature of development.

Much has been written about cooperative farming or about credit cooperatives, but with a primary focus on economic perfor-

mance. Research is badly needed into the elements of success and failure in the experience of developing countries with multi-purpose or comprehensive cooperatives, with a focus on the development of norms for leadership and public administration through the use of this mixed form of political-economic institution.[16]

A second priority area for research concerns the significance for public administration of the nature of local political interest groups outside of the governmental structure. The experience of Japan, China (Taiwan) and the Philippines with committees of local farmers to promote land reform or farm tenancy regulation can yield valuable insight into one type of interest-group participation in processes of local government. But these farmer committees were organized by governments.

An alternative version of the farmer interest group has emerged in Latin America in the form of peasant leagues and syndicates. Among these groups it is possible to distinguish two basically different types: those legitimatized under codes or labor legislation and those organized to promote land tenure rights. . . .

The significance of these different paths to rural political representation lies in the distinction between the peasant as a worker, on the one hand, and as possessor of a land tenure right, on the other. Where the welfare state has arrived ahead of land reform, effective peasant participation in political processes may occur through institutions designed to solve labor problems rather than through the more traditional forms of local government that grew up around a desire to protect land rights.

This difference suggests that in some developing countries, possibly in parts of Africa and the Middle East, as well as in Latin America, new forms of local government will emerge in the search for protection of rights in jobs rather than rights in land. The problems of improving local public administration in this setting depend on prior identification of the units of government that are likely to prove viable.

Before programs to improve rural public administration in developing countries are set in motion, it will be necessary to develop more careful distinctions between the political bases of the governmental units involved. The research needed falls in an area of rural local government that has been badly served by political scientists since the 1930's: At home, rural-urban problems have demanded attention, and abroad, the excitement of independence or new nation-building has diverted attention from local problems. We have dismantled the training and research programs in the United States that yielded a generation of specialists in rural local government between the two World Wars. We are not well-equipped to go abroad and advise on the restructuring needed in local governments whose support must come from the political institutions of industrial society now being grafted onto weak agrarian root stocks.

If rural local government in developing countries proves attractive to research workers from the United States, we may find to our surprise that distressed local governments in the United States will be among the principal beneficiaries. Extremes in fragmentation of farms abroad have a parallel in the extremes in fragmentation of local government at home. It is not only in developing countries that local governments are in pressing need of reform.

1. See Adolf A. Berle, Jr., *Power Without Property* (New York: Harcourt, Brace and Co., 1959); E. Meyers, *Ownership of Jobs: A Comparative Study* (Berkeley and Los Angeles: University of California Press, 1964); Charles A. Reich, "The New Property," *Yale Law Journal*, LXXIII, 5 (April 1964), pp. 733–87; and Andrew Shonfield, *Modern Capitalism: The Changing Balance of Public and Private Power* (London: Oxford University Press, 1965).

2. Matthew D. Edel, "Zinacantan's Ejido: The Effect of Mexican Land Reform on an Indian Community in Chiapas" (Cambridge, Harvard College, Columbia—Cornell—Harvard—Illinois Summer Field Studies Program, 1962). (Mimeographed.)

3. West Pakistan, *Land Reforms in West Pakistan*, I (Lahore, Government of West Pakistan, Oct. 27, 1960); Frithjof Kuhnen, *Landwirtschaft und Anfängliche Industrialisierung, Sozialökonomische Untersuchung in fünf Pakistanischen Dörfern* (Universität Göttingen, Institut für Ausländische Landwirtschaft, 1965).

4. "Seminar on Administration of Land Reform for Rural Development," sponsored by the Eastern Regional Organization for Public Administration (EROPA), Taipei, October 4–10, 1965.

5. Donald C. Rowat (ed.), *The Ombudsman: Citizen's Defender* (London: George Allen and Unwin, 1965).

6. [An excellent examination of this question appears in the same volume as Raup's article; David S. French, "Efficiency vs. Effectiveness: Project Form in Educational Development Programs," *Public Policy 1967*, pp. 59–75. French deals with American aid projects in Ethiopia and demonstrates, we think, the possibly inverse relationship between efficiency and effectiveness. Eds.]

7. Richard R. Nelson, "Uncertainty, Learning, and the Economics of Parallel Research and Development Efforts," *Review of Economics and Statistics*, XLIII, 4 (November 1961).

8. Fred W. Riggs, *Administration in Developing Countries: The Theory of Prismatic Society* (Boston: Houghton Mifflin Co., 1964); and "Bureaucrats and Political Development," in Joseph LaPalombara (ed.), *Bureaucracy and Political Development* (Princeton: Princeton University Press, 1963), pp. 120–167.

9. *The Politics of Scarcity* (Chicago: University of Chicago Press, 1962), p. 156.

10. John D. Powell, "Preliminary Report on the Federacion Campesina de Venezuela" (Madison: University of Wisconsin, Land Tenure Center, September 1964). (Processed.)

11. Dwight B. Heath, "Successes and Shortcomings of Agrarian Reform in Bolivia," *The Progress of Land Reform in Bolivia*, Discussion Paper No. 2 (Madison: University of Wisconsin, Land Tenure Center, May 1963).

12. Frank Bonilla, "Rural Reform in Brazil," American Universities Field Staff, Reports Service, VIII, 4 (East Coast South American Series), October 1961.

13. Taiwan, Joint Commission on Rural Reconstruction, *Land Reform in Free China*, by Hui-Sun Tang (Taipei, 1957).

14. Doreen Warriner, *Land Reform and Development in the Middle East*, 2nd ed. (London: Oxford University Press, 1962), p. 10.

15. José Nun, "A Latin American Phenomenon: The Middle Class Military Coup," *Trends in Social Science Research* (Institute of International Studies, University of California, Berkeley, March 1965).

16. San-eki Nakaoka, "The Agricultural Cooperative in Socialist Egypt—Its Role in a Changing Rural Economy," *The Developing Economies* (Tokyo), III, 2 (June 1965).

THE ALLOCATION OF AUTHORITY IN LAND REFORM PROGRAMS: A COMPARATIVE STUDY OF ADMINISTRATIVE PROCESSES AND OUTPUTS

JOHN D. MONTGOMERY

Harvard University

I

Debate over development policy has usually centered on choices of policy ends (*whether* to pursue policy X) rather than of policy means (*how* best to pursue it, once adopted). As any experienced practitioner of public policy knows, ends and means cannot be separated, but this reality is often overlooked in the heat of the endless arguments over the hypothetical merits of new technology as compared with those of land reform, or of import substitution as compared with mineral extraction. But whether the promised benefits of any policy can be attained really depends on whether it can be carried out.

Land reform is, among other things, an article of faith. Unscathed by pragmatic successes and failures and by doctrinal heresies, it has appeared in nearly every catechism of social justice prepared for the Third World in the last quarter of a century. It has been tried, with various degrees of conviction, in scores of countries. It is thus a rare example of a principle that has been tested and has survived, though its effects have rarely been reported or explained.

Because American foreign aid is so often involved in urging, supporting, advising, and even financing it, there now exists a body of evidence that can offer some tentative answers to several questions heretofore left to the priesthood of populist reformers: how often does it contribute to social justice? Who are the ultimate beneficiaries of most land reforms? Does the style or form of administration affect the social outcomes? Can any government conduct a successful land reform, or does it take an authoritarian regime to overcome the political obstacles to such basic rural change? Once a government embarks upon general reform, what further steps can it take to increase the benefits it distributes to small farmers?

Analyzing the administrative options available for land reform is a difficult task, but not a hopeless one. One means of approaching the problem is to compare various outcomes or outputs of previous experiences with the policies and administrative devices employed. As yet, data on the outcomes of land reform have not been gathered systematically enough to test and compare the intensity or frequency of outcomes associated with different modes and means of policy application. But it is possible to ascertain in at least gross terms on the basis of various country studies whether certain outcomes occurred at all or not and to relate them to different methods used to implement the policy objective.

In most of the 30 case studies prepared for the Spring Review of Land Reform conducted by the U.S. Agency for International Development in 1970, information is given on (a) whether or not the peasants' security of private tenure improved (either through possession of land titles or enforceable rental contracts); (b) whether peasants' incomes increased or not as a direct result of land reform; (c) whether former tenants enjoyed increased political power or not through their increased status as land owners or their increased ability to influence local governmental decisions; and (d) whether or not the bureaucratic agencies conducting the land reform program increased their local or national political power or authority as a result of the operation.[1]

Since the land reform studies prepared for the Review followed a standardized outline, comparable judgments on these outcomes exist for some 25 cases. When

Reprinted by permission of author. Revised version is published in *Administrative Science Quarterly* (March 1972), pp. 62–75.

these outcomes are clustered and analyzed according to the different modes of administration used to carry out the land reform, the implications are striking: the administrative process employed, in particular the allocation of administrative authority, emerges as a distinct and significant independent factor affecting the outputs of land reform programs.

II

Land reform involves at least four administrative operations, each of which is potentially a complex undertaking: initiating changes in ownership of tenancy rights; issuing land titles and enforcing contracts; transferring funds to landlords as compensation, and collecting rents or payments from tenants and new purchasers; and adjudicating disputes over boundaries, inheritances, and rights. These functions may be carried out by any one of three administrative processes. A country may *centralize* land reform functions in the national bureaucracy; it may *decentralize* them by creating new agencies or using several existing ones; or it may *devolve* the responsibility downward by transferring some or all of these functions to local authorities.

A. Nine countries in our study used some existing central bureaucracy to carry out land reform, thus relying upon a single closed system (i.e., one whose members are responsible to its own leadership) to discharge the four functions defined above. Centralized land reform programs like that of Vietnam under Diem, or in the Philippines, the UAR, Iraq, Algeria, Colombia, and Brazil, produced relatively few economic benefits to peasants (doing so only in the UAR); they did little to improve the political position of tenants (except in Indonesia); and they increased the security of land tenure—the minimum aspiration for land reform—in only about half the cases cited above (in Diem's Vietnam, Algeria, and the UAR).[2] In each case, so far as the matter can be judged from the country studies, the bureaucracy emerged from the process relatively strengthened as a social and political force. Thus although the professional central bureaucracy is the most obvious means of carrying out such a major social change as land reform, it is unlikely to produce maximum benefits for the citizens whose plight is the program's ostensible concern. (See Appendix I for data on which these conclusions are based.)

The reason for this outcome can be inferred from the literature on comparative bureaucracy. A centralized bureaucratic instrument is often something of an elite corps, especially in newly independent countries whose civil service is a direct successor to colonial officialdom.[3] Its political orientation is likely to be conservative. It tends to have social links to landlords rather than to peasants; at any rate, its membership is usually at least one generation removed from rural origins, and it is likely to be unresponsive to peasant desires. To entrust land reform to this group runs the risk of a bureaucratic slow-down for want of commitment; it may even encounter outright sabotage if the bureaucracy senses any lack of political will on the part of its own leadership. In either case, its performance is likely to be formal, cautious, and "correct."[4]

A related risk is that the civil service may use the program to advance its own economic or political position. Like any political action group, it is susceptible to corruption in direct ratio to the importance of its decisions.[5] Because land reform actions have important political consequences, a bureaucracy charged with carrying out the reforms can strengthen its relative position by the very fact of possessing the instruments of decision-making.[6] Yet it itself may be fairly invulnerable to reform from external sources because its reward system is internal rather than lateral.[7] In spite of these defects, a common practice among countries undertaking land reform, regardless of the "sincerity" of their purposes, has been to assign functional responsibilities to a central bureaucracy, with the social outcomes described above.

B. The second administrative option for carrying out land reform has been to use several different bureaucratic systems simultaneously to carry out various aspects of the program, without attempting to change the bureaucracy itself ("decentralization"). This approach shares the responsibility among different career services and thus generates an administrative plurality of interests. The social base of the administrators in such cases is more likely to be diversified than that of a single central bureaucracy and their performance is thus subject to at least some political manipulation by the local constituency.

Decentralization has sometimes been

achieved by straight delegation of some of the functions from a national government to autonomous state or province units (as in the case of India and Pakistan, which in turn then usually adopted centralized administrative procedures); sometimes by creating special organs staffed by career civil servants on temporary duty (as was the case in Italy); and sometimes by splitting up the functions among different specialized agencies and using various field offices of the central or local governments (as in Yugoslavia, Ecuador, and presumably now in Vietnam under Thieu).

From the peasant's point of view, the results of this somewhat more flexible, less self-contained administrative approach of "decentralization" have been more satisfactory: two-thirds of the countries taking this approach produced some improvement in tenure security (East—but not West—Pakistan, Yugoslavia, Italy, and Ecuador), and in two cases peasant income was probably increased as a result of the reform (again in East, but not West, Pakistan, and in Yugoslavia). The Thieu regime in Vietnam, which is just beginning its program, may also succeed in improving these two aspects of rural economic life. In these cases, too, the bureaucracy tended to strengthen its political position through the exercise of new administrative authority, but decentralization at least reduced somewhat the concentration of new bureaucratic power. The existence of the competing bureaucracies engaged in a decentralized program may permit the individual citizen to manipulate them somewhat more than he can when dealing with a remote, unitary civil service. (See Appendix II.)

C. The third group of countries made less use of any professional bureaucracy, preferring to bypass it and assign permanent authority over one or more administrative aspects of land reform to local political leaders. The expectation was that local leaders would direct their loyalty toward their own constituents or to traditional groups rather than to a superior hierarchy of officialdom. This "devolvement" of authority would relieve the bureaucracy of the necessity of engaging in detailed fact-finding expeditions and of the responsibility for initiating local actions on behalf of the less privileged majority of tenants, small freeholders, or landless laborers, though this does not necessarily shield the bureaucracy from all local involvement.

A variety of approaches have served the purposes of "devolvement." Korea, for example, followed village precedents and procedures in making land allocations, letting traditional leaders set the pace of reform; but in Taiwan, using a procedure applied in Japan a few years before, newly elected representatives of landlords, tenants, and owner-farmers had to give initial approval to all proposed adjustments in ownership and classification of land. Iran, with limited administrative capabilities, used its central bureaucracy to issue official titles, but only on authorization from local landlord-tenant groups; and even then all boundaries had to be confirmed by adjoining land users and the testimony of village elders. Bolivia allowed individuals and peasant unions to file claims with the local agrarian judge, whose opinion was binding until reviewed by the central agrarian reform agency. Venezuela settled most of its land reform issues on the basis of petitions from local *syndicatos*. Mexico and Guatemala adopted procedures whereby peasants initiated reform proposals, which various local land committees then passed along to national or regional authority for action. In the case of Mexico and Bolivia, this decision usually ratified revolutionary peasant initiatives that had already begun to take place. Chile turned large private holdings over to government ownership, under the management of former tenants, with the provision that a formal election be conducted after five years to determine whether to convert the property to sub-divided private holdings or to continue with the collective operation. In each of these situations an important element of authority was officially transferred down to local levels.

In each instance where "devolvement" took place (Bolivia, Venezuela, Iran, Mexico, Japan, Taiwan, North Vietnam, Korea, Chile, and Guatemala), the peasant farmers enjoyed clearer security rights as a result of land reform; they increased their political power in eight of the ten cases (Bolivia, Mexico, Venezuela, Japan, Taiwan, Korea, Chile, and Guatemala), and their income in eight (Bolivia, Iran, Venezuela, Mexico, Japan, Taiwan, Chile, and Korea). In a few cases the operation was a success but the doctor died: the attack on landlord power led to a counterrevolutionary coup in Guatemala after only two years; in other cases (Iran, for example) the reforms were abandoned or slowed because of political opposition; and in North Vietnam land redistribution was supplanted by collectivization systems on the communist model. But there is no evidence that devolvement is inherently de-stabilizing; indeed, most regimes would doubtless consider it a potential source of support. (See Appendix III.)

Any system of devolvement runs the risk of capture by prestigious local landlords or other notables, but the experience in these countries suggests that this possibility can be countered. Among these 25 countries, in two cases there was no significant landlord class at the time of the reform (Venezuela and Yugoslavia); in three others, most had left their holdings before land reform was undertaken (Algeria, North Vietnam, and Thieu's South Vietnam); and in four the class had already been weakened by internal revolution or military restraint (Bolivia, Mexico, Egypt, and Ecuador). In these cases, no significant threat of local takeover occurred, and neither the administrative decisions regarding land reform nor the outcomes were predetermined by local political forces.

In the majority of our land reforms, however, the landlords were still in possession of their property, and the government therefore had to consider whether and how to counter their influence in support of the reforms. Legislative and administrative controls were introduced for this purpose in ten cases (India, Iran, Japan, Iraq, Chile, South Korea, East and West Pakistan, Taiwan, and Italy); yet in six other cases the landlords were not really weakened except by the passage of time (Philippines, Indonesia, Brazil, Guatemala, Diem's Vietnam, and Colombia). It is significant that devolvement could succeed in both of these situations, regardless of whether or not the landlords had been weakened before land reform took place. As might be expected, centralized processes produced "better" social outputs when there was no landlord class around to hamper the bureaucracy's activities, but devolvement was superior to other administrative procedures in both situations (Table I).[8]

TABLE I

EFFECT OF LANDLORDS' STRENGTH AND ADMINISTRATIVE PROCESS
ON LAND REFORM OUTCOMES

Strength of Landlords	Administrative Process		Peasant Benefits Produced *	Total Possible Benefits	"Batting Average" †
N		N		(N × 3)	
Previously weakened (9)	Centralized	(2)	2	6	.333 ⎫
	Decentralized	(3)	2	9	.222 ⎬ .518
	Devolved	(4)	10	12	.833 ⎭
			14	27	
Not previously weakened (16)	Centralized	(7)	2	21	.095 ⎫
	Decentralized	(3)	2	9	.222 ⎬ .417
	Devolved	(6)	16	18	.888 ⎭
			20	48	

* As summarized in Appendices I, II, and III.
† See note 8 for method of calculation.

One method of protecting local officials engaged in land reform was to pit the national civil servants against local landlords. For example, Japan provided legal and administrative prods to the local committees it established, and used its bureaucratic resources to insure that the intended balance of village forces (5 tenants, 3 landlords, and 2 owner-operators in each committee) was preserved; in Taiwan, the Joint Commission on Rural Reconstruction made similar provisions and placed its technical resources at the disposition of peasant-dominated Farmer Associations; the land reform cadres in North Vietnam served as agents of the New Land Reform Committees; South Korea officials expressed the government's sponsorship of land reform during a period of demoralization of the conservative local leadership; in Guatemala peasant claims were reviewed by a local agrarian committee whose membership was kept sympathetic by the government; in Chile the government expropriated the land quickly enough to reduce the economic power base of the landlords; and even in Iran the bureaucracy could be used to offset the power and influence of local landlords.

In some cases political safeguards also protected the peasants. Local mobilization by political parties took place in Venezuela, Mexico, and Bolivia, and the last vestiges of opposition were politically eliminated in North Vietnam as the redistribution took place. Devolvement has not meant abstention of the central governments. It has required a new posture of administrative and political resources deployed to encourage local popular initiatives. Where the local officials engaged in land reform activities are subject to reelection, recall, or subsequent review of their program decisions, it appears, devolvement can contribute to the development of local self-governing capabilities.[9]

It must surely be disconcerting to advocates of land reform to learn from this survey of the social and political consequences in 25 countries that land reform succeeded in improving peasant security of tenure in only 16 cases, peasant income in only 11, and peasants' political power in only 9; indeed, in 9 of the cases, land reform conferred none of these benefits— while in 15, it increased the bureaucracy's political power. The results take on an entirely different complexion, however, when the intervening variable of administrative process is taken into account, as in Table II (see Appendices for details).

TABLE II

LAND REFORM OUTCOMES AND ADMINISTRATIVE PROCESSES
(PERCENTAGES)

Administrative Processes	Peasants Increased Income	Peasants Increased Political Power	Peasants Increased Tenure Security	Bureaucrats Increased Political Power
Centralized	11	11	22	100
Decentralized	33.3	0	66.6	100
Devolved	80	80	100	10

III

The administrative systems used in these 25 land reforms do not appear to be a mere reflection of other political or social circumstances. Neither the ideology of the governmental leaders nor the type of regime determines the decision to use centralized, decentralized, or devolved administrative systems in carrying out these programs. Some "conservative" governments [10] that undertook land reform were prepared to use a process of devolvement (Taiwan and Korea, for example); while other governments, equally conservative, made use of various special or decentralized bureaucracies (Ecuador and Pakistan, for example); and still others preferred to use central ministerial bureaucracies (Vietnam under Diem, Colombia, and the Philippines). Regimes at the opposite end of the spectrum, reflecting "democratic and revolutionary" ideologies, also employed all three administrative systems: Guatemala, North Vietnam, and Bolivia used devolvement; Yugoslavia and Indonesia decentralized the operation; and Iraq, Algeria, and the UAR followed conventional processes of bureaucratic centralization. "Middleclass modernizing" or "liberal" regimes, whose land reforms have had the least successes in terms of our equity outcomes, have also made use of all three forms of administration: most of the Indian states used their own central ministries; Italy followed a special decentralized approach; and Chile devolved decision-making responsibility on tenant committees.

Similarly, all three of the conventional classifications of regime types represented in our sample made use of the various administrative systems of land reform with no apparent discrimination on constitutional grounds. Among the twelve regimes conventionally classified as conservative, three used a centralized pattern of administration and achieved the predictably poor results; four decentralized the operation, with only marginal benefits accruing to the peasants; while five were able to devolve at least part of these responsibilities to local authority and produce favorable results for the peasants. There were also eleven *radical* or *revolutionary* regimes in our study, of which five used the central bureaucracy, with poor results; one decentralized and conferred noticeable peasant benefits in the process; while five devolved at least some of these responsibilities and achieved good results. Among the seven *liberal* regimes

involved, three centralized the operation, one decentralized it with negligible effect on peasant welfare, and three devolved responsibilities with excellent results. The prospects for devolvement seem to be about equal as among conservative, radical-revolutionary, and liberal regimes—about half in each case—but when devolvement does take place, the outcomes are better in the liberal regimes. (See Table III.) This fact may justify the somewhat greater effort needed in such cases to get land reform started. In any case, it provides grounds for revising the pessimistic views prevailing among political scientists regarding the prospects of land reform in democratic regimes.

TABLE III

REGIME TYPE, ADMINISTRATIVE PROCESS, AND OUTCOME

Type of Regime	Administrative Process		Total Peasant Benefits	"Batting Average"	
Conservative (11)	Centralized	(3)	1	.111	
	Decentralized	(3)	2+	.222	.515
	Devolved	(5)	14	.955	
Radical-Revolutionary (11)	Centralized	(5)	3	.200	
	Decentralized	(1)	2	.666	.485
	Devolved	(5)	11	.733	
Liberal (7)	Centralized	(3)	0	0	
	Decentralized	(1)	0	0	.429
	Devolved	(3)	9	1.000	

Characteristics of political leadership might prove a more powerful predictor of administrative choice and outcome than regimes types, but these characteristics are difficult to classify systematically. One approach would be to classify the land reform programs themselves according to the reasons for their adoption. On the basis of this classification, some conclusions might be drawn regarding the seriousness of purpose on the part of the leadership, assuming that they understood the implications of their choice. But this analysis, too, shows that administration is an independent variable.

Proponents of land reform offer four major political justifications for action. The first reason is to develop rural political support for a faltering or newly established regime or party: conditions which led to programs of the Thieu government in Vietnam

and in Mexico, Egypt, India, Pakistan, Brazil, Chile, Guatemala, Bolivia, Ecuador, Yugoslavia, and Iraq. The second is to anticipate or forestall possible revolution: the case offered in the Philippines, Taiwan, and South Vietnam under Diem. The third reason is to eliminate or weaken political opposition, whether, as in Iran, to counterbalance landlords whose power the Shah distrusted, or, as in Japan, South Korea, and Italy, to outmaneuver a communist opposition. The final reason is ideological purity and consistency: among our countries, Indonesia, Algeria, and North Vietnam undertook land reforms as part of a larger revolution. None of these reasons gives a complete explanation. Land reform is a major political venture, if undertaken seriously, and it may therefore be presumed to relate in most cases to other, more obscure, characteristics of political leadership.

So far as can be judged from the evidence presented in the case studies, regimes that were using land reform to weaken their political opposition were relatively more inclined to devolve responsibilities to local authorities than were other regimes. Whether this was because they found it easier or judged it more efficacious we cannot say from the data. Such regimes on the whole provided more benefits to their peasantries, though this may be a consequence more of the administrative means employed than of the regime's political strategy (means and strategy are presumably not unrelated, however). Unfortunately, there are not enough data to enable us to assess the outcome of land reform motivated by radical ideological objectives. What data we do have suggest that the means employed in land reform affect outcomes more profoundly than the reasons for which it is undertaken. (See Table IV.)

TABLE IV

REASONS FOR ADOPTING LAND REFORM, ADMINISTRATIVE PROCESS,
AND OUTCOMES

Reason	Administrative Process		Total Peasant Benefits	"Batting Average"	
Develop support (13)	Centralized	(4)	2	.166	
	Decentralized	(5)	4	.200	.436
	Devolved	(4)	11	.916	
Forestall revolution (3)	Centralized	(2)	1	.166	
	Decentralized	(0)	—	—	.444
	Devolved	(1)	3	1.000	
Weaken opposition (4)	Centralized	(0)	—	—	
	Decentralized	(1)	0	0	.666
	Devolved	(3)	8	.888	

Economic preconditions to land reform may indicate the urgency of government action. In our sample, they also predicted to some extent the administrative choices involved in land reforms, and hence their social outputs. One index of urgency is the extent of inequality of land distribution; another is the proportion of the labor force employed in agriculture. Presumably when both indicators are high, a nation is vulnerable to serious rural unrest. In order to test the relationships, eighteen of the countries examined here (for the other seven, no adequate data were available) were ranked in order of their presumed "vulnerability" to agrarian unrest. The "vulnerability index" was measured by the extent of cumulative inequality of land ownership (Gini index), plus the proportion of the population engaged in agriculture (Appendix IV), after both raw figures were expressed in standard scores to reduce distortions.

Of the six "most vulnerable" countries on this scale, four chose the route of devolvement. Yugoslavia, at the bottom of the vulnerability ranking, used decentralized instruments, while the Philippines, next to it, chose centralization. And at the middle levels of vulnerability, the options seemed open. No clear pattern emerges except the familiar one of scattered administrative choices with predictable social outcomes (see Table V). It may be significant that so many of the most "vulnerable" countries chose to devolve land reform operations.

Unfortunately none of the evidence now available explains this relationship. Certainly it is not explained by regime types or the political reasons given for undertaking land reforms, which seem randomly distributed among our three "vulnerability" classes. Vulnerability to rural unrest on the basis of land tenure patterns may help explain why political leaders in these situations chose to involve local leaders in the administration of land reform. But it is more significant that the administrative device they chose to use to bring about such involvement is a better predictor of social outcomes than mere "vulnerability" to rural unrest.

TABLE V

VULNERABILITY TO UNREST, ADMINISTRATIVE PROCESS, AND OUTCOME

Vulnerability	Administrative Process		Total Peasant Benefits	"Batting Average"	
Most vulnerable (6)	Centralized	(2)	0	0	
	Decentralized	(0)	0	0	.555
	Devolved	(4)	10	.833	
Moderately vulnerable (6)	Centralized	(4)	3	.250	
	Decentralized	(1)	0	0	.333
	Devolved	(1)	3	1.000	
Least vulnerable (6)	Centralized	(1)	0	0	
	Decentralized	(4)	4	.333	.388
	Devolved	(1)	3	1.000	

Another possibility is that some kind of "political will" to reform explains the successful outcome of such programs. But "political will" cannot be measured except in terms of actual effort.[11] Hung-chao Tai has made an interesting effort to segregate countries according to the "willingness and readiness of the political elite to mobilize all available resources to carry out a reform program" implying a definition of political will that seems to bear some relation to the process variable as suggested here.[12] Mexico, Taiwan, and Iran, for example, whose will he classified as "strong," used various types of devolvement, but the UAR, which he placed in the same class, used a centralized process with predictably less "success" than the others possessing the necessary will. Of the "weak" countries on his scale of political will, Colombia, the Philippines, and the Indian states used centralized processes, again with little "success" as far as peasants are concerned. Pakistan decentralized at least some land reform procedures and achieved satisfactory results in the Eastern province but not in the West. And none of the "weak-willed" countries tried devolvement. Thus Tai's effort to identify political will helps to explain the outcome of land reform programs, but like the vulnerability index, it becomes a better predictor of outputs when "will" is expressed in the choice of administrative process.

It is also possible that the choice of process is related to pre-existing administrative traditions or preferences. But the only consistent effort to classify countries as "centralized" versus "local" in administrative tradition fails to produce satisfactory predictions of the patterns these countries actually used in administering their land reforms. Adelman and Morris[13] indicate that seven of the countries in this study had highly centralized administrative traditions. Four of them used centralized means in carrying out land reform (Algeria, Iraq, UAR, and Indonesia), but two devolved responsibility (Iran and Guatemala) and one (Pakistan) used decentralized techniques. The same authorities report that eight of the countries on our list had decentralized or local governmental units which had, or were gaining, significant political power; and of these, five devolved land reform authority (Bolivia, Chile, Japan, Venezuela, and Mexico), and three treated the operation as a central responsibility (Brazil, Colombia, and the Philippines).

Unfortunately, this index does not separate local self-government tradition from decentralized administration. India, for example, is also listed in the second ("local") category, but its constitution automatically decentralized land reform operations. Thus India relied on state governments which were themselves actually strongly centralized administrative systems. In the end, therefore, land reform in the Indian states was a strongly centralized operation, although Adelman and Morris correctly list India among the countries with a growing potential in local self-government. What is needed to test this precondition is a new index of local self-government tradition.

IV

Conclusions can be drawn from this examination in two distinct areas: suggestions for policy makers dealing with land reforms and other problems of development administration, and suggestions for further research on the social outputs of administrative systems.

Perhaps the first policy question is whether to undertake land reform at all. Many agricultural experts point out that reforms in land ownership alone are unlikely to produce increases in *productivity*. But the findings of this study suggest that with devolvement it is more likely to increase *peasant income* than are the combinations of technical aid and credit institutions ("agrarian reform"). Extensive and effective programs of agrarian reform occurred in sixteen of the land reform cases which we have covered (Philippines, UAR, Algeria, Brazil, Colombia, Indian States, East and West Pakistan, Yugoslavia, Italy, Vietnam (1967), Iran, Venezuela, Japan, Taiwan, and Chile). Of these sixteen cases, only eight resulted in improved peasant income—not a very impressive showing for the effort involved.

Even more significantly, in those countries where substantial agrarian reform took place, the peasant income increased in only one of the six countries that used centralized means of conducting land reform, and in only two of the five decentralized cases, but in all of the five devolved cases. Again, among countries using devolved processes of achieving land reform, there were eight in which peasant income definitely improved, although only five of the countries had introduced significant agrarian programs. There were two of our countries which showed an increase in peasant income without substantial agrarian reform, and both had implemented land reform through devolvement.

Thus if the objective is greater distributive justice through income increases among small farmers, rather than general agricultural productivity increases, programs of devolved land reform show a better record than programs of new agrarian services. Of course there is no reason to assume that both goals could not be served if both types of programs—devolved land reform and new services and technical supports to agriculture—were undertaken.

A second question is whether local institutions have the capacity ("are ready") to assume the sustained responsibilities represented by land reform operations. No clear answer appears from the data presented here, but speculation as to the reasons for success of devolvement may suggest an indirect answer. Devolvement seems to work because of a combination of the following factors that come with public participation in program implementation: (a) easier access to knowledge, (b) more powerful motivations, (c) better communications, and (d) increased community solidarity.

Administratively, the making of decisions about land reform is an easier process when the detailed knowledge necessary for action is already available to decision-makers, and extensive documentation, information standardization, and data processing do not have to be installed in order to act. It is not difficult to imagine what the consequences would be, for example, if all land transfers and title information in the United States had to be gathered in Washington, and final decisions as to title rights had to be made by a central bureaucracy rather than by local jurisdictions.

The immediate purposes of land reform in the Third World do not require the vast documentation used to accomplish title deeds and contracts in the United States, since land matters are already public information carried about in the heads of landlords, tenants, and village notables in the minutest detail. When the Diem government tried to carry out a land reform program that would conform to Western standards in documentation and geodetic technology, it succeeded in expropriating about 453,000 hectares of rice land and purchasing about 230,000 hectares of former French lands from 2,000 large landowners and 450 Frenchmen in 1954, but it could redistribute only about a third of these to small farmers. Still more significantly, what they could not distribute could easily be managed under rental agreements with the villages, which in turn arranged for the farming of small plots.[14]

The bureaucratic system used by the Diem administration "actually prevented most provincial and district officials from developing a sound understanding of rural conditions." This is not a condition exclusive to Vietnam: bureaucratic performance there was "no worse than those of some other Southeast Asian states emerging from colonialism." [15] The principles of work simplification call for the assignment of administrative decisions to those who have the access to information necessary to make them, when possible. Devolvement to local authority simply reduces the number of people who have to gain access to local knowledge and postpones the need for converting this information into Western-style standards of legal and administrative detail. In terms of social justice, speed is more important than elegance for successful land reform.

A second factor explaining the successful outcome of devolvement is associated with the motivation or volition of the respective administrative actors involved. If, as Weber argues, a bureaucracy is characteristically means-oriented, it is the end result that motivates the villagers who want access to the promised lands. No doubt an administrative rewards system can be designed to convert a centralized bureaucracy into an instrument of change, although organizational interests plus the tradition of neutrality make it difficult to commit bureaucracies to novel programs involving social problems.[16] But such reforms are not easily accomplished. The mechanics of administrative reorganization are not well enough understood to insure that any given overhaul will necessarily bring about desired changes in motivation.

Communicating agricultural goals and techniques to farmers is a task difficult to undertake through the use of central bureaucracies, especially when the desired citizen responses involve the expenditure of their personal capital and labor. A natural suspicion exists between farmers and civil servants in many parts of the world, where government agents of all kinds are regarded as the equivalents of policemen and tax collectors rather than as servants of the people. For their part, professional civil servants tend to regard farmers as indolent, tradition-ridden amateurs: a perception which encourages them to resort to the very tactics that confirm the popular suspicion of bureaucrats. Thus the land reform program of the Diem regime in Vietnam did not produce the loyalty that the president had expected. Administrative threats were no more effective in inducing desired innovative behavior on the part of peasants than were the presidential exhortations from Saigon.

A fourth range of speculations concerning the outcomes of devolvement arises from the psychological principle that participation in a government program improves both public understanding of its purposes and loyalty to its processes. Participation reinforces the sense of citizen "efficacy." It also encourages individuals to make better use of the resources made available by the government. Devolvement of land reform operations thus gives substance to local government, converting its activities from structural formalities to common efforts at community betterment. The expected result is a spiraling citizen interest, and presumably a greater commitment to the political process by which government enters into developmental activities.[17]

A more precise analysis of these relationships would serve little purpose here. Doubtless it would be possible to reconstruct the circumstances under which the land reforms we have reviewed above took place, in order to ascertain the extent to which these considerations were present. But even in the absence of such knowledge, it seems clear that decisions regarding the administration of a land reform can take place independently of other objectively definable political circumstances, and that a fairly wide range of choice lies open to development planners.

The research issues raised by this study begin with the evidence available to examine these questions further. The social output indicators used here are crude and impressionistic; although they represent composite views developed in standardized official reports, they lack the precision and richness that would be possible if such second-stage consequences of land reform were made the subject of systematic inquiry. The relationships established here could be much more rigorously explored, using such powerful tools as multi-variate analysis, if the frequency, intensity, and duration of the equity outputs were known.

Much needs to be known as well about the details of a system of devolvement used in various cases since it is likely that the four administrative functions we have examined are not equally susceptible to devolvement or equally important influences on the social outcome. There may also be significant variations in the effectiveness of different organizational devices used for devolvement under various circumstances. Finally, it would be helpful to know more about the political processes by which the administrative systems were chosen in the 25 countries studied here: for example, whether there was any recognition of their respective social benefit potentials, whether administrative alternatives were proposed or considered, and whether any specific administrative traditions served as preconditions to the choice of devolvement.

It would be still more useful if we could extend these findings regarding land reforms to other social and developmental programs to see whether they also fare better using various forms of devolvement.[18] A basic hypothesis might be that interaction between administrative process and administrative effectiveness is closest in programs where success depends upon specific voluntary cooperative behavior of citizens. Developmental programs requiring little action by citizens are obviously easier to manage by administrative action than those depending on sustained or repeated citizen commitment.

Counterparts to devolved land reform operations may well exist in other developing sectors, such as industrialization, the modernization of educational opportuni-

ties, and the improvement of public health standards. Water-use regulation in tertiary irrigation systems would appear to be an obvious candidate for routine, sustained reliance upon local initiatives, coordinated on the appropriate regional basis; and devolvement of educational and service programs in family planning might also produce greater administrative effectiveness in dealing with problems of custom and motivation. But such arguments ultimately rest on grounds of rational efficiency or improved bureaucratic routines, or even on issues of competitive organizational politics, rather than on social equity consequences.

The land reform example might be more suitably applied in other programs designed to confer public benefits on a specific client group, especially those involving the opportunity for self-advancement, such as education, local resource development, or environmental improvement. As in the case of land reform, the problem would be to find how various reciprocal and reinforcing functions and responsibilities may be divided among different bureaucratic and client groups to maximize designated social outputs of a program.

APPENDIX I

STATUS VARIABLES AND POLITICAL AND ECONOMIC OUTCOMES OF LAND REFORM
UNDER CENTRALIZED PROCESSES

Country	Type of Regime (a)	Vulnerability Index Rank (b)	Improved Tenure Security	Improved Peasant Income	Increased Peasant Political Power	Increased Bureaucratic Power
Vietnam (1956–62)	1	7	+	−	−	+
Philippines (1903–65)	1–3	14	− (c)	−	−	+
UAR (1952–70)	2	8 (d)	+	+	−	+
Indonesia (1960–68)	2	−	−	−	+	+
Iraq (1958–70)	2	1	−	−	−	+
Algeria (1963–70)	2	−	(e)	−	−	+
Colombia (1961–70)	1–3	9	−	−	−	+
Brazil (1964–70)	2	6	−	−	−	+
Indian States (1950–61)	3	11	−	−	−	+
9 cases	Extremes	Extremes	2	1	1	9

(a) Lyman-French Index, p. 10a: 1 = Conservative; 2 = Radical Democratic or Revolutionary Appeal; 3 = Modernizing Middle Class
(b) See Appendix IV   (c) See note 2   (d) Egypt only   (e) Collectivized

APPENDIX II

Status Variables and Political and Economic Outcomes of Land Reform Under Decentralized Processes

Country	Type of Regime (a)	Vulnerability Index Rank (b)	Improved Tenure Security	Improved Peasant Income	Increased Peasant Political Power	Increased Bureau- cratic Power
East Pakistan	1	15	+	+	−	+
West Pakistan (1958–61)	1	13	−	−	−	+
Yugoslavia (1919–53)	2	16	+	+	−	+
Italy (1945–70)	3 (d)	18	+	−	−	+
Ecuador (1964–66)	1	10	+	−	−	+
Vietnam (1967–70)	1	—	(c)	(c)	(c)	(c)
6 cases	Mixed	Mixed	4	2	0	6

(a) See Appendix I   (b) See Appendix IV   (c) Undetermined as yet   (d) Supplied by author

APPENDIX III

Status Variables and Political and Economic Outcomes of Land Reform Using Devolvement Processes

Country	Type of Regime (a)	Vulnerability Index Rank (b)	Improved Tenure Security	Improved Peasant Income	Increased Peasant Political Power	Increased Bureau- cratic Power
Bolivia (1953–70)	2	2	+	+	+	−
Iran (1962–70)	1–2	5	+	+	−	+?
Mexico (1915–42)	2–3	4	+	+	+	−
Japan (1946–70)	1–3		+	+	+	−
Taiwan (1949–70)	1		+	+	+	−
North Vietnam (1953–56)	2		+	?	?	−
South Korea (1949–70)	1		+	+	+	−
Guatemala (1952–54)	2	3	+	?	+	−
Venezuela (1960–70)	1	12	+	+	+	−
Chile (1965–70)	3	17	+	+	+	−
10 cases	Mixed	Extremes	10	8	8	0

(a) See Appendix I   (b) See Appendix IV

APPENDIX IV

LAND DISTRIBUTION AND AGRICULTURAL WORK FORCE AS INDICATORS OF
VULNERABILITY TO AGRARIAN UNREST

Country	1 Gini Index of Inequality of Land Ownership in Standard Score	2 Proportion of Labor Force in Agriculture in Standard Score	3 Vulnerability Index (a)	4 Rank Order
Iraq	.761 (1958)	1.349 (1950)	2.110	1
Bolivia	1.114 (1950)	.750 (1950)	1.864	2
Guatemala	.630 (1950)	.484 (1950)	1.114	3
Mexico	1.251 (1930) (d)	−.181 (1958)	1.070	4
Iran	−.672 (1960) (d)	1.282 (1953)	.610	5
Brazil	.488 (1950)	.018 (1950)	.506	6
South Vietnam	−.542 (1935)	.950 (b)	.408	7
Colombia	.562 (1954)	−.381 (1951)	.181	8
Ecuador	.655 (1954)	−.514 (1961)	.141	9
UAR	−.114 (1949)	.218 (1947)	.104	10
India	−.796 (1955)	.684 (1961)	−.112	11
Venezuela	.934 (1956)	−1.378 (1950)	−.444	12
West Pakistan	−.921 (1960)	.285 (c) (1955)	−.636	13
Chile	1.114 (1936)	−2.044 (1952)	−.930	14
East Pakistan	−1.541 (1960)	.285 (c)	−1.256	15
Italy	.803 (1946)	−2.110 (1960)	−1.307	16
Philippines	−1.206 (1948)	−.115 (1959)	−1.321	17
Yugoslavia	−1.994 (1950)	.418 (1953)	−1.576	18

SOURCE: Bruce Russett, *et al*, WORLD HANDBOOK OF POLITICAL AND SOCIAL IN-
DICATORS (New Haven: Yale University Press, 1964), pp. 239–240 and 177–178, and Bruce
Russett, "Inequality and Instability: The Relation of Land Tenure to Politics" in WORLD
POLITICS, No. 3, April 1964. These indices are converted to standard scores.
(a) Column 1 plus column 2
(b) Estimated from S. P. Huntington, POLITICAL ORDER IN CHANGING SOCIETIES
(New Haven: Yale University Press, 1968), Table 6.2
(c) Figure undifferentiated between East and West Pakistan
(d) Estimated from country studies

1. Unless otherwise indicated, data for the analysis that follows come from thirty country studies on the history and effects of land reform prepared for the Spring Review, Agency for International Development, Washington, D.C., June 2–4, 1970. The studies used here are: Clark, Ronald (Bolivia); Dovring, Folke (Mexico); Dovring, Folke (Yugoslavia); Elkinton, Charles (East and West Pakistan); Felstehausen, Herman (Colombia); Foster, Phillips (Algeria); Gayoso, Antonio (Guatemala); Koo, Y. O. (Taiwan); Land Reform Office, Vietnam Bureau, AID (South Vietnam, 2 reforms); McEntire, Davis (Italy); Murrow, R., and K. Sherper (South Korea); Nixon, Jack (Ecuador); Platt, Kenneth (Iran); Platt, Kenneth (UAR); Thiesenhusen, W. C. (Chile); Treakle, Charles (Iraq); USAID/ Brazil (Brazil, the North East); USAID/Philippines (Philippines); Utrecht, E. (Indonesia); Voelkner, Harold (Japan); White, Christine

(North Vietnam); Wing, Harry, Jr. (Venezuela); Wunderlich, Gene (India). Although the use of these reports gives a certain consistency to the judgments presented here, it is possible, since they were prepared for a conference on land reform, that in a few cases the beneficial outcomes may be overstated. Few country studies on administrative processes are available. But see Lawrence I. Hewes, Jr., *Japan: Land and Men* (Ames: Iowa State Univ. Press, 1955) and Dwight B. Heath, Charles J. Erasmus, and Hans C. Buechter, *Land Reform and Social Revolution in Bolivia* (N.Y.: Praeger, 1969) for exceptions.

2. These findings are not incontestable in certain cases. Alex Lachman believes that title security was improved for peasants in the Philippines. (See his paper, "What is Land Reform?" Washington, D.C., Spring Review, June 1970, Table I.) Economic benefits may

be mixed, as appears to be the case in Venezuela where it is reported that the economic position of approximately ⅓ of the peasants was unchanged, about ⅓ gained economic benefits from land reform, and ⅓ suffered financially after the reform. Classification of administrative processes also is not unambiguous. After some hesitance I assigned Venezuela to the "devolvement" list, which departs from the impression conveyed in the USAID country paper. Evidence for this classification is supplied by John Powell, "Agrarian Reform or Agrarian Revolution in Venezuela?" in Arpad Von Lazar and B. Kaufman, *Reform and Revolution, Readings in Latin American Politics* (Boston: Allen & Bacon, 1969).

3. Ralph Braibanti, "Introduction," and Hugh Tinker, "Structure of the British Imperial Heritage," in Ralph Braibanti, ed., *Asian Bureaucratic Systems in the British Imperial Tradition* (Durham: Duke Univ. Press, 1966).

4. Fred W. Riggs, "Bureaucrats and Political Development: A Paradoxical View," in Joseph LaPalombara, ed., *Bureaucracy and Political Development* (Princeton Univ. Press, 1963); and his *Administration in Developing Countries: The Theory of Prismatic Society* (Boston: Houghton Mifflin, 1964).

5. Joseph S. Nye, "Corruption and Political Development: A Cost-Benefit Analysis," *American Political Science Review*, June 1967.

6. A bureaucracy's participation in important reforms automatically gives it superior access to information about land, the technology of land distribution, opportunity for corruption, the privilege of assigning benefits to potentially important individuals and institutions, and close access to political leaders concerned with land as a source of wealth and power. An indication of any of these consequences led to the classification used in Appendix I, II, or III, of "increased bureaucratic power" resulting from the land reform. For a general discussion, cf. Milton J. Esman, "The Politics of Development Administration" in J. D. Montgomery and William Siffin, eds., *Approaches to Development: Politics, Administration, and Change* (N.Y.: McGraw-Hill, 1966).

7. John D. Montgomery, "Sources of Bureaucratic Reform: A Typology of Power and Purpose," in Ralph Braibanti, ed., *Political and Administrative Development* (Durham, N.C.: Duke Univ. Press, 1969).

8. In the scoring of Tables I, II, III, and IV, only peasant benefits were counted. (I.e., bureaucratic strengthening, though potentially harmful to peasants, was not considered "negative" because politics is not a zero-sum game.) Tables do not necessarily have the same N, since data in all cases could not be supplied from existing sources. Each incidence reported of improvement in peasant *security*, *income* and/or *political power* was tallied as

a benefit. "Batting averages" represent the total of benefits reported as a percentage of total possible benefits; this latter number is three times the number of cases in the category since security, income, *and* political power could have been enhanced in each case. In the few cases in the tables where regimes were classified under two categories (see n. 10), the results were scored in each.

9. Harold Voelkner and Jerome T. French consider local political participation as one of several preconditions to successful land reform. *A Dynamic Model for Land Reform Analysis and Public Policy Formulation* (Washington: AID, 1970, processed). Fig. D.

10. To reduce the possibility of bias in regime classification, I have used a three-fold classification taken from Princeton Lyman and Jerome French, *Political Results of Land Reform* (Washington: AID, June 1970). I have collapsed two of their subcategories into their major classes.

11. John D. Montgomery and Stephen A. Marglin, "Measuring the Extent of Governmental Effort in Agriculture: An Approach to the 'Will to Develop,'" in David Hapgood, ed., *Policies for Promoting Agricultural Development* (Cambridge: Center for International Studies, MIT, 1965) and *Indian Administrative Review*, Jan./March, 1969.

12. Hung-chao Tai, *Land Reform in the Developing Countries: Tenure Defects and Political Responses* (Cambridge: Center for International Affairs, Harvard, 1967, processed).

13. Irma Adelman and Cynthia Morris, *Society, Politics and Economic Development, A Quantitative Approach* (Baltimore: Johns Hopkins Univ. Press, 1967), p. 59.

14. Macdonald Salter, "Land Reform in South Vietnam," *Asian Survey*, Vol. 10, No. 8, August 1970, pp. 726–7.

15. John Donnell, "Expanding Political Participation—The Long Haul from Villagism to Nationalism," *Asian Survey*, Vol. 10, No. 8, August 1970, p. 92.

16. Herbert Kaufman, "Administrative Decentralization and Political Power," *Public Administration Review*, 1969: I, 8.

17. My earlier article, "Land Reform as a Means to Political Development in Vietnam," *Orbis*, Spring, 1968 gives an empirical analysis of the political effects and requirements of land reform in that country. It was this study that started my thinking about the comparative analysis presented here.

18. Significant comparative studies relating organization to environment have already been undertaken in industry. An excellent example is Paul R. Lawrence and Jay W. Lorsch, *Organization and Environment, Managing Differentiation and Integration* (Boston: Division of Research, Graduate School of Business Administration, Harvard University, 1967).

CORRUPTION AND POLITICAL DEVELOPMENT
A Cost-Benefit Analysis

J. S. NYE

Harvard University

Private Vices by the dextrous Management of a skilled Politician may be turned into Publick Benefits.   BERNARD MANDEVILLE, 1714

THE STUDY OF CORRUPTION IN
LESS DEVELOPED COUNTRIES

Corruption, some say, is endemic in all governments.[1] Yet it has received remarkably little attention from students of government. Not only is the study of corruption prone to moralism, but it involves one of those aspects of government in which the interests of the politician and the political scientist are likely to conflict. It would probably be rather difficult to obtain (by honest means) a visa to a developing country which is to be the subject of a corruption study.

One of the first charges levelled at the previous regime by the leaders of the coup in the less developed country is "corruption." And generally the charge is accurate. One type of reaction to this among observers is highly moralistic and tends to see corruption as evil. "Throughout the fabric of public life in newly independent States," we are told in a recent work on the subject, "runs the scarlet thread of bribery and corruption . . ." which is like a weed suffocating better plants. Another description of new states informs us that "corruption and nepotism rot good intentions and retard progressive policies." [2]

Others have reacted against this moralistic approach and warn us that we must beware of basing our beliefs about the cause of coups on post-coup rationalizations, and also of judging the social consequences of an act from the motives of the individuals performing it.[3] Under some circumstances Mandeville is right that private vice can cause public benefit. Corruption has probably been, on balance, a positive factor in both Russian and American economic development. At least two very

important aspects of British and American political development—the establishment of the cabinet system in the 18th century and the national integration of millions of immigrants in the 19th century—were based in part on corruption.

As for corruption and stability, an anthropologist has suggested that periodic scandals can sometimes "lead to the affirmation of general principles about how the country should be run, as if there were not posed impossible reconciliations of different interests. These inquiries may not alter what actually happens, but they affirm an ideal condition of unity and justice." [4] However, the "revisionists" who echo Mandeville's aphorism often underestimate tastes for moralism—concern for worthiness of causes as well as utilitarian consequences of behavior. There is always the danger for a corrupt system that someone will question what it profits to gain the world at the price of a soul.

The purpose of this paper is less to settle the difference between "moralists" and "revisionists" about the general effect of corruption on development (although a tentative conclusion is presented) than to suggest a means to make the debate more fruitful. After discussing the problem in the usual general terms of possibility, we shall turn to more specific hypotheses about probability.

This paper is concerned with the *effects* of corruption, but a word should be said about causes to dispel any impression that corruption is a uniquely Afro-Asian-Latin American problem. I assume no European or American monopoly of morals. After all, Lord Bryce saw corruption as a major American flaw and noted its outbreak in "virulent form" in the new states in Eu-

From *American Political Science Review* (June 1967), pp. 417–427. Reprinted by permission.

rope.[5] Yet behavior that will be considered corrupt is likely to be more prominent in less developed countries because of a variety of conditions involved in their underdevelopment—great inequality in distribution of wealth; political office as the primary means of gaining access to wealth; conflict between changing moral codes; the weakness of social and governmental enforcement mechanisms; and the absence of a strong sense of national community.[6]

The weakness of the legitimacy of governmental institutions is also a contributing factor, though to attribute this entirely to the prevalence of a cash nexus or the divergence of moral codes under previous colonial governments or to the mere newness of the states concerned may be inadequate in the light of the experience with corruption of older, non-colonial less developed states such as Thailand or Liberia. Regardless of causes, however, the conditions of less developed countries are such that corruption is likely to have different effects than in more developed countries.

Most researchers on developing areas gather some information on corruption, and this paper will suggest hypotheses about the costs and benefits of corruption for development that may lure some of this information into the open. However, in view of the fact that generalizations about corruption and development tend to be disguised descriptions of a particular area in which the generalizer has done field work, I will state at the outset that generalizations in this paper are unevenly based on field work in East Africa and Central America and on secondary sources for other areas.

Definitions pose a problem. Indeed, if we define political development as "rational, modern, honest government," then it cannot coexist with corruption in the same time period; and if corruption is endemic in government, a politically developed society cannot exist. "Political development" is not an entirely satisfactory term since it has an evaluative as well as a descriptive content. At least in the case of economic development, there is general agreement on the units and scale by which to measure (growth of per capita income). In politics, however, there is agreement neither on the units nor on a single scale to measure development.[7] Emphasis on some scales rather

than others tends to reflect an author's interests.

In this author's view, the term "political development" is best used to refer to the recurring problem of relating governmental structures and processes to social change. It seems useful to use one term to refer to the type of change which seems to be occurring in our age ("modernization") and another to refer to capacity of political structures and processes to cope with social change, to the extent it exists, in any period.[8] We generally assume that this means structures and processes which are regarded as legitimate by relevant sectors of the population and effective in producing outputs desired by relevant sectors of the population. I assume that legitimacy and effectiveness are linked in the "long run" but can compensate for each other in the "short run."[9] What constitutes a relevant sector of the population will vary with the period and with social changes within a period. In the modern period we tend to assume that at least a veneer of broad participation is essential for establishing or maintaining legitimacy. In other words, in the current period, political development and political modernization may come close to involving the same things.

In this paper, political development (or decay) will mean growth (or decline) in the capacity of a society's governmental structures and processes to maintain their legitimacy over time (i.e., presumably in the face of social change). This allows us to see development as a moving equilibrium and avoid some of the limitations of equating development and modernization. Of course, this definition does not solve all the concept's problems. Unless we treat development entirely *ex post facto,* there will still be differences over evaluation (legitimate in whose eyes?) and measurement (national integration, administrative capacity, institutionalization?) as well as what constitutes a "long" and "short" run.

Thus we will find that forms of corruption which have beneficial effects on economic development may be detrimental for political development; or may promote one form of political development (i.e., defined one way or measured along one scale) but be detrimental to another. We shall have to continue to beware of variations in what we mean by political development. (Alternatively, those who reject the term "political development" can still read the paper as relating corruption to three problems of change discussed below.)

The definition of corruption also poses serious problems. Broadly defined as perversion or a change from good to bad, it covers a wide range of behavior from venality to ideological erosion. For instance, we might describe the revolutionary student who returns from Paris to a former French African country and accepts a (perfectly legal) overpaid civil service post as "corrupted." But used this broadly the term is more relevant to moral evaluation than political analysis. I will use a narrower definition which can be made operational.

Corruption is behavior which deviates from the formal duties of a public role because of private-regarding (personal, close family, private clique) pecuniary or status gains; or violates rules against the exercise of certain types of private-regarding influence.[10] This includes such behavior as bribery (use of a reward to pervert the judgment of a person in a position of trust); nepotism (bestowal of patronage by reason of ascriptive relationship rather than merit); and misappropriation (illegal appropriation of public resources for private-regarding uses).

This definition does not include much behavior that might nonetheless be regarded as offensive to moral standards. It also excludes any consideration of whether the behavior is in the public interest, since building the study of the effects of the behavior into the definition makes analysis of the relationship between corruption and development difficult. Similarly, it avoids the question of whether non-Western societies regard the behavior as corrupt, preferring to treat that also as a separate variable.

To build such relativism into the definition is to make specific behavior which can be compared between countries hard to identify. Moreover, in most less developed countries, there are two standards regarding such behavior, one indigenous and one more or less Western, and the formal duties and rules concerning most public roles tend to be expressed in terms of the latter.[11] In short, while this definition of corruption is not entirely satisfactory in terms of inclusiveness of behavior and the handling of relativity of standards, it has the merit of denoting specific behavior generally called corrupt by Western standards (which are at least partly relevant in most developing countries) and thus allowing us to ask what effects this specific behavior has under differing conditions.

POSSIBLE BENEFITS AND COSTS

Discussion of the relation of corruption to development tends to be phrased in general terms. Usually the argument between moralists and revisionists tends to be about the possibility that corruption (type unspecified) *can* be beneficial for development. Leaving aside questions of probability, one can argue that corruption can be beneficial to political development, as here defined, by contributing to the solution of three major problems involved: economic development, national integration, and governmental capacity.

Economic Development

If corruption helps promote economic development which is generally necessary to maintain a capacity to preserve legitimacy in the face of social change, then (by definition) it is beneficial for political development.

There seem to be at least three major ways in which some kinds of corruption might promote economic development.

Capital formation. Where private capital is scarce and government lacks a capacity to tax a surplus out of peasants or workers openly, corruption may be an important source of capital formation. There seems to be little question about the effectiveness of this form of taxation—Trujillo reputedly accumulated $500 million and Nkrumah and relatives probably more than $10 million.[12] The real question is then whether the accumulated capital is then put to uses which promote economic development or winds up in Swiss banks.

Cutting red tape. In many new countries the association of profit with imperialism has led to a systematic bias against the market mechanism. Given inadequate administrative resources in most new states, it can be argued that corruption helps to mitigate the consequences of ideologically determined economic devices which may not be wholly appropriate for the countries concerned.[13] Even where the quality of

bureaucrats is high, as in India, some observers believe that "too much checking on
corruption can delay development. Trying
to run a development economy with triple
checking is impossible." [14] Corruption on
the part of factory managers in the Soviet
Union is sometimes credited with providing
a flexibility that makes central planning
more effective.

Entrepreneurship and incentives. If Schumpeter is correct that the entrepreneur is a
vital factor in economic growth and if
there is an ideological bias against private
incentives in a country, then corruption
may provide one of the major means by
which a developing country can make use
of this factor. This becomes even more true
if, as is often the case, the personal characteristics associated with entrepreneurship
have a higher incidence among minority
groups. Corruption may provide the means
of overcoming discrimination against members of a minority group, and allow the entrepreneur from a minority to gain access
to the political decisions necessary for him
to provide his skills. In East Africa, for
instance, corruption may be prolonging the
effective life of an important economic asset—the Asian minority entrepreneur—beyond what political conditions would otherwise allow.

National Integration

It seems fair to assume that a society's political structures will be better able to cope
with change and preserve their legitimacy
if the members share a sense of community. Indeed, integration is sometimes used
as one of the main scales for measuring
political development.

Elite integration. Corruption may help
overcome divisions in a ruling elite that
might otherwise result in destructive conflict. One observer believes that it helped
bridge the gap between the groups based
on power and those based on wealth that
appeared in the early nationalist period in
West Africa and allowed the groups to
"assimilate each other." Certainly in Central America, corruption has been a major
factor in the succession mechanism by integrating the leaders of the new coup into
the existing upper class. Whether this is
beneficial for political development or not

is another question involving particular
circumstances, different evaluation of the
importance of continuity, and the question
of the relevant period for measurement.

Integration of non-elites. Corruption may
help to ease the transition from traditional
life to modern. It can be argued that the
man who has lived under "ascriptive, particularistic and diffuse" conditions cares
far less about the rational impartiality of
the government and its laws than he does
about its awesomeness and seeming inhu-
manity. The vast gap between literate official and illiterate peasant which is often
characteristic of the countryside may be
bridged if the peasant approaches the official bearing traditional gifts or their (marginally corrupt) money equivalent. For the
new urban resident, a political machine
based on corruption may provide a com-
prehensible point at which to relate to government by other than purely ethnic or
tribal means. In McMullan's words, a degree of low-level corruption can "soften
relations of officials and people" or in Shils'
words it "humanizes government and makes
it less awesome." [15]

However, what is integrative for one
group may be disintegrative for another.
The "traditional" or "transitional" man may
care far more that he has a means to get
his son out of jail than that the system as
a whole be incorruptible, but for "modern"
groups such as students and middle classes
(who have profited from achievement and
universalism) the absence of honesty may
destroy the legitimacy of the system. Finally, it is worth noting again Gluckman's
statement that the scandals associated with
corruption can sometimes have the effect
of strengthening a value system as a whole.

Governmental Capacity

The capacity of the political structures of
many new states to cope with change is
frequently limited by weakness of their
new institutions and (often despite apparent centralization) the fragmentation of
power in a country. Moreover, there is
little "elasticity of power"—i.e., power does
not expand or contract easily with a change
of man or situation.[16]

To use a somewhat simplified scheme of
motivations, one could say that the leaders
in such a country have to rely (in various

combinations) on ideal, coercive or material incentives to aggregate enough power to govern. Legal material incentives may have to be augmented by corrupt ones. Those who place great faith in ideal incentives (such as Wraith and Simpkins) see the use of corrupt material incentives as destructive ("these countries depend considerably on enthusiasm and on youthful pride of achievement . . .") [17] of governmental capacity.

With a lower evaluation of the role of ideal incentives, however, corrupt material incentives may become a functional equivalent for violence. In Mexico, for instance, Needler has described the important role which corruption played in the transition from the violent phases of the revolution to its institutionalized form.[18] At the local level, Greenstone notes that while patronage and corruption was one factor that contributed to an initial decline in governmental capacity in East Africa, corrupt material incentives may provide the glue for reassembling sufficient power to govern.[19]

Governmental capacity can be increased by the creation of supporting institutions such as political parties. Financing political parties tends to be a problem in developed as well as less developed countries, but it is a particular problem in poor countries. Broad-based mass financing is difficult to maintain after independence.[20] In some cases the major alternatives to corrupt proceeds as a means of party finance are party decay or reliance on outside funds. Needless to say, not all such investments are successful. The nearly $12 million diverted from Nigeria's Western Region Marketing Board into Action Group coffers from 1959 to 1962 (and probably equivalent amounts in other regions) [21] seem to have been wasted in terms of institution-building; but on the other hand, investment in India's Congress Party or Mexico's *Partido Revolucionario Institucional* has been more profitable for political development.

Those who dispute the possible benefits of corruption could argue that it involves countervailing costs that interfere with the solution of each of the three problems. They could argue that corruption is economically wasteful, politically destabilizing, and destructive of governmental capacity.

Waste of Resources

Although corruption may help promote economic development, it can also hinder it or direct it in socially less desirable directions.

Capital outflow. As we mentioned above, capital accumulated by corruption that winds up in Swiss banks is a net loss for the developing country. These costs can be considerable. For instance, one source estimates that from 1954 to 1959, three Latin American dictators (Peron, Perez Jimenez, and Batista) removed a total of $1.15 billion from their countries.[22] It is no wonder that another source believes that economic development in some Latin American countries has been "checked" by corruption.[23]

Investment distortions. Investment may be channeled into sectors such as construction not because of economic profitability, but because they are more susceptible to hiding corrupt fees through cost-plus contracts and use of suppliers' credits. This was the case, for instance, in Venezuela under Perez Jimenez and in Ghana under Nkrumah.

Waste of skills. "If the top political elite of a country consumes its time and energy in trying to get rich by corrupt means, it is not likely that the development plans will be fulfilled." [24] Moreover, the costs in terms of time and energy spent attempting to set some limits to corruption can also be expensive. For instance, in Burma, U Nu's creation of a Bureau of Special Investigation to check corruption actually reduced administrative efficiency.[25]

Aid foregone. Another possible wastage, the opportunity costs of aid foregone or withdrawn by outside donors because of disgust with corruption in a developing country could be a serious cost in the sense that developing countries are highly dependent on external sources of capital. Thus far, however, there has not been a marked correlation between honesty of governments and their per capita receipt of aid. If corruption is a consideration with donors (presumably it weighs more heavily with multilateral institutions), it is not yet a primary one.

Instability

By destroying the legitimacy of political structures in the eyes of those who have power to do something about the situation, corruption can contribute to instability and possible national disintegration. But it is not clear that instability is always inimical to political development.

Social revolution. An argument can be made that a full social revolution (whatever its short-run costs) can speed the development of new political structures better able to preserve their legitimacy in the face of social change. Thus, in this view if corruption led to social revolution, this might be a beneficial effect for political development. But it is not clear that corruption of the old regime is a primary cause of social revolution. Such revolutions are comparatively rare and often depend heavily on catalytic events (such as external wars).

Military takeovers. If corruption causes a loss of legitimacy in the eyes of those with guns, it may be a direct cause of instability and the disintegration of existing political institutions. But the consequences for political development are again ambiguous. Much depends on differing evaluations of the ability of military regimes (which tend to comprise people and procedures oriented toward modernity) to maintain legitimacy in a democratic age either by self-transformation into political regimes or by being willing and able to foster new political institutions to which power can be returned. To the extent that this tends to be difficult, then if corruption leads to military takeover, it has hindered political development.[26]

The degree to which corruption is itself a major cause of military takeovers is, however, open to some question. Despite its prominence in post-coup rationalizations, one might suspect that it is only a secondary cause in most cases. Perhaps more significant is military leaders' total distaste for the messiness of politics—whether honest or not—and a tendency to blame civilian politicians for failures to meet overly optimistic popular aspirations which would be impossible of fulfillment even by a government of angels.[27] Indeed, to the extent that corruption contributes to governmental

effectiveness in meeting these aspirations, it may enhance stability.

Crozier sees "revulsion against civilian incompetence and corruption" as a major cause of coups in several Asian countries including Burma, but he also states that the main cause of Ne Win's return to power was the Shan demand for a federal rather than unitary state.[28] Similarly, corruption is sometimes blamed for the first coup in Nigeria, but the post-electoral crisis in the Western region and the fear of permanent Northern domination was probably a more important and direct cause. In Ghana, corruption may have played a more important role in causing the coup, but not so much because of revulsion at dishonesty, as the fact that corruption had reached an extent where it contributed to an economic situation in which real wages had fallen. Nonetheless, its impact in relation to other factors should not be overestimated.[29]

Upsetting ethnic balances. Corruption can sometimes exacerbate problems of national integration in developing countries. If a corrupt leader must be fired, it may upset ethnic arithmetic as happened in both Kenya and Zambia in 1966. Of course this can be manipulated as a deliberate political weapon. In Western Nigeria in 1959, an anti-corruption officer was appointed but his jurisdiction was subject to approval by the cabinet, which meant that no case could be investigated "unless the party leader decided that a man needed to be challenged." [30] But as a weapon, charging corruption is a risky device. Efforts by southern politicians in Uganda to use it in 1966 precipitated a pre-emptive coup by the northern Prime Minister in alliance with the predominantly northern army.

Reduction of Governmental Capacity

While it may not be the sole or major cause, corruption can contribute to the loss of governmental capacity in developing countries.

Reduction of administrative capacity. Corruption may alienate modern-oriented civil servants (a scarce resource) and cause them to leave a country or withdraw or reduce their efforts. In addition to the obvious costs, this may involve considerable opportunity costs in the form of restriction of governmental programs because of fears that a new program (for instance, administration of new taxes) might be ineffective in practice. While this is a real cost, it is worth noting that efficient bureaucracy is not always a necessary condition for economic or political development (at least in the early stages), and in some cases can even hinder it.[31]

Loss of legitimacy. It is often alleged that corruption squanders the most important asset a new country has—the legitimacy of its government. This is a serious cost but it must be analyzed in terms of groups. As we have seen, what may enhance legitimacy for the student or civil servant may not enhance it for the tradition-oriented man. It is interesting, for instance, that there is some evidence that in Tanganyika petty corruption at low levels seems to have increased during the year following the replacement of an "illegitimate" colonial regime by a "legitimate" nationalist one.[32] The loss of legitimacy as a cost must be coupled with assessment of the power or importance of the group in whose eyes legitimacy is lost. If they are young army officers, it can be important indeed.

PROBABILITIES

Thus far I have been discussing *possible* benefits and costs. I have established that under some circumstances corruption can have beneficial effects on at least three major development problems. Also, I have evaluated the importance of several frequently alleged countervailing costs. It remains to offer hypotheses about the *probabilities* of benefits outweighing costs. In general terms, such probabilities will vary with at least three conditions: (1) a tolerant culture and dominant groups; (2) a degree of security on the part of the members of the elite being corrupted; (3) the existence of societal and institutional checks and restraints on corrupt behavior.

(1) Attitudes toward corruption vary greatly. In certain West African countries, observers have reported little widespread sense of indignation about corruption.[33] The Philippines, with its American colonial heritage of corruption, and appreciation of the politics of compromise, seems able to tolerate a higher level of corruption than formerly-Dutch Indonesia. According to Higgins, the Indonesian attitude to corruption (which began on a large scale only in 1954) is that it is sinful. He attributes the civil war of 1958 to corruption and argues that in the Philippines, "anomalies" are taken more for granted.[34]

Not only is the general level of tolerance of corruption relevant; variations of attitude within a country can be as important (or more so) than differences between countries. Very often, traditional sectors of the populace are likely to be more tolerant of corruption than some of the modern sectors (students, army, civil service). Thus the hypothesis must take into account not only the tolerant nature of the culture, but also the relative power of groups representing more and less tolerant sub-cultures in a country. In Nigeria, tolerance was by many accounts considerable among the population at large, but not among the young army officers who overthrew the old regime.

(2) Another condition which increases the probability that the benefits of corruption will outweigh the costs is a degree of security (and perception thereof) by the members of the elites indulging in corrupt practices. Too great insecurity means that any capital formed by corruption will tend to be exported rather than invested at home. In Nicaragua, for instance, it is argued that the sense of security of the Somoza family encouraged them in internal investments in economic projects and the strengthening of their political party, which led to impressive economic growth and diminished direct reliance on the army. In contrast are the numerous cases of capital outflow mentioned above. One might add that this sense of security, including the whole capitalist ethic, which is rare in less developed countries today, makes comparison with capital formation by the "robber barons" of the American 19th century of dubious relevance to less developed countries today.

(3) It is probable that for the benefits of corruption to outweigh the costs depends on its being limited in various ways, much as the beneficial effects of inflation for economic growth tend to depend on limits. These limits depend upon the existence of societal or institutional restraints on corruption. These can be external to the leaders, e.g., the existence of an independent press, and honest elections; or internalized conceptions of public interest by a

ruling group such as Leys argues that 18th century English aristocrats held.[35] In Mandeville's words, "Vice is beneficial found when it's by Justice lopt and bound." [36]

Given the characteristics of less developed countries, one can see that the general probability of the presence of one or more of these conditions (and thus of benefits outweighing costs) is not high. But to conclude merely that the moralists are more right than wrong (though for the wrong reasons) is insufficient because the whole issue remains unsatisfactory if left in these general terms. Though corruption may not prove beneficial for resolution of development problems in general, it may prove to be the only means to solution of a particular problem.

If a country has some overriding problem, some "obstacle to development"— for instance, if capital can be formed by no other means, or ethnic hatred threatens all legal activities aimed at its alleviation— then it is possible that corruption is beneficial for development despite the high costs and risks involved. While there are dangers in identifying "obstacles to development," [37] and while the corruption that is beneficial to the solution of one problem may be detrimental to another, we need to get away from general statements which are difficult to test and which provide us with no means of ordering the vast number of variables involved. We are more likely to advance this argument if we distinguish the roles of different types of corruption in relation to different types of development problems.

The matrix in Table 1 relates three types of corruption to three types of development problems, first assuming favorable and then assuming unfavorable conditions described above. Favorable conditions (F) means a tolerant culture or dominance of more tolerant groups, relative security of the elite corrupted, and societal/institutional checks. Unfavorable conditions (U) means intolerant culture or groups, insecure elite, and few societal/institutional checks. The development problems are those discussed above: economic development, national integration, and governmental capacity.

The scores are a priori judgments that the costs of a particular type of corruption are likely to outweigh the benefits for a particular development problem or sub-problem. They represent a series of tentative hypotheses to be clarified or refuted by data. Under economic development, the specific sub-problems discussed are whether capital accumulation is promoted (benefit) without capital flight (cost); whether cutting bureaucratic red tape (benefit) outweighs distortion of rational criteria (cost); whether the attraction of unused scarce skills such as entrepreneurship (benefit) is greater than the wastage of scarce skills of, say, politicians and civil servants (cost).

Under the problem of national integration are the sub-problems of whether a particular type of corruption tends to make the elite more cohesive (benefit) or seriously splits them (cost); and whether it tends to humanize government and make national identification easier for the non-elites (benefit) or alienates them (cost). Under the problem of governmental capacity are the sub-problems of whether the additional power aggregated by corruption (benefit) outweighs possible damage to administrative efficiency (cost); and whether it enhances (benefit) or seriously weakens the governmental legitimacy (cost).

Level of Beneficiary

Shils argues that "freedom from corruption at the highest levels is a necessity for the maintenance of public respect of Government . . ." whereas a modicum of corruption at lower levels is probably not too injurious.[38] On the other hand, McMullan reports that West Africans show little sense of indignation about often fantastic stories of corruption by leaders, and impressions from Mexico indicate that petty corruption most saps morale.[39] In India, Bayley notes that "although corruption at the top attracts the most attention in public forums, and involves the largest amount of money in separate transactions, corruption at the very bottom levels is the more apparent and obvious and in total amounts of money involved may very well rival corruption at the top." [40]

The matrix in Table 1 suggests that under unfavorable conditions neither type of corruption is likely to be beneficial in general, although top level corruption may enhance governmental power more than it weakens administrative efficiency. It also suggests that under favorable conditions, top level corruption may be beneficial but bottom level corruption probably is not (except for non-elite integration). If these judgments are accurate, it suggests that

TABLE 1
CORRUPTION COST-BENEFIT MATRIX

Types of Corruption	Political Conditions	Development Problems							General Probability that Costs Outweigh Benefits
		Economic Development			National Integration		Governmental Capacity		
		(a) Capital	(b) Bureaucracy	(c) Skills	(d) Elite	(e) Non-elite	(f) Effectiveness	(g) Legitimacy	
Level									
top	F	low	uncertain	uncertain/low	low	uncertain	low	low	low/uncertain
bottom	F	high	uncertain	uncertain/high	uncertain	low	high	low	high
top	U	high	high	uncertain/low	high	high	low	high	high
bottom	U	high	uncertain	uncertain/high	little relevance	high	high	high	high
Inducements									
modern	F	uncertain	uncertain/low	low	low	low	low/uncertain	uncertain	low/uncertain
traditional	F	high/uncertain	uncertain	high	high	uncertain	high	uncertain	high
modern	U	high	uncertain	uncertain/low	high	high	low/uncertain	high	high
traditional	U	high/uncertain	uncertain	high	high	uncertain	high	high	high
Deviation									
extensive	F	uncertain	high	uncertain	uncertain	low	uncertain/low	uncertain/high	high
marginal	F	uncertain	low	uncertain/low	low	low	low	low	low
extensive	U	uncertain	high	uncertain	high	high	uncertain	high	high
marginal	U	uncertain	low	uncertain/low	high	high	low	high	high

NOTES: F favorable political conditions (cultural tolerance, elite security, checks)
U unfavorable political conditions
High high probability that costs exceed benefits
Low low probability that costs exceed benefits
Uncertain little relationship or ambiguous relationship

countries with favorable conditions, like India, which have considerable bottom level corruption but pride themselves on the relative honesty of the higher levels, may be falling between two stools.

The rationale of the scoring is as follows: (a) Capital. Bottom level corruption with smaller size of each inducement will probably increase consumption more than capital formation. While top level corruption may represent the latter, whether it is invested productively rather than sent overseas depends on favorable political conditions. (b) Bureaucracy. Other factors seem more important in determining whether expediting is more important than distortion; except that those with the power of the top levels will probably distort investment criteria considerably in conditions of uncertainty—witness the selling of investment licenses (alleged) under a previous government in Guatemala. (c) Skills. Whether top level corruption permits the use of more skills than it wastes depends upon their supply. Where they exist as with Asians in East Africa or "Turcos" in Honduras, it is probably beneficial. Corruption of those at lower levels of power may be more likely to waste energies than to be important in permission of use of new skills simply because their power is limited.

(d) Elite integration. It is difficult to see a clear relation between bottom level corruption and elite integration. At the higher levels under unfavorable conditions, e.g., a powerful intolerant part of the elite such as students or army, corruption would probably have a more divisive than cohesive effect. Under favorable conditions it might be more cohesive. (e) Non-elite integration. Under unfavorable conditions it seems likely that both types of corruption would tend to alienate more than enhance identification, whereas under favorable conditions corruption by the lower levels that the populace deals with most frequently might have the humanizing effect mentioned above, and alienation would be slight in the tolerant culture. Top level corruption might have the same effect though the connection is less clear because of the lesser degree of direct contact.

(f) Effectiveness. Bottom level corruption is more likely to disperse rather than aggregate power by making governmental machinery less responsive than otherwise might be the case; whereas at top levels the ability to change the behavior of important power holders by corrupt inducements is likely to outweigh the loss of efficiency, even under unfavorable conditions. (g) Legitimacy. Whether corruption enhances or reduces governmental legitimacy depends more on favorable conditions than on level of corruption. Much depends on another factor, visibility of corrupt behavior, which does not always have a clear relationship to level of corruption.

Inducements

Another distinction which can be made between types of corruption is the nature of the inducement used, for instance the extent to which they reflect the values of the traditional society or the values of the modern sector. A traditional inducement such as status in one's clan or tribe may be more tolerable to those who share the ascriptive affinity, but others outside the ascriptive relationship would prefer the use of money which would give them equality of access to the corruptee. Weiner writes of India that "from a political point of view, equal opportunity to corrupt is often more important than the amount of corruption, and therefore . . . an increase in *bakshish* is in the long run less serious than an increase in corruption by ascriptive criteria." [41]

As scored here, our matrix suggests that under favorable political conditions (e.g., India?) Weiner's hypothesis is probably correct but would not be correct under unfavorable conditions. (a) Capital. Modern inducements (i.e., money) probably lead to capital formation (at top levels) which may be invested under favorable conditions or be sent abroad under unfavorable conditions. Traditional inducements (kin status) do not promote capital formation (and may even interfere with it) but probably have little effect on capital flight. (b) Bureaucracy. What edge modern inducements may have in expediting procedure may be offset by distortion of criteria, so the relation between type of inducement and this problem is scored as uncertain. (c) Skills. Assuming the existence of untapped skills (as above), modern inducements increase the access to power while traditional ones decrease it.

(d) Elite integration. Under favorable conditions modern inducements are unlikely to divide elites more than make them cohere, but traditional inducements tend to preserve and emphasize ethnic divisions in the elites. Under unfavorable conditions, both types of inducements tend to be divisive. (e) Non-elite integration. Whether modern inducements promote identification or alienation varies with political conditions in the expected way, but the effect of traditional inducements is more ambiguous and probably varies from positive to negative according to the prevalence of traditional as against modern values in the particular country in question.

(f) Effectiveness. Modern inducements probably give the government greater range to aggregate more sources of power than traditional inducements do. The probabilities will vary not only with political conditions but also by the opportunity costs— whether there is an efficient administrative machine to be damaged or not. (g) Legitimacy. Under favorable conditions whether traditional or modern inducements will decrease legitimacy more than they enhance it remains uncertain because it will vary with the (above mentioned) degree of existence of modern and traditional values in a society. Under unfavorable conditions, both will likely have higher costs than benefits.

Deviation

We can also distinguish types of corruption by whether the corrupt behavior involves extensive deviation from the formal duties of a public role or marginal deviation. This is not the same thing as a scale of corrupt inducements, since the size of the inducements may bear little relation to the degree of deviation. For instance, it is alleged that in one Central American country under an insecure recent regime, a business could get the government to reverse a decision for as little as $2,000, whereas in a neighboring country the mere expediting of a decision cost $50,000. Such a distinction between types of corruption by extent of deviation is not uncommon among practitioners who use terms like "speed-up money" or "honest graft" in their rationalizations.[42]

(a) Capital. It is difficult to see that the extensiveness of the deviation (except insofar as it affects the scale of inducement) has much to do with the probabilities of capital formation or flight. (b) Bureaucracy. On the other hand, marginal devia-

tions (by definition) are unlikely to involve high costs in distortion of criteria and even under unfavorable conditions may help expedite matters. Extensive deviations are likely to have high costs in terms of rational criteria regardless of conditions. (c) Skills. It is not clear that extensive deviations call forth more unused skills than they waste administrative skills; nor is the matter completely clear with marginal deviations, though the costs of administrative skills wasted may be lower because the tasks are simpler.

(d) Elite integration. Under unfavorable conditions, the effects of corruption on elite cohesiveness are likely to be negative regardless of the extent of deviations, though they might be less negative for marginal deviations. Under favorable conditions, marginal deviations are likely to have low costs, but the effect of extensive deviations will be uncertain, varying with other factors such as existing cohesiveness of the elite and the nature of the extensive deviations. (e) Non-elite integration. Under unfavorable conditions, corruption is likely to have more alienative than identification effects regardless of the nature of the deviations. Under favorable conditions, marginal deviation will not have high costs in terms of alienation, and extensive deviation may have special appeal to those who are seeking human and "reversible" government more than impartial or "rational" government.

(f) Effectiveness. It is difficult to see that extensive deviations alone would increase governmental power more than weaken administrative efficiency, but with marginal deviation, the extent of the latter would be sufficiently small that the benefits would probably outweigh the costs. (g) Legitimacy. Under unfavorable conditions either type of corruption would be more likely to weaken than to enhance legitimacy, but under favorable conditions the lesser challenge to rationality might make marginal corruption less detrimental than extensive— though this would depend on the proportion and dominance of groups in society placing emphasis on modern values.

CONCLUSION

The scoring of the matrix suggests that we can refine the general statements about corruption and political development to read,

"It is probable that the costs of corruption in less developed countries will exceed its benefits except for top level corruption involving modern inducements and marginal deviations and except for situations where corruption provides the only solution to an important obstacle to development." As our matrix shows, corruption can provide the solution to several of the more limited problems of development. Whether this is beneficial to development as a whole depends on how important the problems are and what alternatives exist. It is also interesting to note that while the three conditions we have identified seem to be necessary for corruption to be beneficial in general terms, they are not necessary for it to be beneficial in the solution of a number of particular problems.

At this point, however, not enough information is at hand to justify great confidence in the exact conclusions reached here. More important is the suggestion of the use of this or a similar matrix to advance the discussion of the relationship between corruption and development. The matrix can be expanded or elaborated in a number of ways if the data seem to justify it. Additional development problems can be added, as can additional types of corruption (e.g., by scale, visibility, income effects, and so forth). The above categories can be made more precise by adding possibilities; for instance intermediate as well as top and bottom levels of corruption, or distinctions between politicians and civil servants at top, bottom, and intermediate levels.

Despite the problems of systematic field research on corruption in developing countries mentioned above, there is probably much more data on corruption and development gleaned during field work on other topics than we realize. What we need to advance the study of the problem is to refute and replace *specific* a priori hypotheses with propositions based on such data rather than with the generalities of the moralists. Corruption in developing countries is too important a phenomenon to be left to moralists.

1. C. J. Friedrich, *Man and His Government* (New York, 1963), p. 167. See also "Political Pathology," *Political Quarterly*, 37 (January–March, 1966), 70–85.

2. Ronald Wraith and Edgar Simpkins, *Corruption in Developing Countries* (London, 1963), pp. 11, 12; K. T. Young, Jr., "New Politics in New States," *Foreign Affairs*, 39 (April, 1961), p. 498.

3. See, for example: Nathaniel Leff, "Economic Development Through Bureaucratic Corruption," *American Behavioral Scientist*, 8 (November, 1964), 8–14; David H. Bayley, "The Effects of Corruption in a Developing Nation," *Western Political Quarterly*, 19 (December, 1966), 719–732; J. J. Van Klaveren in a "Comment" in *Comparative Studies in Society and History*, 6 (January, 1964), p. 195, even argues that "recent experience in the so-called underdeveloped countries has most vividly brought home the fact that corruption is not a mass of incoherent phenomena, but a political system, capable of being steered with tolerable precision by those in power."

4. Max Gluckman, *Custom and Conflict in Africa* (Oxford, 1955), p. 135.

5. James Bryce, *Modern Democracies* (New York, 1921), Vol. II, p. 509.

6. Colin Leys, "What Is the Problem About Corruption?" *Journal of Modern African Studies*, 3, 2 (1965), 224–225; Ralph Braibanti, "Reflections on Bureaucratic Corruption," *Public Administration*, 40 (Winter, 1962), 365–371.

7. Nor, by the nature of the subject, is there likely to be. In Pye's words, "no single scale can be used for measuring political development": Lucian Pye (ed.), *Communications and Political Development* (Princeton, 1963). See also Lucian Pye, "The Concept of Political Development," *The Annals*, 358 (March, 1965), 1–19; Samuel Huntington, "Political Development and Political Decay," *World Politics*, 17 (April, 1965), 386–430; Robert Packenham, "Political Development Doctrines in the American Foreign Aid Program," *World Politics*, 18 (January, 1966), 194–235.

8. See Huntington, *op. cit.*, p. 389.

9. S. M. Lipset, *Political Man* (Garden City, 1959), pp. 72–75.

10. The second part of the definition is taken from Edward C. Banfield, *Political Influence* (Glencoe, Ill.: Free Press, 1961), p. 315.

11. See, for example: M. G. Smith, "Historical and Cultural Conditions of Political Corruption Among the Hausa," *Comparative Studies in Society and History*, 6 (January, 1964), p. 194; Lloyd Fallers, "The Predicament of the Modern African Chief: An Instance from Uganda," *American Anthropologist*, 57 (1955), 290–305. I agree with Bayley on this point: *op. cit.*, pp. 720–722.

12. A. Terry Rambo, "The Dominican Republic," in Martin Needler (ed.), *Political Systems of Latin America* (Princeton, 1964), p. 172; *New York Times*, March 5, 1966.

Ayeh Kumi's quoted statement has almost certainly greatly underestimated his own assets.

13. On the economic problems of "African socialism," see Elliot Berg, "Socialism and Economic Development in Tropical Africa," *Quarterly Journal of Economics,* 78 (November, 1964), 549–573.

14. Barbara Ward, addressing the Harvard Center for International Affairs, Cambridge, Mass., March 3, 1966.

15. M. McMullan, "A Theory of Corruption," *Sociological Review* (Keele), 9 (July, 1961), p. 196; Edward Shils, *Political Development in the New States* (The Hague, 1962), p. 385.

16. See Herbert Werlin, "The Nairobi City Council: A Study in Comparative Local Government," *Comparative Studies in Society and History,* 7 (January, 1966), p. 185.

17. Wraith and Simpkins, *op. cit.,* p. 172.

18. Martin Needler, "The Political Development of Mexico," *American Political Science Review,* 55 (June, 1960), pp. 310–311.

19. J. David Greenstone, "Corruption and Self Interest in Kampala and Nairobi," *Comparative Studies in Society and History,* 7 (January, 1966), 199–210.

20. See J. S. Nye, "The Impact of Independence on Two African Nationalist Parties," in J. Butler and A. Castagno (eds.), *Boston University Papers on Africa* (New York, 1967), pp. 224–245.

21. Richard L. Sklar, "Contradictions in the Nigerian Political System," *Journal of Modern African Studies,* 3, 2 (1965), p. 206.

22. Edwin Lieuwen, *Arms and Politics in Latin America* (New York, 1960), p. 149.

23. F. Benham and H. A. Holley, *A Short Introduction to the Economy of Latin America* (London, 1960), p. 10.

24. Leys, *op. cit.,* p. 229.

25. Brian Crozier, *The Morning After: A Study of Independence* (London, 1963), p. 82.

26. In Pye's words, the military "can contribute to only a limited part of national development," *Aspects of Political Development* (Boston, 1966), p. 187.

27. "Have no fear," General Mobutu told the Congo people, "My Government is not composed of politicians." Mobutu alleged that political corruption cost the Congo $43 million: *East Africa and Rhodesia,* January 13, 1966; *Africa Report,* January 1966, p. 23.

28. Crozier, *op. cit.,* pp. 62, 74.

29. For two interpretations, see Martin Kilson, "Behind Nigeria's Revolts"; Immanuel Wallerstein, "Autopsy of Nkrumah's Ghana," *New Leader,* January 31, pp. 9–12; March 14, 1966, pp. 3–5.

30. Henry Bretton, *Power and Stability in Nigeria* (New York, 1962), p. 79.

31. Bert Hoselitz, "Levels of Economic Performance and Bureaucratic Structures," in Joseph LaPalombara (ed.), *Bureaucracy and Political Development* (Princeton, 1963), pp. 193–195. See also Nathaniel Leff, *loc. cit.,* 8–14.

32. See *Tanganyika Standard,* May 15, 1963.

33. McMullan, *op. cit.,* p. 195.

34. Benjamin Higgins, *Economic Development* (New York, 1959), p. 62.

35. Leys, *op. cit.,* p. 227. See also Eric McKitrick, "The Study of Corruption," *Political Science Quarterly,* 72 (December, 1957), 502–514, for limits on corruption in urban America.

36. Bernard Mandeville, *The Fable of the Bees,* Vol. I (Oxford: Clarendon Press, by F. B. Kaye, 1924), p. 37.

37. See Albert O. Hirschman, "Obstacles to Development: A Classification and a Quasi-Vanishing Act" [reprinted on pages 55–62 above].

38. Shils, *op. cit.,* p. 385.

39. McMullan, *op. cit.,* p. 195; Oscar Lewis, *The Children of Sanchez* (New York, 1961).

40. Bayley, *op. cit.,* p. 724.

41. Myron Weiner, *The Politics of Scarcity* (Chicago: University of Chicago Press, 1962), p. 236.

42. Cf. William Riordan, *Plunkitt of Tammany Hall* (New York, 1948), p. 4.

PART IV

MEASURES
AND MODELS FOR
DEVELOPMENT

Our discussion will be adequate if it has as much clearness as the subject-matter admits of, for precision is not to be sought for alike in all discussions. . . . We must be content, then, . . . to indicate the truth roughly and in outline, and in speaking about things which are only for the most part true and with premises of the same kind to reach conclusions that are no better. . . . It is the mark of an educated man to look for precision in each class of things just so far as the nature of the subject admits.

ARISTOTLE, "THE ETHICS" [1]

THE PHILOSOPHICAL DEBATE alluded to in Part I, between essentialist and existential approaches to knowledge, carries over into questions of quantification and analysis in social science. Precision and clarity are virtues to be attained wherever and whenever possible, but we should not expect that they will be equally attainable in all matters. It would be a mark of unsophistication to use "sophisticated" mathematical modes of analysis and explanation, however elegant, on problems that do not lend themselves to such treatment. Like other social scientists, especially those oriented to policy problems, we desire to attain the greatest clarity and precision possible, and this commonly involves quantitative analysis. But we would be ever mindful of Aristotle's caveat, because we wish to contribute to an existential social science that can deal with problems of choice. Otherwise, one is likely to subscribe to a neo-Pythagorean social science that has essences determining outcomes, leaving little scope for action to shape events in a more desired way.[2]

[1] Book I, Ch. 3, cited in Sheldon Wolin, *Politics and Vision* (1964), p. 59.
[2] This question deserves fuller treatment than we can give it here in a work concerned with development. Again, the contrasting positions can be traced back to Aristotle and Plato, though actually it goes back to Pythagoras, who believed and taught that underlying the disorderly appearance of the real world was a fundamental order based on

These issues are important, though not necessarily central, to an understanding of development. Given the considerable interest in models and quantitative analysis, we would like at least to address ourselves to these questions here.

THE USE OF NUMBERS IN SOCIAL SCIENCE

There should be no aversion to the use of quantitative methods in social science, but a number of reservations—philosophical, practical, and methodological—need to be expressed. We think that a critical discussion is in order and can be entertained without fear of producing a complete rejection of quantification, because, first, there is ample advocacy within social science for quantitative analysis, and second, as long as social scientists are working on policy problems, there will be persistent pressures from decision-makers for such analysis, to minimize the appearance at least of subjective considerations.

We would agree with Kenneth Arrow that "any intuitive knowledge can always be reduced to mathematical terms." [3] Indeed, we see such efforts as possibly useful attempts at the objectification of knowledge. But whereas Arrow stresses the adjective "any," we would emphasize the verb "reduce." The auxiliary verbs "can be" point out that this is a matter of choice. Presumably it is made only where the benefits of simplification, which permits certain quantitative manipulation, exceed the costs of reductionism and the distortion this entails. The use of numbers in analysis is, then, something instrumental, not justified for its own sake. This is an important epistemological premise.[4]

There are, after all, other methods for introducing rigor into analysis. Logical methods and criteria are surely centrally important to successful social science. Other than numerical systems can be employed in analysis, for example, the notation system used in linguistic analysis,[5] though these can often be augmented or even extended by quantitative methods. It is not clear, however, that these methods

---

numbers. All true or ultimate relationships could, he thought, be expressed in numerical terms. Consequently, he and his followers searched to discover the "truth" about the real world through quantitative analysis. For a brief exposition on this, see B. A. C. Fuller, *History of Greek Philosophy*, Vol. I, (New York: Holt and Co.), pp. 42–47. Plato adopted this perspective and applied it to politics. See discussion in Wolin, *op. cit.*, p. 49, and Hayward Alker, Jr., *Mathematics and Politics* (1965), pp. 6–7. Alker cites the view of A. N. Whitehead that "the Platonic world of ideas [or forms] is the refined, revised form of the Pythagorean doctrine that number lies at the base of the real world." In *Science and the Modern World* (1959), p. 33.

Aristotle, as we know, rejected this perspective. Though he contributed significantly to the development of mathematics, he applied it more to categories than to concepts. Much of his work went into classification of phenomena and analysis of the variations in consequences from certain common elements, while he also worked to improve logical reasoning, which brought some of the rigor of quantitative analysis to qualitative problems. His was an existential approach in contrast to Plato's Pythagorean approach, which assumed that underlying events there was an immutable "reality" that could be *revealed* through the *manipulation* of *numbers*. We find that a good many contemporary social scientists take a similar ontological and epistemological position; hence the designation "neo-Pythagorean."

[3] See p. 90 in Harold Lasswell and Daniel Lerner (eds.), *The Policy Sciences* (1951).

[4] Lasswell and Kaplan suggest that social inquiry may profit from a relaxation of the demand for precise quantificative determinations from the outset, since "numerical determination marks the successful close of inquiry, not its indispensable prerequisite." *Power and Society: A Framework for Political Inquiry* (1950), p. xvii.

[5] See Clyde Kluckhohn's commentary on this in Lasswell and Lerner, *op. cit.*, p. 130.

are invariably appropriate to the "shape" of the phenomena under consideration. When certain mathematical terms are applied to economics, for example, this implies that economic phenomena are related to one another in the same way as spatial relationships in geometry or rates of change in calculus, but this is a tenuous assumption.[6] Were one to apply comparable quantification in the new political economy, similar assumptions would be implied.

That the numbers available for analysis of Third World problems are commonly incomplete or unreliable poses practical problems. Even economic data, which are generally more extensive than social and political data, are likely to be spotty in underdeveloped countries (except for trade statistics); and demographic data cover their populations less thoroughly and frequently have less longitudinal depth than in more developed countries. Where censuses are taken or national income accounts published, they may be distorted for political reasons, as the Nultys reported was the case in Pakistan or as has been true in Nigeria. These practical considerations are separate from the question of the competence and conscientiousness of the staff compiling the statistics.

These problems are probably no more limiting in quantitative analysis than the fact that the data have been gathered primarily according to externally derived constructs, such as employment or marital status.[7] To contribute more effectively to development, data should be acquired and organized essentially in terms of various needs and capabilities, rather than in terms of aspects and traits which when manipulated statistically are detached from the persons or aggregates they are supposed to represent. Dissected traits grouped according to standardized constructs are unlikely to provide much basis for choice or action. A coefficient of determination describes covariation; it does not "explain" anything except by statistical inference.

One needs to be concerned also with various methodological problems associated with the use of numbers. Some problems can be avoided, such as those stemming from the use of "high-powered" statistical techniques on data that are too crude or unreliable to warrant them. Corrections applied to adjust for non-random sampling or non-normal distributions are likely to be adding to an unstable statistical house of cards. To talk about "probable error" in such circumstances is seldom justified. Statistical tests of "significance" are particularly prone to misleading inferences. They reveal nothing about the substantive significance of a relationship, and because they are largely a function of the size of the sample, truly significant results can be discarded (because of a small sample) while spurious results are accepted (because of a large one.) [8] There is good reason for having tests that help one

---

[6] We would call readers' attention to the essay by G. Routh, "The Evolution of an Economist," *Monthly Labor Review* (February 1967), pp. 18–22. Routh is responding to the assertion by Paul Samuelson that mathematics is language and that, in economics, it cannot be any worse or better than prose. Routh points out that mathematics and prose are not interchangeable, any more than language and painting, or language and music. Mathematical economists can *assume* the economy into a shape that can be expressed mathematically by the reification of economic entities. Where predictive capabilities are

thereby gained, the process is justified, but this should not be taken to mean that the phenomena "really" have geometrical or mathematical shapes or structures.

[7] On this, see discussion in G. Myrdal, *Asian Drama* (1968), pp. 16–20. It is very nice for scholars doing comparative analysis to have consistent categories of data, but international efforts to standardize them may well have had the effect of making them less useful for national needs.

[8] For some very cogent comments on this and related subjects in statistics, see Edward R. Tufte, "Improving Data Analysis in Polit-

guard against unjustified inferences from data. Indeed, statistical sampling theory is the most developed application of the rule of "optimal ignorance." But the use of designations like "test of significance" and "coefficient of determination" is deceptive. Fortunately, one can use these techniques without overstating their meaning if one is attuned to their limitations.

One methodological difficulty is less ameliorable, and this goes by the name "multicollinearity." Where several independent variables are presumed to be operative on a dependent variable, and they are themselves related to one another, this leads to unstable and possibly spurious estimations of their effect on the latter. This is not an uncommon problem since, as Hubert Blalock has written, "in non-experimental research such independent variables are quite likely to be inter-correlated." [9] His conclusion bears on the reality which quantitative methods are supposed to explicate: that it is highly complex and interactive is to say that multi-collinearity is more than a statistical problem; it poses a basic problem of episte-mology.

While recognizing how ubiquitous this problem is, we share the preference expressed by Edward Tufte for multiple regression analysis.[10] Below we comment on several illuminating uses of factor analysis, path correlations, causal modeling, and the like, but the basic regression technique occupies a useful middle ground between overly simple correlation analysis and other techniques that are likely to overpower their data base. Assessment of *ceteris paribus* effects is one valuable output of regression analysis; its coefficients indicate the direction and strength of associations between variables in the absence of intervention. The identification of "deviant cases" on the basis of analyzing *residuals* is another. As we suggested in Part I, when studying development problems, we are as interested in exceptions as in the rule: What cases depart from the usual pattern, especially in preferred directions? Analysis of these can provide clues to how the apparent grip of "normal" develop-ment (or stagnation) can be broken and how impetus can be given toward effect-ing more desired combinations of events.

We are quite sympathetic to what Tukey and Wilk call "data analysis" as con-trasted with "statistical theory." [11] The former attempts to lay open the data, "to display the unanticipated," whereas the latter gives almost no guidance on this; "indeed, it is not clear how the informality and flexibility appropriate to the exploratory character of exposure can be fitted into any of the structures of formal statistics so far proposed." [12] These authors advocate use of quite simple analytical techniques, especially graphic presentations such as scattergrams. This is to be

ical Science," *World Politics* (July 1969), pp. 641–654. We regret that space limitations have prevented us from including this and a number of other contributions in this area. See also his forthcoming book, *Data Analysis in Political Science*.

[9] "Correlated Independent Variables: The Problem of Multicollinearity," *Social Forces* (December 1963), p. 238.

[10] "Improving Data Analysis in Political Science," pp. 650–652. We appreciate that this technique is not without shortcomings, the most serious being multicollinearity. The usual assumption of linearity in regression analysis can be accommodated for by using curvilinear

or other equations, though this courts the kinds of misunderstanding discussed by Routh (see n. 6 above). One way of making regres-sion analysis more useful in policy studies is to employ regression discontinuity designs such as those discussed by D. T. Campbell in "Reforms as Experiments," *American Psy-chologist* (1969), pp. 419–425.

[11] J. W. Tukey and M. B. Wilk, "Data Analysis and Statistics: Techniques and Ap-proaches," in Edward Tufte (ed.), *The Quan-titative Analysis of Social Problems* (1970), pp. 370–390.

[12] *Ibid.*, p. 371.

preferred inasmuch as numbers are more usefully probed for clues than manipulated for proofs.

Most use of numbers pertains to *ex post* analysis, very little treats the problems of choice *ex ante*. To note this is not to deprecate *ex post* uses. They can be useful in *ex ante* analysis by describing situations of choice in terms of what has happened before and by estimating the probability of different outcomes in response to familiar interventions (or no intervention). What should be clear is that short of certainty, choices and outcomes are always somewhat problematic. Though a certain choice or outcome may have a probability of .8 under certain conditions, the fact is that one may use one's resources to affect the choice or alter the outcome, to raise the probability of a desired choice or outcome or to reduce it if undesired. Some idea of probabilities in the absence of intervention is needed, but these are subject to modification in the give-and-take of the real world.

Being interested in assessing alternative choices, we are very much concerned with probabilities. The anticipated value of any future event or outcome is its value if obtained, discounted by the probability of attainment, which is almost always less than 1.0. If, speaking symbolically, something has an attributed value of, say, ten units, and if there is only a 20 percent likelihood (.2 probability) of achieving it under prevailing conditions, the anticipated future value is two units, and one cannot justify expending more than two units of effort or resources toward it. If, however, the likelihood of attainment could be raised to 50 percent by an expenditure of four units, this would be quite desirable. Seldom are probabilities quite fixed in advance, though one's effort may not be able to affect outcomes sufficiently to be warranted. The interaction of value and probability, with respect to efforts and consequences, is at the heart of choice and thus is central in an existential approach to social science.[13]

When all is said and done, however, the use of numbers cannot replace the careful and critical use of language as an analytical tool for social scientists. In this we would agree with the formulations of Richard Bernhard below, that because of the limitations inherent in quantitative analysis, one should be wary of accepting proofs in mathematical terms alone. These are basically void of substance, and even when they manifest a good statistical "fit," they may not be telling us something "true" about the phenomena under consideration. For capturing and assessing relationships in the real world, even though concepts can also distort empirical analysis, the most versatile analytical instrument is still language. Readers unpersuaded of this may want to read Bernhard's analysis (pages 497–506 below) before proceeding with us to consider the measurement of some developmental relationships.

MEASURING DEVELOPMENTAL RELATIONSHIPS

Measurement has been defined as "the business of pinning numbers on things."[14] This view appropriately emphasizes that, when measuring phenomena, one is not

---

[13] It can be inferred from this that we are interested in the application of statistical decision theory where feasible. It has been applied mainly to business choices thus far, but provides a useful analytical framework for policy. For a summary of this approach, see

Howard Raiffa, *Decision Analysis: Introductory Lectures on Choices under Uncertainty* (1968).

[14] This is S. S. Stevens' definition, cited by Alker, *op. cit.*, p. 19.

"discovering" intrinsic numerical values but rather attaching values instrumentally for purposes of description and analysis. The difference between qualitative and quantitative measurement is not underscored in this definition. The ways in which numbers can be used are not dichotomized, but rather constitute something of a continuum, from nominal to ordinal to interval to ratio measurement. The first use simply classifies, to answer the question "what?" while the second indicates whether one thing is "more" or "less" than another. The latter uses give information on "how much?" Certainly one would prefer being able to answer this question since it subsumes the others. But we are mindful of Aristotle's caution and would be satisfied with whatever mode of measurement can be used without misrepresentation of the phenomena involved.

Given our concern with development and our equation of it with gains in productivity, we have one of the most difficult dependent variables there is to measure. There has been great difficulty in measuring productivity in economic terms, where presumably the denominator of money can make inputs and outputs commensurable. Part of the problem stems from agreeing on the definition of productivity in economics, whether it refers to single factor productivity, as of labor or capital, to total factor productivity, or whether it is a residual remaining after increases in physical inputs have been accounted for. In our discussion, we have used the term "aggregate productivity" to refer to the total amount of satisfaction people derive from their economic, social, and political interaction, that is, production and exchange. This is something which is certainly difficult to measure in any absolute sense, but it remains the primary problem for persons concerned with development to unravel. Addressing efforts to the more rigorous solution of simpler problems holds little attraction.

Some social scientists would contend that our ultimate dependent variable is inherently beyond analysis of any sort since it involves if not measurement, at least comparison of inter-personal utilities, of the benefits and costs which different persons receive from alternative policies or structural conditions. There are economists in particular who maintain that it is impossible to make any judgments about the satisfactions or dissatisfactions which different persons receive as income of any sort. This problem is handled in some few instances by Pareto's rule, that welfare is increased unambiguously only where someone gains without others losing thereby. But this condition is satisfied too seldom for the rule to be of much use, so the larger question must be addressed frontally.

Surely, there are situations in which the difference between costs, on one hand, and benefits, on the other, is so narrow—and their distribution so wide—that there is no basis for concluding that either exceeds the other. To recognize that one cannot arrive at unfailingly unambiguous conclusions should not lead to the position that one eschews all such judgments.[15] To use an analogy with statistics, the "con-

[15] We would concur with the position of J. E. Meade on this: "If there is any meaning in saying that to take $1 from a millionaire and to give it to a starving man does more to satisfy the starving man than to dissatisfy the millionaire, then logically we must admit that the feelings of different men are commensurable. It may be that in innumerable cases, there is too little evidence even to guess whether $1 means more to A than to B; but this must be because we have not got the necessary information and not because it is nonsense to attempt to compare A's feelings with B's." See his introduction to Meade and Charles Hitch, *An Introduction to Economic Analysis and Policy* (1938). Robert Lekachman has noted that most economists found arguments for a more nearly equal distribution of income persuasive until the 1920s, but now "welfare economists no longer be-

fidence" one places in a judgment that there is or is not a net gain in productivity resulting from a policy or an infrastructural investment is a function of the *magnitude* of the *estimated difference* between costs and benefits and of their *distribution* within the population. If the difference does not appear to be very great, and the benefits and costs are distributed within and among sectors that are relatively homogeneous in factor endowment, one cannot say with much confidence that any improvement has been made.

If, on the other hand, the margin of difference appears relatively large and the distribution of benefits is primarily to underendowed sectors, while the costs are distributed among relatively well endowed sectors, it should be possible with some degree of confidence to conclude that a net gain in aggregate productivity had been achieved. (In marginal utility terms, the losses of the latter sectors would not be judged equivalent to the gains of the former.) There is a trade-off between the magnitude of the difference achieved and the direction of distributional effects. While there is no formula for calculating this, in principle it can be seen as a matter of confidence levels. One might reserve judgment on policies or programs that entailed uncertain or small margins of benefit or that had ambiguous consequences for the level and distribution of productive factors. In more extreme cases, however, though analysts might differ as to whether the probability was 80, or 90, or 95 percent that some significant increase in productivity had resulted (or would result), in this range, one could conclude with some confidence that improvements were being made. To refuse to make any judgments about productivity, even in such reasonably clear-cut cases, because one cannot make judgments about every case is like saying one will make no inferences from statistical data, even in terms of confidence levels, because one cannot say positively that every statistical result is or is not "significant."

The formal methods of cost-benefit analysis should have something to say about productivity; however, most applications are not of much use to us. Generally they assume all other structures of production as constant and accept the level and distribution of factors of production as givens, thus they assess productivity in "growth" terms, not "developmental" ones.[16] It should be possible to undertake cost-benefit analyses with reference to structural change, but this is bound to vitiate the quantitative precision that is one of the most attractive features of such analysis. Rather than dwell on this method, which certainly has its uses but which can be better employed by economists than by political economists, let us suggest a different approach.

Given the difficulties in measuring *how much* cost and benefit result from changes in policy or structure, one can focus on *who* benefits and *who* bears the costs of

---

lieve that interpersonal judgments and comparisons can be made, at least by scientists. But if they cannot be made, then there is no objective way to say, for example, that a tax change which redistributes income from rich to poor is more likely to improve welfare than a shift which takes income from the poor and gives it to the rich." This he calls a nonsense conclusion. See his introduction to David Mermelstein (ed.), *Economics: Mainstream Readings and Radical Critiques* (1970), p. xii.

[16] Hirschman's conclusions about "the centrality of side-effects" in development projects greatly limit the utility of such analysis. See his comments in *Development Projects Observed*, pp. 162 and 179. We would note also Guy Hunter's observation that rates of change going on in the world make 1990 a vision or a guess, and any forecasting of costs and benefits claiming accuracy over, say, a 20-year period has a spurious look. *Modernizing Peasant Societies*, Oxford University Press (1969), p. 125 n.

change. This requires disaggregation rather than aggregation in analysis and involves identification of the sectors and resources affected favorably or adversely. Such analysis does not yield an unambiguous outcome, because there are no absolute criteria by which to judge the pattern traced. But such a pattern should make clear the relative distribution of costs and benefits, with as much identification as possible of magnitudes. These would indicate the number and status of beneficiaries compared to the persons concomitantly disadvantaged; one can hope that in many cases they would also indicate extents or degrees of advantage and deprivation. On the basis of such analysis, decision-makers or the public at large could assess with greater clarity whether they thought changes to be made or already made represent an advance toward greater aggregate productivity.

There are many trade-offs to be weighed. Are some greater net benefits in the future to be preferred over net benefits in the present? If a choice must be made between these two alternatives, do political gains for an underprivileged minority outweigh economic benefits for more numerous but only somewhat more advantaged "middle sectors"? There are no scientific answers to these questions. People can legitimately differ about the "value" of benefiting one generation vis-à-vis another, or they can sincerely disagree over how the "greatest good for the greatest number" is achieved. We cannot provide solutions, but we can point to the kind of considerations and the kind of information that would sharpen policy deliberations, by focusing attention on the problems of assessing aggregate productivity and by making narrowly and perhaps excessively quantitative analysis seem less satisfactory. These questions can only be answered, more or less adequately, through political processes, where judgments about the preferred shape of society can be made and where resources are allocated to alter the status quo or preserve it. We would see explicit analyses of distributional effects playing an important role in such consideration if they were made available by policy analysts.[17]

We think that the problems of measuring productivity directly can be somewhat bypassed by considering the various elements which can contribute to it in the context of development: market integration, factor endowments, infrastructure, organization, and entrepreneurship. There are various quantitative methods that have been used insightfully to shed light on development processes and that we would like to note for readers interested in such work.

The extent of economic *market integration* can be determined rather precisely by an intersectoral input-output analysis as well as by household expenditure studies, which determine the proportion of goods and services acquired from outside the household or local community. Such studies have been done for Ghana by R. S. Szereszewski with particular reference to their indications of development.[18]

[17] This approach may be faulted by mathematical economists as sacrificing the rigor which cost-benefit analysis offers, if admittedly over narrower terrain. We are persuaded, however, by James Buchanan's argument in *Cost and Choice* (1969) that neo-classical economics' measurement of cost in "objective" terms is mistaken insofar as one wants to understand and predict people's economic or other choices. Measurement of cost in terms of "factor prices" at market value cannot be equated in practice with the subjective valuation placed on real opportunities foregone by making a particular choice. It is these latter opportunity costs, Buchanan argues, that are uppermost in the minds of choosers, not objective factor costs. Buchanan calls into question the meaning and value of standard economic cost-benefit calculations, while giving rigor and significance to the concept of cost as it bears on the analysis of choice.

[18] See *Structural Changes in the Economy of Ghana, 1891–1911*, and also chap. 3 in Birmingham, et al., *A Study of Contemporary Ghana. Volume I: The Economy of Ghana* (1966).

An instructive study of political market integration has been done for Norway by Stein Rokkan, using electoral time-series data.[19] He employs a model of political center and periphery, looking at registration, party competition, and voting to determine changes in political participation, in response to extension of the franchise but also other developmental influences. (Our discussion below of work by Adelman and Morris touches upon social market integration and on market integration in general.)

The productive consequences of changes in *factor endowments,* such as that of information, can be examined longitudinally with time-series data, as Ito has done above for the case of Japan, or cross-sectionally, as Peaslee has done. A very imaginative and statistically rigorous examination, attempting to assess the relative productivity of different factors, is that undertaken by Anne O. Krueger with a view to guiding development policy.[20] She writes in her introduction:

> It would be highly useful to know how much of the difference in per capita incomes between a developed and a less-developed country is attributable to less capital (or land and natural resources) per head, how much to lower skill levels, and how much to other factors. Although all may affect relative income levels, it is important for analysis and policy whether disparities in resources account for 20 percent of the difference, or whether they account for 90 percent. For if most of the disparities are attributable (at least in a proximate sense) to uneven resource endowments per head, models of resource accumulation should be the basis for analyses of development. If, however, resource disparities explain little of the differences in income levels between countries, economists must search anew for a theory of output determination, for the central question of economic development must then become the reason for differences in outputs with comparable inputs. Models focusing upon technology differences, "dual" economies and the like would then appear appropriate.[21]

Using econometric techniques with some limiting assumptions, Krueger finds that factor endowments indeed account statistically for most of the variation in per capita incomes, but that more than half the variation is attributable just to differences in human capital alone. This does not imply that development expenditures should be concentrated exclusively on human capital formation or that present patterns of expenditure for education have been optimal. But it does suggest some priority for this factor in development plans, especially considering the longer "gestation period" for this kind of investment. "A planning horizon of five to ten years would almost certainly result in few, if any, resources devoted to education." [22] This would, according to her analysis, be a mistake.

A number of analytical methods suitable for studying the productivity of *infrastructure* are shown in the last section of Part III: the *comparative analysis* of regime strategies employing different mixes of political and administrative infrastructure; *field work* and *survey research* to ascertain inducements and disincentives for popular participation in the national political market through a political party; exploration of *historical analogies* to consider functions and functional equivalents of local government in rural settings; *quantitative analysis* of case studies to determine whether policy outputs were associated with administrative mechanisms; and construction of a *matrix* to explore the logical possibilities for positive or negative

[19] "Electoral Mobilization, Party Competition, and National Integration," in Joseph La-Palombara and Myron Weiner (eds.), *Political Parties and Political Development* (1966), pp. 246–256.

[20] "Factor Endowments and Per Capita Income Differences Among Countries," *Economic Journal* (September 1968), pp. 641–659.

[21] *Ibid.,* p. 641.

[22] *Ibid.,* p. 657.

consequences from corruption under different conditions. All of these authors sought to contribute, and to invite others to contribute, to cumulative research that would have a bearing on development policy with respect to political and administrative organization.

A highly ambitious and stimulating study by Irma Adelman and Cynthia Taft Morris should be considered in this connection. They sought, using the technique of factor analysis, to assess the association of social and political factors with per capita GNP as a measure of economic development.[23] One of the criticisms that has been made of their work is that, given their methodology, they were proceeding without any theoretical basis. As exploratory work, we find the work valuable, and it both contributes to and is in part explained by the political economy of development. Adelman and Morris consider twenty-two social and political variables in seventy-four countries during the period 1957–1962, letting their computer program ascertain the strongest associations among these variables with respect to GNP per capita. Four compound "factors" are constructed by the program.

The first of these (factor I), which accounts for 42 percent of the variance observed in per capita income, can best be understood in terms of *market integration* in socio-political terms. Income was found to be higher: the smaller is the "traditional" sector, the less salient are particularized kinship forms (tribe, clan, extended family), the greater the extent of literacy and mass communication, the greater the degree of linguistic homogeneity, the larger the size of an indigenous (linking) middle class, and the degree of modernization. The second factor (factor II), accounting for 19 percent of the variance, is, we think, misconceived in the evaluation of the results, being identified with "Westernization" when it represents to our minds the development and extension of *political and administrative infrastructure,* particularly those forms which increase political factor endowments and opportunities for popular participation. Income was found to be higher: the more effective democratic political institutions are, the greater the freedom of political opposition and the factionalization of political parties, the more parties are based on ideological platforms rather than simply on appeals for national unity, the weaker the military in political affairs, the greater the efficiency of public administration, and the greater the degree of decentralization of political power. Two other factors were found to have relatively little explanatory power, factor III including elite and leadership factors (5% of the variance), and factor IV representing social and political stability (1.4% of the variance).[24]

Separate regional analyses were made and they strengthened but also modified the conclusions based on the whole sample. For African countries, with the lowest average income per capita, factor I took on much greater significance, accounting for over three-quarters of the variance in income. This suggests that market integration is the basic condition for economic development and that other factors are

[23] "A Factor Analysis of the Interrelationship between Social and Political Variables and Per Capita Gross National Product," *Quarterly Journal of Economics* (November 1965), pp. 555–578. This is presented in greater detail in their book, *Society, Politics and Economic Development: A Quantitative Approach* (1967).

[24] Adelman and Morris postulate that factor IV received such a low weight because the study covered a relatively short period. They would expect it to be more important in variations in income over a longer run. A point they make is that changes associated with factor I lead to social and political instability, so factor IV is somewhat ambiguous. Some instability, though presumably not too much, might be more beneficial for economic development, than "stability" per se.

relatively less important until this condition is relatively satisfied. (No other factors account for more than 2 percent of the variance in African countries' per capita income.) Factor I accounts for just over half and factor II for nearly a quarter of the variance in Asian countries' incomes, with the other factors negligible. Greater market integration having been achieved, political and administrative infrastructure are relatively more important there than in Africa. Latin American countries, which have still higher per capita incomes, show factor I accounting for 38 percent of the variance, with factor II "explaining" another 21 percent, though in this region, the second factor includes leadership variables that show more salience than in the other regions.

The policy inferences which Adelman and Morris draw from their data are consistent with the model we have proposed. They suggest that foreign aid to the least developed countries focus on what we call integration of markets, especially through education and physical infrastructure. Countries at a somewhat higher stage of development would benefit relatively more from the extension of political and administrative infrastructure, with the most advanced of the underdeveloped countries having more need for generalized resources (program rather than project aid) because leadership and stability are more important at this stage. We find this work by Adelman and Morris, though it might be considered "essentialist" in its methodology, quite fruitful, perhaps because the authors are engaged in it to derive implications for development policy.

There are many ways to study the element of *organization* in development. We would like to discuss the findings of Nie, Powell, and Prewitt concerning organization and political participation, derived from the more complicated technique of causal modeling using path correlations.[25] They find that practically all of the development-related differences in mass participation can be explained by differences in social status and organizational involvement; indeed, citizens in five countries studied who were of similar social class and organizational involvement participated in politics to the same extent without any significant differences by nation. What they want to understand better is the relationship among status, organization, and participation.

Quite different causal patterns are found by statistical analysis. Whereas 60 percent of the effects of *social status* on participation are mediated through attitudinal variables and another 30 percent "pass through" organizational involvement, 60 percent of the effects of *organizational involvement* go directly into participation without any intervening factors. We would quote the authors' conclusions here at some length:

Organizational involvement may represent an alternative channel for political participation for socially disadvantaged groups. The rural peasant, the industrial laborer, the disadvantaged black may become politically active through his organizational involvement even though he may otherwise lack the status resources for political participation. . . . We have argued that economic development changes both the class and organizational structures of a society. This is true, but other factors may also promote such changes. The class structure is, of course, intimately tied to the long-term development of human and capital resources. Governments may establish massive education programs

[25] Norman H. Nie, G. Bingham Powell, Jr., and Kenneth Prewitt, "Social Structure and Political Participation: Developmental Relationships: I and II," *American Political Science Review* (June and September 1969), pp. 361–378 and 808–832. We are considering here findings from Part II of the report. The five countries from which data are drawn and analyzed are the United States, United Kingdom, Germany, Italy, and Mexico.

and engage in forceful income redistribution. However, obviously major changes in the status structure, involving occupation, education, and income patterns, are extremely difficult to bring about. We suspect that the organizational structure may be susceptible to more direct and short-term manipulation. . . . It appears that the richness and complexity of organizational life might be altered somewhat independently of economic development. Deliberate government policies, for instance, can increase the number of citizens who are politically active. . . . all social strata in the society would participate in those political processes which presumably lead to control of political leadership and through this control to influence over public policy. Group mobilization could attract into political life larger numbers of those persons who presently are political isolates. These citizens need not have the enabling antecedents, such as higher levels of education, now thought to be necessary conditions for political participation. Alterations in the organizational structure, then, can serve to correct the tendency for even the most democratically organized societies to allow a disproportionate amount of political influence to be exercised by the well-to-do. . . . It is probably no coincidence that those nations in which both political parties and governmental bureaucracies have been most active in encouraging secondary group formation show less upper class domination of the organized life of the society. What must be concluded is that processes of economic development will not automatically help redress class participation imbalances through the growth of secondary groups.[26]

Readers are referred to the original article for the authors' analysis of their data, for their methodological techniques and their full set of conclusions. Here we would point to the implications of their quantitative analysis which support the emphasis to be placed upon *organization* in the political economy of development.

Very little quantitative analysis has dealt with *entrepreneurship* as an element in development. To understand the contribution it makes, one must look at it retrospectively and examine how leaders mobilized resources, formulated programs, created organizations, or established infrastructure, bringing together the factors of economic, social, and political production in new and more productive ways. Historical studies of leadership are legion, and many are quite instructive from a political economy viewpoint. The account by John Womack of Zapata's leadership in the Mexican Revolution and of the strategy pursued by Zapata's successor, Gildardo Magaña, is excellent for its analysis of sectors, interests, resources, and the interplay of strategies in what was a three-, four- or more-cornered political competition.[27] Two chapters stand out in the volume on *Political Parties and Political Development* as analyses of political entrepreneurship, demonstrated by Ataturk in Turkey and Nasser in Egypt.[28] A less successful example of entrepreneurship is that of Kwame Nkrumah in Ghana; we find quite informative an analysis of this by Jitendra Mohan, who employs more of a Marxian than a conventional social science approach. Mohan shows how the failure to establish truly productive political and administrative infrastructure reaching down to the grass roots, despite appearances of a strong party and a strong state apparatus, left Nkrumah vulnerable as he kept expending political capital without adequately replenishing it.[29] Studies such as these provide insights into the exercise of entrepreneurship and the kinds of consequences to be expected from different choices.

One work we know of has applied very interesting quantitative methods, albeit somewhat complicated ones, to the study of entrepreneurship.[30] Cornelius traces

[26] *Ibid.,* pp. 819 and 826–827.

[27] *Zapata and the Mexican Revolution.*

[28] LaPalombara and Weiner, *op. cit.,* chapters by Dankwart Rustow and Leonard Binder.

[29] "Nkrumah and Nkrumahism," in Ralph Miliband and John Saville (eds.), *Socialist Register, 1967* (1967), pp. 191–228.

[30] Wayne A. Cornelius, Jr., "Nation-Building, Participation, and Distribution: in Gabriel A. Almond and Scott C. Flanagan (eds.), *Developmental Episodes in Comparative Politics: Crisis, Choice, and Change* (forthcoming).

the strategy of Lázaro Cárdenas to mobilize the agrarian and labor sectors both during his campaign for the Mexican presidency and after assuming that office, in order to offset the power and resources of other sectors in the country. Using measures of issue-distance among contending elites (sector leaderships) and of their respective political power (resources) at different points in time, he is able to show how the balance was shifted to favor more the large underendowed sectors of peasants and workers. The analysis shows the significance of entrepreneurial efforts at organizing peasants and workers for political action, establishing and maintaining information flows to and from these sectors, and raising their endowments of economic factors through land reform and industrial relations policies. The methodology employed by Cornelius may not be applicable for all situations, but we would hope to see such measures developed and refined to deal with even such difficult analytical problems as entrepreneurship.

There are quantitative studies, as we have shown, that attempt to measure some of the developmental relationships outlined in the political economy of development. These studies provide some criteria for development strategies, though clearly it is important that many more studies must be made, to test the model further and refine it, if it is to be generally supported. For now, it does not appear possible to do more than point directions for policy, suggesting priorities and probable interactions. We cannot designate quantitative limits, for example, to the productivity of market integration, though this inability need not be a cause for rejection of the approach. It would be foolish to formulate a general proposition on the subject since judgments of productivity will always be highly contextual. One needs always to identify the respective gains and losses of groups from a change in the status quo so that any verdicts about aggregate productivity are viewed in light of who is benefiting and who is not.[31] It would appear that priorities rather than prescriptions will by and large result from quantitative analysis at the macro level of the various elements of development.

Almost no rigorous analysis has been done at the micro level by scholars of development. To be sure, there are hundreds and more of briefing papers and memoranda that project different courses of action and estimate their costs and advantages *ex ante,* but these have been undertaken by and for governments and are almost all hidden away from public knowledge. Social scientists do not have the benefit of such analyses in refining their own understanding of phenomena, and have almost never undertaken such analyses themselves. Retrospective analysis has its payoff insofar as one can learn from the past and particularly from the consequences of past miscalculations. But an understanding of economic, social, and political processes that permits one to intervene in them so as to move in a preferred direction requires more *ex ante* analysis. In this, anticipated effects and interactions are specified and then checked against the course of events to develop models of social change and social control. In such an effort, the primary problem lies not so much in the area of quantification as in determining the most

[31] For example, an overall benefit-cost ratio of 2:1 for a project needs to be seen in terms of the distribution of effects if one is to go beyond simply the generation of resources (valued at current market prices) and deal with developmental potentials raised or not by the project. One qualification would be that it should be possible to estimate project benefits using shadow prices based on relative equalization of purchasing power. This would be a very useful adaptation of the benefit-cost method of analysis and should be possible with computer techniques.

salient elements to be considered and the relationships among them to be examined. This takes us from the question of measurement to the more basic question of models in social science.

MODELS AND ANALYSIS OF DEVELOPMENT

Models may be used in either essentialist or existential social science. In the first tradition, we have "ideal type" analysis and variations on this theme, which can be traced from Plato through Weber to contemporary social science. Disclaimers may be made—that the ideal type has no empirical referent or reality—but the imputation is made that the "essence" of this type has some determinant impact on outcomes; legal-rational bureaucracies, or mobilization systems, or single-party regimes are thought to yield because of their nature certain kinds of consequences. This analytical approach may be linked with neo-Pythagorean assumptions: that there is some fundamental numerical relationship among parts "out there" in the real world and that a model will reveal these relationships.

Actually, existential social science has even more need of models because of its ontological view of the world—as being in flux, with outcomes determined *ex post* but not necessarily *ex ante,* and as being shaped by individuals and groups according to their needs, values, and capabilities.[32] There is causation to be studied and understood, but the task is not to be simplified by definitional solutions. An instrumental view of knowledge and analysis in fact places a premium on developing models and theories. Without them, one cannot improve one's ability to influence events. This does not mean, however, that one can regard any intellectual ordering or rationalization of the world as true in some ultimate sense. Rather, any superimposition of order on the world through intellectual effort can only be judged as more or less useful than other formulations or models.

It follows from this view that, as Tukey and Wilk have put it, "models must be used but must never be believed," models being described as means of intellectual guidance that imply neither belief nor reality.[33] To analyze and to measure interactions or outcomes, some prior structure must be assumed; to achieve some predictive capability, one needs to know what are the most significant factors affecting outcomes. Not all structures or factors are equally illuminating, however. The search in social science is for better models than those presently available, and we think this will lead to existential models. In these, one assumes no preexisting, necessary, universal, or immutable coefficients or parameters, but considers instead how they might be altered in a desired direction.[34]

[32] This view of reality (ontology) has been perhaps best expressed by John Dewey. Our affinity with his philosophy has probably been apparent already to any students of his thought. See, among other of his works, *Reconstruction in Philosophy* (1920), and *The Quest for Certainty* (1930). There is some basis for describing his philosophy as "pragmatism" or "empiricism," but the designation he preferred and which we find most apt is "instrumentalism."

[33] *Op. cit.,* pp. 372 and 385–386. Without

models, we are most certainly lost, they write, but were we to accept them unquestioningly we would be equally lost in a different morass.

[34] We would support the view of A. R. Louch that economic theory, for example, does not describe the necessary nature of an economy; rather, an economy results from policy. Economic "laws" are to be seen as formulations of policy, need, and value, with "no reason to suppose they cannot or do not need to be altered. . . . When formulae for an economy are thought of as reflecting

One develops improved models, we would suggest, by studying the interactions and exchanges in the real world. This requires the rediscovery or revival of observation in social science. Perhaps we overstate the extent to which it has been forgotten or derogated, but it is curious that social and political scientists in recent years should have thought they could study society and politics without observing them, looking instead to U.N. Statistical Handbooks or census tracts. Numbers from these sources capture only aspects of people and groups and their relationships. Working from some of this data is like trying to envision prehistoric animals from petrified footprints, or if the data are better, like trying to put together a skeleton from fossil bones. None of the data can reconstruct the organism. Where the phenomena one is interested in no longer exist, such methods may be the only ones feasible. But they are pale reflections of a reality that might better be studied directly as much as possible.[35]

It is true that there are many restrictions on observing the policy process and on ascertaining all the aims of policy-makers. These difficulties can be offset somewhat by participant observation, though one should not assume that this will obviate them all.[36] The kind of observation we are pointing to is the study of consequences of choices, such as Albert Hirschman made in *Development Projects Observed*. This is feasible and represents the kind of work on development that is greatly needed. As Hirschman's analysis shows, one can learn things of general value through "immersion in the particular," as he puts it. Knowledge gained in this way can make theoretical contributions, contrary to some prevailing views, and it has the advantage of being keyed to empirical problems.

The emphasis in recent years on comparative analysis, with its possibilities for large sample, cross-sectional quantitative analysis, has lowered the esteem and deference paid to case studies. We would, however, echo Lucian Pye's words "in praise of description." [37] In doing so we do not downgrade the role of analysis— quite the contrary. But we see case studies as permitting the necessary attention to the contexts of choices and their consequences, as well as to the longitudinal course of events. Cross-sectional studies using quantitative measurements that manipulate aspects or abstractions cannot capture the nuances or depth of relationships that decisively affect outcomes.

Analysis growing out of case studies offers, we think, promise for developing the kind of social science theory relevant to policy, as well as the kind of insights which statistical comparative analysis with its abstractions and analytical variables is likely to obscure. We would point to two studies, by an economist and a political scientist, that serve development theory well. In his analysis of the Chilean experience over the past several decades, Tom Davis finds the prevailing theory of eco-

---

theories, trouble ensues. Matters of policy are elevated into unalterable law." One cannot say, Louch argues, that the market must work this way "and don't tamper with it." See *Explanation and Human Action* (1969), p. 197.

[35] It may not appear a fair comparison, but we would ask, What studies of American politics have matched the work of Alexis deToqueville on *Democracy in America* despite the subsequent refinement in quantitative tech-

niques and the immense aggregation of data for analysis?

[36] See discussion of observation in Webb, Campbell, Schwartz, and Seechrist, *Unobtrusive Measures* (1966), chapters 5 and 6, esp. pp. 114–115 on problems of participant observation.

[37] See his essay on "Description, Analysis, and Sensitivity to Change," *op. cit.,* esp. pp. 246–247. This is an excellent statement, which we would commend to all readers.

nomic growth, focused as it is on physical capital as the limiting factor, quite inadequate.[38]

This theory rests on the idea that there exists a "reserve army" of unemployed and underemployed who could be put to work, if capital were forthcoming, in factories employing modern technology and at wages only slightly in excess of workers' opportunity cost in disguised unemployment. Davis finds this assumption, of a homogeneous labor factor with an abundance of unutilized skills, unfounded. The implications of his analysis deserve consideration in other national contexts, though in each case the conditions would have to be examined to see how applicable the model Davis sketches would be. We would note further that, in accounting for the phenomena observed in Chile, Davis uses an approach very close to the political economy perspective we have been elaborating.

Another "revisionist" contribution to development theory is that by Robert Price, who examines the role of the military vis-à-vis national development in the case of Ghana.[39] The essentialist models of the military, proposed in books by Johnson, Finer, and Janowitz, which treat it as inherently "modernizing" because of its organizational structure and its technological training and values, are quite wrong in the case of Ghana. And the refinement proposed by Huntington, identifying the impact of the military as being conservative or progressive depending on the *type* of society in which it functions, is not much better.[40] Price shows how reference-group theory accounts quite well for the role of the military in Ghana while ruling after Nkrumah's overthrow; its pro-British and pro-Western orientation impeded nationalistic policies which would have accelerated modernization and development. This theory would appear relevant in many situations apart from that in Ghana, where its utility can be demonstrated. Moreover, we find it valuable because it extends and makes more concrete the analysis of *status* as a resource, tracing as it does the political effects of differing valuations put on the esteem and deference of others.

In both of these studies, the authors were alert to discrepancies between the outcomes observed and those that would be predicted on the basis of conventional generalizations about capital investment or military behavior. These divergences were taken, not as "proving a rule," but as posing problems to be understood in their own terms. To account for the discrepancies, Davis and Price did not manufacture analytical variables or direct their attention elsewhere (in search of "comparisons") as though either abstractions or other cases would explain the cases at hand. Rather, the authors looked at the economic, social, and political interaction taking place and tried to comprehend the purposes of participants in it. Such attention to situational

---

[38] "Changing Conceptions of the Development Problem: The Chilean Example," *Economic Development and Cultural Change* (October 1965), pp. 21–32.

[39] "A Theoretical Approach to Military Rule in New States: Reference-Group Theory and the Ghanaian Case," *World Politics* (April 1971), pp. 399–430.

[40] See article for citations. Price says of the Huntington model: "The credibility of this model is strained by the assumption that military men at all times and in all places will have the same orientation toward political participation; positive toward the middle class and negative toward the masses. What is needed is an analytic approach that can differentiate the military from other organizations and social groups within a society, as does the formal organizational model, and, at the same time, differentiate among military organizations in different societies. . . . Such an approach would avoid the pitfall of assigning a modernizing role to military rule in all cases, but would not demand the banning of organizational factors from the explanatory picture altogether" (*ibid.*, pp. 400–401).

details and dynamics produces, we think, more of theoretical value than analyses that aim more self-consciously at theory-building but take little account of the perspectives and aims of actors.[41]

There has been posed in social science an antinomy between *rigor* and *relevance,* with the former seen as taking precedence in efforts to reach more "scientific" conclusions. But this is like preferring the criterion of *reliability* of measurement to that of *validity.* Just as one would be ill-advised to purchase reliability of measures at the price of their validity, attaining rigor at the expense of relevance has little to commend it. A good case can be made for trying to make valid measures more reliable rather than for working the other way around. Similarly, it makes sense to try to increase the rigor of social science inquiry pertaining to real world problems rather than seek to make rigorous inquiry more relevant.

To be sure, the matter need not be posed too starkly. Rigor and relevance are not mutually exclusive qualities. It is eminently desirable that we have inter-subjectively verifiable knowledge about contemporary problems of public policy and private choice. One should consider the trade-off according to some marginal rate of substitution: how much rigor would or should be given up for a gain in relevance, or vice versa? One can imagine a *production possibility curve* for social science representing various combinations of rigor and relevance.[42] By making advances in rigor or relevance—but preferably in both—it would be possible to establish new, more productive boundaries for social science.

We think the first step toward moving this frontier outward is to emphasize more relevant kinds of social science analysis. In particular we are mindful of Kenneth Boulding's warning about abstracting and separating the various aspects of the "sociosphere." We are concerned with developing a model of economic, social, and political interaction that relates the most salient factors within one framework. In this way, choices can be informed by consideration of more than the set of factors examined by any one discipline, since there clearly are interactions *among* the sets— as well as within them—that need to be analyzed for purposes of choice and action.

At the same time, with a view toward achieving greater rigor of analysis, we would focus on factors that have observable or ascertainable manifestations, avoiding what Occam called "suprasensible" explanations of sensible effects. All the resources we deal with have their origin in the activities or attitudes of persons.[43] Sectors and infrastructure are no less "real" though they are analytically identified. The persons or patterns of activity considered under sectoral or infrastructural rubrics are not changeless, nor are they in practice confined to single activities or purposes. This

[41] This concern is stated forcefully, if somewhat differently, by Joseph LaPalombara in "Macrotheories and Microapplications in Comparative Politics: A Widening Chasm," *Comparative Politics,* October 1968, pp. 52–78.

[42] We would probably draw the curve in standard form—concave to the origin—for the sake of illustration; but we suspect it may be convex, which would account for social scientists' tendency to work at either extreme, where they must give up relatively more of what they have (rigor or relevance) to get some of the other.

[43] We would note here a reference made in our previous work to Bentley's view that "if we can get our social life stated in terms of activity and of nothing else, we have not indeed succeeded in measuring it, but we have at least reached a foundation upon which a coherent system of measurement can be built up." Ilchman and Uphoff, *op. cit.,* p. 277. Resources such as status and legitimacy though not tangible in the material sense are nonetheless real in terms of behavioral consequences. Thus we see them as usefully included under the rubric of "activity." They are to be ascertained by innovative survey research methods as well as by methods which account for compliance differentials.

complicates and makes more situational the tasks of definition and measurement. But these analytical categories are tangible and thus identifiable, and they pertain to the basic problem for social science—especially with respect to development—the determination and evaluation of productivity in its various aspects.

We share the common aspiration for quantification of variables, but our enthusiasm is tempered by the dictum put well by Giovanni Sartori, *"concept formation stands prior to quantification."* [44] Surely, agreement on conceptual terms of analysis depends to some extent on their susceptibility to "operationalization," which generally but not necessarily entails quantification. But acceptance of concepts or models *because* they are readily amenable to quantitative applications offers little prospect for a social science comprehending and serving the basic concern of productivity. First priority goes to developing concepts and models that can stake out the boundaries and focus on the central factors of analysis. Thus, our concern has been primarily with the formulation of a framework for the analysis of choice pertaining to productivity.[45]

There are, it should be remembered, inherent limitations on the use of quantification in economic, social, or political analysis. The essay below, by Richard Bernhard, explores these epistemologically, but the point is put succinctly by Sartori: "We seldom, if ever, obtain isomorphic correspondences between empirical relations among things and formal relations among numbers." [46] As Bernhard contends—citing Keynes, Marshall, and others—language still constitutes the most general and most powerful tool for analysis in social science.[47] This realization underscores the importance of choosing among terms and approaches those which can yield relevant knowledge, since any of them may be used in quantitative analysis—but not with equal benefit.

In addressing developmental problems, then, we must employ words and terms which represent the realities of economic, social and political existence. Of necessity, some simplifications of that reality must be made in the form of a model of developmental change. This model, however, cannot purchase much simplification without paying dearly in the coin of relevance to policy choices. Reducing social systems to a set of equations has the merit of elegance but only rarely that of relevance. The

[44] "Concept Misformation in Comparative Politics," *American Political Science Review*, December 1970, p. 1038 (italics in original). Sartori prefaces his statement with that of J. J. Spengler, that the mathematical development of economics "always lagged behind its qualitative and conceptual improvement." Cf. "Quantification in Economics: Its History," in Daniel Lerner, ed., *Quantity and Quality* (1961), p. 176.

[45] We recognize that by applying basically economic concepts to other forms of analysis, we might be charged with "conceptual stretching." Cf. Sartori, *ibid.*, pp. 1034 ff. We think the new political economy can withstand the charge because, to continue Sartori's metaphor, the concepts are quite elastic and accommodate readily to situational definitions— for example, the prevailing criteria for conferring esteem and deference, or the group categories for political activity (sectors).

[46] *Ibid.*, p. 1037. We have characterized confidence in this isomorphism as "neo-Pythagoreanism." N. Georgescu-Roegen examines a related problem of "arithromorphism" in *Analytical Economics: Issues and Problems* (1966). Neither these authors nor we deprecate quantitative analysis *per se*, but rather argue for its reasonable use.

[47] We again cite Sartori, who disparages the social scientist whose sophisticated statistical methods race ahead of his concepts and theory —"the man who refuses to discuss heat unless he is given a thermometer." He sympathizes instead with "the man who realizes the limitations of not having a thermometer and still manages to say a great deal simply by saying hot and cold, warmer and cooler." He notes later a statement by Richard Rose ("a scholar well versed in quantitative analysis") that "all the most interesting variables are nominal." *Op. cit.*, pp. 1033 and 1045. Nominal variables are basically qualitative, though ordinal valuations or rankings are possible.

new political economy admittedly entails some complexity, but we think no more than necessary to encompass the contingency of human choices and their consequences.[48]

In the political economy of development, we delineate basic elements contributing to productivity: extending and diversifying *patterns of exchange,* augmenting endowments of the *factors of production,* aggregating resources and structuring their flow through *organization,* and promoting all of these through *entrepreneurship.* The model is partly inductive and partly deductive, deriving from the detailed analysis of one country's development experience (Ghana) and from an extended analysis of one discipline's learning about development (economics). What encourages us to propose the model is that it fits with—and we think it integrates—the empirical and conceptual work of a good number of other social scientists.

Most developmental effects must for the present be inferred from various indicators of change. Such indicators would be: (a) *market integration:* changes in the scope of trade, travel and migration, transportation facilities, education, communications, political participation (e.g. voting), administrative activity, and shared criteria of status;[49] reduction in social discrimination according to race, class, age, etc.; increase in literacy or the use of a *lingua franca;* (b) *resource endowments:* increased possession—particularly by the less well-endowed—of land, skills, and capital (fixed or liquid); attributes conferring higher status (e.g., education, better health, more "modern" life-styles, social amenities, or money income); knowledge of various sorts; and opportunities to participate in or influence the exercise of authority; (c) *organization:* number and scope of organizations, especially involving the less well-endowed, considering number of members, amounts of resources aggregated, internal communication and cohesion, plus at the aggregate level some measures of "institutionalization";[50] and (d) *entrepreneurship:* this poses the greatest difficulties in measurement, ones not unique to the new political economy, as seen from the entry on "Entrepreneurship" in the *International Encyclopedia of the Social Sciences;*[51] Schumpeter is cited as saying that "it can never be understood *ex ante,*" and Aitken infers that "the typical characteristics of entrepreneurship differ" according to different cultures; clearly, operationalization of the study of this element is still in its early stages.[52]

An enumeration of the variables relating to the basic elements of development reveals considerable overlapping of effects from different factors such as income, education, reduction in discrimination, and political participation. It would serve no

[48] In his review of *The Political Economy of Change,* Raymond Hopkins finds the model's variables "too disaggregated, too complex, and too ambiguous to be measured," though he finds other features commendable. Hopkins suggests that had we "attempted to build a formal model, as is done, for instance, in computer simulations, [our] complex disaggregations would have been abandoned in favor of fewer, more critical disaggregations." We cannot abandon disaggregation as readily as Hopkins because of our concern with the assessment of chocies, not with a maximum attainable R^2 across some large N of cases. See "Securing Authority: The View from the Top," World Politics, January 1972, pp. 279–280. Hopkins makes some appropriate criticisms, though like all authors we find the reviewer misunderstanding various intended points.

[49] This could include the interpersonal identification which Daniel Lerner identifies as "empathy" in *The Passing of Traditional Society, op. cit.*

[50] See S. P. Huntington, "Political Development and Political Decay," *World Politics,* April 1965, pp. 384–430.

[51] (1968), Vol. 5, pp. 87–91.

[52] We have commented previously on this subject, emphasizing the study of opportunity structures in preference to psychological or cultural variables. See Ilchman and Uphoff, *op. cit.,* pp. 262–267.

purpose to insist that one separate, for example, the "market integration" and "factor endowment" effects of education—or dissect the augmentation, respectively, of economic, social, and political resources from a given amount and kind of education. What is needed is a look at education—or land reform, or economic policies, or administrative structures—in terms of how each form or amount contributes to those elements which can increase a society's aggregate production possibilities, especially as its less well-endowed members are affected.[53]

The emphasis in this approach on productivity does not provide formulas for choice so much as it directs attention to the substantive effects of choice. One cannot "prove" that a certain policy is objectively more productive so as to satisfy someone who places different values on inter-sectoral outcomes. A judgment that one course of action is *more* productive than another according to specified objectives, such as raising income, status, or political power of certain groups, is, however, tenable. Ordinal estimates are a form of measurement that can reasonably be aspired to in development policy analysis. There can be reasonably objective assessment of the *modal* effects of a policy: which sectors get what or lose what as a result of it. Comparison of x benefit for sector A with y benefit for sector B can only be made with reference to some chosen set of objectives. For developmental purposes, one is likely to assign weights that alter the simple measures of aggregate physical or monetary amounts.

Consider the following illustration. A fertilizer program yielding increased production worth 100,000 rupees from one hundred farmers with annual incomes of 5,000 rupees may be judged less desirable than one yielding 90,000 rupees' worth from three hundred farmers with incomes of only 1,000 rupees. The 1,000-rupee increases in the incomes of the first group amount to a 16 percent gain, while the 300-rupee increases for the second group boost their income by 30 percent. The costs of reaching the three hundred will be greater than those for the one hundred, and under certain circumstances, it may be socially or politically desirable to get a maximum physical increase in production in the shortest period of time. But in developmental terms, bringing the three hundred along the road to higher productivity is more important than advancing the one hundred still farther.

The importance of considering these distributional questions comes not simply from a concern with welfare but from an appreciation of the link between distribution at one period and production in the next.[54] This is to say that information on distri-

---

[53] For example, in assessing a rural credit program, the model shows the importance of having criteria of performance that extend the "developmental" impact of the activity. If the standard measure of effectiveness—rate of loan recovery—is used, this encourages credit officers to lend mostly to farmers who are already well-endowed, in preference to the rest, who are poor "risks." But it is their productivity which needs most to be raised in developmental terms. Similarly, in choosing locations for school construction, one ought to consider which locations will contribute most in relation to the existing distribution of informational resources, so that schools are not built simply to maximize enrollment for a given level of economic expenditure. The productivity (in terms of eliciting under-

developed resources) of adding, say, thirty schoolleavers per year to a community varies according to the size of the community and its present level of educational attainment. Concentrating enrollment increases in the least educationally developed areas may be no more productive than doing this in the most developed areas; some "mix" of locations will upon consideration in these terms probably be judged most productive. The point is that evaluations of development programs should go beyond quantitative "growth" criteria.

[54] As stated in Part II, we reject the argument that development is primarily a consequence of capital formation, and that this—through personal savings—is maximized by unequal distributions of income.

bution is in many contexts more important than that on aggregate amounts. And whereas cardinal measurement is usually needed for comparison of the latter, ordinal and even nominal measurement can serve in the assessment of distributional effects. At present, the data base for distributional analysis is very weak, most statistics having been gathered and analyzed in aggregate terms. This has suited both economists' theories and the more advantaged sectors' interests. But increasingly it is apparent that neither deserve the deference that has been paid to them in the name of development.

The political economy of development is presented not as a theory of development but still only as a model, which people can examine, test, and elaborate. There is no claim that it represents some incontrovertible truth about development, because the subject is unavoidably freighted with preferences and value judgments. The crux of the model is the nexus between production and distribution, in social and political as well as economic activity. The analysis, still largely deductive, points most clearly to the centrality of the *factors of production* conceived of in supradisciplinary terms; to those who have, it shall be given, from those who have not, it shall be taken away.

The process of development is not seen in terms of distributing or redistributing *income* but rather in terms of allocating or reallocating *factors of production,* though this can require changes in income distribution. Distribution is important not so much for its own sake as for the sake of productivity, With greater factor endowments, people by their contributions to economic, social, and political processes will be able to increase the total of "goods" produced therefrom and to *earn* a larger share of these.

This is the problem and the promise of development—that a community's potential for satisfying the needs and wants of its members be enhanced, through individual, group, and public action. The latter is the critical element, we believe, because individual or group action alone can do little to alter factor allocations. Public policy may reinforce the existing distribution, for reasons already considered, if the well-endowed sectors are able to monopolize the political process. Significant shifts are likely to be achieved only through political leadership at various levels, which mobilizes and organizes political resources with a view to using *authority* on behalf of developmental change. Thus, the political economy of development poses for all —practitioners and academics, statesmen and scholars—the challenge of conceiving and raising in aggregate terms the productivity of politics.

MATHEMATICS, MODELS, AND LANGUAGE IN THE SOCIAL SCIENCES

RICHARD C. BERNHARD

University of Utah

Mathematics is often said to be the queen of the sciences. Is she queen of the social sciences as well? Can everything that is significant in the social universe be converted into numerical quantities? Must the whole subject matter of the social sciences be formulated in mathematical symbols?

The role of mathematics in the social

Reprinted by permission of author. An earlier and shorter version of this article appeared in National Institute of Social and Behavioral Science, *Symposia Series* (1960), No. 3, pp. 1–5.

sciences has been discussed in numerous articles and monographs, but several basic issues remain unresolved. These still unresolved issues involve nothing less than the validity of much of the data used in our models of the social system. In other words, what is involved is the relevance of our data for understanding the social universe and for solving our problems. It is extraordinarily difficult to resist the temptation to look upon social and economic data as 18th and 19th century natural scientists looked upon their data and their formulations. Objective data and the observational relationships that scientists formulate may easily be given credit for a definitiveness that only later is revealed as incomplete, inadequate, or even deceptive. To be aware of the nature and limitations of the data with which the social scientist works requires constant vigilance. Without this, we may seriously entertain propositions that range from the innocently inadequate to the preposterous error.

I

A discussion of the role of mathematics and language in the social sciences will be greatly facilitated if, at the outset, there is a general statement of the nature of science and mathematics—as these terms will be used here.

Science is a part of man's endeavor to understand the universe about him. In this sense, it is a sister of art, literature, philosophy, and religion. As Einstein said, "All religions, arts and sciences are branches of the same tree." [1] In a more technical sense, science is the endeavor to formulate invariant relationships of observational data, that is, invariant relationships between specific measurements. It is the endeavor to show, with the greatest possible exactitude, the relationship between various entities of the world about us as these entities are measured by the scientist. This is the concept of science that one finds among men such as Einstein, Schrödinger, Planck, Bohr, Heisenberg, and others.[2]

Mathematics is considered by a number of eminent authorities to be a specialized language, a form of logic, a symbolism for expressing numerical or other formal relationships. "Mathematics deals exclusively with the relations of concepts to each other without consideration of their relation to

experience." [3] This is the way Einstein describes the scope of mathematics.

The distinction between mathematics and science involves a fundamental difference: science concerns matters where measurements or observations are employed; mathematics is concerned with purely logical relationships. Thus, the propositions of science differ from the propositions of mathematics in that mathematics can be *perfectly exact;* science cannot. "As far as the laws of mathematics refer to reality, they are not certain; and as far as they are certain, they do not refer to reality." [4] Conceptions and formulations of relationship, even in physics are always subject to revision.[5] Social scientists should never assume because they put their relationships into mathematical notation that they have escaped this inherent infirmity of all science.

The distinction between mathematics and empirical science reveals the error in the popular notion that confusion can be avoided by resorting to mathematics. Fourier's dictum that "mathematical analysis . . . has no marks to express confused notions" is false.[6] The whole development of physical science is the continuous replacement of one set of mathematical concepts by others when ambiguity is discovered. All scientific concepts, definitions, and laws are, as Heisenberg says, *"a part of the human language that has been formed from the interplay between the world and ourselves."* [7] It is really a bit preposterous to suppose that mathematical procedures are a sure prophylactic against errors of human reason and understanding.

II

Mathematics' role in the physical sciences is fairly clear and well settled. There are, perhaps, still those who look upon mathematics as the Pythagoreans did, as an expression of nature or as the expression of an ultimate reality.[8] In this view, nature's secrets are supposed to be revealed by the study of mathematics. The predominant opinion of natural scientists now is that mathematics is a language for expressing relatively simple relationships with the utmost precision, a way of expressing them that permits the maximum chain of logical deduction.[9]

In the social sciences, the role of mathematics has not been so clearly established.

The term *mathematical* covers a multitude of different characteristics of our expositions. It is often like another term, *dynamic,* in being just an appellation given gratuitously to signify approval. Out of deference to the rather diffuse, general usage of the word, we shall consider two different instances in which the treatment is commonly said to be mathematical. One is the use of reasoning in mathematical symbols to unravel the consequences of certain assumptions. This is the method of developing, or discovering, the logical results of certain propositions by using the instrument of formal symbols. The second case, often described as being mathematical, comprises all those instances when quantitative measurements are employed in one way or another in the analysis. Thus both the use of abstract symbols in reasoning and the use of measurements are considered a use of mathematics in the social sciences.

III

The use of mathematical models, conceptual frameworks, laws, world pictures, or theories in the physical sciences is well established. Sometimes these models are as simple as a representation of the structure of a molecule; sometimes they are as highly abstract as the kinetic theory of gases, laws of light, electromagnetism, and gravity. All may be put under the designation of models, though they are often called laws. In economics, where the application of this type of mathematical formulation has possibly gone further than in other social sciences, models range from formulations of the relationship between quantity sold and price (the demand) to formulations of the entire economy in a magnificent Walrasian system of type equations. There is, therefore, a resemblance between the natural and the social scientist's models. But there are also differences.

Models, laws, or relationships, even in the physical sciences, are creations of the human intellect, not dictations by Nature; [10] but they are formulated on the basis of extremely accurate measurements and on a careful checking of logical deductions from the model by experimental results. The model must predict accurately. From models formulated in mathematical language, a large number of specific consequences may be deduced; and these logical consequences are subject to verification (to known degrees of precision) by experiment.

Models in the social sciences are often mathematical formulations using type equations without specific numerical content. The most eminent of these is the Walrasian synthesis, a logical structure of great intricacy and beauty, but by itself not based on measurements nor leading to the experimental verification of deductions from its postulates. Other models, much less elegant in structure and more modest in aim, do purport to be based on measurements and do submit themselves for experimental verification. Statistical demand curves have been formulated; relationships of money to prices and employment have been devised; the relationship of inputs of materials to outputs of goods and services in a nation's industries have been studied; the strategy in simple games has been reduced to rules; and, more recently, the selection of the best choice among a variety of technically possible alternatives with given prices has become subject to precise determination by methods called "linear programming."

Social scientists are, therefore, attempting to use the same techniques as the natural scientists, with some modest success; but the gap between the accomplishments of the natural scientists in their use of models and the social scientists remains preposterously large. The question is whether the gap can be narrowed by more expansive use of abstract mathematical models of phenomena in the social world. Or is it a gap, that, by the nature of the social world, is bound to remain? Does this tool of science have limited uses in social matters? One way to answer these questions is to examine the measurements on which social scientists rely. Can they be put to the same use as measurements in the physical sciences?

IV

The measurements employed in the social sciences are often the result of the most haphazard, fortuitous process of collection. Statistics as a by-product of the administration of some law or as a by-product of some industry's accounting system—these form too large a part of our data, particularly in economics. The relevance of the information collected in this manner is often less than perfect, so there are frequent violations of the principle of scientific work which holds that the greatest care must be taken in obtaining data that have a direct bearing on the problem in hand. The design of the experiment is crucial. Much of the data that comes as a by-product is also defective in not being very accurate.

Social scientists should be thoroughly familiar with the exact manner in which their data were originally gathered so that they can evaluate both the relevance and the accuracy. Such familiarity will make them cautious when working with defective information, if that is all that is available. Social scientists should be experimentalists in knowing the origin of their figures and also logicians thoroughly versed in the principles of statistical inference. If they have this discernment in full measure, they become advocates for discrimination in what information is collected. Science depends on accurate, relevant facts, not on large compilations collected with the discrimination of a department of sanitation.

All the above is mentioned merely by way of confessional so that we do not need to consider this state of affairs in what follows. Here we wish to consider the use of measurements assumed to be made carefully and with proper consideration of the use to which the measurements are to be put.

v

The role of precise measurements in the social sciences involves several fundamental issues. One is whether the whole range of phenomena of the social world can be expressed in numerical quantities. Can the social universe be formulated completely, or adequately, by measurements? Can all things that are important be reduced to quantities? Among economists, political scientists, sociologists, and psychologists, there are some who assume that no matter is scientific or worthy of intellectual respect unless it is measured and expressed in numbers. Despite the persistence of those holding this view, the proposition has, I believe, the weight of authority

against it—authority both of natural and social scientists.

The existence of causal factors which cannot be reduced to measurable quantities led Marshall to depreciate the importance of what measurements are possible. He wrote:

Every economic fact . . . stands in relation as cause and effect to many other facts: and since it *never* happens that all of them can be expressed in numbers, the application of exact mathematical methods to those which can is nearly always a waste of time, while in the large majority of cases it is positively misleading.[11]

Marshall was aware of the importance of what we call institutional factors and aware of the constant changes in these factors.[12] Institutional arrangements in the business or social world, the state of technology, laws, customs, fashions, motives, hopes and expectations, beliefs and values—and changes in any of these factors—cannot be formulated in mathematical symbols, yet all these influence the social world. The social scientist has, therefore, the agonizingly arduous task of having to work with both measurable and non-measurable causes; and the task is complicated by the inordinately complicated causal interrelationship of the factors that are somewhat amenable to measurement. Various devices are used to put aside the effects of causes that are not measurable—arbitrary time lags, trends, residual causes, and assumed random elements; but the arbitrary nature of these devices is quite foreign to the natural sciences and of very dubious validity.[13] At times it is assumed that, by using those causal factors that are measurable, one can nevertheless make predictions based on probability. This is, indeed, a strange application of probability analysis.

VI

The inability to put all the causal factors with which the social scientist works into mathematical form limits the extent to which mathematical models (that is, precise theoretical formulations) can be used. This is not the only infirmity of theoretical models. A rigorous examination of the nature of measurements reveals that the best of data has a strictly limited significance. As was said at the outset, social scientists are often like 19th century physical scientists in regarding their facts and relationships as absolutely valid and unquestionable. Now atomic physicists are not so sure. Their data is, they know, a function of their measuring devices. "Quantum mechanics does not describe a situation in an objective external world, but a definite experimental arrangement for observing a section of the external world." [14] Note the statement of limitation, "a section of the external world."

The most accurate measurement is a partial, incomplete picture. It is *that aspect of the event we have chosen to look at.* It is nothing more than what we have decided to count. This means that we decide, deliberately or unawares, to ignore many other aspects. Every term, every concept, is a classification—a more or less precise specification of some entity. Every measurement of an entity has its significance limited by the manner in which the classification was set up *and the entity designated.* The design of the experiment conditions the meaning of the data obtained in it. Our definition, or our design, determines what we measure and the way we measure. No measurement gives more than this predetermined, limited amount of information.

The man who formulated the quantum theory commented on this matter at some length.[15]

Any scientific treatment of a given material demands the introduction of a certain order into the material dealt with. . . . Order, however, demands classification; and to this extent any given science is faced by the problem of classifying the available material according to some principle. . . . There is no one definite principle available *a priori* and enabling a classification suitable for every purpose to be made. This applies equally to every science.

All measurements are, thus, based on some *classification, which is nothing more than an abstraction of a very few elements from the immense wealth of information involved in each event.* If we take any term of economics and examine its meaning carefully, we will find that there is an arbitrary restriction in its content. This arbitrary element—the specification of what the category is to include and what it is to exclude—sets definite limits to the meaning of our measurements. The terms commodity, industry, firm, market, price, monopoly, competition, welfare, money, investment, saving, national income are all instances of classification in which from one to several features are used to determine what is to be included under each term. And any data we have on these entities—any "facts" about them—have no greater meaning than what is warranted by our specifications in drawing the classification.

There is, indeed, no escape from this arbitrary process of classification; but we should be aware of what we are doing, and conscious of the tentative nature of our system of classification. We should not act as though we were dealing with sacred, inspired doctrine when expounding our terms and concepts. In this respect, the physical sciences and the social sciences are similar. Both are based on systems of classifying which make a selection from the infinite variety of sense impressions— or recordings on our measuring devices— that could be registered in careful observation of the simplest phenomenon. But the physical scientists are significantly different, first, in being more sure that their categories are adequate for the specific purpose they have in mind, second, in that there are only a relatively limited number of important aspects to observe and measure, and, third, that the phenomena are not going to change because of a new idea or belief, a law, an invention—or simply because someone is watching the event.

Formulating specifications for a commodity, a relevant market, an industry, or income can be an exhausting experience *when one is doing this in full awareness of the complexity of actual events.* The experience is salutary. It should teach us to take a more provisional view of our formulations. It should also teach us that all measurements have a limited significance. We should respect this limit in dealing with all our concepts and magnitudes; but we often forget it. The economist has, to take one example, a concept of the firm. This is a fairly rigorous concept; but the logical consequences which follow from this concept do not correspond at all well with the facts of observation.[16] The chain of reasoning has been carried much further than the original concept warrants.

VII

Given the inherent infirmities of data, every science must proceed to formulate relationships, theories, world pictures, models —or whatever name they go by. How useful is it to formulate extremely precise mathematical models in the social sciences? Physical scientists do this, as we have seen; and they succeed in deducing a marvelous series of precise consequences which are verified by observation. (If not verified, the model is quickly scrapped for a better.) Should not social scientists try to do the same? Here again the judgment of many authorities, some the most skilled mathematicians ever to study economics, is against the use of long chains of reasoning from formal principles or models. Keynes insisted that:

Too large a proportion of recent "mathematical" economics are mere concoctions, as imprecise as the initial assumptions they rest on, which allow the author to lose sight of the complexities and interdependencies of the real world in a maze of pretentious and unhelpful symbols.[17]

In his biography of Marshall, Keynes added a footnote commenting on the difference between the use of logical deductions in physics and in economics. "Economic interpretation in its highest form," he wrote, requires an "amalgam of logic and intuition and the wide knowledge of facts, most of which are not precise." [18] Marshall, who also had outstanding talents as a mathematician, realized that the concepts of economics would not support much logical elaboration. "It is obvious," he said, "that there is no room in economics for long trains of deductive reasoning." [19] He reached this conclusion because "the forces of which economics has to take account are more numerous, less definite, less well known, and more diverse in character than those of mechanics; while the material on which they act is more uncertain and less homogeneous." [20] After considerable experience in obtaining measurements and in testing the validity of inferences from data, a sophisticated statistician cautioned all those using "facts" that "statistical techniques are instruments in our hands and—like all instruments of measurement—constantly to be suspected by the investigator of playing him false." [21] This is wisdom born of experience!

VIII

The argument of the last sections has been, first, that not all important causes in the social world are subject to measurement; second, that all measurements give a definitely limited amount of information about an event and that this circumstance restricts the relevance of any data. Further, we are never sure in the social sciences that all the important aspects of a situation are covered by the measurements we have obtained. The utmost caution must, therefore, be used before a model "can be used as a substitute for reality itself." [22]

The fascination of mathematical models is intense, whether the concepts employed can be measured or whether they are purely formal, so that a great deal of labor is devoted to them. The difficulty or the impossibility of checking the working of models against observations (because of inaccessible or inaccurate data) permits the game to be played without that restriction imposed in the natural sciences where the most beautiful and dearly loved theoretical model can survive only if it can stand up under the most exacting tests. The exuberant growth of concepts and models in economics, and their sterility, have been observed by certain economists. Professor Boulding cited one of the most venerable of these—marginal cost-marginal revenue—and asked "why a system of analysis so self-consistent, so obedient to the great scientific principle of parsimony, so elegant, so persistent in academic teaching, and so admirably adapted to the understanding of students and to regurgitation in examinations, should be so confoundedly useless." [23]

The results of elaborate, deductive mathematical analysis based on models, not substantial enough to support an elaborate superstructure, are shown by Robertson in a number of papers. The logical consequences drawn from the economist's model of a business firm,[24] the "behavior" of a model of the consumer,[25] the popular model for determining income, employment and prices [26]—all this is shown with the utmost suavity and good humor. But what stands revealed is rather pathetic. Robertson modestly pleads for less mathematics and geometry and more common sense. He wants more fruit and less foliage.

Professor Williams, like Robertson, does not investigate in detail the methodological problems, but instead shows clearly the results in economic analysis of sacrificing relevance in use to purely logical consistency.

The great paradox of classical economics is that, whereas it began with dynamics, providing the rationale for revolutionary changes, it would end up in a tight system of static equilibrium theory, which in striving for logical consistency became increasingly remote from reality.[27]

The most dangerous policy maker is the man who knows the answer, because he feels he can take it literally from his theory.[28]

IX

The attitude of the physical scientists toward their theoretical formulations is in striking contrast to the attitude which is characteristic of social scientists. Anyone who reads in these two fields cannot but note a fundamentally different outlook. The physical scientist has seen much alteration in the knowledge about which he once felt sure; his experiments reveal facts that do not fit into a completely consistent scheme of things; and he is acutely aware that his measurements give him a limited amount of information. Reality for him is an infinitely remote goal, an eternal pursuit. The social scientist has less reason for assurance but has, by contrast, much more confidence in his system and in his measurements. An unexpressed but not uncommon assumption is that by means of science we shall eventually be able to obtain a complete understanding and control of all nature, including life itself and human desires and aspirations. With further development of scientific laws and with more measurements, science will be able to take charge of man and direct him to a predetermined "heaven" wherein all evils will be eliminated, from toothache and crime to scarcity and even the difficulties of artistic creation and scientific discovery. Exact measurement and the formulation of scientific laws are going to do the trick.

Psychologists and sociologists seem to be a bit more prone to this point of view than economists, but it can be found among economists too, especially those who are going to make a science of welfare. Belief in such supreme, latent powers of science is valid only on the assumption that life and nature can be summed up completely in mechanical principles, in exact mathematical equations for all relationships. For science to treat all problems, there would have to be an exact determination of the precise cause and effect of everything from the mass and position of an atom to the yearnings in the heart. Those who hold this view are strict Newtonians in their philosophy.

Modern physicists realize that they cannot give a complete picture of nature. Total knowledge, the goal of those who would control man by what they conceive as scientific knowledge, is impossible, they are convinced. According to Planck, "it is certain that scientific progress will never enable us to grasp the real world in its totality." [29] Born says that "there are two objectionable types of believers: those who believe the incredible and those who believe that 'belief' must be discarded and replaced by 'the scientific method.' " [30] According to Oppenheimer, "perhaps only a malignant end can follow the systematic belief that total knowledge is possible; that all that is potential can exist as actual." [31]

X

The preoccupation with mathematical formulations in economics and in other social sciences has had one definite destructive effect. The esteem for mathematics has resulted in the neglect of another instrument for stating relationships, namely, the *effective* use of language. Language is also a flexible instrument for expressing ideas and relationships in the social sciences. In one of Keynes' earliest publications, he mentions the problem of instruments for expressing a rigorous analysis. Conceding the advantages of the exact mathematical notation in certain uses, he says:

But there are advantages also in writing the English of Hume . . . it is possible, under cover of a careful formalism, to make statements [using symbols], which, if expressed in plain language, the mind would immediately repudiate. There is much to be said, therefore, in favor of understanding the substance of what you are saying *all the time*, and of never reducing the substantives of your argument to the mental status of an *x* or *y*.[32]

In this opinion, Keynes was consistent throughout his life. The same judgment is given in his *General Theory of Employment, Interest and Money:*

It is a great fault of symbolic pseudo-mathematical methods of formalising a system of economic analysis . . . that they expressly assume strict independence between the factors involved and lose all their cogency and authority if this hypothesis is disallowed; whereas, in ordinary discourse, where we are not blindly manipulating but know all the time what we are doing and what the words mean, we can keep "at the back of our heads" the necessary reserves and qualifications and the adjustments which we shall have to make later on, in a way in which we cannot keep complicated partial differentials "at the back" of several pages of algebra which assume they all vanish.[33]

Precision and clarity in using our language is, however, as arduous as the accurate use of mathematical symbols, perhaps more difficult. It is usually assumed that we all know how to communicate in our mother tongue; but Keynes knew, and great legal scholars like Holmes and Cardozo knew, that exact expression is a skilled craft that requires the most arduous labor.[34] Few realize the work involved in accurate use of words, and tradition dictates that we don't comment on another man's use of these symbols the way a scientist would check another's mathematical manipulation. We may complain that someone is hard to understand; but the burden is still on the reader to make some sense out of it, not on the writer to be clear.

Concepts stated in English have more of the complex texture of the world. They are less abstract than mathematical symbols, so we will be more cautious in basing highly involved analysis on them when this is dangerous. Even verbal symbols are likely to trick us at times, so we must be cautious with them, too; but they do provide some assurance that deductions will be exposed to general criticism.

XI

There has been no time to describe the enormous amount of work that is still to be done, both in providing better statistical

data and in using the tools of statistical analysis to check, with the utmost rigor, popular casual explanations and each "very obvious inductive generalization." [35] Appearances can be deceptive, and scientific relationships are often more subtle than they appear. For this work, scientific analysis of the highest caliber is required,[36] and on it depends any further progress in our subject. Here we have been concerned only with the deceptive feeling of contentment and satisfaction that social scientists often feel when they get a figure, when they invent symbols, or devise a mathematical model. The sciences should not be content with symbols and models. In that direction lies scholasticism. Mathematics is a queen; but that is within her own realm. Outside it, she is a servant and should be kept in a servant's status, whether in the world of the physicist, the biologist, or the social scientist.

1. Albert Einstein, *Out of My Later Years* (New York: Philosophical Library, 1950), p. 9. Others have expressed the same idea. Max Planck wrote: "Actually there is a continuous chain from physics and chemistry to biology and anthropology and thence to the social and intellectual sciences; a chain which cannot be broken at any point save capriciously." *The Philosophy of Physics* (London: Allen & Unwin, 1936), p. 81. See also: Max Born, *Natural Philosophy of Cause and Chance* (Oxford University Press, 1949), p. 128; Erwin Schrödinger, *Science and Humanism* (Cambridge University Press, 1951), p. 2; J. R. Oppenheimer, "The Age of Science, 1900–1950," *Scientific American,* September 1950, p. 21.
2. "Science is the attempt to make the chaotic diversity of our sense experience correspond to a logically uniform system of thought." Albert Einstein, *op. cit.,* p. 98. "Science is nothing else than the endeavor to construct . . . invariants where they are not obvious." Max Born, *op. cit.,* p. 104. According to Max Planck, science "consists in the task of introducing order and regularity into the wealth of heterogeneous experiences conveyed by the various fields of the sense world." *Scientific Autobiography* (New York: Philosophical Library, 1949), p. 88.
3. Albert Einstein, *op. cit.,* p. 41.
4. Albert Einstein, "Geometry and Experience," *Sidelights on Relativity* (London: Methuen, 1922), p. 28. This essay has been reprinted in *Ideas and Opinions by Albert Einstein* (New York: Crown Publishers, 1954), p. 233. Others have expressed the same idea. See, for example, Max Planck's

The Philosophy of Physics, pp. 41–53; and *Scientific Autobiography,* pp. 121–125.

5. See Einstein's essay, "Maxwell's Influence on the Development of the Conception of Physical Reality," *James Clerk Maxwell Essays* (Cambridge University Press, 1931), p. 66.

6. Professor Stigler comments on this common belief in his lecture, "The Mathematical Method in Economics," and cites a very confused idea concealed in mathematical analysis. See: George J. Stigler, *Five Lectures on Economic Problems* (London: Macmillan and Co., 1949), pp. 39–40.

7. Werner Heisenberg, *Physics and Philosophy* (New York: Harper, 1958), p. 108 (emphasis added).

8. "Things were not only related to or expressible by numbers; they *were* numbers." Ernest Cassirer, *An Essay on Man,* p. 266. Erwin Schrödinger also describes this view in his book, *Nature and the Greeks* (Cambridge University Press, 1954), chap. 3. For a statement of the more contemporary issue, see Max Born, *Experiment and Theory in Physics* (Cambridge University Press, 1944).

9. See Werner Heisenberg, *op. cit.,* pp. 171–2.

10. This proposition may seem surprising or false to many people who think of laws of nature being somehow given by Nature, with man only discovering what Nature wrote. How widely the proposition is accepted in physics may be seen from the following quotations and references. Einstein has said: "Physics constitutes a logical system of thought which is in a state of evolution, whose basis cannot be distilled, as it were, from experience by an inductive method, but can only be arrived at by free invention." "Physics and Reality," reprinted in *Ideas and Opinions,* p. 322. See also pp. 307, 226. Werner Heisenberg has written: "When we represent a group of connections by a closed and coherent set of concepts, axioms, definitions and laws which in turn is represented by a mathematical scheme we have in fact isolated and idealized this group of connections with the purpose of clarification. But even if complete clarity has been achieved in this way, it is not known how accurately the set of concepts describes reality. These idealizations may be called a part of the human language that has been formed from the interplay between the world and ourselves." *Physics and Philosophy,* pp. 107–8. Similar statements may be found in *The Philosophy of Physics* by Max Planck, pp. 12–13, and 15; *Natural Philosophy of Cause and Chance* by Max Born, p. 208; *Atomic Physics and Human Knowledge* by Niels Bohr, p. 65; and *Nature and the Greeks* by Erwin Schrödinger, *passim.*

11. *Memorial of Alfred Marshall,* edited by A. C. Pigou (London: Macmillan, 1925), p. 422. At another time, he wrote: "The longer I live the more convinced I am that—except in purely abstract problems—the statistical side must never be separated even for an instant from the non-statistical" (*ibid.,* p. 428). In a letter to Professor Edgeworth, he wrote: "Economic theory is, in my opinion, as mischievous an imposter when it claims to be economics proper as is mere crude unanalysed history" (*ibid.,* p. 437).

12. Alfred Marshall, *Principles of Economics,* 8th ed., p. 783. A. C. Pigou is of the same opinion as Marshall on this matter; see *Alfred Marshall and Current Thought* (London: Macmillan, 1953), p. 15. Sir Dennis Robertson makes frequent mention of the economic factors that cannot be expressed in mathematical symbols; see, among others, his *Economic Commentaries* (London: Staples Press, 1956), p. 23; *Utility and All That* (London: Allen & Unwin, 1952), p. 41; and Frank Knight is deeply absorbed by the problem of the "divergence between theoretical conditions and reality"; see in particular his "Preface to the Re-Issue" of *Risk, Uncertainty and Profit* (London School of Economics and Political Science Reprints, No. 16).

13. For discussion, see J. M. Keynes on a review of a Tinbergen work, *Economic Journal,* 49 (1939), 558 ff.

14. Max Born, *Natural Philosophy of Cause and Chance,* p. 108. See also, Bohr, *op. cit.,* p. 61.

15. Max Planck, *The Philosophy of Physics,* pp. 12–13. The same point has been clearly stated by Ernest Cassirer in his *Essay on Man,* p. 264. Cassirer, like Einstein, emphasizes that each system of classification is a work of creative art.

16. On this matter, see Sir Dennis H. Robertson's chapter, "Some Recent (1950–55) Writings on the Theory of Pricing," in his book, *Economic Commentaries.*

17. *General Theory of Employment, Interest and Money,* p. 298.

18. *Memorials of Alfred Marshall,* p. 25 n. This is from the famous footnote in which Keynes tells of Planck relating that, as a student, he found economics too difficult! Keynes continues this footnote, saying that this highest form of economic art "is, quite truly, overwhelmingly difficult for those whose gift mainly consists in the power to imagine and pursue to their furthest points the implications and prior conditions of comparatively simple facts which are known with a high degree of precision."

19. *Principles of Economics,* p. 781.

20. *Ibid.,* p. 772.

21. M. J. Moroney, *Facts from Figures* (Penguin Books, 1953), p. 416.

22. This phrase is from Dr. Evsey D. Domar's "Comment" on the section "Methodological Developments" by Richard Ruggles in *A Survey of Contemporary Economics*, Vol. II, edited by Bernard F. Haley; a physical scientist would probably not use the word reality in such a way. For him, the question would be whether the model was adequate for some specific purpose.

23. Kenneth E. Boulding, *The Skills of the Economist* (Cleveland: Howard Allen, 1958), pp. 41–42.

24. D. H. Robertson, "Some Recent (1950–55) Writings on the Theory of Pricing"; *Utility and All That*, pp. 73–76; "Those Empty Boxes," *Economic Journal*, 34 (1924), reprinted in *Readings in Price Theory*, published by the American Economics Association (Chicago: Irwin, 1952).

25. D. H. Robertson, *Utility and All That*, pp. 13–42 and 70–73; *Economic Commentaries*, pp. 42–58.

26. D. H. Robertson, *Utility and All That*, pp. 83–115.

27. John H. Williams, "An Economist's Confession," *American Economic Review*, March 1952, Vol. XLII, No. 1, p. 4.

28. *Ibid.*, p. 12.

29. *The Philosophy of Physics*, p. 31.

30. *Natural Philosophy of Cause and Chance*, p. 209.

31. J. Robert Oppenheimer, *Science and the Common Understanding* (New York: Simon and Schuster, 1953, 1954), p. 95.

32. J. M. Keynes, *A Treatise on Probability* (London: Macmillan, 1921), p. 19 n.

33. Pp. 297–8.

34. The failure to emphasize sufficiently the difficulty of clear, accurate writing is the only point with which I would disagree in Professor Stigler's lecture, "The Mathematical Method in Economics" (*Five Lectures on Economic Problems*).

35. This phrase is that of Professor J. R. Hicks asserting that "the economic systems of modern times are liable to fluctuations of a particular sort, which can properly be called cyclical." See: *A Contribution to the Theory of the Trade Cycle* (Oxford University Press, 1950), p. 1. Eminent statisticians, on the basis of empirical analysis, disagree.

36. For examples of generalizations put to the test of statistical analysis, see: M. G. Kendall, "The Analysis of Economic Time-Series," *Journal of The Royal Statistical Society*, Vol. 116, Part I, 1953; M. G. Kendall, *Advanced Theory of Statistics* (London: Charles Griffin, 1946), Vol. II, p. 381; C. Udny Yule and M. G. Kendall, *An Introduction to the Theory of Statistics*, 14th ed. (London: Charles Griffin, 1953), pp. 641–2; M. J. Moroney, *Facts from Figures, passim*.